Understanding Microsoft Teams Administration

Configure, Customize, and Manage the Teams Experience

Second Edition

Balu N Ilag
Durgesh Tripathy
Vijay Ireddy

Apress®

Understanding Microsoft Teams Administration: Configure, Customize, and Manage the Teams Experience, Second Edition

Balu N Ilag
Tracy, CA, USA

Durgesh Tripathy
Bengaluru, Karnataka, India

Vijay Ireddy
Plano, Texas, TX, USA

ISBN-13 (pbk): 979-8-8688-0013-9
https://doi.org/10.1007/979-8-8688-0014-6

ISBN-13 (electronic): 979-8-8688-0014-6

Managing Director, Apress Media LLC: Welmoed Spahr
Acquisitions Editor: Smriti Srivastava
Development Editor: Laura Berendson
Editorial Project Manager: Jessica Vakili

Cover designed by eStudioCalamar

Cover image designed by by XiaoXiao Sun (@smile_97) on Unsplash

Distributed to the book trade worldwide by Springer Science+Business Media New York, 1 New York Plaza, Suite 4600, New York, NY 10004-1562, USA. Phone 1-800-SPRINGER, fax (201) 348-4505, e-mail orders-ny@springer-sbm.com, or visit www.springeronline.com. Apress Media, LLC is a California LLC and the sole member (owner) is Springer Science + Business Media Finance Inc (SSBM Finance Inc). SSBM Finance Inc is a **Delaware** corporation.

For information on translations, please e-mail booktranslations@springernature.com; for reprint, paperback, or audio rights, please e-mail bookpermissions@springernature.com.

Apress titles may be purchased in bulk for academic, corporate, or promotional use. eBook versions and licenses are also available for most titles. For more information, reference our Print and eBook Bulk Sales web page at http://www.apress.com/bulk-sales.

Any source code or other supplementary material referenced by the author in this book is available to readers on GitHub. For more detailed information, please visit https://www.apress.com/gp/services/source-code.

Paper in this product is recyclable

This book is dedicated to our cherished family members, who have been our steadfast pillars of strength through the ups and downs of this book-writing journey. Your unwavering support and love have fueled our spirit and determination, making every challenge surmountable and every victory sweet.

Your collective support has been the foundation upon which this work stands, and for that, we are eternally grateful.

Table of Contents

About the Authors

 **Balu N Ilag** is a luminary in the realm of unified communications and collaboration technologies. With an impressive career spanning 17 years, Balu has carved a niche for himself in messaging, telecom, and modern workplace collaboration. He currently serves as an Office 365 and collaboration specialist at Juniper Networks, where he wears multiple hats—from product administration and development to strategic guidance for enterprise customers.

Balu holds a plethora of distinguished certifications that reinforce his expertise in the field. He is a Microsoft Certified Trainer (MCT), a Microsoft 365 Certified Teams Administrator Associate, and a Microsoft Certified Solutions Expert (MCSE) in communication and productivity. These credentials not only highlight his grasp over Microsoft technologies but also signify his commitment to continuous learning and excellence.

An avid writer, Balu has authored an array of blog posts on his site `www.bloguc.com` that serve as a treasure trove of insights on unified communication and collaboration technologies. Whether you're looking for a comprehensive how-to guide or best practices for troubleshooting, chances are Balu has penned a blog post about it. His writings reflect his deep understanding of the complexities involved in modern workplace technologies, making them an invaluable resource for professionals and enthusiasts alike.

Durgesh Tripathy has more than 14 years of experience in the field of technology. He likes to learn new technology and its core. He spends most of his time learning and reading books.

His field of expertise comprises Microsoft Technologies such as Directory Services, Networking, Telephony, Windows Core Services, and many more, along with Core Java and Web Technologies. His keen interest in Mathematics and its use to resolve real-life issues is what fascinates him the most using AI and ML and how this can be implemented to enhance existing infrastructure and productivity rather be in Development, Cyber-Security or Infra Management.

Vijay Ireddy is a highly skilled technology professional passionate about innovation and digital transformation. He has extensive experience and a range of Microsoft and UC certifications, including Teams Administrator Associate, Support Specialist, and Collaboration Communication System Engineer.

As a modern communications architect at Cyclotron, Vijay works with organizations to evaluate their existing communication and collaboration platforms and help them transition to the modern Microsoft Teams platform. He has a proven track record of implementing Microsoft Teams with industry-specific best practices while ensuring governance and security. He is dedicated to delivering effective solutions that meet each organization's unique needs and to staying up-to-date with the latest technological advancements to help his clients achieve their business goals.

About the Technical Reviewer

Vikas Sukhija has nearly two decades of IT infrastructure experience. He is certified in various Microsoft and related technologies; in fact, he has been awarded the Microsoft Most Valuable Professional title eight times.

Vikas is a lifelong learner, always eager to explore new technologies and expand his knowledge. He keeps himself up-to-date with the latest trends and developments in the field, ensuring that his work reflects current best practices and industry standards. His commitment to continuous improvement and his passion for sharing knowledge make him an invaluable resource for technical content creators and readers alike.

With a strong foundation in Microsoft technologies, Vikas has continuously expanded his knowledge and skills throughout his career, adapting to the ever-evolving landscape of cloud. His deep understanding of the Microsoft ecosystem, including Windows Server, SQL Server, Exchange Server , Active Directory, and other technologies, allows him to provide comprehensive and insightful reviews of technical materials.

Vikas's passion for automation and scripting led him to specialize in PowerShell and Python, where he has honed his skills in developing efficient and robust scripts for various administrative tasks. His expertise in PowerShell/Python ranges from simple automation scripts to complex solutions, empowering organizations to streamline their processes and enhance productivity.

His contributions can be found on his blogs and Facebook page:

http://TechWizard.cloud

http://SysCloudPro.com

https://www.facebook.com/TechWizard.cloud

Acknowledgments

Writing this book has been a monumental undertaking, and it would not have been possible without the contributions, support, and encouragement of numerous individuals and organizations.

First and foremost, we extend our heartfelt gratitude to **Microsoft**. The wealth of information provided through their official documentation and the `learn.microsoft.com` learning platform has been invaluable in the creation of this second edition.

We'd also like to extend our deepest appreciation to the **Microsoft MVP community**. Your knowledge and insights have enriched the content immeasurably, and your continuous efforts to build a better technological ecosystem inspire us every day.

Special thanks go to **LinkedIn Learning** for offering a platform that bridges the gap between learners and experts and for its resources that have augmented our research and perspectives.

We'd also like to extend a special thank-you to the **IT management team at Juniper Networks**. Your encouragement and the flexibility have been invaluable gifts, making it possible for us to dedicate the time and effort required to bring this book to life.

On the production side, a massive thank-you goes to our **technical reviewer** and **content editor**. Your meticulous eyes have made this book what it is—precise, accurate, and comprehensive. We also want to thank **Smriti Srivastava** and **Shobana Srinivasan**, who have been exceptional in managing the book's production. Your cooperation has been invaluable, and your hard work has not gone unnoticed.

Lastly, but certainly not least, we reserve our most heartfelt acknowledgment for our **family members**. Your unconditional love and support have been our rock, enabling us to devote the time and energy needed to bring this project to fruition.

Thank you, everyone, for making the second edition of *Understanding Microsoft Teams Administration* a collaborative effort and a repository of collective wisdom.

Introduction

Welcome to the second edition of *Understanding Microsoft Teams Administration*, a comprehensive guide designed to delve deep into the administrative landscape of Microsoft Teams—the platform revolutionizing how organizations communicate, collaborate, and get work done.

What Is Microsoft Teams Administration?

Microsoft Teams administration refers to the practice of managing and configuring the Microsoft Teams platform within an organization. This extends beyond mere technicalities; it involves a delicate interplay of user management, security settings, compliance protocols, app management, and overall governance. The role of a Teams administrator is pivotal for the effective and secure deployment, maintenance, and customization of the platform to suit an organization's unique requirements.

Why Is Teams Administration Important?

The significance of adept Teams administration cannot be overstated, and here's why:

- **User management:** One of the first steps in Teams administration involves controlling who has access to what within the platform. From creating teams and assigning roles to setting permissions, effective user management ensures streamlined collaboration.

- **Security and compliance:** Ensuring that sensitive information remains confidential is paramount. Teams administration helps set up security policies, manage data retention, and integrate with other security solutions, thereby aiding in compliance with regulatory standards.

- **Governance and policies:** Setting the rules of engagement for Teams usage—naming conventions, usage guidelines, and a code of conduct—assists in maintaining organizational coherence and responsibility.

- **App management:** Controlling which apps can be integrated and how they function within the Teams environment is a critical aspect. This involves scrutinizing app installations and monitoring app usage to maintain both compliance and performance.

- **Monitoring and troubleshooting:** Keeping an eye on the health of the Teams environment helps in preemptive problem-solving and ensures the platform runs smoothly.

- **Adoption and training:** The final pillar involves equipping users with the knowledge and resources to utilize Teams effectively. This drives the platform's adoption as a central collaboration tool within an organization.

Special Focus: Microsoft Teams for Education

This edition includes a segment dedicated to Microsoft Teams for Education—a specialized version of Teams tailored to meet the unique needs of educational institutions. This brings teachers and students together in a virtual space, ripe with opportunities for effective communication and learning.

What Will You Gain?

Effective Teams administration is the linchpin for establishing a secure, well-managed, and efficient collaborative environment. This book aims to equip you with the skills, best practices, and knowledge to optimize your organization's investment in Microsoft Teams. Whether your team is scattered across different time zones or just down the hall, effective administration will make the difference between mere communication and effective collaboration.

Welcome aboard this educational journey to unlock the full potential of Microsoft Teams. Let's begin.

Staying Updated: Navigating the Ever-Evolving Landscape of Microsoft Teams

As Microsoft Teams continues to develop, bringing new features and updating existing ones, it's important to have the most current information at your fingertips. While this book offers comprehensive coverage up to September 2023, we encourage readers to refer to the Microsoft Teams documentation (`https://learn.microsoft.com/en-us/microsoftteams`) for the latest features and updates. Additionally, our blog at `https://bloguc.com` regularly features updated content and insights into Microsoft Teams. Should you be unable to find a specific feature, option, or tab mentioned in this book, these resources can be invaluable. Moreover, for any queries or further assistance, feel free to reach out to us through the 'Contact Us' feature on our blog, and we will be more than happy to assist you.

CHAPTER 1

Microsoft Teams Overview

These days, the modern workforce has evolved to be more focused on team contributions than individual ones. As technology makes it easier to have remote and global teams, all users must be able to connect with each other. Microsoft Teams provides all that the modern workforce requires. Teams is a complete meeting solution, supporting sharing, voice, and videoconferencing and allowing users to meet from anywhere. Users can use Teams for all types of meetings—spontaneous or scheduled, formal or informal—with internal and external participants.

Specifically, Microsoft Teams is a unified communication and collaboration tool built on a cloud platform that combines various services for collaboration, such as chat, meetings, calling, and files. Teams is tightly integrated with Microsoft 365 and combines multiple workloads into a unified communication and collaboration system. Teams also offers integration capabilities for additional tools and third-party applications.

This chapter covers several introductory topics to get you started with Teams. At the end of this chapter, you will be able to describe the following:

- What Microsoft Teams is and what it is used for

- Microsoft Teams architecture and the different components involved

- How Microsoft Teams stores data and interacts with SharePoint Online and OneDrive for Business

- Where Teams stores chat conversations and how Teams interacts with Exchange

- Live events and their architecture

- What Microsoft Stream is used for and its architecture

- Teams Phone System overview and voice communication capabilities

- Teams licensing requirements and add-on licenses

- Teams integration with Microsoft 365 and third-party applications

© Balu N Ilag, Durgesh Tripathy, Vijay Ireddy 2024
B. N. Ilag et al., *Understanding Microsoft Teams Administration*,
https://doi.org/10.1007/979-8-8688-0014-6_1

What Is Microsoft Teams?

Microsoft Teams is a center for teamwork, offering chat, meeting, calling, content, Microsoft 365 applications, and third-party and custom applications all in one place. The definition of a *team* within Teams is "a collection of people, content, and tools surrounding different projects and outcomes within an organization," according to Microsoft. (See `https://learn.microsoft.com/en-us/microsoftteams/teams-channels-overview` for more information.)

Teams is a single product that provides extensive capabilities, starting with a conversation platform that allows team members to communicate via voice and video calls, with content sharing and application integration opportunities that teams and team members require to be successful in their technical journey.

Microsoft Teams Architecture

Microsoft Teams brings together Microsoft 365 services and intelligent communications in a single platform. Before using Microsoft Teams, you, as an administrator, support person, or even end user, must understand the design and how Teams services work together to provide a unified experience.

Understanding the Microsoft Teams architecture is crucial to managing teams and answering users' questions. One question users often ask is, "Where is my Teams data stored?" In Microsoft Teams, each feature stores data in a different service. Hence, it is also essential to understand Teams data storage.

The Microsoft Teams architecture is designed to provide a reliable and scalable collaboration platform for users. It comprises different components working together to enable seamless communication, collaboration, and data sharing. The following is an overview of the Microsoft Teams architecture:

- **Client applications:** Microsoft Teams is accessible through various client applications, including desktop applications for Windows and macOS, web browsers, and mobile apps for iOS and Android. These clients provide the user interface for interacting with Teams' features and functionalities.

- **Front-end services:** The front-end services handle user authentication, presence information, chat messages, and channel messages. They manage user requests and handle real-time communication features such as chat, voice, and video calls. The front-end services also provide the user interface elements, including channels, tabs, and notifications.

- **Back-end services:** The back-end services handle the processing and storage of data in Microsoft Teams. They manage tasks such as user provisioning, authentication and authorization, data storage, and retrieval. The back-end services ensure the security, scalability, and reliability of the platform.

- **Data store:** Microsoft Teams uses multiple data stores to store different types of data. The primary data store is Azure Cosmos DB, a globally distributed NoSQL database service. It provides high scalability, low latency, and strong consistency for storing chat messages, channel conversations, and other persistent data. Additionally, Teams leverages Azure Storage for storing file attachments, media, and other binary data.

- **Integration with Office 365 services:** Microsoft Teams integrates with various Office 365 services to enhance its collaboration capabilities. These services include SharePoint Online for document storage and collaboration, Exchange Online for email integration and calendar management, and OneDrive for Business for individual file storage.

- **Azure Active Directory (AAD):** Azure AD is the identity and access management service used by Microsoft Teams. It manages user authentication, authorization, and access control for Teams and ensures secure access to the platform's resources.

- **Media processing:** Microsoft Teams employs media processing services for handling audio and video streams during meetings and calls. These services facilitate real-time audio and video encoding, decoding, and transmission, ensuring optimal call quality.

- **Network infrastructure:** Microsoft Teams relies on Microsoft's global network infrastructure, including data centers and content delivery networks (CDNs), to deliver fast and reliable performance to users worldwide. The network infrastructure supports real-time communication, content delivery, and data synchronization.

It's important to note that the exact architecture and data store location may vary based on factors such as geographic location, deployment model (cloud or hybrid), and organizational requirements. Microsoft continuously updates and enhances the Teams architecture to improve performance, security, and the user experience. Office 365 and Microsoft 365 are used interchangeably, and there is some overlap between the two. Basically, Office 365 focuses primarily on productivity applications and cloud storage, and Microsoft 365 provides a broader set of tools and services, including Office 365, along with security and management features. Microsoft 365 is designed to offer a comprehensive solution for organizations looking for a unified productivity and security platform.

Teams Architecture Overview

It is essential to understand how Teams was architected and what is happening behind the scenes. As Figure 1-1 shows, from an architecture perspective, Microsoft Teams brings together Microsoft 365 services and intelligent communications (intelligent communications is the next-generation Skype service).

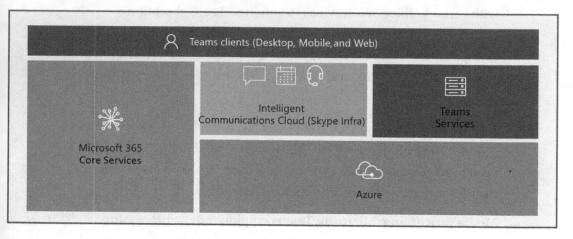

Figure 1-1. *Teams high-level architecture*

Components include Microsoft 365 Core Services such as Exchange Online, SharePoint, and OneNote; Microsoft 365 apps; and the intelligent communication cloud. These components enable all communication capabilities including persistent chat, meetings, and audio and video calls. Teams services are the services that the Microsoft

4

engineering team built to create Microsoft Teams. They orchestrate the layer that brings together all the other pieces, for example, attaching a Microsoft 365 group to a team created for easy membership management.

This is important because whenever someone creates a team, two things happen on the back end. First, creating a new team creates a Microsoft 365 group for membership management (that's how Teams manages membership); second, Teams creates a SharePoint team site for file sharing. This means every team has a Microsoft 365 group as well as a SharePoint team site. All these features build on the same scalable Azure infrastructure that Microsoft used in Teams. On the top are the Teams clients, which are available for all platforms, such as the Teams web app, Teams desktop client (Windows and macOS), Teams mobile app (iOS and Android), VDI, and the Teams Linux client.

In many cases, the Teams client sits on top of the Teams layer, which is more efficient because it directly talks to the Microsoft 365 services.

To help you deploy a Teams client in your organization, Microsoft has added the Microsoft Teams client to Microsoft 365 apps. In addition, Microsoft Teams has a semi-annual update channel.

What Is the Intelligent Communications Cloud?

You might be wondering what the intelligent communications cloud is and what it consists of. The *intelligent communications cloud* was formerly known as the next-generation Skype service; it is where the messaging, calling, meeting, people, configuration, and identity services reside (see Figure 1-2). It represents the next-generation evolution of Skype services that Teams uses for messaging and voice over IP (VoIP) calling. The intelligent communications cloud also contains the PSTN telephone network integration system, and another critical service is a unified presence for Teams.

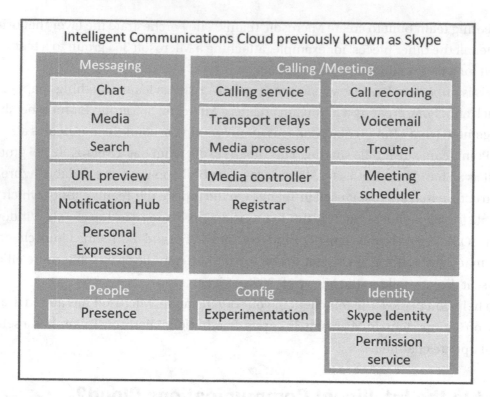

Figure 1-2. *Microsoft Teams next-generation services*

Note   There is no unified presence between Microsoft Teams and Skype for Business On-Premise.

The messaging stack handles messaging as well as media, which means images attached in chat go to blob storage. This stack also takes care of search functions and URL previews (when a user puts a URL in Teams chat, it shows a preview from the URL preview service). Notifications for tracking activity that happens in the team and personal expression services for emojis and stickers are handled in the messaging stack.

The calling and meeting stack includes call recording, calling, voice mail, Trouter, and meeting scheduler services.

The presence server gives user presence or availability information. The configuration service for experimentation and Identity for Skype (consumer) have different tokens than the Active Directory token for authorization and permission services.

Microsoft 365 Services Used by Teams

Figure 1-3 shows the Microsoft 365 components. Applications include OneNote, PowerApps, Planner, PowerPoint, Word, and Excel. Platform services include Exchange for email and calendars in Teams (this is the same as the Outlook calendar, as Teams uses graphs to retrieve the calendar). Additional features include Modern Groups, also known as Microsoft 365 groups, SharePoint for content collaboration, Stream (on SharePoint) for voice recording, OneDrive for Business for file sharing, and Information Protection, which provides a shield for these services. The final component is Power BI for data analytics.

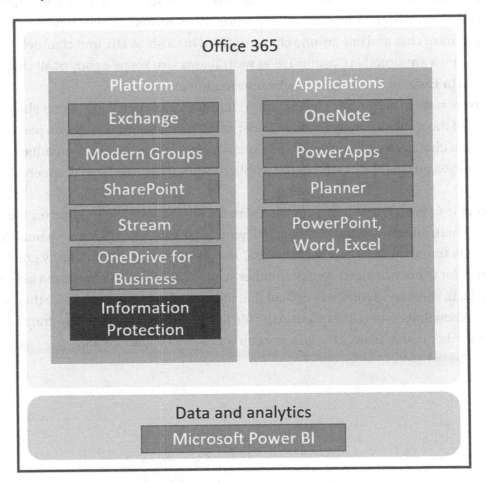

Figure 1-3. *Microsoft 365 services and Teams*

Microsoft 365 provides a great set of services and applications, but there is nothing that synthesizes all of the functionalities in one place as one application. Microsoft envisions Teams as the application that makes the whole greater than the sum of its parts. That's why Microsoft built Teams this way, to be the hub of Microsoft 365.

Microsoft Teams Capabilities and Their Data Storage Locations

Those supporting Teams users frequently get asked by users where their Teams data is stored, including conversations (chats), files that users shared, images, and others. Teams chat is persistent, which means it is stored in its entirety, and it uses its own storage. Group chat and one-to-one chat are stored in Cosmos DB, and channel conversations are stored in Cosmos DB as well. Teams also keeps a copy of all chat messages in Exchange, mainly to enable information protection.

If users have a one-to-one chat or group chat, Teams keeps a copy of that chat in the mailbox of the individuals (in a hidden folder of the user's mailbox) who are part of that chat. If you chat in channel teams, Teams keeps a copy of that chat in the mailbox of the Microsoft 365 group (in a hidden folder within the group mailbox) that is attached to that team.

Specific to files, Teams leverages OneDrive for Business and SharePoint for file storing. There are two scenarios shown in Figure 1-4. First, a file shared with one-to-one chat is stored on OneDrive for Business, and permission is automatically granted by Teams for users who need access. Another scenario is when a file is shared between channels. In this case, Teams will upload that file to the SharePoint team site that is created when that team is created, and the file permission is automatically granted to every member of that team. This is important for content collaboration.

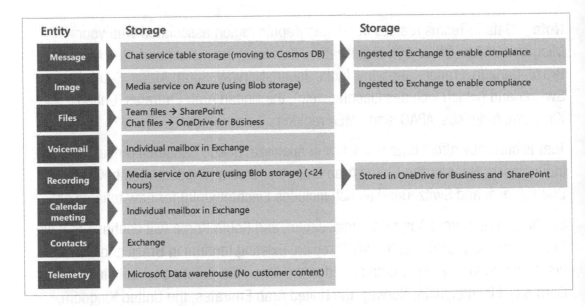

Figure 1-4. *Teams activity and data storage locations*

Voicemail is another critical feature that most enterprise users utilize. Voicemail is stored in the Exchange mailbox of the user who receives the voicemail, similar to Skype for Business. Calendars and Teams contacts are also stored in Exchange. A calendar is stored in an Exchange unified group mailbox that is created with the team, and a user's calendar is stored in an individual mailbox.

Where are users' meeting recordings stored? Whenever a user records a meeting, it is first stored in the same media storage where images are stored. The recording is then encoded and made available on Microsoft Stream for content collaboration. When Microsoft launched Teams, recordings were embedded and stored on the classic Stream. Microsoft merged the powerful capabilities of Stream and SharePoint to bring in Stream on SharePoint to use native video capabilities in Microsoft 365. With the new architecture, all the meeting recordings scheduled within a user calendar, including ad hoc meetings, one-to-one calls, external calls, PSTN calls, and group calls, are stored in OneDrive for Business for the user who initiated the recording. All the meeting recordings scheduled within a channel calendar are stored in the SharePoint document library of the team.

The Teams telemetry is stored in the Microsoft data warehouse without any customer content such as email address and contact numbers.

Note   Data in Teams resides in the geographic region associated with your
Microsoft 365 or Office 365 organization. Currently, Teams supports the Australia,
Brazil, Canada, France, Germany, India, Japan, Norway, South Africa, South Korea,
Switzerland (which includes Liechtenstein), the United Arab Emirates, United
Kingdom, Americas, APAC, and EMEA regions.

Teams currently offers data residency in Australia, Brazil, Canada, France, Germany,
India, Japan, Norway, the United Arab Emirates, United Kingdom, South Korea,
South Africa, and Switzerland (which includes Liechtenstein) for new tenants only.

Existing tenants from Australia, India, Japan, and South Korea will continue to have
their Teams data stored in the APAC region. Existing tenants in Brazil and Canada
will continue to have their data stored in the Americas. Existing tenants in France,
Germany, Liechtenstein, Norway, the United Arab Emirates, the United Kingdom,
South Africa, and Switzerland will have their data stored in the EMEA region.

Now that you understand how many components are involved in the Teams
architecture, the next important question comes from the technical community: how
does Microsoft Teams intermingle with Microsoft 365 technologies?

Teams delivers multiple functionalities, including persistent chat, online meetings,
voice and video calls, calendars, content sharing, and many more. All these features
come from underlying technologies, but as an admin, you must know how this
technology interaction works. When a user creates a team, on the back end it creates a
new Microsoft 365 group, SharePoint Online site, and document library to store team
files. Exchange Online shares a mailbox with the calendar, and a OneNote notebook is
automatically provisioned for the team.

Microsoft Teams Logical Architecture

In Figure 1-1, you saw the different components of Teams and how they communicate
with each other. Figure 1-5 demonstrates the logical architecture of Teams. The Teams
client is the interface to access Teams services in real time for communication and
collaboration for teams. The Teams connector provides a novel way to integrate third-
party apps.

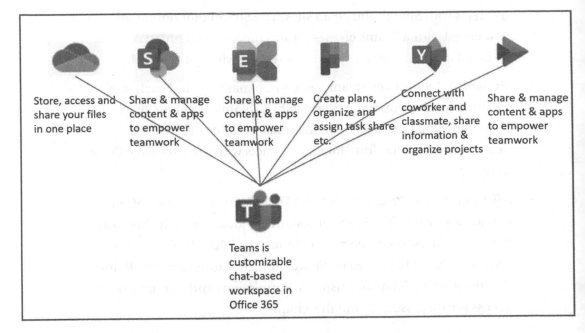

Figure 1-5. *Teams interaction with underlying services*

Microsoft 365 Groups and Teams are tightly integrated. For example, when a user creates a team from an existing Microsoft 365 group, that group's membership, site, mailbox, and notebook, if any, are merged in Teams. If the Microsoft 365 Groups and Teams integration breaks, then the Office group will not materialize in Teams. That is why Microsoft 365 and Teams are tightly integrated.

- *OneDrive for Business:* OneDrive for Business is mainly used for storing personal user documents until they are shared with others. From a Teams perspective, when a user shares a file in one-to-one chat, which is stored on OneDrive for Business, permission is automatically granted by Teams for the user who needs access. OneDrive for Business also stores recordings initiated in ad hoc or scheduled meetings, group calls, one-on-one calls, and external calls.

- *SharePoint Online:* This is mainly used to store Teams files that are shared within channel and team sites. When a team creates a SharePoint site, it is automatically provisioned. Once a file is shared within a team, the access permission is automatically granted by Teams to all team members. The Teams file tab therefore directly interacts with SharePoint Team sites. The SharePoint online site associated with a Teams channel stores meetings recorded or initiated in an ad hoc or scheduled meeting within a channel.

- *Exchange Online:* Every team has a group mailbox, and each team member has an individual user mailbox. Teams meetings scheduled by an individual are stored on their mailbox and calendar. The Teams calendar therefore directly interacts with the Exchange Online mailbox.

- *Microsoft classic Stream/Stream on SharePoint:* The classic Stream service was used for creating and sharing videos securely. Microsoft is retiring the classic Stream on February 15, 2024. All the videos are now created in Stream on SharePoint and stored in SharePoint Online and OneDrive for Business. Permissions and role-based access are discussed later in this chapter.

Microsoft Teams Depends on Other Services

You just saw how the Teams logical architecture works with Microsoft 365 services. Teams does have specific dependencies with other services (see Figure 1-6); for example, Teams chat features directly interact with the chat service in Microsoft 365, one-to-one chat is stored in the user mailbox, and group chat is stored in the Teams group mailbox. Chat is therefore dependent on Exchange Online. Teams files and wikis are dependent on SharePoint team sites. Teams meetings and calls are dependent on next-generation Skype calling and meeting services, meeting calendars are stored in the user's mailbox, and files (one-to-one sharing) depend on OneDrive for Business.

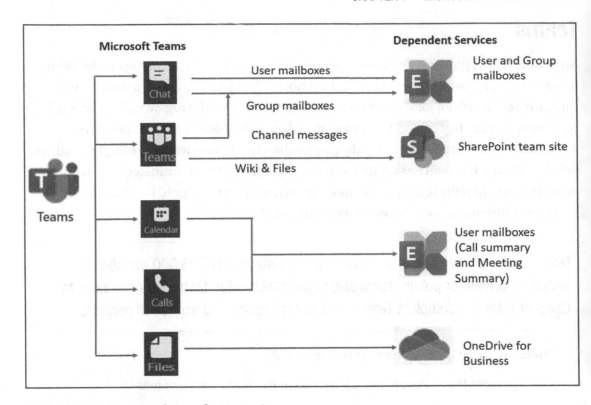

Figure 1-6. *Teams-dependent services*

Note   SharePoint Online is a requirement for using OneDrive for Business. Users cannot store and share files on the channel without SharePoint Online and OneDrive for Business.

Teams and Channels

Let's talk more about teams and channels.

Teams

Microsoft Teams provides a tool set that a team requires to execute project tasks. When a user creates a team, they will be asked to choose the option to create a private team (only invited users can join) or a public team (anyone from the organization can join). As a team owner, they can add members and designate them as a team owner for administration. We recommend adding more than two team owners to mitigate a single point of failure. If a team has a single owner and that owner is terminated or leaves the organization, then the team will not have an owner to administer it. For this reason, having a minimum of two owners is recommended.

Note   As of this writing, a team can have a maximum of 25,000 members, including private or public teams and organization-wide teams. You can refer to Chapter 8 for the complete Teams feature limitations and expiration periods.

There are three types of teams (see Figure 1-7).

- *Private team:* People need permission to join this type of team.

- *Public team:* Anyone in your organization can join this type of team.

- *Org-wide team:* Everyone in your organization automatically joins this team.

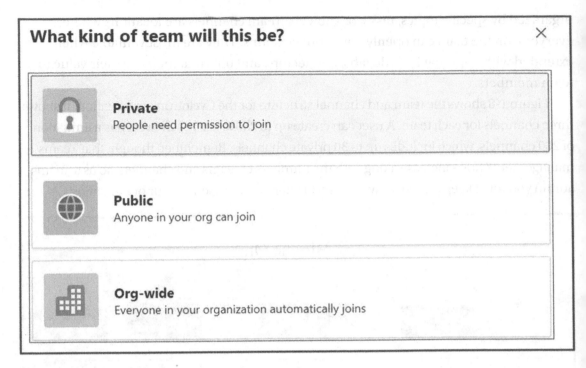

Figure 1-7. *Team types*

Note   Regular users cannot create organization-wide teams. Only global administrators can create org-wide teams, and currently, an org-wide team is limited to organizations with no more than 10,000 users. There is also a limit of five org-wide teams per tenant, and this limit includes archived teams.

Team creation and management are covered in Chapter 2.

Channels

A team is a collection people who gather to perform a project for their organization. That project might have multiple subtasks, so performing these individual tasks requires conversations, calls, or meetings. Each task might have separate documentation requirements. To maintain these separate tasks, Teams provides a dedicated section called a *channel*. Channels are dedicated sections within a team that keep conversations organized by specific topics, tasks, or subjects. Team channels are locations where everyone on the team can openly have conversations. They are most valuable when extended with apps that include tabs, connectors, and bots that increase their value to team members.

Figure 1-8 shows the team and channel structure for the Cyclotron organization. It shows three channels for each team. A user can create up to 250 teams; each team has a limitation of 200 channels, which includes up to 30 private channels. Remember, though, that Teams management efforts increase along with the numbers of teams and channels, so as a Teams admin you must keep track of how teams and channels are used in your organization.

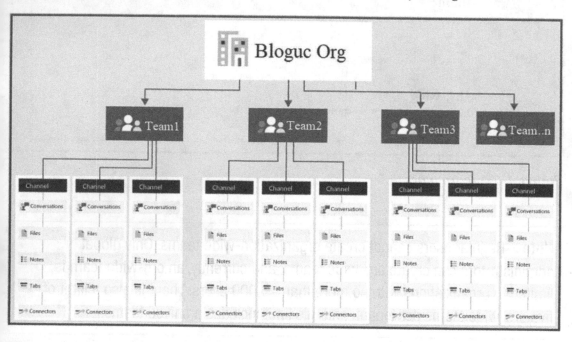

Figure 1-8. *Team and channel structure*

There are three types of channels (see Figure 1-9).

- *Standard channel:* The standard type of channel is accessible to everyone on the team, including team members and guest members.

- *Private channel:* Private channels are accessible only to a specific group of people within the team.

- *Shared channel:* Shared channels are accessible to external users by Azure AD B2B Direct Connect. The external members of the channel have access only to the shared channel resources.

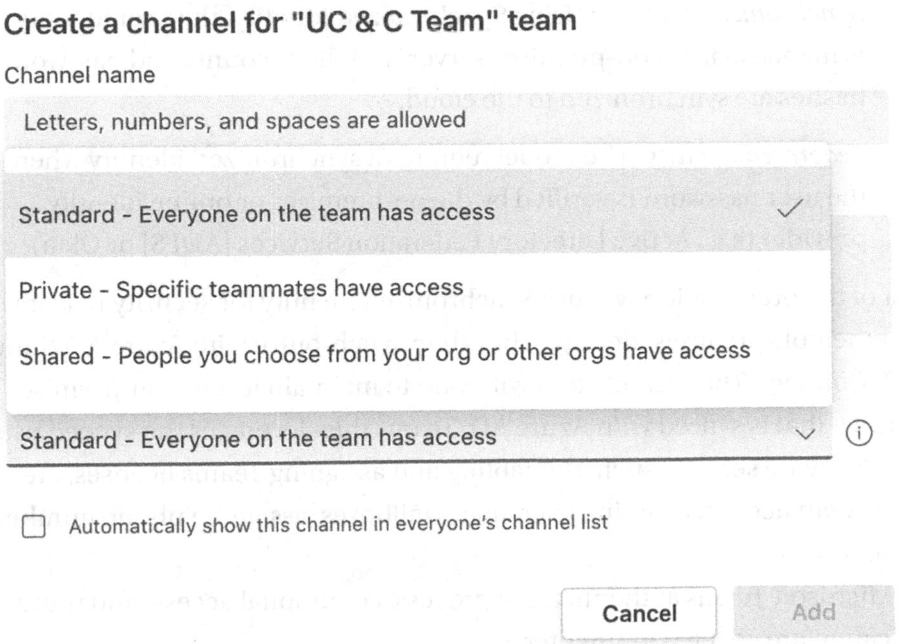

Create a channel for "UC & C Team" team

Channel name

Letters, numbers, and spaces are allowed

Standard - Everyone on the team has access   ✓

Private - Specific teammates have access

Shared - People you choose from your org or other orgs have access

Standard - Everyone on the team has access   ⌄   ⓘ

☐   Automatically show this channel in everyone's channel list

Cancel   Add

Figure 1-9. *Team channel types and their uses*

Channel use and management are covered in Chapter 2.

How Does Microsoft Teams Manage Identities?

Microsoft Teams is a cloud-only service, which means users who access Teams must have a cloud identity. It does not mean teams require a cloud-only identity. Teams does support all identity models that are available with Microsoft 365. Teams leverage identities stored in Azure Active Directory (Azure AD), which combines core directory services, application access management, and identity protection into a single solution.

Today Microsoft Teams supports all the identity models that are available in Microsoft 365, including Cloud Identity, Synchronized Identity, and Federated Identity.

- *Cloud Identity model:* Using the Cloud Identity model, a user is created and managed in Office/Microsoft 365 and stored in Azure AD, and the password is verified by Azure AD.

- *Synchronized Identity:* Using Synchronized Identity, the user identity is managed in an on-premises server, and the accounts and password hashes are synchronized to the cloud.

- *Federated Identity:* The model requires a synchronized identity where the user password is verified by the on-premises or online identity provider (e.g., Active Directory Federation Services [ADFS] or Okta).

Most of the organization will use Synchronized Identity for security reasons, as users maintain their on-premises identity. They then synchronize with Azure AD through Azure AD Connect. The organization will want to maintain its own on-premises identity as the source that is synced with Azure AD. Teams then leverages the synced user identity to provide services such as enabling and assigning Teams licenses, creating a Phone System license, enabling Exchange mailboxes, assigning phone numbers, and so on.

The Microsoft Teams authentication process, conditional access, and multifactor authentication are covered in Chapter 2.

Tabs, Files, and Connectors in Teams

The channel tabs, files, and connectors improve the user experience and allow users to configure their frequently used applications to expedite application access.

Tabs

Tabs allow team members to access services and content in a dedicated space within a channel or in a chat. Tabs let a team work directly with tools and data and have conversations about those tools and data, all within the context of the channel or chat.

Team owners, as well as team members, can add tabs in the team channel (standard, private, and shared), channel chat, and private chat (one-to-one and group) to use Microsoft cloud applications and third-party applications in the team to manage the information they use frequently. For example, Microsoft Planner is a useful tool to plan and prioritize project tasks. Adding a planner as a tab allows users to access their assigned project tasks within the team.

Files

Files allow users to upload new files and share them with team members or access existing files uploaded by another team member in Teams.

Remember, in every channel, the Conversations and Files tabs are created by default. In every private chat, the Conversations, Files, Organization, and Activity tabs are created by default. Apart from the built-in tabs, the team owner and members can design and add custom tabs. Refer to the Microsoft official documentation to learn how to design a custom tab: `https://docs.microsoft.com/en-us/microsoftteams/built-in-custom-tabs`.

Connectors

Connectors are used in Teams to get the service updates and content from the third-party services into a Teams channel. These connectors are used to quickly get the information from third-party services in real time and into a Teams channel workspace for easy access. See also `https://learn.microsoft.com/en-us/microsoftteams/office-365-custom-connectors`.

Microsoft Stream and Live Event

Microsoft Stream is a Microsoft enterprise video solution that is part of Office/Microsoft 365. Using Stream, customers can securely create and deliver videos to their organization. Microsoft provides a portal to upload, share, and discover videos that can be used for things such as executive communication or training and support. Microsoft Stream allows users to upload videos, search groups and videos, broadcast their live events, and categorize and organize videos. Users can also create a group and stream that allows users to embed video in Microsoft Teams. The classic Stream was a stand-alone product isolated from the rest of the M365 services. The classic Stream supported live events and meeting recordings by embedding videos and links into M365 Apps links, Teams, and Yammer. To deeply connect Stream to Microsoft 365 collaborative apps and services, Microsoft introduced Stream (on SharePoint). Stream (on SharePoint) will make enterprise video an integral part of Microsoft 365. All the videos are now available as files within SharePoint/OneDrive for Business, and tools are available in the UI to work with the videos.

The intelligent video experience built into Stream (on SharePoint) will allow users to build, discover, edit, upload, and manage the videos just like any other file in a SharePoint site; the built-in tools and services within the Stream (on SharePoint) allow users to generate transcripts, use closed captions, and add chapters manually to enable users to navigate to the focused topic quickly. The tool also allows users to collaborate on the video with comments and add custom titles, thumbnails, and descriptions.

Stream on SharePoint has advanced video-sharing capabilities like files within SharePoint. Based on the organization's sharing permissions, the videos can be shared internally, with guests, or with external users. Stream on SharePoint carries forward the analytics features available with the classic Stream. Features such as trends of viewership, unique visitors over a period, which part of the video is more visited, usage insights, popular content, and overall data usage and traffic are available. With Stream on SharePoint, security and compliance are built in. As the data resides in SharePoint, video availability will be in more than one regional data center with support for multigeographic locations for data storage. Similar to SharePoint files, basic information governance such as retention, DLP, legal, and eDiscovery for videos are available. The Microsoft Graph Files API is also available for basic video operations.

Recordings on Stream (on SharePoint)

Microsoft Teams has rich capabilities of audio, video, and desktop sharing in calls and meetings. These meetings or calls can be recorded for future viewing. These recordings can be initiated from one-on-one calls, scheduled/ad hoc meetings, VoIP calls with external people, or scheduled/ad hoc meetings within a Teams channel and shared securely within the organization. Depending on the type of meeting and calls, the recording is stored on OneDrive for Business or SharePoint.

By default, the channel meetings will be stored in the recordings folder in the Files tab of the channel/Document library of the channel in the SharePoint site in Teams. All the users in the channel are granted permission to view the recording. All the recordings from nonchannel meetings, group calls, and one-on-one calls are stored in the recording folder in the OneDrive for Business directory of the person who started the recording. The recording opens up in Stream (on SharePoint) irrespective of where it's stored. Stream (on SharePoint) allows users to use the tools to edit, modify, and share videos.

There are many ways users can share videos within an organization. Each meeting type has role-based access and default permissions. The details of permissions and role-based access will be explained later in the book.

For organizations that are still using Stream (classic), Microsoft recommends migrating the content from Stream (classic) to Stream (on SharePoint). The migration tool from Microsoft can help with the process and is available at `https://aka.ms/ StreamMigration`. As of August 15, 2023, no new videos can be uploaded to Stream (classic), which is set to retire on February 13, 2024. The embed code will stop working on February 15, 2025.

Microsoft Stream Architecture

The architecture of Microsoft Stream, which is integrated with SharePoint, involves multiple components working together to provide a robust video streaming and sharing platform. Here is an overview of the Microsoft Stream architecture:

- **User interface:** Microsoft Stream offers a user-friendly interface accessible through web browsers and mobile applications. Users can upload, view, search, and interact with videos using the intuitive interface.

- **Azure Media Services:** Microsoft Stream leverages Azure Media Services, a cloud-based media processing and streaming platform, for video encoding, transcoding, and adaptive streaming. Azure Media Services ensures that videos are delivered in various formats and resolutions to provide optimal viewing experiences across different devices and network conditions.

- **Storage and content delivery:** Videos uploaded to Microsoft Stream are stored in Azure Storage, which provides scalable and durable storage for video assets. Azure Content Delivery Network (CDN) is used to deliver videos efficiently to users worldwide, reducing latency and improving playback performance.

- **SharePoint integration:** Microsoft Stream is tightly integrated with SharePoint, a document management and collaboration platform. The integration allows videos to be stored and managed within SharePoint document libraries. Users can access and search for videos directly within SharePoint sites, enhancing content discoverability and collaboration.

- **Video processing pipeline:** When a video is uploaded to Microsoft Stream, it goes through a processing pipeline that includes tasks such as video encoding, thumbnail generation, metadata extraction, and transcript generation. These processes enable features such as automatic video indexing, transcription search, and thumbnail previews.

- **Security and permissions:** Microsoft Stream leverages Azure Active Directory (AAD) for user authentication and authorization. It honors SharePoint permissions, ensuring that access to videos is controlled based on user roles and permissions. Administrators can configure security settings, including restrictions on sharing and external access, to maintain data privacy and compliance.

- **Integration with Office 365 services:** Microsoft Stream integrates with other Office 365 services, such as Microsoft Teams and Yammer, allowing users to share and discuss videos within these collaboration tools. Integration with Microsoft PowerPoint enables users to embed videos directly into presentations.

- **Search and discovery:** Microsoft Stream incorporates robust search capabilities, making it easy for users to find videos based on titles, descriptions, tags, and even spoken words within the video content. Users can also browse videos by categories, channels, and creators, improving content discovery and navigation.

Overall, the architecture of Microsoft Stream combines the capabilities of Azure Media Services, Azure Storage, SharePoint, and other Office 365 services to provide a secure, scalable, and feature-rich video streaming and sharing platform. The integration with SharePoint enhances content management and collaboration, while Azure Media Services ensures high-quality video encoding and delivery.

How Can I Access Stream (on SharePoint)?

Users can access and interact with a stream through the Stream portal at `https://stream.office.com/`. The new Stream mobile app is available on iOS and Android. These mobile-based applications can be used to view and replay recordings.

Where Is My Stream Data Residing?

Microsoft Stream presently hosts data in regions including the United States, Europe, Asia Pacific, Australia, India, United Kingdom, Canada, and the U.S. Government Community Cloud (GCC). Remember, if your tenant is located in one of these regions, then your organization's Stream data will also be located in that region. However, if a user lives in a region not listed, then Microsoft hosts Stream data in the closest tenant region. Microsoft is planning to host Stream data in a few other regions, including but not limited to China, Germany, and GCC-High/GCC-DoD.

Tip   To learn the data storage location in Stream, simply log in to Stream and then click About Microsoft Stream.

Microsoft Teams Live Event

Microsoft Teams provides unified communication and collaboration capabilities, including persistent chat, calling, meetings, and live events. Teams meetings are interactive meetings in which both the presenter and attendees can interact with optimal voice and video with application sharing. Teams meetings are limited to 1,000 attendees, though. When your organization wants to host a larger meeting, such as a broadcast events or organization-wide events with thousands of online attendees, that's where live events come in handy. Microsoft Teams, through live events, provides an option that enables users to expand their meeting attendees by broadcasting video and meeting content online to large audiences of up to 20,000 attendees.

A live event is created for one-to-many communications (one organizer or presenter to many attendees), where the host of the event conducts the interactions. Attendees, or the audience, views the content shared by the host or presenter. The attendees can watch the live or recorded events in Yammer, Teams, and Microsoft Stream, and they can also interact with the presenters using moderated questions and answers (Q&As) or a Yammer conversation.

Live Event Architecture

Figure 1-10 displays the high-level architecture of live events. The organizer organizes the live event in either Teams, Yammer, or Stream, depending on the production method chosen. It will be in Teams if all presenters are using the Teams client. If the production type chosen is an external app or device, the presenter can use a production app or tools like a media mixer, microphones, speakers, and so on. When more professional video equipment is used and the producer is using Teams or Stream to produce live events, all this content is sent over Office/Microsoft 365, which uses Azure Media Services, where it goes through the CDN to customers.

In Figure 1-10, you can see the certified third-party enterprise content delivery network (eCDN) providers (Kollective, Hive, Peer5, Ramp, and Riverbed), and the content can be viewed by all the attendees via the Teams client, Yammer, or Stream.

Note   eCDN use is not mandatory; however, it will help to save your enterprise's bandwidth.

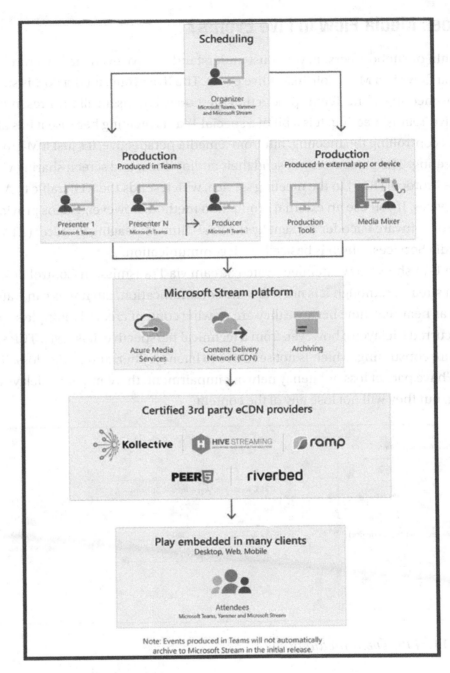

Figure 1-10. *Live event architecture*

How Does Media Flow in Live Events?

As an admin or support person, you must understand the live event architecture and how media flows in a Microsoft Teams live event. The live events media flow is similar to a Teams meeting. If the Teams production method was chosen, all the presenters will join a native Teams meeting. It is a bit of a special Teams meeting because it has all the presenters controlling the meeting, but from a media perspective, it's just a Microsoft Teams meeting. The presenters will send their audio, video, and screen sharing via Real-Time Protocol (RTP) to the meeting service, which sends the RTP traffic to Azure Media Services. If you use an external production method, however, videos provided by hardware or software encoder are sent by the Real-Time Messaging Protocol (RTMP) to Azure Media Services, which is basically RTP communication.

Figure 1-11 shows how attendees watch Stream via Transmission Control Protocol (TCP) as a stream. Although it is not real-time communication, attendees can watch a live event as near real-time because they are viewing content created multiple seconds after it occurred (delayed); however, from a technical perspective, it is just a TCP stream that they are consuming, which is not sensitive to latency, jitter, and packet loss. If attendees have packet loss or latency network impairment, there might be delays in streaming, but they will not lose any of the content.

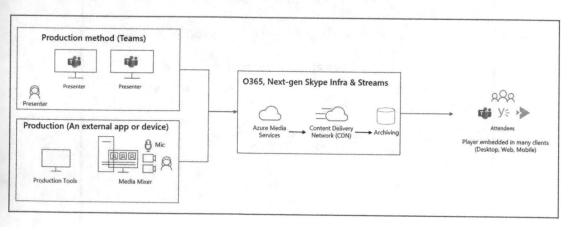

Figure 1-11. *Live event media flow*

How Does Microsoft Teams Live Events Work?

Live events are online meetings with audiences of up to thousands of concurrent viewers, where the presenter team shares audio, video, and content, and the audience views that content. In live meetings, there are specific key roles that perform different activities to run the live event successfully, and every role has different permissions assigned. Here is detailed information about each role:

- **Tenant admin:** The tenant admin has nothing to do with live event operation; however, the tenant admin can configure the live events settings for the tenant and set the right permissions.

- **Organizer:** The organizer of a live event is the person who schedules the event and ensures the event is set up with the right permissions for attendees and the event group, who will manage the event.

- **Producer:** The producer is a host of the meeting. This person is part of the event group, so they are invited to the event by the organizer. It is the producer's responsibility to ensure attendees have a great viewing experience by controlling the media sources that are sent to the live event. The producer actually decides whose audio and video goes live in the event.

- **Presenter:** The presenter is the person who presents audio, video, or a screen in the live event, or they might moderate the Q&A.

- **Attendee:** An attendee just views or watches the event live or on demand, either anonymously or authenticated. Attendees can participate in the Q&A.

You can schedule live events using different options. As a user or admin, you can schedule the live event in the Teams client, Yammer, or Stream. Producer options for the live event are using the Microsoft Teams client or using the external (third-party) encoder as the source used for production methods. If you are unable to schedule a live event and get an error message that indicates you do not have a live event meeting policy assigned, contact your organization admin to be able to schedule a live event.

How Does the Live Event Production Method Work?

You can produce a live event using two different methods: using Teams or using an external app or device.

Using the Teams Live Event

In a Teams live event, all audio, video, and content captured from a producer or presenter are joined into a Teams regular meeting. For example, presenters and the producer both join a Teams meeting and share audio, video, and content (see Figure 1-12).

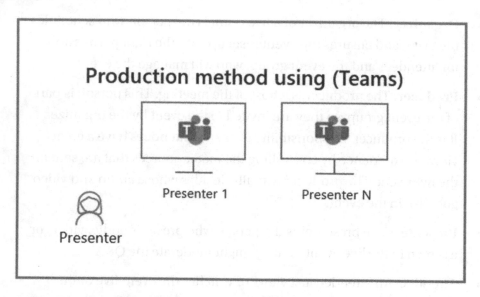

Figure 1-12. *Live event production through Teams*

Using an External App or Device

In an externally coded live event, audio and video come from an external hardware or software encoder (see Figure 1-13). All media comes in one stream and goes into the live event meeting; then it is broadcast to all attendees. Learn more about external encoders by visiting https://learn.microsoft.com/en-us/microsoftteams/teams-encoder-setup.

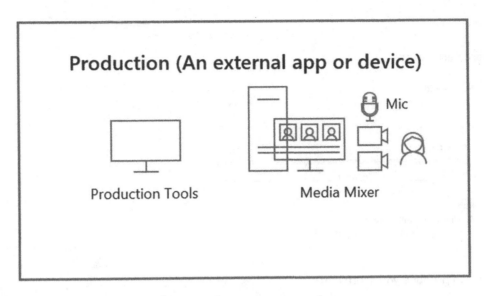

Figure 1-13. *Live event production through external apps*

How Do I Use Live Events Effectively with Minimum Knowledge?

Live events can be scheduled quickly in Teams, and users can present and produce live events from a macOS or Windows Teams client with one or more presenters, including application sharing. You can present from a Teams room system, or a presenter can join via phone dial-in to a live event using Teams audio conferencing. You, as a live event organizer, can control access to the public, including everyone from an organization or specific groups or people.

Organizing a live event is simple; you start by scheduling the event. As shown in Figure 1-14, scheduling a live event in Teams is straightforward. Just click Meeting, choose Live event, and set permissions such as public, org-wide, or people and group.

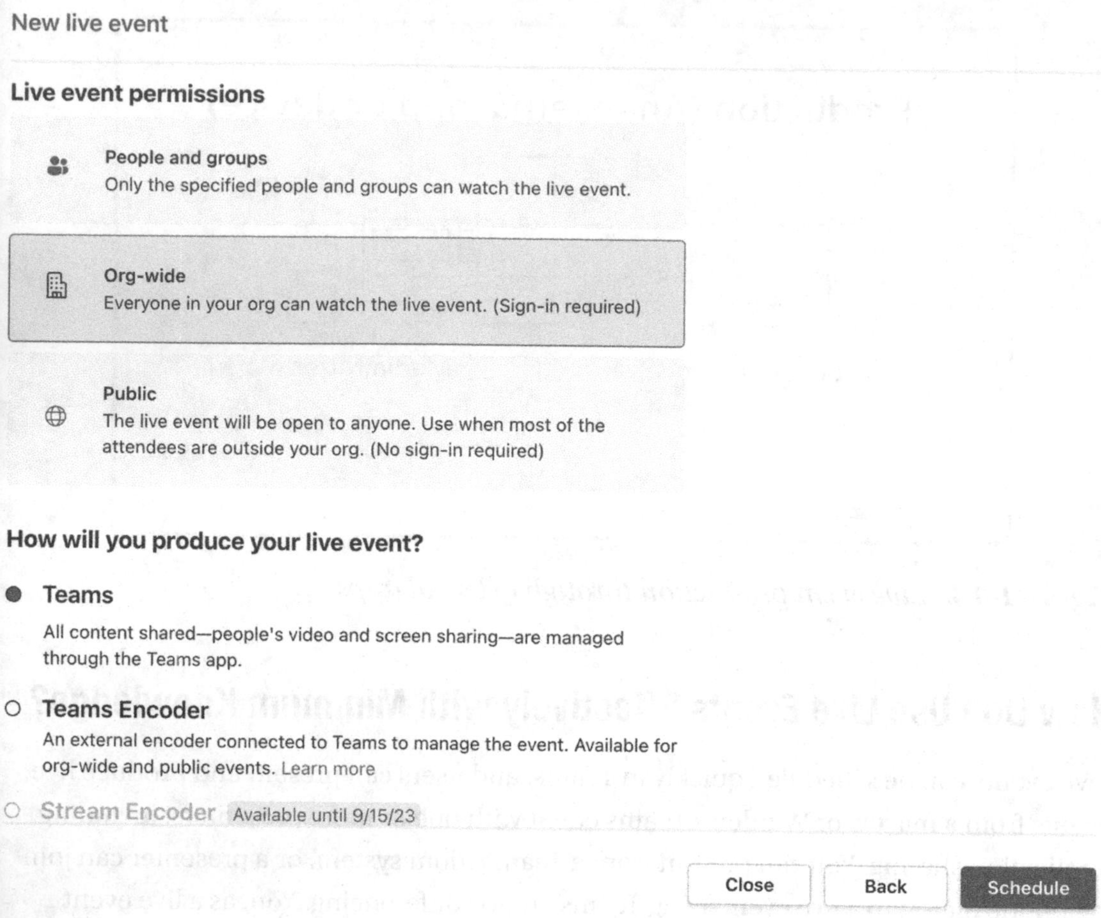

New live event

Live event permissions

👥 **People and groups**
Only the specified people and groups can watch the live event.

🏢 **Org-wide**
Everyone in your org can watch the live event. (Sign-in required)

🌐 **Public**
The live event will be open to anyone. Use when most of the attendees are outside your org. (No sign-in required)

How will you produce your live event?

● **Teams**
All content shared—people's video and screen sharing—are managed through the Teams app.

○ **Teams Encoder**
An external encoder connected to Teams to manage the event. Available for org-wide and public events. Learn more

○ Stream Encoder Available until 9/15/23

[Close]   [Back]   [Schedule]

Figure 1-14. Scheduling a live event

The next step is to set the production type by selecting a quick-start or third-party production, and then click Schedule to get the event scheduled. The examples in this book use the Teams meeting as a production type, as shown in Figure 1-15.

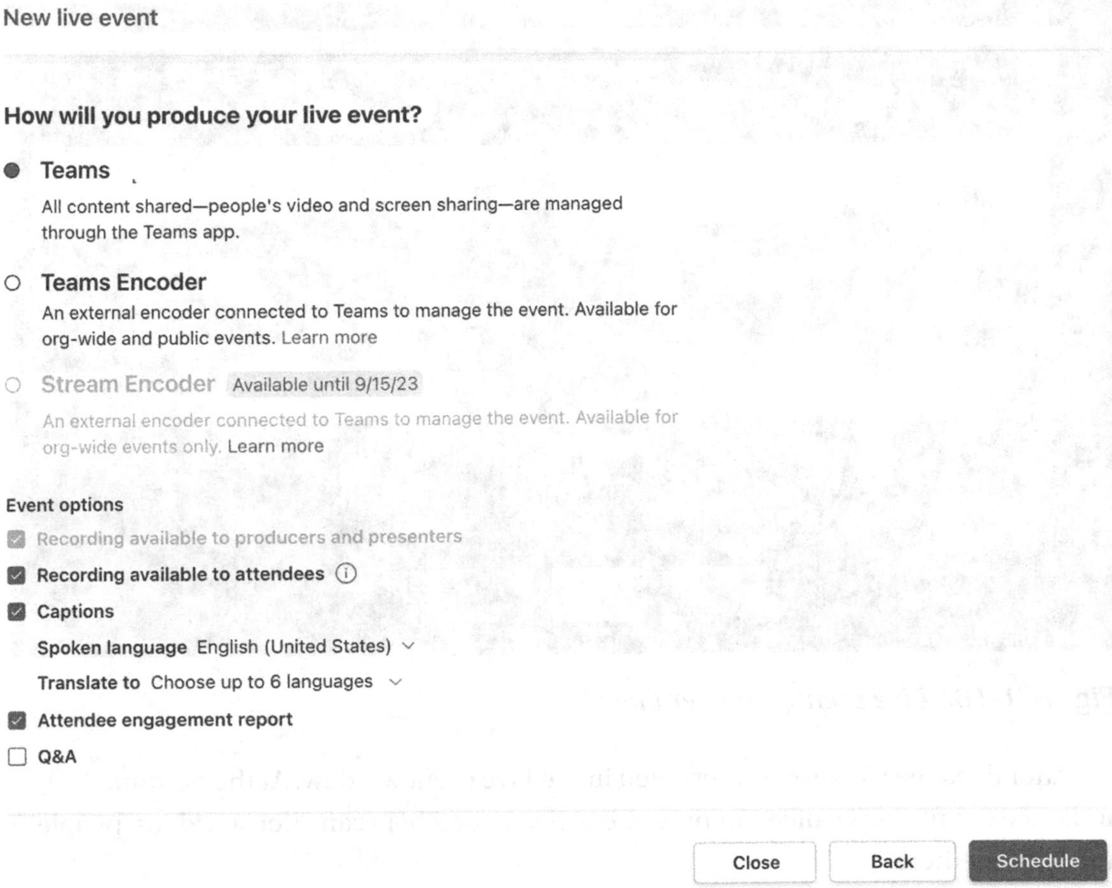

New live event

How will you produce your live event?

● **Teams**
All content shared—people's video and screen sharing—are managed through the Teams app.

○ **Teams Encoder**
An external encoder connected to Teams to manage the event. Available for org-wide and public events. Learn more

○ Stream Encoder   Available until 9/15/23
An external encoder connected to Teams to manage the event. Available for org-wide events only. Learn more

Event options

☑ Recording available to producers and presenters

☑ **Recording available to attendees** ⓘ

☑ **Captions**

Spoken language English (United States) ⌄

Translate to Choose up to 6 languages ⌄

☑ **Attendee engagement report**

☐ Q&A

[Close]   [Back]   [Schedule]

Figure 1-15. *Live event production type*

After the live event is scheduled, the event team can join the event. Figure 1-16 shows the producer view. At the top, you can see two windows, Queue and Live event. On the left you can always queue contents to follow, like presenting a slide after a video. Once the presentation is ready to begin, click Send Live so everyone can see it.

Figure 1-16. *Live event producer view*

Attendees see whatever is presented in the Live event window. At the bottom, audience members see different presenters. Event members can choose videos, people, and content there.

If the presenter decides to schedule a meeting with the Q&A Manager to allow users to ask questions, then they can open or hide the Q&A Manager or keep it open all the time. The producer can send broadcast messages or share links during the session.

Teams Voice and Video Call and Meetings

Let's discuss Teams voice and video calls as well as meetings.

Teams Voice and Video Calls

Microsoft Teams provides voice and video call capabilities with desktop sharing so that users can elevate their chat conversation to voice and video calls. Teams allows users to have a private, one-to-one call or group calls. This voice and video calling happens through VoIP. Teams voice and video calling has some network requirements, which are covered in Chapter 3 as part of organization preparation and readiness.

Users can make calls to their colleague as internal users, as well as external users, including guests, federated, and external phone calls. All of the following user types can leverage voice and video call capabilities:

- **Teams call with internal users:** These include corporate users who have an account in the same tenant, for example, `bilag@bloguc.com` or `balu@cyclotron.com`.

- **Call with guest users:** Guest users are invited to join one or two teams in your organization. That's why they are called guest users. Users who have a guest account in the same tenant can utilize calls and chat in Teams.

- **Call with federated (external) users:** Federated users are users of a different organization with federation configured between both organizations, where both organizations are using Teams, for example, `bloguc.com`, `cyclotron.com`, and `microsoft.com`.

- **Phone (PSTN) call (audio only):** Teams allows users to make phone calls (voice only) using PSTN. However, the user must have enabled enterprise voice to make a phone call.

Microsoft Teams Meetings

Meetings provide a rich set of capabilities using various devices. Teams meetings provide premeeting, in-meeting, and postmeeting opportunities to collaborate with members.

Microsoft Teams provides a better meeting experience by allowing users to organize easily, prepare, and follow up using pre- and postmeeting experiences like collaboration before the meeting using chat and Meet Now. Users can be more engaged and productive by sharing content from desktop (Mac and Windows) or mobile devices and by adding video to meetings for face-to-face video. Finally, Teams meetings offer excellent audio and video quality and reliability from desktop (Windows and Mac) and mobile devices, phones, or conference rooms. The meeting organizer can also invite external users to join via a web browser. All this meeting experience builds on the foundation of the next-generation Skype infrastructure and Microsoft 365 services including Exchange, SharePoint, Stream, Microsoft AI, and Cortana.

For example, when a user schedules a Teams meeting to discuss project work, they will have the opportunity to engage in premeeting collaboration. For example, before the meeting, they can use the chat that is automatically created for that meeting to discuss the agenda and share files. Members of the team can join from all kinds of different devices, such as desktops (Windows or Mac), Android phones, and iOS phones. Office users can join from a Surface hub, if available. They can also share links, audio, video, and desktops so that everyone can see project materials. Also, they can record meetings so that users who were not able to join live can review the recording as well as any notes created during the meeting and continue collaborating in chat.

Teams meetings have some network requirements, and the network has a high impact on user experience, so it is essential to get the network right to have the best experience possible. Network assessment and bandwidth planning details are covered in Chapter 3.

There are different types of meetings that you can create in Microsoft Teams, depending on the nature of the meeting.

- **Private meeting:** This is for when the user wants to have a meeting with individual people but does not want the meeting to be visible to others.

- **Channel meeting:** When channel meetings are scheduled in the Teams team, all team members are automatically invited, and they will have access to the discussion and meeting recording if that meeting is recorded.

- **Ad hoc meeting (Meet Now):** For use when the user wants to meet immediately without previously scheduling a meeting.

Teams meetings have a meeting life cycle that includes after the experience before, during, and after the meeting.

- **Premeeting:** Users can have contextual conversations in Teams, set up meeting options, and prepare and discuss content before the scheduled Teams meeting.

- **During meeting:** Users can use face-to-face video, follow the action, share content, use applications within a meeting, record the meeting with transcription, and join from a Teams room quickly.

- **Postmeeting:** Users can play back meetings with transcription recordings and meeting chat, and they can share notes and engage in postmeeting chat and collaboration.

Microsoft Teams offers a range of meeting capabilities and features designed to optimize the meeting experience for users. Here's an overview of these features:

- **Scheduling and invitations:** Users can schedule meetings directly within Teams or through integration with Outlook. Meeting invitations can be sent to participants, including internal and external attendees, with details such as date, time, agenda, and meeting links.

- **Joining meetings:** Participants can join meetings through various options, including clicking the meeting link in the invitation, using the Teams app on desktop or mobile devices, or joining via web browser as a guest.

- **Audio and videoconferencing:** Teams supports high-quality audio and videoconferencing, enabling participants to have real-time conversations and collaborate effectively. Participants can choose to join with audio only, enable video, or share their screen during the meeting.

- **Meeting controls:** Meeting organizers have access to a range of controls to manage the meeting, such as muting/unmuting participants, managing video visibility, and controlling participant permissions for screen sharing and chat.

- **Collaboration and content sharing:** Teams offers seamless collaboration through features such as real-time co-authoring of documents, screen sharing, and virtual whiteboarding. Participants can share their screen, present PowerPoint slides, collaborate on shared documents, and use the whiteboard for brainstorming and annotation.

- **Meeting recording:** Teams allows meeting organizers to record meetings, capturing audio, video, and shared content. The recordings can be shared with participants for later reference or with those who were unable to attend the meeting.

- **Live captions and transcription:** Teams supports live captions during meetings, providing real-time text captions that can enhance accessibility and comprehension. Transcription services can also be enabled to provide a recorded text version of the meeting for reference.

- **Meeting notes:** Users can capture and share meeting notes directly within Teams, using apps like OneNote or the built-in Wiki tab. This allows participants to collaborate on shared notes, capture action items, and maintain a record of discussions.

Teams meeting call quality is optimized through various mechanisms, including the following:

- **Intelligent network optimization:** Teams uses intelligent algorithms to adapt to network conditions, optimizing audio and video quality based on available bandwidth and network congestion.

- **Adaptive bitrate technology:** Teams dynamically adjusts the video quality based on the user's network connection, ensuring smooth video playback and minimizing buffering.

- **Network resiliency:** Teams leverages Microsoft's global network infrastructure, which includes data centers and content delivery networks, to provide reliable and resilient connectivity for meetings.

Premeeting collaboration experiences in Teams involve activities such as sharing meeting agendas, documents, and resources before the scheduled meeting. Participants can collaborate on shared files, make annotations, and provide feedback to ensure a productive discussion during the meeting.

Postmeeting collaboration experiences allow participants to continue discussions, access meeting recordings or transcripts, and review shared notes. Teams provides a persistent chat history for each meeting, allowing participants to refer to previous conversations and follow up on action items.

Overall, Microsoft Teams offers a comprehensive set of meeting capabilities that enable effective communication, collaboration, and productivity. Its features optimize the meeting experience, ensure call quality, and support premeeting and postmeeting collaboration to enhance the overall teamwork and productivity of users.

Who Can Attend the Teams Meeting?

As mentioned earlier, Teams allows internal (within the organization) and external (outside organization) participants, but there are more than just these two attendee types, and Teams allows all of them to join a Teams meeting. Depending on what type of attendee they are, however, they will have different information and options in the meeting.

- **Internal users:** These are corporate users who have an account in the same tenant, for example, balu@cyclotron.com.

- **Guest users:** These users are invited to join one or two teams in your organization; that's why they are called guest users. Users who have a guest account in the same tenant can join the Teams meeting.

- **Federated users:** Federated users are users of a different organization with federation configured between both organizations. Both organizations are using Teams, for example, cyclotron.com and microsoft.com.

- **Anonymous users:** Anonymous users have no account at all or an account in a tenant without a federation.

Remember that attendee type is determined at the meeting join time, and the user cannot change attendee type. For example, if a federated user forgot to sign in, that user will be treated as an anonymous user when they join a meeting. To join the meeting as a federated user, that user must leave the meeting and rejoin as federated by signing in.

Note   It is not possible to promote users from one attendee type to a different attendee type. However, it is possible to demote or promote attendees as presenters or attendees in a Teams meeting.

Teams meetings, including audio conferencing details, are covered in Chapter 4. External access (federation) and guest access details are covered in Chapter 5.

Teams Phone System Overview

Microsoft Teams provides cloud voice facilities that are provided from Microsoft 365 cloud services; additionally, it provides private branch exchange (PBX) functionality and options for connecting Teams infrastructure to PSTN. The Phone System is the terminology that Microsoft uses for call control and PBX functionality.

What Does the Phone System Require?

The Phone System provides call control and PBX Phone System capabilities that allow an organization to connect the Teams infrastructure to a PSTN provider so that Teams users can make phone calls to external PSTN numbers. PSTN is essential because it is reliable and universal, and most important, it is deeply integrated with human life. Wherever users go, a phone is there, even when they are in an elevator or in the field somewhere.

Using the Phone System in Teams allows users to place and receive phone calls, transfer calls, and mute or unmute phone calls. Calling functionality in Teams supports the required Phone System features, such as call answering and initiating (by name and number) with an integrated dial pad, call holding and retrieving, call forwarding and simultaneous ringing, call history, voicemail, and emergency calls. Users can also use a different range of devices to establish calls, including mobile devices, headsets connected to a computer, and IP phones.

Now you understand why calling and the Phone System is required in Teams. However, you should learn about the different components involved in Teams calling and Phone System that combine to provide complete Teams Phone System capabilities.

- **Phone System:** Teams Phone System is an add-on license on top of the Teams license that provides phone calling capabilities in Microsoft Teams. It turns on everything from simultaneous ringing to call queues to emergency calls.

- **Calling plans:** These provide a way to connect Teams Phone System to the PSTN using Microsoft as a service provider through a Calling Plans license.

- **Operator Connect partners:** These provide a way to connect Teams' Phone System to the PSTN using Microsoft-certified Operator Connect partners as a service provider through a Phone System license and calling rates defined by the Operator Connect partners.

- **Direct routing:** If an organization wants to continue with its existing PSTN service provider and wants to connect that on-premises session border controller (SBC) to the Teams Phone System, that can be achieved in Phone System through the Teams direct routing functionality. It is another way to connect to the PSTN, where customers interface with existing PSTN services to Teams through an on-premises SBC.

- **Teams Phone Mobile:** With Teams Phone Mobile, a user's SIM-enabled phone number can also be used as a Teams phone number. The operators for Teams Phone Mobile are available in the Teams admin center.

- **PSTN:** The PSTN is the aggregate of the world's circuit-switched telephone networks that are operated by national, regional, or local telephone operators, providing infrastructure and services for public telecommunication. The PSTN needs to integrate Teams modern software with modern coding technique.

Teams Phone System details, including phone number management, direct routing, phone number porting, and call queues, are covered in Chapter 4.

Microsoft Teams Licensing Requirement Overview

Microsoft has designed Teams licensing to provide maximum flexibility for the organization. After using basic Teams features including chat, internal calls, and content sharing, you as an admin can buy add-on licenses for more features, such as audio conferencing, phone system, calling plans, and Microsoft Teams rooms.

Table 1-1 shows all Microsoft 365 subscriptions that include Microsoft Teams.

Table 1-1. *Teams Licenses*

Small Business Plans	Enterprise Plans	Education Plans	Developer Plans
Microsoft Essentials	Office 365/Microsoft 365 Enterprise E1	Office 365/Microsoft 365 A1	Office/Microsoft 365 Developer
Microsoft 365 Business Basic	Office 365/Microsoft 365 Enterprise E3	Office 365/Microsoft 365 A3	
Microsoft 365 Business Standard	Office 365/Microsoft 365 Enterprise E5	Office 365/Microsoft 365 A5	
	Microsoft 365 Enterprise F1		
	Office 365/Microsoft 365 Enterprise F3		

Note   All supported subscription plans are eligible for access to the Teams web client, desktop clients, and mobile apps.

Here are the answers to some common questions:

- Is Teams Meeting included in all Microsoft 365 subscriptions?
    - Yes, Teams Meeting is included in all the Office 365/Microsoft 365 subscriptions.
- What Teams license do I need to use for Teams audio conferencing?

    Audio conferencing is included in the E5 license with unlimited toll dial-in and 60 minutes/user/month dial-out to Zone A countries. For all the other subscriptions, audio conferencing is available for free as a stand-alone license with unlimited toll dial-in and 60 minutes/user/month dial-out to U.S. and Canada phone numbers.

- Do I need a separate license to use the Teams Phone System and calling?

  - Yes, you need an add-on Microsoft Teams phone license or E5 license that includes a Microsoft Teams Phone on top of that. To use phone calling, you need the Calling Plans/Operator Connect service. For Calling Plans/Operator Connect, each user will need Phone System licenses and additionally for calling plans, each user needs a domestic and international calling plan to allow them to make and receive phone calls.

- Is a Microsoft Stream license included in all Microsoft 365 subscriptions?

  - A Microsoft Stream license, which provides the ability to record Teams meetings, requires E1, E2, E3, A1, A3, A5, Microsoft 365 Business Basic, Business Standard, or Microsoft Teams Essential. Remember, this is the case for both the organizer and the user who initiates the recording.

- Do I need any license to schedule a live event?

  - Yes, to schedule a live event, you need the following licenses:

    - An Exchange Online mailbox

    - An Office/Microsoft 365 Enterprise E1, E3, or E5 license or an Office/Microsoft 365 A3 or A5 license

    - A Microsoft Teams license

    - A Microsoft Stream license

By default, Teams is turned on for all organizations. Administrators can assign user licenses to control individual access to Teams and allow or block which content sources are used.

Teams Integration with a Third-Party Application

Microsoft Teams provides greater customization within the Teams client by changing color themes and notifications within Teams for the channel tab, connector, bot, and Microsoft apps, as well third-party apps integration. All this communication, collaboration, and customization happens securely with compliance capabilities.

Microsoft Teams provides a default set of apps published by Microsoft and by third parties that are designed to connect users, support productivity, and integrate commonly used business services into Teams. For example, users can use the Planner app to build and manage team tasks in Teams. These apps are available to organizations through the Teams Store. By default, all apps, including custom apps that your organization has submitted through the Teams Store approval process, are turned on for all users. Although all Microsoft apps and all custom apps are available by default, you can turn the availability of individual apps off. For efficiency, an organization-wide setting is available that allows you to turn all custom apps on or off for your entire organization.

Teams apps are a way to collect one or more capabilities into an app package that can be installed, upgraded, and uninstalled. The capabilities include the following:

- Bots

- Messaging extensions

- Tabs

- Connectors

Apps let you find content from your favorite services and share it right in Teams. They help you do things such as pin services at the top of a channel, chat with bots, or share and assign tasks. Microsoft recommends that you add featured apps such as Planner in your initial Teams rollout. Add other apps, bots, and connectors as you increase Teams adoption.

Managing apps policy and administration is covered in Chapter 5.

Summary

In this introductory chapter, we provided a comprehensive overview of Microsoft Teams, the cornerstone of collaborative work in the modern digital workspace. We delved into the architecture of Teams, highlighting its various components and how they interact to create a unified communication platform. Our journey started with an exploration of the symbiotic relationship between Teams, SharePoint Online, and OneDrive for Business. We examined how these services work in tandem to facilitate seamless file sharing and collaboration within Teams.

Subsequently, we ventured into the relationship between Teams and Exchange, examining how they integrate to bring email and calendar functionalities into the Teams interface. This consolidation allows for streamlined communication and scheduling within the same platform.

We also introduced the concept of live events, presenting the architecture and how it uses Microsoft Stream to broadcast video and meeting content to large online audiences. We further detailed Microsoft Stream's architecture and how it powers video streaming in Teams.

A crucial segment of this chapter focused on the Teams Phone System. We detailed its ability to provide voice communication capabilities, replacing traditional telephony hardware with a cloud-based system integrated into Teams. In terms of licensing requirements, we outlined the necessary licenses needed to deploy Teams within an organization, including add-on licenses for additional functionalities.

Finally, we discussed the powerful integration possibilities that Teams offers, enabling connections with a myriad of Microsoft 365 services and third-party applications. This feature reinforces the versatility of Teams, making it a central hub for all workplace tools and applications.

Upon completion of this chapter, you should have a robust understanding of Microsoft Teams and its essential functionalities. This foundation will serve as a steppingstone as we delve deeper into Teams' capabilities in subsequent chapters.

CHAPTER 2

Managing and Controlling Microsoft Teams

Balu N Ilag[a], Durgesh Tripathy

[a] Tracy, CA, USA

As a Microsoft Teams administrator, you play a pivotal role in setting up, managing, and optimizing the collaborative environment within your organization. This chapter provides an overview of the various policies and functionalities you can control, ensuring smooth collaboration, data security, and user-friendliness. Managing and administrating the Microsoft Teams experience involves overseeing a variety of tasks and functionalities to ensure a smooth, secure, and efficient collaborative environment for users within your organization.

We'll cover the following in this chapter:

- **Microsoft Teams Authentication process:** We'll cover how Microsoft Teams user authentication works and the Microsoft Teams sign-in process.

- **Teams and channels:** We'll cover how to deploy and manage teams and channels and how to manage the Teams desktop client.

- **Live events and Streams:** We'll show how to configure and manage live events and Microsoft Stream.

- **Administrative tools:** We'll show how to manage Teams using the Microsoft Teams admin center.

- **Messaging policies:** As an administrator, you can create and modify messaging policies that govern chat behaviors and options. This includes settings such as read receipts, URL previews, editing and deletion permissions, and GIF settings, among others.

© Balu N Ilag, Durgesh Tripathy, Vijay Ireddy 2024
B. N. Ilag et al., *Understanding Microsoft Teams Administration*,
https://doi.org/10.1007/979-8-8688-0014-6_2

- **Teams policies for channel creation and discovery:** Admins design policies to manage team creation and set up parameters that influence who can create teams, the naming conventions used, and how teams can be discovered by users.

- **Organization-wide settings for Teams:** These settings affect all teams within the organization, impacting features such as guest access, Teams for Education settings, and Teams Live events.

- **Private channel creation management:** Administrators manage who can create private channels, allowing for controlled, private collaboration within Teams without creating entirely new teams.

- **Email integration control:** Admins can enable or disable the ability to send emails to a channel in Teams, providing another way for users to share information.

- **File-sharing functions:** You can control the file-sharing functions from the Teams client, such as cloud storage options and the use of third-party storage providers.

- **Channel moderation setup:** Admins can set up channel moderation in Teams to control who can start new posts and control whether team members can reply.

- **Understanding the Teams admin center:** The Teams admin center is the primary portal for managing and configuring Teams; it provides tools for managing the entire life cycle of Teams from creation to archiving.

- **Additional tools:** We'll also cover Microsoft Azure Active Directory Center, the Microsoft 365 admin center, and the Microsoft 365 Security and Compliance Centers.

- **Teams management through PowerShell:** We'll also cover PowerShell in this chapter.

As a Teams administrator, understanding these tools and policies will enable you to create an environment that fosters collaboration, respects user needs, and aligns with organizational policies and compliance requirements. This knowledge is crucial to leverage the full potential of Microsoft Teams, driving efficiency and productivity within your organization.

Microsoft Teams Authentication

How does Microsoft Teams user authentication work? Microsoft Teams uses Azure AD as the identity service to authenticate Teams users. Azure AD is purely a cloud-based identity and access management service for Office 365, but that doesn't mean you cannot use the on-premises Active Directory Domain Service (ADDS) identity service. You as an admin need to synchronize your on-premises user identities to Azure AD so that the user identities will be available in the Azure AD cloud, and then it will authenticate users using their user principal name (UPN) and password. For example, my UPN is balu@cyclotron.com, and I can sign into Teams using my password.

Azure AD is a crucial part of the overall deployment of Teams and how it works. The million-dollar question is, what is Azure AD, and how does Teams leverage it?

As mentioned, Azure AD is the cloud-based identity and access management service for Microsoft Office 365 services. Microsoft Teams leverages identities stored in Azure AD for collaboration and communication purposes. From a license requirements standpoint, Teams and Azure AD are included in a large number of licensing bundles, including small business plans like Office 365 Business; enterprise plans like Microsoft 365 Enterprise E1, E3, and E5; education plans like Office 365 Education; and developer plans like Office 365 Developer.

Another critical question is, how do I manage cloud identity with Azure AD? Because Teams is a cloud-only service and highly dependent on Azure AD, as a Teams admin you must know how cloud identity is managed in your Teams deployments and specifically how Teams credentials are managed and securely stored. Azure AD provides managed identities, which offers access to Azure and Office 365 resources for custom applications and services including Teams. The facility provides Azure services with an automatically managed identity in Azure AD. You can use this identity to authenticate to any service that supports Azure AD authentication, such as Teams, Exchange Online, SharePoint, OneDrive, and Yammer.

Now that you know the importance of Azure AD, how do you make sure the access permissions that users have are protected? Because Azure AD allows users to collaborate with internal users (within the organization) as well as external users (users outside the organization, like vendors or partners), it's crucial that you as an admin regularly review users' access to ensure that only the right people have access to cloud resources. This can be achieved through an Azure AD feature called *access reviews*, which enables organizations to effectively manage group memberships, access to enterprise applications, and role assignments.

Note   Using the Azure AD access review feature requires an Azure AD Premium P2 license.

Microsoft Teams Sign-in Process

Microsoft Teams, like other Microsoft 365 services, uses Azure AD for authentication. As mentioned, Azure AD is Microsoft's cloud-based identity and access management service. Microsoft Teams leverages Azure AD for authentication, and it uses Modern Authentication for sign-in and to protect login credentials. What is Modern Authentication, and why does Teams use it? It allows Teams apps to understand that users have previously registered and logged in with their credentials (like their work or institutional email and password) somewhere else, so they are not required to enter credentials again to initiate the Teams app.

Remember, Teams has clients for Windows, macOS, iOS, Linux, and Android, so the user experience might be different for each client platform. Another reason for the experience variation is the authentication method that an organization chooses. Usually there are two authentication methods: single-factor authentication (based on the user account and password) and multifactor authentication (involving more than one factor, such as verification over the phone or with a PIN along with a user account and password). The user experience will differ depending on the authentication method.

As a Teams admin, you must understand the different login experiences for Windows and Mac users.

Figure 2-1 shows a logical representation of the sign-in process with a call flow.

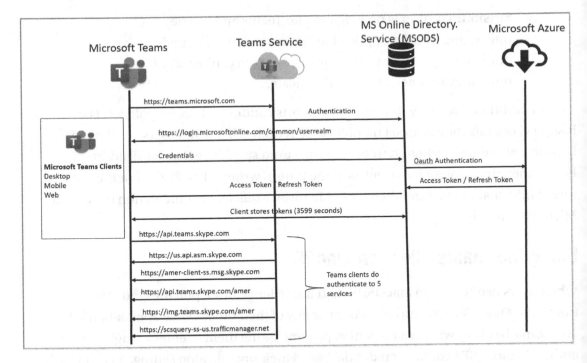

Figure 2-1. *Teams client sign-in process*

Here's a simplified explanation of the sign-in process:

1. **User sign-in:** When a user tries to sign into Microsoft Teams, the application directs the user to Azure AD for sign-in. The user enters their username and password in the sign-in page hosted by Azure AD.

2. **Authentication:** Azure AD verifies the user's credentials against the stored user information. If multifactor authentication (MFA) is enabled for the user's account, Azure AD will also prompt for additional verification, such as a phone call, text message, or mobile app notification.

3. **Authorization:** If the user's credentials are correct, Azure AD issues a security token, known as an *access token*, back to the Teams application. This token contains information about the user's identity, the application, and permissions or scopes.

4. **Access:** The Teams application uses this access token to authorize the user and grant them access to the service.

5. **Session:** The user is now signed into Teams and can begin interacting with the application. Their session will remain active until they sign out or until their access token expires, at which point they may need to re-authenticate.

For additional security, Teams also supports conditional access policies. For instance, organizations can set up policies to require MFA when users are signing in from unfamiliar locations or block sign-ins from specific regions or IP addresses. Remember, this content is current as of the time of writing (late 2023). For the most recent information, you should refer to Microsoft's official documentation or contact Microsoft directly.

Using the Teams Client on macOS

When users use Teams on macOS, their Teams client cannot pull the credentials from their Office 365 enterprise account or any of their other Office applications. As an alternative, they will get a credential prompt asking them to enter a single-factor authentication (SFA) or MFA credential based their organization setting. As soon as they enter the required credential, Teams will sign them in, and they won't have to enter their credential again. Instead, Teams will allow them to automatically sign in on the same macOS desktop.

Using Teams on a Windows Machine

When users are using Teams on a Windows desktop, their Teams client will be able pull the credentials from their Office 365 enterprise account or any of their other Office applications (where they are already logged in), so users are not required to enter their credentials. If a user is not signed on to their Office 365 enterprise account anywhere else, when they start Teams, they are asked to provide either SFA or MFA, depending on what their organization requires.

Specific to the Windows Teams client, when users using their domain-joined desktop log in to Teams, they might be asked to go through an additional authentication prompt depending on whether their organization has chosen to require MFA or their desktop already requires MFA to sign in. If their desktop has previously required MFA to sign in, then users will automatically be signed into Teams as soon as it opens.

Note   If a user signs out (by clicking their avatar at the top of the app and then signing out) from the Teams app after completing the Modern Authentication process, to log in again, they need to enter their login credentials to start the Teams app.

Keep in mind that Modern Authentication is offered for each organization that uses Microsoft Teams, so if users are unable to complete the login process, there could be a problem with their Microsoft 365 tenant, domain, or enterprise account. If federation is used, for example, authentication happens with a client on-premises AD via secure AUTH, ping, or OKTA (these are the third-party identity providers).

Step-by-Step Teams Client Login Process

Here is the login process:

1. First, the user enters a login credential in the Teams client, and the application directs the user to Azure AD for sign-in. The user enters their username and password on the sign-in page hosted by Azure AD.

2. The Teams client resolves the DNS record to `teams.microsoft.com`. Once it resolves, the Teams client connects to Teams services.

    A. **Name:** s-0005.s-msedge.net

    B. **Addresses:** 2620:1ec:42::132, 52.113.194.132

    C. **Aliases:** teams.microsoft.com, teams.office.com, teams-mira-afd.trafficmanager.net and teams-office-com.s-0005.s-msedge.net

3. Teams services redirect the Teams client to Azure AD to get a token from Azure AD. If the user's credentials are correct, Azure AD issues a security token, known as an *access token*, to the Teams application. This token contains information about the user's identity, the application, and permissions or scopes.

4. Azure AD gives the client access token to the Teams application. Then the Teams application uses this access token to authorize the user and grant them access to the service.

5. The Teams client gives the access token to the Teams cloud service.

6. The Teams user is logged in to Teams services. The user is now signed in to Teams and can begin interacting with the application. Their session will remain active until they sign out or until their access token expires, at which point they may need to re-authenticate.

Managing and Configuring MFA and Conditional Access for Teams

What is conditional access in authentication? Azure AD conditional access is a Microsoft security feature that helps you control and secure access to your cloud apps, based on specific conditions from a central location. It is essentially an "if-then" policy execution framework for access control. When a user tries to access a resource, conditional access policies are evaluated to determine whether the request is allowed, is denied, or requires additional authentication steps.

As you learned, Microsoft Teams leverages Azure AD for authentication, and there are two different kinds of authentication: SFA and MFA. However, an organization can consider securing the authentication by allowing Teams access through specific conditions such as the use of a specific operating system or version, client version, network subnet, and so on. That's where conditional access policies come in handy. Fundamentally, a conditional access policy is a set of regulations for access control based on several specifications such as client version, service, registration procedure, location, compliance status, and so on. Conditional access is used to decide whether the user's access to the organization's data is allowed. By using conditional access policies, you as an admin can apply the right access controls when needed to both keep your organization secure and allow users to access applications.

Here's a simple explanation of how Azure AD conditional access works:

- **Conditions:** These are the circumstances under which the policy applies. Conditions can include user or group membership, IP location information, whether the device is marked as compliant or not, and the perceived risk level of the sign-in attempt, among others.

- **Assignments:** After defining the conditions, the administrator assigns what should happen if these conditions are met. This involves defining users and groups, cloud apps, and conditions such as sign-in risk levels, device platforms, and more.

- **Access controls:** If the conditions are met, then certain controls are applied that are defined under access controls. Controls can either allow access, require additional authentication challenges (such as multifactor authentication), limit access, or even block access entirely.

For instance, you might set a policy that requires users to authenticate via MFA if they are trying to access sensitive resources and are not on the corporate network. This dynamic, risk-based approach to access control helps to secure your organization's resources while ensuring that valid users can stay productive and don't get locked out of their work.

Note   Conditional access policies are applicable to all Microsoft Modern Authentication–enabled applications including Teams, Exchange Online, and SharePoint Online.

How Conditional Access Flow Works

Azure AD conditional access allows users to work from anywhere securely through condition-based access. It allows IT admins to define access rules based on their organizational requirements to allow access for applications through different conditions. It is designed to enforce access policies based on specific conditions when users attempt to access applications such as Microsoft Teams. Here's how it might look for Teams:

1. **Access request:** A user tries to access Microsoft Teams, through the desktop app, web app, or mobile app.

2. **Authentication:** The user authenticates themselves via Azure AD. This could be via username and password, MFA, biometric data, or other means.

3. **Policy evaluation:** Once the user is authenticated, Azure AD checks all conditional access policies applicable to the user. It assesses the user's role, location, device status, sign-in risk, etc., and checks them against the conditions set in the policies.

4. **Enforce requirements:** If the user and their context meet the conditions of a policy, Azure AD then checks whether the user fulfils the requirements of that policy. For example, the policy may require the user to use a device that is compliant with company policies, complete MFA, or connect from a trusted network.

5. **Access decision:** Azure AD then makes a decision to either grant or deny access based on the requirements of the policy. The access can be granted fully, granted with limitations (like read-only access), or completely denied.

6. **Access to Teams:** If Azure AD grants access, the user can access Microsoft Teams with the level of access granted by the policy (e.g., full or limited). If access is denied, the user cannot access Teams.

This flow ensures that access to Microsoft Teams is granted in a secure manner, only under conditions that align with the organization's security policies. It provides a balance between security and productivity by enforcing security requirements without hindering user access to the tools they need for their work. Figure 2-2 shows signals on the right side: the access condition based on user and locations, device used with version, application used with app version, and real-time risk. The access attempt gets verified, and based on the signals, the access attempt is allowed or MFA is required for a blocked access attempt. If access is allowed, the user connects their application client to the back-end service.

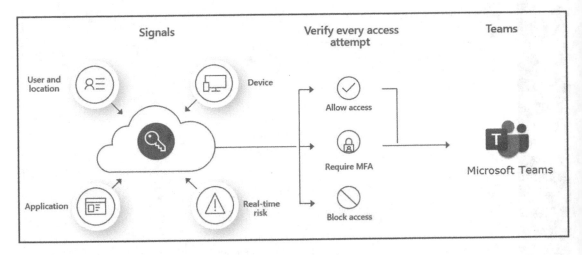

Figure 2-2. *Azure AD conditional access*

Managing Teams and Channels

In Chapter 1 you learned about teams and channels and their structure, as well as how to create organization-wide teams. We will now address how to manage teams and channels.

Before undertaking team management, you should understand how to create teams and channels effectively. To create a team, log in to Microsoft Teams and follow these steps:

1. Open the Teams app, log in, and click Teams, as shown in Figure 2-3. Then select "Join or create a team."

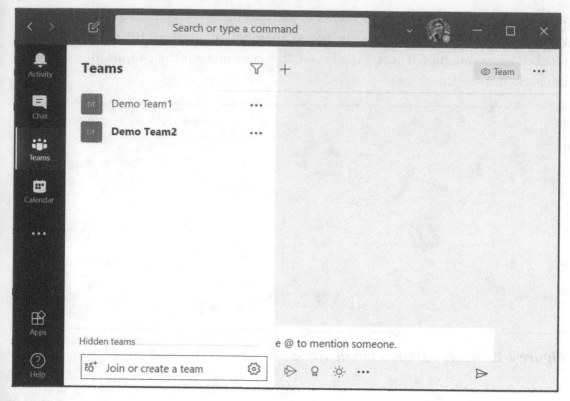

Figure 2-3. *Creating or joining teams*

2. Once the "Join or create team" page opens, click "Create team," as shown in Figure 2-4.

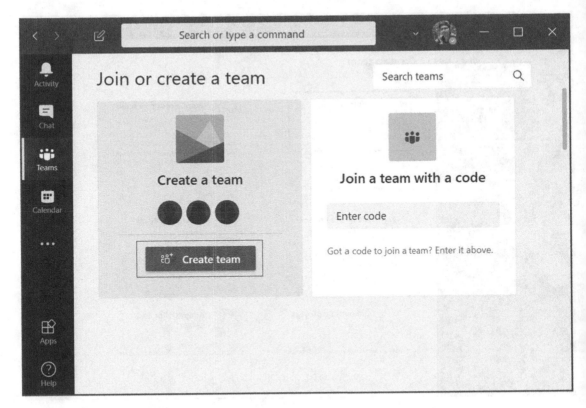

Figure 2-4. *Create team button*

3. Once you click "Create team," it will display options to create a
    team from scratch or create a team using an existing Office 365
    group. In Figure 2-5, we're building a team from scratch.

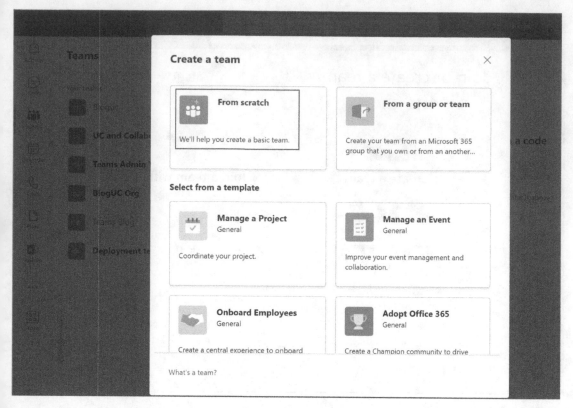

Figure 2-5. *Selecting an option to create a team from scratch or using an existing Office 365 group*

4. After selecting "From scratch," you will be asked to choose what kind of team you will create, private or public. Remember for private teams, users need permission to join; for public teams, anyone in the organization can join without team owner permission. Figure 2-6 shows the selection of a private team.

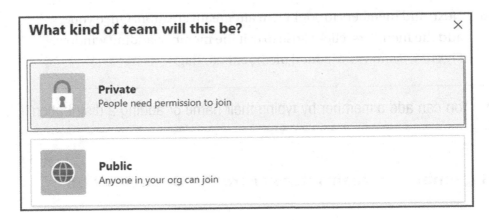

Figure 2-6. *The team type can be private or public*

5. Next, provide an appropriate name and description for your team. Figure 2-7 shows the name Teams Administration Book Revision project and an appropriate description. Click Create; Teams will take some time to create the new team. Remember, creating a team means it will also create an Office 365 group, SharePoint Team site, and Exchange mailbox. Provisioning all these requires some time.

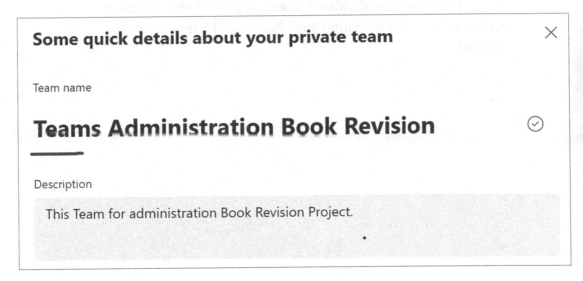

Figure 2-7. *Team name and description*

6. Next, add members to your team after team creation. Once you add the members, click Close to exit the member-adding window. Figure 2-8 shows the added member Balu Ilag.

Note   You can add a member by typing their name or adding a distribution list.

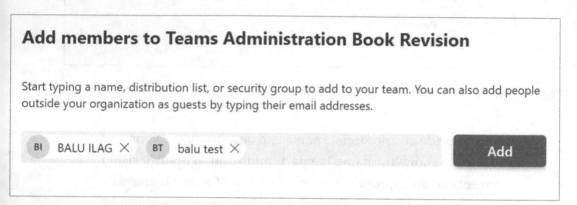

Figure 2-8. *Adding a team member*

7. Now you will can see that the team has been created, and a default channel was also added, called General. Figure 2-9 shows a team named Teams Administration Book Revision with the General channel.

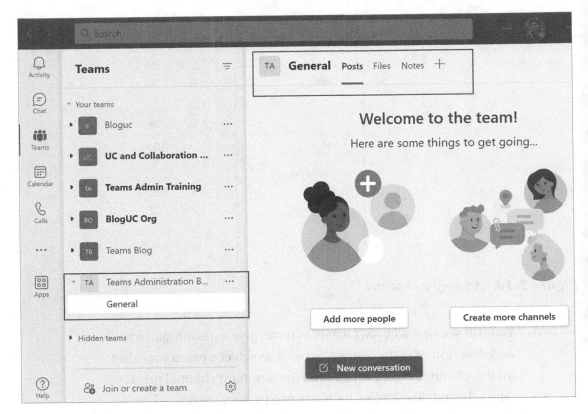

Figure 2-9. *Team created with General channel*

Note   Creating a new team will automatically create a General channel that you cannot disable or delete.

Creating a Channel in a Team

Creating a team and channels in Microsoft Teams is a relatively simple process. Here's how you do it:

1. Navigate to the team for which you want to create a new channel and then click the three dots next to the team name.

2. From that list, select "Add channel" to create a channel, as shown in Figure 2-10.

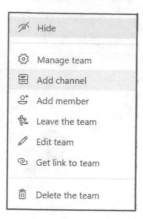

Figure 2-10. *Adding a channel*

3. You will see new windows where you can give a meaningful name and description to the channel, as well as select a privacy mode for the channel. Figure 2-11 shows the Standard channel privacy type selected. Remember, there are two privacy modes.

    • *Standard channel:* This privacy mode allows anyone (team members) to access this channel's content within the team. These channels are open and available to all members of the team. They are best for topics that everyone in the team needs to see. For example, in a team dedicated to a project, there might be standard channels for Design, Development, Marketing, etc.

    • *Private channel:* A private channel is a subset of a team and can be accessed only by certain members of the team. Private channels are useful for sensitive discussions or when a project or topic involves a subgroup of the larger team. For example, in a team dedicated to a project, there might be a private channel called Project Leaders, where only the leadership team can access and discuss higher-level strategies.

- *Shared channel:* Microsoft Teams' shared channels offer spaces where collaboration can take place with individuals who may not belong to the same team. Access to these channels is limited to those who have been designated as owners or members. Although individuals with guest status in your organization's Azure Active Directory cannot be included in a shared channel, Azure AD B2B Direct Connect provides a mechanism for inviting people outside your organization to participate in a shared channel.

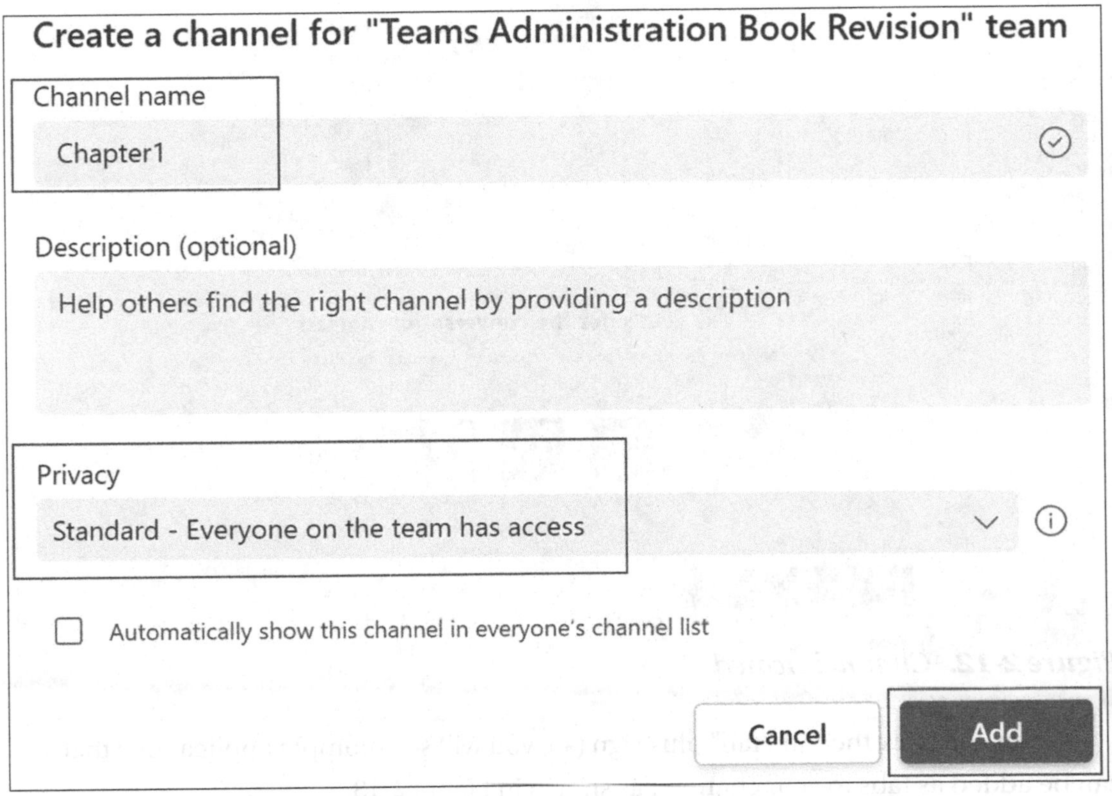

Create a channel for "Teams Administration Book Revision" team

Channel name

Chapter1

Description (optional)

Help others find the right channel by providing a description

Privacy

Standard - Everyone on the team has access

☐ Automatically show this channel in everyone's channel list

Cancel   Add

Figure 2-11. *Creating a channel and selecting a privacy mode*

Click Add to create the channel. Figure 2-12 shows the newly created channel and default features available to use. After channel creation, it will show the Posts and Files wiki tabs. You can add additional tabs by clicking the plus sign.

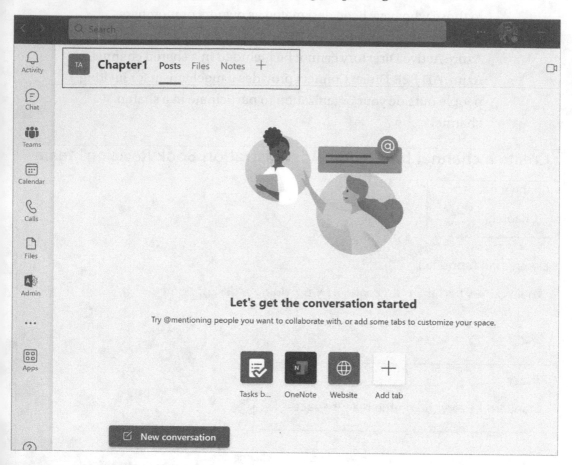

Figure 2-12. *Channel created*

When you click the "Add tab" plus sign (+), you will see multiple applications that can be added as tabs to your channel, as shown in Figure 2-13.

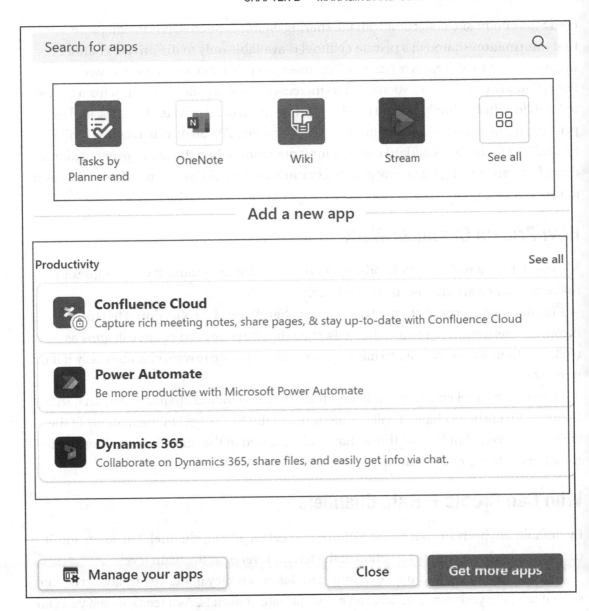

Figure 2-13. *Applications to add as tabs*

The other channel privacy mode is private. This type of channel focuses on private collaboration within a team. Private channels are different than standard channels, and they are already rolled out and available in Teams for use. It is important to notice from an architecture perspective that things are a bit different for private channels; for example, information that is shared in a private channel is stored differently than information stored in a standard channel because each private channel has its own SharePoint site collection with file sharing enabled. Microsoft is making sure that information shared in a private channel is available only to the private channel members, not to all Teams members. Because each private channel has its own SharePoint site collection, Microsoft has increased the site collection count from 500,000 to 2 million. Individually, a team can hold a maximum of 30 private channels, and every private channel can hold a maximum of 250 members. The 30 private channel limit is in addition to the 200 standard channel limit per team. When the team owner creates a team from an existing team, any private channels in the existing team will not carry over to the new team.

How Private Channels Work

Microsoft took a while to made private channels available because it was complex to make sure a private channel is truly private.

Remember, a private channel has its own SharePoint site collection. That means if your Teams has more private channels, then the site collection count will grow as well. It is therefore important to inform your users to create private channels only if it is necessary.

Private channel chat is also different than chat in standard channels. Any chat that happens in a private channel will not be stored in the Exchange Online mailbox of the Office 365 group, but instead those chats will be stored in the individual mailbox of the members of that private channel.

Who Can Create Private Channels

By default, anybody in your organization can create a private channel. You as an admin can control private channel creation at the tenant level or at the team level.

For the tenant level, you as an admin can define a policy in the Teams admin center so that users in your organization can create private channels. As a team owner, you can also control private channel creation in your team by clicking More Options, selecting Manage Team, and then clicking Settings. Clear the check mark next to the "Allow members to create private channels" check box, as shown in Figure 2-14.

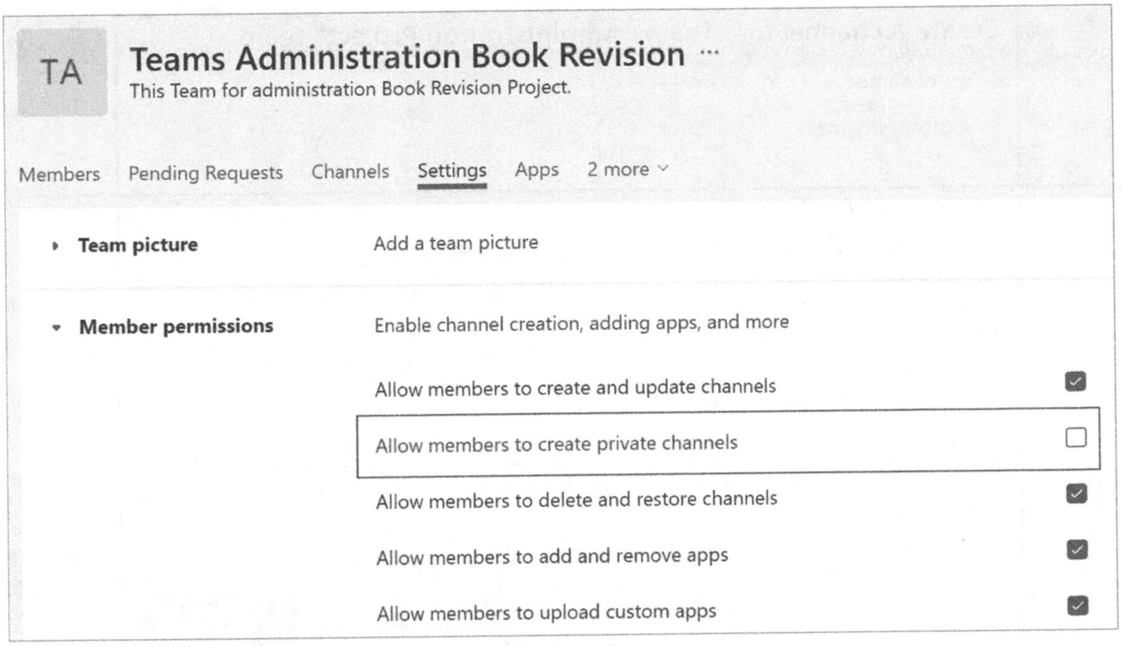

Figure 2-14. *Private channel restriction setting (user level)*

Creating a Private Channel

A private channel is accessible to specific people or a group that is added as a member of that private channel inside the team. To create a private channel, log in to the Teams app and expand the team under which you want to create the private channel. Click the more options icon (...) that is next to the team name, and you will see multiple options. Select Add Channel to create a channel, as shown in Figure 2-10. On the next screen, add a meaningful name and description to identify the private channel. Select "Private – Accessible only to a specific group of people within the team" to make the channel a private channel, as shown in Figure 2-15.

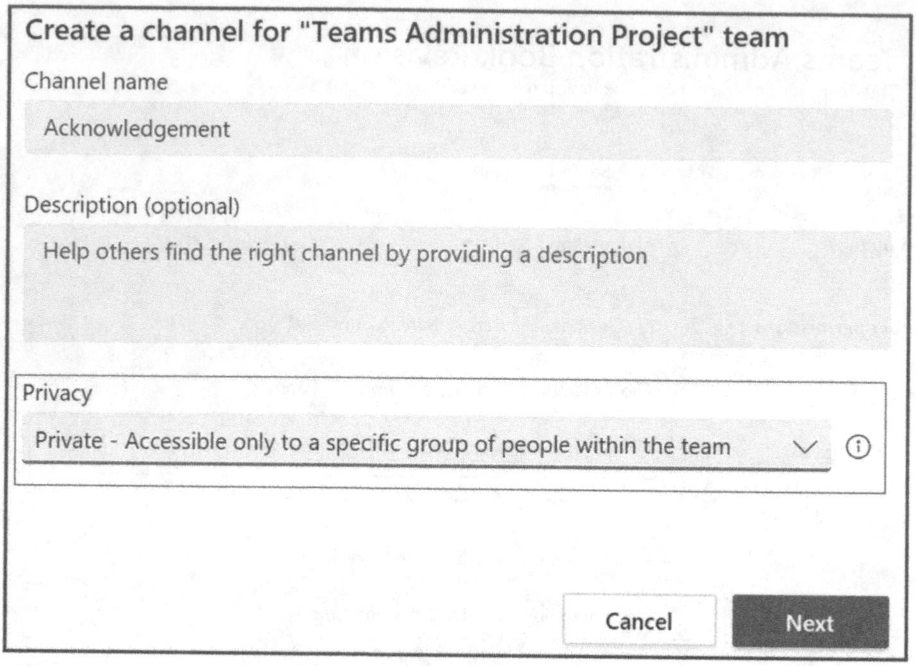

Figure 2-15. *Give a meaningful name and description to the private channel*

After assigning a name and selecting the privacy type, on the next screen you need to add the members for the private channel. Because this is a private channel, only the people you add here will see this channel in Teams. If you want to add members later, just click Skip button, as shown in Figure 2-16.

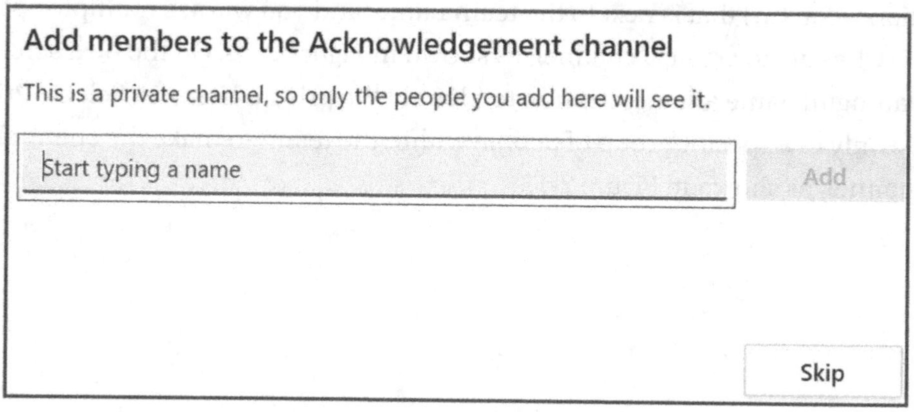

Figure 2-16. *Adding members to a private channel*

You will see the private channel has been created. Next to the channel name, you will see a lock icon that indicates that this is a private channel. Figure 2-17 shows that the Acknowledgement channel is a private channel.

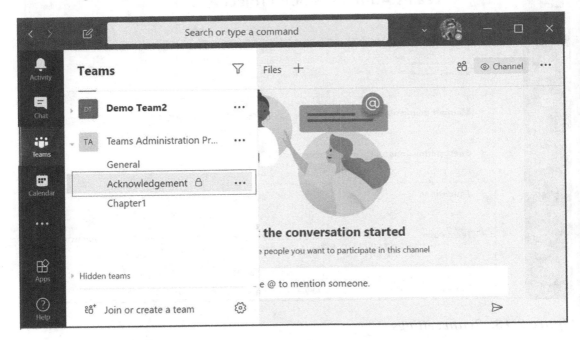

Figure 2-17. *Private channel with a lock icon next to its name*

Team Management Options

You as a team owner can manage your team settings. Figure 2-18 shows the team management settings that are available, including membership, guest access, and more.

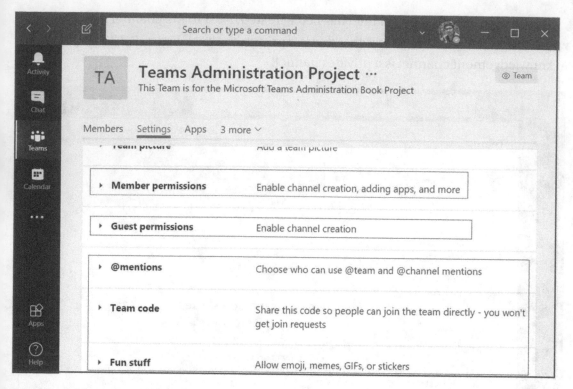

Figure 2-18. *Team settings*

Using the guest permissions settings, you can manage guest access for creating, updating, and deleting channels, as shown in Figure 2-19.

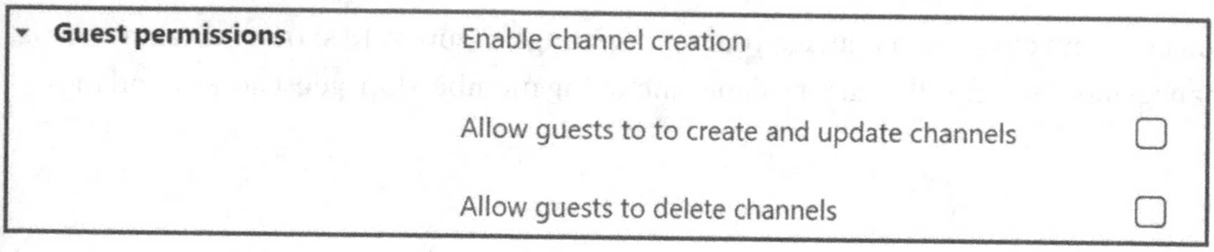

▾ **Guest permissions**	Enable channel creation	
	Allow guests to to create and update channels	☐
	Allow guests to delete channels	☐

Figure 2-19. *Guest permissions settings*

The team owner can manage member permissions such as who can create or add apps, update channels, create private channels, and so on. Figure 2-20 shows all the available member permissions settings.

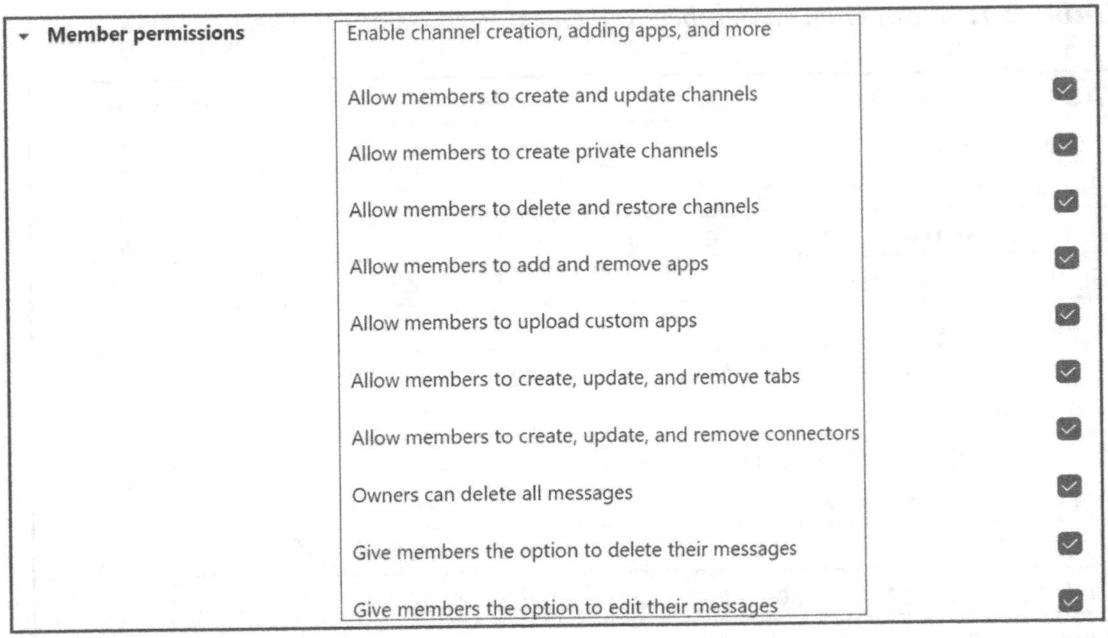

Figure 2-20. Member permissions to control member access

Every team has two roles: users and administrators. Users can be either owners, members, or guests of a team. The team owner is the person who creates the team. Team owners have authority to make any member of their team a co-owner when they invite them to the team or at any point after they have joined the team. It is best practice to have multiple team owners, which allows owners to share the responsibilities of managing team settings and membership, such as adding and removing members, adding guests, changing team settings, and handling administrative tasks. Team members are simply the individuals who the owners invite to join their team. Members can talk with other team members in conversations. They can view and usually upload and change files. They also can participate in the usual sorts of collaboration that team owners have permitted. Guests are individuals from outside of your organization, such as vendors, partners, or consultants, that a team owner invites to join the team. Guests have fewer capabilities than team members or team owners, but there is still a lot they can do.

Table 2-1 shows the different permissions that the team owner, members, and guests have to execute tasks. The listed permissions are based on the Teams desktop client; when using the Teams mobile client, you might see some differences.

Table 2-1. *Team Owner, Member, and Guest Permissions to Execute Tasks*

Ability to execute tasks	Owner	Member	Guest
Create a channel	✓	✓	✓
Participate in a private chat	✓	✓	✓
Participate in a channel conversation	✓	✓	✓
Share a channel file	✓	✓	✓
Share a chat file	✓	✓	✗
Add apps (such as tabs, bots, or connectors)	✓	✓	✗
Can be invited via any work or school account for Office 365	✗	✗	✓
Create a team	✓	✓	✗
Delete or edit posted messages	✓	✓	✓
Discover and join public teams	✓	✓	✗
View org chart	✓	✓	✗
Add or remove members and guests	✓	✗	✗
Edit or delete a team	✓	✗	✗
Set team permissions for channels, tabs, and connectors	✓	✗	✗
Change the team picture	✓	✗	✗
Add guests to a team	✓	✗	✗
Auto-show channels for the whole team	✓	✗	✗
Control @[team name] mentions	✓	✗	✗
Allow @channel or @[channel name] mentions	✓	✗	✗
Allow usage of emoji, GIFs, and memes	✓	✗	✗
Renew a team	✓	✗	✗
Archive or restore a team	✓	✗	✗

> **Note**   As you know, a team can be created from an existing Office 365 group. If this is the case, permissions are inherited from that group.
>
> All users who have Exchange Online mailboxes can create a team.

Deploying and Managing Teams Clients

Microsoft Teams clients are available for all platforms, such as web clients, desktop (Windows, Mac, and Linux), and mobile (Android and iOS). So far, all clients require an active Internet connection and do not support an offline or cached mode, although this might change in the future. As a Teams admin, you will need to provide an installation method to distribute the Microsoft Teams client to computers and devices in your organization. For example, you can use System Center Configuration Manager (SCCM) for Windows operating systems or JAMF Pro for macOS.

Installing Teams Client on Desktop and Mobile

You can download the Teams desktop client (Windows or macOS) or mobile client by visiting https://teams.microsoft.com/downloads.

The Teams desktop client comes with a stand-alone (.exe) installer for user installation and works with MSI for Admin client rollouts. It is also available by default as part of Office 365 ProPlus. There is no special licensing for Teams clients. The desktop clients provide real-time communications support (audio, video, and content sharing) for team meetings, group calling, and private one-to-one calls. Also, Teams desktop clients can be downloaded and installed by an end user directly from the Microsoft Teams download site if the user has the appropriate local permissions.

> **Note**   Admin rights are not required to install the Teams client on a Windows machine, but they are required to install the Teams client on a macOS machine. Besides manual installation, admins can perform a bulk deployment of the Teams desktop client to selected users or computers in their organization. Microsoft

has provided MSI files (for both 32-bit and 64-bit) that let admins use Microsoft System Center Configuration Manager, Group Policy, or any third-party distribution mechanism for broad deployment. These files can be used to remotely deploy Teams so that users do not have to manually download the Teams app.

Distribution of the client through software deployment is only for the initial installation of Microsoft Team clients and not for future updates.

Getting the Teams Client Download for All Devices

Teams clients have a stand-alone application (.exe) installer for individual user installation available at https://teams.microsoft.com/downloads. When users visit the Teams download site, they will find all desktop (Windows 32- and 64-bit, macOS, and Linux DEB/RPM 64-bit) and mobile (iOS and Android) clients, as shown in Figure 2-21.

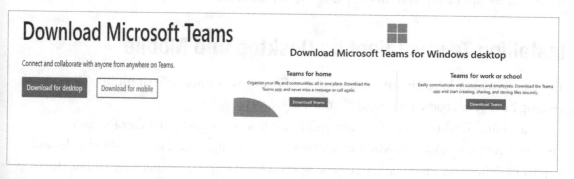

Figure 2-21. *Getting the Teams client for all devices*

The Microsoft Teams client is part of Office 365 ProPlus, which means when you install Office 365, the Teams client comes with it. The Teams client is part of update channels, including the Monthly channel and Semi-Annual channel. For more information, you can visit the Microsoft documentation for deploying Teams at https://learn.microsoft.com/en-us/microsoftteams/get-clients.

Teams Desktop Client Software and Hardware Requirements

For the best experience, a Windows desktop running Teams must meet the software and hardware requirements listed in Table 2-2.

Table 2-2. *Teams Client Hardware and Software Requirements*

Component	Requirement
Computer and processor	Minimum 1.1 GHz or faster, two core
Memory	4.0 GB RAM
Hard disk	3.0 GB of available disk space
Display	1024 x 768 screen resolution
Graphics hardware	Windows OS: Graphics hardware acceleration requires DirectX 9 or later, with WDDM 2.0 or higher for Windows 10 (or WDDM 1.3 or higher for Windows 10 Fall Creators Update)
Operating system	Windows 11, Windows 10 (excluding Windows 10 LTSC for Teams desktop app), Windows 10 on ARM, Windows 8.1, Windows Server 2019, Windows Server 2016, Windows Server 2012 R2. Note: We recommend using the latest Windows version and security patches available.
.NET version	Requires .NET 4.5 CLR or later
Video	USB 2.0 video camera
Devices	Standard laptop camera, microphone, and speakers
Video calls and meetings	Requires two-core processor. For higher video/screen share resolution and frame rate, a four-core processor or better is recommended. Background video effects require Windows 10 or a processor with AVX2 instruction set. Joining a meeting using proximity detection in Microsoft Teams Rooms requires Bluetooth LE. Bluetooth LE on Windows requires Bluetooth to be enabled on the client device and requires the 64-bit version of the Teams client. This feature is not available on 32-bit Teams clients.

You might be wondering if you need to allow admin permission for a user to install the Teams client. The answer is no; you don't need admin permission to install the Teams client.

Teams Desktop Client for Windows

When a Microsoft Teams call is initialized by a user for the first time, the user might notice a warning with the Windows firewall settings that prompts users to allow communication. However, the user might be instructed to ignore this message because despite the warning, when it is dismissed, the call will still work. On Windows, the Teams desktop client requires .NET Framework 4.5 or later. If this is not installed on the computer, the Teams installer will offer to install it automatically.

Where Can I Find the Teams Client Installation?

The Teams client can be installed on a per-user basis. This means if a computer is shared and more than one user accesses the same computer, every individual accessing the computer can install the Teams client on their own login profile. The Teams client is installed to the directories listed here and updated in separate directories. Figure 2-22 shows the Teams directory.

- Teams application

    - %LocalAppData%\Microsoft\Teams

    - %LocalAppData%\Microsoft\TeamsMeetingAddin

    - %AppData%\Microsoft\Teams

- Update directories

    - %LocalAppData%\SquirrelTemp

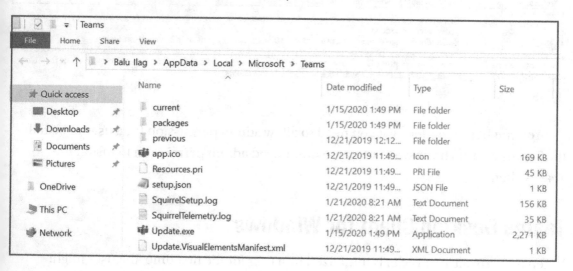

Figure 2-22. Teams installation directory

Note   For Teams admin control of installation, all of the directories just mentioned can be accessed and controlled.

Microsoft Teams Desktop Client MSI Deployment

The Microsoft Teams desktop client can be deployed to computers in your organization by using the Microsoft Teams MSI package. The Teams MSI package will place an installer in Program Files, which will in turn install the Teams Machine-Wide Installer on each user profile logged into a machine.

Microsoft allows for Teams (MSI) client rollout through existing standard deployment processes such as Group Policy, SCCM, Intune, or third-party tools. You as an admin must determine which computers already have the Teams client installed and which are newly built with an operating system. Usually, you can add the Teams client in the operating system build so that all newly built computers will have the Teams client installed.

Deploying the Teams MSI Client

As an admin, you can use MSI deployment for the Teams client; however, you cannot deploy the client updates. When the Teams client is deployed, the Teams MSI installer is located in the Program Files directory. Whenever a new user signs in, Teams will be installed and then started automatically. After the Teams client starts, the user is signed in, and the update process begins. If the Teams version is new enough, the user will be able to use the Teams client (the update happens in the background). If the Teams version is old, the Teams client will update itself, but the user will have to wait for the update to be completed.

The Teams MSI installer also allows you to disable client autostart. Once the Teams client rollout is complete, all users will have the Teams client on their computer, and it automatically starts when they log in to their computer. However, if end users don't want Teams client to start automatically, the MSI installer allows you to disable the initial automatic launch of Teams. Also, the Teams client shortcut will be placed on the user's desktop.

Note   Once the user manually starts the Teams client, it will automatically start at startup.

To disable the Teams client autostart for the 32-bit version, run this command at the command prompt: `msiexec /i Teams_windows.msi OPTIONS="noAutoStart=true"`. For the 64-bit version, run this command at the command prompt: `msiexec /i Teams_windows_x64.msi OPTIONS="noAutoStart=true"`.

Note   If you run the MSI manually, be sure to run it with elevated permissions. Even if you run it as an administrator, without running it with elevated permissions, the installer will not be able to configure the option to disable autostart.

Managing the Teams Desktop Client

Microsoft has made Teams client management simple.

Uninstalling Teams Completely from a Computer

If the Teams client is installed but not working correctly or you want to uninstall the Teams client for any other reason, make sure to uninstall the client completely; otherwise, the MSI installer won't install the Teams client again. To completely uninstall the Teams client on your computer, first uninstall the Teams client from every user profile that was installed earlier using Start ➤ Control Panel ➤ Program Files. Locate Microsoft Teams, and then click Uninstall. After uninstallation, delete the Teams directory recursively under `%LocalAppData%\Microsoft\Teams`.

Microsoft has provided a cleanup script for the uninstallation steps for SCCM, which you can get from `https://aka.ms/AA2jisb`.

Updating the Teams Client

Microsoft designed the Teams client to be updated automatically so that users will always have an updated client with the latest bug fixes, feature improvements, and new capabilities. Hence, you as an admin cannot control or manage Teams client updates.

The Teams client update process includes multiple checks. For example, when a user signs into Teams, validation occurs. If the Teams client version is not up-to-date (more than three versions old), then Teams updates are made before the client can sign in.

If the Teams client is not outdated, the user can sign in and use the client, but the Teams client will check for new updates after 15 minutes in the background. If an updated version is available, Teams will download the updated Teams full client package. It will be installed when the Teams client is idle for 30 minutes. After the Teams client installs the updated version, it will restart and send a notification to the user indicating that the Teams client has been updated.

As per Microsoft, Teams client updates are expected every two weeks, excluding hotfixes, which are deployed whenever required.

Note   If the Teams client is older than three versions, the Teams client cannot sign in before the client updates.

Managing Teams Client Configuration

Currently, the Microsoft Teams client behavior is controlled via policies that are defined and managed in the Teams admin portal and PowerShell. As of now, there are no options to manage the Teams client via Group Policy or the registry keys. For example, the features that Teams client displays, including voice and video calls, are controlled via the Teams admin center policies for all the clients. As another example, Outlook add-ins can be enabled or disabled through the Teams admin center meeting policies. However, there is nothing that can be managed or controlled via Group Policy or a registry key. Microsoft might or might not change this behavior in the future.

When the Microsoft Teams Outlook Add-in Is Not Installed

When a Microsoft Teams desktop client installs on a computer, the Teams meeting add-ins in Outlook are added automatically, allowing users to schedule Teams meetings. However, if somehow the Teams meeting add-ins are not visible, the user cannot schedule Teams meetings using Outlook. This happens because Teams might fail to initialize the add-in. To resolve this, follow these steps. Note that these steps are required only the first time to initialize the add-ins.

1. Make sure Outlook is open before the Teams client is started. You can simply close both the Teams client and the Outlook client (you can use Task Manager to completely close `teams.exe` and `outlook.exe`; see Figure 2-23).

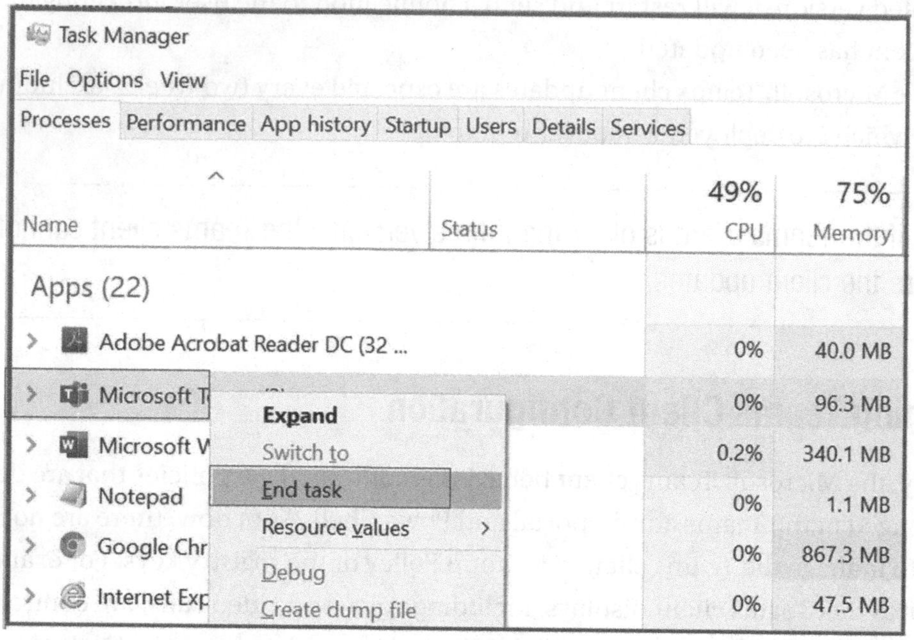

Figure 2-23. *Closing the Teams client completely*

2. Open or start Outlook first and then start the Teams client.

Most important, the Teams outlook add-in will be disabled depending on the Teams upgrade coexistence mode selected for the tenant or the specific user in the Teams admin center. For example, if a user's Teams upgrade mode selected Skype for Business Only, then the Teams meeting add-in will not show in Outlook. Also, as mentioned earlier, the meeting add-in can be disabled via Meeting Policy in the Teams admin center.

For Mac operating systems, users can install the Teams client by using a PKG installation file for macOS computers. Administrative access is required to install the Mac client. The macOS client is installed in the /Applications folder. To install Teams using the PKG file, perform the following steps:

1. Visit the Teams download page at `https://teams.microsoft.`
   `com/downloads#allDevicesSection`. Under Desktop, click Mac to
   download the file.

2. Double-click the PKG file.

3. Follow the installation wizard to complete the installation.

4. Teams will be installed to the `/Applications` folder; it is a
   machine-wide installation.

On Linux operating systems, the Teams client for Linux is available for users as native Linux packages in `.deb` and `.rpm` formats. To download the Linux DEB (64-bit) or RPM (64-bit) client, visit `https://teams.microsoft.com/downloads#allDevicesSection`, click Linux DEB or RPM, and then install it.

Virtual Desktop Infrastructure (VDI) is virtualization technology that hosts a desktop operating system and applications on a centralized server in a data center. With VDI, users can enjoy a fully personalized desktop experience with a fully secured and compliant centralized source.

Deploying the Teams Mobile Client

As previously mentioned, Microsoft Teams mobile apps are available for Android and iOS. Users can download the mobile apps through the Apple App Store and the Google Play Store. Currently there are two supported mobile platforms for Microsoft Teams mobile apps: Android (5.0 or later) and iOS (10.0 or later). Once the mobile app has been installed on a supported mobile platform, the Teams mobile app itself will be supported provided the version is within three months of the current release.

Note   Teams mobile app distribution is not currently supported using a mobile device management (MDM) solution. Microsoft might support Teams mobile app distribution through MDM in the future.

Monitoring Teams Client Usage

As a Teams admin, when you roll out the Teams desktop and mobile clients in your organization, the next important step is to monitor the Teams client usage per the operating system or device. You can monitor the Teams client device usage using the Teams admin portal.

To get a Teams client device usage report, log in to the Office 365 admin center portal by visiting https://admin.microsoft.com/Adminportal/Home. Click Report and then select Usage. On the Usage page, select Microsoft Teams and choose Device Usage. Figure 2-24 shows an example Teams client device report. On the report page, you can choose Users or Distribution; Figure 2-24 shows the Teams device distribution report.

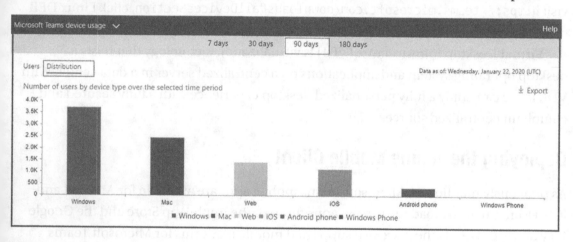

Figure 2-24. *Teams client device usage report*

The Teams device report is available for different durations, including 7 days, 30 days, 90 days, and 180 days. The report will allow you to receive per-user basis usage as well.

Configuring and Managing Live Events and Microsoft Stream

Microsoft Teams provides different formats for interactive and large broadcast events such as Teams meetings and live events within your organization, with both internal and external meeting participants. As an admin, you must understand the configuration, settings, and policies that can be used in Teams Live events and Microsoft Stream.

Chapter 1 covered topics like what live events and Microsoft Stream are, their architecture, live event scheduling, how Stream stores users' meeting recordings, how users can access the recordings, and so on. If you are still new to live events and Microsoft Stream, review Chapter 1 before continuing.

In this section, you are going to learn the step-by-step process for configuring policies and settings so that you as an admin can provide your users with the optimal user experience during live events and when using Microsoft Stream for meeting video recording and sharing content.

After learning about these topics, you will be able to do the following:

- Configure live event settings

- Manage and create live event policies

- Manage Microsoft Stream

Overview of Live Events

Microsoft Teams Live events are a scalable and ideal solution for online meetings for an audience up to 20,000 with four-hour duration. Microsoft Teams Live events are ideal for webinars, presentations, conferences, or company-wide announcements. Live events are highly customizable and offer various roles such as organizer, producer, presenter, and attendee each with specific capabilities and permissions. Live events scale online meetings to audiences with thousands of concurrent viewers. In the background, Teams leverages artificial intelligence for meeting assistance for features such as captions and translation. Captions are useful when attendees have audio limitations or need language translation. Optionally you can enable Q&A Manager and Yammer social feed integration to interact with audience members. You can record the event with video and after the live event provide an attendee engagement report for consumption insights, such as how many people joined and how long they stayed with an event.

Live events work very well because they enable high-quality, adaptive video streaming that can be consumed on any Teams-enabled devices, including Windows, macOS, and mobile devices, and devices that don't have the Teams client installed through a browser. Live events are delivered with minimal lag from worldwide Microsoft data centers, so no matter where your tenant is located and users are located, live events always find a shorter path for users to connect to the event to avoid latency. Also, large organizations can use a third-party eCDN partner to save corporate bandwidth.

With limited knowledge, anyone can use live events, and they can be scheduled easily in Teams. Users can present and produce live events from the macOS or Windows Teams client with one or more presenters, including application sharing. You can present from the Teams room system, or presenters can dial in from a phone line to a live event using Teams audio conferencing. As a live event organizer, you can control access to the event for everyone from an organization to specific groups or people.

Before configuring live event policies and settings, an admin must know who can use and schedule live events based on license requirements and permissions. To use live events, users must have a user account in Azure AD; the user cannot be a guest or from another organization. Apart from the Azure AD account, users must have a Microsoft 365 Enterprise E1, E3, or E5 license or a Microsoft 365 A3 or A5 license. Users must also have permission to create live events in the Microsoft Teams admin center and in Microsoft Stream for events produced using an external broadcasting app or device. Finally, users must have private meeting scheduling, screen sharing, and IP video sharing turned on in a Teams meeting policy with an Exchange Online mailbox.

Configuring and Managing Live Events Settings

Teams Live events settings allow you to control organization-wide settings for all live events that are scheduled. An admin can decide to include a support URL when live events are held and set up a third-party video distribution provider for all live events organized and scheduled by people in an organization.

Settings for the live events that are organized within your organization can be configured in the Microsoft Teams admin center. Remember, live event settings will be applied to all live events that are going to be created in the organization.

Microsoft has provided two different ways to configure Live event settings: using the Teams admin center and using PowerShell.

Configuring Live Event Settings Using the Teams Admin Center

To configure live event settings using the Teams admin center, follow these steps:

1. Log in to the Microsoft Teams admin center with your admin credential (you must have Teams service admin or global admin permission configure live event settings).

2. After you log in to the Teams admin center, navigate to Meetings and then select Live Events Settings (see Figure 2-25). If you have an internal support URL, replace the default URL with the support URL that will be shown to the attendees who will participate in the live event. You can also enable third-party video distribution providers.

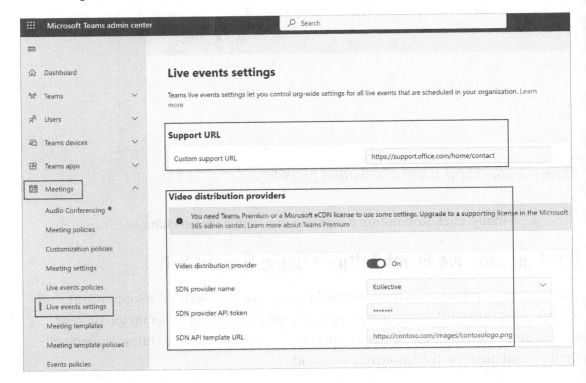

Figure 2-25. *Live event settings*

If you have a third-party distribution provider, select the appropriate one. The example shown in Figure 2-26 has Kollective selected as the provider. Enter the software-defined networking (SDN) provider API token you received from your provider and then enter the SDN template URL you received from your provider. There currently are five distribution providers: Microsoft eCDN, Hive, Kollective, Riverbed, and Ramp.

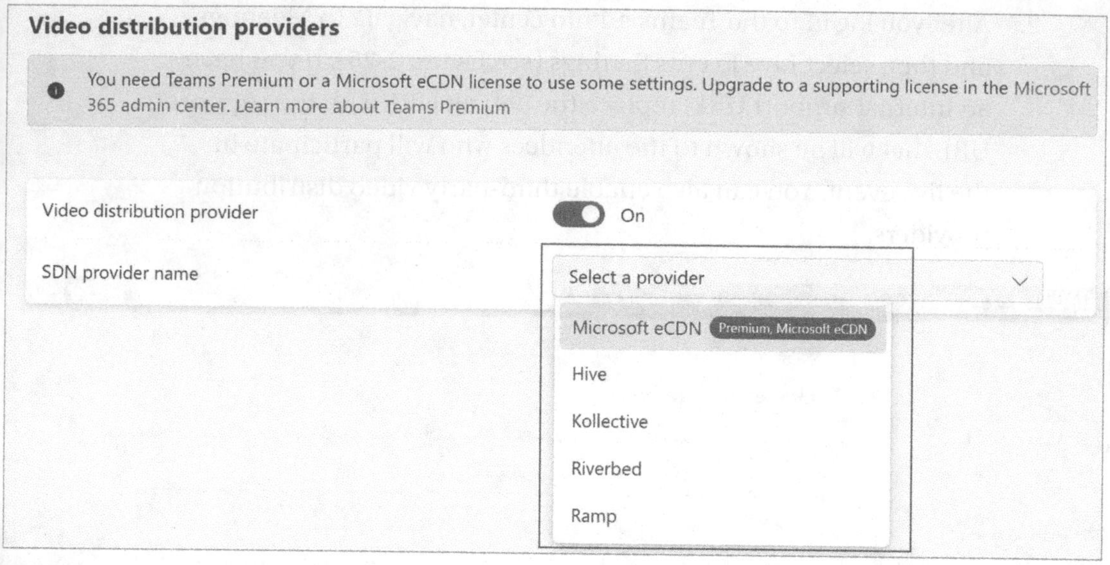

Figure 2-26. *Third-party distribution providers*

3. Finally, click Save button to commit the configuration changes.

Configuring Live Event Settings Using PowerShell

Perform the following steps to configure the live event settings for the support URL and a third-party distribution provider using Windows PowerShell. To set up the support URL using PowerShell, you should connect to the Microsoft Teams Online PowerShell module and then run the following command:

```
Set-CsTeamsMeetingBroadcastConfiguration -SupportURL "Org Support URL"
```

Here's an example:

```
Set-CsTeamsMeetingBroadcastConfiguration -SupportURL "https://bloguc.com/
Support"
```

Next, if you want to configure your third-party video provider using Windows PowerShell, you must first acquire a provider API token and API template from your provider contact. Once you have that information, you should run the following command (in this example, the provider is Kollective Streaming):

```
Set-CsTeamsMeetingBroadcastConfiguration -AllowSdnProviderForBroadcast
Meeting $True -SdnProviderName Kollective -SdnLicenseId {license ID GUID
provided by Hive} -SdnApiTemplateUrl "{API template URL provided by Hive}"
```

> **Note**   If you want to create live events using an external encoder or device, you must first configure your eCDN third-party provider with the Microsoft Stream admin center as well.

Configuring and Managing Live Events Policies

As an admin, you can modify existing live event policies or create new policies. A live event policy allows admins to control which users in the organization can host live events, as well as which features are going to be available in the events they create. By default, a Global (Org-wide default) live events policy is available. Admins can modify this policy or create one or more custom live event policies. After a custom policy is created, it should be assigned to a user or groups of users within the organization.

> **Note**   The live event Global (Org-wide default) policy is already assigned to every individual in your organization. If you have not created and assigned any custom policy, all users will receive the default policy.

Figure 2-27 shows the default policy with these settings: live event scheduling is enabled for Teams users, live captions and subtitles are turned off, everyone in the organization can join live events, and the recording setting is set to always record.

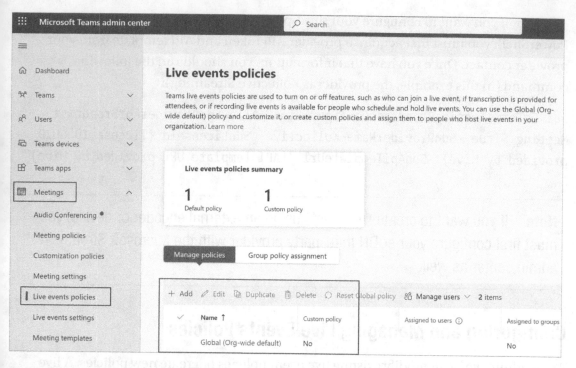

Figure 2-27. Default Global (Org-wide) policy in live event

Microsoft has provided two different ways to configure live event policies: using the Teams admin center and using PowerShell.

Creating a New Live Event Policy Using the Teams Admin Center

Log in to the Teams admin center, navigate to the Meetings tab, and then select Live Event Policies. You can choose to create or manage/edit live event policies. When doing so, you can manage the following options:

- *Global policy:* This organization-wide policy is the existing default policy. You can click Edit to make changes to this policy.

- *New policy:* This option is used to create a new custom policy.

- *Choose existing policy:* By selecting this option, along with an existing policy and the Edit button, you can make changes to that policy.

Creating a New Policy

Follow this procedure to create a new live event policy. Log in to the Teams admin center, navigate to Meetings, and click Live Event Policies. Click the +Add button, and then enter the required inputs, as shown in Figure 2-28.

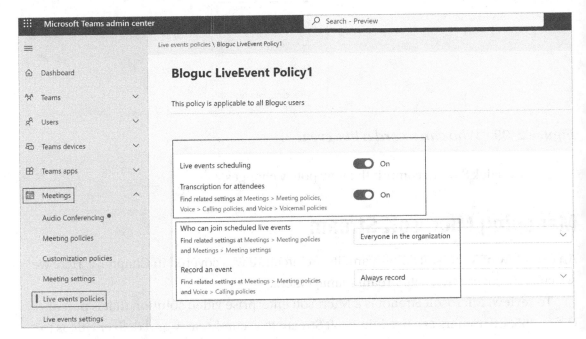

Figure 2-28.   *Creating a new live event policy*

On the new event page, type a meaningful name for your policy, and optionally type a description. This example uses the name Cyclotron LiveEvent Policy1 and includes a description. Next, customize the following settings according to your preferences for this new policy:

- *Allow scheduling:* You must allow this so that the users will able to schedule live events.

- *Allow transcription for attendees:* This allows transcription.

- *Who can join scheduled live events:* Select from Everyone, Everyone in the organization, and Specific users or groups. In this example, Everyone In The Organization is selected.

- *Who can record an event:* Select from Always record, Never record, and Organizer can record. Figure 2-29 shows "Always record" as the selected setting.

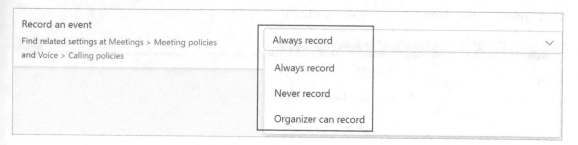

Figure 2-29. *Who can record a live event*

Finally, click Save to commit the new policy changes.

Managing Microsoft Stream

An overview of Microsoft Stream and its architecture was covered in Chapter 1. Here we specifically cover Microsoft Stream management.

To review, Microsoft Stream is a Microsoft enterprise video solution that is part of Office 365. Customers can use Microsoft Stream to securely carry and deliver videos to their organization. Stream supports live events through Teams, Stream, and Yammer. Microsoft provides a portal to upload, share, and discover videos such as executive communication or training and support videos. Microsoft Stream allows users to upload videos, search groups and videos, broadcast their live events, and provide a way to categorize and organize videos. Users can also create a group, and Stream allows users to embed video in Microsoft Teams.

Stream supports Teams video recording, as when a user records a Teams meeting by clicking the record button in a Teams meeting. That recording goes over Stream, and all of the sources are fully integrated with Stream, including automatic transcripts, a search function, and the enterprise security that customers expect from Microsoft Office 365 services.

There are two ways to access Microsoft Stream.

- You can access Microsoft Stream by visiting `https://web.microsoftstream.com`.

- You can access Stream using the Office portal. Log in to `office.com`. Click the Office 365 app launcher icon, select All Apps, and then select Stream. Alternatively, go to `stream.microsoft.com` and sign in with your work or school credentials.

When you log in to Microsoft Stream, you can see the Discover, My Content, and Create options. Under Discover, the Videos, Channels, People, and Groups settings are available for your organization, as shown in Figure 2-30.

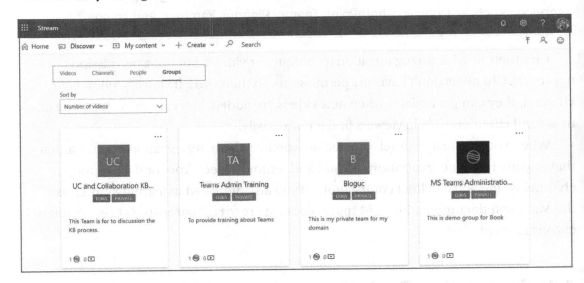

Figure 2-30. *Microsoft Stream Groups view*

Organizing and Managing Groups and Channels in Stream

When you create a group in Stream, it actually creates a group in Office 365, which means groups in Stream are built on top of Office 365 Groups. When you make a group in Stream, it creates a new Office 365 group that can be used across Office 365, giving the group an email address, calendar, group site, and so on. If you already use Office 365 Groups in your organization from Microsoft Teams, SharePoint, Viva (Yammer), Planner, and so on, you can start using those groups in Stream right away.

In Microsoft Stream, you can use channels and groups to organize and grant permission to your videos. Specifically, groups in Stream are used to control video access and organize videos. Each group has both owners and members. Each group gets its own video portal, with a highlights page showing trending and new content within the group. A group's videos can be further organized by creating channels within the group. It is best practice to put a video into one or several groups to help viewers find it more easily.

Important   Remember, deleting a group in Stream will also permanently delete the Office 365 Group and everything associated with the group. This includes videos, conversations, files, and content for all the Office 365 group-enabled services such as Outlook, SharePoint, Teams, Planner, Yammer, and so on.

Channels provide an organization technique for videos, but not a permission approach. Channels don't have any permissions on their own. If viewers follow your channel, they can get updates when new videos are added. You can put a video into one or several channels to help viewers find it more easily.

When you create a channel, you decide whether it's an organization-wide channel that anyone in your organization can add and remove videos from or if it's a group channel where you can limit contributors. If you are interested in learning more, visit the Microsoft documentation at https://docs.microsoft.com/en-us/stream/groups-channels-overview.

Administrative Tools

The following sections cover the administrative tools.

Managing Teams Using the Microsoft Teams Admin Center

The Microsoft Teams admin center is one place where most of the Teams service-side configuration and management resides. Using the Teams admin center, admins can manage the Teams services the way an organization wants to manage the Teams experience for its users. This is similar to other Office 365 applications. There are multiple admin tools available; however, from a graphical user interface (GUI) perspective, there are three main admin tools, including the Microsoft Teams admin center. This is where you manage all Teams-related settings and policies for communications and Teams-specific features such as Teams meetings, messaging and calling policies, Teams organization-wide settings, guest and external access, application permissions, and so on.

This section will provide extensive details about Microsoft Teams administration including all that the Teams admin center provides.

Accessing the Teams Admin Center

Admins can access the Teams admin center through the Office 365 portal or by directly visiting the Teams admin center at https://admin.teams.microsoft.com/.

In addition to the previously mentioned GUI tools, you can use PowerShell to manage the Teams experience. Microsoft provides a Teams module as well, and to some extent you can use the Microsoft Teams graph API. It's entirely up to you to use whichever solution is suitable for the Teams management perspective in your organization.

Understanding the Teams Admin Role

Many organizations that use Teams have more than one admin managing the Teams workload and supporting the Teams functionality. In many cases, you don't want to have same the access permissions for every admin, and that's where the Teams admin role comes in.

A Teams admin has four different roles that you can designate to Teams administrators who need different levels of access for managing Microsoft Teams. That gives every Teams admin the correct required permissions. The following are the roles that are available to manage Teams:

- *Teams Administrator (Service):* This admin role can manage the Teams service and manage and create Office 365 groups.

- *Teams Communications Administrator:* This admin role can manage calling and meeting features within the Teams service.

- *Teams Communications Support Engineer:* This admin role can troubleshoot communication issues within Teams using advanced tools.

- *Teams Communications Support Specialist:* This admin role can troubleshoot communications issues within Teams using basic tools.

- *Teams Device Administrator:* This role can manage device configuration and updates, review device health and status of connected peripherals, set up and apply configuration profiles, and restart devices.

If you are interested in learning more about each role and its capabilities, visit https://docs.microsoft.com/en-us/microsoftteams/using-admin-roles.

Teams Administration Through the Teams Admin Center

The Microsoft Teams admin center is an online portal designed specifically for IT administrators to manage the Teams platform across their organization. It provides admins with a central place to handle settings, users, teams, and policies, enabling efficient and effective management of the Teams environment.

Key Uses of the Microsoft Teams Admin Center

Here are some of the core functions and tasks you can accomplish using the Microsoft Teams admin center:

- *Manage teams:* Admins can view and manage all teams in the organization, including creating new teams, changing team settings, managing membership, and deleting teams. They can also manage team templates to streamline the process of creating new teams.

- *Manage users:* This includes adding and removing users, assigning roles and permissions, and managing user settings.

- *Manage policies:* Admins can create and manage various policies that govern the features and capabilities available to users, such as meeting policies, messaging policies, app setup policies, and live events policies.

- *Manage meeting settings:* These include global settings for meetings like default meeting settings, meeting expiration times, and cloud recording options.

- *Analytics and reporting:* The admin center provides extensive analytics and reporting options, helping admins monitor usage, performance, and user activity. This includes call quality, user activity reports, and device usage reports.

- *Manage voice and calling features:* Admins can manage Teams calling features such as call queues, auto attendants, call park policies, and more.

- *Manage apps:* Admins can manage the apps available to users, set up app permission policies, and control app setup policies.

- *Manage devices:* Admins can manage certified Teams devices, monitor device health, and update device settings from the admin center.

To log in to Microsoft Teams admin center, you must have one of the role permissions just covered or the Office 365 Global admin permission. When you log in to the Teams admin center, you will see different views based on your access permissions. For example, if you have Teams Communication Support Engineer or Teams Communications Support Specialist role permissions, you will see only the Users and Call Quality Dashboard options on the Teams admin center dashboard.

I have logged in to the Teams admin center (`https://admin.teams.microsoft.com/`) using my Teams Admin (Service) role permission to see all admin tools and options to manage Teams for my demo tenant. Figure 2-31 shows the ideal Teams admin dashboard that a Teams admin can see.

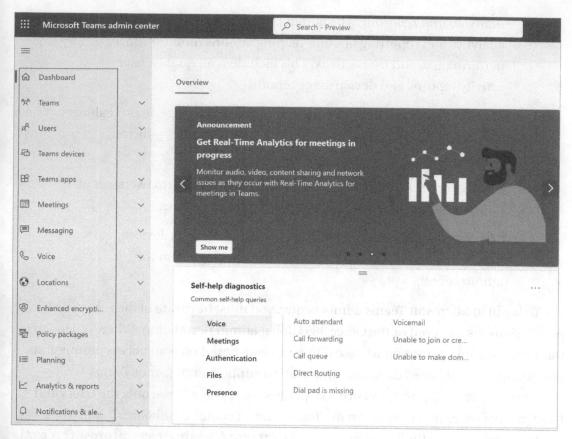

Figure 2-31. *Teams admin center dashboard*

Admin Center: Teams Tab

The first management tab shown in the Teams admin center is Teams. By using this tab you can manage your organization's teams and channels that users have created. This includes creating new teams, managing existing ones, setting up team permissions, and even deleting teams when necessary.

Manage Teams

When you click Manage Teams, you will see a global view of the teams that have been created in your organization. As an admin, you can manage every team from this tab. You can also add or create teams. For example, you can see seven teams created in Figure 2-32. To manage Teams, follow these steps:

1. In the left navigation pane, go to Teams ➤ Manage Teams.

2. Here, you can view all existing teams, their members, privacy settings, and more.

3. Click a team name to view more detailed settings and to modify the team's settings.

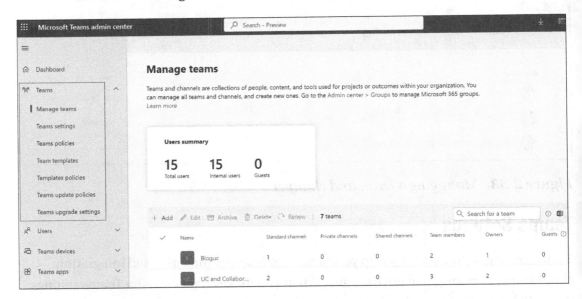

Figure 2-32. *The Manage Teams tab*

To manage an individual team, click the team name to open a management page for the team. You can add or remove members, modify channels, and change settings. Also, you can edit the team name and description and modify the team's privacy settings. In this example, clicking the Teams Admin Training team displays the management options shown in Figure 2-33.

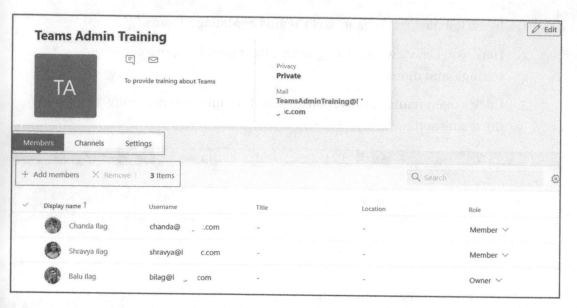

Figure 2-33.   Managing a team and channel

Teams Settings

Teams settings allow you to set up your teams for features such as email integration, cloud storage options, and device setup. When you make changes to the Teams settings, they will be applied to all the teams within your organization.

You can enable and manage different organization-wide Teams settings including notifications and feeds, email integration, files, organization, devices, and directory search (search by name). Let's understand each setting in detail.

Notification and Feeds

The notification and feeds settings allow you to manage the way that Teams handles suggested and trending feeds. Once you enable this setting, users will see the suggested feeds in their activity feeds.

Tagging control how tags are used across your organization. Tags can be added to one or multiple team members and used in @mentions by anyone on the team to notify people who are assigned that tag of a conversation.

To enable notification and feeds, follow these steps:

1. Log in to the Teams admin center, navigate to Teams, and then select Teams Settings.

2. Under Notification and Feeds, turn on the "Suggested feeds can appear in a user's activity feed" option, as shown in Figure 2-34.

3. Under Tagging, set who can manage tags and more.

4. Once you have made the required changes, click Save to commit the changes.

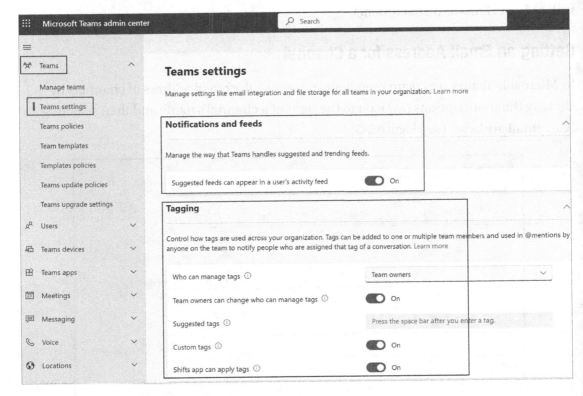

Figure 2-34. *Notifications and feeds and tagging*

Email Integration

Email integration is one of the most popular integration features among users. You as a Teams admin can use the Teams admin center to configure email integration. This is useful when you are integrating Teams into existing messaging workflows to provide information through email to team members. It is possible to retrieve email addresses for any individual channel within a team. Messages sent to these email addresses are then posted as conversation messages to the conversations of the channel, and other members can download the original message or add comments to the messages content.

Remember, the maximum message length for Teams messages is 24 KB, which can be reached quickly when creating an email. Therefore, if you just want to post basic information into a channel, you should use a text-only email. Otherwise, only the first part of the email is displayed as a team's conversation, and all team members who want to read the message must download and open it using an electronic mail (EML) format. EML files can contain plain ASCII text for the headers and the main message body as well as hyperlinks and attachments.

Getting an Email Address for a Channel

In Microsoft Teams, any team member can retrieve the email address of channels by clicking the more options (**...**) icon to the right of a channel's name and then selecting "Get email address" (see Figure 2-35).

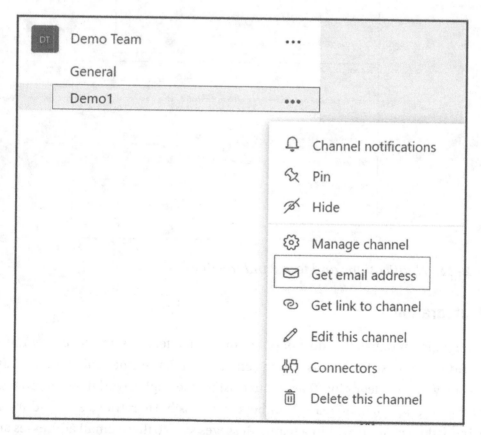

Figure 2-35. *Retrieving the email address of a channel*

The format of these channel email addresses makes them difficult to recognize because they appear similar to this demo address: `ChannelName - TeamName <UniqueID.TenantName.onmicrosoft.com@amer.teams.ms>`. Here's an example: `Demo1 - Demo Team fb181c9a.bloguc.com@amer.teams.ms`.

For ease of management, team owners and users can remove the email address, or they can modify advanced settings to restrict message delivery to team members and certain domains only.

Note   When an email is sent to the channel's email address, the email is stored as an EML file in the folder Email Messages in the channel's document library. All participants of a channel can download the files and open them in their preferred viewer for EML files.

Enabling and Managing Email Integration

Email integration lets people send an email to a Teams channel and have the contents of the email displayed in a conversation for all team members to view. This feature is very useful. To enable email integration, follow these steps:

1. Log in to the Teams admin center, navigate to Teams, and then select Teams Settings.

2. Under Email Integration, turn on the "Users can send emails to a channel email address" option.

3. Add the SMTP domains from which channel emails will be accepted. Once you have made the required changes, click Save to commit the changes. As an example, Figure 2-36 shows the `bloguc1.com` and `bloguc2.com` SMTP domains added to accept the channel emails.

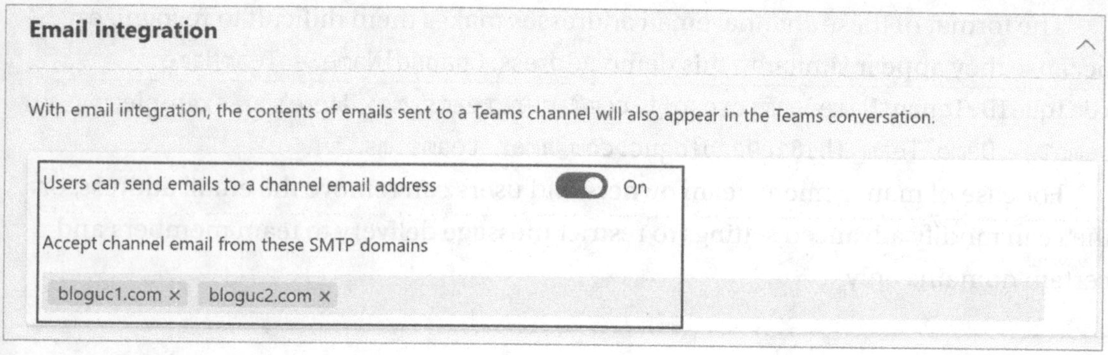

Email integration   ∧

With email integration, the contents of emails sent to a Teams channel will also appear in the Teams conversation.

Users can send emails to a channel email address   ⬤ On

Accept channel email from these SMTP domains

bloguc1.com ×   bloguc2.com ×

Figure 2-36. Email integration

Files (Enabling and Managing File Sharing and Cloud File Storage)

Now that you have learned about the different file storage options Teams uses, to enable file storage, follow this procedure:

1. Log in to the Teams admin center, navigate to Teams, and then select Teams Settings.

2. Under Files, turn on or off the options for Citrix files, Dropbox, Box, Google Drive, and Egnyte.

3. Once you have made the required changes, click Save to commit the changes. As an example, Figure 2-37 shows that the Bloguc organization allows all four types of file storage.

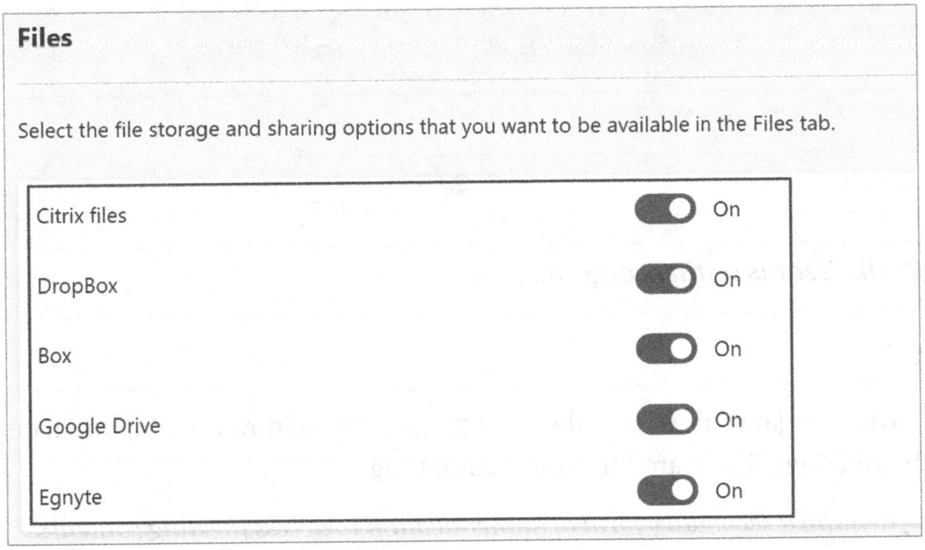

Files

Select the file storage and sharing options that you want to be available in the Files tab.

Citrix files	On
DropBox	On
Box	On
Google Drive	On
Egnyte	On

Figure 2-37. *Teams settings for files*

Organization Settings

In Teams, the Organization tab allows Teams users to see others in their organization's hierarchy. The Show Organization tab in chats allows users to show or hide the Organization tab in chats that shows additional data about a chat partner. An admin can manage enabling or disabling Organization tab details per your organization's requirements. To enable the Organization tab, follow these steps:

1. Log in to the Teams admin center, navigate to Teams, and then select Teams Settings.

2. Under Organization, turn on the Show Organization Tab In Chats option.

3. Once you have made the required changes, click Save to commit the changes. The example in Figure 2-38 shows that the Bloguc organization allows the Organization tab to be displayed in chat.

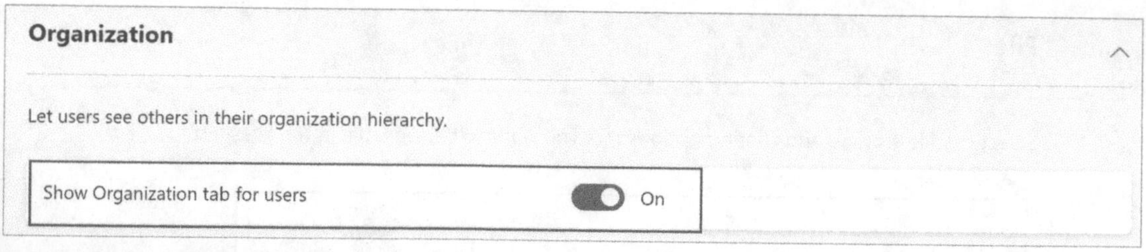

Organization   ∧

Let users see others in their organization hierarchy.

Show Organization tab for users   🔵 On

Figure 2-38. Teams settings organization

Devices

Teams provides organization-wide device settings to set up how meeting room devices operate in meetings. There are three different settings.

- *Require a secondary form of authentication to access meeting content:* This setting controls whether users must provide a second form of authentication before entering a meeting. This setting is especially useful when using Surface Hub devices, where users can possibly join a meeting with the identity of a different user who is already logged on. You want this setting to provide an additional security verification before users can access possibly sensitive content. This is especially helpful when using shared devices, such as Surface Hubs, where users often forget to sign off after using a device.

- *Set content PIN:* This setting requires users to enter a PIN before accessing documents from a team. This also is a useful setting for multiuser devices, where users could access the session of a different user who was already logged on. You want to protect access to possibly sensitive content on shared devices, similar to the secondary security verification.

- *Resource accounts can send messages:* This setting allows resource accounts to send messages to participants. You want to allow automatic messages by resources, or you might restrict communication of these accounts. This setting can be helpful when configuring workflows for resources.

To enable devices settings, follow this procedure:

1. Log in to the Teams admin center, navigate to Teams, and then select Teams Settings.

2. Under Devices, select the following settings:

   a. *Require a secondary form of authentication to access meeting content:* Full Access

   b. *Set content PIN:* Required For Outside Scheduled Meetings

   c. *Resource accounts can send messages:* Select On or Off

3. Once you have made the required changes, click Save to commit the changes. As an example, Figure 2-39 shows the Bloguc organization's device settings.

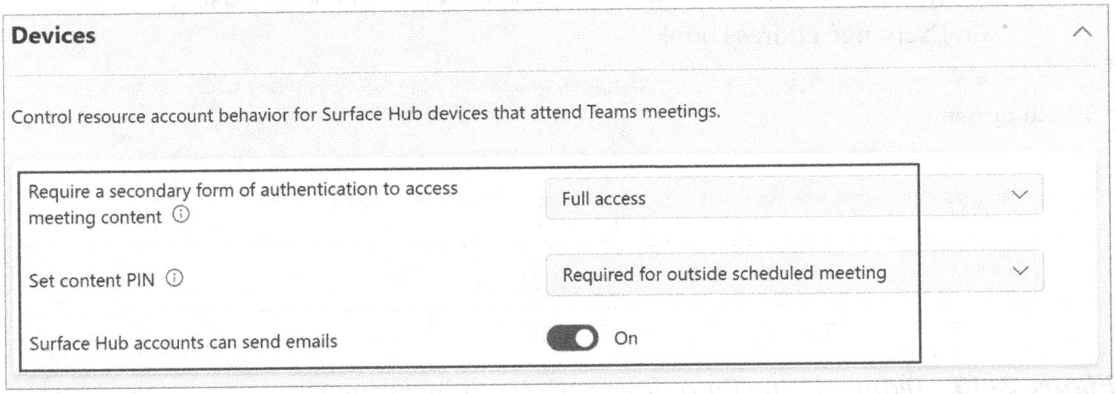

Devices

Control resource account behavior for Surface Hub devices that attend Teams meetings.

Require a secondary form of authentication to access meeting content ⓘ	Full access ⌄
Set content PIN ⓘ	Required for outside scheduled meeting ⌄
Surface Hub accounts can send emails	🔵 On

Figure 2-39. Teams settings for devices

Search by Name

Using Microsoft Teams scope directory search, you as an admin can create virtual boundaries that control how users communicate with each other within the organization. Microsoft Teams provides custom views of the directory of organization users. Most important, the Information Barrier policies support these custom views. Once the policies have been enabled, the results returned by searches for other users (e.g., to initiate a chat or to add members to a team) will be scoped according to the configured policies.

Users will not be able to search or discover teams when scope search is in effect. Note that in the case of Exchange hybrid environments, this feature will work only with Exchange Online mailboxes (not with on-premises mailboxes).

To turn on the scope directory search, you need to use Information Barrier policies to configure your organization into virtual subgroups. To configure a scope directory search using an Exchange address book policy in your tenant, follow these steps:

1. Log in to the Teams admin center, navigate to Teams, and then select Teams Settings.

2. Under Search By Name, turn on the "Scope directory search using an exchange address book policy" option.

3. Once you have made the required changes, click Save to commit the changes. The example shown in Figure 2-40 shows that the Bloguc organization has enabled the scope directory search using an Exchange address book.

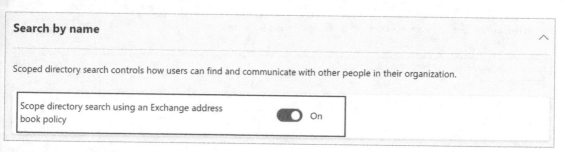

Figure 2-40. *Teams setting for a directory search by name*

Note   If it was not already turned on, you can turn on the scope directory search as a prerequisite to using Information Barrier.

Remember, after enabling scope directory search, before you can set up or define Information Barrier policies, you need to wait at least 24 hours.

Safety and Communications

Role-based chat permissions control the amount of supervision a user needs while chatting with others. Before you turn this on, turn on chat and assign chat permission roles to users.

1. Log in to the Teams admin center, navigate to Teams, and then select Teams Settings.

2. Under "Safety and communications," turn on the "Role-based chat permissions" option.

3. Once you have made the required changes, click Save to commit the changes. The example shown in Figure 2-41 shows that the role-based chat permission enabled.

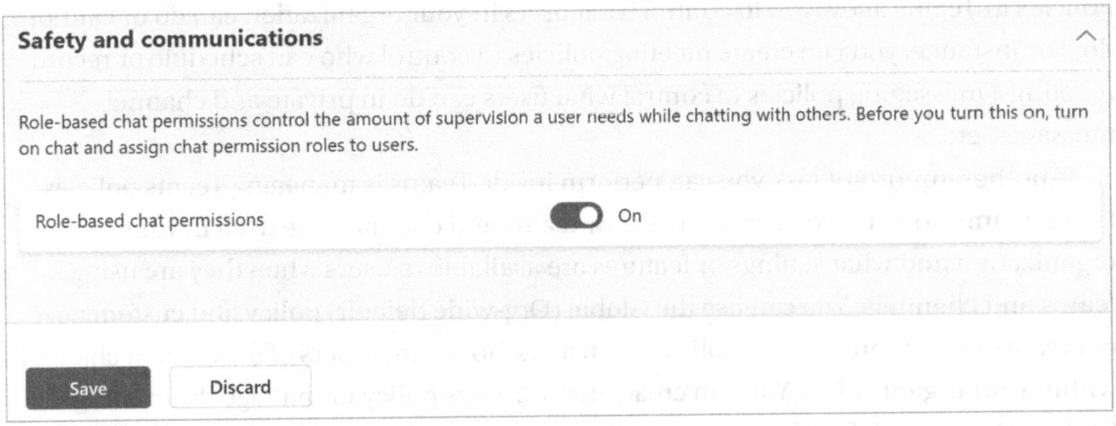

Safety and communications

Role-based chat permissions control the amount of supervision a user needs while chatting with others. Before you turn this on, turn on chat and assign chat permission roles to users.

Role-based chat permissions   ● On

Save   Discard

Figure 2-41. Teams "Safety and communications" settings

Best Practices for Email Integration

Channel email addresses are lengthy and contain the Teams domain, which make them difficult to remember. It is a best practice for users to create contact objects for the channel addresses or for Exchange administrators to create mail contacts that provide an easily recognized mail address in their own organization custom domain. For example, bloguc.com, for my Demo Team, has few channels. One channel named Demo1 in the team Demo Team has the email address Demo1 - Demo Team fb181c9a.bloguc.com@ amer.teams.ms.

When you create a mail contact with the alias demo1-team@bloguc.com and set its external email address to 123ab345.1.bloguc.onmicrosoft.com@amer.teams.ms, all email sent from internal users to the preceding email address will be forwarded to the team's channel.

Remember, users can remove and reactivate a channel's email address, in which case a new address is generated, and the old address cannot be reused. This invalidates the mail contact's external address, which in turn must be changed when this occurs.

Teams Policies

Let's talk about Teams policies.

Creating and Managing Teams Policies

Policies in Teams allow you to control what users in your organization can do or cannot do. For instance, you can create meeting policies to control who can schedule or record meetings, messaging policies to control what users can do in private and channel messages, etc.

Another important task you can perform inside Teams is managing Teams policies. Using Teams policies, you can control how teams and channels are used in your organization and what settings or features are available to users when they are using teams and channels. You can use the Global (Org-wide default) policy and customize it or create one or more custom policies for users who are members of a team or a channel within your organization. You can create new a Teams policy or manage the existing Global (Org-wide default) or custom policy.

Creating a New Teams Policy

To create a Teams policy, log in to the Teams admin center, navigate to Teams, and select Teams Policies. Click +Add. Once the new Teams policy form opens, enter a meaningful name and description and turn on or off the discovery of private teams and the creation of channels. Figure 2-42 shows new Teams policy settings.

Microsoft added private channels, so they modified the Teams default policies. By default, anybody in your organization can create a private channel with the exception of guests. This default behavior can be controlled at the tenant level in the Teams Global policy.

- *Create private channels:* Team owners and members with permission can create private channels for a specific group of users in your organization. Only people added to the private channel can read and write messages.

- *Create shared channels:* Team owners can create shared channels for people within and outside the organization. Only people added to the shared channel can read and write messages.

- *Invite external users to shared channels:* Owners of a shared channel can invite external users to join the channel, if Azure AD external sharing policies are configured. If the channel has been shared with an external member or team, they will continue to have access to the channel even if this control is turned off.

- *Join external shared channels:* Users and teams can be invited to external shared channels, if Azure AD external sharing policies are configured. If a team in your organization is part of an external shared channel, new team members will have access to the channel even if this control is turned off.

Admins can modify this behavior and assign custom policy to targeted users to allow or block private channel creation.

Note   Consider the increased SharePoint workload before allowing private channel creation for everyone in your organization.

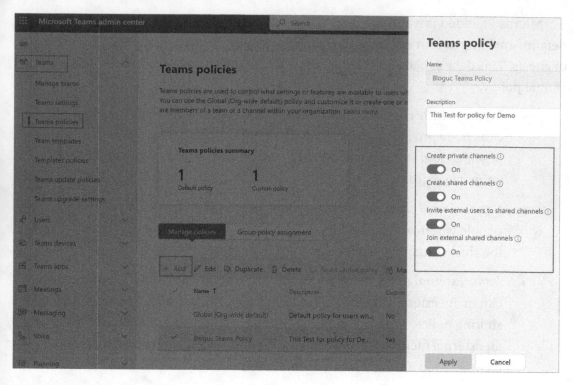

Figure 2-42. *Creating a new Teams policy*

Teams Templates

Teams templates make it easy to create new teams by providing a predefined template of channels, apps, and settings. You can use the default templates provided by Microsoft or create your own. Refer to Figure 2-43. Users can easily go to the Teams client and create a team using template.

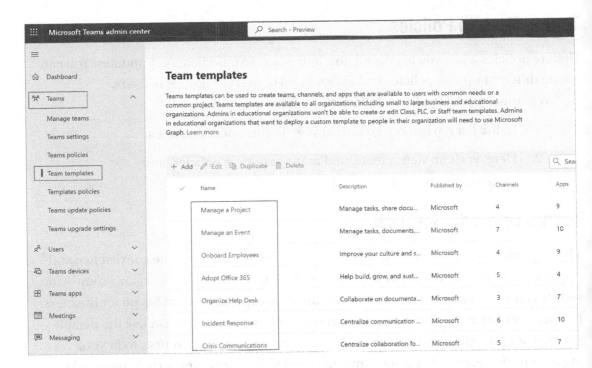

Figure 2-43. *Teams temples*

You can find details about the predefined templates here:

https://learn.microsoft.com/en-us/microsoftteams/get-started-with-teams-templates-in-the-admin-console#pre-built-team-templates-in-the-teams-admin-center

Template Policy

You can set what templates can been seen by users. To hide a template, go to "Template policy," click Add, select which template you need to hide, and click Hide. We can create multiple policies and assign them to users. In the user policy, you will be able to see the template policy. Also, you can create a new template by clicking the +Add button.

Template Policies

Templates policies let you create and set up policies that control what templates people in your organization can see. You can use the Global (Org-wide default) policy and customize it, or you can create custom policies. Also, you can assign newly created policies to users.

Teams Update Policies

Update policies allow you to control how and when Teams clients get updates. You can create different update policies and assign them to users or groups of users.

To manage update policies, follow these steps:

1.   In the left navigation, go to Teams ➤ Teams update policies.

2.   Here, you can view, create, and manage update policies, and assign them to users.

Teams Upgrade Settings

The upgrade settings in the Teams admin center help you control the coexistence and upgrade experience from Skype for Business to Teams. The upgrade organization-wide settings allow Teams admins to set up the upgrade experience from Skype for Business to Microsoft Teams for their organization users. As an admin, you can use the default settings or make changes to the coexistence mode and app preferences to fit your organizational needs. Migrating or moving from Skype for Business (on-premises) to Teams is more than a practical migration. Basically, this move signifies a change in how users communicate and collaborate, and change is not always easy. The perfect upgrade method should address the technical aspects of your upgrade as well as encourage user acceptance and adoption of Teams, driving a positive user experience and business outcome understanding.

For comprehensive migration and upgrade details, refer to Chapter 6. The material here is simply an overview of Teams upgrade settings.

Once you are planning the transition from Skype for Business to Teams, you will need to become familiar with the various upgrade modes, notions, and terminology applicable to upgrading from Skype for Business to Teams. Figure 2-44 shows a default view of the Teams upgrade settings.

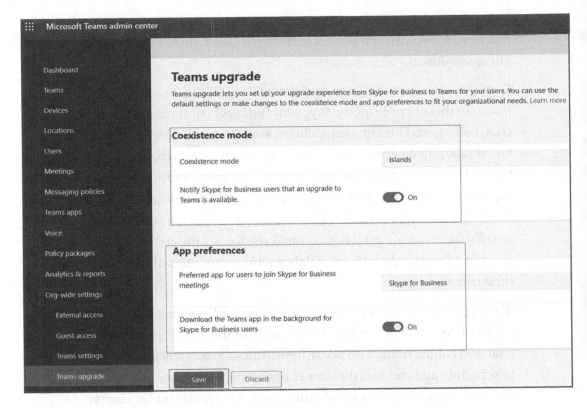

Figure 2-44. *Teams upgrade settings*

First let's understand the various upgrade modes available in the Teams admin center before making an upgrade plan.

- *Islands mode:* In the Islands upgrade coexistence mode for Teams, every client will use both Skype for Business and Microsoft Teams, operating side by side. The Skype for Business client talks to Skype for Business, and the Microsoft Teams client talks to Teams. Users are always expected to run both clients and can communicate natively in the client from which the communication was initiated.

- *Skype for Business Only mode:* Using this Teams upgrade coexistence mode, users continue using Skype for Business as they are, and there are no Teams capabilities allowed such as chat, meeting, and calling capabilities. They do not use Teams for teams and channels. This mode can be used prior to starting a managed deployment of Teams to prevent users from starting to use Teams ahead of their readiness.

113

This can also be used to enable authenticated participation in Teams meetings for Skype for Business users, if the users are licensed for Microsoft Teams.

- *Skype for Business with Teams collaboration (SfBWithTeamsCollab) mode:* In this upgrade mode, Skype for Business continues to support chat, calling, and meeting capabilities, and Microsoft Teams is used for collaboration capabilities such as teams and channels, access to files in Office 365, and added applications. Teams communications capabilities, including private chat, calling, and scheduling meetings, are off by default in this mode. This mode is a valid first step for organizations still relying on Skype for Business that want to provide a first insight into the collaboration capabilities of Teams for their users.

- *Skype for Business with Teams collaboration and meetings (SfBWithTeamsCollabAndMeetings) mode:* In this mode, private chat and calling remain on Skype for Business. Users will use Teams to schedule and conduct their meetings along with team- and channel-based conversations in this mode. This mode is also known as Meetings First mode. This coexistence mode is especially useful for organizations with Skype for Business on-premises deployments with Enterprise Voice, who are likely to take some time to upgrade to Teams and want to benefit from the superior Teams meetings capabilities as soon as possible.

- *Teams Only:* In this mode, a Teams Only user (also called an *upgraded user*) has access to all the capabilities of Teams. They might retain the Skype for Business client to join meetings on Skype for Business that have been organized by nonupgraded users or external parties. An upgraded user can continue to communicate with other users in the organization who are still using Skype for Business by using the interoperability capabilities between Teams and Skype for Business (if these Skype for Business users are not in Islands mode). However, an upgraded user cannot initiate a Skype for Business chat, call, or meeting. As soon as your organization is ready for some or all users to use Teams as their only communications and collaboration tool, you can upgrade those users to Teams Only mode.

Note   Even if the Skype for Business Only mode is meant to have the collaboration features of Teams disabled, in the current implementation, teams and channels are not automatically turned off for the user. This can be achieved by using the App Permissions policy to hide teams and channels.

Figure 2-45 shows details for all five upgrade modes.

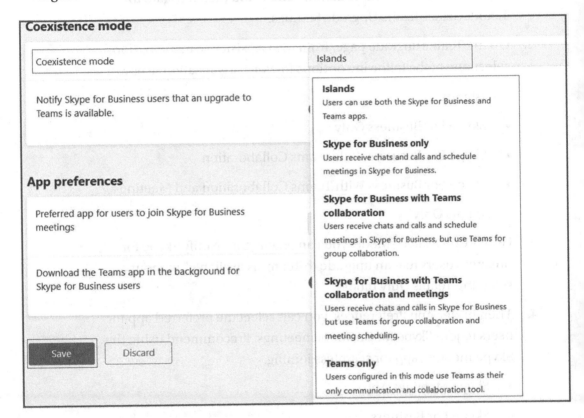

Figure 2-45.   *Teams coexistence modes*

Setting Teams Upgrade Mode

Before enabling Teams upgrade mode for users, you as an admin must undertake extensive planning and preparation, including the readiness of network infrastructure to allow Teams media traffic, the setup of your firewall to allow Teams traffic seamlessly, the Teams client deployment, and adoption. Once you are ready for the changeover from

Skype for Business to Teams, you will need to choose the appropriate upgrade path and coexistence modes for a smooth transition to Microsoft Teams in your organization.

You can use the same coexistence mode for all the users and upgrade to Microsoft Teams all at once, or you can do the migration by region, site, or group by configuring different coexistence modes for different groups of users.

To set the coexistence mode for your organization's users, follow these steps:

1. Log in to Microsoft Teams admin center, and then navigate to Teams. Select Teams Upgrade Settings.

2. On the Teams upgrade page, from the Coexistence mode options, select one of the following options for your organization users:

   - Islands

   - Skype For Business Only

   - Skype For Business With Teams Collaboration

   - Skype For Business With Teams Collaboration and Meetings

   - Teams Only

3. Under Coexistence Mode, you can enable the "Notify Skype for business users that an upgrade to Teams is available" without selecting Teams Only mode.

4. Then under App Preferences, you can select the preferred app for users to join Skype for Business meetings. I recommend using the Skype meeting app for seamless joining.

   - Skype Meetings App

   - Skype For Business

5. Turn on the "Download the teams app in the background for Skype for business users," which will download the Teams app on their machine.

6. Click Save to save the changes.

Note Microsoft has announced that all new Office 365 tenants are onboarded directly to Microsoft Teams for chat, meetings, and calling. Therefore, you will not see the options to select a coexistence mode if you have a newly provisioned tenant.

Setting Upgrade Options for an Individual User Using the Teams Admin Center

You learned about the Teams coexistence modes and how to enable an upgrade mode for a whole tenant, but what if you want to set different coexistence modes for different users? This can be achieved through the Teams admin center. To set a coexistence mode for an individual user, follow these steps:

1. Log in to the Microsoft Teams admin center and then navigate to and select Users. Locate the user for whom you would like to set the upgrade options. For this example, I have selected Chanda Ilag as the user to whom to assign a coexistence mode.

2. On the user page, on the Account tab, under Teams Upgrade, click Edit.

3. In the Teams Upgrade window, select one of the following options for the selected user:

   - Use Org-wide Settings

   - Islands

   - Skype For Business Only

   - Skype For Business With Teams collaboration

   - Skype For Business With Teams collaboration And Meetings

   - *Teams Only*

4. At the end, click Apply. The example in Figure 2-46 shows Teams Only assigned to user Chanda Ilag.

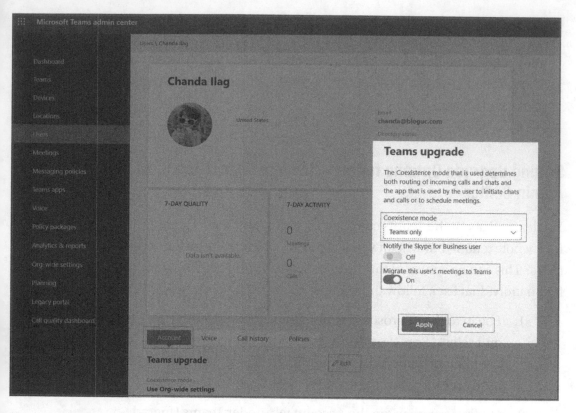

Figure 2-46. *Assigning a Teams upgrade mode*

Note   If you select any coexistence mode (except Use Org-wide Settings), you will have the option to enable notifications in the user's Skype for Business app, which will inform the user that the upgrade to Teams is coming soon. Enabling this for the user is done by turning on the "Notify the Skype for business user" option.

Selecting Teams Upgrade Mode Using PowerShell

As a Teams admin, you can use Windows PowerShell to assign a Teams coexistence mode to users. PowerShell is a decent option for automation as well. To manage the transition from Skype for Business to Teams, you can use the `Grant-CsTeams UpgradePolicy` command, which enables admins to apply `TeamsUpgradePolicy` to individual users or to configure the default settings for an entire organization. For example, to configure the user chanda@bloguc.com to Teams in SfBWithTeamsCollab mode and to notify the user, run the following command:

```
Grant-CsTeamsUpgradePolicy -PolicyName SfBWithTeamsCollabWithNotify
-Identity "chanda@bloguc.com"
```

Another example is to configure a TeamsOnly policy for the entire organization by running the following command:

```
Grant-CsTeamsUpgradePolicy -PolicyName TeamsOnly -Global
```

The next example shows how to remove a Teams upgrade policy:

```
Grant-CsTeamsUpgradePolicy -PolicyName $null -Identity chanda@bloguc.com
```

Admin Center: Users Tab

The Users tab within the Microsoft Teams admin center is a one-stop portal for managing individual users and their corresponding settings. Let's delve deeper into its key functionalities including managing users, regulating guest access, and controlling external access.

As an admin, most of your time will be spent managing users. In the Teams admin center, the Users tab allows you to manage all your users with different settings such as audio conferencing settings, the policies assigned to them, phone numbers, and other features for users in your organization who use Teams. Figure 2-47 shows a list of users and their different settings.

If you want to manage other user settings, such as by adding or deleting users, changing passwords, or assigning licenses, you need to visit the Office 365 admin center and navigate to Users.

User Management

The User Management function empowers admins to handle a myriad of settings, policies, and functionalities for each individual within the organization. To begin managing users, navigate to the Microsoft Teams admin center, select Users, and then Manage Users.

Here, you can take charge of several user-related tasks such as adding or deleting policies, assigning phone, check user-specific call analytics, and more. Additionally, you can handle audio conferencing settings, allocate phone numbers, and manage various Teams policies for each person.

Essentially, this section ensures you have full control over user-level features and functionalities.

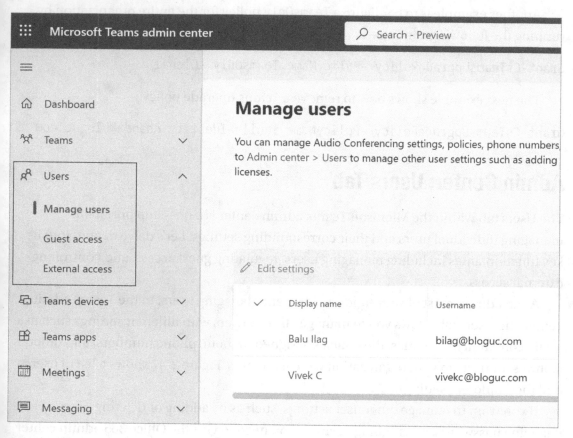

Figure 2-47. *Users and their different settings*

Guest Access

With guest access, you can regulate how guests interact and collaborate with your organization's users. This feature allows you to extend an invitation to individuals outside your organization, granting them access to specific teams. These guests can join meetings and engage in chats with your users. The guest access feature provides a controlled environment for external collaboration, while keeping your data secure.

Microsoft Teams offers external collaboration through two methods: guest access and external access, also known as federation access. We already learned about external access, so now we will cover guest access in detail.

Guest access permits teams in your organization to work together with users outside your organization by allowing them access to existing teams and channels on one or more of your tenants. Someone with an organization or consumer email account, such as Outlook, Hotmail, Gmail, or any other domain, can participate as a guest in Teams with full access to team chats, meetings, and files. Guest access is an org-wide setting in the Teams admin center and is turned off by default. Allowing guest access in Teams requires guest access in Teams, Azure AD, and Office 365 services. Before guest access is allowed and users add guests in their teams, as an admin you need to secure the environment so that guests will get specific access to what they need, not full access to everything.

The formal definition of guest access is access for users or individuals who do not have identity in your organization. For example, in the Bloguc.com organization, a user added abc@microsoft.com to their team as a guest. That means a Microsoft user is added to the Bloguc organization as a guest. The guest organization (Microsoft) will control the authentication layer, and the Bloguc organization controls the authorization layer that determines what the guest can access.

Don't confuse external access and guest access. Guest access gives access permission to an individual. External access gives access permission to an entire domain. Guest access uses your existing licenses when using certain features. Teams doesn't restrict the number of guests you can add. However, the total number of guests that can be added to your tenant is based on what your Azure AD licensing allows, typically five guests per Azure AD licensed user. External access allows you to communicate with users from other domains that are already using Teams. Therefore, they need to provide their own licenses to use Teams.

Adding Guest Users in Microsoft Teams

When a guest user wants access, they first need to get invited through email or invited/added in Azure as a guest user. Once the guest user accepts the invite, they get added to Azure AD in the cloud only. Remember, there is no on-premises data access. An invited guest account is not governed because there is no password to maintain. Guest authentication happens through its own tenant because it is federated with the Office 365 tenant.

Other than Azure AD tenants, a user like Google (Gmail) can also get invited for guest access. Once they are accepted and sign in to Gmail, no secondary authentication is required. Office 365 gets federated to that organization. Pretty much everything that is based on Security Assertion Markup Language (SAML) or Web Service (Ws)-federated is permitted to have guest access in Teams. Guest authentication is therefore managed by the guest's own organization tenant, and access is governed done by Teams, where the users gets specific access as a guest user.

Enabling and Managing Guest Access in Teams

As an admin, you can add guests in your tenant, and you can manage their access as well. As a security and Teams administrator, you have the capability to disable or enable guest access for Teams using the Teams admin portal and Windows PowerShell with the Teams service administrator role permission or global admin permission.

You can add guests at the tenant level, set and manage guest user policies and permissions, and view reports on guest user activity. These controls are available through the Microsoft Teams admin center. Guest user content and activities are under the same compliance and auditing protection as the rest of Office 365.

Note   Even if you activate guest access in Teams, you have to make sure that guest access is enabled in Azure AD and SharePoint as well.

Guest access is enabled and managed via four separate levels of permissions. All the authorization levels apply to your Office 365 tenant. As mentioned previously, every authorization level controls the guest experience, as demonstrated here:

- *Azure AD:* Guest access in Microsoft Teams depends on the Azure AD business-to-business (B2B) platform. This authorization level controls the guest experience at the directory, tenant, and application levels.

- *Office 365 groups:* This controls the guest experience in Office 365 Groups and Microsoft Teams.

- *Microsoft Teams:* This controls the guest experience in Microsoft Teams only.

- *SharePoint Online and OneDrive for Business:* This controls the guest experience in SharePoint Online, OneDrive for Business, Office 365 Groups, and Microsoft Teams.

An admin has the flexibility to set up guest access for organization tenant. For example, if you don't want to allow guest users in Microsoft Teams but want to allow them in general in your organization, such as for SharePoint or OneDrive for Business, just turn off guest access in Microsoft Teams. In another scenario, you could enable guest access at the Azure AD, Teams, and groups levels, but then disable the adding of guest users on selected teams that match one or more measures, such as a data classification of confidential. SharePoint Online and OneDrive for Business have their own guest access settings that do not rely on Office 365 Groups.

Note   Theoretically a guest user is a new user object in your Azure AD tenant. On the first line, you can allow or restrict the creation of new guest objects in your tenant, and then you can control whether guest access is allowed or if there are additional dependencies to access different locations, such as Teams, Office 365 Groups, and SharePoint.

Any guest access setting changes could take 2 to 24 hours to take effect, so be patient when you modify any org-wide settings.

You can also use Windows PowerShell commands to set up guest access in Teams. Remember, for Teams settings, you have to use the Skype for Business Online PowerShell module with Teams service admin or global admin permission. The most used and useful command for guest access is `Set-CsTeamsClientConfiguration`.

Open Windows PowerShell and connect to the Skype for Business Online tenant and run commands to enable various levels of guest access in Teams. To allow guest users globally, run the following command:

```
Set-CsTeamsClientConfiguration -AllowGuestUser $True -Identity Global
```

To allow private calling for guests, run this command:

```
Set-CsTeamsGuestCallingConfiguration -Identity Global -AllowPrivateCalling
$false
```

To allow Meet Now for guests, run the following command:

```
Set-CsTeamsGuestMeetingConfiguration -Identity Global -AllowMeetNow
$false -AllowIPVideo $false
```

To allow messaging settings like memes for guests, run this command:

```
Set-CsTeamsGuestMessagingConfiguration -AllowMemes $False
```

If you want to limit guest user capabilities in a subset of teams, you can use the Microsoft Teams PowerShell module and the Set-Team command. This lets you configure the same limitations as the Teams admin center, but instead of restricting it for all teams, you can focus on a single team. This can be useful if you need to create a team for your external consultants to exchange information without disrupting the existing structure.

Managing Guest Access Setting

As a Teams admin, you can enable and disable guest access settings, manage calling settings for guests, manage what meeting features are available to guests during meetings hosted by people in your organization, and manage messaging features for guests in channel conversations and chats. Figure 2-48 shows the guest access settings and what to enable.

Note Admin can enable or disable guest access permission based on your requirements.

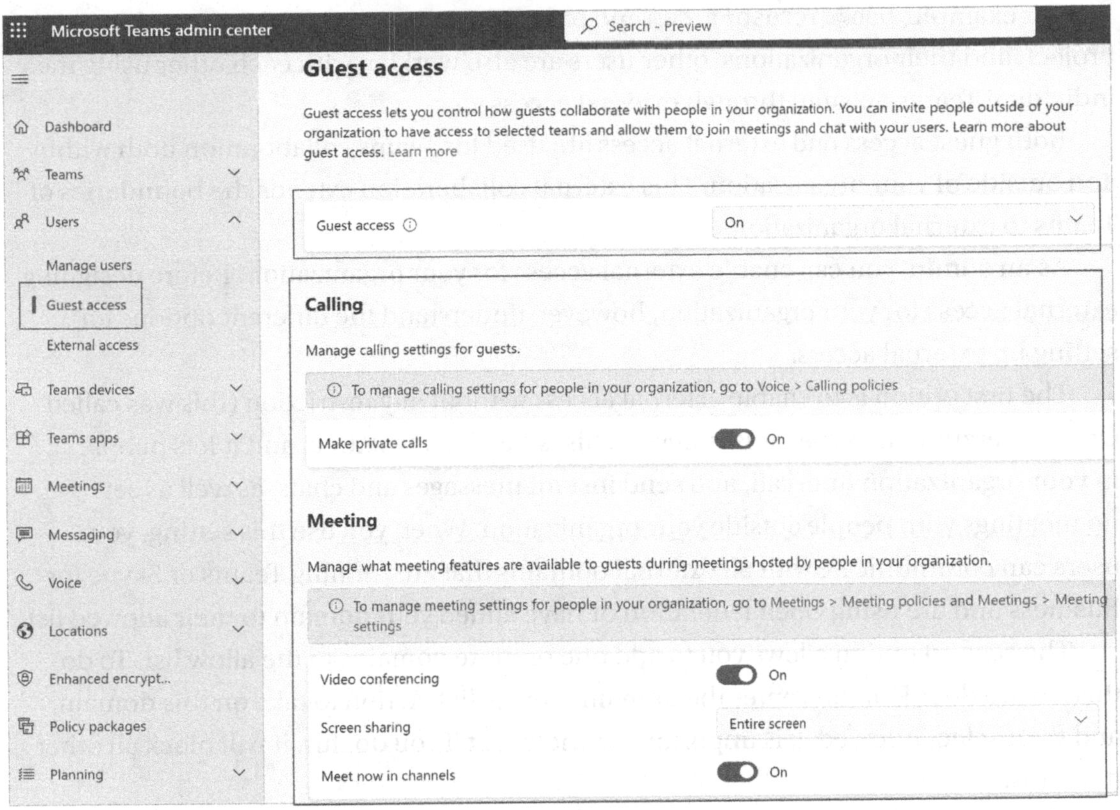

Figure 2-48. *Guest access settings*

External Access

External access (federation) in Microsoft Teams allows your Teams users to communicate with users who are outside of your organization. By using external access, your users can send messages to or receive messages from users in specific external domains.

Note   External (federation) access always uses peer-to-peer sessions; it is not used for group chat or team or channel conversations.

For example, bob@microsoft.com and balu@bloguc.com are working together on a project, and their organizations' other users are also working with each other using their individual Teams account through external access.

Both guest access and external access are used for Teams collaboration both within and outside of your organization. This external collaboration extends the boundaries of Teams to external organizations.

As an admin, you can enable external access for your organization. Before designing external access for your organization, however, understand the different options for setting up external access.

The first option is to enable external access without any restriction (this was called Open federation in Skype for Business). This is the default setting, and it lets people in your organization find, call, and send instant messages and chats, as well as set up meetings with people outside your organization. When you use this setting, your users can communicate with all external domains that are running Teams or Skype for Business and are using Open federation or have added your domain to their allowed list.

The second option allows you to add one or more domains to the allow list. To do this, click Add A Domain, enter the domain name, click Action to take on this domain, and then select Allowed. It is important to know that if you do this, it will block all other domains.

The third option is adding one or more domains to the block list. To do this, click Add A Domain, enter the domain name, click Action to take on this domain, and then select Blocked. It is important to know that if you do this, it will allow all other domains.

Here's how you can use external access in Teams:

- **Communicate across domains:** External access allows your Teams and Skype for Business users to communicate with other users that are outside of your organization.

- **Chat and calling:** Your users can engage in one-on-one chats and make calls with users in the external domain.

- **Share files:** While you can't directly share files with external users in a chat, you can share files from your Teams with external users if they are added as guests to the Team.

- **Participate in Teams:** External users can't be added to Teams, but they can participate in Teams as guests if they have a Microsoft 365 or Office 365 account.

This function allows your users to add apps when hosting meetings or chats with external participants. Simultaneously, your users can utilize third-party apps shared by external participants when they partake in externally hosted meetings or chats.

It's important to note that the data policies of the hosting user's organization, along with the data sharing practices of any third-party apps shared by that user's organization, will be applied in such interactions. Figure 2-49 shows external access settings. In the external access setting page, the admin can customize the settings based on their organization requirements; the available settings are to allow all external domains, add a specific domain and block all external domains, block only specific domains, or block all external domain settings.

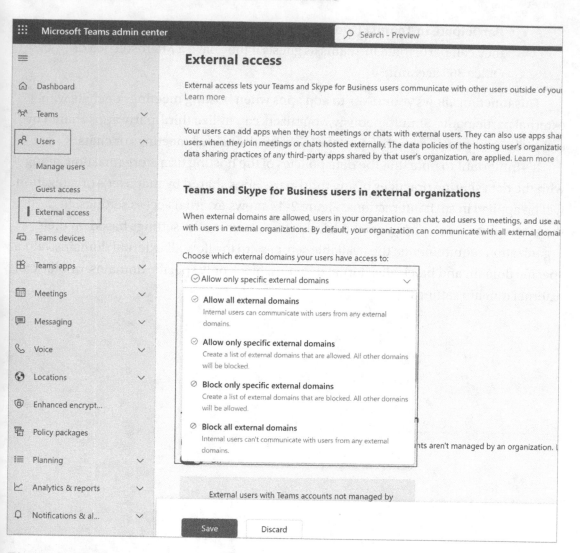

Figure 2-49. *External access settings*

In essence, the Users tab in the Teams admin center gives you extensive control over user settings, enhancing your ability to manage a safe and productive Teams environment. By understanding and utilizing these functionalities, you can create a customized and secure collaborative space for both your internal users and your external guests.

Admin Center: Teams Devices Tab

Let's explain the Devices tab.

Managing and Deploying a Teams Phone Endpoint

Microsoft Teams Phone is a flexible telephony solution that seamlessly integrates with Microsoft Teams, enabling users to make and receive calls on various devices such as IP phones, conference phones, or Teams Rooms devices. To efficiently manage and deploy these phone endpoints, administrators can use the Teams admin center.

Microsoft Teams has clients available for the desktop (Windows and macOS), mobile platforms (Android and iOS), Linux clients, and web clients. The end user using Teams on any of these devices will have the same experience. Apart from desktop, mobile, and web clients, there are different devices available that support Teams, such as desk phones, conference rooms, and common area phones. Teams does have native Teams phone and conference rooms available that you can use in meeting rooms and common areas. However, you need to set up a resource account for these room devices.

Store

When navigating a Teams device, the first thing you notice is the store. This is a Teams-certified device store. From here the admin can purchase new devices. Figure 2-50 shows the Teams device store.

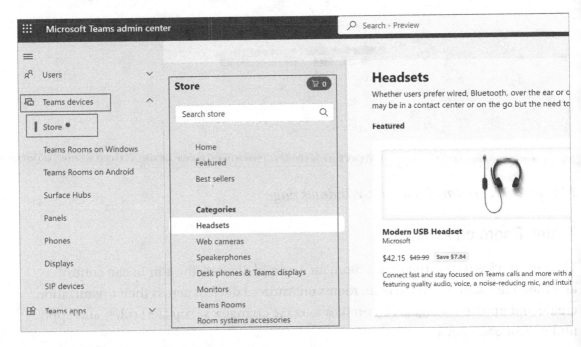

Figure 2-50. *Teams device store*

Teams Room on Windows

The next device type is the team room on Windows. As a Teams device admin, you can control and manage team rooms on Windows devices such as consoles, microphones, cameras, and displays, in your organization. You can configure settings, view activity information, manage updates, set up alert rules, and perform diagnostics to help with troubleshooting. You will see the status for each device. Figure 2-51 shows the Teams Rooms on Windows page, where the admin can manage them.

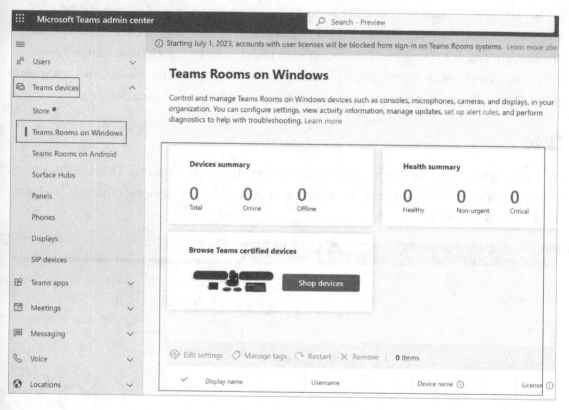

Figure 2-51. *Teams Rooms on Windows page*

Teams Room on Android

The next device type is the Teams room for Android devices; the admin can control and manage Teams-certified team rooms on Android devices across their organization, create and upload configuration profiles to make changes, set up alert rules, and apply updates for each device.

Surface Hubs

Another device type is Surface Hubs. This offers an all-in-one digital whiteboard, meetings platform, and collaborative computing experience. The Teams device admin can manage Surface Hubs from the Surface Hubs page.

Panels

The next device type is Panels. These types of devices are mounted outside of conference rooms, typically next to room entrances. They show room availability, room name, and reservations. Figure 2-52 shows Panels page, where the admin can manage Teams panel devices.

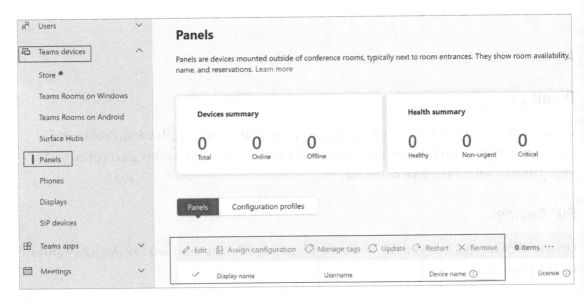

Figure 2-52. *Teams Panels page*

Phones

The next device type is Phones. As an admin, you control and manage Teams-certified phones across your organization, create and upload configuration profiles for each type of phone you have, make changes to their settings, set up alert rules, and apply software updates.

You will see all the phone devices under Phones such as user phones, common area phones, and conference phones. Additionally, you can create a configuration profile that is assigned to phone devices. Figure 2-53 shows the Teams Phones page, where the admin can manage Teams phone devices.

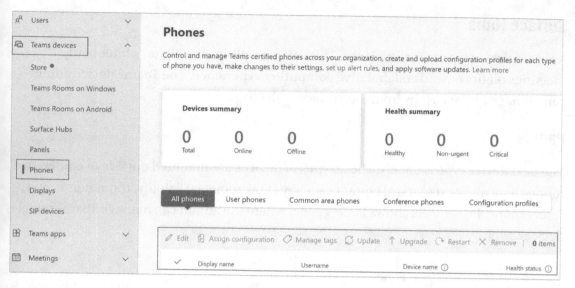

Figure 2-53. *Phone devices in the Teams admin center*

Displays

On the Display tab, you can manage display devices in your organization, create and upload configuration profiles so you can make setting changes, set up alert rules, and apply updates for each type of device.

SIP Devices

On the SIP Devices tab, you can control and manage Teams-certified SIP devices across your organization.

Creating and Managing Configuration Profiles in Teams

Admins can create and assign configuration profiles to a device or groups of devices to manage them. Device management settings include device status, device updates, restart, monitor diagnostics for devices, and device inventory. These are all management tasks that admins can perform using the Teams admin center.

To manage settings and features for Teams devices in your organization, you can use configuration profiles. As an admin, you can create or upload configuration profiles to include settings and features that you would like to enable or disable and then assign a profile to a device or groups of devices. To set up a profile, you need to create a profile configuration with custom settings, such as general setting with device lock setting, language, time/date format, time daylight saving, device setting with display screen saver, office hours for device, and network setting with DHCP enabled, hostname, IP address, subnet mask, DNS, and gateway.

Note   Out of the box there will no configuration profiles. Admins have to create configuration profiles to assign profiles to devices or groups of devices.

Creating a Configuration Profile to Manage Devices

To create a configuration profile, follow these steps:

1. Log in to the Microsoft Teams admin center. In the left navigation pane, select Teams Devices and click Phones.

2. On the Phones page, select Configuration Profiles, and then click Add.

3. On the Devices/New page, enter the name of the configuration profile and an optional description. Assign a meaningful name so that the profile configuration can be easily identified.

   a. In the General section, select if you will enable Device Lock and PIN, Language, Timezone, Date Format, and Time Format. Figure 2-54 shows a sample configuration.

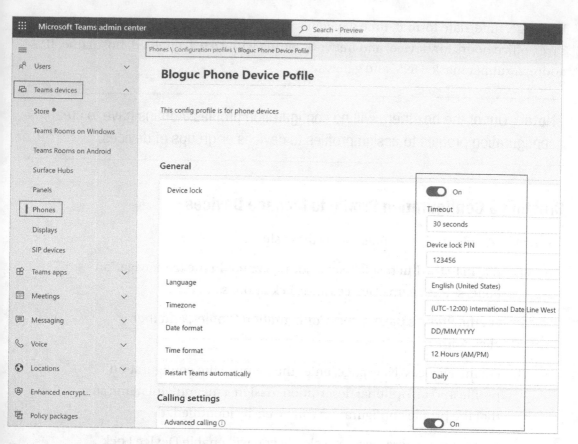

Figure 2-54. Phone configuration

b. Licensing for common area devices was expanded to include some new features (voicemail, call-forward settings, call park, call queues, auto attendants, Intune enrollment into Endpoint Manager). As you can probably imagine, the basic default common area phone user interface is not going to give you the flexibility to use all these features. Figure 2-42 shows the calling setting option with the advanced calling feature.

c. In the Device Settings section, select whether you will enable the display of a screen saver, brightness, backlight timeout, contrast, silent mode, office hours, power saving, and screen capture. Figure 2-55 shows sample device settings.

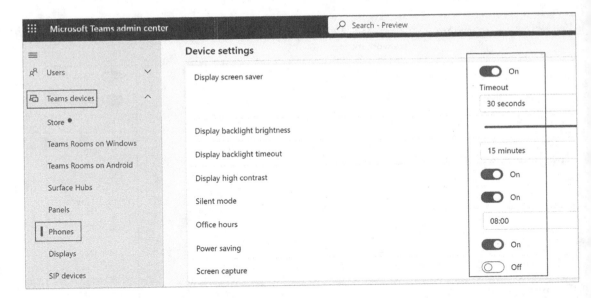

Figure 2-55. *Device config profile settings*

    d.   Under Network Settings, select if you will enable DHCP or logging and if you will configure Host Name, Domain Name, IP Address, Subnet Mask, Default Gateway, Primary DNS, Secondary DNS, Device's Default Admin Password, and Network PC Port. Figure 2-56 shows a sample profile configuration with network settings.

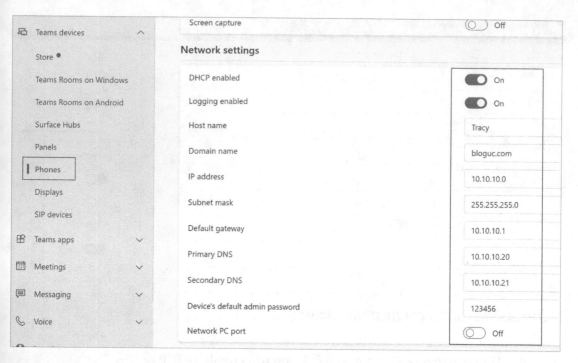

Figure 2-56. *Configuration profile network settings*

4.   Once you complete the configuration profile settings, click Save
     to commit the profile configuration. The next step is to assign the
     configuration to a device or group of devices.

Assigning the Configuration Profile to Devices

After creating the configuration profile, you need to assign it to the appropriate devices.
To assign a configuration profile, follow these steps:

1.   In the Microsoft Teams admin center, on the Phones page, select
     Configuration Profiles.

2.   Select the policy (just select the check mark) you want to apply
     (e.g., Bloguc VVX & Trion Phone in Figure 2-57), and then click
     Assign To Device.

3.   On the "Assign devices to a configuration profile" page, select
     the appropriate devices and then click Apply. Figure 2-57 shows
     assignment of the configuration profile to a phone device.

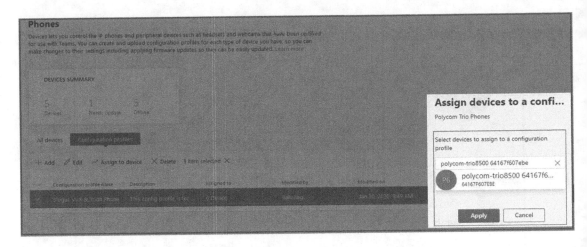

Figure 2-57. *Assigning a configuration profile to a device*

After a configuration profile is assigned, the settings of this profile will be applied to the selected devices.

Managing for Phone Inventory

You can manage phone inventory, including viewing and managing all phones. This includes admin tasks such as updating phones, restarting phones for maintenance, and monitoring and diagnostics. You can also create and assign configuration profiles. Figure 2-58 shows the available management options.

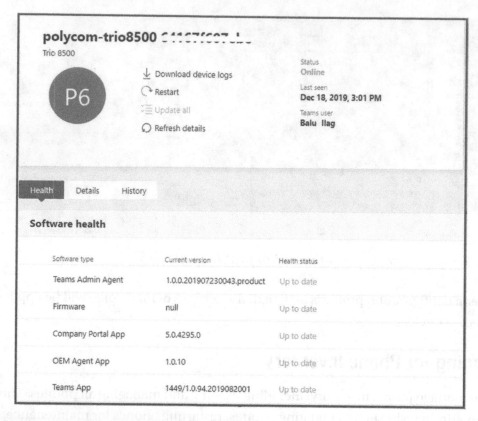

Figure 2-58. Phone management options

Configuring and Managing Microsoft Teams Rooms

Let's look at configuring and managing rooms.

Managing Microsoft Teams Rooms

Microsoft Teams Rooms (MTR), previously known as Skype Room Systems, offers a complete meeting experience, bringing HD video, audio, and content sharing to meetings of all sizes, from small huddle areas to large conference rooms. Before configuring an MTR resource account, an admin must understand the environments, room size, layout, and purpose. You can then identify the capabilities you want each room to have in the future. When you create an inventory of the equipment and capabilities in each existing room, your requirements for that room feed into your device selection planning to create a rich conferencing solution. The audio and video capabilities that are needed for each room, as well as the room size and purpose, all play an important role in deciding which solution will be optimal for each room. You must also check and confirm that the room doesn't have excessive echo, noisy air conditioning, or furniture getting in the way of the equipment. You should also confirm there is enough power for the screens and rooms.

As an MTR admin, your role is critical in ensuring that your organization gets the maximum benefit from its MTR system, providing an excellent meeting experience for all users. Remember, though, that each organization's specific needs and requirements may necessitate additional responsibilities. Always ensure you're following your organization's guidelines and best practices. Please always review the Microsoft documentation for the most current and accurate information.

As an MTR admin, you will have various responsibilities to ensure a seamless meeting experience.

- **Configuration and setup:** Configure and set up MTR devices according to the room layout and user requirements. This includes setting up the AV devices and screens and ensuring the MTR console is correctly configured with the MTR app.

- **Software updates:** Regularly check for and apply software updates to the MTR devices. This is crucial for maintaining security and gaining new features or improvements.

- **Monitoring and troubleshooting:** Use the Teams admin center or other monitoring tools to regularly check the status and health of the MTR devices. Promptly troubleshoot and resolve any issues that arise.

- **User training:** Provide training and support to users on how to use the MTR system for their meetings.

- **Policies and access control:** Implement and enforce policies for room usage. Also, manage the room calendar settings in Microsoft 365 to control who can book the room.

- **Maintenance:** Regularly clean and maintain the physical equipment. Test the equipment regularly to ensure it's working correctly.

It is a best practice to make sure to have a plan for monitoring, administration, and management tasks on an ongoing basis. It is important to decide who will undertake these tasks early in your deployment. In planning for operations, factors you need to consider are deciding who will manage team rooms and which help-desk queue will handle calls regarding them. As part of Teams room management, important administrative considerations include the following:

- As an admin, have a proper plan for managing and configuring the local accounts that are created by the MTR application installer.

- You can consider using Microsoft Azure Monitor to monitor the MTR deployment and report on availability, hardware and software errors, and the MTR application version. As of this writing, this monitoring facility is not available, but Microsoft plans to provide such monitoring in the future.

- An additional consideration is whether rooms will be domain-joined or a workgroup member. Domain-joined deployment includes multiple advantages, such as granting domain users and groups administrative rights and importing your organization's private root certificate chain automatically. We recommend joining your Teams room to the domain so that you don't have to manually install the root certificate.

After addressing these considerations, you can start preparing to host accounts for rooms. Remember, every MTR device requires a dedicated and unique resource account that must be enabled for both Microsoft Teams or Skype for Business Online and additionally for Exchange Online. This account must have a room mailbox hosted on Exchange Online and be enabled as a meeting room in the Teams or Skype for Business deployment. In Exchange, you need to configure calendar processing so that the device can automatically accept incoming meeting requests.

Note   Meeting scheduling features will not work without a device account.

There are several best practices to adopt when managing MTR rooms. Create a resource account for a Teams room with a meaningful display name and description to easily locate the Microsoft Teams room. The display name is important because users will see it when searching for and adding MTR systems to their meetings. As an example, you could use the following convention: city initials, followed by room name and maximum capacity. The Lincoln room with an eight-person capacity in San Jose might have the display name SJ-LN-8.

Creating a Microsoft Teams Room Account

To create a new room mailbox, use the following Exchange Online PowerShell module:

```
New-Mailbox -Name "Bloguc Sunnyvale Room 1" -Alias Bl-SVL-6-01 -Room
-EnableRoomMailbox -Account $true -MicrosoftOnlineServicesID <Account>
-RoomMailboxPassword (ConvertTo-SecureString -String '**********'
-AsPlainText -Force)
```

Here's an example of configuring the settings on the room mailbox named Bloguc MTR Room1:

```
Set-CalendarProcessing -Identity "Bl-SVL-6-01" -AutomateProcessing
AutoAccept -AddOrganizerToSubject $false -DeleteComments $false
-DeleteSubject $false -RemovePrivateProperty $false -AddAdditionalResponse
$true -AdditionalResponse "This is a Microsoft Teams Meeting room!"
```

Once the Teams room account is ready, you can proceed to room device installation. Once your Teams Rooms system is physically deployed and the supported peripheral devices are connected, including screens, speakers, microphones, console panels, and so on, the next matter is providing the Teams account and the login to the Teams room using the resource account and password that you created earlier, in our example, Bl-svl-6-01@bloguc.com. You use a script to create a Teams account (see https://docs.microsoft.com/en-us/microsoftteams/rooms/rooms-configure-accounts).

To sign in, you first need to configure the Teams Rooms application to assign the Microsoft Teams Rooms resource account and password created earlier. That enables the Microsoft Teams Rooms system to sign into Microsoft Teams or Skype for Business and Exchange. It is important to leverage certified USB audio and video peripherals linked elsewhere in the document. Not doing so can result in unpredictable behavior. Additionally, the account also needs a rooms license or add-on license assigned.

As an admin, you can manually configure each Microsoft Teams Rooms system. Alternatively, you can use a centrally stored XML configuration file to manage the application settings and leverage a startup Group Policy object (GPO) script to reapply the configuration you want, each time the Microsoft Teams Rooms system boots. To leverage a centrally stored configuration, however, your room must be domain-joined.

After room deployment, you can run multiple tests to make sure everything works as per your expectations. Frequently check the call quality using the call quality dashboard.

Admin Center: Teams Apps Tab

The Teams Apps tab in the Microsoft Teams admin center provides a consolidated view of all the Teams apps within your organization. It allows Teams administrators to manage and control these apps effectively. Here's a rundown of the capabilities available in the Apps tab:

- **Manage apps:** Here, you can view all the apps available for your organization in Teams. This includes Microsoft's own apps, third-party apps, and custom apps built by your organization. For each app, you can see its name, publisher, status, and other details. Also, you can view, manage, and upload custom apps developed specifically for your organization.

- **Permission policies:** You can control what apps are available to which users. For instance, you can allow everyone in your organization to use a certain app, or you can restrict its use to certain departments or teams.

- **Setup policies:** These policies let you control which apps and shortcuts appear in the Teams app bar for your users. For example, you could add a shortcut to a frequently used app for a specific department.

- **Teams apps:** Monitor the usage of Teams apps in your organization.

- **App catalog:** View the catalog of apps that are available for your organization to install.

- **Manage app setup policies:** Configure and assign policies to set up teams with pre-installed apps that are pinned to the app bar in the Teams desktop and web clients.

Managing applications as an admin is not difficult; however, you must know how to set up and assign policies. The following sections contain detailed information about managing Teams apps.

Permission Policies

The Microsoft Teams admin center has app permission policy settings that control what apps are available to Teams users in your organization. You can use the Global (Org-wide) default policy and customize it, or you can create one or more policies to meet the needs of your organization. Basically, you can allow Microsoft apps, third-party apps, or tenant apps.

Using app permission policies, you can block or allow apps either organization-wide or for specific users. When you block an app, all interactions with that app are disabled, and it will no longer appear in Teams. For example, you can use app permission policies to disable an app that creates a permission or data loss risk to your organization, gradually roll out new third-party or custom-built apps to specific users, and simplify the user experience, especially when you start rolling out Teams across your organization.

Out of the box, you will see the Global (Org-wide default) policy, which is designed to allow all Microsoft apps, third-party apps, and tenant apps to all users in your organization. This policy is assigned and applicable to all users by default (unless a custom policy is assigned). Figure 2-59 shows the default policy.

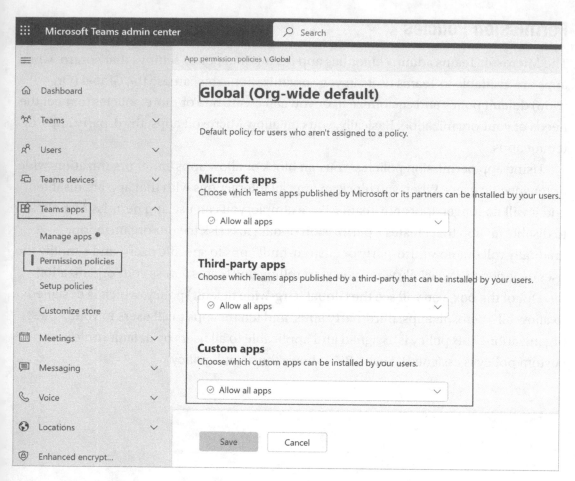

Figure 2-59. *Teams global app permission policy*

Managing Organization-wide App Settings

As a Teams admin, you can use organization-wide app settings to control which apps are available across your organization. Organization-wide app settings govern behavior for all users and override any other app permission policies assigned to users. You can use them to control malicious or problematic apps.

To manage org-wide app settings, log in to the Teams admin center and navigate to Teams Apps and select Manage Apps. Click Org-wide App Settings shown on the left side of the page. Once the Org-wide App Setting window opens, you can configure the settings you want to use. Figure 2-60 shows that tailored apps, third-party apps, and custom apps are allowed, and no apps are blocked. However, one setting that is not enabled is "Auto installed approved apps," which is a newly added feature by Microsoft.

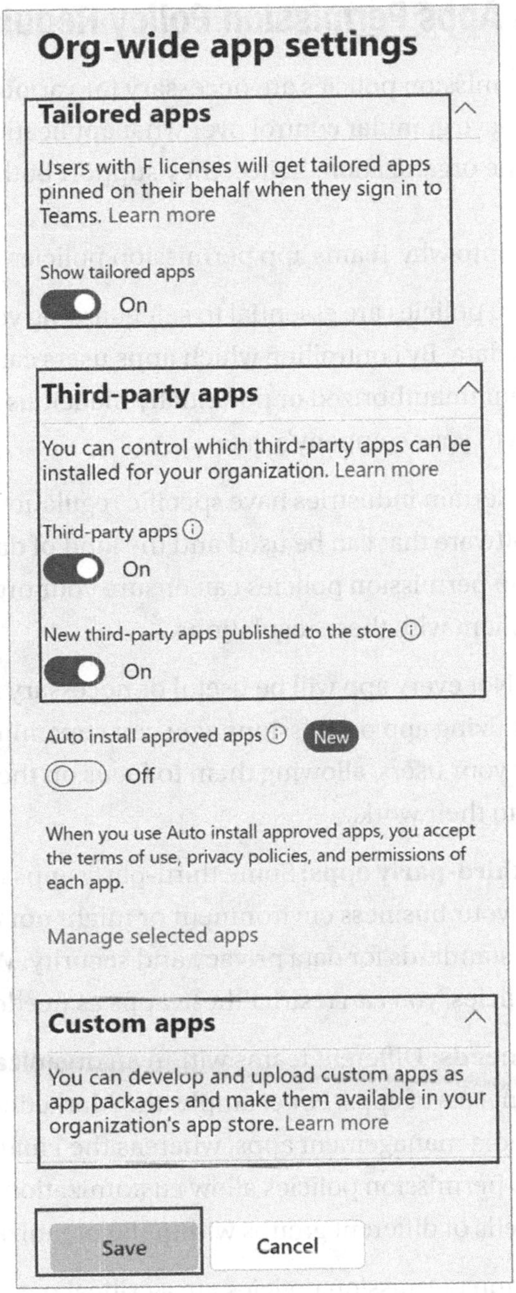

Org-wide app settings

Tailored apps ∧

Users with F licenses will get tailored apps pinned on their behalf when they sign in to Teams. Learn more

Show tailored apps

⚫◯ On

Third-party apps ∧

You can control which third-party apps can be installed for your organization. Learn more

Third-party apps ⓘ

⚫◯ On

New third-party apps published to the store ⓘ

⚫◯ On

Auto install approved apps ⓘ (New)

◯ Off

When you use Auto install approved apps, you accept the terms of use, privacy policies, and permissions of each app.

Manage selected apps

Custom apps ∧

You can develop and upload custom apps as app packages and make them available in your organization's app store. Learn more

Save   Cancel

Figure 2-60. *App Org-wide settings*

Why Is the Teams Apps Permission Policy Required?

Microsoft Teams app permission policies are necessary for various reasons. They allow administrators to have granular control over what applications can be accessed or installed by users in the organization; hence, they support both productivity and security.

Here's a deeper dive into why Teams app permission policies are essential:

- **Security:** These policies are essential to safeguarding your organization's data. By controlling which apps users can install and use, you prevent unauthorized or potentially malicious apps from gaining access to your company's data.

- **Compliance:** Certain industries have specific regulations regarding the types of software that can be used and the kind of data they can access. App permission policies can ensure your organization remains compliant with these regulations.

- **Productivity:** Not every app will be useful or necessary for every user. By customizing app permissions, you can streamline the Teams experience for your users, allowing them to focus on the tools that are most relevant to their work.

- **Control over third-party apps:** Some third-party apps might not be suitable for your business environment or might not meet your organization's standards for data privacy and security. With app permission policies, you can restrict these apps as needed.

- **User-specific needs:** Different teams within an organization may require different sets of apps. For example, the Marketing team might need social media management apps, whereas the Finance team might not. App permission policies allow customization according to the specific needs of different groups within the organization.

To sum it up, Teams app permission policies are a critical part of managing your organization's Teams environment, providing the flexibility to support a diverse set of user needs while maintaining data security and compliance.

Creating a Teams App Permission Policy

Admins create a custom app policy to control the apps that are available for different groups of users in an organization. You can create and assign separate custom policies based on whether apps are published by Microsoft or third parties or whether they are custom apps for your organization. It's important to know that after you create a custom policy, you can't change it if third-party apps are disabled in org-wide settings.

As an admin, you can be very specific about which applications you allow (Microsoft, third-party, or tenant apps) or block. You can allow all apps or just specific apps and block all apps such as Microsoft apps, third-party published apps, and tenant apps, or those published by your organization.

1. To create a custom app policy, log in to the Microsoft Teams admin center, and then navigate to Teams Apps. Select Permission Policies and then click +Add to create a new policy.

2. Once the app permission policy page opens, enter a name and description for the policy (e.g., **Bloguc App Policy1**).

3. The default setting for Microsoft apps is "Allow all apps."

4. Then, under Third-Party Apps, select "Allow specific apps and block all others," as shown in Figure 2-61. You then have to add the apps that you want to allow.

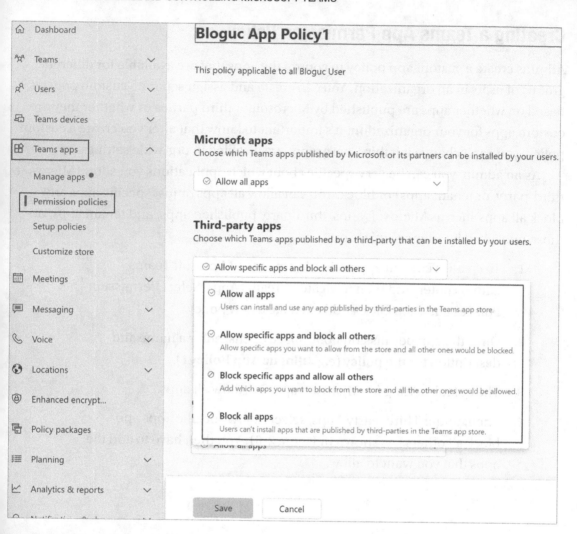

Figure 2-61. *Allowing specific apps and blocking all others*

5. Select "Allow apps" and then search for the app(s) that you want to allow. Make your selections and then click Add. The search results are filtered to the app publisher (Microsoft apps, third-party apps, or tenant apps). The example in Figure 2-62 shows that Workplace from Facebook is allowed.

6. Once you have chosen the list of apps, select Allow. Similarly, if you selected "Block specific apps and allow all others," search for and add the apps that you want to block.

7. Click Save to save the app policy. For the example shown in
    Figure 2-62, the Bloguc organization requirement is to allow all
    Microsoft apps and custom apps but block all third-party apps
    except Twitter apps.

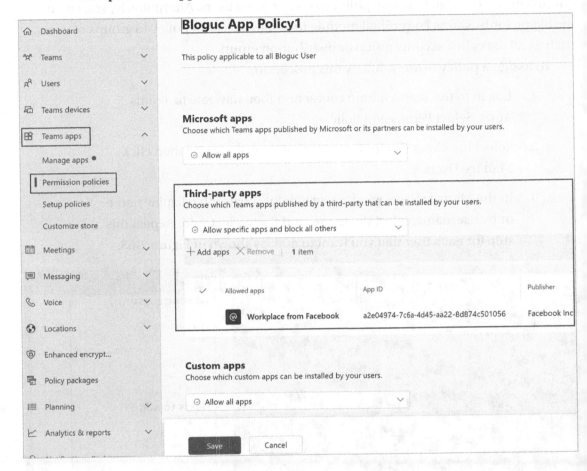

Figure 2-62. *Teams app permission policy*

Note   All allowed apps will show in Teams client apps, and users can add to their teams and use them.

Assigning the App Permission Policy to Users

Once you create a custom policy, the next thing you need to do is to assign the policy to users so that the policy takes effect. As an admin, you can use the Microsoft Teams admin center to assign a custom policy to one or more users. Alternatively, you can use the Skype for Business PowerShell module to assign a custom policy to groups of users, such as all users in a security group or distribution group.

To assign a policy to users, follow this procedure:

1. Log in to the Teams admin center and then navigate to Teams Apps. Select Permission Policies.

2. Select the check box for the custom policy name and then click Manage Users.

3. In the Manage Users window, search for the user by display name or by username, select the name, and then select Add. Repeat this step for each user that you want to add, as shown in Figure 2-63.

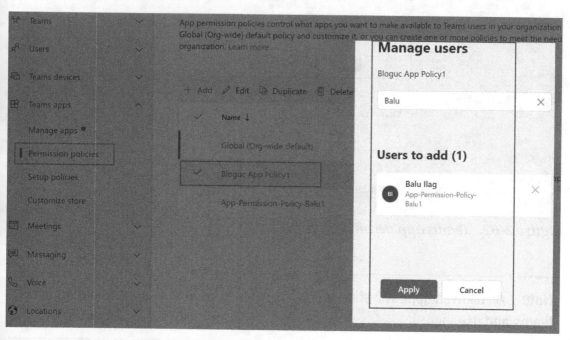

Figure 2-63. *Assigning a policy to a user*

4. Once you add the required users, click Apply to commit the change and assign the policy to those users.

You can assign custom app permissions to users on the Users tab in the Teams admin center. Simply log in to the Teams admin center, navigate to Users, and select the users. Click Edit Settings and then under App Permission Policy, select the app permission policy you want to assign; click Apply.

Assigning a Custom App Permission Policy Using PowerShell

As previously mentioned, you can assign a custom app permission policy to multiple users with PowerShell for automation. For example, you might want to assign a policy to all users in a security group. You can do this by connecting to the Azure AD PowerShell module and the Skype for Business Online PowerShell module and using the Grant-CsTeamsAppPermissionPolicy command.

For example, if you want to assign a custom app permission policy called Bloguc App Policy1 to all users in the Bloguc IT group, you would run the following command:

```
$group = Get-AzureADGroup -SearchString "Bloguc IT Group"
$members = Get-AzureADGroupMember -ObjectId $group.ObjectId -All $true |
Where-Object {$_.ObjectType -eq "User"}
$members | ForEach-Object { Grant-CsTeamsAppPermissionPolicy -PolicyName
"Bloguc App Policy1" -Identity $_.EmailAddress}
```

Depending on the number of members in the group, this command could take several minutes to execute.

Setup Policies

In Teams apps, the next type of policy is a setup policy. This is actually where you as an admin can control how apps will appear in the Teams client for users. You can use app setup policies to customize Microsoft Teams to highlight the apps that are most important for your users. You can select the apps to pin to the apps bar and the order in which they appear. App setup policies let you showcase apps that users in your organization need, including those built by third parties or by developers in your organization.

Figure 2-64 shows the default Teams app setup policy. You can see the app names such as Activity, Chat, Teams, Calendar, Calling, and Files. All these apps will be displayed in the Teams client in the same order as shown under "Setup policies."

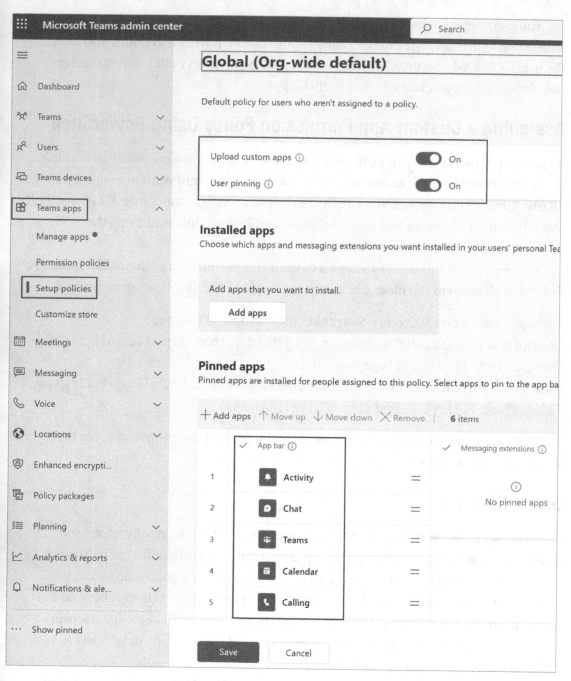

Figure 2-64. *Setting setup policies*

Figure 2-65 shows the result as it appears in the Teams client. The app bar displays on the side of the Teams desktop client and at the bottom for the Teams mobile clients.

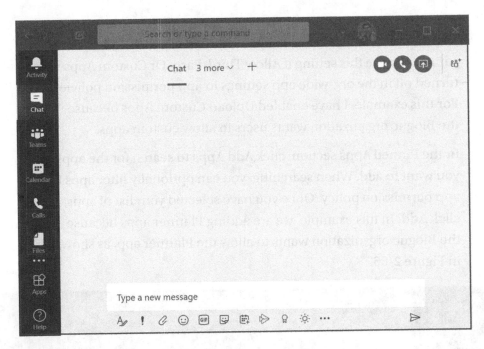

Figure 2-65. *Teams apps set in a Teams setup policy*

Managing the Teams Setup Policy

Microsoft Teams setup policies are rules that admins can configure to control what apps, bots, and other features should be pinned and visible in Microsoft Teams for end users. These policies help admins tailor the Teams experience to a user's role within the organization, making them more productive by having the necessary tools readily available.

In the Microsoft Teams admin center, setup policies can be found under Teams apps ➤ Setup policies. As part of managing Teams setup policies, you can create a custom app setup policy and add any Microsoft or custom apps as pinned apps. For example, the Bloguc organization wants to allow its users to see Planner as a pinned app in their Teams client. To add an app in a Teams app setup policy, follow these steps:

1. Log in to the Teams admin center, navigate to Teams Apps, and select Setup Policies. On the App Setup Policies page, select Add and then enter a name and description for the app setup policy.

2.   Turn the Upload Custom Apps setting on or off, depending on
     whether you want to let users upload custom apps to Teams. You
     cannot change this setting if Allow Third-Party Or Custom Apps is
     turned off in the org-wide app settings in app permission policies.
     For this example, I have enabled Upload Custom Apps because
     the Bloguc organization wants users to allow custom apps.

3.   In the Pinned Apps section, click Add Apps to search for the apps
     you want to add. When searching, you can optionally filter apps by
     app permission policy. Once you have selected your list of apps,
     click Add. In this example, we are adding Planner apps because
     the Bloguc organization wants to allow the Planner app, as shown
     in Figure 2-66.

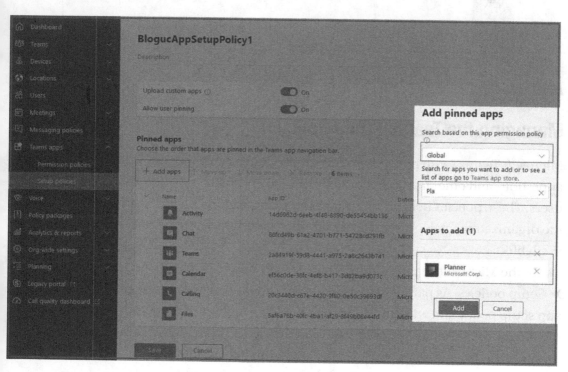

Figure 2-66. *Adding apps to pinned apps*

Once you click Add, the Planner apps will be included under "Pinned apps," as shown in Figure 2-67.

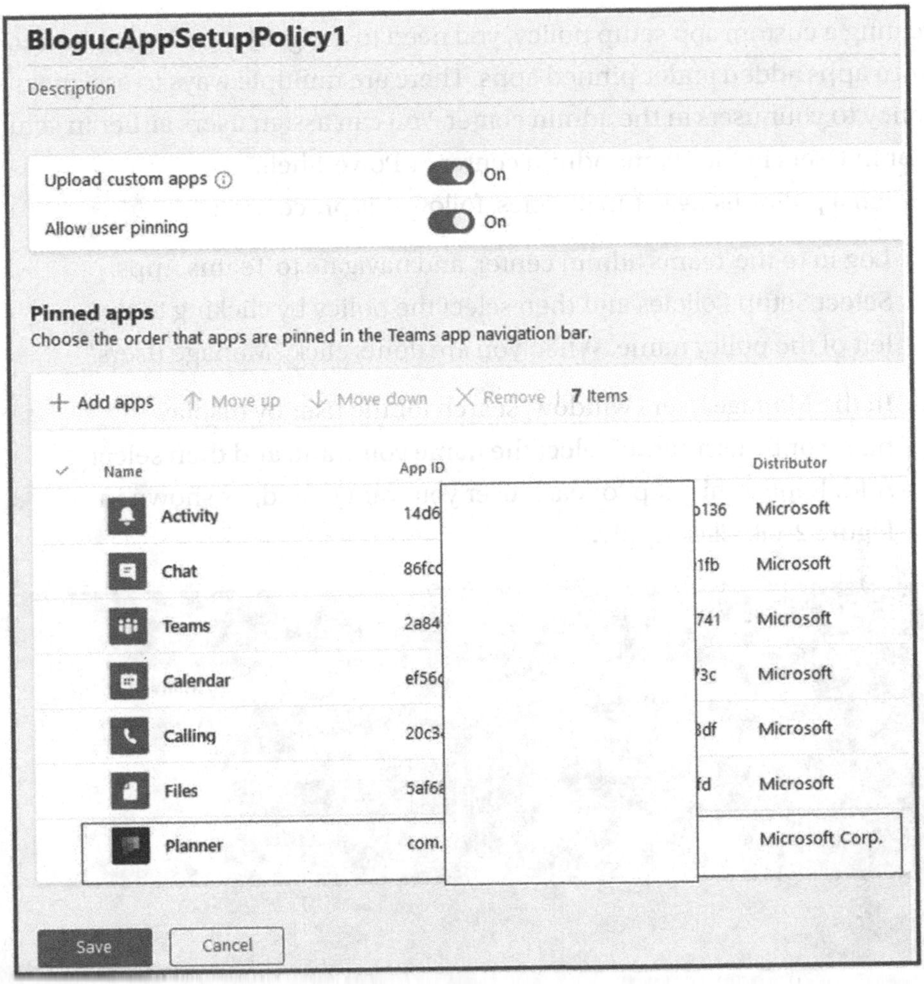

BlogucAppSetupPolicy1

Description

Upload custom apps (i)   On

Allow user pinning   On

Pinned apps
Choose the order that apps are pinned in the Teams app navigation bar.

+ Add apps   ↑ Move up   ↓ Move down   ✕ Remove | **7** Items

	Name	App ID		Distributor
🔔	Activity	14d6	136	Microsoft
💬	Chat	86fc	1fb	Microsoft
👥	Teams	2a84	741	Microsoft
📅	Calendar	ef56	3c	Microsoft
📞	Calling	20c3	8df	Microsoft
📁	Files	5af6	fd	Microsoft
▦	Planner	com.		Microsoft Corp.

Save   Cancel

Figure 2-67. *An app added to pinned apps*

By leveraging setup policies, you can guide your team's workflows and increase productivity by making the most commonly used apps readily accessible. You can have multiple policies for different teams based on their specific needs. It's a powerful way to customize the Teams experience for your users.

Assigning a Custom App Setup Policy to Users from the Teams Admin Center and PowerShell

After creating a custom app setup policy, you need to assign the policy to users to show the custom apps added under pinned apps. There are multiple ways to assign an app setup policy to your users in the admin center. You can assign users either in setup policies or in Users in the Teams admin center or PowerShell.

To assign a policy using setup policies, follow this procedure:

1. Log in to the Teams admin center, and navigate to Teams Apps. Select Setup Policies and then select the policy by clicking to the left of the policy name. When you are done, click "Manage users."

2. In the Manage Users window, search for the user by display name or by username, select the name you want, and then select Add. Repeat this step for each user you want to add, as shown in Figure 2-68. Click Apply.

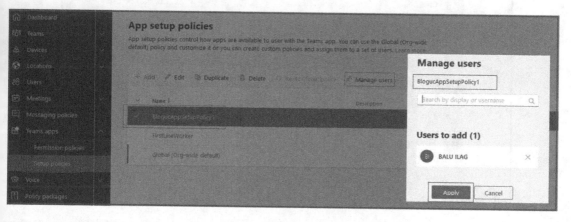

Figure 2-68. *Assigning an app setup policy to a user*

3. Once you are done adding users, click Save.

You can also perform the following steps if you want to assign users within the Users pane. Log in to the Teams admin center and then navigate to Users. Select the appropriate user and click Edit Settings. Under "App setup policy," select the app setup policy you want to assign, and then click Apply.

Assigning a Custom App Setup Policy to Users Using PowerShell

As an admin, you might want to assign an app setup policy to multiple users that you have already identified. For example, you might want to assign a policy to all users in an IT group. You can do this by connecting to the Azure AD PowerShell for Graph module and the Skype for Business Online PowerShell module.

For example, to assign an app setup policy called BlogucAppSetupPolicy1 to all users in the Bloguc IT group, you should execute the following PowerShell commands:

```
## Get the GroupObjectId of the particular group: ##
$group = Get-AzureADGroup -SearchString "**Bloguc IT**"
## Get the members of the specified group: ##
$members = Get-AzureADGroupMember -ObjectId $group.ObjectId -All $true |
Where-Object {$_.ObjectType -eq "User"}
## Assign all users in the group to a particular app setup policy: ##
$members | ForEach-Object { Grant-CsTeamsAppSetupPolicy -PolicyName
"**BlogucAppSetupPolicy1**" -Identity $_.EmailAddress}
```

Depending on the number of members in the Bloguc IT group, this command could take several minutes to execute.

These capabilities make it easier to manage the integration of apps into Teams, enhance security, and improve the Teams experience for your users. By having control over what apps are available and to whom, you can help ensure that your organization gets the maximum benefit from Teams while reducing the risks associated with unmanaged app usage. Always make sure to refer to the latest Microsoft documentation to get the most current and accurate information about managing apps in Teams.

Admin Center: Meetings Tab

The Meetings tab in the Microsoft Teams admin center is a centralized place for admins to manage and customize the meeting experiences for their organization. It offers a wide range of settings and configurations that can be tailored to suit the unique needs of your organization. You will find all the meeting and live event settings and policies under Meeting in the Teams admin center, as shown in Figure 2-69.

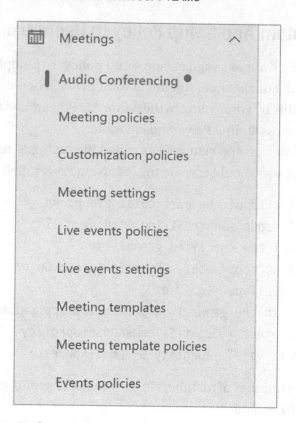

Figure 2-69. *Meeting policy*

Here's what you can do on the Meetings tab:

Audio conferencing: The Audio Conferencing tab controls phone numbers and features available to users with audio conferencing. You can use the Global (Org-wide) default policy and customize it, or you can create one or more policies to meet the needs of your organization.

Meeting policies: Here, you can define what features are available to users during Teams meetings. You can control things such as screen sharing, recording permissions, video settings, and much more.

Customization policies: Use the customization policies tab to customize the look of your organization's Teams meetings. You can use the Global (Org-wide default) policy or create custom policies and assign them to a set of users. Remember this policy setting is available only with Teams Premium.

Meeting Settings: This is where global meeting settings are defined, including settings for third-party apps, cloud recording, transcription services, and the use of Microsoft Whiteboard.

Live Events Policies: This section allows you to define the settings for live events, including permissions and features for presenters and attendees.

Live Events Settings: Here you can manage global settings for live events, including permissions for third-party apps and default roles for attendees.

Meeting templates: Meeting templates can be used to create meetings that are available to users with common needs or a common project. Meeting templates are available to all organizations including small to large business and educational organizations. Remember this policy setting is available only with Teams premium.

Meeting templates policies: Meeting templates policies let you create and set up policies that control what templates people in your organization can see. You can use the Global (Org-wide default) policy and customize it, or you can create custom policies. Remember this policy setting is available only with Teams premium.

Event Policies: Teams Events Policies are used to configure event settings on Teams, starting with webinars. You can use the Global (Org wide default) policy and customize it, or you can create custom policies and assign them to people who create, run, and manage events in your organization.

Why Is Teams Meeting So Important?

Meetings play a crucial role in today's business environment, especially with remote work becoming increasingly prevalent. Effective meetings can help in the following ways:

Improve communication: They provide a platform for open discussion and immediate feedback. This helps to ensure that everyone is on the same page and any misunderstandings can be cleared up promptly.

Facilitate collaboration: Meetings bring people together to work toward common goals. They encourage teamwork and foster a culture of collaboration.

Drive decision-making: They offer an opportunity for decision-makers to come together to discuss, debate, and make important decisions.

Boost productivity: Regular meetings keep everyone updated about the ongoing projects, work progress, and next steps, which helps in maintaining momentum and productivity.

Detailed Information for All the Meeting Policies

Microsoft Teams meetings are one of the most used and best features Teams provides. We already covered the basic details of Teams meetings in Chapter 1. If you are new to Teams meeting, we encourage you to review Chapter 1. Once you are aware of how to set up teams, channels, and applications within Microsoft Teams, the next step you can take is to add and customize settings and policies for meetings, including audio conferencing, video, and application sharing.

Users can schedule and join Teams meetings from a variety of clients. For example, using audio conferencing, users can attend meetings from land lines or mobile phones by dialing in to the meeting. As a Teams admin, you can enable or disable certain types of meetings in addition to disabling modalities such as video or screen sharing, according to organization regulations. Because there is integration between Teams and Office 365 tools such as Microsoft Outlook, you can use an add-in to schedule Teams meetings directly from your calendar. Based on your organization's needs and requirements, you can configure the appropriate settings for meetings and conferencing that your employees are going to use in Microsoft Teams. Because Teams offers so many options and advantages, it is important for you as an admin to review and confirm that your environment is properly configured to provide your users with the best possible experience.

Audio Conferencing

Audio conferencing policies allows admins to manage phone numbers and features available to users with audio conferencing. You can use the Global (Org-wide) default policy and customize it, or you can create one or more policies to meet the needs of your organization. Figure 2-70 shows an audio conferencing policy example.

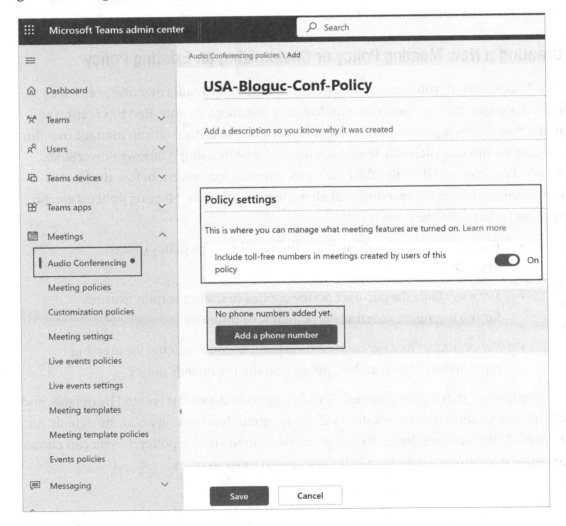

Figure 2-70. *Meeting audio conferencing*

Meeting Policies

Meeting policies are used to control what features are available to users when they join Microsoft Teams meetings. You can use the Global (Org-wide default) policy and customize it or create one or more custom meeting policies for people who host meetings in your organization. Along with meeting policies, you can permit or restrict the features that will be available to users during meetings and audio conferencing. You must first decide if you are going to customize the initial meeting policies and whether you need multiple meeting policies. Then you must determine which groups of users receive which meeting policies. By default, there are six policies available including Global (Org-wide default), AllOn, AllOff, Restricted Anonymous access, Restricted Anonymous No Recording, and Kiosk.

Creating a New Meeting Policy or Customizing an Existing Policy

As a Teams admin, you must create or customize default Teams meeting policies as per your organization's requirements. Meeting features are controlled by creating and managing meeting policies, which are then assigned to users. You can manage meeting policies within the Microsoft Teams admin center or by using Windows PowerShell. Applied policies will directly affect the users' meeting experience before the start of the meeting, during the meeting, and after the meeting ends. Meeting policies can be applied in three different ways:

- *Per organizer:* All meeting participants inherit the policy of the organizer.

- *Per user:* Only the per-user policy applies to restrict certain features for the organizer, meeting participants, or both.

- *Per organizer and per user:* Certain features are restricted for meeting participants based on their policy and the organizer's policy.

Remember that a policy named Global (Org-wide default) is created by default, and all the users within the organization will be assigned this meeting policy by default. As a Teams admin, you can decide if changes must be made to this policy, or you can choose to create one or more custom policies and assign those to users.

Creating a New Meeting Policy

In a meeting policy there are six sections: Meeting scheduling, Meeting join & lobby, Meeting engagement, Content sharing, Recording & transcription, Audio & Video, and Watermark. To create a new meeting policy, follow these steps:

1. First, log in to the Teams admin center. From the left-hand navigation menu, select Meetings, and then click Meeting Policies. Click +Add to create a new meeting policy.

2. Once the New Meeting Policy page opens, enter a meaningful name for the new policy, and optionally enter a description. In the Meeting scheduling section, select whether to turn the following options on or off. For example, I gave the policy name **USA-Bloguc-Meeting-Policy**.

   - **Private meeting scheduling:** By default, this setting is on. When this setting On, meeting organizers allow users to schedule private meetings.

   - **Meet now in private meetings:** By default, this setting is on. This option controls whether a user can start an instant private meeting.

   - **Channel meeting scheduling:** By default, this setting is on. When this setting is On, meeting organizers allow users to schedule channel meetings within channels that the users belong to.

   - **Meet now in channel meetings:** By default, this setting is on. When this setting is On, meeting organizers allow users to start instant meetings within channels that the users belong to.

   - **Outlook Add-In:** By default, this setting is on. When this setting is On, meeting organizers allow users to schedule private meetings from Outlook. This option is important because users can schedule Teams meetings through Outlook using add-in.

   - **Meeting registration:** By default, this setting is on. When this setting is On, meeting organizers can require registration to join a meeting.

- **Who can register:** By default, this setting is Everyone. This setting determines who can register for meetings (if Meeting registration is On): Everyone or People in my organization.

- **Attendance report:** By default, this setting is Everyone, unless organizers opt out. This setting gives meeting organizers the ability to see the toggle that turns on or off attendance reports within the Meeting options.

- **Who is in the report:** By default, this setting is Everyone, but participants can opt out. This setting controls whether participants in the meeting can opt in or out of offering their attendance information in the attendance report.

- **Attendance summary:** By default, this setting is "Show everything." This setting controls whether to show attendance time information, such as join times, leave times, and in-meeting duration, for each meeting participant.

Figure 2-71 shows all of those options turned on in the "Meeting scheduling" section.

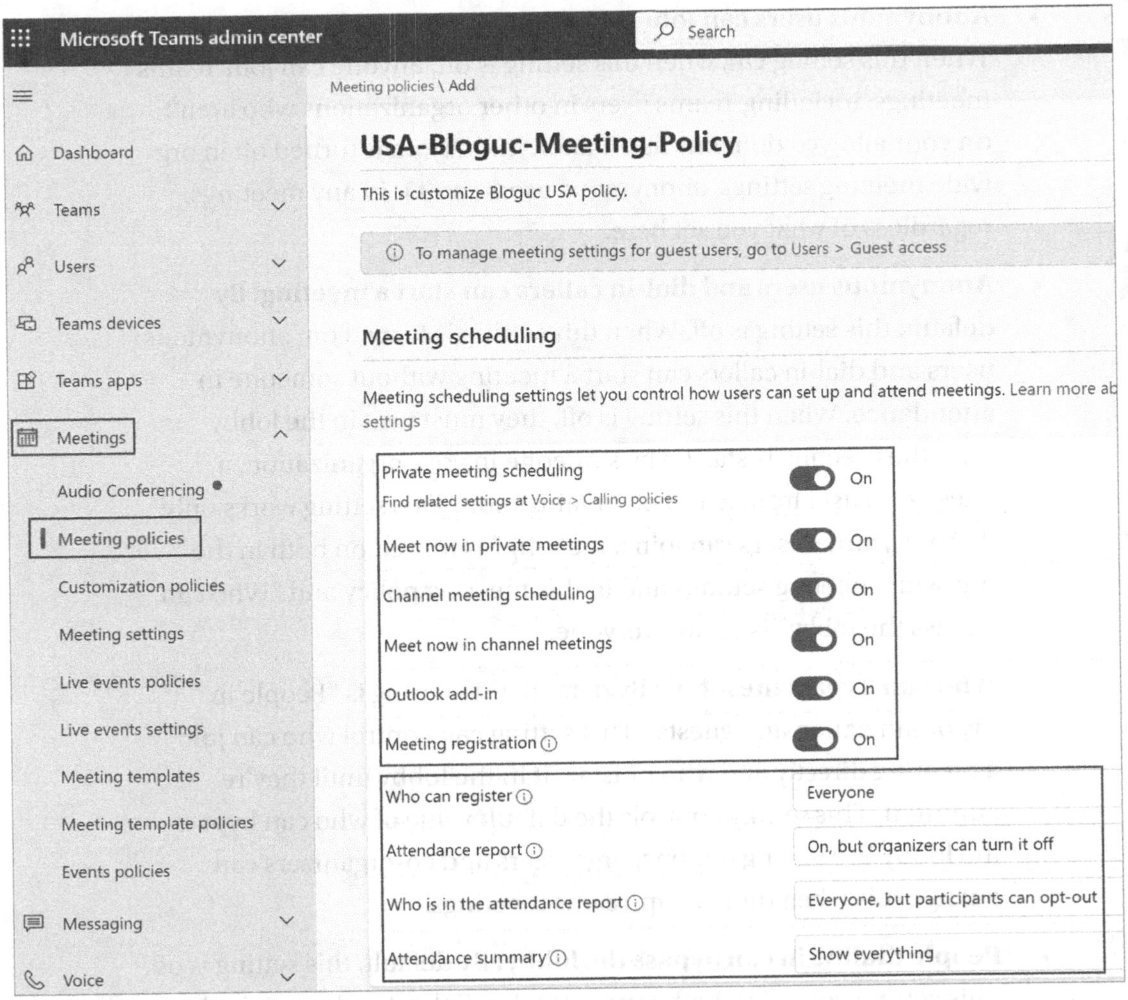

Figure 2-71. *Meeting policies, scheduling option*

For example, Meet Now in channel meetings is a policy setting that is applied before starting the meetings, and it has a per-user model. This policy controls whether the user can start a meeting in a Teams channel without the meeting having been previously scheduled. If you turn this setting on, when a user posts a message in a Teams channel, the user can select Meet Now to initialize an ad hoc meeting in the channel.

The next policy setting options are "Meeting join and lobby" and "Meeting engagement." The "Meeting join and lobby" settings let you control how people join meetings and allow you to manage the lobby for Teams meetings. The "Meeting engagement" policy settings let you control how people interact in meetings. Figure 2-72 shows all of those options turned on in the "Meeting scheduling" section.

- **Anonymous users can join a meeting:** By default, this setting is on. When this setting On, when this setting is on, anyone can join Teams meetings, including Teams users in other organizations who aren't on your allowed domains list. If anonymous join is turned off in org-wide meeting settings, anonymous users can't join any meetings, regardless of what you set here.

- **Anonymous users and dial-in callers can start a meeting:** By default, this setting is off. When this setting is turned on, anonymous users and dial-in callers can start a meeting without someone in attendance. When this setting is off, they must wait in the lobby until the meeting is started by someone in your organization, a guest, or a user from a trusted organization. This setting works only if "Anonymous users can join a meeting" is turned on both in the org-wide meeting settings and in this meeting policy and "Who can bypass the lobby" is set to Everyone.

- **Who can bypass the lobby:** By default, this setting is "People in my organization and guests." This setting can control who can join a meeting directly and who must wait in the lobby until they're admitted. This setting controls the default value of who can bypass the lobby in Meeting options; organizers and co-organizers can change this when they set up Teams meetings.

- **People dialing in can bypass the lobby:** By default, this setting is off. This setting controls whether people who dial in by phone join the meeting directly or wait in the lobby, regardless of who can bypass the lobby setting. When this setting is turned off, dial-in callers must wait in the lobby until they're admitted. This setting controls the default value for Meeting options; organizers and co-organizers can change this when they set up Teams meetings.

- **Meeting chat:** By default, this setting is on for everyone. This setting controls which meeting attendees can participate in the meeting chat. When turned off for anonymous participants, they can read the chat but not post messages.

- **Q&A:** By default, this setting is on. When this setting is On, organizers can enable a question and answer experience for their meetings.

- **Reactions:** By default, this setting is on. This setting controls whether users can use live reactions such as Like, Love, Applause, Laugh, and Surprise in Teams meetings.

  Figure 2-72 shows all of those options for meeting join and lobby and meeting engagement section.

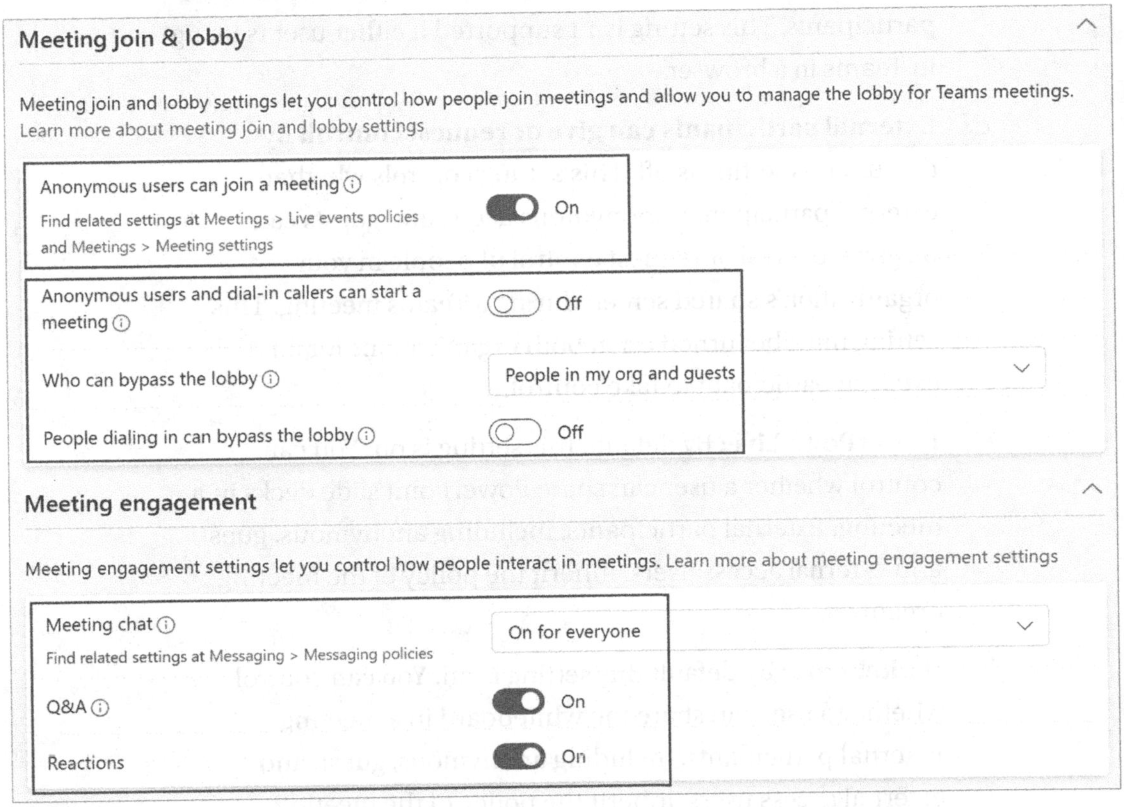

Meeting join & lobby

Meeting join and lobby settings let you control how people join meetings and allow you to manage the lobby for Teams meetings. Learn more about meeting join and lobby settings

Anonymous users can join a meeting ⓘ Find related settings at Meetings > Live events policies and Meetings > Meeting settings	On
Anonymous users and dial-in callers can start a meeting ⓘ	Off
Who can bypass the lobby ⓘ	People in my org and guests
People dialing in can bypass the lobby ⓘ	Off

Meeting engagement

Meeting engagement settings let you control how people interact in meetings. Learn more about meeting engagement settings

Meeting chat ⓘ Find related settings at Messaging > Messaging policies	On for everyone
Q&A ⓘ	On
Reactions	On

Figure 2-72. *Meeting policies: meeting join and engagement option*

- The next policy setting option is "Content sharing settings," which allows you to control the different types of content that can be used during Teams meetings that are held in your organization.

  a. **Who can present:** By default this setting is Everyone. You can control who can be a presenter in Teams meetings. Organizers and co-organizers can change this when they set up Teams meetings.

b. **Screen sharing mode:** By default this setting is set to "Entire screen." You can control whether desktop and window sharing is allowed in the user's meeting.

c. **Participants can give or request control:** By default, this setting is on. You can control whether the user can give control of the shared desktop or window to other meeting participants. This setting isn't supported if either user is using in Teams in a browser.

d. **External participants can give or request control:** By default, this setting is off. This setting controls whether external participants, anonymous users, and guests can be given control or request control of people in your organization's shared screen during a Teams meeting. This setting must be turned on in both organizations for an external participant to take control.

e. **PowerPoint Live:** By default, this setting is on. You can control whether a user can share PowerPoint slide decks in a meeting. External participants, including anonymous, guest, and external access users, inherit the policy of the meeting organizer.

f. **Whiteboard:** By default this setting is on. You can control whether a user can share the whiteboard in a meeting. External participants, including anonymous, guest, and external access users, inherit the policy of the meeting organizer.

g. **Shared notes:** By default this setting is on. When this setting is on, attendees can create shared meeting notes through the meeting details.

Figure 2-73 shows the content sharing settings and the ways the settings can change based your organization needs.

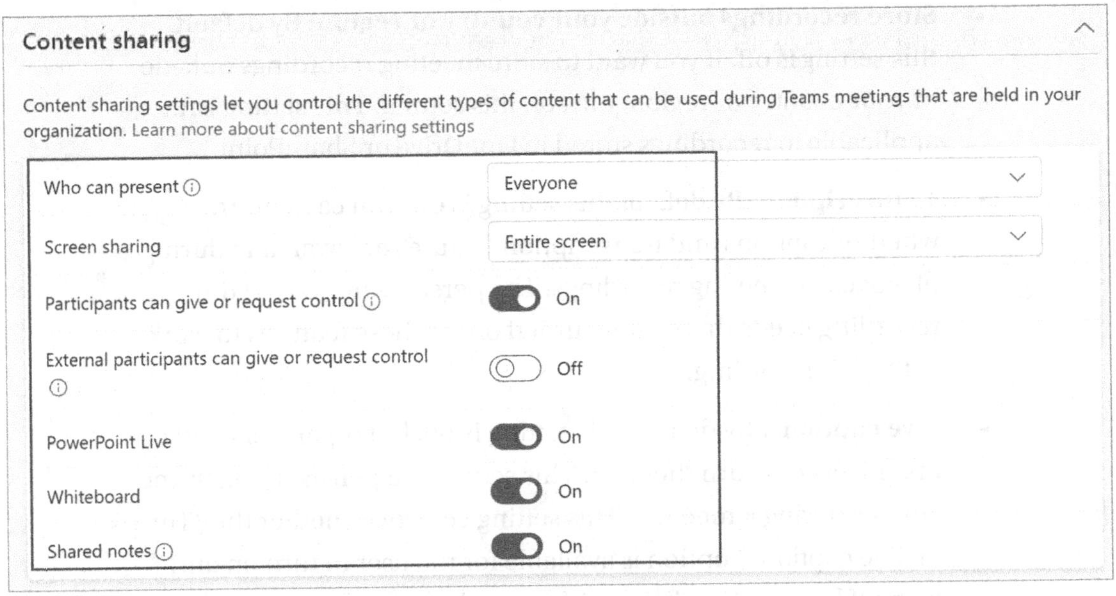

Content sharing

Content sharing settings let you control the different types of content that can be used during Teams meetings that are held in your organization. Learn more about content sharing settings

Who can present ⓘ	Everyone ∨
Screen sharing	Entire screen ∨
Participants can give or request control ⓘ	🔵 On
External participants can give or request control ⓘ	⚪ Off
PowerPoint Live	🔵 On
Whiteboard	🔵 On
Shared notes ⓘ	🔵 On

Figure 2-73. Meeting policies: Content sharing

- The next setting is "Recording and transcription." Recording and transcription settings let you control how these features are used in a Teams meeting. As part of recording and transcription, you can customize the following setting options. Figure 2-74 shows the recording and transcription settings:

  - **Meeting recording:** By default this setting is on. When this setting is on, users can record their Teams meetings and group calls to capture audio, video, and screen sharing activity. The meeting organizer and recording initiator need to have recording permissions to record the meeting.

  - **Recordings automatically expire:** By default this setting is on. When this setting is on, meeting recordings automatically expire in the number of days shown in the "Default expiration time" setting.

  - **Default expiration time:** By default, expiration set as 120 days. The default expiration time for new meeting recordings is from 1 to 99999 days. Recordings that automatically expire must also be turned On.

- **Store recordings outside your country or region:** By default this setting is off. If you want to store meeting recordings outside of your country or region, turn on this setting. This setting isn't applicable to recordings stored in OneDrive or SharePoint.

- **Transcription:** By default this setting is on. You can control whether captions and transcription features are available during playback of meeting recordings. The person who started the recording needs this setting turned on for these features to work with their recording.

- **Live captions:** By default this setting is off, but organizers and co-organizers can turn them on. This setting is a per-user policy and applies during a meeting. This setting controls whether the "Turn on live captions" option is available for the user to turn on and turn off live captions in meetings that the user attends.

Recording & transcription   ∧

Recording and transcription settings let you control how these features are used in a Teams meeting. Learn more about recording and transcription settings

Meeting recording Find related settings at Voice > Calling policies and Meetings > Live events policies	◉	On
Recordings automatically expire ⓘ	◉	On

Default expiration time	120

Store recordings outside of your country or region ⓘ	◯	Off
Transcription ⓘ Find related settings at Voice > Calling policies, Meetings > Live events policies, and Voice > Voicemail policies	◯	Off
Live captions Find related settings at Voice > Calling policies	Off, but organizers and co-organizers can turn them on ∨	

Figure 2-74. Meeting policies: Recording and transcription

- The next and last settings are in the "Audio & Video and watermark" section. Audio and video settings allow you turn on or off features that are used during Teams meetings. An additional setting is to add a watermark to content and videos shared in Teams meetings to protect confidential data.

  - **Mode for IP audio:** By default this setting is set to Outgoing, and incoming audio is enabled. This setting controls whether incoming and outgoing audio can be turned on in meetings and group calls.

  - **Mode for IP video:** By default this setting is set to Outgoing, and incoming audio is enabled. This setting controls whether incoming and outgoing video can be turned on in meetings and group calls.

  - **IP Video:** By default this setting is on. This setting controls whether video can be turned on in meetings hosted by a user and in one-on-one and group calls started by a user. On Teams mobile clients, this setting controls whether users can share photos and videos in a meeting.

  - **Local broadcasting:** By default this setting is off. Use NDI or SDI technology to capture and deliver broadcast-quality audio and video over your network.

  - **Media bit rate (Kbs):** By default, this value is set as 50000. This setting determines the media bit rate for audio, video, and video-based app sharing transmissions in calls and meetings for the user. It's applied to both the uplink and downlink media traversal for users in the call or meeting. This setting gives you granular control over managing bandwidth in your organization.

  - **Network configuration lookup:** By default this setting is off. When it is on, roaming policies in network topology are checked.

  - **Participants can use video effects:** By default this setting is set to all video effects. You can control if participants can customize their camera feed with video background images and filters.

171

- **Live streaming:** By default this setting set as off. This determines whether you provide support for your users to stream their Teams meetings to large audiences through the Real-Time Messaging Protocol (RTMP).

- **Watermark videos:** By default this setting is off. This setting controls watermarks on attendee videos.

- **Watermark shared content:** By default this setting set as off. This setting controls watermarks on content shared on the screen in a meeting.

Figure 2-75 shows the "Audio & video" meeting settings and Watermark setting.

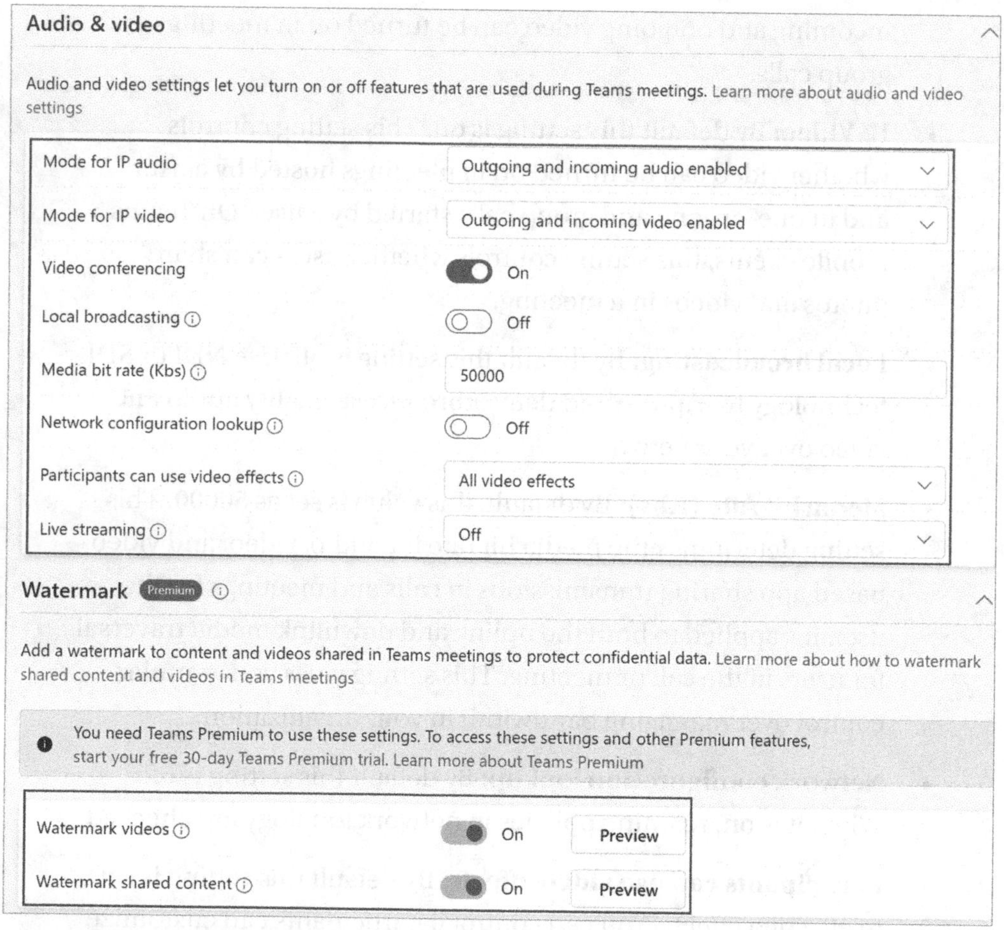

Figure 2-75. *"Audio & video" settings and Watermark setting options*

Meeting Policy Assignment

Once you create a meeting policy, the next thing you have to do is to assign the policy to a user or group of users for it to take effect. There are two ways to assign a policy to a user using the Teams admin center in both the Users and Meeting Policies sections.

- To assign a policy using the Meeting Policies tab, simply log in to the Teams admin center, navigate to Meetings, and select Meeting Policies. Select the required meeting policy and then click Manage Users. In the "Manage users" drop-down window, select "Assign users" and start entering a username. Once the full username shows, click Add and then click Apply to apply the policy. Figure 2-76 shows user Balu Ilag added to the applied policy.

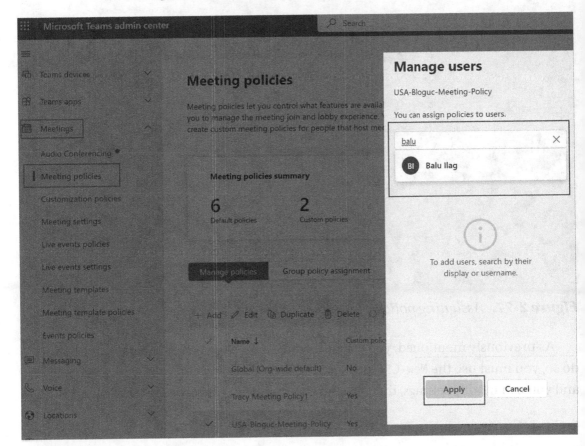

Figure 2-76. *Policy assigned to user*

- To assign a policy using the Users section in the Teams admin center, log in to the Teams admin center, and then navigate to Users. Select the users to whom you want to apply the policy and then click the Policies section. Under Edit User Policies, select the appropriate meeting policy, and then click Apply, as shown in Figure 2-77.

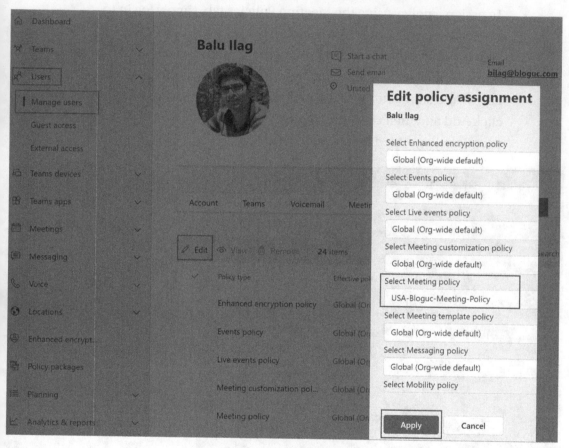

Figure 2-77. *Assigning policies from the Users tab*

As previously mentioned, you can also create a meeting policy using PowerShell. To do so, you must use the New-CSTeamsMeetingPolicy cmdlet. Once the policy is ready and you can modify settings, then use the command Set-CsTeamsMeetingPolicy.

In this example, we create a new meeting policy with the identity BlogucMeetingPolicy1. In this example, two different property values are configured: AutoAdmittedUsers is set to Everyone, and AllowMeetNow is set to False. All other policy properties will use the default values.

```
New-CsTeamsMeetingPolicy -Identity BlogucMeetingPolicy1 -AutoAdmittedUsers
"Everyone" -AllowMeetNow $False
```

As an example, consider the setting titled AllowTranscription. This setting controls whether meetings can include real-time or post-meeting captions and transcriptions. If you want to enable this setting on an existing meeting policy titled BlogucMeetingPolicy1, you should run the following command:

```
Set-CsTeamsMeetingPolicy -Identity BlogucMeetingPolicy1 -AllowTranscription
$True
```

Customization Policies

Customize your meetings with your organization's logo, colors, or other visuals. Customization policies are available for meeting organizers with a Teams Premium or Advanced Communications license. Figure 2-78 shows the customization policies.

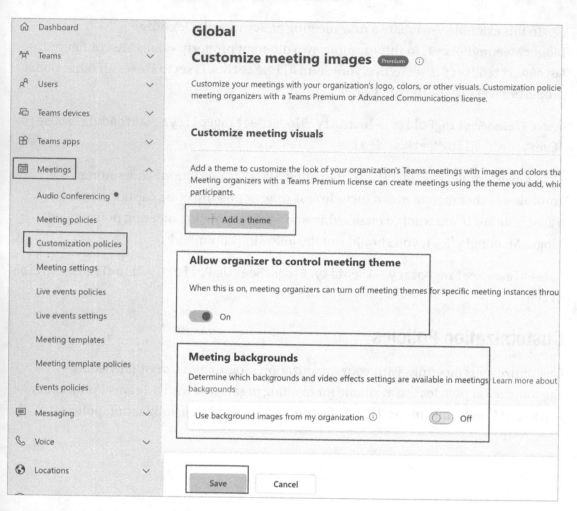

Figure 2-78. Customization policy

Managing Meeting Settings

Meeting settings allow you to customize meeting invitations, set up cross-cloud relationships, and manage network settings for all Teams meetings in your organization. Microsoft Teams provides meeting settings that determine whether anonymous users can join Teams meetings, customize meeting invitations, enable quality of service (QoS), and set port ranges for real-time traffic. If you change any of these meeting settings, the changes will be applied to all Teams meetings that users schedule within your organization. There are three main settings.

Participants

This option determines whether anonymous participants can join a meeting. Anonymous participants are users who can join without logging in, as long as they have the link for the meeting. An admin can turn on this feature per the organization requirements. To enable anonymous users to join a meeting, log in to the Teams admin center and navigate to Meetings. Select Meeting Settings, and under Participants, turn on the "Anonymous users can join a meeting" option. Another option is "Anonymous users can interact with apps in meetings."

Email Invitation

Microsoft allows organizations to customize meeting invitations with their company log and support as well as legal URLs. Based on the organization's needs and requirements, the meeting invitations can be customized and previewed before being applied to an organization's settings. For example, Bloguc customized meeting invitations by adding their organization's logo, links to their support website and legal disclaimer, and a text-only footer. To customize meeting invitations, log in to the Teams admin center and navigate to Meetings. Select Meeting Settings, and under Email Invitation you can add a logo URL, legal URL, help URL, and footer text. Figure 2-79 shows a preview for email invitation settings.

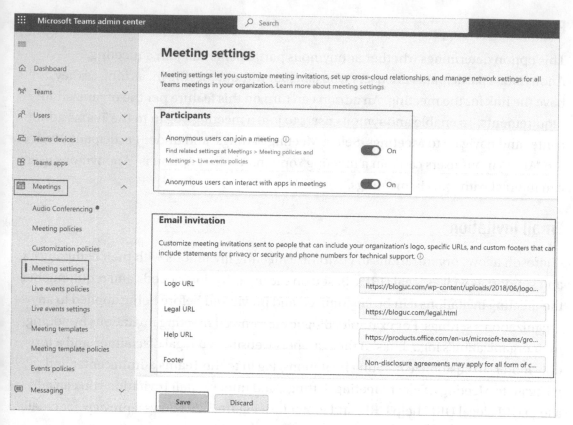

Figure 2-79. Participant setting and email invitation customization

Network

If you are using QoS to prioritize network traffic, you can enable QoS markers and set port ranges for each type of media traffic. It is important to note that if you enable QoS or change settings in the Microsoft Teams admin center for the Microsoft Teams service, you will also need to apply matching settings to all user devices and all internal network devices to fully implement the changes to QoS. When you turn on "Insert Quality of Service (QoS) markers for real-time media traffic," all the real-time media traffic for meetings will be marked. If they have this marking, the network packets can be prioritized.

It is important to use port ranges to specify which ports to use for specific types of media traffic. Setting this to automatic mode would use any available ports within the 1024–65535 range. I recommend using the Specify Port Ranges option and using a smaller port range. Figure 2-80 shows all the recommended starting and ending port numbers with their media types.

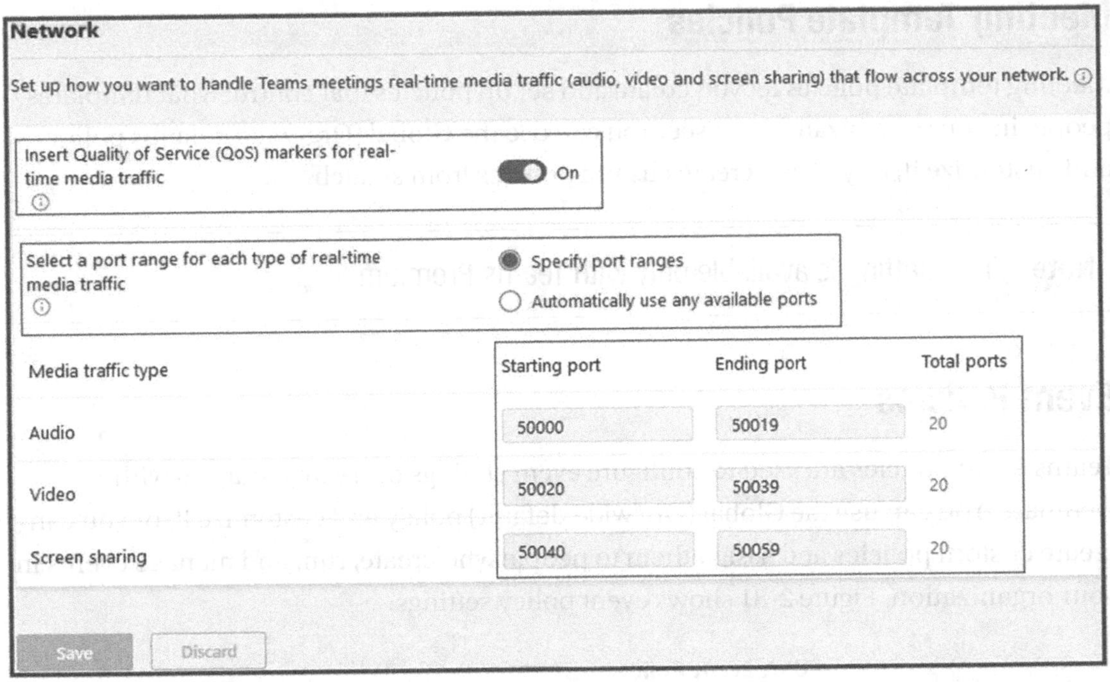

Figure 2-80. *Network and QoS settings*

In summary, the Meetings tab in the Teams admin center is a comprehensive toolkit for managing and optimizing the meeting experiences within your organization. Given the importance of meetings in driving effective collaboration, decision-making, and productivity, it's crucial to manage these settings to fit your organizational needs.

Note   The Live Event Policies and Live Event settings were described in the "Overview of Live Events" section in this chapter.

Meeting Templates

Meeting templates can be used to create meetings that are available to users with common needs or a common project. Meeting templates are available to all organizations including small to large business and educational organizations.

Note   This setting is available only with Teams Premium.

Meeting Template Policies

Meeting template policies let you create and set up policies that control what templates people in your organization can see. You can use the Global (Org-wide default) policy and customize it, or you can create custom policies from scratch.

Note   This setting is available only with Teams Premium.

Event Policies

Teams event policies are used to configure event settings on Teams, starting with webinars. You can use the Global (Org wide default) policy and customize it, or you can create custom policies and assign them to people who create, run, and manage events in your organization. Figure 2-81 shows event policy settings.

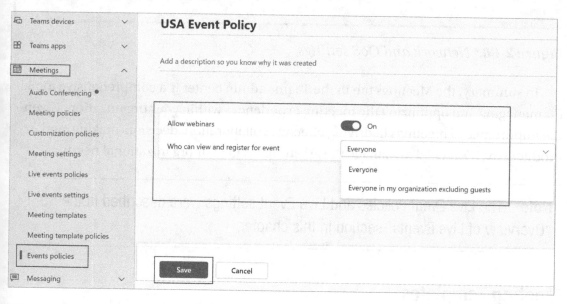

Figure 2-81. *Teams events policy*

Admin Center: Messaging Policies Tab

Microsoft Teams provides optimal chat capability through one-to-one chat, group chat, or channel chat. For this reason, Teams is often called a *chat-based workspace*. Teams not only provides chat capability but also provides granular control to manage the Teams chat experience through Teams messaging policies that are used to control chat and channel messaging features for users such as the ability to delete sent messages, access to memes and stickers, or the ability for users to remove other users from a group chat.

Out of the box, all users are assigned to the Global (Org-wide default) policy. A Teams admin can create additional custom policies and assign them to individual users, but a user can be assigned to only one messaging policy at a time. Also, messaging policies can be used to activate or deactivate messaging features and to configure or enforce messaging settings. All messaging policies are managed from the Microsoft Teams admin center and through the PowerShell commands.

Note   Any user can have only one messaging policy assigned at a time, regardless of policy type.

Some of these settings, such as using Giphys, can also be configured at the team level by team.

Creating New Messaging Policies

Messaging policies are used to control what chat and channel messaging features are available to users in Teams. You can use the Global (Org-wide default) policy or create one or more custom messaging policies for people in your organization.

By default, there will be one Global (Org-Wide default) messaging policy available that has been assigned to every user in your organization. If different settings for individual users are required, such as when an organization wants to deny regular users the ability to delete sent messages, a Teams admin must create a new messaging policy and assign it to a user.

To create a new messaging policy in the Teams admin center and assign it to a user, follow these steps:

1. Log in to the Teams admin center. In the left navigation pane, select Messaging Policies. Click +Add. In the top section under Messaging policies/Add window, enter the following information:

   - *New Messaging Policy:* A name for the policy.

- *Description:* A description for the policy.

- Turn on or off all settings as required, including allowing or blocking deletion of sent messages, read receipts, chat, Giphy content rating, URL preview, and so on. Figure 2-82 shows recommended settings, but the admin can customize the policy.

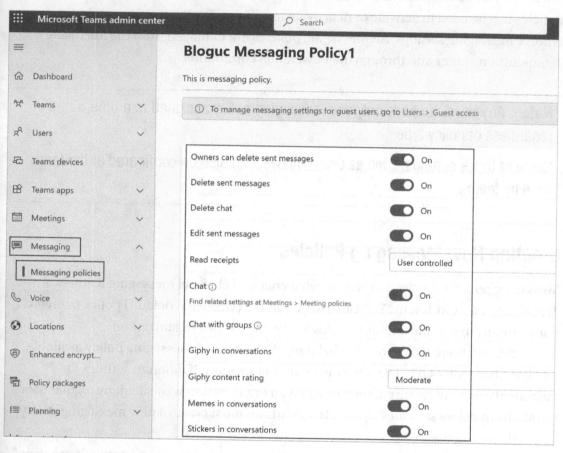

Figure 2-82. Messaging policy

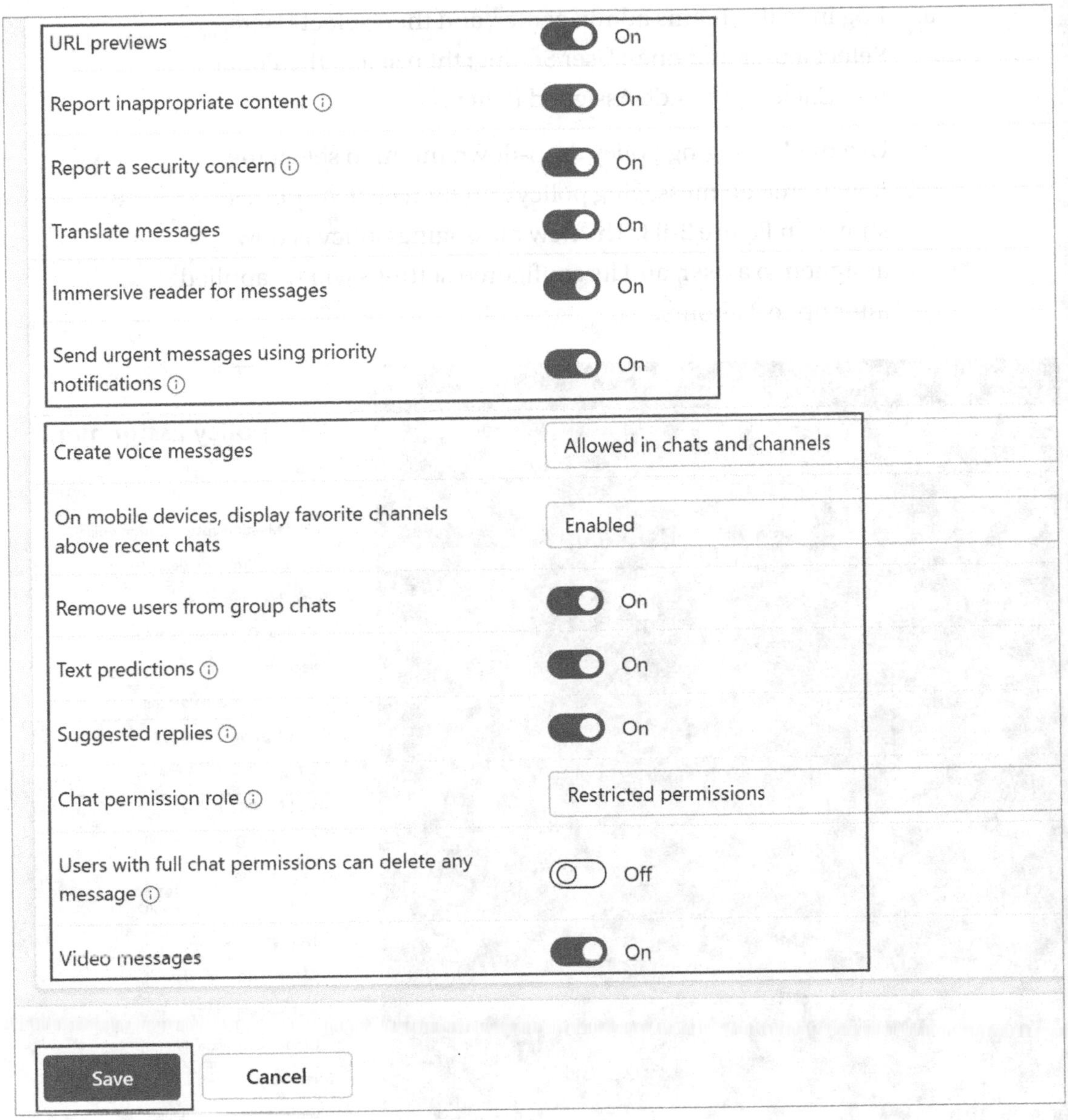

URL previews	◉ On
Report inappropriate content ⓘ	◉ On
Report a security concern ⓘ	◉ On
Translate messages	◉ On
Immersive reader for messages	◉ On
Send urgent messages using priority notifications ⓘ	◉ On

Create voice messages	Allowed in chats and channels
On mobile devices, display favorite channels above recent chats	Enabled
Remove users from group chats	◉ On
Text predictions ⓘ	◉ On
Suggested replies ⓘ	◉ On
Chat permission role ⓘ	Restricted permissions
Users with full chat permissions can delete any message ⓘ	◯ Off
Video messages	◉ On

Save   Cancel

Figure 2-82. (*continued*)

2. Once you have selected the desired settings, click Save to commit the policy setting and create the new messaging policy.

3. After a new messaging policy is created, it will be displayed in the Messaging Policies window, where it is ready for assignment to individual users. To assign the newly created policy to a user, you should perform the following steps:

a. Log in to the Teams admin center, and then select Users.
    Select a user and open User Setting; then select the Policies
    tab. Click Edit beside Assigned Policies.

b. Use the Messaging Policy drop-down menu to select the
    newly created messaging policy and then click Apply, as
    shown in Figure 2-83. The new messaging policy is now
    assigned to a user, and its configured settings will be applied
    after up to 24 hours.

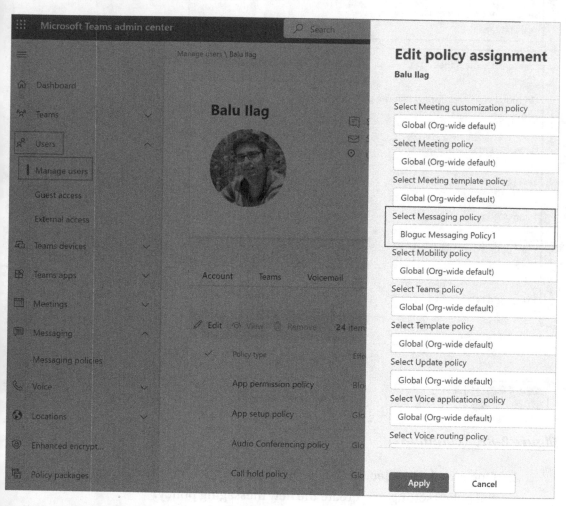

Figure 2-83. *Messaging policy assigned to user*

Modifying or Deleting Message Policies

When changes to an existing messaging policy are required or if the "Global policy" settings need to be changed, they can be edited, or in the case of custom policies, they can be deleted.

Note The default Global (Org-wide default) policy cannot be deleted, but it can be reset to default settings.

To modify policies or delete them, you should log in to the Teams admin center and then select Messaging Policies. Select the box for the policy that you want to modify or delete. You should then select one of the following options, as shown in Figure 2-84:

- Click Edit to delete the policy.

- Click Duplicate to create a copy of the selected policy with a "copy" suffix.

- Click Delete to remove the policy.

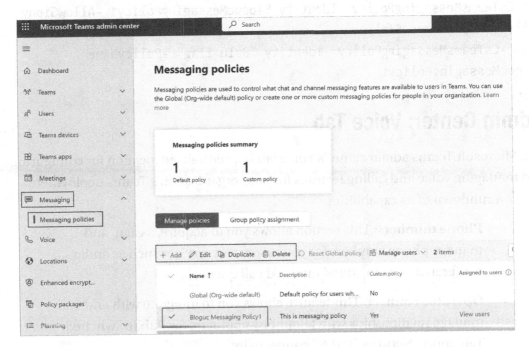

Figure 2-84. Modifying the messaging policy

Managing Messaging Policies Using PowerShell

As mentioned earlier, you can create and manage Teams messaging policies using PowerShell. The required commands to work with messaging policies are available in the Skype for Business Online module. Here is a list of the commands:

- `Get-CsTeamsMessagingPolicy`

- `New-CsTeamsMessagingPolicy`

- `Set-CsTeamsMessagingPolicy`

- `Grant-CsTeamsMessagingPolicy`

- `Remove-CsTeamsMessagingPolicy`

Here are examples to get the Global (Org-wide default) policy, create a new policy, modify a policy, and grant a policy to the user, respectively:

```
Get-CsTeamsMessagingPolicy Global
New-CsTeamsMessagingPolicy -Identity BlogucMessagingPolicy1 -AllowGiphy
$false -AllowMemes $false
Set-CsTeamsMessagingPolicy -Identity BlogucMessagingPolicy1 -AllowGiphy
$false -AllowMemes $false
Grant-CsTeamsMessagingPolicy -identity "Balu Ilag" -PolicyName
BlogucMessagingPolicy1
```

Admin Center: Voice Tab

The Microsoft Teams admin center's Voice tab is a centralized location for configuring and managing voice and calling features for your organization's Teams deployment. Here's a rundown of its capabilities:

- **Phone numbers:** This section allows you to acquire, assign, and manage phone numbers for your users and services such as audio conferencing, auto attendants, and call queues.

- **Operator connect:** This feature allows you to integrate with and manage relationships with telephony operators for Public Switched Telephone Network (PSTN) connectivity.

- **Direct routing:** This feature allows you to integrate Microsoft Teams with your existing telephony infrastructure via Session Border Controllers (SBCs) and manage settings related to voice routes and PSTN usage records.

- **Calling policies:** This is where you define what calling features are available to Teams users. You can create and manage policies and assign them to users or groups.

- **Call hold policies:** These policies control the music or audio file that's played when a Teams user puts a call on hold.

- **Call park policies:** This capability lets you manage settings related to the "call park" feature, which allows users to put a call on hold and then retrieve it on a different device.

- **Caller ID policies:** These policies let you control how a user's phone number is displayed to others during a call, including options to display an alternate number or block the display of the number.

- **Dial plans:** Dial plans are sets of normalization rules that translate dialed phone numbers into a standard format for routing and authorization.

- **Emergency policies:** This section lets you manage settings related to emergency calling features, including dynamic location updates for emergency services.

- **Mobility policies:** These policies control what Teams Phone Mobile features are available to users.

- **Voice routing policies:** These policies are used to manage the routing of calls made through Direct Routing, including prioritization of PSTN usages and routing to specific SBCs.

- **Voicemail policies:** These control the available features for the voicemail service in Teams, including transcription, message duration, and other settings.

Each of these features provides a critical part of managing the overall voice and calling experience in Teams, ensuring users can communicate effectively and that the organization's telephony requirements are met.

The Voice tab includes several settings related to calling and phone usage for Microsoft Teams, as shown in Figure 2-85.

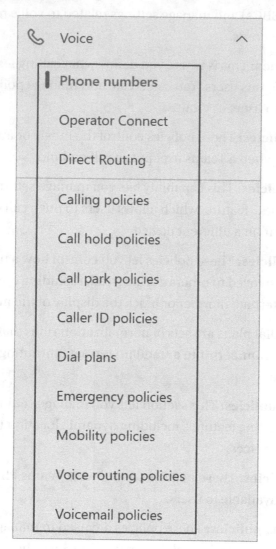

Figure 2-85. *Teams Voice features*

Phone Numbers

To set up calling features for users and services in your organization, you can get new numbers or port existing ones from a service provider. You can manage phone numbers including assigning, unassigning, and releasing phone numbers for people or for services such as audio conferencing, auto attendants, or call queues.

Phone Number Management

The Microsoft Teams admin center allows Teams admins to port their existing on-premise phone numbers, search for new numbers, and acquire new phone numbers from Microsoft 365 Phone System. In addition to acquiring new numbers, you can assign these new numbers to end users and resource accounts. Admins can manage locations for emergency calling and assign them to users. This means when you assign phone numbers to end users, they have their emergency location configured. When they make a call to emergency services, this location address can help them to get help quickly. Admins can see all order histories as well as updates to their records.

To add new phone numbers, follow this procedure:

1. Log in to the Teams admin center, and navigate to Voice. Select Phone Numbers and then click +Add to add a new phone number.

2. On the Phone Numbers/Get Phone Number page, enter the order name and a description.

3. Under Location And Quantity, select the country or region and then select appropriate number type and search location (if you have not added a location then you need add a location first to search). Specify the quantity and then click Next. In the example shown in Figure 2-86, the order name is Demo Order, the selected country is United States, the number type is user number, the location is HQ, the area code is 209, and the quantity is five. The number acquisition process takes some time, so be patient.

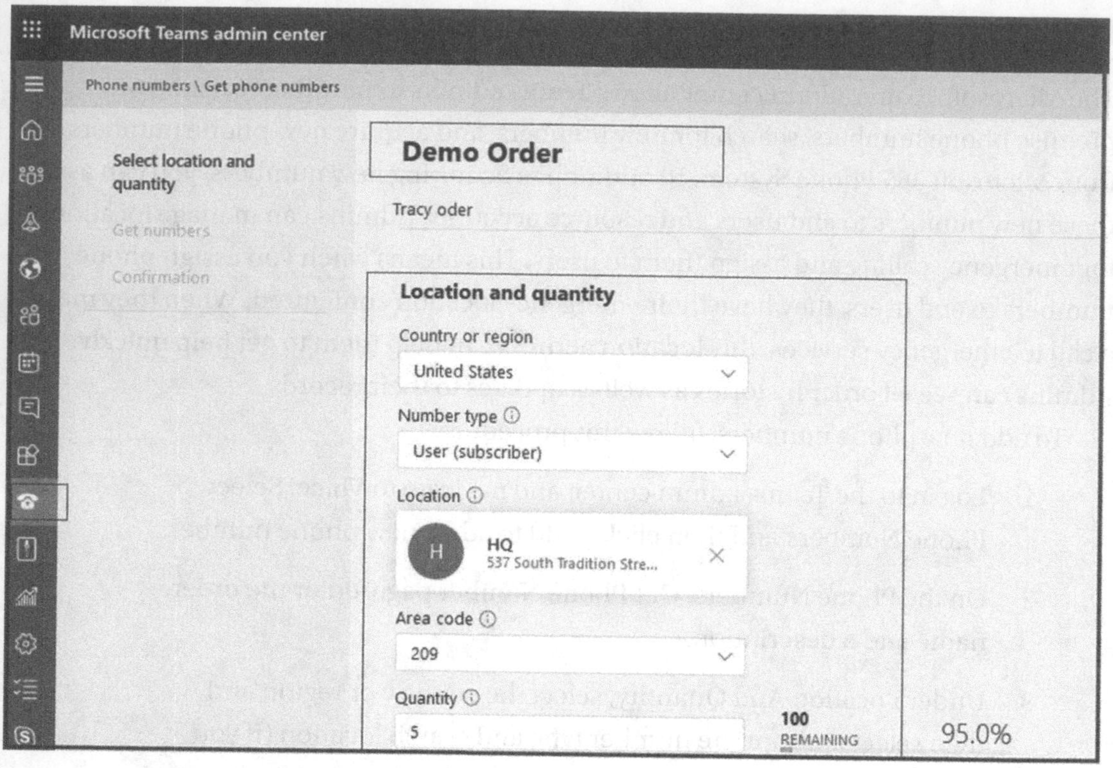

Figure 2-86. *Phone numbers*

4. On the next page, you will see the new number added and finally
   confirm.

Note   If you are trying to acquire phone numbers without Phone System licenses,
you will end up getting an error, because to acquire phone numbers and use them,
you must have Phone System licenses.

Porting Phone Numbers

Admins have the ability to port phone numbers from an existing service provider into
the Microsoft 365 Cloud Teams service. There are two processes for porting the phone
numbers. The first is automated porting, which is supported for U.S.-based numbers
only (Microsoft-developed API with carrier and partners to be able to automate the
whole process from end to end). The other porting option is through a service desk,
which is available for all porting scenarios through support.

To port through a service desk, you as the Teams admin can download a form that the service desk provides, fill it out, sign it, scan it, and email it to Microsoft.

1. To port a phone number, log in to the Teams admin center, and navigate to Voice. Select Phone Numbers and then click Port to port phone numbers.

2. On the Porting page, review the information before you start transferring your phone numbers. After you review it, we will walk you through the steps you need to complete the transfer of your numbers from your current service provider to Microsoft. When you're ready, click Next to continue (see Figure 2-87).

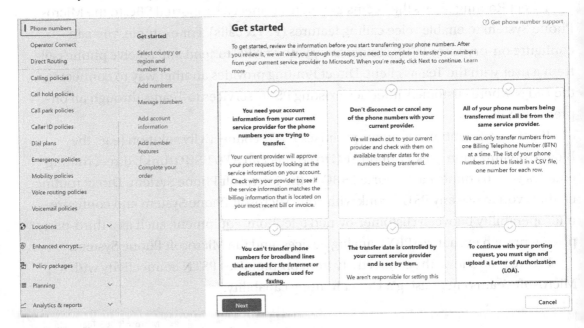

Figure 2-87. *Porting the number*

You can check the order history.

Operator Connect

Operator Connect allows you to manage partnerships with your phone operators. You can manage operators you already have a relationship with or view all operators to set up a partnership with a new operator.

191

Direct Routing

Microsoft Teams Direct Routing is a feature that allows organizations to connect their on-premises telecom infrastructure (like a PBX or SIP trunk) to Microsoft Teams. In other words, it connects your phone system to the Microsoft Teams environment using a Session Border Controller (SBC). This enables users to make and receive calls within Microsoft Teams using the organization's existing telecom provider.

The benefit of Direct Routing is that it gives organizations greater control over their telephony solutions, such as the ability to use existing contracts with telecom providers, add capacity as needed, or implement advanced features that may not be supported by Microsoft's Calling Plans.

Direct Routing allows the Teams admin to connect a supported SBC to the Microsoft Phone System to enable voice calling features (PSTN calls). For example, you can configure on-premises PSTN connectivity with an SBC to send and receive phone calls from a user with the Teams client. Direct Routing provides another way to connect to the PSTN where customers interface existing PSTN services to Teams through an on-premises SBC.

If your organization has an on-premises PSTN connectivity solution (e.g., the Bloguc organization uses a ribbon SBC to connect an AT&T SIP trunk), direct routing enables you to connect a supported SBC to the Microsoft Phone System. Direct routing enables you to use any PSTN trunk with your Microsoft Phone System and configure interoperability between customer-owned telephony equipment, such as a third-party private branch exchange (PBX), analog devices, and the Microsoft Phone System.

Figure 2-88 shows the connectivity from on-premises PSTN connectivity with a Microsoft Teams client using a Direct Routing capability.

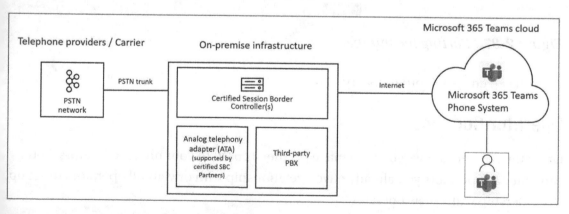

Figure 2-88. *Teams Direct Routing high-level connectivity*

Scenarios in Which You Can Use Direct Routing

As mentioned earlier, Direct Routing provides a way for the Teams admin to connect a supported SBC to the Microsoft Phone System to enable voice calling features (PSTN calls). Direct Routing can be deployed in organizations that want to leverage on-premises PSTN within the following scenarios:

- The Microsoft Calling Plan is not available in the organization's country or region. Thus far, the Microsoft Calling Plan is available in only some countries. You can visit https://docs.microsoft.com/en-us/microsoftteams/country-and-region-availability-for-audio-conferencing-and-calling-plans/country-and-region-availability-for-audio-conferencing-and-calling-plans to see where Calling Plan is available.

- The organization requires a connection to third-party analog devices or call centers.

- The organization has an existing contract with a PSTN carrier and wants to continue to use on-premises PSTN.

Prerequisites for Planning or Deploying Direct Routing

As a Teams admin, you should confirm you have the infrastructure requirements in place to deploy a Direct Routing solution in your organization. There are multiple requirements that you must be aware of and understand before planning or implementing Teams Direct Routing.

- The first step is to check your existing SBC for supportability. Microsoft has published a supported SBC vendor list with their product and software version. Validate your SBC, as it must be one from a supported SBC vendor. Read more details at https://docs.microsoft.com/en-US/microsoftteams/direct-routing-border-controllers.

- SBC must have one or more telephony trunks connected. The SBC can also be connected to third-party PBXs or analog telephony adapters. On the other end, the SBC will be connected to the Microsoft Phone System through Direct Routing; for example, select PSTN carrier ➤ SBC ➤ Microsoft Teams Office 365 Cloud.

193

- You must have an Office 365 tenant where your organization's Teams users are located or homed.

- To use Direct Routing capabilities, users must be homed in Microsoft Teams. In a hybrid environment, on-premises Skype for Business users cannot be enabled for Direct Routing voice in Microsoft Teams.

- Your domains must be configured to your organization's Office 365 tenant; for example, Bloguc.com means the SBC FQDN looks like this: `sbc1.bloguc.com`. The default `*.onmicrosoft.com` domain cannot be used.

- The SBC must have a public DNS FQDN and a public IP address interface that will be used to connect SBC to Teams Office 365 Cloud.

- The SBC connection to the Teams Office 365 Cloud is secured, so you must have a public trusted certificate for the SBC that will be used for communication with Direct Routing.

- The SBC public IP address interface must be allowed to communicate to Teams Direct Routing over certain ports and protocols. This is the firewall requirement mentioned here.

  - `sip.pstnhub.microsoft.com`: Global FQDN; must be tried first.

  - `sip2.pstnhub.microsoft.com`: Secondary FQDN; geographically maps to the second priority region.

  - `sip3.pstnhub.microsoft.com`: Tertiary FQDN; geographically maps to the third-priority region.

  - Firewall IP addresses and ports for Direct Routing and Microsoft Teams media should be opened. Table 2-3 identifies the ports that should be opened.

Table 2-3. *Traffic Types and Related Ports*

Traffic Type	From	To	Source Port	Destination Port
SIP/TLS	SIP Proxy	SBC	1024–65535	Defined on the SBC
SIP/TLS	SBC	SIP Proxy	Defined on the SBC	5061

- The Media Transport Profile should allow TCP/RTP/SAVP and UDP/ RTP/SAVP. The media traffic flows to and from a separate service in the Microsoft Office 365 Cloud. The IP range for Media traffic should include 52.112.0.0 /14 (IP addresses from 52.112.0.1–52.115.255.254).

- Specific to the Media traffic codec perspective:

  - The Direct Routing interface on the leg between the SBC and Cloud Media Processor (without media bypass) or between the Teams client and the SBC (if media bypass is enabled) can use the following codecs:

    - Non-media bypass (SBC to Cloud Media Processor): SILK, G.711, G.722, G.729

    - Media bypass (SBC to Teams client): SILK, G.711, G.722, G.729, OPUS

- On the leg between the Cloud Media Processor and the Microsoft Teams client, media flows directly between the Teams client and the SBC, where either SILK or G.722 is used.

- Teams Direct Routing licensing requirement. Users of Direct Routing must have the following licenses assigned in Office 365 to use Teams Direct Routing capabilities:

  - Microsoft 365 Phone System (either part of E5 or add-on license on top of E1 or E5).

  - Microsoft Teams (from Microsoft 365 subscription plan, like E1, E3, E5, etc.).

  - Microsoft 365 Audio Conferencing (either part of E5 subscription or add-on license on top of E1 and E3) is required in scenarios where a Teams user in a call wants to add a PSTN user in a call through the Audio Conferencing service.

Now that you aware of the requirements, let's move on to configuring Teams Direct Routing.

Configuring Microsoft Teams Direct Routing

For Teams Direct Routing configuration, as of this writing, Teams admins can perform Direct Routing configuration through the PowerShell command line, such as using New-CSOnlinePSTNGateway only. There is no option to configure Direct Routing through the Team admin center. Microsoft will be adding a Direct Routing configuration capability for Teams admins in the Teams admin center portal to perform the configuration of Direct Routing and control the PSTN trunk definitions to support customers' on-premises PSTN connectivity with Microsoft 365. Using the Teams admin center portal, admins will include voice route support and assigning on-premises telephone numbers (TNs); however, as of this writing, it is not available through the admin portal but can be done using the Teams PowerShell command line. I am assuming when you read this book you will see a Teams Direct Routing configuration option in the Teams admin center portal.

Let's configure Teams Direct Routing using Teams PowerShell:

1. Connect the SBC to the Teams Direct Routing service of the Phone System using Teams PowerShell.

a. To do so, first connect Teams Online PowerShell using the following PowerShell command:

```
$credential = Get-Credential
Connect-MicrosoftTeams -Credential $credential
```

b. After you are connected to Microsoft Teams PowerShell, run the following command to pair the SBC to the Office 365 tenant:

```
New-CsOnlinePSTNGateway -Fqdn <SBC FQDN> -SipSignallingPort
<SBC SIP Port> -MaxConcurrentSessions <Max Concurrent
Sessions the SBC can handle> -Enabled $true
```

Here's an example:

```
New-CsOnlinePSTNGateway -Fqdn sbc1.bloguc.com -SipSignallingPort
5061 -MaxConcurrentSessions 50 -Enabled $true
```

Note   It is recommended that you set a maximum call limit in the SBC, using information that can be found in the SBC documentation. The limit will trigger a notification if the SBC is at capacity.

2. After pairing with the SBC, you must validate the SBC setting is expected. If not, then modify it using the Set-CsOnlinePSTNGateway command. Figure 2-89 shows an example of PSTN gateway details.

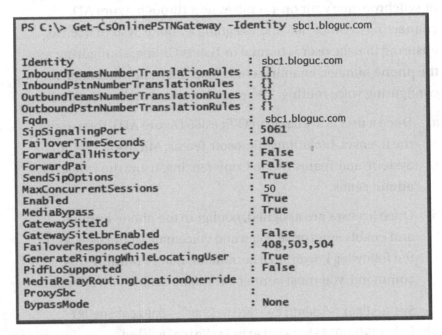

```
PS C:\> Get-CsOnlinePSTNGateway -Identity sbc1.bloguc.com


Identity                              : sbc1.bloguc.com
InboundTeamsNumberTranslationRules    : {}
InboundPstnNumberTranslationRules     : {}
OutbundTeamsNumberTranslationRules    : {}
OutboundPstnNumberTranslationRules    : {}
Fqdn                                  :   sbc1.bloguc.com
SipSignalingPort                      : 5061
FailoverTimeSeconds                   : 10
ForwardCallHistory                    : False
ForwardPai                            : False
SendSipOptions                        : True
MaxConcurrentSessions                 :   50
Enabled                               : True
MediaBypass                           : True
GatewaySiteId                         :
GatewaySiteLbrEnabled                 : False
FailoverResponseCodes                 : 408,503,504
GenerateRingingWhileLocatingUser      : True
PidfLoSupported                       : False
MediaRelayRoutingLocationOverride     :
ProxySbc                              :
BypassMode                            : None
```

Figure 2-89. *Validating PSTN gateway details*

Note   Validate if SendSipOptions is set to True or not. If not, then modify it to True because it is important to send option requests from SBC. When Direct Routing sees incoming SIP Options, it will start sending outgoing SIP Options messages to the SBC FQDN configured in the Contact header field in the incoming Options message.

3. Once an Online PSTN gateway is created, work with your SBC vendor to configure your SBC for Teams Direct Routing. That includes installing a certificate on SBC, adding a new public IP interface or network address translation (NAT) and FQDN on your SBC, opening communication between the SBC public IP interface and the Teams SIP proxy, actual call routing configuration, and so on.

4. The next thing you need to do is enable users for Teams Direct Routing. That includes creating a user in Office 365 or synchronizing your on-premises user through Azure AD, connecting to Office 365 and assigning a Phone System license, ensuring that the user is homed in Teams Online, configuring the phone number, enabling enterprise voice and voicemail, and configuring voice routing. The route is automatically validated.

   a. Once a user is available in Office 365 (Azure AD), then assign the licenses, including Microsoft Teams, Microsoft Phone System, and Teams Audio Conferencing, using the Office 365 admin center.

   b. Once licenses are assigned, configure the phone number and enable enterprise voice and voicemail for the user using the following PowerShell command. Before running this command, you must connect to Teams Online PowerShell.

   ```
   Set-CsUser -Identity "Balu Ilag" -OnPremLineURI
   tel:+12092034567 -EnterpriseVoiceEnabled
   $true -HostedVoiceMail $true
   ```

Note   If the user's phone number is managed on-premises, use on-premises Skype for Business Management Shell or Control Panel to configure the user's phone number.

---

c. Create and assign a voice routing policy to the user
    including an Online voice routing policy. To create a voice
    routing policy, PSTN usages, and so on, refer the Microsoft
    documentation at `https://docs.microsoft.com/en-US/`
    `microsoftteams/direct-routing-configure`.

d. Once the Online Voice routing policy is available, connect
    to Skype for Business Online PowerShell and assign
    the online voice routing policy to the user. Refer to the
    following PowerShell command to assign the online voice
    routing policy:

```
Grant-CsOnlineVoiceRoutingPolicy -Identity "Balu Ilag"
-PolicyName "Bloguc-CA-International"
```

Managing Teams Direct Routing

The Teams Direct Routing dashboard is the place where you see all your SBC
configurations. Basically, this enumerates all the SBC configurations in the tenant
with multiple data points on connectivity and quality with usage information. Every
option has its help information associated with it, which helps the administrator check,
test, and remediate any issues. The example in Figure 2-90 shows the Direct Routing
dashboard with three SBCs. Two out of three SBCs are shown as active; however, there
was no call made in the last 24 hours, so it displays as orange. There is one inactive SBC
(`sbc3.bloguc.com`); the red mark means the SBC does have an issue that the admin has
to address.

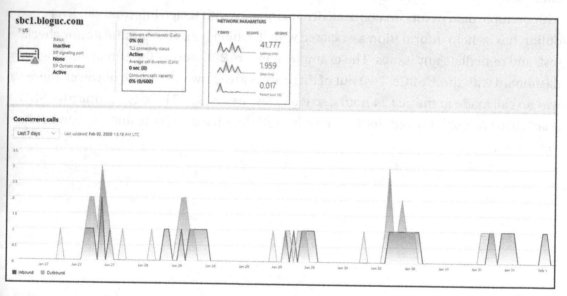

Direct Routing

Direct Routing lets you connect a supported Session Border Controller (SBC) to Microsoft Phone System to enable voice calling features. For example, you can configure on-premises PSTN connectivity with an SBC to send and receive calls from a user with the Teams app. Learn more

DIRECT ROUTING SUMMARY

3	3
Total SBCs	SBCs with issues

3 Items

SBC	Network effectiveness (Calls) ⓘ	Average call duration (Calls) ⓘ	TLS connectivity status ⓘ	SIP options status ⓘ	Concurrent calls capacity ⓘ
sbc1.bloguc.com	ⓘ 0% (0)	0 sec (0)	Active	Active	Within limits
sbc2.bloguc.com	ⓘ 0% (0)	0 sec (0)	Active	Active	Within limits
sbc3.bloguc.com	ⓘ 0% (0)	0 sec (0)	ⓘ Inactive	⚠ Warning	Within limits

Figure 2-90. *Teams Direct Routing dashboard*

When you click sbc1.bloguc.com, it shows the statistics regarding calls, network parameters, and concurrent calls happening through this SBC, as displayed in Figure 2-91.

Figure 2-91. *Teams Direct Routing SBC view*

Best Practices for Implementing Teams Direct Routing

Here are some best practices for implementing Teams Direct Routing:

- **Ensure you have the necessary license and subscription:** Before you begin, you must have the right Office 365 license with Microsoft Teams and Phone System add-on. Understanding what is covered in your subscription can help you anticipate costs and configure the system accurately.

- **Choose the right SBC:** The SBC is an essential element in Direct Routing as it acts as an intermediary between your telecom provider and Teams. Microsoft has a list of certified SBCs. Choose one that suits your needs and budget.

- **Plan and configure network infrastructure:** Your network should have sufficient capacity to handle voice traffic. In addition, latency, packet loss, and jitter should be minimized to provide good call quality. You should also set up quality of service (QoS) rules to prioritize voice traffic.

- **Secure the connection:** Be sure to secure the connection between your SBC and Microsoft Teams. This could be achieved through Transport Layer Security (TLS) and secure Real-Time Transport Protocol (SRTP).

- **Number management:** Make sure you have a clear plan for managing and assigning telephone numbers to users. If you're porting numbers from an existing system, carefully plan the porting process to minimize disruption.

- **Emergency services:** Be aware of the rules in your country regarding provision of location information for emergency calls. You'll need to configure emergency addresses and locations in the Microsoft Teams admin center.

- **Test before going live:** Always thoroughly test your setup before going live. Make a few test calls to ensure that inbound and outbound calling works correctly. Test call quality and make sure that all call handling features work as expected.

- **Provide training:** Microsoft Teams might be new to many users. Ensure you provide adequate training and documentation to help them understand how to make and receive calls and use call handling features.

- **Monitoring and troubleshooting:** After implementation, use the Call Quality Dashboard and other monitoring tools provided by Microsoft to keep an eye on your system. This will help you spot any potential issues before they become major problems.

- **Create a disaster recovery plan:** While Teams and Direct Routing are quite reliable, it's always good to have a plan in place in case something goes wrong. This could involve having a backup SBC or having a failover procedure to an existing PBX or other phone system.

By following these best practices, you can ensure a smooth implementation of Microsoft Teams Direct Routing and provide your users with a high-quality and reliable voice service.

Calling Policies

Calling policies are used to control what calling features are available to people in Teams. You can use the Global (Org-wide default) policy and customize it or create one or more custom calling policies for people who have phone numbers in your organization.

Calling Policy Settings

The following are the settings:

- *Make Private call:* This setting controls all calling capabilities in Teams. Turn this setting off to turn off all calling functionality in Teams.

- *Cloud recording for calling:* This setting controls whether users can record calls. This setting is off by default.

- *Transcription:* This setting controls whether the transcription of calls is available for your users. This setting is off by default.

- *Routing for PSTN calls:* This setting controls how inbound PSTN calls should be routed. These PSTN calls can be sent to voicemail, sent to unanswered settings, or use default call routing, or you can allow your users to decide. "Use default settings" is on by default.

- *Routing for federated calls:* This setting controls how inbound federated calls should be routed. These federated calls can be sent to voicemail, sent to unanswered settings, or use default call routing. "Use default settings" is on by default. Federated calls are calls that don't originate from the PSTN and that are outside your tenant.

- *Call forwarding and simultaneous ringing to people in your organization:* This setting controls whether incoming calls can be forwarded to other users or can ring another person in your organization at the same time. This setting is on by default.

- *Call forwarding and simultaneous ringing to external phone numbers:* This setting controls whether incoming calls can be forwarded to an external number or can ring an external number at the same time. This setting is on by default.

- *Voicemail for inbound calls:* This setting enables inbound calls to be sent to voicemail. The default setting is "Let users decide." Valid options are as follows:

  - *On Voicemail:* This is always available for inbound calls.

  - *Off Voicemail:* This isn't available for inbound calls.

  - *Let users decide:* Users can determine whether they want voicemail to be available.

- *Inbound calls can be routed to call groups:* This setting controls whether incoming calls can be forwarded to a call group. This setting is turned on by default.

- *Delegation for inbound and outbound calls:* This setting enables inbound calls to be routed to delegates, allowing delegates to make outbound calls on behalf of the users for whom they have delegated permissions. This setting is turned on by default.

- *Prevent toll bypass and send calls through the PSTN:* Turning on this setting sends calls through the Public Switched Telephone Network (PSTN) and incurs charges rather than sending them through the network and bypassing the tolls. This setting is off by default.

- *Music on hold for PSTN calls:* This setting allows you to turn on or turn off music on hold when a PSTN caller is placed on hold. It's turned on by default. This setting doesn't apply to call park and boss delegate features.

- *Busy on busy during calls:* Busy on busy during calls (also called *busy options*) lets you configure how incoming calls are handled when a user is already in a call or conference or has a call placed on hold. New or incoming calls can be rejected with a busy signal or can be routed accordingly to the user's unanswered settings. Regardless of how their busy options are configured, users in a call or conference or those with a call on hold are not prevented from initiating new calls or conferences. This setting is set to *Off* by default.

  - *Off:* No busy option is enabled, and new or incoming calls can still go to the user while the user is already in a call.

  - *On:* New or incoming calls will be rejected with a busy signal.

  - *Use unanswered settings:* The user's unanswered settings will be used, such as routing to voicemail or forwarding to another user.

  - *Let users decide:* Users can determine their busy options choice from call settings in the Teams app.

- *Web PSTN calling:* This setting enables users to call PSTN numbers using the Teams web client. This setting is on by default.

- *Real-time captions in Teams calls:* This setting controls whether real-time captions in Teams calls are available for your users. This setting is turned on by default.

- *Automatically answer incoming meeting invites:* This setting controls whether incoming meeting invites are automatically answered. It's turned off by default. Keep in mind that this setting applies only to incoming meeting invites. It doesn't apply to other types of calls.

- *Spam filtering:* This setting allows you to control the type of spam filtering available on incoming calls. This setting is on by default. This setting has three options.

  - *On:* Spam filtering is fully enabled. Both Basic and Captcha Interactive Voice Response (IVR) checks are performed. If the call is considered spam, the user gets a "Spam Likely" notification in Teams.

  - *On without IVR:* Spam filtering is partially enabled. Captcha IVR checks are disabled. A "Spam Likely" notification appears. A call might get dropped if it gets a high score from Basic checks.

  - *Off:* Spam filtering is completely disabled. No checks are performed. A "Spam Likely" notification doesn't appear.

- *SIP devices can be used for calls:* This setting enables users to use a SIP device to make and receive calls. This setting is turned off by default.

- *Open apps in browser for incoming PSTN calls:* This setting controls whether apps are automatically opened in the browser for incoming PSTN calls to your users. This can be used to pass the phone number of an inbound caller to an app to find the associated customer record while the call is taking place. This setting is off by default.

If turned on, a link to the app needs to be given in the "URL to open apps in browser for incoming PSTN calls" box. You can use the {phone} placeholder to pass the phone number (in E.164 format) to the provided URL. Or, you can give a generic URL without any placeholder. This setting simply launches the listed URL. Figure 2-92 shows the calling policy settings.

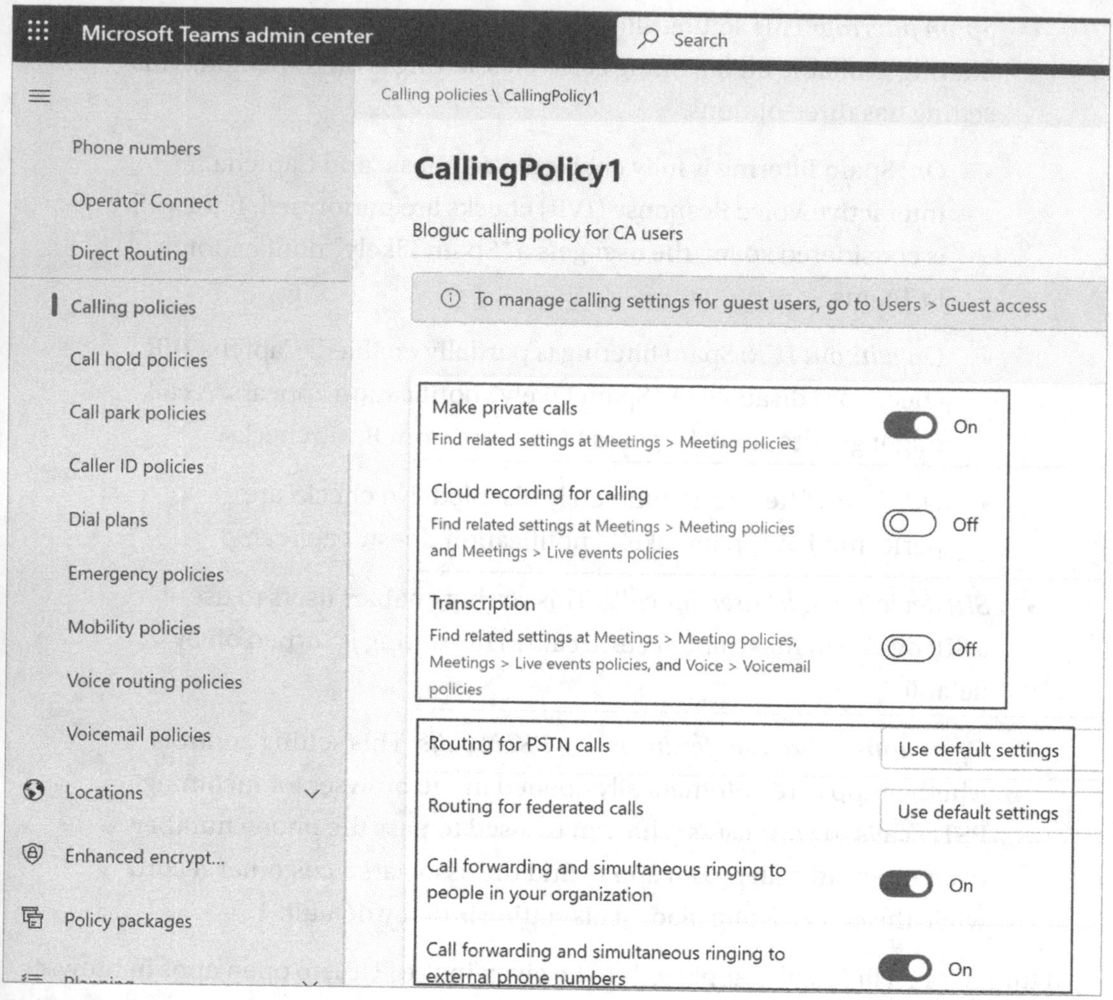

Figure 2-92. Teams Calling Policy settings

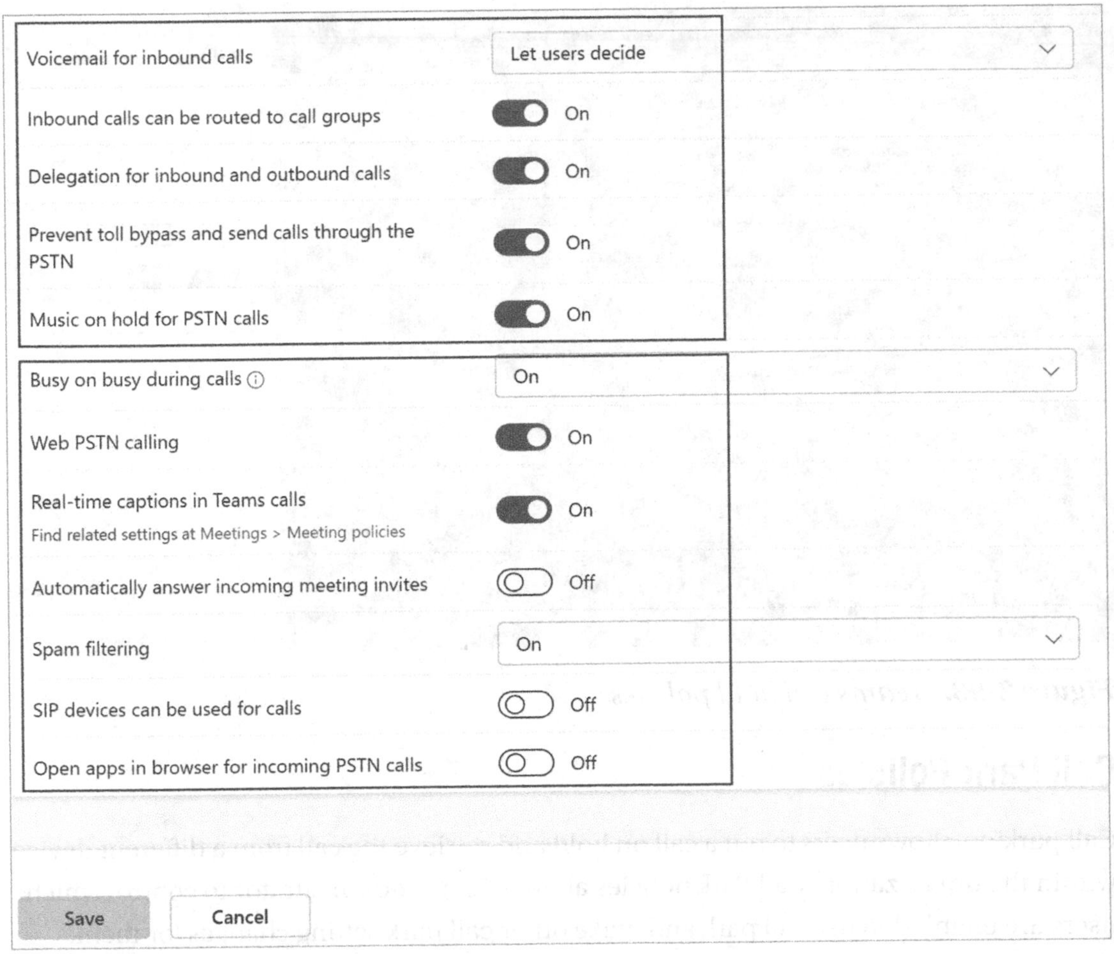

Voicemail for inbound calls	Let users decide ⌄
Inbound calls can be routed to call groups	⬤ On
Delegation for inbound and outbound calls	⬤ On
Prevent toll bypass and send calls through the PSTN	⬤ On
Music on hold for PSTN calls	⬤ On

Busy on busy during calls ⓘ	On ⌄
Web PSTN calling	⬤ On
Real-time captions in Teams calls Find related settings at Meetings > Meeting policies	⬤ On
Automatically answer incoming meeting invites	◯ Off
Spam filtering	On ⌄
SIP devices can be used for calls	◯ Off
Open apps in browser for incoming PSTN calls	◯ Off

Save   Cancel

Figure 2-92. (*continued*)

Call Hold Policies

Call hold policies are used to control the audio file that's played when a Teams user puts a caller on hold. You can use the Global (Org-wide default) policy or create custom call hold policies for users that have phone numbers in your organization. Figure 2-93 shows the custom call hold policy settings.

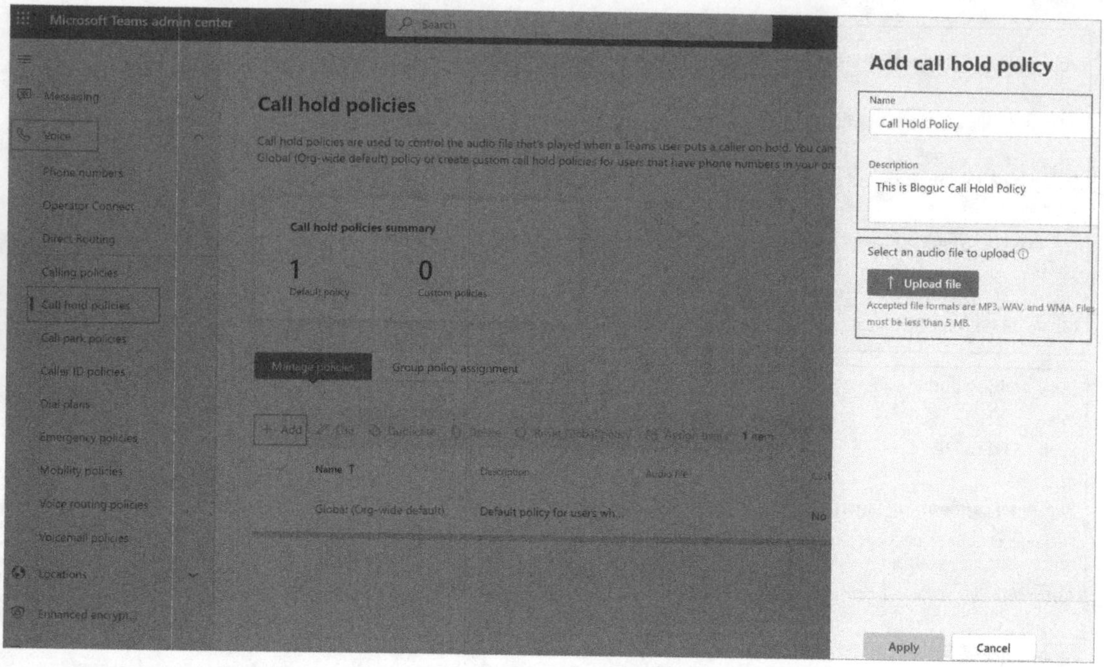

Figure 2-93. *Teams call hold policies*

Call Park Policies

Call parking allows users to put a call on hold and retrieve the call from a different device within the organization. Call Park policies allow a Teams administrator to control which users are enabled to use call park and make other call park setting changes for them. You can use the Global (Org-wide default) policy and customize it or create one or more custom policies and assign them to users.

It is important to know that the call park feature is available in Teams-only mode. That enables a user to place a call on hold in the Teams service in the cloud. For example, a user's phone battery is running low, so the user decides to park a call and then retrieve the call from a Teams desk phone. To park and retrieve calls, a user must be an Enterprise Voice user, and the Teams administrator must have granted the user a call park policy. The call park feature is disabled by default, but an admin can enable it for users and create user groups using the call park policy. Figure 2-94 shows Call Park policy with available options. You can configure call park options through PowerShell such as with New-CsTeamsCallParkPolicy. Here's an example:

```
New-CsTeamsCallParkPolicy -Identity "HelpdeskPolicy" -AllowCallPark
$true -PickupRangeStart 500 -PickupRangeEnd 1500 -ParkTimeoutSeconds 600
```

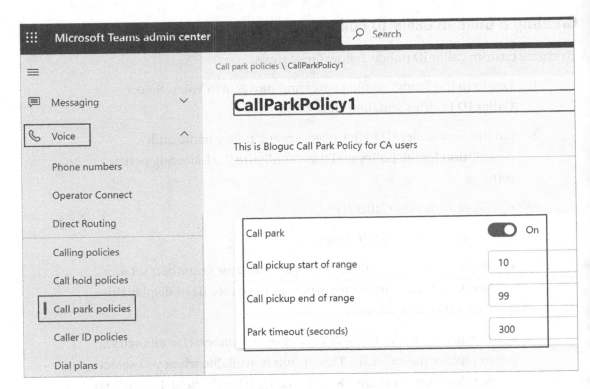

Figure 2-94. Teams call park policies

Caller ID Policies

Caller ID policies are used to change or block the caller ID (also called a calling line ID) for users. By default, the user's phone number is displayed when a call is made to a PSTN phone number such as a landline or mobile phone. You can use the Global (Org-wide default) policy and customize it or create a custom policy that provides an alternate number to display or to block any number from being displayed.

Caller ID is set up by default so that when a Teams user calls a PSTN phone, their phone number is displayed. Likewise, the phone numbers of PSTN callers can be seen when they call a Teams user. A Teams admin can manage caller ID policies in the Microsoft Teams admin center in the Voice section, under Caller ID Policies. You can select the Global (Org-wide default) policy or create custom policies according to your organization preferences and then assign them to users. If you do not create a policy, the users within the organization will by default have the Global policy assigned.

Creating a Custom Caller ID Policy

To create custom caller ID policy, follow these steps:

1. Log in to the Teams admin center and navigate to Voice. Select
    Caller ID Policies and then click +Add.

2. On the New Caller ID Policy page, enter a policy name and
    description for the policy and then configure the following policy
    settings:

    -   *Block Incoming Caller ID*

    -   *Override The Caller ID Policy*

    -   *Replace The Caller ID With:* Display the user's number; set a
        service phone number to display as the caller ID or display the
        caller ID as anonymous.

    -   *Replace the Caller ID With This Service Number:* Use this setting
        to replace the caller ID. This option is available when you select
        Service Number in the "Replace caller ID with" field. Figure 2-95
        shows these Caller ID settings.

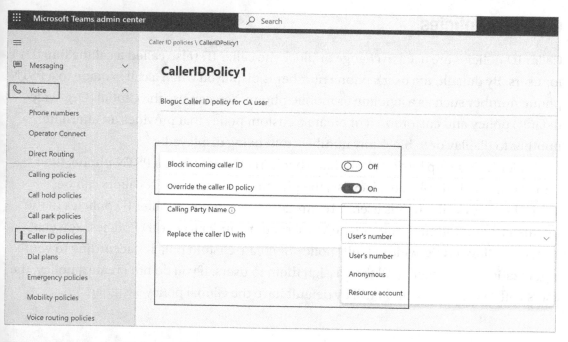

Figure 2-95. *Caller ID policy*

3. Once you are done configuring the caller ID settings, click Save.

4. Assign the policy to a user or group.

Dial Plans

A dial plan is a configuration applied to a user's phone in Microsoft Teams that influences how the phone number is interpreted and dialed out. Dial plans can be user-level or service-level (applied to everyone in your organization).

Microsoft Teams uses the E.164 format by default for phone numbers, but with dial plans, you can support other formats that might be more familiar or intuitive to your users. This is particularly useful for organizations that operate in countries where the local dialing habit might be different from the E.164 standard.

Here are some ways a dial plan is useful:

- **User experience:** Dial plans can make the dialing process more intuitive for your users. For instance, they might be used to dialing local numbers without the area code. A dial plan can be configured to automatically add the area code when they dial a local number.

- **Support for extension dialing:** Dial plans can be used to support extension dialing within your organization. For instance, a user might dial a four-digit extension, and the dial plan can translate this into a full phone number.

- **Normalization rules:** Dial plans consist of normalization rules that define how phone numbers expressed in various formats are interpreted (normalized) to the standard E.164 format. This provides flexibility and ensures consistency in how numbers are dialed within your organization.

- **Efficiency:** With a dial plan, users don't have to remember to dial in a specific format. They can dial as they usually would, and the dial plan will ensure the number is correctly interpreted. This can increase efficiency and reduce errors in dialing.

However, configuring and managing dial plans can be complex, particularly for large organizations. It's important to carefully plan your dial plan configuration to ensure it meets the needs of your users and aligns with your overall telephony strategy. Basically, using PowerShell you write a regular expression (RegEx), which is used to translate a dialed number to something that can be routed over PSTN.

Now, however, dial plans are available in the Teams admin center. There is a Global (Org-wide) dial plan that will be applied to all users in the Teams tenant or those who don't have custom dial plan applied. A custom dial plan allows you to codify users' dialing habits for each city or country, similar to handling voice routing policies.

Another important thing to understand is that normalization follows precedence. This means the first rule gets applied first if it matches; otherwise, it will go to the next one, and so on. If nothing matches, then it will give an error with no match found and call processing will stop, resulting in a failed phone call. That is why dial plans are essential in phone call routing.

Fundamentally, a dial plan is a set of rules that translate a phone number that a user dials into a standard E.164 number for call authorization and routing. You can use the Global (Org-wide default) dial plan that is created or create one or more custom dial plans for people in your organization. You can use the Global (Org-wide default) dial-plan policy as a basis to modify or create a custom dial-plan. Figure 2-96 shows a default dial plan.

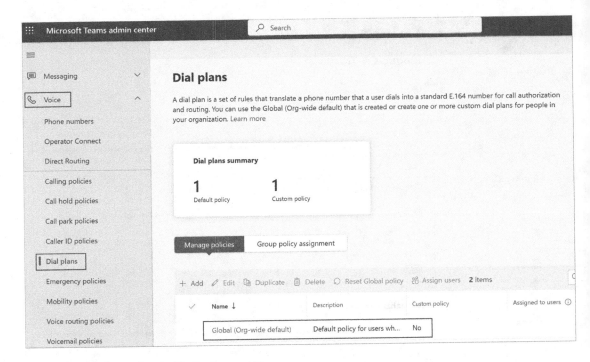

Figure 2-96. *Default dial plan policy*

Creating a Custom Dial Plan

To create custom dial plan, follow this procedure:

1. Log in to the Teams admin center, and then navigate to Voice. Select Dial Plans and then click +Add. Enter a name and description for the dial plan.

2. On the Dial Plan/Add page, under Dial Plan Details, specify an external dialing prefix if users need to dial one or more additional leading digits (e.g., 9) to get an external line. To do this, in the External Dialing Prefix box, enter an external dialing prefix (e.g., 9). The prefix can be up to four characters (including #, *, and 0–9). In Figure 2-97 the external dialing prefix is set to 9.

3. Set the Optimized Device Dialing option to on. If you specify an external dialing prefix, you must also turn on this setting to apply the prefix so that calls can be made outside your organization. This setting is shown in Figure 2-97.

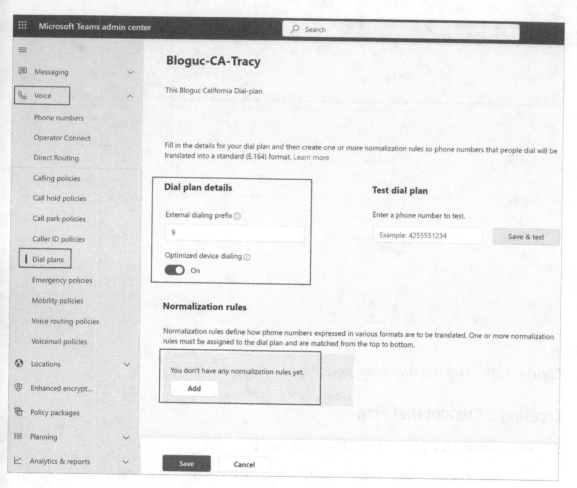

Figure 2-97. *Configuring a dial plan*

4. Under Normalization Rules, configure and associate one or more normalization rules for the dial plan. Each dial plan must have at least one normalization rule associated with it. To do this, follow this procedure.

   a. To create a new normalization rule and associate it with the dial plan, click Add. You can then define the rule. Figure 2-98 shows a normalization rule named NorthAmerica-West.

b. To edit a normalization rule that is already associated with the dial plan, select the rule by clicking to the left of the rule name, and then click Edit. Make the changes you want, and then click Save.

c. To remove a normalization rule from the dial plan, select the rule by clicking to the left of the rule name, and then click Remove.

5. Arrange the normalization rules in the order you want. Click Move Up or Move Down to change the position of rules in the list and then click Save to commit the changes.

6. After creating a dial plan, you must test it. Under "Test dial plan," enter a phone number, and then click Test. Figure 2-98 shows five digits tested to make sure it normalizes correctly with E.164 format. For example, here the result shows +12096566625.

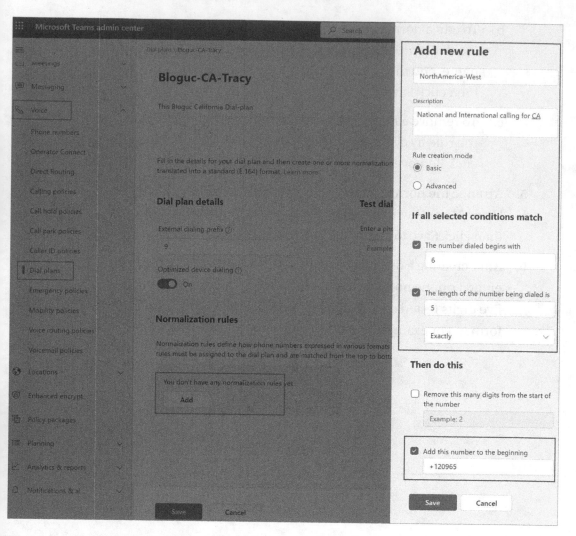

Figure 2-98. *Normalization rule*

Normalization Rule Types

Microsoft Teams provides two different types of normalization: basic and advanced. When you create a new dial plan, it will give you these two options. Basic is a basic option for conditions without regular expression, and it is an advanced option for complex dial plans with multiple conditions using regular expressions. Figure 2-99 shows the normalization rule type. Choose the normalization rule type that best fits your requirements.

Once your dial plan is ready, you as an admin can test the dial plan by dialing numbers, such as five-digit dialing, four-digit dialing, and so on. The next step is then to assign the dial plan to the user, by clicking Manage Users and then typing the username and assigning the dial plan to the end user.

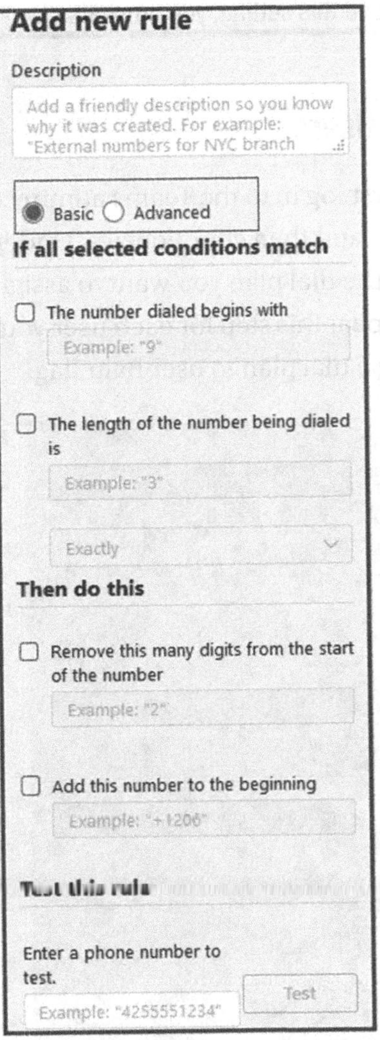

Figure 2-99. Normalization type selection

WHAT IS THE EXTERNAL DIALING PREFIX?

You can put in an external access prefix of up to four characters (including #, *, and 0–9) if users need to dial one or more additional leading digits (e.g., 9) to get an external line outside your organization. When you use this setting, you must also turn on optimized device dialing.

Assigning a Dial Plan to Users

To add users to a dial plan, first log in to the Teams admin center, and then navigate to Users. Select the desired user, and then click Policies. Under Assigned Policies, click Edit. Under Dial Plan, select the dial plan you want to assign. When you are finished adding users, click Apply. Repeat this step for each user you want to add. The example in Figure 2-100 shows assigning a dial plan to user Balu Ilag.

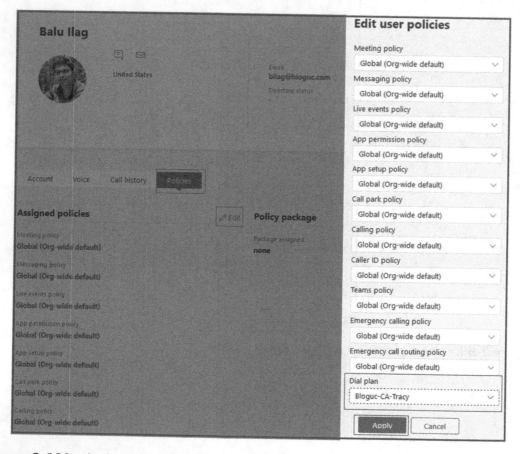

Figure 2-100. *Assigning a dial plan to a user*

Dial Plan Management and Creation Through Windows PowerShell

As a Teams admin, you have to manage dial plans and use them for call troubleshooting. Microsoft has provided multiple PowerShell commands that help you to manage dial plans. Before even running PowerShell commands, you must first connect your Windows PowerShell module to your Microsoft Teams tenant to the Microsoft 365 organization. You must have Microsoft Teams PowerShell module installed; you can use this link to Install Teams PowerShell module: https://learn.microsoft.com/en-us/microsoftteams/teams-powershell-install.

You can do that using the following PowerShell command, assuming you are not using MFA.

```
# When using Teams PowerShell Module
Install-Module -Name MicrosoftTeams -Force -AllowClobber
# Connect to Microsoft Teams
    Import-Module MicrosoftTeams
    $credential = Get-Credential
    Connect-MicrosoftTeams -Credential $credential
```

After connecting to Teams PowerShell module, run the next command to create a new dial plan:

```
New-CsTenantDialPlan -Identity Blouc-CA-Tracy -Description "Dial Plan
for CA Tracy" -NormalizationRules <pslistmodifier> -ExternalAccessPrefix
9 -SimpleName "Dial-Plan-for-CA-Tracy"
```

If you want to edit existing dial plan settings, then use this PowerShell command:

```
Set-CsTenantDialPlan -Identity Bloguc-CA-Tracy -NormalizationRules
<pslistmodifier> -ExternalAccessPrefix 9 -SimpleName "Dial-Plan-for-
CA-Tracy"
```

To assign users to a dial plan, use this PowerShell command:

```
Grant-CsTenantDialPlan -Identity bilag@bloguc.com -PolicyName
Bloguc-CA-Tracy
```

If you want to delete a dial plan, then use this PowerShell command:

```
Remove-CsTenantDialPlan -Identity Bloguc-CA-Tracy -force
```

Sometimes you need to see what dial plan is assigned to a user. To do that, use the next PowerShell command:

```
Get-CsEffectiveTenantDialPlan -Identity bilag@bloguc.com
```

Another important task that you can achieve through PowerShell commands is to test the effective tenant dial plan using a dialed number and user account. To do so, use this PowerShell command:

```
Test-CsEffectiveTenantDialPlan -DialedNumber 14255550199 -Identity
bilag@bloguc.com
```

If you want to add a normalization rule to the existing tenant dial plan, use the following PowerShell command:

```
$nr1=New-CsVoiceNormalizationRule -Parent Global -Description 'Organization
extension dialing' -Pattern '^(\\d{3})$' -Translation '+140855551$1' -Name
NR1 -IsInternalExtension $false -InMemory
Set-CsTenantDialPlan -Identity Bloguc-CA-Tracy -NormalizationRules
@{add=$nr1}
```

If you want to remove a normalization rule from the existing tenant dial plan, use this PowerShell command:

```
$nr1=New-CsVoiceNormalizationRule -Parent Global/NR1 -InMemory
Set-CsTenantDialPlan -Identity Bloguc-CA-Tracy -NormalizationRules
@{remove=$nr1}
```

To find all users who have been granted the Bloguc-CA-Tracy tenant dial plan, use this command:

```
Get-CsOnlineUser | Where-Object {$_.TenantDialPlan -eq "Bloguc-CA-Tracy"}
```

Refer to the PowerShell reference documents for more information: https://learn. microsoft.com/en-US/microsoftteams/create-and-manage-dial-plans#using-powershell.

Emergency Policies

Emergency calling policies are used to control how users in your organization can use dynamic emergency calling features. You can use the Global (Org-wide default) policy and customize it or create one or more custom policies for those people within your organization.

Emergency Calling Policies

As a Teams admin, you can manage emergency calling policies by going to the Teams admin center and then navigating to Voice. You can then use Emergency Policies and Calling Policies in the Microsoft Teams admin center or Windows PowerShell.

For users, you can use the Global (Org-wide default) policy or create and assign custom policies. Users will automatically get the Global policy unless you create and assign a custom policy. Keep in mind that you can edit the settings in the Global policy, but you cannot rename or delete it. For network sites, you create and assign custom policies.

If you assigned an emergency calling policy to a network site and to a user and if that user is at that network site, the policy that is assigned to the network site overrides the policy that is assigned to the user.

Using the Microsoft Teams Admin Center

Follow these steps:

1. Log in to the Teams admin center, and then navigate to Voice. Select Emergency Policies, and then click the "Calling policies" tab and click +Add.

2. On the next screen, enter a name and description for the policy and then set how you want to notify people in your organization, typically the security desk, when an emergency call is made. To do this, under Notification Mode, select one of the following options:

   - *Send notification only:* A Teams chat message is sent to the users and groups that you specify.

   - *Conferenced in but are muted:* A Teams chat message is sent to the users and groups that you specify, and they can listen (but not participate) in the conversation between the caller and the PSAP operator.

- *Conferenced in and are unmuted:* A Teams chat message is sent
  to the users and groups that you specify, and they can listen as
  well as participate in the conversation between the caller and the
  PSAP operator.

  In the example shown in Figure 2-101, "Conference in but are
  muted" is selected.

3. Enter the dial-out number for notifications and then search
   for and select one or more users or groups, such as your
   organization's security desk, to notify when an emergency call is
   made. The notification can be sent to email addresses of users,
   distribution groups, and security groups. A maximum of 50 users
   can be notified. Figure 2-101 shows an example emergency
   calling policy.

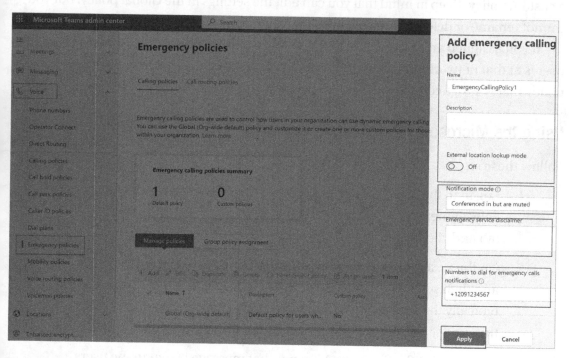

Figure 2-101. *Emergency calling policy*

4. Once all settings are complete, click Apply.

You can also set the emergency calling policy using PowerShell, using this command:

```
New-CsTeamsEmergencyCallingPolicy -Identity EmergencyCallingPolicy1
-Description "EMS Group HQ" -NotificationGroup "bilag@bloguc.com"
-NotificationDialOutNumber "1234567890" -NotificationMode NotificationOnly
-ExternalLocationLookupMode $true
```

Assigning a Custom Emergency Calling Policy to Users in a Group

After creating an emergency calling policy, the next thing you need to do is assign a custom emergency calling policy to multiple users that you've already identified using the Teams admin center or PowerShell.

Assigning an Emergency Calling Policy Using Teams Admin Center

Log in to the Teams admin center and navigate to Users. Select the user and then click Policies. Under Assigned Policies, click Edit. Under Emergency Calling Policy, select the newly created policy. Finally, click Save to commit the changes. In our example, the policy name is EmergencyCallingPolicy1.

Note   You can assign an emergency calling policy to users through the Emergency Calling Policy page itself by clicking Manage User.

Tip   As a best practice, assign an emergency call routing policy to users as well as to a network site to cover those who are not at the network site location.

Assigning Emergency Calling Policy Using PowerShell

For example, you might want to assign a policy to all users in a security group. You can do this by connecting to the Azure AD PowerShell for Graph module and the Teams PowerShell module. In this example, we assign a policy called Operations Emergency Calling Policy to all users in the Bloguc Security group.

```
Group = Get-AzureADGroup -SearchString "Bloguc Security Group"
$members = Get-AzureADGroupMember -ObjectId $group.ObjectId -All $true |
Where-Object {$_.ObjectType -eq "User"}
$members | ForEach-Object { Grant-CsTeamsChannelsPolicy -PolicyName
"EmergencyCallingPolicy1" -Identity $_.UserPrincipalName}
```

Note   Depending on the number of members in the group, this command might take several minutes to execute.

Assigning an Emergency Calling Policy to the Network Site

This is an important requirement. To assign an emergency calling policy to the network, run the following PowerShell command, which uses the Set-CsTenantNetworkSite command to assign an emergency calling policy to a network site:

```
Set-CsTenantNetworkSite -identity "site1" -EmergencyCallingPolicy
"Bloguc Emergency Calling Policy 1"
```

Emergency Call Routing Policies

After creating an emergency calling policy, you next need to create emergency call routing policies. These policies are used to set up emergency numbers and then specify how those emergency calls are routed. You can use the Global (Org-wide default) policy and customize it or create one or more custom policies for those users within your organization.

However, before creating an emergency call routing policy, you must understand why you are creating these policies. For example, if you have deployed Phone System Direct Routing in your organization, you can use emergency call routing policies in Microsoft Teams to set up emergency numbers and specify how emergency calls are routed. An emergency call routing policy determines whether enhanced emergency services are enabled for users who are assigned the policy, the numbers used to call emergency services (e.g., the 911 calling service in the United States), and how calls to emergency services are routed. Out of the box, the Global (Org-wide default) policy is available, or you can create and assign custom policies. Users will automatically get the Global policy unless you create and assign a custom policy.

Note   Remember, you can edit the settings in the Global policy, but you can't rename or delete it. For network sites, you create and assign custom policies.

Creating and Managing Emergency Call Routing Policy

Admins can create an emergency call routing policy using the Teams admin center as well as PowerShell. To create an emergency call routing policy using the Teams admin center, follow these steps:

1. Log in to the Teams admin center and navigate to Voice. Select Emergency Policies, and then click the Call Routing Policies tab. Click +Add.

2. On the Emergency Call Routing Policy page, enter a meaningful name and description for the policy

3. To enable enhanced emergency services, turn on the Enhanced Emergency Services option. When enhanced emergency services are enabled, Teams retrieves the policy and location information from the service and includes that information as part of the emergency call. Figure 2-102 shows the enhanced emergency services enabled.

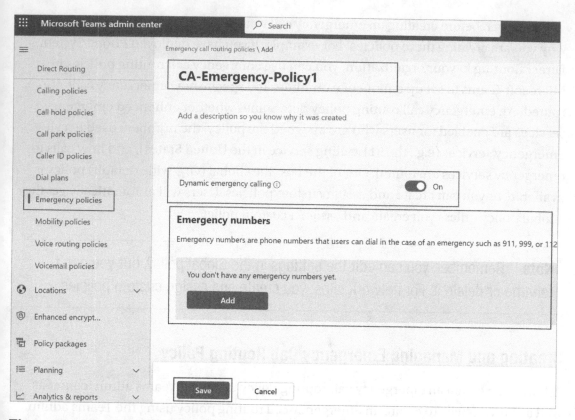

Figure 2-102.   *Emergency call routing policy*

4. The next thing you need to do to identify one or more emergency numbers. To do this, under Emergency Numbers, do the following:

   a. *Emergency dial string:* Enter the emergency dial string. This dial string indicates that a call is an emergency call. Refer to Figure 2-103, which shows 911 as the dial string.

   b. *Emergency dial mask:* For each emergency number, you can specify zero or more emergency dial masks. A dial mask is the number that you want to translate into the value of the emergency dial string. This allows for alternate emergency numbers to be dialed and still have the call reach emergency services. For example, you can add 112 as the emergency dial mask, which is the emergency service number for most of

Europe, and you can add 911 as the emergency dial string. A Teams user from Europe who is visiting might not know that 911 is the emergency number in the United States, and when they dial 112, the call will be made to 911. To define multiple dial masks, separate each value by a semicolon (e.g., 112;212). See Figure 2-103.

c.   *PSTN usage record:* Select the PSTN usage record. The PSTN usage determines which route is used to route emergency calls from users who are authorized to use them. The route associated with this usage should point to a Session Initiation Protocol (SIP) trunk dedicated to emergency calls or to an Emergency Location Identification Number (ELIN) gateway that routes emergency calls to the nearest PSAP. See Figure 2-103.

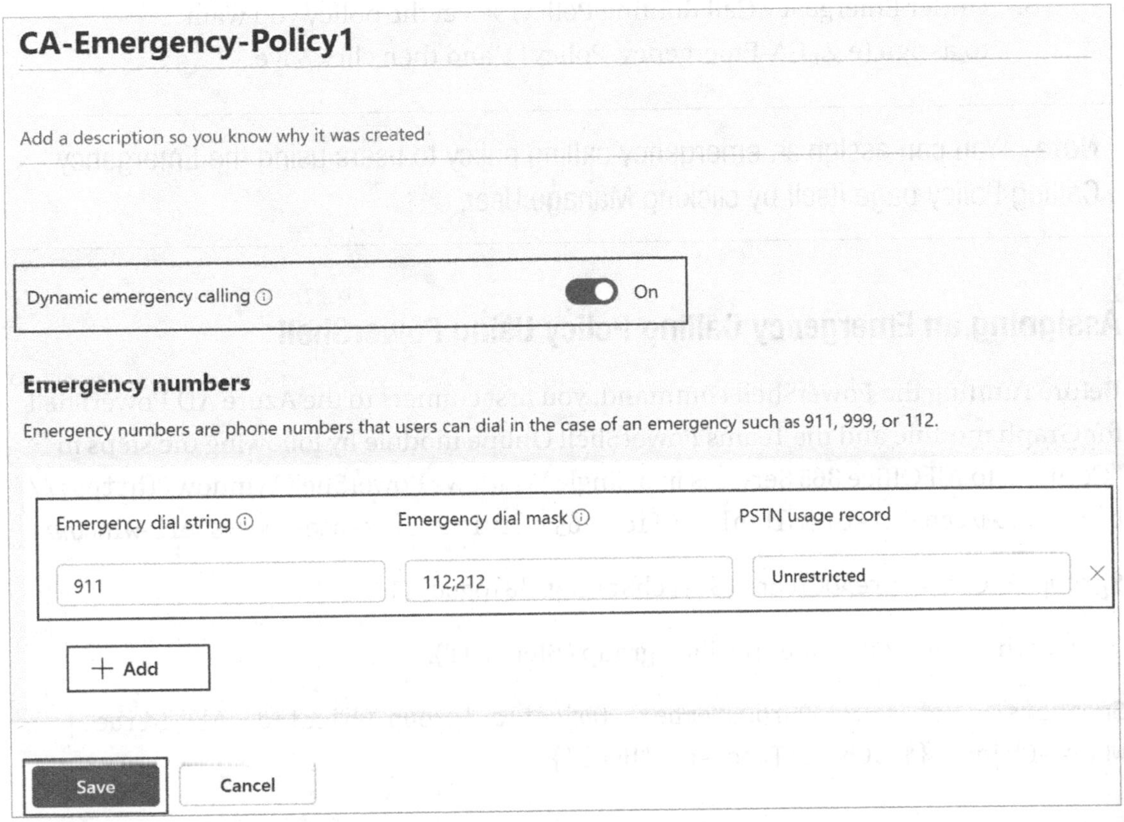

Figure 2-103. Emergency numbers

5. Once you are finished adding all emergency numbers, click
   Save. Remember, Figure 2-103 shows an example, not a real
   policy that you can follow. You as an admin need to come up
   with an emergency string and dial mask before creating the
   emergency number.

Emergency Call Routing Policy to Users Using the Teams Admin Center and PowerShell

To assign an emergency routing policy to users using the Teams admin center, follow this
procedure:

1. Log in to the Teams admin center, and then navigate to Users.
   Select the user and then click Policies.

2. Under Assigned Policies, click Edit.

3. Under Emergency Call Routing Policy, select the policy you want
   to assign (e.g., CA-Emergency-Policy1), and then click Save.

Note   You can assign an emergency calling policy to users using the Emergency
Calling Policy page itself by clicking Manage User.

Assigning an Emergency Calling Policy Using PowerShell

Before running the PowerShell command, you first connect to the Azure AD PowerShell
for Graph module and the Teams PowerShell Online module by following the steps in
"Connect to All Office 365 Services in a Single Windows PowerShell Window" (https://
bloguc.com/connect-to-multiple-office-365-services-in-a-one-powershell-window/).

```
$group = Get-AzureADGroup -SearchString "Bloguc IT"
```

Get the members of the specified group (Bloguc IT).

```
$members = Get-AzureADGroupMember -ObjectId $group.ObjectId -All $true |
Where-Object {$_.ObjectType -eq "User"}
```

Then assign all users in the group to a particular Teams policy. In this example, it's EmergencyCallRoutingPolicy1. First connect the Teams PowerShell module.

```
# When using Teams PowerShell Module
    Import-Module MicrosoftTeams
    $credential = Get-Credential
    Connect-MicrosoftTeams -Credential $credential
# Then run the command.
$members | ForEach-Object { Grant-CsTeamsEmergencyCallRoutingPolicy
-PolicyName "CA-Emergency-Policy1" -Identity $_.UserPrincipalName}
```

Note   Depending on the number of members in the group, this command could take several minutes to execute.

Assigning a Custom Emergency Call Routing Policy to a Network Site

It is important to assign an emergency call routing policy to the network site using the Set-CsTenantNetworkSite command to use a network site or subnet with the same policy. This example shows how to assign a policy called EmergencyCallRoutingPolicy1 to the BlogucSite1 site.

```
Set-CsTenantNetworkSite -Identity "BlogucSite1" -EmergencyCallRoutingPolicy
"CA-Emergency-Policy1"
```

Mobility Policies

Mobility policies control the Teams Phone Mobile features that are available to users in Teams. You can use the Global (Org-wide default) policy or create one or more custom mobility policies for people in your organization. Figure 2-104 shows the Teams mobility policy. You can use a default global policy or create a new custom policy.

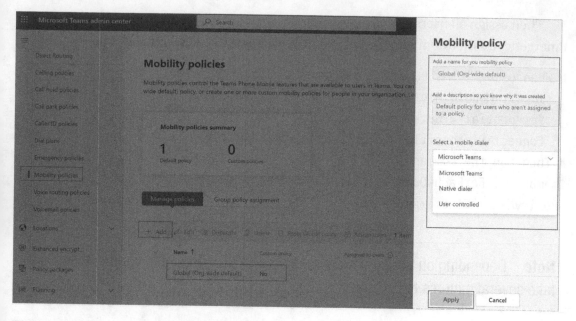

Figure 2-104.   *Teams mobility policy*

Voice Routing Policies

Voice routing policies in Microsoft Teams determine how calls are routed. These policies specify a set of Public Switched Telephone Network (PSTN) usages that define which voice routes are assigned to users who are homed online.

Setting up a voice routing policy involves creating and assigning PSTN usages, creating voice routes, and then creating the policy itself.

To create and manage Teams Voice routing policy in the Teams admin center, you would do the following:

1. Log in to the Teams admin center.

2. Navigate to Voice, click Voice Routing Policies, and then click +Add to create a new voice routing policy. You can use a global policy; however, creating a new custom policy for each calling scenarios is recommended.

3. On the next page, give a meaningful name and description and
    then click "Add PSTN usage records." On the next page, click +Add
    to create a new PSTN usage record. Give a meaningful name,
    check the newly created PSTN record, and click "Save and apply."
    For example, use "CA-National-Usage." Figure 2-105 shows the
    voice route policy and PSTN usage creation settings.

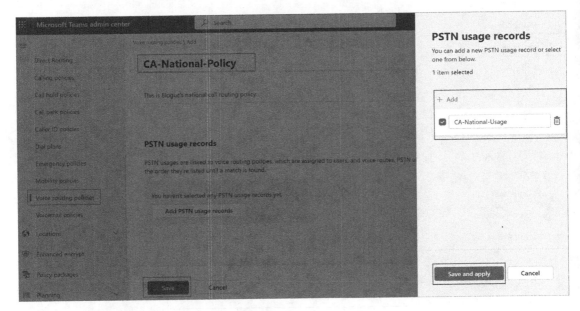

Figure 2-105. *Teams voice routing policy*

4. The next thing you need to create is a voice route. The voice route
    option is available in the Teams admin center; click Voice ➤
    Direct Routing ➤ Voice route.

5. Then click +Add to create new route. Figure 2-106 shows the voice
    route creation; you need to give a meaningful name, add the
    SBC, and then select the appropriate PSTN Usage. For example,
    Figure 2-106 shows CA-National-Usage.

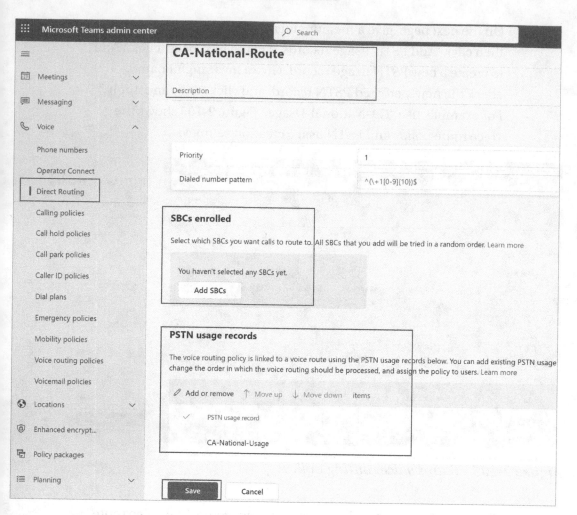

Figure 2-106.   *Teams voice routing policy*

Creating Voice Routing Policies Using PowerShell

Here's how to use PowerShell.

Creating PSTN Usages

PSTN usages are labels that you assign to voice routes. They don't describe or define a route but are just a way to group routes. To create a PSTN usage, you use the New-CsPstnUsage cmdlet.

```
# When using Teams PowerShell Module
    Import-Module MicrosoftTeams
    $credential = Get-Credential
    Connect-MicrosoftTeams -Credential $credential
```

Here's an example:

```
New-CsPstnUsage -Identity Global -Usage "CA-National-Usage"
```

Creating Voice Routes

Voice routes contain instructions on how to route calls to specific numbers or number patterns. To create a voice route, you use the New-CsVoiceRoute cmdlet. Here's an example:

```
New-CsVoiceRoute -Identity "CA-National-Route" -NumberPattern
"^\+1209(\d{7})$" -PstnUsages @{Add="CA-National-Route"} -PstnGatewayList
@{Add="sbc1.bloguc.com"}
```

This command creates a new voice route that applies to numbers that match the specified pattern and sends them through the specified gateway. The PstnUsages parameter associates this route with the previously created PSTN usage.

Creating Voice Routing Policies

Voice routing policies tie PSTN usages to users. To create a voice routing policy, you use the New-CsVoiceRoutingPolicy cmdlet. Here's an example:

```
New-CsVoiceRoutingPolicy -Identity "CA-National-Policy" -PstnUsages
@{Add="NationalRoute"}
```

This command creates a new voice routing policy and assigns it the LocalRoute PSTN usage.

Assigning Voice Routing Policies to Users

After creating the voice routing policy, you can assign it to users. Here's an example:

```
Grant-CsVoiceRoutingPolicy -Identity "bilag@bloguc.com" -PolicyName
"NationalPolicy"
```

This command assigns the LocalPolicy voice routing policy to the user with the email address bilag@bloguc.com.

It's important to note that these are just basic examples. Real-world routing scenarios can be much more complex and might involve multiple usages, routes, and policies. Always plan your configuration carefully to ensure it meets your specific needs.

Remember that changes in PowerShell might take up to 15 minutes or more than that to propagate through Microsoft Teams.

Voicemail Policies

Voicemail policies control the available features for the voicemail service in Teams. You can use the Global (Org-wide default) policy and customize it or create custom voicemail policies for users in your organization. Figure 2-107 shows the voicemail policy settings including that users can edit call answering rules, maximum voicemail recording length, primary and secondary prompt language, voicemail transcription, translation for transcription, etc.

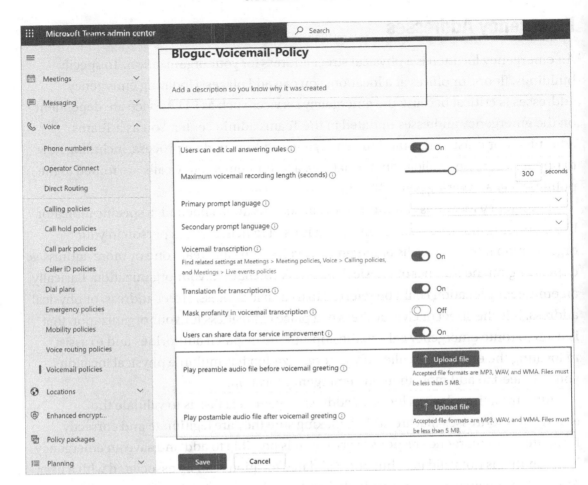

Figure 2-107. *Teams voicemail policy*

Admin Center: Locations Tab

In the Teams admin center, when you navigate locations, you will see three different options. Reporting labels is a way to upload your existing network's IP subnets with their physical office addresses to identify the site correctly in Teams reports and the Call Quality dashboard. Emergency addresses allows you to update physical office addresses that can be used for emergency services like Enhanced 911. Network topology itself offers a way to update network details including central and branch office designations with network site subnets and bandwidth details. Read each option carefully to understand Teams networking.

Emergency Addresses

An emergency location is a physical street address for your organization. To specify buildings, floors, or offices at a location, you can add places. Updating emergency addresses is critical because the emergency services such as 911 service are dependent on the emergency addresses updated in the Teams admin center. You as a Teams administrator must understand the emergency address update process, including how to update addresses, validation, formatting, and how emergency calls are routed to the public safety answering point (PSAP).

Emergency locations contain a physical address and, if needed, a specific indicator, like a building, floor, cubical or office, that is used to help locate a person in your organization if that user calls emergency services. You can create one or more addresses, depending on the number of physical locations you have in your organization. Basically, an emergency location could be referred to as a civic address, street address, or physical address. It is the street or civic address of a place of business for your organization that is used to route emergency calls to the appropriate dispatch authorities and to assist in locating the emergency caller. If your organization has multiple physical locations, you will need to add more than one emergency location.

After updating physical location addresses, your next task is to validate the emergency addresses that are added, making sure they are legitimate and correctly formatted for emergency response services. It is possible to add and save an emergency location that is not validated, but only validated locations can be associated with a user. After an emergency location is validated and saved, you can assign it to a user. You can also modify an emergency location that is saved and validated.

When an emergency location is assigned to a user, you will assign a location ID that references the location. The location ID includes the referenced emergency address (the street or civic address). A default place is included with an emergency location for cases in which in-building specifiers are not needed.

When a Teams user dials an emergency number, how the call is routed to the serving PSAP varies by country or region. In some countries or regions, such as the United States and the United Kingdom, the calls are first screened to determine the current location of the user before connecting the call to the appropriate dispatch center. In other areas, calls are routed directly to the dispatch center serving the phone number associated with the emergency caller.

To add an emergency address, follow these steps:

1. First, list all emergency locations, meaning all the physical addresses of your organization offices.

2. Once you are ready to add emergency locations, log in to the Teams admin center and navigate to Locations ➤ Emergency Addresses. Click +Add and then type the name of your location. Select the country and then type the address starting with office number, road, city, state, and area code. The example in Figure 2-108 shows the Bloguc HQ office address.

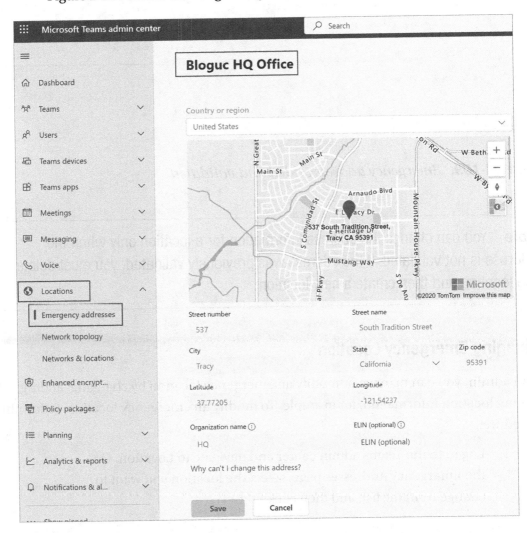

Figure 2-108. *Updating emergency addresses*

Microsoft made address searching easier by allowing you to select Correct when you type the address. Once you click Save, it will automatically validate the address. After an address is added, this window shows the address status. Figure 2-109 shows the Bloguc HQ office address and its validation status.

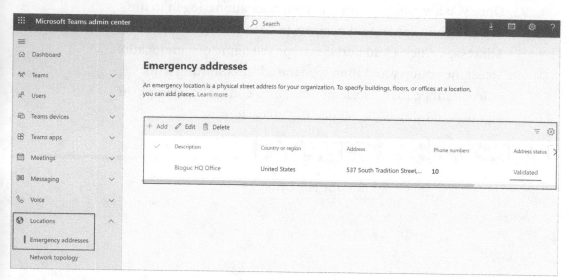

Figure 2-109. *Emergency address added and validated*

Note   You can change the address information for a location only when the address is not validated. If the address was previously validated, you must delete the location and then create a new location.

Managing Emergency Location

As an admin, you can manage or modify an emergency location by changing, adding, or deleting location information, for example. To modify an emergency location, follow this procedure:

1. Log in to the Teams admin center and navigate to Location. On the Emergency Addresses page, select the location you want to change from the list, and then click Edit.

2. Make your changes.

3. Click Save.

To remove or delete an emergency location, visit the Emergency Addresses page in the Microsoft Teams admin center. Find and select the location you want to remove from the list of locations, and then click Delete.

Network Topology

You can use network topology to define the network regions, sites, and subnets that are used to determine the emergency call routing and calling policies that are to be used for a given location.

Inside the network topology you can add network sites and trusted IP addresses that are going to be used in call admission control, location-based routing, and so on. A network region contains a collection of network sites. You can add new network regions that can be used globally for all network sites. Follow this procedure to add a network site:

1. Log in to the Teams admin center and navigate to Location. On the Network Topology page, select Network Sites and then click Add.

2. Once the Add Network Site page opens, enter a network site name and description, and then set whether location based routing is enabled for this site. Select an emergency location, and finally click New to add the subnet. Figure 2-110 illustrates adding a network site.

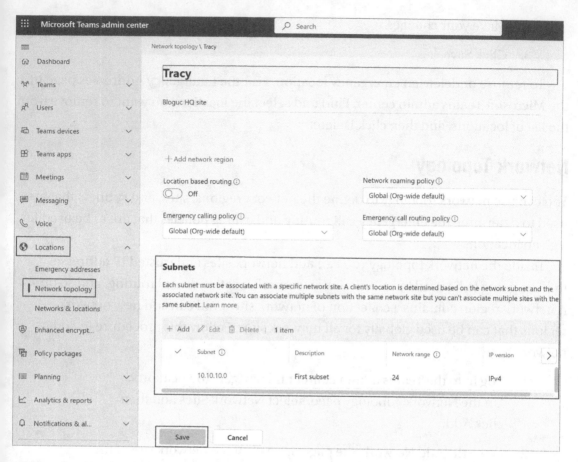

Figure 2-110. *Network site*

Click +New to add a new subnet with a subnet mask and IP version (see Figure 2-111).

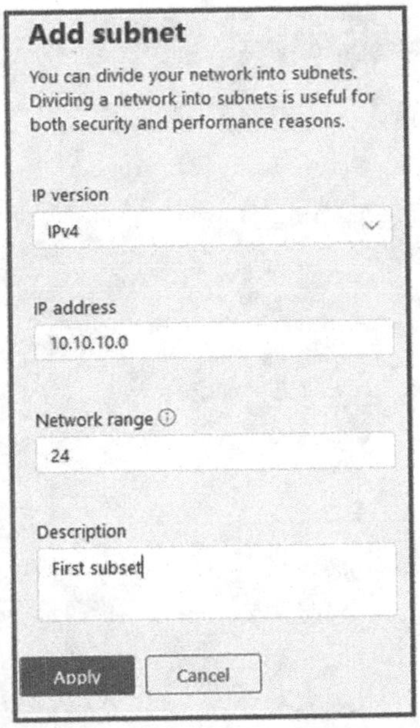

Figure 2-111. *Adding a subnet*

Adding Trusted Ips

Trusted external IP addresses are the external IP addresses of the enterprise network and are exempt from certain designated security options. To add trusted IP addresses on the Network Topology page, you can select Trusted IPs and then click Add. Enter the IP version, IP address, network range, and description, as shown in Figure 2-112. Trusted IP addresses are required to implement a location-based routing (LBR) service, as LBR checks to discover the internal subnet where the user's endpoint is located. If the user's external IP address doesn't match any IP address defined in the trusted IP address list, the endpoint is categorized as being at an unfamiliar location, and any PSTN calls to or from a user who is enabled for location-based routing are blocked.

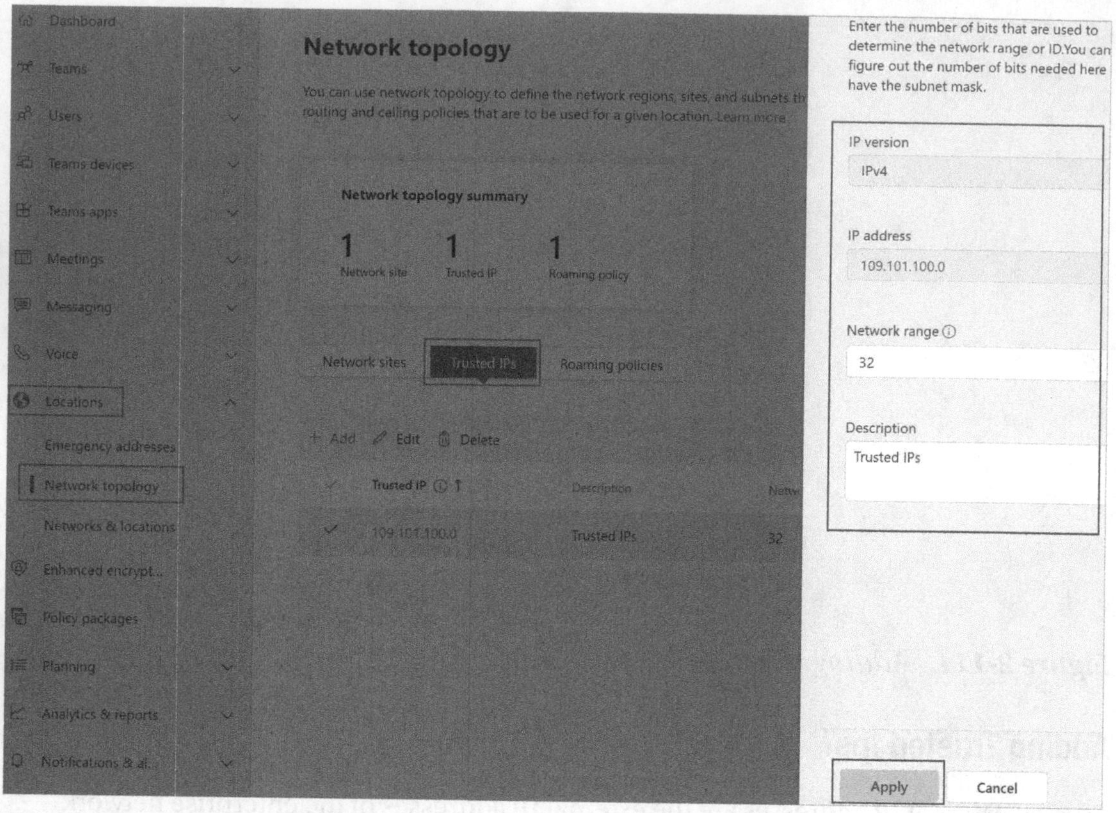

Figure 2-112. Adding a trusted IP

Roaming Policies

You can manage video and media settings with the network roaming policy.

In addition to managing video and media settings with meeting policies, you can now dynamically control the use of the following attributes used by the Microsoft Teams client by using the TeamsNetworkRoamingPolicy: IP Video and Media bit rate settings. Figure 2-113 shows the roaming policy with the "Media bit rate (Kbs)" config option.

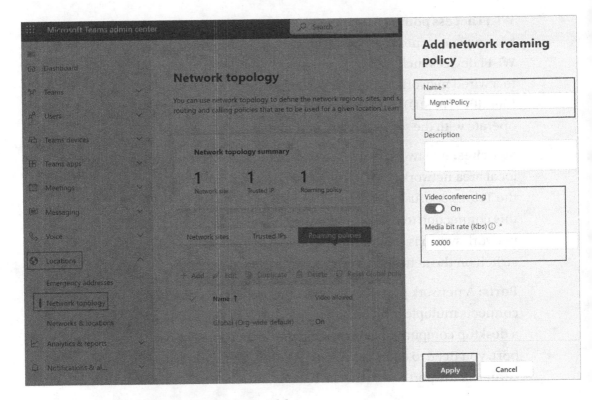

Figure 2-113. *Adding a trusted IP address*

Networks and Locations

In the Microsoft Teams admin center, under Networks and Locations, you can view
and manage information about your organization's network. This includes subnets,
Wi-Fi access points, switches, and ports, which together help the Teams client to obtain
emergency addresses from the locations associated with different network identifiers.
For a client to obtain a location, you as Teams admin must fill the location information
server (LIS) with network identifiers (subnets, WAPs, switches, ports) and emergency
locations. You can do this in the Microsoft Teams admin center or by using PowerShell.

Here's a breakdown of each component:

> **Subnets:** A network subnet defines a segment of the IP network
> that contains the addresses of one or more endpoints. Each
> subnet must be associated with an emergency location, and the
> subnet ID must match the client network.

Wi-Fi access points: A wireless access point (WAP), also referred to as an access point (AP), is a networking device that allows other Wi-Fi devices such as PCs, laptops, and mobile phones to connect to a wired network. Each WAP is assigned a Basic Service Set Identifier (BSSID) used for grouping wireless network devices that operate with the same network parameters.

Switches: A network switch is a device that connects multiple local area network (LAN) devices, such as desktops running the Teams app, using Ethernet connections. The devices use this connection to receive and transfer data to each other. Each network switch is stamped with a chassis ID, which identifies the switch on the network.

Ports: A network port is a physical Ethernet connection that connects multiple local area network (LAN) devices such as a desktop computer that is running the Teams app. For each port, you need to enter the chassis ID of the network switch that connects the port to a switch in Teams.

Admin Center: Enhanced Encryption Policies

Enhanced encryption policies are used to control if users in your organization can use enhanced encryption settings in Teams. You can use the Global (Org-wide default) policy, or you can create one or more custom policies and then assign them to users. As part of the enhanced encryption, you as an admin can create a custom policy and enable one-on-one Teams calls that are end-to-end encrypted if both participants turn on this setting. Some features won't be available, including recording and transcription. Chat messages are secured by Teams data encryption. End-to-end encryption is part of Team premium license. Figure 2-114 shows three default policies and an option to create custom policies.

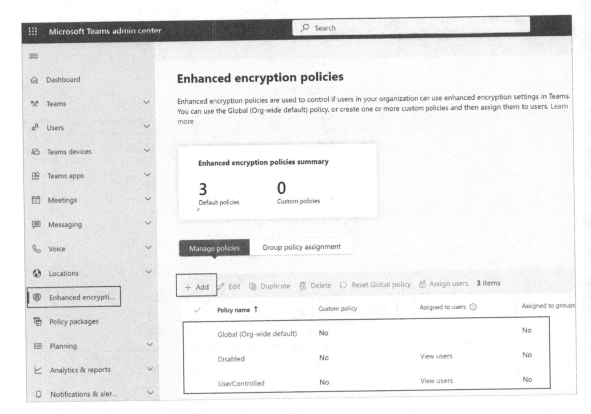

Figure 2-114. *Enhanced encryption policy*

Admin Center: Policy Packages

A policy package is a collection of predefined policies and settings that can be customized and applied to a group of users that have similar roles within your organization. You'll need Teams Premium or an Advanced Communications license to add, edit, duplicate, or manage users for custom policy packages. Figure 2-115 shows 14 policy packages that are available by default. However, you cannot create a custom policy package without a Teams Premium license. You can use an existing policy package and group policy assignment option.

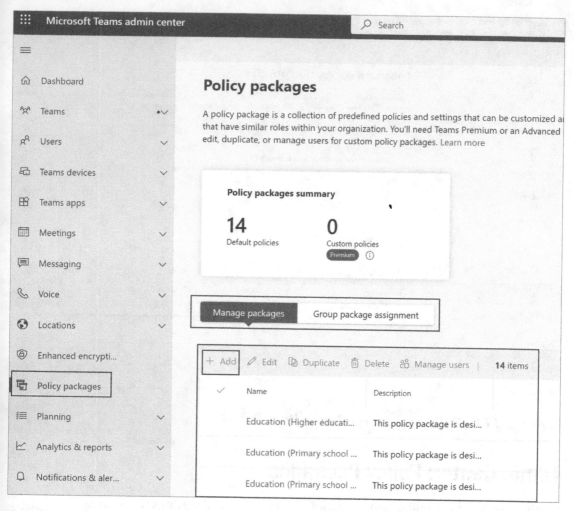

Figure 2-115. *Policy packages*

Admin Center: Planning

In the Microsoft Teams admin center, the Planning tab provides tools and resources to help you plan for deploying Teams in your organization. As a Teams admin, you need to ensure your existing environment is ready for handling the Teams workload and added media traffic before deploying Microsoft Teams in a production environment. You should check that the existing network infrastructure of an organization will meet the requirements needed for Teams collaboration and real-time communication.

In this discussion, we'll explore how to leverage Teams Advisor for optimal Teams deployment planning. It's crucial to guarantee sufficient bandwidth, complete access to necessary IP addresses, and the appropriate configuration of ports when deploying Microsoft Teams within your network. Furthermore, fulfilling the performance demands for real-time media is a pivotal aspect of this planning process.

Advisor for Teams

Teams Advisor is a tool that helps you roll out Teams by providing a recommended deployment plan based on your organization's needs. The Teams Advisor generates a plan with a list of tasks that guide you through deploying Teams. It focuses on different workloads, including chat, teams, channels, apps, meetings, conferencing, and PSTN calling.

For example, if you're planning to deploy Teams for the first time in your organization, you could use the Teams Advisor to create a deployment plan. The Advisor would provide a list of tasks and step-by-step instructions to help you prepare your organization, configure settings, and train your users.

What Advisor for Teams Can Do

There are multiple things that Advisor for Teams can provide, and here we cover a few of them. Customers can select what workload they want to roll out and who they are rolling it out with. A tenant readiness assessment is provided based on common friction points that FastTrack has helped customers solve. Teams is created with the project team and populated with success resources to get started quickly.

Using Advisor for Teams

To use Advisor for Teams, you need to log in to the Teams admin center and then select Planning. Select Advisor for Teams and then click Add to select a workload to roll out in your organization. If this is the first workload you roll out, start with chat, teams, channels, and apps. Based on your selection, if a service management team doesn't exist, a team will be created with a channel dedicated to that workload. Prepopulated success resources listed under Details will be added into the team. Should you need to add additional workloads, you can at any time once the team is created. Repeat the same process to add another workload as Meetings and Conferencing. After adding both workloads, you will see them under Deployment Team, as shown in Figure 2-116.

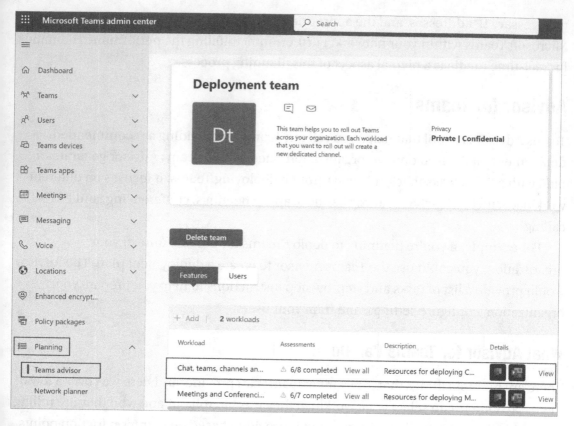

Figure 2-116.   *Two workloads*

On the Users tab, you add users who can execute the deployment tasks.

Advisor for Teams has two core workloads covered. The first one includes chat, teams, channels, and apps; the second one is Meetings and Conferencing. Advisor for Teams runs the assessment and then highlights the areas that require more attention. As an example, Figure 2-117 shows two areas that need more attention: Office 365 Group Naming Standard Configured and Office 365 Group Expiration Configured. The rest of the tasks shown are completed.

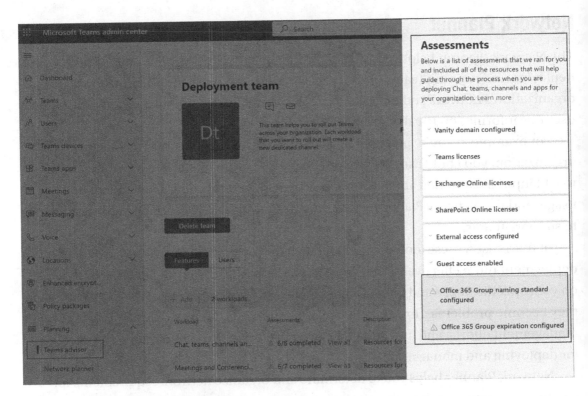

Figure 2-117. Advisor for Teams assessment

Advisor also gives recommended plans—basically step-by-step guidance—of how to best deploy this workload in Teams. This workload detail looks familiar, as it is actually coming from a planner. This is the plan that Microsoft Teams creates for the deployment team with all the details about how to deploy these workloads in Microsoft Teams.

On the Advisor for Teams main screen, you can see the deployment status as well. Advisor for Teams can open in your Teams and shows both the channels. Clicking the individual channel and Planner tab, you can see all the tasks for that workload. Because it is a shared workspace for deployment Teams, all the members can update the tasks.

Before starting Teams deployment, you must add all the project team members who are going to execute deployment tasks. Adding a member is easy; you can open the deployment team in Teams and add multiple members who are going to execute tasks.

Network Planner

The Network Planner helps you calculate and manage network requirements for deploying and running Teams in your organization. You input information about your organization's network and the Teams features you plan to use, and the Network Planner uses this information to calculate network requirements.

For example, if you're planning to introduce Teams meetings and calling in your organization, you could use the Network Planner to estimate the network impact. You would input information about your offices, network connections, and anticipated usage, and the Network Planner would provide an estimate of the bandwidth you'll need to support Teams.

In both cases, these tools are intended to help you plan and manage your Teams deployment more effectively. They provide guidance and recommendations based on your specific needs and help you anticipate and address potential issues before they become problems. However, they're not a substitute for broader planning and management efforts, and they should be used in conjunction with other best practices for deploying and managing Teams.

Network Planner helps you to determine and organize network requirements for connecting people who use Teams across your organization in a few steps. By providing your networking details and Teams usage, you get calculations and the network requirements you need when deploying Teams and cloud voice across organizational physical locations.

Using Network Planner, an admin can create representations of the organization using sites and Microsoft-recommended personas (office workers, remote workers, and Teams room system devices) and then generate reports and calculate bandwidth requirements for Teams usage.

To use Network Planner, you must have global administrator, Teams admin, or Teams communication administrator role permission. You can access the Network Planner tool through the Microsoft Teams admin center. Select Planning and then Network Planner.

When you click Add, it will allow you to create a Network Planner name. By default, there will be three user personas, but you can add custom persons on the Network Planner page. Click the Users tab, and then on the Add Persona page, provide the persona name and description. In the Permissions section, select from the following services: Audio, Video, Screen Sharing, File Sharing, Conference Audio, Conference Video, Conference Screen Sharing, and PSTN.

Building a Network Planner Plan

Network Planner helps you to determine and organize network requirements for connecting people who use Teams across your organization in a few steps. To build your network plan, follow these steps:

1. Log in to the Microsoft Teams admin center, navigate to Planning, and select Network Planner.

2. On the Network Planner page, under Network Plans, click Add, as shown in Figure 2-118.

3. On the Network Plan name page, enter the name for the network plan (e.g., Bloguc BW Planning 2020 in Figure 2-118) and an optional description, and click Apply.

Figure 2-118. *Assigning a network plan name*

4. The newly created network plan will appear in the Network Plans section. Select the plan you created. On the plan page, in the Network Sites section, select Add A Network Site. On the Add A Network Site page, enter the following information:

   - Name of the network site

   - Network site address

   - Network settings: IP address subnet and network range

   - Express route or WAN connection

   - Internet egress

   - Internet link capacity

   - PSTN egress (VoIP only or local)

   - An optional description

5. Once you enter all details, as shown in Figure 2-119, click Save to commit the changes.

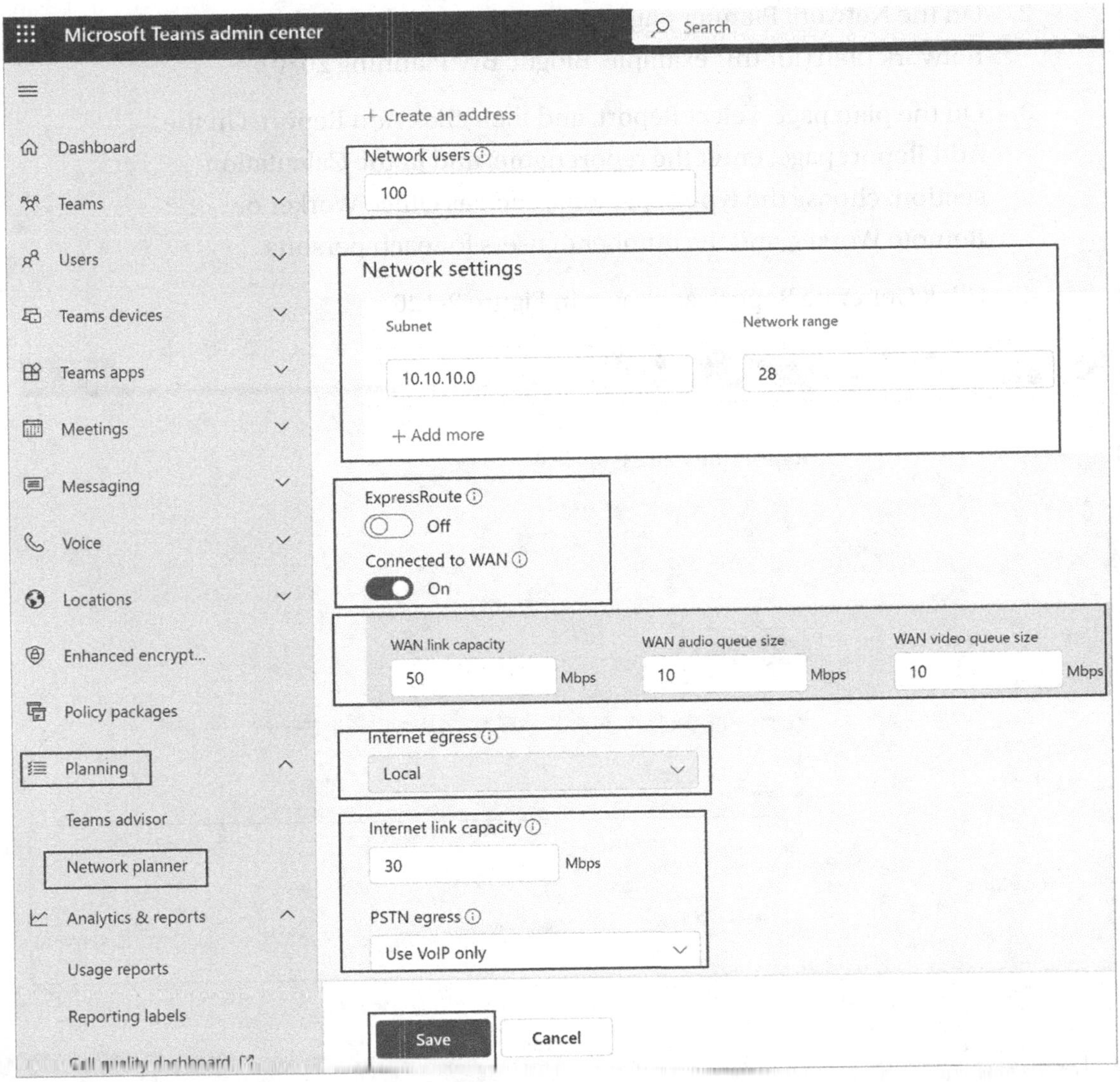

Figure 2-119. Adding a network site and subnet

Creating a Report

After creating a plan, you run the report to see the required bandwidth for the number of users per site. To create a report based on your network plan, perform the following steps:

1. Log in to the Microsoft Teams admin center. Navigate to Planning and then select Network Planner.

2. On the Network Planner page, under Network Plans, select your network plan (for this example, Bloguc BW Planning 2020).

3. On the plan page, select Report, and then click Add Report. On the Add Report page, enter the report name, and in the Calculation section, choose the type of persona, such as Office Worker or Remote Worker, and the number of users for each persona.

4. Click Generate Report, as shown in Figure 2-120.

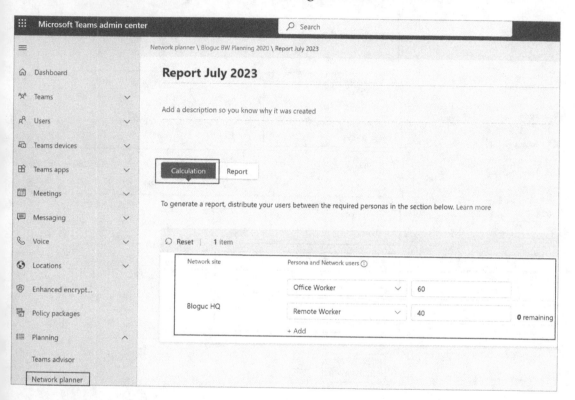

Figure 2-120. *Generating a report*

5. On the report page, review the report, including the type of service and required bandwidth for different services, such as audio, video, screenshare, Office 365 server traffic, and PSTN. Figure 2-121 shows the Network Planner report.

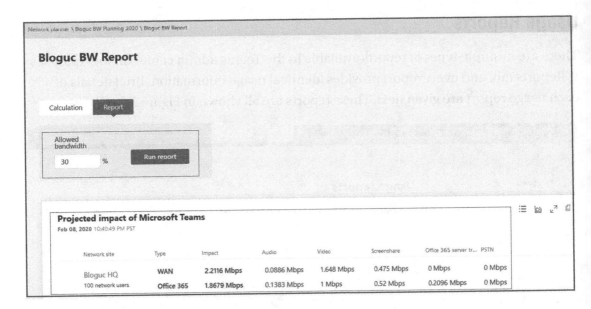

Figure 2-121. *Network Planner report*

Admin Center: Analytics and Reports

Teams reporting is important because it will improve the overall Teams deployment experience in your environment and how users will use Teams. Teams reporting provides user-level reporting and live event usage reports in the Teams admin center. The Analytics & Reports tab in the Teams admin center allows you to understand how your users are using Microsoft Teams, which features they are using, and their usage levels, which is important information for admins because it allows you to prioritize the training and readiness efforts.

To implement Microsoft Teams in the organization effectively, it is essential that you as a Teams admin generate reports that display usage activity in Teams, including the number of active users and channels. The Teams usage report helps you to understand users' adoption and verify how many users across your organization are using Teams to communicate and collaborate. Teams usage reports are available in the Microsoft Teams admin center. These reports provide usage information for teams, including the number of active users and channels, guests, and messages in each team.

Usage Reports

There are multiple types of reports available in the Teams admin center on the Analytics & Reports tab, and every report provides identical usage information. Brief details of each usage report are given next. These reports are all shown in Figure 2-122.

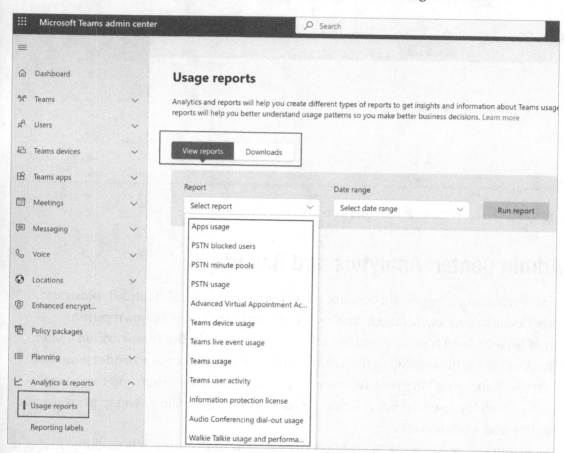

Figure 2-122. *Available reports in the Teams admin center*

- *Apps usage:* The Teams app usage report in the Microsoft Teams admin center provides you with insights about which apps users are using in Teams. You can gain insights into the app activity in your organization for different Microsoft (Viva learning, Shifts, etc.), third-party (Polly, Trello etc.), and line-of-business (LOB) Teams apps.

- *PSTN Blocked Users:* This report offers details of the display name, the phone number, the reason, the type of action, and the date and time of the action.

- *PSTN Minute Pools:* The Teams PSTN minute pools report in the Microsoft Teams admin center gives you an overview of audio conferencing and calling activity in your organization by showing you the number of minutes consumed during the current month. You can see a breakdown of activity including the license used for calls, total minutes available, used minutes, and license usage by location.

- *PSTN Usage:* This report offers usage information on Calling Plans as well as Direct Routing. The Teams PSTN and SMS usage report in the Microsoft Teams admin center gives you an overview of calling and audio conferencing activity in your organization. You can view detailed calling activity for Calling Plans if you use Microsoft as your telephony carrier and for Direct Routing if you use your own telephony carrier. The Calling Plans tab shows information including the number of minutes that users spent in inbound and outbound PSTN calls and the cost of these calls.

  - *Calling Plans:* This includes information on time stamp, username, phone number, call type, called to and called from, duration of the call, number type, charge, domestic or international call, conference ID, and capability (license).

  - *Direct Routing:* This includes information on time stamp, display name, SIP address, phone number, called to and called from, duration of the call, invite time, time of the call start, duration, failure time, number type, media bypass, SBC FQDN, event type, Azure region, final SIP code, final Microsoft subcode, final SIP phrase, and correlation ID.

- *Advanced Virtual Appointment:* The Advanced Virtual Appointments activity report in the Microsoft Teams admin center provides user activity information for advanced Virtual Appointments capabilities that are available with Teams Premium. To view the report, you must be a Global admin, Teams admin, Global reader, or Report reader, and your organization must be using advanced Virtual Appointments capabilities.

- *Teams Device Usage:* This report gives information on whether users are using Windows, Mac, iOS, or Android devices to access the Teams app.

- *Teams device usage*: The Microsoft 365 Reports dashboard shows you the activity overview across the products in your organization. It enables you to drill in to individual product-level reports to give you more granular insight about the activities within each product. Check out the Reports overview topic. In the Microsoft Teams device usage report, you can gain insights into the types of devices on which the Microsoft Teams apps is being used in your organization.

- *Teams Live Event Usage:* This report provides information on total views of a live event; starting time; the status of the event; which users had a role as organizer, presenter, and producer; the recording setting; and the production type.

- *Teams Usage:* This report offers information about active users, active users in teams and channels, active channels, messages, privacy setting of teams, and guests in a team.

- *Teams User Activity*: This report provides information on one-to-one calls, messages that the user has posted in a team chat or in a private chat, and the last activity date of a user.

- *Audio Conferencing Dial-out report:* The Audio Conferencing dial-out usage report in the Teams admin center gives you an overview of usage and dollars spent for the audio conferencing dial-out service. This report allows admins to consume user-level data in terms of communication credits spent and dial-out minutes used. It will help admins determine the future communication credits needed going forward from any point in time.

- *Walkie Talkie Usage and Performance Report:* The Walkie Talkie usage and performance report in the Microsoft Teams admin center gives you an overview of Walkie Talkie activity in your organization. The report provides information such as the number of push-to-talk (PTT) transmissions made and received, channel activity, transmission duration, and device and participant details.

Use this report to gain insight into Walkie Talkie usage trends and performance in your organization. To access the report, you must be a Global admin, Teams admin, Global reader, or Report reader.

Accessing Teams Reports

Now that you have seen how important the information is that Teams reports provide, the logical question is how you access these reports. To access the Teams usage reports, you should have one of the following roles: Microsoft/Office 365 global admin, Teams Service admin, or Skype for Business admin. All of these reports are accessed via the Microsoft Teams admin center. Some of the most useful and accessed reports are covered next.

Reporting Labels

Reporting labels are used to give an IP subnet a name that links it to a physical location such as offices, buildings, or organizational sites within your organization. They are used by the Call Quality Dashboard or call analytics to make it easier to see the name of a place instead of just an IP subnet in reports. You can upload a text file (`.csv` or `.tsv`) that has a list of physical locations and their associated network subnets.

To upload the locations data, log in to the Teams admin center, then navigate to Analytics and Reports, and then select Reporting Labels. Next, click Upload, as shown in Figure 2-123.

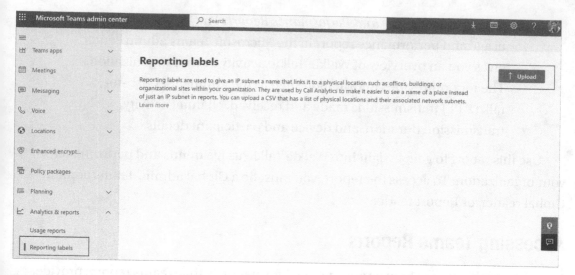

Figure 2-123. *Upload Locations Data option*

Once you click Upload Locations Data, you will see a new window where you can upload the location information with IP subnets using a labels file in .csv or .tsv format. I recommend downloading the existing template and then updating it and uploading it so that you will see any error while uploading the file.

Admin Center: Call Quality Dashboard

The Call Quality Dashboard (CQD) provides an overall view for analyzing Teams call quality. It supports Teams admins and network engineers in troubleshooting call quality problems with specific calls and helps them optimize a network. The users' individual call details are not visible in CQD, but the overall quality of calls made using Teams is captured. Another important use of CQD is to assess details about the audio and video call quality users are getting using Teams. It provides reports about call quality metrics that give you insights into overall call quality, server–client and client–client streams, and voice quality service-level agreements.

Using the Call Quality Dashboard

Microsoft Teams has extensive reporting and analytical capabilities that help admins to measure the overall call quality. When users report poor call quality, Teams and network admins can together check the CQD to see if an overall site-related issue could be a contributing cause of the call quality problems. Microsoft has labeled many of the dimensions and measures as first or second. In the CQD, the main logic determines which endpoint involved in the stream or call is labeled as first.

- The first will always be considered the Teams Cloud service because the purely cloud-based Teams service means their server endpoints include Audio Video Multi-Control Unit (AV MCU), Mediation Server, transport relay, and so on. If a Teams service is involved in the stream or call, consider it as first.

- The second will always be a client endpoint unless the stream is between two server endpoints.

- If both endpoints are the same type, such as client–client, the order for which is first or second is based on the internal ordering of the user agent category. This ensures the ordering is consistent.

Note   The first and second classification is separate from which endpoint is the caller or the person being called. The First Is Caller dimension can be used to help identify which endpoint was the caller or the person being called.

Accessing the Call Quality Dashboard

There are two CQD dashboards for Teams: one is a preview, and the other one is generally available. As an admin, you can access CQD through the Teams admin center, as well as directly by browsing to the CQD URL. Using the Teams admin center, log in to the Teams admin center and then navigate to and select Call Quality Dashboard. That will open a new browser tab for the Microsoft Call Quality Dashboard. To see the CQD, however, you need to sign in again. Once you sign in, you will see the CQD. Figure 2-124 shows the CQD displaying the overall call quality. You will see options to display the server–client call quality, client–client call quality, and voice quality SLA.

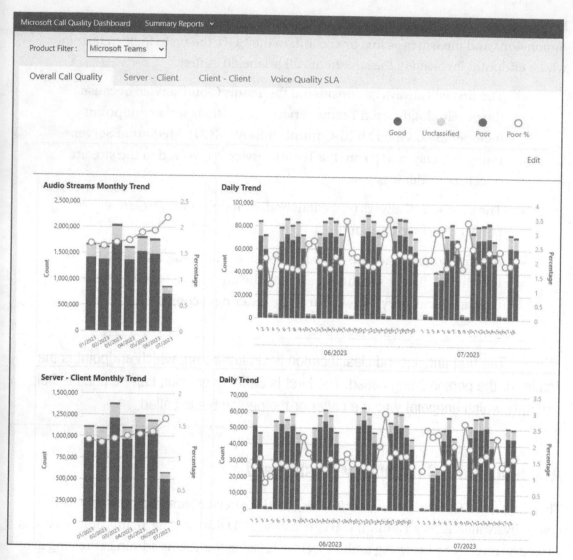

Figure 2-124. *Call Quality Dashboard*

You can see the CQD by directly browsing to https://cqd.teams.microsoft.com/ spd/#/Dashboard.

Displaying the List of Call Quality Reports

CQD provides multiple types of reports. Figure 2-125 shows the list of CQD reports on the Summary Reports tab. You can easily access each type of report by clicking its report name. To see the summary report, log in to the Teams admin center and then navigate to the CQD and then click it. It will open in a new browser tab.

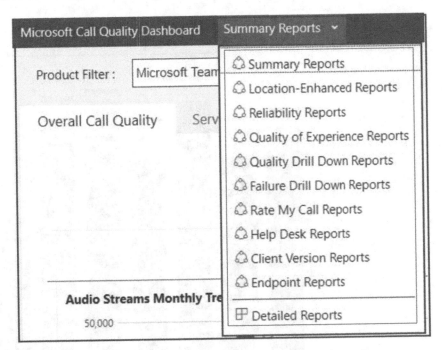

Figure 2-125. *Summary Reports tab*

Currently detailed reports are in preview. When you click Detailed Report, it opens and displays as a preview. To directly access the detailed report, simply visit https://cqd.teams.microsoft.com/cqd/. Figure 2-126 shows an example of a detailed report.

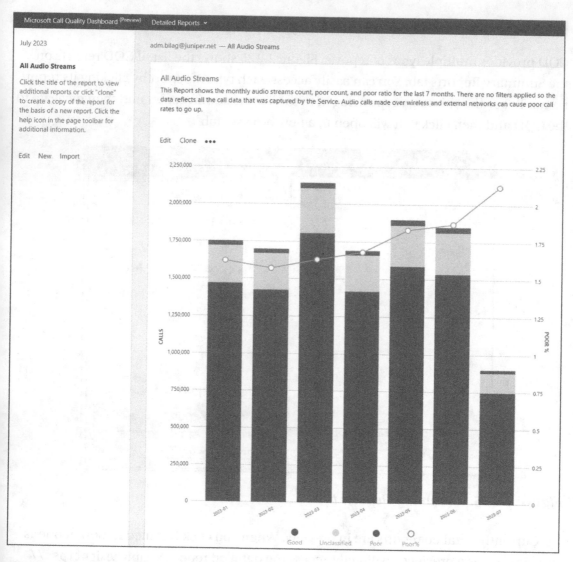

Figure 2-126. *Detailed report for all audio streams*

Click the title of the report to view additional reports or click Clone to create a copy of the report to use as the basis of a new report. For help, click the help icon on the page toolbar for additional information.

The All Audio Streams report in Figure 2-126 shows the monthly audio streams count ratio of and audio for the last seven months. There are no filters applied, so the data reflects all the call data captured by the Teams service. Audio calls made over wireless and external networks can cause poor call rates to go up.

Additional Tools for Teams Dependent Service Management

The following are additional tools.

Microsoft Azure Active Directory Center

In this section, you will learn about Azure AD usage within Teams. As a Teams admin, you must understand the role of directory services and identity management and that these came from Azure AD for Teams. Fundamentally, Azure AD is the cloud-based identity and access management service for Office 365. As such, it is an essential part of Microsoft Teams because Teams leverages identities stored in Azure AD for collaboration and communication. The license requirements for using Azure AD identities and for accessing Teams are included in a large number of different licensing packages, such as Small Business Plans like Office 365 Business, Enterprise Plans like Office 365 Enterprise E1/E3/E5, Education Plans like Office 365 Education, and Developer Plans like Office 365 Developer. This means almost every Office 365 plan includes Azure AD.

Microsoft Azure Active Directory (Azure AD) is a cloud-based identity and access management service, which helps your employees sign in and access resources in the following:

- External resources, such as Microsoft Office 365, the Azure portal, and thousands of other SaaS applications

- Internal resources, such as apps on your corporate network and intranet, along with any cloud apps developed by your own organization

Managing Microsoft Teams Identify

Managing identities in Microsoft Teams is closely linked with Azure Active Directory (Azure AD) as Teams relies on Azure AD for its identity service. This encompasses user identities, including guest users, bots, and system accounts. Here's how the identity management process typically works:

- **User provisioning:** When a user is created in Azure AD, they are automatically provisioned in Teams if they are licensed for it. The user details, such as name, email, etc., are pulled from Azure AD.

265

- **User authentication:** Teams uses Azure AD for authenticating users. This includes not only primary authentication when users sign in, but also MFA and conditional access policies to provide additional layers of security.

- **Role-based access control (RBAC):** Azure AD also provides role-based access control to Teams, allowing you to assign roles to users with specific permissions. For example, Teams has roles such as Owners, Members, and Guests, each with different levels of permissions.

- **Guest access:** Teams supports guest access, which lets you add individuals to your teams who are outside your organization. Guest users are added to Azure AD and sign into Teams using their own credentials, and their identity is managed in Azure AD.

- **Security and compliance:** Teams, in conjunction with Azure AD, provides various security and compliance features such as data loss prevention (DLP), eDiscovery, legal hold, and more.

Managing identity is the biggest challenge for any cloud application deployment, and Teams is no exception. When designing and deploying cloud applications, one of the biggest challenges is how to manage the login credentials in the application for authenticating to cloud services while keeping users' credentials secure. Azure AD resolves this problem with a feature called *managed identities*, which provides access to Azure and Office 365 resources for custom applications and services. As previously mentioned, Microsoft Teams leverages Azure AD for identity management. The feature provides Azure services with an automatically managed identity in Azure AD. As an admin, you can use this identity to authenticate to any service that supports Azure AD authentication, such as Microsoft Teams, Exchange Online, SharePoint, OneDrive, and Yammer without any credentials in the application code.

Azure AD has multiple features that provide granular control to Teams admins, such as Azure AD access review, which allows organizations to efficiently manage group memberships, access to enterprise applications, and role assignments. Conditional access is the set of rules for access control based on various specifications such as client, service, registration procedure, location, compliance status, and so on. Conditional access is used to choose whether the user's has access to the organization data.

In addition, Teams provides additional settings for managing user experiences and policies at the team and channel levels, which include things such as team creation policies, app setup policies, meeting policies, etc.

Remember that the ability to manage identities in Microsoft Teams, such as creating and assigning roles, implementing policies, etc., requires administrative privileges. Administrators can access these controls via the Microsoft Teams admin center or through PowerShell commands.

Accessing Azure AD

Accessing the Azure AD portal can be done with these simple steps:

1. **Open a web browser:** Open your preferred web browser.

2. **Navigate to the Azure portal:** Type in the following URL into your web browser: `https://portal.azure.com/`. Or log in to the Microsoft 365 admin center by browsing to `http://portal.office.com/` and then clicking Admin or directly visiting the admin portal URL at `https://admin.microsoft.com/Adminportal/Home`. Then click Azure AD.

3. **Sign into your account:** Click the Sign In button. You'll be directed to the Microsoft sign-in page.

4. **Enter your credentials:** Type in your Microsoft credentials, which is typically your email or phone number, and click Next. Then enter your password.

Note   If you have MFA enabled, you will need to verify your identity using the method you've set up (e.g., a phone call, text message, or an app notification).

---

5. **Access the Azure Active Directory:** Once logged in, you'll see the main Azure dashboard. On the left side, there's a navigation pane. Look for Azure Active Directory and click it. If it's not visible, click All Services, and search for *Azure Active Directory*. You can also pin Azure Active Directory to the sidebar for easy access in the future.

6. **Explore Azure Active Directory:** Now you should be in the Azure
    AD interface, where you can manage users and groups, handle
    identity protection and security, define user settings, etc.

Once the Microsoft 365 admin center page opens, click Show All to show all the
admin tools and then select Azure Active Directory. Once the Azure AD admin center
page opens, click Azure Active Directory to show the Azure AD capabilities.

Using Azure AD, as an admin you can manage users, groups, organizational
relationships, roles and administrators, devices, and so on. Figure 2-127 shows the Azure
AD admin center for the Bloguc organization.

Complete details about Azure AD are outside the scope of this book. I provide the
summary of Azure AD here, though, because Microsoft Teams leverages Azure AD for
identity management.

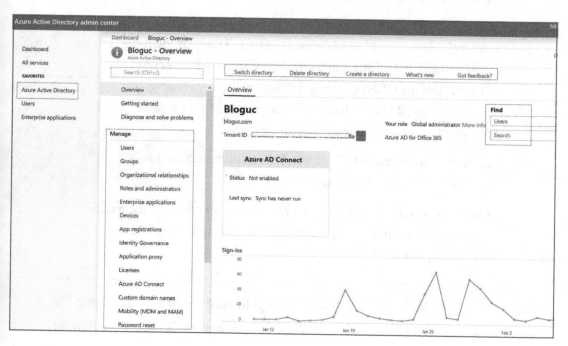

Figure 2-127. *Azure Active Directory admin center*

Microsoft 365 Admin Center

The Microsoft 365 admin center is the main portal where administrators can manage all their Microsoft services. It allows them to set up users, manage licenses, configure security settings, manage resources, and access support, among other administrative tasks.

You can create users or Office 365 groups and manage them through the Microsoft 365 admin center. Figure 2-128 shows the Microsoft 365 admin center. Again, complete details of the Microsoft 365 admin center are outside the scope of this book. I provide brief information about the Microsoft 365 admin center here because Teams and add-on Phone System licenses are assigned and managed, and Teams usage reports are available through the Microsoft 365 admin center.

Accessing Microsoft 365 Admin Center

Accessing the Microsoft 365 admin center can be done as follows:

1. **Open a web browser:** Open your preferred web browser.

2. **Navigate to the Microsoft 365 admin center:** Enter the following URL into your web browser: `https://admin.microsoft.com/`.

3. **Sign into your account:** Click the Sign In button. You'll be directed to the Microsoft sign-in page.

4. **Enter your credentials:** Enter your email, phone, or Skype credentials. These credentials must be associated with an account that has administrative privileges in Microsoft 365. Then, click Next. Enter your password and click Sign in.

Note   If you have MFA enabled, you will need to verify your identity using the method you've set up (e.g., a phone call, text message, or an app notification).

---

5. **Access the Microsoft 365 admin center:** Once you sign in, you'll be directed to the main dashboard of the Microsoft 365 admin center.

6. **Explore the Microsoft 365 admin center:** From here, you can manage users and groups, billing, licenses, admin centers for all Microsoft services, and a whole lot more. You can use the Microsoft 365 admin center to assign Teams, Exchange, SharePoint licenses, and user management.

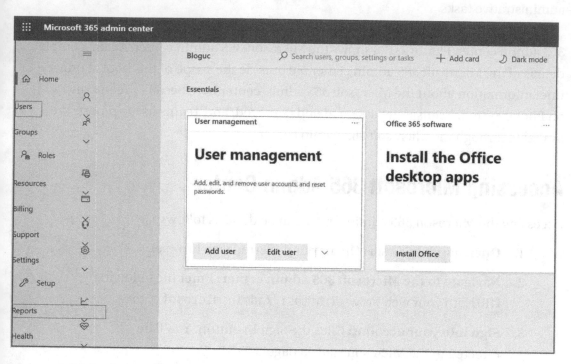

Figure 2-128. *Microsoft 365 admin center*

Remember, not all users in a Microsoft 365 organization have access to the admin center. You need to have administrator privileges for your organization to access the admin center. If you don't have admin privileges, you'll see a message that you don't have permission to access the page. In such cases, you should contact your organization's IT administrator.

Accessing Teams Reports in the Microsoft 365 Admin Center in the Reports Dashboard

The Microsoft 365 admin center is a portal where administrators can manage all Microsoft services, including users, groups, billing, licenses, and a wide range of settings and configurations.

Under the Reports section in the Microsoft 365 admin center, administrators can gain insights into how users in the organization are utilizing Microsoft 365 services. There is a Usage section under Reports that allows you to view different usage data.

Here are some of the types of usage reports you might see:

- **Microsoft 365 active users:** This report shows the number of active users that perform an activity using any Microsoft 365 or Office 365 product.

- **Microsoft 365 services usage:** Here you can see the usage details of individual Microsoft services such as Exchange (email), OneDrive, SharePoint, Teams, and Yammer.

- **Email activity:** This report shows statistics on email usage, including the volume of sent/received mail, and the number of active users.

- **OneDrive activity:** This report gives details about how users in your organization are using OneDrive, such as file count, storage used, and sharing activity.

- **SharePoint activity:** This report provides insights into how users are utilizing SharePoint, including file usage, active sites, and storage metrics.

- **Teams activity:** You can get insights on how your organization is using Teams, such as the number of active users, meeting participation, and calling and chat usage.

- **Yammer activity:** This report will tell you about Yammer usage, including the number of posts, reads, and likes.

The reports provide information about how your Teams deployment is being used and how users are taking advantage of Teams for their collaboration and communication needs. While you are managing a Microsoft Teams environment as an admin within your organization, you will need to generate the usage report from the Microsoft 365 admin center to see how the users in your organization are using Microsoft Teams. These usage and activity reports provide you with comprehensive information to choose where to prioritize training and communication efforts. Using the Microsoft 365 admin center, you can view two activity reports: the Microsoft Teams device usage report and the Microsoft Teams user activity report.

1. To view the Teams user activity and device usage reports, log in to the Microsoft 365 admin center, select Reports, and then select Usage.

2. Once the Usage page opens, click "Select a report," and then click Microsoft Teams. Select Device Usage or User Activity to choose the report you want to view.

3. You can then analyze the report, as shown in Figure 2-129.

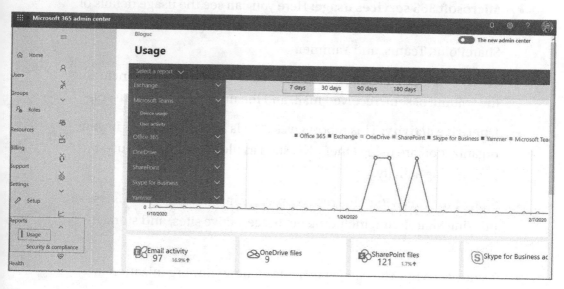

Figure 2-129. *Teams usage reports*

Remember that to view the activity reports, you need one of the following admin role permissions:

- Global administrator

- Exchange administrator

- SharePoint administrator

- Reports reader (the Reports reader role can be assigned to a non-IT user who you would like to have access to these reports by assigning this role)

Remember, these reports can be filtered and adjusted by date range and other factors, and many of them can be downloaded for offline use or further analysis. Please note that your ability to view certain reports might depend on your role and permissions within the organization.

Microsoft 365 Security and Compliance Centers

The Microsoft 365 Security Center and the Microsoft 365 Compliance Center are specialized dashboards that offer administrators unified experiences to manage and enhance the security and compliance of their organizations.

Microsoft 365 Security Center

The Microsoft 365 Security Center is designed to help you manage and enhance the security posture of your organization. It's a central place where you can monitor and respond to security incidents and set up security policies across Microsoft 365.

Here's what you can do in the Security Center:

- **Threat management:** Monitor and manage real-time threat incidents across your Microsoft 365 organization.

- **Alerts dashboard:** View and manage security alerts.

- **Secure score:** Evaluate your organization's security posture by giving you visibility into your existing security settings and providing recommendations to enhance security.

- **Security policies:** Configure various security policies like Safe Links, Safe Attachments, Anti-Spam, and more.

- **Investigate risks:** Use advanced hunting to query across your data to identify potential risks.

- **Manage Devices:** If integrated with Microsoft Endpoint Manager, you can manage the security of devices used within your organization.

Microsoft 365 Compliance Center

The Microsoft 365 Compliance Center is a specialized dashboard for managing the compliance needs of your organization. It gives you a centralized place to access solutions that help you comply with standards, regulations, and laws.

Here's what you can do in the Compliance Center:

- **Compliance Manager:** Understand, manage, and improve your organization's compliance posture with regard to various regulations and standards such as GDPR, ISO 27001, etc.

- **Data subject requests:** Respond to data subject requests for GDPR and other regulations.

- **Data classification:** Classify your data based on sensitivity labels and retain it using retention labels.

- **Data loss prevention (DLP):** Create, manage, and monitor DLP policies to protect sensitive information.

- **eDiscovery:** Search for content across Microsoft 365 for legal and compliance purposes.

- **Audit logs:** Access and search the audit log for user and administrator activities across Microsoft 365.

- **Insider risk management:** Identify risky activities within your organization and take appropriate action.

The advanced security capabilities of Microsoft Teams help you create policies to secure your information and protect company data. Microsoft provides and displays the latest features that enable secure collaboration while helping customers meet their obligations under national, regional, and industry-specific regulations. Microsoft Teams is one of the fastest growing apps in Microsoft history.

As a Teams admin and compliance and information security admin in your organization, you must be aware of what Teams provides to securely maintain the data that Microsoft Teams generates. When the data are generated, admins' concerns are who is accessing the Teams data and how it can be secured and accessed by the right set of users who need the data.

Microsoft is heavily investing in securing the Teams data, and Teams is a first-party application that applies all the security, compliance, and identity investments that Microsoft has already made in information protection and compliance.

Most people believe that ineffective communication is the cause for workplace failures. There is a long list of applications that provide communication and collaboration, but they are lacking the facet of helping people come together, be more productive, and allow them to do everything that they want to do. That's where Microsoft Teams comes in.

Microsoft Teams is a hub for teamwork, as everything that a team requires is in one place such as chats with threaded conversation, meetings with voice and video conferencing and application sharing, calls with voice and video and PSTN phone calls, files for collaboration, and applications and workflows that allow users to create and integrate your application in one frame. These features are all crucial for teamwork, and Microsoft Teams provides everything that users need to do their day-to-day work in more productive ways.

To understand the Teams security and compliance capabilities, it is important to separate queues such as identity and access management, information protection, the ability to discover content and respond to it, the application of data governance policies for the type of content that exists, the duration, and finally the ability to manage risks.

Remember, access to these centers requires the necessary permissions and privileges, so not all users will be able to access or perform all tasks in these centers.

Understanding Identity and Access Management for Teams

Identity and access management (IAM) in the context of Microsoft Teams is a set of business processes and supporting technologies that help ensure the right people have access to the right parts of Teams. It is closely tied to Azure AD, the identity provider for Microsoft 365 that includes Teams.

Here are some key aspects of IAM for Teams:

- **Identity:** An identity is the digital representation of a user in an organization. In Teams, a user's identity includes their username, password, roles, groups, and other attributes. Identities in Teams are managed via Azure AD. When a user is created in Azure AD and assigned a Teams license, they become a Teams user.

- **Authentication:** Authentication is the process of validating a user's identity. When a user signs into Teams, they're authenticated by Azure AD. Azure AD supports various types of authentication methods, including password-based, MFA, and more.

- **Authorization:** Authorization is the process of determining what a user can do in Teams after they've been authenticated. For example, a user might be authorized to join a team, create a channel, or initiate a meeting. In Teams, authorization is managed through various settings and policies in the Teams admin center.

- **Access management:** Access management involves defining and managing the access that users have in Teams. This includes things such as setting up guest access (allowing people outside the organization to join Teams), setting up sharing policies (controlling how users in Teams can share files and content), and setting up meeting policies (controlling who can create meetings, who can join, etc.).

- **RBAC:** In Teams, roles are used to control what users can do. There are several built-in roles in Teams, including Owner, Member, and Guest, each with different levels of permissions. Owners have the most permissions, including the ability to add and remove members, update team settings, and more. Members have fewer permissions but can still interact fully within the team, and Guests have the fewest permissions.

- **Security:** Teams leverages the security features of Azure AD to protect user identities and data. This includes features such as MFA, conditional access policies, identity protection, and more.

Understanding IAM for Teams can help ensure that the right people have the right access in Teams, enhancing both productivity and security.

Identities are key for any application or system. If bad actors compromise an identity, your data and content are at risk. Because Teams leverages Azure AD for identity, the investments and improvements that have occurred in Azure are directly applied to Microsoft Teams.

Does Teams have robust authentication? Teams has solid authentication because Teams uses smart protection policies and risk assessment to block threats. As an admin, you need to ensure that your organization's users have strong passwords and have MFA enabled. Once you have enabled MFA for SharePoint Online and Exchange Online, you automatically endorsed it for Teams because Teams used SharePoint and Exchange extensively. When users try to log in to Teams, they will challenge for the two-factor workflow or whether you have a PIN enabled; both have the same workflow.

Another aspect is what to authorize a user to access. This is specifically based on a policy that is defined in conditional access in Azure AD, and Microsoft Teams is part of this feature as well. Conditional access flow is based on the signal that comes from the devices, applications, and users. Microsoft determines a risk score, and as an admin you configure the policies that determine who can access the Teams application.

Remember, the conditional access policies prevent access for authenticated users from unmanaged devices. Understanding IAM for Teams can help ensure that the right people have the right access in Teams, enhancing both productivity and security.

Accessing the Office 365 Security & Compliance Center

As a Teams admin and compliance and information security admin, you must be aware of what the Microsoft 365 Security & Compliance Center provides for Teams to securely maintain the data that Microsoft Teams generates. You can also use classification labels, data loss prevention (DLP), information governance, and so on. To access the Office 365 Security & Compliance Center, log in to Office 365 admin center and then click Security & Compliance to open the Office 365 Security & Compliance Center, as shown in Figure 2-130. You can also directly access the Security & Compliance Center by visiting https://compliance.microsoft.com/.

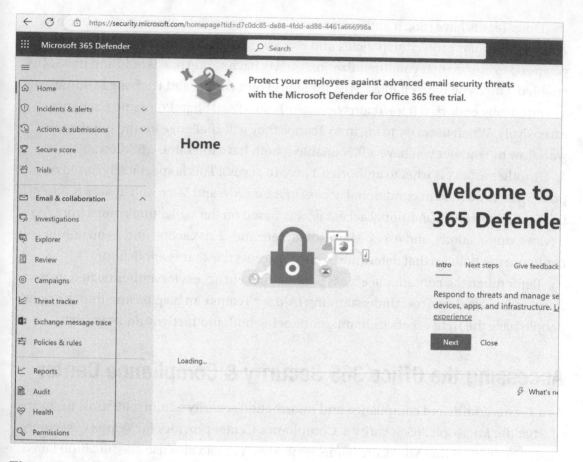

Figure 2-130.   *Microsoft 365 Security Center*

Figure 2-131 shows Microsoft 365 Compliance Center.

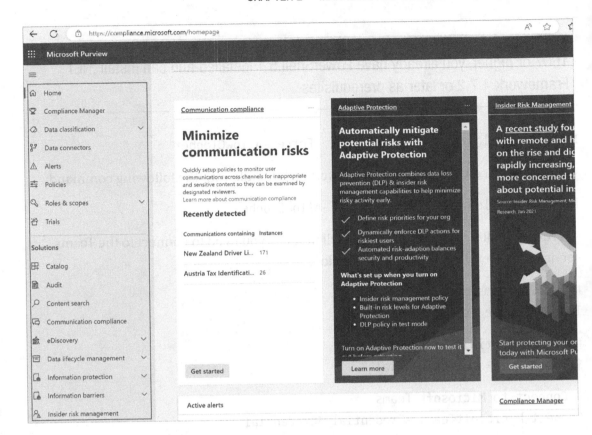

Figure 2-131.   Microsoft 365 Compliance Center

Topics such as managing sensitivity labels and data loss prevention policies, managing eDiscovery cases and supervision policies, configuring alert policies for events in Microsoft Teams, and creating retention policies and information barriers are covered in Chapter 5.

Teams Management Through PowerShell

PowerShell is a powerful command-line shell and scripting language that provides Teams administrators with control and automation of Teams management tasks. Teams administrators can use the Teams PowerShell module to manage various aspects of Teams, including managing Teams settings, policies, users, and more.

Before you use PowerShell for Teams, you need to install the Teams PowerShell module. To do this, open PowerShell as an administrator and run the following command:

Note   Update to Windows PowerShell 5.1. If you're on Windows 10 version 1607 or higher, you already have PowerShell 5.1 installed and can install .NET Framework 4.7.2 or later as prerequisites.

```
Install-Module -Name PowerShellGet -Force -AllowClobber
```

Then, you can install the Teams PowerShell module with the following command:

```
Install-Module -Name Teams -Force -AllowClobber
```

After installing the Teams PowerShell module, you need to connect to the Teams service in PowerShell. Here is how you do it:

```
# Import Teams module
Import-Module Teams

# Get credential
$credential = Get-Credential

# Connect to Microsoft Teams
Connect-MicrosoftTeams -Credential $credential
```

Once connected, you can use various cmdlets to manage Teams. Here are some commonly used PowerShell cmdlets for Teams:

Get-Team: Retrieves all the teams a user is part of

```
Get-Team -User user@bloguc.com
```

New-Team: Creates a new team

```
New-Team -DisplayName "New Team" -Description
"Description of the new team"
```

Add-TeamUser: Adds a user to a team

```
Add-TeamUser -GroupId teamGroupId -User
user@bloguc.com -Role Member
```

Remove-TeamUser: Removes a user from a team

```
Remove-TeamUser -GroupId teamGroupId -Use user@bloguc.com
```

Set-Team: Modifies the settings of a team

```
Set-Team -GroupId teamGroupId -DisplayName "Updated Team Name"
```

Get-TeamChannel: Retrieves all the channels for a team

```
Get-TeamChannel -GroupId teamGroupId
```

New-TeamChannel: Creates a new channel in a team

```
New-TeamChannel -GroupId teamGroupId -DisplayName "New Channel
Name" -Description "Description of the new channel"
```

Phone Number Assignment

Assigning a phone number to a user involves acquiring a phone number from Microsoft or porting your existing numbers and then assigning it to a user. You can use the Set-CsPhoneNumberAssignment cmdlet to assign a phone number to a user with Direct Routing:

```
Set-CsPhoneNumberAssignment -Identity user@bloguc.com -PhoneNumber
+12091234567 -PhoneNumberType DirectRouting
```

Voice Policy Assignment

Voice policies define what calling features are available to users. The Grant-CsTeamsCallingPolicy cmdlet can be used to assign a voice policy to a user:

```
Grant-CsTeamsCallingPolicy -Identity user@example.com -PolicyName
"Calling Policy Name"
```

Dial Plan Assignment

Dial plans are used to normalize phone numbers for users. You can assign a dial plan to a user with the Grant-CsDialPlan cmdlet:

```
Grant-CsDialPlan -Identity user@example.com -PolicyName "Dial Plan Name"
```

Unassign

To unassign a policy or a phone number from a user, you can use the Remove cmdlet:

```
Remove-CsPhoneNumberAssignment -Identity user@example.com -PhoneNumber
+12065551234
Remove-CsTeamsCallingPolicy -Identity user@example.com
Remove-CsDialPlan -Identity bilag@bloguc.com
```

Teams Meeting Management

Here are some cmdlets for managing Teams meetings.

To get information about Teams meeting policies, use this:

```
Get-CsTeamsMeetingPolicy -Identity "Meeting Policy Name"
```

To assign a Teams meeting policy to a user, use this:

```
Grant-CsTeamsMeetingPolicy -Identity user@example.com -PolicyName "Meeting
Policy Name"
```

Teams Live Event Management

Here are some cmdlets for managing Teams Live events.

To get information about Teams Live event policies, use this:

```
Get-CsTeamsLiveEventPolicy -Identity "Live Event Policy Name"
```

To assign a Teams Live event policy to a user, use this:

```
Grant-CsTeamsLiveEventPolicy -Identity user@example.com -PolicyName "Live
Event Policy Name"
```

Teams Room System Management

Here are some cmdlets for managing Teams Rooms.

To get information about Teams room devices, use this:

```
Get-CsTeamsRoom -Identity "Room System Name"
```

To set properties of a Teams room device, use this:

```
Set-CsTeamsRoom -Identity "Room System Name" -DisplayName "New Room Name"
```

Remember, you should replace bilag@bloguc.com, +12091234567, Policy Name, Dial Plan Name, and Room System Name with actual values. Be sure to also check Microsoft's documentation to understand the requirements and impacts of these commands.

PowerShell provides Teams administrators with granular control over Teams management tasks and can be a very efficient way of managing Teams, especially for large organizations or for repetitive tasks. PowerShell can also be used to automate various Teams management tasks by writing scripts that run these cmdlets in sequence or on a schedule.

Summary

This chapter provided a comprehensive overview of the diverse tools available for managing and controlling Microsoft Teams. It underscores the significance of the Teams admin center as the primary portal for administering Teams and outlines its various functionalities, from managing teams, channels, and apps to adjusting settings and policies.

In addition to the Teams admin center, the chapter discussed the role of the Microsoft 365 admin center in managing users and groups, licensing, and organization-wide settings. It highlighted the seamless integration of these platforms, enabling efficient user and resource management across Microsoft 365 services.

Next, the chapter explored Azure AD and its integral role in Teams management. Azure AD's central position in handling user identities, authentication, and access control was thoroughly discussed. The chapter elucidates how Azure AD policies can impact Teams, including user sign-ins, guest access, and group memberships.

Following Azure AD, the chapter delved into the use of PowerShell for Teams administration. It illustrated how administrators can leverage PowerShell to automate repetitive tasks, carry out bulk operations, and implement advanced management tasks that are not possible through the admin centers. A variety of common PowerShell commands for Teams were also presented as examples.

Finally, the chapter wrapped up with a detailed examination of the Microsoft Security & Compliance Centers. It explained how these tools are used to enforce security and compliance across Teams and the entire Microsoft 365 suite. The features of these centers, such as threat management, data loss prevention, data governance, and audit log investigations, were thoroughly explained.

In conclusion, this chapter gave administrators a comprehensive toolkit for managing and controlling Microsoft Teams effectively. From day-to-day tasks such as user and team management to advanced security and compliance enforcement, administrators now understand how to utilize these tools to ensure a secure and productive Teams environment.

CHAPTER 3

Organization Readiness for Microsoft Teams

In the era of modern collaboration, Microsoft Teams has emerged as a powerful platform offering a multitude of features for seamless communication and collaboration. With its advanced audio and video calling capabilities, real-time conversations, and content sharing, Teams has revolutionized the way organizations work together. Microsoft's meticulous approach in building Teams from the ground up, incorporating the latest codec and media stack support, ensures optimal call quality for users. However, to fully leverage the potential of Teams, organizations must ensure their network infrastructure is prepared to handle the signaling and media traffic generated by Teams. Sufficient bandwidth for audio and video media traffic is crucial for delivering a smooth user experience. Without a properly provisioned and ready infrastructure, Teams may not perform as expected, leading to user frustrations and diminished productivity.

In this chapter, we delve into the critical aspects that organizations need to consider to ensure their readiness for Teams. We explore the network infrastructure requirements, including signaling and media traffic considerations, and we provide insights into provisioning the right bandwidth to support Teams' audio and video communication. We discuss the significance of preparing the network infrastructure to enable optimal call quality and seamless collaboration.

By addressing the organization's readiness for Teams, organizations can proactively eliminate potential roadblocks and ensure a smooth deployment and adoption of the platform. We explore best practices, recommendations, and practical steps to assess and optimize network infrastructure, enabling organizations to unlock the full potential of Microsoft Teams and empower their teams to collaborate effectively, regardless of geographical boundaries. This chapter serves as a comprehensive guide for organizations seeking to maximize the benefits of Microsoft Teams. By focusing

© Balu N Ilag, Durgesh Tripathy, Vijay Ireddy 2024
B. N. Ilag et al., *Understanding Microsoft Teams Administration*,
https://doi.org/10.1007/979-8-8688-0014-6_3

on organization readiness, IT professionals and decision-makers can ensure a robust and reliable environment for Teams, elevating collaboration, productivity, and user satisfaction within their organization.

Microsoft Teams offers a wide array of features, including audio and video calls, meetings, content sharing, and real-time conversations. Microsoft has invested significant effort in building Teams from the ground up, incorporating the latest codec and media stack support. As a result, Teams delivers commendable call quality. However, to ensure an optimal Teams experience, it is essential to have a network infrastructure that seamlessly handles Teams signaling and media traffic while providing sufficient bandwidth for audio and video transmissions. While Teams is designed to deliver optimal call quality, it heavily relies on a well-provisioned infrastructure. If your infrastructure is not correctly set up or prepared for Teams, the platform may not perform as intended, leading to a subpar experience for end users.

To avoid such issues, it is crucial to prioritize infrastructure readiness for Teams deployment. This involves evaluating and optimizing the network infrastructure, ensuring adequate bandwidth allocation, and configuring proper quality of service (QoS) settings. By proactively addressing these considerations, organizations can create an environment that supports the full functionality and performance of Microsoft Teams, enhancing collaboration and minimizing user frustrations. Ultimately, a properly provisioned and ready infrastructure for Teams is key to unlocking its potential and enabling seamless communication and collaboration among team members. By acknowledging the importance of infrastructure readiness, organizations can ensure a positive user experience, drive productivity, and maximize the benefits of Microsoft Teams within their workforce.

Preparing the infrastructure is, therefore, essential. Before starting Teams deployment, you as a Teams admin must ensure that all Teams network requirements are completed, including infrastructure and network readiness. You can then plan for starting the actual deployment. Microsoft did a better job of consolidating all the Teams (Office 365) IP subnets and port and protocol requirements in one document (`https://learn.microsoft.com/en-us/microsoft-365/enterprise/urls-and-ip-address-ranges?view=o365-worldwide#skype-for-business-online-and-microsoft-teams`), which you can refer to in completing these requirements.

So far, you have learned about Teams fundamentals, team and channel architecture, live events, identity, and Teams management tools. This chapter covers detailed information on network assessment and bandwidth planning for Teams, how to deploy and manage QoS, and how to deploy a virtual private network (VPN) split tunnel for Microsoft Teams media traffic. Before the deployment of Microsoft Teams in a production environment, you, as an admin, need to determine whether the existing network meets the networking requirements of Microsoft Teams. Make sure you have the required bandwidth, access to all required IP addresses, and correct ports opened. You also need to ensure you meet the performance requirements for Teams real-time media traffic, such as audio, video, and application sharing.

Network Assessment and Bandwidth Planning for Teams

Assessing the network and planning the bandwidth for Microsoft Teams are crucial steps in ensuring a smooth and reliable communication experience within the platform. These processes involve evaluating the organization's network infrastructure, identifying potential bottlenecks or limitations, and determining the required bandwidth to support Teams' audio and video traffic.

Network assessment is the evaluation of the organization's existing network infrastructure to assess its readiness for supporting Microsoft Teams. It involves analyzing various factors that impact network performance, such as network capacity, latency, jitter, packet loss, and overall network health. The purpose of the assessment is to identify any network issues that may hinder Teams' performance and to implement appropriate measures to address them.

Bandwidth planning is the process of determining the amount of network bandwidth required to support the audio and video traffic generated by Microsoft Teams. It involves estimating the bandwidth needs based on factors such as the number of concurrent users, their usage patterns, and the types of activities they engage in (e.g., audio calls, video calls, screen sharing). Bandwidth planning ensures that the network can handle the anticipated traffic volume without degradation in call quality or performance.

To conduct a network assessment and bandwidth planning for Microsoft Teams, the following requirements should be considered:

- **Network monitoring tools:** Implement network monitoring tools to gather data on network performance metrics such as latency, jitter, and packet loss. These tools help identify areas of concern and provide insights into the network's capabilities.

- **Testing scenarios:** Simulate various usage scenarios within Microsoft Teams, including audio and video calls, screen sharing, and file transfers. These tests help assess the network's ability to handle different types of traffic and identify any bottlenecks or performance issues.

- **Quality of service (QoS) configuration:** Configure QoS settings to prioritize Teams' traffic over other network traffic. This ensures that audio and video calls receive the necessary bandwidth and are not impacted by competing network activities.

- **Network capacity planning:** Evaluate the organization's current network capacity and determine if any upgrades or optimizations are required to accommodate Teams' traffic. Consider factors such as the number of users, their geographical distribution, and potential growth projections.

- **Collaboration with network administrators:** Collaborate with network administrators to gather insights into the network infrastructure, understand its limitations, and work together to address any identified issues.

Network assessment and bandwidth planning are essential for a successful deployment of Microsoft Teams. They help organizations identify and mitigate potential network-related challenges that could impact call quality, user experience, and overall performance. By ensuring a robust and well-prepared network infrastructure, organizations can provide their users with a reliable and seamless communication and collaboration platform, optimizing productivity and enhancing the value of Microsoft Teams within their organization.

Before doing a network assessment and bandwidth planning for Microsoft Teams, you must know what different types of traffic Teams generates. At a high level, Teams produces and supports two types of traffic: Teams signaling traffic, also known as *gesturing*, and Teams media traffic, known as *real-time media traffic*. Teams is a purely cloud-hosted service that allows it to operate in three types of network traffic directions.

- **Teams signaling traffic:** Teams data traffic between the Teams service (Office 365 Online environment) and the Teams client for signaling, presence, chat, file upload and download, and OneNote synchronization).

- **Teams media traffic:**

  - Teams one-to-one real-time communications media traffic for audio, video, and application (desktop) sharing.

  - Teams conferencing real-time media communications traffic for audio, video, and application (desktop) sharing.

If any of the Teams network traffic directions are affected, then it will affect Teams communication. Teams traffic flows between the Teams clients directly in one-to-one call situations or between the Office 365 environment and the Teams clients for meetings.

To ensure the optimal traffic flow for both one-to-one and conference scenarios in Microsoft Teams, it is crucial for administrators to enable seamless communication between the organization's internal network segments. This includes establishing an uninterrupted traffic flow between different sites over a wide-area network (WAN) and between the network sites and the Office 365 environment. For instance, let's consider the example of the Bloguc organization. They have central offices located in Tracy, California, and Denver, Colorado, with branch offices in India. To facilitate effective communication, traffic between the central and branch offices is allowed to flow freely over the WAN without any restrictions. Additionally, these offices have direct connectivity to the Teams services in Office 365 via the Internet.

To ensure smooth traffic flow, the organization has taken measures to allow all necessary Teams IP subnets, ports/protocols, fully qualified domain names (FQDNs), and URLs. By permitting these essential communication elements, the organization ensures that there are no interruptions or interference in the flow of Teams-related traffic. By implementing these configurations, the Bloguc organization enables their users to seamlessly connect and collaborate within Microsoft Teams, irrespective of their geographical locations. This unrestricted traffic flow allows for efficient communication, smooth meeting experiences, and optimal utilization of Teams' features and capabilities.

Overall, by allowing seamless traffic flow and ensuring compatibility between network segments and the Office 365 environment, organizations can create an enhanced user experience and maximize the benefits of Microsoft Teams for their workforce.

Note   Actively blocking specific ports or not opening the correct ports will lead to a degraded Teams experience.

Carrying Out a Network Assessment Before Teams Deployment

You have learned what type of traffic Teams generates, the traffic directions, and how it potentially affects the user experience. A network assessment is essential before Teams deployment because it will evaluate the existing network infrastructure and pinpoint the network impairments that could cause poor call quality. Also, the assessment will identify the performance-linked problems that can be introduced into the environment through latency and packet loss. Issues such as these will result in a negative experience in Teams audio and video scenarios, where real-time streams are essential.

Network assessment has several different aspects.

- It assesses the existing network configuration that might affect Teams traffic, while evaluating the existing network environment for hard limitations such as blocked IP addresses, faulty name resolution through DNS, and blocked ports. These problems are easy to spot because specific Teams features will simply not work at all when IP addresses or ports are blocked.

- Point-in-time problems, like bandwidth, latency, or packet-loss issues, are more complicated, because they might appear only under special conditions; for example, the Bloguc organization HQ office might have a high number of users who are using audio and video communication at the same time. Thus, when planning the network requirements for a Teams deployment, you must calculate the maximum number of concurrent users, including a sufficient buffer and bandwidth.

There are several best practices for preparing your environment for Microsoft Teams.

- You must allow seamless connectivity from your corporate network where the user resides to the Microsoft Teams service, which is in Office 365. Also, make sure that all required DNS names are resolved correctly, and Teams service IP addresses must be reachable.

- Make sure the network connection quality of an established connection is optimal through measuring in values, such as latency, jitter, and packet-loss rates. Also, the existing networking hardware must provide a stable connection with minimum network hops by keeping as few active networking devices between a Teams client and Office 365 as possible. Each active networking device adds additional latency and raises the chance of connectivity quality issues. So, optimizing the network path by eliminating the unnecessary network devices or hops will expedite packet flow and untimely improve call quality.

- Make sure to keep enough bandwidth available for Teams communication to Office 365 services. Remember, the required bandwidth of Teams depends on the required functionalities and number of Teams clients in an organization location. You must analyze the maximum number of concurrent participants and then multiply this number with the provided utilized Teams functionalities. For example, Bloguc has 100 users in the HQ office, and the available bandwidth is 100 MB. At any point in time 30 users will be on calls, so the available bandwidth must be sufficient for 30 users' calls.

- The Teams client can be connected over any network, either wired or wireless. Teams clients connected over a wireless connection, such as corporate Wi-Fi networks and hotspots, are more vulnerable for high latency and possibly higher packet loss because wireless networks usually are not necessarily designed or configured to support real-time media or not prepared for real-time services, such as Teams audio and video communication. For the wireless network, implementing QoS or Wi-Fi Multimedia (WMM) will ensure that media traffic is getting prioritized appropriately over the Wi-Fi networks. You can work with your organization network engineer to plan and optimize the Wi-Fi bands and access point placement. Implement band steering, and ensure the access points that are next to each other are on channels that do not overlap. Furthermore, the network coverage must provide enough bandwidth even between wireless access points and on the edges.

- One of the significant network impairments is the intrusion detection system (IDS) and intrusion prevention system (IPS) feature on the firewalls that can analyze the payload of data packages for the attack signatures. If any organization network environment uses IDS and IPS solutions, then make sure all network traffic between your organization and the Teams services (Office 365) is whitelisted and excluded from any kind of scanning.

- Another best practice for Network Address Translation (NAT) pool size provides access to multiple internal systems by using a single public IP address. When multiple users and devices access Office 365 using NAT or Port Address Translation (PAT), you, as a Teams admin, must ensure that the devices hidden behind each publicly routable IP address do not exceed the supported number. You might need to check with your network engineer, who can help you to understand NAT configuration.

- Most of the time, the organization uses VPN that offers an encryption tunnel between endpoints, like remote users and the corporate network. Generally, VPNs are not designed to support real-time media traffic and introduce an extra layer of encryption on top of media traffic that is already encrypted. This adds overhead. Additionally, connectivity to the Teams service (Office 365) might not be efficient because of hair-pinning traffic through a VPN device. For VPNs, the suggestion is to provide an alternate path that bypasses the VPN tunnel for Teams traffic. This is generally known as split-tunnel VPN. We will cover the VPN split tunnel in detail in this chapter.

- Finally, verifying overall network health is equally critical, so identify the network health and quality baseline before Teams deployment in your organization. After planning on the Teams implementation in your organization using the existing network, you should ensure there is sufficient bandwidth, accessibility to all required IP addresses, correct configuration of ports, and that the performance requirements for Teams real-time media are met.

Network Bandwidth Requirements for Microsoft Teams Calling Scenarios

Network bandwidth requirements for Microsoft Teams meetings and calls depend on various factors, including the type of communication (audio or video), the number of participants, and the activities involved, such as desktop sharing or content sharing. While these requirements can vary, the following are general guidelines for network bandwidth needed for different Teams communication scenarios:

Teams audio call:

- Recommended minimum bandwidth: 30 to 50 kilobits per second (Kbps) per user.

- This is the typical bandwidth requirement for a standard audio call between two participants. It may increase slightly depending on the quality of audio and any additional audio features in use (e.g., background noise suppression).

Teams video call:

- Recommended minimum bandwidth:

  - **For one-to-one video calls:** 300 to 500 Kbps per user for standard definition (SD) video.

  - **For group video calls:** 1.2 megabits per second (Mbps) for 720p HD video and 1.5 Mbps for 1080p Full HD video.

- These bandwidth recommendations apply to each participant in the video call. For example, in a four-person video call, the total bandwidth requirement will be four times the recommended minimum per user.

Teams desktop sharing:

- Recommended minimum bandwidth: 50 to 150 Kbps per user.
- Desktop sharing involves transmitting the screen contents to participants, including any applications or documents being shared. The bandwidth requirement can vary based on the complexity of the shared content and the frequency of screen updates.

It's important to note that these bandwidth requirements are for smooth and optimal performance. Actual bandwidth usage may vary based on factors such as network congestion, device capabilities, and other network activities running simultaneously.

To ensure a high-quality experience, it is recommended to have a reliable Internet connection with sufficient bandwidth. Additionally, implementing QoS settings on the network can help prioritize Teams traffic over other network activities, ensuring a smooth communication experience. Organizations with larger deployments or higher user densities may need to consider additional network capacity and scaling requirements to accommodate multiple concurrent meetings and calls.

Regularly monitoring and assessing your network's performance and bandwidth utilization can help identify any bottlenecks or issues and make necessary adjustments to ensure a seamless Microsoft Teams experience for all users.

So far, you have learned about network assessment and network best practices. Next, you need to understand the importance of network quality between your organization's network and Microsoft Teams cloud service and the required bandwidth for each Teams calling scenario. When assessing the existing network environment, first complete the Teams IP address, port/protocol, URLs, and faulty name resolution through DNS requirements, because specific Teams features will not work at all when Teams service IP addresses or ports are blocked. Additionally, finding the bandwidth, latency, or packet-loss issues is more complicated because they might appear only under particular circumstances. Refer to Table 3-1, which shows the recommended network capabilities and accepted latency, burst packet loss, packet loss, jitter, and packet reordering. For example, Teams call quality will be best when you have less than 50 ms latency between your organization network and Microsoft Edge router along with packet loss and jitter values under the limit.

Table 3-1. *Accepted Limits for Network Values*

Network (Value)	Teams client to Microsoft Edge N/W (without SfB Hybrid)	Customer Edge N/W to Microsoft Edge (with SfB Hybrid)
Latency (one way)	< 50ms	< 30ms
Latency (RTT or Round-trip Time)	< 100ms	< 60ms
Burst packet loss	<10% during any 200ms interval	<1% during any 200ms interval
Packet loss	<1% during any 15s interval	<0.1% during any 15s interval
Packet inter-arrival Jitter	<30ms during any 15s interval	<15ms during any 15s interval
Packet reorder	<0.05% out-of-order packets	<0.01% out-of-order packets

Because Microsoft Teams supports multiple features, each feature has different bandwidth requirements; for example, Teams one-to-one audio calling requires 30 Kb bandwidth for upstream and downstream. Table 3-2 shows call scenarios and required network bandwidth for your Teams clients to optimally use Teams features.

Table 3-2. *Teams Call Scenarios with Required Bandwidth*

Teams call/ conference scenarios	Required Bandwidth (up/down)
One-to-one audio calling	30 kbps
One-to-one audio calling and screen sharing	130 kbps
One-to-one video calling with resolution 360p at 30fps	500 kbps
One-to-one High Definition (HD) quality video calling with resolution of HD 720p at 30fps	1.2 Mbps
One-to-one HD quality video calling with resolution of HD 1080p at 30fps	1.5 Mbps
Group (more than 2 participant) Video calling	500kbps/1Mbps
HD Group video calling (540p videos on 1080p screen)	1Mbps/2Mbps

For network assessment, you can use the Network Planner and Network Testing Companion tools.

Network Planner

In the context of Microsoft Teams, the Network Planner is a tool designed to help organizations assess their network readiness and plan for optimal network performance when using Teams. It focuses on network quality perspectives and provides insights into network requirements for a smooth Teams experience.

The Network Planner helps organizations understand and address potential network challenges that may impact the audio, video, and screen sharing quality in Teams meetings. It provides guidance on network capacity, latency, and network paths to ensure that Teams can function optimally.

Here are some key aspects of the Network Planner in Microsoft Teams:

- **Network assessment:** The Network Planner conducts a network assessment to evaluate the suitability of your network infrastructure for Teams usage. It measures key network parameters such as available bandwidth, network latency, and network paths to determine whether they meet the recommended requirements for Teams.

- **Bandwidth planning:** The Network Planner helps organizations estimate the bandwidth requirements for different Teams activities, such as audio calls, video calls, and screen sharing. It provides insights into the expected bandwidth usage, allowing organizations to allocate sufficient network resources for a seamless Teams experience.

- **Latency analysis:** Latency refers to the delay in data transmission across a network. The Network Planner assesses network latency and helps identify any potential latency issues that could impact real-time communication in Teams meetings. It provides recommendations to reduce latency and improve call quality.

- **Network path analysis:** The Network Planner examines the network paths between users and the Teams services to identify potential bottlenecks or areas of concern. It helps organizations understand the network paths used by Teams traffic and suggests optimizations to ensure smooth connectivity and minimize disruptions.

- **Reports and recommendations:** Based on the assessment results, the Network Planner generates reports and recommendations to help organizations address network quality issues. It provides actionable insights and guidance on network configuration changes, network optimizations, and network infrastructure upgrades to enhance the overall Teams experience.

By leveraging the Network Planner, organizations can proactively assess and plan their network infrastructure to meet the specific requirements of Microsoft Teams. It enables IT administrators to identify and address network quality issues, ensuring that users can have reliable and high-quality audio and video communication in Teams meetings. Using Network Planner, an admin can create representations of an organization using sites and Microsoft-recommended personas (office workers, remote workers, and Teams room system devices) and then generate reports and calculate bandwidth requirements for Teams usage. To use the Network Planner, you must have global administrator, Teams admin, or Teams communication administrator role permissions.

Adding a Plan

You can access the Network Planner tool, shown in Figure 3-1, by going to the Microsoft Teams admin center and navigating to Planning. Select "Network planner."

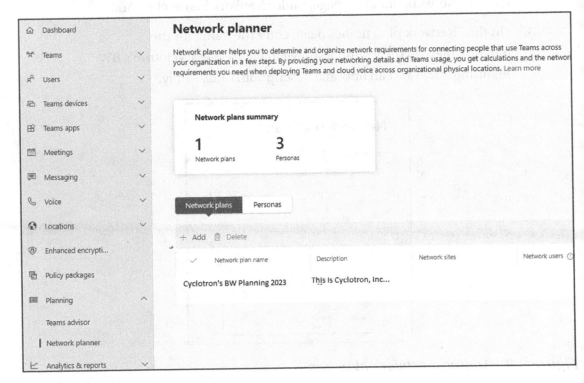

Figure 3-1. *Network planner*

When you click Add, it will allow you to create a Network Planner name. By default, there will be three user personas; you can add custom personas on the "Network planner" page by clicking the Users tab. On the Add Persona page, provide the persona name and description. In the Permissions section, select from the following services: Audio, Video, Screen Sharing, File Sharing, Conference Audio, Conference Video, Conference Screen Sharing, and PSTN.

Developing a Network Planner Plan

The Network Planner helps you to determine and organize network requirements for connecting people who use Teams across your organization in a few steps. To build your network plan, follow these steps:

1. Log in to the Microsoft Teams admin center and then navigate to Planning. Select "Network planner."

2. On the "Network planner" page, under Network Plans, click Add.

3. On the "Network plan name" page, enter the name for the network plan (in the example shown in Figure 3-2, Cyclotron's BW Planning 2023) and an optional description. Click Apply.

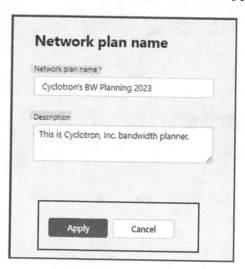

Figure 3-2. *Adding a network plan name*

4. The newly created network plan will appear in the Network Plans section. Select the plan you created. On the plan page, in the Network Sites section, click Add A Network Site. On the Add A Network Site page, shown in Figure 3-3, enter the following information:

   - Name of the network site

   - Network site address

   - Network settings: IP address subnet and network range

   - Express route or WAN connection

   - Internet egress

   - Internet link capacity

   - PSTN egress (VoIP only or local)

   - An optional description

5. Once you enter all the details, click Save to commit the changes.

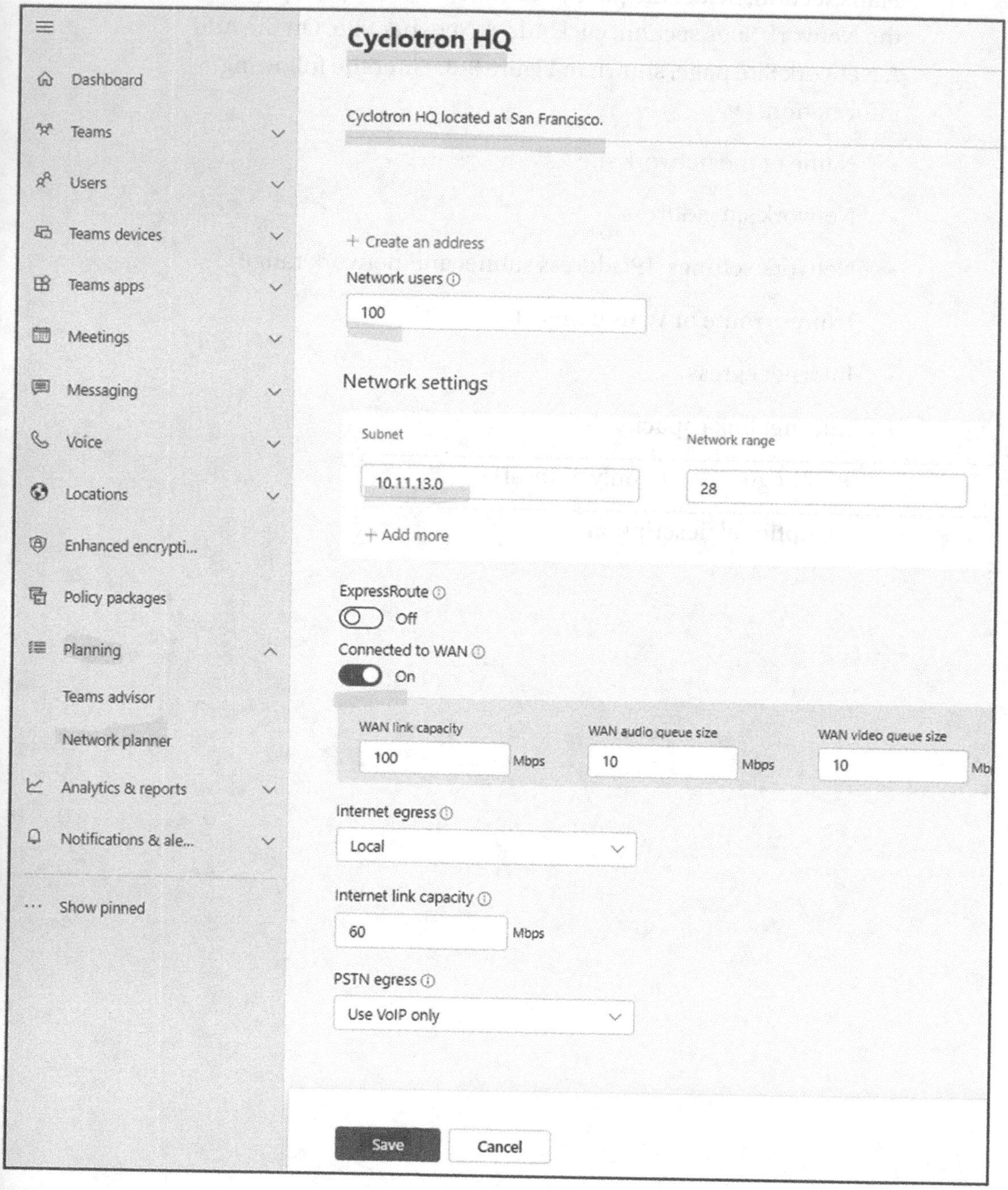

Figure 3-3. *Adding a network site and subnet*

After creating a plan, the next thing you have to do is create a report based on your network plan and view the projected impact of Teams media traffic such as audio, video, meetings, and PSTN calls. To do so, log in to the Teams admin center, navigate to Planning, and then select Network Planner. On the Network Planner page, in the Network Plans section, select your network plan (given a meaningful name). On the plan page, select Report, and then click Add Report.

On the Add Report page, enter the report name (Cyclotron's BW Report in our example), and in the Calculation section, select the type of persona, such as Office Worker or Remote Worker and the number of each persona type, and then click Generate Report. On the report page, review the report including type of service and required bandwidth for different services, such as audio, video, desktop sharing, Office 365 server traffic, and PSTN.

Microsoft Teams Network Assessment Tool

The Microsoft Teams Network Assessment Tool is a utility designed to help assess network connectivity and performance for Microsoft 365 services, including Microsoft Teams. It allows you to simulate network traffic and measure the quality of the network connection between your client devices and Microsoft's datacenters.

The Microsoft Teams Network Assessment Tool is used to test the quality of your network connection to the Teams service. It's crucial to ensure that your network meets the minimum requirements for a good user experience with Teams.

This tool checks the following:

- Network connectivity to the Teams service

- UDP port connectivity

- Network performance statistics such as jitter, latency, packet loss, and round-trip time

The information it provides can be valuable for troubleshooting network problems that might be affecting Teams audio and video quality.

Microsoft Teams Network Assessment Tool Capabilities

Let's look at the tool's capabilities.

Network Connectivity Checker

The Microsoft Teams Network Assessment Tool also possesses the capability to confirm whether the network connectivity between the user's location and the Microsoft Network is properly set up for additional services necessary for Microsoft Teams calls. These essential services encompass the following, along with their associated protocols:

- Call Controller (HTTP and UDP)
- Conversation Service (HTTP)
- Chat Service (HTTP)
- Trouter Service (HTTP)
- Broker Service (HTTP)

The specific addresses and ports for these services can be found at `https://support.office.com/en-us/article/Office-365-URLs-and-IP-address-ranges-8548a211-3fe7-47cb-abb1-355ea5aa88a2#bkmk_teams`.

Network Quality Checker

The Microsoft Network Assessment Tool allows users to conduct a basic network performance test to evaluate the network's compatibility for a Microsoft Teams call. This tool examines the connection to a Microsoft relay server by broadcasting a series of RTP media packets to the server and back for a duration defined by the user. In this process, the client attempts to allocate with the relay load-balancer (VIP). Similar to a Teams call, priority is given to UDP relay connections over TCP/HTTPS relay connections. To ensure this, the checker initiates UDP relay allocations slightly ahead of TCP/HTTPS allocations. If the relay allocations are successful, the tool proceeds to transmit media packets to the forwarded relay instance (DIP). The tool then periodically (approximately every five seconds) reports the following:

- Timestamp
- Packet loss rate
- Round-trip latency
- Jitter

- Media Path local IP/port

- Media path reflexive (NAT translated) IP/port

- Media path remote IP/port

- Status of proxy usage for media flow (applicable only to TCP/HTTPS relay connection)

As with the relay connectivity check, a default relay load-balancer relay (VIP) FQDN for Worldwide Office 365 Endpoints is used by default, but users have the option to enter a custom FQDN in the configuration file. The checker performs DNS resolution to acquire a relay load-balancer IP address, although users can specify connectivity checks to a particular load-balancer relay IP address in the configuration file. If a relay IP address is input, the relay FQDN (either default or custom) is ignored. Users can also designate the source port range on their client machine for relay connection. Unlike the connectivity checker, users can opt to disable either UDP or TCP connections to the relay, but not both. Users can also alter the UDP/TCP relay instance (DIP) ports for media packet transmission. The quality checker can be halted at any moment by pressing Ctrl+C; this will conclude the checker after the next set of metrics is displayed on the console.

Prerequisites for the Teams Network Assessment Tool

There are some prerequisites for this tool. Your operating system must be Windows 8 or later, and most importantly, you must have a local administrator account permission to install the Network Assessment Tool.

Installing the Teams Network Assessment Tool

Installation is very straightforward; however, to install this tool, a user must have administrator rights to the computer. You can download the tool at `https://www.microsoft.com/en-us/download/confirmation.aspx?id=103017`. After downloading, run the downloaded executable to install. The install location is `%ProgramFiles(x86)%\Microsoft Teams Network Assessment Tool`, and the tool itself is `NetworkAssessmentTool.exe`. Follow the prompts and install the tool; after a successful install, your screen will look like Figure 3-4.

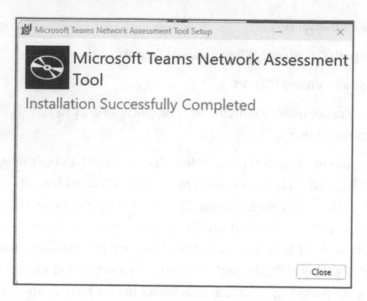

Figure 3-4. *Installing the Teams Network Assessment Tool*

After installation, to start the Teams Network Assessment Tool, open the command prompt with administrative privileges and then go to the path where the tool installed, which is `%ProgramFiles(x86)%\Microsoft Teams Network Assessment Tool`.

Using the Teams Network Assessment Tool

This tool is self-explanatory. After you install this tool, you can simply open the command prompt with administrative privileges and then browse to the tool installer directory, which is `%ProgramFiles(x86)%\Microsoft Teams Network Assessment Tool`. Then from a command prompt, view the options in the tool by running `NetworkAssessmentTool.exe /?` or `NetworkAssessmentTool.exe /usage`. Figure 3-5 shows the usage options.

```
Administrator: Command Prompt

C:\>cd C:\Program Files (x86)\Microsoft Teams Network Assessment Tool

C:\Program Files (x86)\Microsoft Teams Network Assessment Tool>NetworkAssessmentTool.exe /?
Microsoft Teams - Network Assessment Tool

Usage:
    NetworkAssessmentTool.exe [options]
    [options]:
        <no option>               Perform connectivity checks.
        /qualitycheck             Perform quality checks with relay.
        /infraconnectivitytest    Perform HTTP stack infra tests.
        /interfaces               Dumps the list of the interfaces found.
        /location                 Perform lldp and geolocation checks.
        /usage or /?              Print usage text.

C:\Program Files (x86)\Microsoft Teams Network Assessment Tool>
```

Figure 3-5. *Teams Network Assessment Tool*

For a Teams connectivity check, from a command prompt, execute the tool by simply running NetworkAssessmentTool.exe.

Here is the exact command:

C:\Program Files (x86)\Microsoft Teams Network Assessment Tool>Network AssessmentTool.exe

You will get detailed reports about the connectivity check test, as shown in Figure 3-6.

```
C:\Program Files (x86)\Microsoft Teams Network Assessment Tool>NetworkAssessmentTool.exe
Microsoft Teams - Network Assessment Tool

Starting Relay Connectivity Check:
UDP, PseudoTLS, FullTLS, HTTPS connectivity will be checked to this relay (VIP) FQDN: worldaz.tr.teams.microsoft.com
If user wants to check connectivity to a particular relay (VIP) IP, please specify in NetworkAssessment.exe.config.

Connectivity check source port range: 50000 - 50019

Relay : 52.115.63.231   is the relay load balancer (VIP)
Relay : 52.115.63.231   is reachable using Protocol UDP and Port 3478
Relay : 52.115.63.231   is QOS (Media Priority) enabled
Relay : 52.115.63.231   is the relay load balancer (VIP)
Relay : 52.115.63.231   is reachable using Protocol PseudoTLS and Port 443
Relay : 52.115.63.231   is the relay load balancer (VIP)

Starting Service Connectivity Check:
Relay : 52.115.63.231   is reachable using Protocol FullTLS and Port 443
Relay : 52.115.63.231   is the relay load balancer (VIP)
Relay : 52.115.63.231   is reachable using Protocol HTTPS and Port 443
Relay : 52.115.63.242   is the actual relay instance (DIP)
Relay : 52.115.63.242   is reachable using Protocol UDP and Port 3478
Relay : 52.115.63.242   is the actual relay instance (DIP)
Relay : 52.115.63.242   is reachable using Protocol UDP and Port 3479
Relay : 52.115.63.242   is the actual relay instance (DIP)
Relay : 52.115.63.242   is reachable using Protocol UDP and Port 3480
Relay : 52.115.63.242   is the actual relay instance (DIP)
Relay : 52.115.63.242   is reachable using Protocol UDP and Port 3481

Relay connectivity and Qos (Media Priority) check is successful for all relays.
```

Figure 3-6. *Network connectivity and quality test*

For network quality checker usage, from a command prompt, execute the tool by running `NetworkAssessmentTool.exe /qualitycheck`.

Here is the command:

```
C:\Program Files (x86)\Microsoft Teams Network Assessment
Tool>NetworkAssessmentTool.exe /qualitycheck
```

This command initiates the media flow by starting the Teams call and then waiting for the call to end after 300 seconds, displaying call quality metrics every five seconds or so. Figure 3-7 shows the call quality metrics.

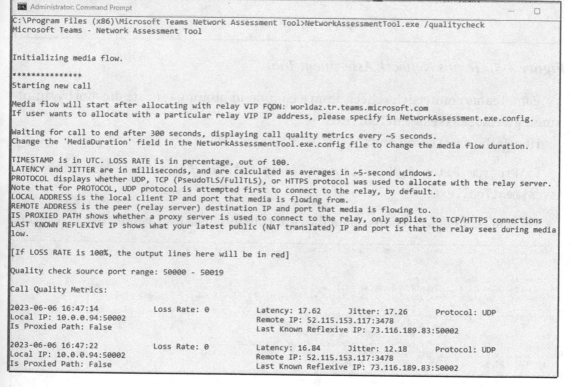

Figure 3-7. *Media quality checks*

The next thing you can test is the infrastructure connectivity; the test `infraconnectivitytest` performs HTTPS stack infra tests. Here is the command:

```
C:\Program Files (x86)\Microsoft Teams Network Assessment
Tool>NetworkAssessmentTool.exe/infraconnectivitytest
```

This command checks multiple HTTP stack infra connectivity tests such as the following:

- Checking connectivity to `https://go.trouter.teams.microsoft.com/`

- Checking connectivity to `https://config.teams.microsoft.com/config/`

- Checking connectivity to `https://ic3.events.data.microsoft.com/Collector/3.0/`

- Checking connectivity to `https://api.flightproxy.teams.microsoft.com/api/v1/health`

The report, shown in Figure 3-8, summarizes the HTTP connectivity checks, results, and status.

```
Administrator: Command Prompt                                                    —   □   ×
C:\Program Files (x86)\Microsoft Teams Network Assessment Tool>NetworkAssessmentTool.exe /infraconnectivitytest
Microsoft Teams - Network Assessment Tool

2023-06-06 14:01:36.325 [#71c822d5-S] T#80416 [DEBUG2] [auf.log_config] Log console updated, adding log console
2023-06-06 14:01:36.325 [#40548b1b-S] T#80416 [DEBUG4] [auf.log_config] Not persisting log config, disabled
2023-06-06 14:01:36.325 [#13504ed8-S] T#80416 [ERROR] [auf.log_config] Text file logging not allowed in public clients
2023-06-06 14:01:36.325 [#6d7ac071-S] T#80416 [DEBUG2] [auf] Rotating log file: ....\....log
2023-06-06 14:01:36.325 [#8b56a8d8-S] T#80416 [DEBUG1] [auf] Opening log file ....\....log
2023-06-06 14:01:36.325 [#46925e77-S] T#80416 [DEBUG1] [auf] Current time: Local=2023-06-06T14:01:36.328 ; Utc=2023-06-0
6T21:01:36.328 ; tzBias=-25200s
2023-06-06 14:01:36.325 [#46925e77-S] T#80416 [DEBUG1] [auf] Current time: Local=2023-06-06T14:01:36.329 ; Utc=2023-06-0
6T21:01:36.329 ; tzBias=-25200s
2023-06-06 14:01:36.361 [#4cc62021-S] T#80416 [DEBUG2] [auf.log_config] Log file updated, adding log file MaxSize=104857
600 MaxRotations=10 Encryption=1 File=c....log
2023-06-06 14:01:36.361 [#46925e77-S] T#80416 [DEBUG1] [auf] Current time: Local=2023-06-06T14:01:36.361 ; Utc=2023-06-0
6T21:01:36.361 ; tzBias=-25200s
2023-06-06 14:01:36.361 [#40548b1b-S] T#80416 [DEBUG4] [auf.log_config] Not persisting log config, disabled

====
Checking connectivity to https://go.trouter.teams.microsoft.com/
2023-06-06 14:01:36.368 [#8420e817-S] T#80416 [DEBUG4] [httpstack.Init] Init
2023-06-06 14:01:36.368 [#d0cc8b0a-S] T#80416 [DEBUG4] [auf] auf::init() from C:\a_work\1\s\RootTools\roottools\auf\incl
ude\auf\auf_init.hpp:Tue Feb 21 16:53:06 2023 g_aufUp=1
2023-06-06 14:01:36.371 [#5ba7ec71-S] T#80416 [DEBUG4] [spl.EcsConfig] Pushed keys: {}
2023-06-06 14:01:36.371 [#4d0fb7a0-S] T#80416 [DEBUG4] [auf] Spawning new worker (concurrency 0, cur count 0)
2023-06-06 14:01:36.371 [#af4d0c25-S] T#19100 [DEBUG4] [auf] New worker is created
2023-06-06 14:01:36.372 [#518a18f3-S] T#34888 [DEBUG4] [spl] Created thread 34888.
2023-06-06 14:01:36.372 [#c15bb53a-S] T#34888 [DEBUG4] [spl] threadWinEntry: Thread is at Win32 priority 0.
2023-06-06 14:01:36.373 [#4be6c0a9-S] T#80416 [DEBUG2] [httpstack] Configured backend RT, will use RT
2023-06-06 14:01:36.373 [#f576d4a0-S] T#80416 [DEBUG3] [httpstack.rt.Backend] @00dd7478: Created version 2023.09.00.20
2023-06-06 14:01:36.373 [#6e93c25d-S] T#80416 [DEBUG4] [httpstack] @00dfc248: Created
2023-06-06 14:01:36.373 [#e0ae1e2a-S] T#80416 [DEBUG2] [httpstack.Request] @0782e060: RQ1: Open GET "https://go.trouter.
teams.microsoft.com/..."
```

Figure 3-8. *Infra connectivity test*

Figure 3-8 also shows the different HTTP stack infra tests and their results and status information.

Deploying and Managing Quality of Service

Microsoft Teams provides real-time communication, including persistent chat, audio and video calls (VoIP), conferences, desktop sharing, PSTN calls, content sharing, and so on. These capabilities, however, will increase the traffic on your existing network. It is increasingly important for you as a Teams admin to balance network performance with QoS. All of these modalities include signaling and media traffic, and this real-time traffic is latency sensitive. Microsoft Teams is a latency-sensitive application; to provide an optimal user experience using Teams audio, video, and application sharing, you must prioritize the Teams real-time media traffic against lower-priority traffic.

Quality of service (QoS) is a networking technology feature that can manage data traffic to reduce packet loss, latency, and jitter on the network. This can be crucial for applications such as Microsoft Teams, where network performance can greatly impact the user experience. Teams uses different sets of ports for signaling, audio, video, and desktop sharing, and these can be configured with different QoS values.

To set up QoS for Microsoft Teams, you need to perform the following steps:

1. **Define the QoS policy:** You first need to define the QoS policies in your network infrastructure (routers, switches, etc.). This usually involves defining differentiated services code point (DSCP) values for each type of traffic. For Microsoft Teams, you may use the following recommended values:

   - **Audio:** DSCP 46, port range 50000 to 50019

   - **Video:** DSCP 34, port range 50020 to 50039

   - **Desktop sharing:** DSCP 18, port range 50040 to 50059

   - **Signaling:** DSCP 26, port range 50000 to 50059

2. **Configure QoS on Windows:** You will need to configure the Group Policy settings in Windows to enforce these QoS policies. The policy settings are located under Computer Configuration ➤ Windows Settings ➤ Policy-based QoS.

   You need to create a new policy for each type of traffic (audio, video, desktop sharing, signaling) with the corresponding DSCP and port range values. In the application name field, specify Teams.exe to apply these policies to Microsoft Teams.

3. **Configure QoS on macOS:** macOS does not have built-in support for DSCP marking. Therefore, you'll need to use third-party tools or a network device to perform DSCP marking for macOS devices. One approach is to use the network router or switch to classify the traffic based on its source port and apply the appropriate DSCP values.

There are different ways to prioritize network traffic, but the most common way is by using Differentiated Services Code Point (DSCP) markings. DSCP values can be applied or tagged based on port ranges and via Group Policy objects (GPOs). Because Microsoft Teams is available across the platform, including Windows, macOS, iOS, Android, and so on, applying port ranges via GPO will not work for non-Windows devices. It is a best practice that you use DSCP tagging based on port ranges on the network layer because it will work for all devices, including macOS, iOS, and Android devices. In fact, a combination of GPOs for Windows and DSCP tagging at the network layer will work better.

QoS is more beneficial when you configure it from end to end, meaning from the user computer to network switches to routers to the cloud (Office 365 Service), because any part of the path that fails to support QoS can degrade the quality of the entire call.

Microsoft Teams is a cloud-only service, so you don't have end-to-end control over the network. When network traffic leaves your management network, you will be dependent on the Internet, where you don't have much control. Basically, the interconnect network will be an unmanaged network Internet connection, illustrated in Figure 3-9. One option available to address end-to-end QoS is Microsoft Azure ExpressRoute, which requires an additional investment.

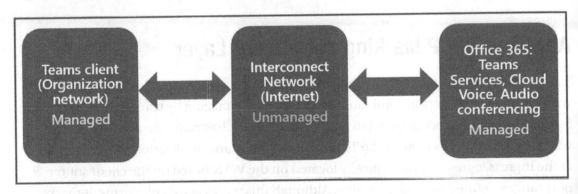

Figure 3-9. *Managed and unmanaged networks*

Even though you will not have end-to-end control on the network, it is highly recommended that you implement QoS on the portion of the network that you have control over, which is your on-premises network. This will increase the quality of real-time communication workloads throughout your deployment and improve chokepoints in your existing deployment.

Deploying Quality of Service for Microsoft Teams

For Teams traffic, you should use GPOs and DSCP marking using port ranges to accommodate Windows and non-Windows devices. This chapter covers only the QoS configuration at the endpoint level as well as the network layer. It is a best practice to use a GPO to grab the majority of clients and to use port-based DSCP tagging to ensure that mobile, Mac, and other clients will still get QoS treatment (at least partially).

Table 3-3 shows the DSCP values and client source port ranges that are recommended for Microsoft Teams media traffic.

Table 3-3. *Teams Media Category with Client Source Port Ranges*

Client Source Port Range	Protocol	Media Category	DSCP Value	DSCP Class
50,000–50,019	TCP/UDP	Audio	46	Expedited Forwarding (EF)
50,020–50,039	TCP/UDP	Video	34	Assured Forwarding (AF41)
50,040–50,059	TCP/UDP	Application/ Desktop Sharing	18	Assured Forwarding (AF21)

Applying DSCP Marking at Network Layer

To implement DSCP marking on network devices, you as a Teams admin need to work with network engineers to configure port-based DSCP tagging by using access control lists (ACLs) on network devices (switches and routers); basically, the network engineer will configure devices to mark the Teams audio, video, and application sharing traffic at the ingress/egress routers typically located on the WAN based on the client source port ranges defined for each modality. Although this works across platforms, it marks traffic only at the WAN edge, not all the way to the client computer; therefore, this incurs management overhead.

To set this up, you can discuss and share Teams client source port ranges with DSCP classes and values with your network engineer.

DSCP Marking at Endpoint Level Using Policy-Based QoS

QoS policies are applied to a user login session or a computer as part of a GPO that you have linked to an Active Directory container, such as a domain, site, or organizational unit (OU). QoS traffic management occurs below the application layer, which means your existing applications do not need to be modified to benefit from the advantages that are provided by QoS policies.

For Microsoft Teams, we need to set up QoS policies for computer configuration so that whoever logs in to a computer and uses the Teams client will have the policy applied.

The following is the GPO path: Default Domain Policy ➤ Computer Configuration ➤ Policies ➤ Windows Settings ➤ Policy-Based QoS.

Follow these steps to implement policy-based QoS for Teams.

1. First, define the Teams client source port ranges on the Teams admin center. Log in to the Teams admin center, then go to a meeting, and finally go to the meeting settings under Network (https://admin.teams.microsoft.com/meetings/settings).

    a. Turn on "Insert Quality of Service (QoS) markers for real-time media traffic," as shown in Figure 3-10.

    b. Select "Select a port range for each type of real-time media traffic," as shown in Figure 3-10.

    c. Update starting and ending port ranges with media traffic type. Figure 3-10 shows the media port ranges.

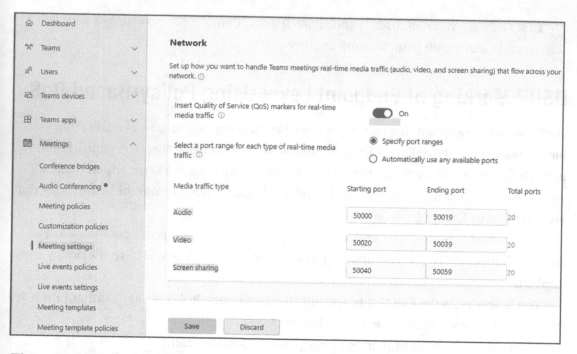

Figure 3-10. Configuring media port ranges

You can set up a port range using PowerShell as well.

2.   Configure a separate GPO for each modality.

After defining the port ranges in the Teams admin center, you must create QoS policies that specify the DSCP values to be associated with each port range. Basically, restricting a set of ports to a specific type of traffic does not result in packets traveling through those ports being marked with the appropriate DSCP value. In addition to defining port ranges, you must also create QoS policies that specify the DSCP value to be associated with each port range. This DSCP value's association with a port range can be achieved via GPO, which is called *policy-based QoS*. With QoS policy, you can configure and enforce QoS policies that cannot be configured on routers and switches. A QoS policy provides the following advantages:

- QoS policies are easier to configure by using a user-level QoS policy on a domain controller and propagating the policy to the user's computer.

- QoS policies are flexible. Regardless of where or how a computer connects to the network, QoS policy is applied. The computer can connect using Wi-Fi or Ethernet from any location.

- Some QoS functions, such as throttling, are better performed when they are closer to the source. QoS policy moves such QoS functions closest to the source.

If you already have all the port ranges and DSCP values with media category type, then proceed to the next step. If not, then decide on port ranges and follow step 2 for configuring port ranges. Microsoft outlines the complete steps and port ranges at https://docs.microsoft.com/en-us/microsoftteams/qos-in-teams.

a. You must have consolidated all your computer objects to a single OU. For example, the Bloguc organization consolidated all computers under the PC OU to apply the GPO correctly. You can apply a single GPO to multiple OUs; however, for better management, consolidate objects into one OU and then apply the policy.

b. Log in to the domain controller or computer that has Group Policy Management installed.

c. Open the Group Policy Management tool (Run ➤ gpmc.msc) and then right-click the OU (Computer). Click Create A GPO In This Domain And Link It Here to create a new GPO such as TeamsClient-QoS. You must have the required permission (domain admin or the like) to create and link the policy object permission.

d. Select the newly created GPO and right-click it. Select Edit to Open Group Policy Management Editor. Expand Computer Configuration ➤ Policies ➤ Windows Settings. Right-click Policy-based QoS, then select Create New Policy, as shown in Figure 3-11.

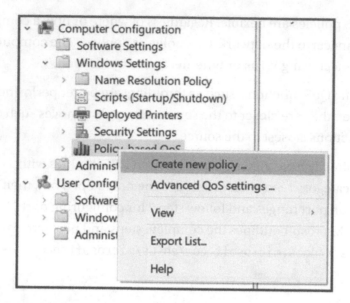

Figure 3-11. *Policy-based QoS*

    e. On the Policy-based QoS page, shown in Figure 3-12, give the policy a name, such as Teams Audio. Select the Specify DSCP Value check box and enter the value **46**. Click Next.

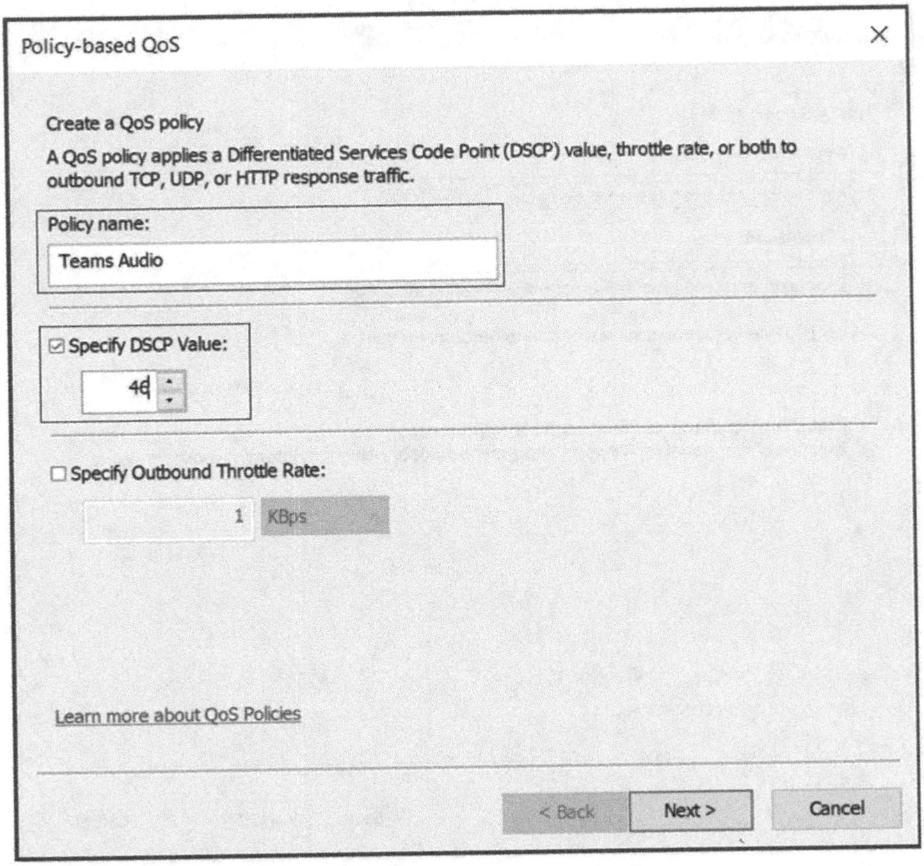

Figure 3-12. *Specifying the policy name and DSCP values*

 f. On the next page, shown in Figure 3-13, select the Only
  Applications With This Executable Name option, and enter
  Teams.exe. Click Next.

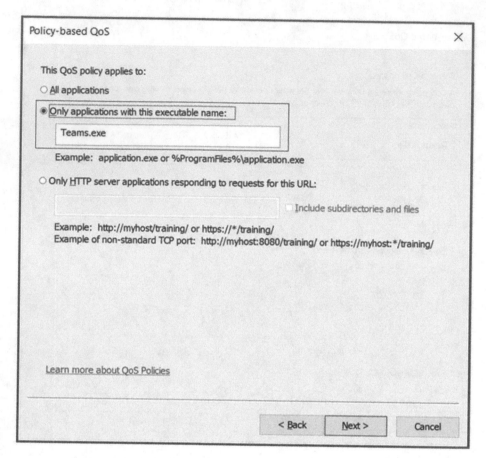

Figure 3-13. *Application name*

Note   This simply ensures that the Teams.exe application will match packets from the specified port range with the specified DSCP code.

    g. On the next page, make sure that both the Any Source IP Address and Any Destination IP Address options are selected, as shown in Figure 3-14. Click Next.

Note   These two settings ensure that packets will be managed regardless of which computer (IP address) sent those packets and which computer (IP address) will receive those packets.

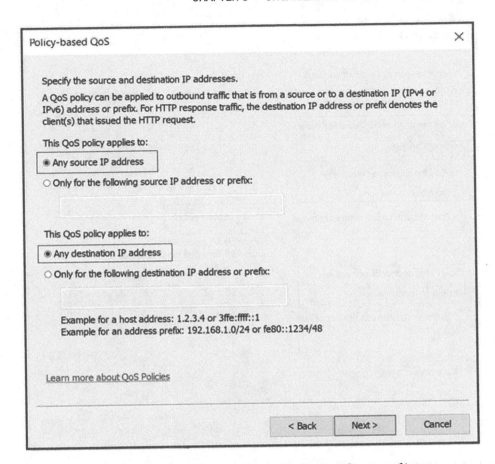

Figure 3-14. *Selecting the IP addresses that the QoS policy applies to*

h.   On the next page, for the Select the Protocol This QoS Policy
Applies To setting, select TCP and UDP. Select From This Source
Port Number Or Range. Also, enter a port range reserved for
audio transmissions (50000–50019) and select To Any Destination
Port. Figure 3-15 shows protocol and port range configuration
information.

Note   Transmission Control Protocol (TCP) and User Datagram Protocol (UDP) are
the two networking protocols most commonly used by the Microsoft Teams service
and its client applications.

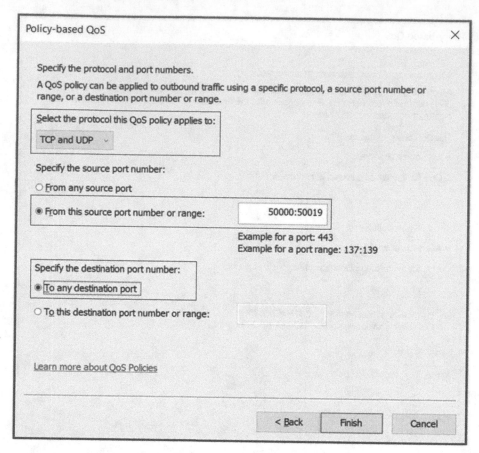

Figure 3-15. *Defining the source port number or range*

    i.   Follow steps e to h and create new policy objects as Teams Video
         and Teams Sharing with the given port ranges and DSCP values.

   ii.   After you are finished configuring all policy objects, it will look
         like Figure 3-16.

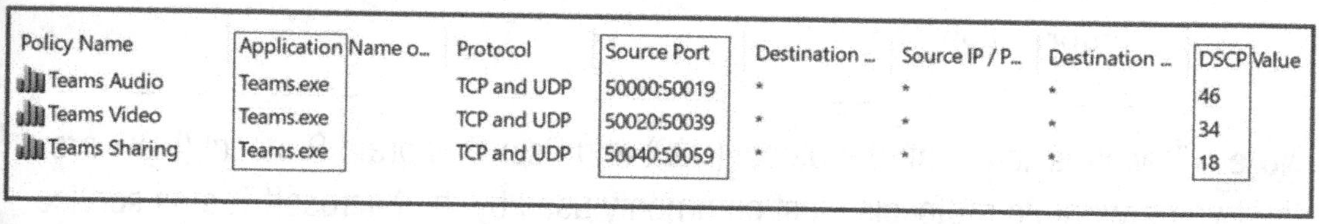

Policy Name	Application	Name o...	Protocol	Source Port	Destination ...	Source IP / P...	Destination ...	DSCP Value
Teams Audio	Teams.exe		TCP and UDP	50000:50019	*	*	*	46
Teams Video	Teams.exe		TCP and UDP	50020:50039	*	*	*	34
Teams Sharing	Teams.exe		TCP and UDP	50040:50059	*	*	*	18

Figure 3-16. *All policies*

3.   Finally, test the QoS. As a best practice, you must validate QoS
configuration and DSCP tagging on a quarterly basis.

Verifying QoS Policies Are Applied

After QoS policy configuration, you must verify all QoS settings. There are multiple ways
to verify the QoS.

- **Using Registry on the Windows local computer:** Once the GPO
  pushed and applied to the computer, you can force the GPO to the
  local computer by running the command gpudate.exe /force. Then
  visit the Registry path Computer\HKEY_LOCAL_MACHINE\SOFTWARE\
  Policies\Microsoft\Windows\QoS\Teams Audio to verify that QoS
  policies have been applied. Figure 3-17 shows Teams Audio, Teams
  Video, and Teams Sharing policies with port ranges and DSCP values.

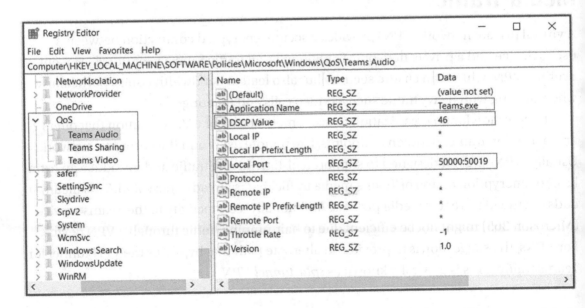

Figure 3-17. Verifying QoS using local computer registry

- **Validate QoS tagging using packet capture:** You need Wireshark
  as a network packet capturing tool. Start a Teams audio/video
  meeting and capture the network traffic via the Wireshark tool (it is a
  freeware tool that you can download and install on your computer).

Figure 3-18 shows Teams audio traffic (the source is 10.0.0.207 and destination is 104.42.192.49) protocol UDP with the port number 50018. This packet shows DSCP marked as EF (expedite forwarding as DSCP 46). Verify the two-way traffic to get QoS benefits.

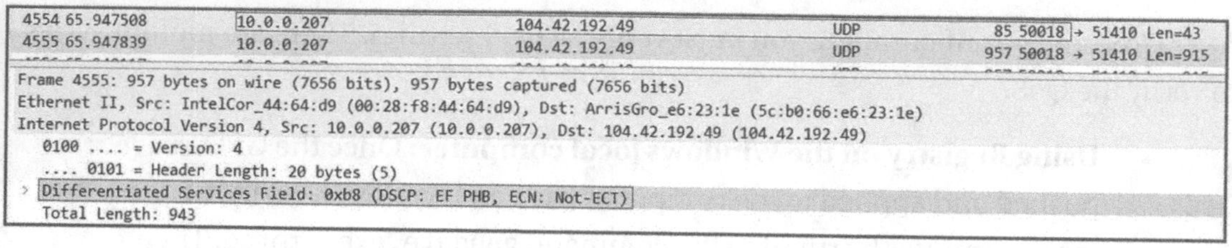

```
4554 65.947508        10.0.0.207            104.42.192.49              UDP          85 50018 → 51410 Len=43
4555 65.947839        10.0.0.207            104.42.192.49              UDP         957 50018 → 51410 Len=915
Frame 4555: 957 bytes on wire (7656 bits), 957 bytes captured (7656 bits)
Ethernet II, Src: IntelCor_44:64:d9 (00:28:f8:44:64:d9), Dst: ArrisGro_e6:23:1e (5c:b0:66:e6:23:1e)
Internet Protocol Version 4, Src: 10.0.0.207 (10.0.0.207), Dst: 104.42.192.49 (104.42.192.49)
    0100 .... = Version: 4
    .... 0101 = Header Length: 20 bytes (5)
>   Differentiated Services Field: 0xb8 (DSCP: EF PHB, ECN: Not-ECT)
    Total Length: 943
```

Figure 3-18. *Validating QoS tagging*

Deploying VPN Split Tunnel for Microsoft Teams Media Traffic

A virtual private network (VPN) provides a secure, encrypted connection between a user's device and a private network. Traditionally, all traffic from a user's device is sent over the VPN, which can ensure security but also lead to bandwidth issues, particularly when dealing with heavy traffic such as video calls and meetings.

It's common for an organization to use remote access or a VPN solution that offers an encryption tunnel between endpoints, like remote users and the corporate network. Usually, VPNs are not designed to support real-time media traffic and introduce an extra layer of encryption on top of Teams media traffic that is already encrypted. This means it adds overhead to Teams media packets. Additionally, connectivity to the Teams service (Microsoft 365) might not be efficient due to hair-pinning traffic through a VPN device. For VPNs, the suggestion is to provide an alternate path that bypasses the VPN tunnel for Teams traffic. This is generally known as *split-tunnel VPN*.

Understanding Split-Tunnel VPN for Teams Media Traffic

With split tunneling, only traffic destined for the private network is sent over the VPN. Other traffic goes directly over the public Internet. This has several benefits for Microsoft Teams:

- **Bandwidth optimization:** Since only necessary traffic is sent over the VPN, it reduces the overall bandwidth consumption on the VPN connection. This means less congestion and better performance for Teams calls and meetings.

- **Better performance:** Teams is a latency-sensitive application, meaning it performs better with lower network delays. By sending Teams traffic directly over the Internet, it can take a more direct and faster route to Microsoft's servers, reducing latency.

- **Scalability:** Since less traffic is sent over the VPN, it can support more users without needing to upgrade the VPN infrastructure.

- **Reduced load on VPN gateways:** Offloading Teams traffic from the VPN connection reduces the load on the VPN gateways, increasing their longevity and decreasing maintenance costs.

Because there are multiple VPN solutions available in the market and every solution vendor might have a different process to implement split-tunnel VPN, this topic covers general recommendations as to what should be configured on the VPN solutions. There are multiple rationales for which you, as a Teams admin, must implement split-tunnel VPN.

- For Microsoft Teams conversation and collaboration features, VPN or remote access connections are usually acceptable because the network qualities are frequently not visible to the end user. If a chat message arrives a second or two later, there would be only a minor impact. The same is not applicable for keeping a bidirectional conversation in real time, like a Teams audio call.

- Microsoft Teams uses a number of codecs, and they have different packetization times. However, VPN solutions add another layer of encryption and decryption, which greatly increases network latency on these packets getting to their destination in a timely manner. When these Teams media packets are delayed or received out of order, jitter increases, and the receiving endpoint will attempt to fill in and stretch the audio to fill in the gaps, which usually results in undesired audio effects such as robotic noise, voice speed up, and so on.

- A VPN solution contributes to intermittent difficulties such as random network disconnections, which will cause the Microsoft Teams session to disconnect (disruption of the signaling path) or media quality issues. This would generally indicate a need for increased capacity on the VPN solution. However, when the VPN solution was designed, this likely wasn't factored in, and the media usage is degrading the overall VPN experience for other applications as well.

- Clients who have configured their VPN solution to exclude Microsoft Teams traffic or implement split-tunnel VPN have seen great returns in user satisfaction not specific to the Teams audio and video experience. For this purpose, we strongly recommend leveraging the steps that follow to complete a split-tunnel VPN for Teams media traffic over VPN solutions.

Some Recommendations Before Implementing VPN Split Tunnelling

Before implementing split tunneling, it's important to understand your organization's security requirements, as it can increase exposure to Internet-based threats. For example, at Cyclotron, Inc., we have implemented VPN split tunnelling, which has improved our Teams call quality drastically over VPN connections.

Here are some recommendations:

- **Security assessment:** Conduct a risk assessment before implementing split tunneling to ensure it aligns with your organization's security policy.

- **Traffic monitoring:** Regularly monitor network traffic to detect any abnormal behavior or potential security threats.

- **Selective split tunneling:** Rather than implementing split tunneling for all traffic, consider only implementing it for Teams media traffic to balance performance with security.

- **VPN choice:** Choose a VPN solution that fits your organization's needs, both in terms of features and scalability.

- **Network optimization:** Regularly review and optimize your network to ensure it continues to support the needs of your organization as they evolve.

- **Microsoft recommendations:** Follow Microsoft's guidance for implementing VPN split tunneling with Teams. They provide documentation and support that can be invaluable during the process.

Remember that while split tunneling can improve performance, it may not be suitable for all organizations, particularly those with strict security requirements. Always weigh the benefits against the potential risks before implementing.

Split-Tunnel VPN Architecture

A VPN split tunnel architecture for Microsoft Teams media traffic would involve both your private network (with the VPN server) and the public internet. Here's a basic layout:

- **User device:** This is the starting point of the network traffic. It could be a laptop, desktop, or mobile device running the Microsoft Teams client.

- **VPN client:** Installed on the user device, the VPN client handles creating the secure connection to the VPN server and managing the split tunnel.

- **VPN server:** This server resides within your organization's private network and manages the incoming VPN connections. The VPN server also applies the split tunnel rules.

- **Private network:** This is your organization's internal network, where private resources (such as file servers, intranet websites, etc.) reside. Traffic to these resources goes over the VPN.

- **Public Internet:** Traffic not destined for the private network, such as Microsoft Teams media traffic, goes directly over the public internet.

When a Microsoft Teams call or meeting is started, the following happens:

- Signaling traffic (used to initiate the call or meeting) is sent from the Teams client on the user device to the Teams service over the Internet, bypassing the VPN.

- Once the call or meeting is established, the media traffic (audio, video, and screen sharing) also goes directly from the Teams client to the Teams service over the internet, bypassing the VPN.

- Other traffic, such as access to file servers or other private resources, is sent over the VPN to the private network.

This setup ensures that Teams media traffic takes the most direct path to the Teams service, reducing latency and improving call quality. It also reduces the load on the VPN server, freeing up bandwidth for other traffic.

In this scenario, the VPN client and VPN server are configured to allow Microsoft Teams traffic (based on specific ports and/or IPs) to bypass the VPN while sending other traffic over the VPN. This is often done through firewall rules or specific VPN configuration settings.

For this setup to work, both the VPN solution and the network infrastructure must support split tunneling, and the VPN client must be correctly configured on the user devices. It's also important to note that while this architecture can improve Teams performance, it can potentially expose Teams traffic to Internet-based threats, so appropriate security measures should be taken.

The VPN split tunneling solution for Microsoft Teams provides optimal call quality to the end user who uses Teams over VPN. In a split-tunnel VPN configuration, all IP addresses that are used by the Microsoft Teams services (Office 365) environment are excluded so that traffic to and from those IP addresses is not included in the VPN tunnel. This means the split-tunnel VPN must work exactly the same way as the external Teams client should. Most VPN solution providers support split-tunnel VPN; you must check the configuration for your VPN solution by checking the vendor documentation. Figure 3-19 shows how split-tunnel VPN works.

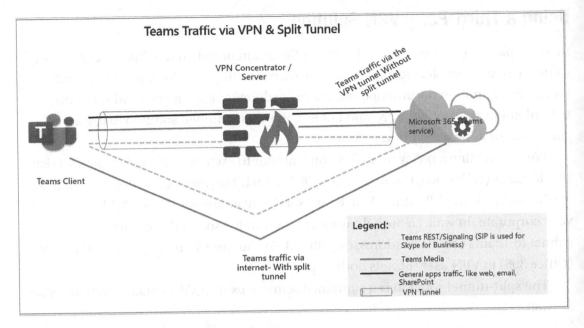

Figure 3-19. *Split-tunnel VPN traffic flow*

All Microsoft Teams signaling and media traffic split from the VPN secure tunnel, as shown in Figure 3-19, and go through Microsoft Teams service (Office 365). To redirect users away from the VPN solution for Teams, it must first be configured to support a split tunnel, which is a popular feature of today's VPN appliances. Split-tunnel VPN allows Teams traffic without going through the VPN tunnel. For example, the external web traffic from the Teams site (`teams.microsoft.com`) does not traverse over the VPN solution. Without split tunnel, the default VPN configuration will force all the Teams traffic through the VPN tunnel.

Implementing Split-Tunnel VPN

There might be different way to achieve a VPN split tunnel for Teams media and signaling traffic, such as using a firewall or third-party VPN solution. I have mentioned here one of the ways that is commonly used to configure VPN split tunneling using a third-party VPN.

Using a Third-Party VPN Solution

In this topic, we cover split-tunnel VPN configuration based on the Pulse secure VPN solution as an example. I strongly recommend contacting your VPN vendor for split-tunnel configuration documentation. There are different approaches and solutions to implement split-tunnel VPN, and I present here a combined solution to use a VPN concentrator and your corporate firewall.

We are creating a policy on a VPN concentrator to exclude Microsoft Teams service IP addresses (Office 365) traffic from the VPN tunnel. This means denying signaling and media traffic via the VPN tunnel for Teams service IP addresses (Office 365). Then, using your corporate firewall, create a deny rule to deny traffic sourced from the VPN user subnet to Teams service IP addresses (Office 365) and from Teams service IP addresses (Office 365) to VPN user subnets both ways.

The split-tunnel solution is a combined solution using a VPN concentrator and your firewall.

1. First, get all Teams service IP addresses, including optimized required and allow required. Refer to the Microsoft documentation for Teams service IP addresses at https://docs.microsoft.com/en-us/Office365/Enterprise/urls-and-ip-address-ranges.

2. Create a policy on a VPN concentrator, which will exclude traffic via VPN tunnel for all Teams service IP addresses (refer to the preceding URL for Teams IP addresses). In other words, deny traffic or split tunnel to these Teams IP addresses from your VPN tunnel and assign this policy to all other policies and users.

3. Now work with your network firewall team and do this. Split Teams conferencing (media) traffic to external (not via VPN tunnel).

Remember, all-conference modality traffic is involved through a multicontrol unit (MCU) running on Teams service (Office 365). First, create the following firewall rules:

- Create a firewall rule that will block traffic going from VPN user subnets to Teams service IP addresses or subnets (Office 365). Refer to the earlier Microsoft documentation link.

- Create another firewall rule that will block traffic going from Teams service IP addresses or subnets (Office 365) to the VPN user subnet.

To implement split-tunnel VPN for Teams one-to-one call traffic, you must create more rules on your corporate firewall.

Apart from the Teams conferencing traffic, you can enable the blockage of the UDP/TCP source port for Teams audio, video, and application sharing. Basically, Microsoft Teams, by default, has a limited scope of UDP/TCP ports it will be using as the source ports for communication. If you block these source ports from entering the VPN tunnel, then the media should go via the external split from the VPN tunnel. That will ensure that even two users both connected via VPN and their Teams media traffic will not allow hair-pinning via their VPN connection but go directly from one Internet connection to the other.

The sample firewall rules look like this:

- Create a firewall rule source address from the VPN_Users subnet to the destination as Any with the application Stun and Teams (if allowed) and Service port (UDP/TCP port ranges of audio, video, and application sharing).

- Create another firewall rule source from any address to the destination VPN_Users subnet with the application Stun and Teams (if allowed) and Service port (UDP/TCP port ranges of audio, video, and application sharing).

You can get Teams audio/video and application sharing client port ranges from the Teams admin center. Log in to the Teams admin center, and go to a meeting. In Meeting Settings, under Network, select Get New Image.

DOES THIS TOPIC APPLY TO SKYPE FOR BUSINESS ONLINE?

Yes, this applies to Skype for Business Online as well, because Microsoft Teams and Skype for Business Online share the same IP subnets and ports.

Verifying VPN Split Tunneling

To verify the VPN split tunnel, you must connect using the external network (wired or wireless) and then connect the VPN, which has the split tunnel implemented.

1. Make a Teams one-to-one call and capture network traces using Wireshark or Network Monitor. Verify the Teams media (UDP) traffic going between your local IP address and other third-party local IP addresses (not via VPN IP addresses).

2. Join the Teams meeting, and capture network traces using Wireshark or Network Monitor. Verify the Teams media (UDP) traffic going between your local IP address and Teams service IP address (Office 365) transport relay and not via VPN IP addresses.

Note   For the Teams service IP addresses or subnet block rule on the firewall, set the action to Reset instead of denying. That allows for a faster Teams client sign-in.

Providing optimal experience to the end-user community is our main goal, and using VPN split tunneling helps to achieve this through blocking the Teams client from connecting via VPN tunnel. The media will then always go through externally, not via VPN tunnel, which will eliminate extra hops, double encryption, and so on.

Security and Compliance Requirements for Teams Deployment

Before deploying Microsoft Teams in an organization, it is crucial to understand and meet the necessary security and compliance requirements.

- **Data security:** Teams is built on the Office 365 hyper-scale, enterprise-grade cloud, delivering the advanced security and compliance capabilities. Data in Teams resides in Exchange, SharePoint, and OneDrive for Business, so protection, detection, and response capabilities cover the security spectrum.

- **Identity and access management:** It is important to ensure only authorized individuals have access to your Teams data. This involves setting up appropriate user authentication and authorization methods such as multifactor authentication (MFA), single sign-on (SSO), and conditional access.

- **Data compliance:** Teams is Tier-C compliant including standards such as ISO 27001, ISO 27018, SSAE16 SOC 1, and SOC 2, HIPAA, and EU Model Clauses (EUMC). Data residency commitments also apply to Teams.

- **Data governance and retention:** Organizations must set up data retention policies according to their needs and the regulatory landscape of their industry. Teams allows admins to set up granular data retention policies.

- **Audit logs:** Teams provides a unified audit log in the Security & Compliance Center for events, and teams-related information is logged into the Office 365 audit log for review.

- **Privacy and transparency:** Teams follows the Office 365 Privacy and Trust Center commitments such as access control, auditing and compliance, certification and compliance, and more.

Benefits of Security and Compliance Planning

Thorough security and compliance planning before deploying Microsoft Teams provides several benefits.

- **Risk mitigation:** By understanding and addressing potential security risks up front, organizations can significantly reduce the chance of data breaches and other security incidents.

- **Regulatory compliance:** Compliance planning helps organizations meet industry-specific regulatory requirements, such as HIPAA for healthcare or the GDPR for EU data protection, avoiding potential legal issues and penalties.

- **Trust and reputation:** Having strong security and compliance measures in place helps build trust with customers, partners, and employees, thereby enhancing the organization's reputation.

- **Data protection:** Proper data governance and retention policies ensure that organizational data is properly stored, managed, and protected.

- **Operational efficiency:** A well-planned security and compliance strategy can streamline operations, making it easier to manage and monitor Teams deployment.

- **Cost savings:** By avoiding potential security incidents and regulatory fines, organizations can save significant costs in the long term.

By meeting the security and compliance requirements for Teams deployment, organizations can ensure they get the most out of the platform while minimizing potential risks and issues.

Training and Change Management for Teams Deployment

A successful transition to Microsoft Teams requires not only technical readiness but also comprehensive training and effective change management strategies.

- **Understanding Teams:** Before initiating training, ensure that everyone in the organization understands the purpose, value, and benefits of Teams. This can be done through seminars, workshops, and introductory meetings.

- **Training programs:** Develop detailed training programs for different user groups. This could include live training sessions, online courses, tutorial videos, and quick reference guides. Training should cover all aspects of Teams, from basic functionality to advanced features.

- **Change management:** Implementing a new tool like Teams can cause disruption. Effective change management strategies can help manage this transition smoothly. This could involve regular communication updates, providing ample resources for self-learning, and appointing "champions" or power users who can help others in their team.

- **Support and feedback:** After deployment, provide ongoing support to address any issues or challenges that users might face. Establish clear channels for users to provide feedback or ask questions.

Benefits of Training and Change Management

Effective training and change management during Teams deployment offer several benefits:

- **Higher adoption rates:** Proper training ensures users understand how to use Teams effectively, leading to higher adoption rates.

- **Improved productivity:** When employees understand how to use all the features of Teams, they can leverage the platform to work more efficiently and collaboratively.

- **Reduced resistance:** Change can often meet resistance in an organization. Effective change management can help ease this transition and reduce resistance to the new tool.

- **Lower support costs:** When users are well-trained, they will encounter fewer issues, resulting in lower support costs.

- **Feedback loop:** Establishing clear channels for feedback helps the organization understand the challenges users are facing and how the deployment can be improved.

- **Employee satisfaction:** When employees feel supported during the transition and understand how to use the new tool, it can lead to higher overall job satisfaction.

In conclusion, training and change management are crucial elements of successful Teams deployment. They help ensure that the organization can effectively use the platform, leading to higher productivity and collaboration.

Microsoft Teams Adoption Strategy

Creating an effective adoption strategy is critical to ensure your organization gets the most from Microsoft Teams. The adoption process involves more than just technical deployment; it's about driving a change in how people work and collaborate. The following are the key steps to creating a successful adoption strategy.

Identify Business Objectives and Use Cases

This involves the following:

1. Understand what your organization wants to achieve with Microsoft Teams. Is it to streamline communications, enhance collaboration, reduce emails, or all of the above? Next, identify specific use cases that align with these objectives. Use cases could be department-specific or project-specific. They provide concrete examples of how Teams can be used to improve processes and productivity.

2. Define success metrics. Set clear, measurable goals to track the success of your Teams deployment. These could include user engagement metrics (such as the number of active users or the frequency of use), productivity metrics (such as the reduction in email usage or faster project completion times), and satisfaction metrics gathered through user surveys.

3. Develop a champions program. Identify and recruit enthusiastic individuals from different departments to be Teams "champions." These individuals will receive additional training and will play a crucial role in driving Teams adoption within their respective departments. They can provide peer support, share success stories, and give feedback from the ground level.

Prepare a Training Plan

Based on your use cases and user roles, prepare a comprehensive training plan. The training could be in the form of workshops, webinars, one-on-one sessions, online courses, and self-help resources. Remember that training is not a one-time event; refresher courses, tips, and tricks, and updates about new features should be provided regularly.

1. **Communicate:** Keep all users informed about the rollout plan, training schedules, and where they can get help if needed. This ongoing communication helps to manage expectations, reduce resistance to change, and increase user confidence.

2. **Pilot and iterate:** Consider running a pilot with a small group of users before a full-scale rollout. The pilot will help you identify potential issues, understand user feedback, and make necessary adjustments before deploying Teams across the organization.

3. **Launch and monitor:** After successful testing and iteration, launch Teams to the entire organization. Post-launch, monitor the success metrics you've defined and take corrective actions if needed. Keep channels for feedback open and make sure users are supported throughout their journey.

4. **Celebrate success:** Recognizing and celebrating success is an important part of the adoption strategy. It could be sharing success stories, acknowledging active users or departments, or celebrating milestones like 100 percent deployment.

Remember, a successful Teams adoption strategy is not just about deploying the technology. It's about changing habits and driving a new way of working that aligns with your organization's culture and objectives. Be patient and persistent. Change takes time, and the journey to full adoption is a marathon, not a sprint.

Summary

This chapter underscored the pivotal role of network preparedness and bandwidth planning in facilitating a smooth Microsoft Teams deployment. It elaborated on the integral steps required to assess the network's current state, the potential adjustments needed, and the planning of bandwidth in accordance with calling scenarios and meetings.

Network assessment provides a detailed examination of the existing network infrastructure, revealing its readiness to support the implementation of Microsoft Teams. Highlighting the importance of a robust and stable network, the chapter furnished insights on potential enhancements needed to ensure optimum performance.

Bandwidth planning defines how effectively Teams can operate, particularly in regard to calling scenarios and meetings. The chapter illustrated the bandwidth requirements, demonstrating the relationship between the quality of calls and meetings and the network's capacity.

In this chapter, you learned detailed information about network assessment and bandwidth planning for Teams, how to deploy and manage QoS, and how to deploy split-tunnel VPN for Microsoft Teams media traffic. Before the deployment of Microsoft Teams in a production environment, you, as an admin, need to evaluate if the existing network meets the networking requirements of Microsoft Teams. Make sure you have the required bandwidth, access to all required IP addresses, the correct ports opened, and that you are meeting the performance requirements for Teams real-time media traffic such as audio, video, and application sharing.

This detailed investigation of organizational readiness sets the stage perfectly for our next chapter. Moving from the foundation of a reliable network and effective bandwidth planning, we will now venture into the intricacies of managing Teams' audio conferencing and phone system. This will help us explore the impressive potential of Teams as a comprehensive communication and collaboration platform.

CHAPTER 4

Teams Audio Conferencing and Phone System Management

Balu N Igala*, Vijay Ireddy

ᵃ Tracy, CA, USA

Microsoft Teams provides different capabilities, such as persistent chat, audio and video calls, conferences (dial-in and client join), and phone systems (inbound/outbound PSTN calls). So far, you have learned how Teams features work, how the components interact, and management aspects. This chapter covers Teams conference management, including audio conferencing (dial-in), Teams Webinars, Teams Premium, and VoIP for internal and external attendees. It also covers Teams Phone System management, including Teams Direct Routing, Operator Connect, Calling Plans, Teams Phone Mobile, E911, and voice routing policies.

The Microsoft Teams Phone System is a cloud-based phone system with advanced features for call control and PBX capabilities. It replaces on-premises PBX systems and provides the following functionalities:

- **Call control:** Allows users to make, receive, and transfer calls to and from landlines and mobile phones on the public switched telephone network (PSTN) right from Teams.

- **Voicemail:** Offers integrated voicemail services with transcription features.

- **Call queues:** Directs incoming calls to the next available attendant or distributes them to a group.

© Balu N Ilag, Durgesh Tripathy, Vijay Ireddy 2024
B. N. Ilag et al., *Understanding Microsoft Teams Administration*,
https://doi.org/10.1007/979-8-8688-0014-6_4

- **Auto attendants:** Offers automated systems that answer calls, ask questions, and route the call based on the answers.

- **Call park:** Allows users to put a call on hold and then retrieve the call from another phone.

- **Emergency calling:** Offers support for dialing emergency services.

- **E9-1-1 dialing:** Offers enhanced emergency calling that provides the user's callback number and location to the emergency responders.

- **Caller ID:** Display and control of the caller's phone number.

- **Direct Routing:** Connects Teams to your existing telephony provider to allow the routing of calls via a direct path.

- **Interoperability:** Integrates with third-party systems, such as analog devices and on-premises call centers.

Audio conferencing in Microsoft Teams allows users in a Teams meeting to join over a regular phone line if they're not on a device with Teams installed or if their Internet connection is poor. It provides the following:

- **Dial-in numbers:** It offers a range of numbers, local to multiple countries, that participants can dial to join Teams meetings.

- **Dial-out:** Participants in a meeting can add someone by dialing their number.

- **PIN-protected meetings:** For security, some meetings require a PIN to join via audio conferencing.

- **Dynamic conference IDs:** This provides each meeting with a unique ID, reducing the chance of overlapping or unauthorized access.

After this chapter, you will be able to do the following tasks:

- Plan and manage Teams conferences.

- Use Teams Webinars and Teams Premium

- Plan a Teams Phone System planning.

- Configure and manage Teams Direct Routing

- Configure and manage Microsoft Calling Plan

- Configure and manage Operator Connect

- Configure and manage Teams Phone Mobile

- Configure and manage the call queue and Auto Attendant

- Configure and manage the Teams emergency service

- Manage a phone number and voice routing policy

- Manage a voice routing policy (dial plan, voice routing policy, and PSTN usage)

Planning and Managing Teams Conferences

Let's talk about conferences.

Microsoft Teams Conferences

This section explains how you can collaborate using Teams. You can easily prepare, organize, and follow up by using before and after meeting experiences, such as collaborating before the meeting using chat and Meet Now. Users can be more involved and productive by sharing content from their desktop (Mac and Windows) or mobile devices and adding video to meetings for face-to-face video interactions. Teams meetings work fine with great audio and video quality and reliability when joining from desktops (Windows and Mac), mobile devices, phones, or rooms.

Users can also invite external attendees to join Teams meetings through a web browser with any plug-in. Why do Teams meetings work fine with internal and external participants? The main reason is that Teams is built on a base of the next-generation Skype infrastructure, media services, and Office 365 services, including Exchange, SharePoint, Microsoft Stream, Microsoft Artificial Intelligence service, and Cortana.

Teams also provide an extra layer of engagement before, during, and after meetings. For example, before a meeting, you can have a background conversation in Teams and prepare and discuss content, set up meeting options to manage meeting permissions and settings, and then schedule a Teams meeting. Throughout a meeting, you can use face-to-face video, follow the action, share content, record the session with transcription, use applications integrated with Teams meetings, use live captions, and quickly join from a Teams room. After a meeting, you can play back the meeting with transcription, share notes, and have a post-meeting chat for collaboration. This makes Teams meetings uniquely reliable and reduces quality complaints drastically.

First, you must understand how to use Teams meetings in your organization effectively.

Organizing Teams Meetings Efficiently

Log in to the Teams client and click Calendar. You will see the day's upcoming meetings when it switches to meeting view. You can switch the calendar to daily, weekly, or monthly views. Figure 4-1 shows the daily and weekly views.

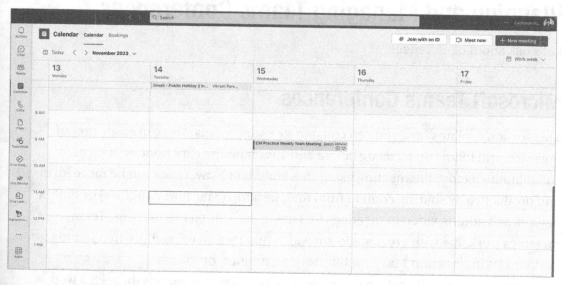

Figure 4-1. *Calendar daily and weekly views*

To schedule a meeting, click New Meeting to open the meeting page.

You can enter a title, location, and start and end times on the meeting schedule page. You can indicate if it is recurring or a one-time meeting and use scheduling assistance to see team members' free/busy information. Here you specify the time zone in which the meeting will be held. You can also select a channel to meet in so all members get invited, or you can choose individual people or a distribution list for meetings. You can add an agenda for the meeting, and other participants can review and edit it before joining the meeting. Once you have added the desired information, click Save to schedule the meeting, as shown in Figure 4-2.

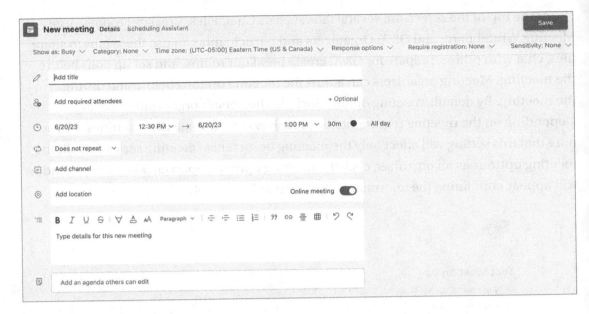

Figure 4-2. *Setting up a new meeting*

At this point, the meeting has been created and shown on the calendar. You can see all the details about the meeting: title, time, and who has scheduled it. You can also see the status of the attendees who have accepted the meeting. This information is not only for the organizer but all attendees.

Once the meeting is scheduled, you can start a chat with all participants before the meeting, where you can discuss the agenda or share any files that attendees should review before the meeting. You can join the meeting in the same conversation by clicking Join, as shown in Figure 4-3.

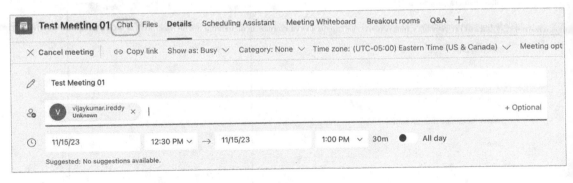

Figure 4-3. *Chat with participants option*

At the top of the screen are several tabs such as Chat, Files, Breakout rooms, Apps, Meeting Whiteboard, and Q&A. Organizers and participants can use these tabs to share files, chat with others, prepare for Q&A, create breakout rooms, and set up polls before the meeting. Meeting organizers can adjust the meeting options before and during the meeting. By default, meeting options include the default organization settings. Depending on the meeting requirements, organizers can change these settings. Please note that this setting will affect only the meeting occurrence/meeting series. To edit the meeting options as an organizer, click the meeting options. Upon clicking, a new window will appear containing the information specified in Figure 4-4.

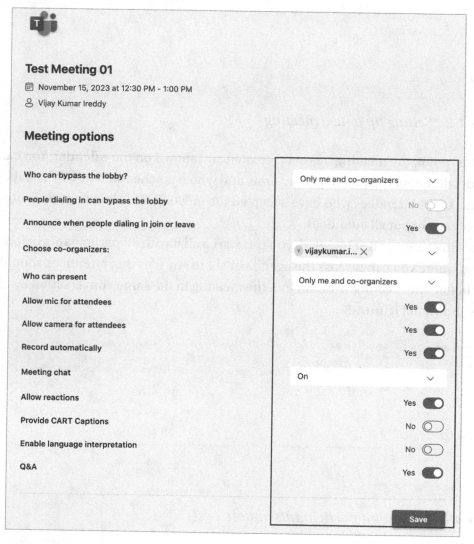

Figure 4-4. *Adjusting the meeting options*

To meet specific needs, organizers can adjust meeting options. For example, in the given meeting example, the organizer wants to include co-organizers, keep all participants in the lobby until allowed into the meeting, and only allow organizers or co-organizers to admit the participants, and the meeting recording is turned on automatically.

You can join the meeting by clicking Join in the Teams client calendar or Outlook Calendar. You can turn on video, view a preview, control audio, and change the audio or video device. Figure 4-5 illustrates joining my test meeting.

Figure 4-5. *Joining a meeting*

When joining audio in Teams, you have several options to choose from. You can use your computer's default audio setting or select your preferred microphone and speakers. You can also make a Teams call to your phone by entering your phone number (note that this feature requires an Audio Conference License). If there are Teams rooms or certified devices nearby, they will be detected automatically. Lastly, you have the choice not to use any audio at all.

To enable video in your meeting, turn on the video icon and select the Effects and Avatars option. Please note that avatars are currently in public preview. Within the effects options, you can choose from default background effects or upload your custom images. Additionally, Teams offers video enhancement features such as soft focus, brightness adjustment, and mirror image to improve the video quality in low-lighting scenarios.

To use an avatar during your Teams meeting, create one using the Avatar app in the Teams app store. Then, when joining the video, select the Avatar option instead of your video. It's important to note that you can choose only one, either your avatar or your video but not both. For a visual example, refer to Figure 4-6, which shows joining a meeting using an avatar.

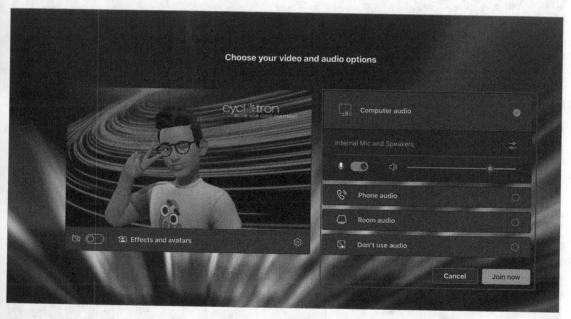

Figure 4-6. *Joining a meeting using an avatar*

Tip   Teams settings don't have the option to set up default devices to join audio and video for your meetings. However, Teams AI is intuitive and can recognize your preferred method of joining meetings. For instance, if you previously connected multiple meetings via an avatar and room audio, it will suggest using the same way for future meetings.

Once you are ready to join the meeting, click Join to enter the meeting. Once in the meeting, you can use several controls, including turning your camera on or off, muting or unmuting your microphone, sharing a presentation and desktop, and other things. In the upper-right corner, other items manage participants and access chat. Figure 4-7 shows these meeting controls.

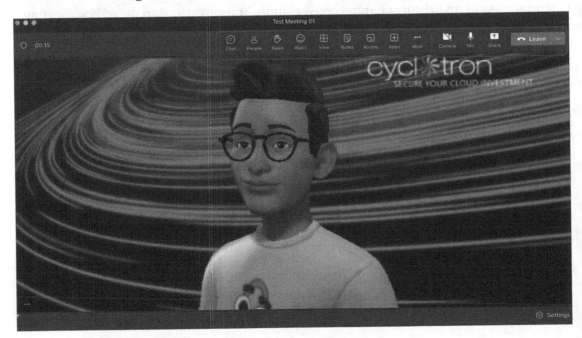

Figure 4-7. *Meeting controls*

During the meeting, you will see several meeting controls. You can use the sharing options to share your screen, window, PowerPoint Live, Excel Live, and whiteboard. Each sharing method has its benefits. If you want to display your entire screen and other desktop activities, choose "share your screen," as it enables seamless sharing of multiple windows. If you share only a single application, consider sharing via "window." Teams meetings offer rich collaboration capabilities through PowerPoint and Excel presentations. PowerPoint Live and Excel Live allow participants to move through the presentation at their own pace. Finally, the whiteboard feature and annotation features enable real-time collaboration among participants.

After a meeting, you can access a recording, any shared presentation files, and a transcript of all the discussions. The recording is stored in the OneDrive of the person who started the recording and can be viewed by all internal meeting participants in Teams. Please note that the recording is available only if the meeting was recorded.

There are two broad meeting types: channel meetings and private meetings. Channel meetings exist within a channel, making them visible to all channel members. Pre- and post-meeting features stay within the channel. You can add nonmembers of a team to the channel meetings, but they will not have access to chat because it is visible to channel members only. A channel meeting can be scheduled from the Teams client calendar view or an existing channel conversation. You can also start an ad hoc meeting from a current channel conversation instead of through a reply. Just create an ad hoc meeting and start.

Private meetings can start from an existing chat conversation with chat participants. They are visible to invited people only, and the pre-meeting and post-meeting experiences are accessible via chat. You can schedule a private meeting with the Teams client or the Outlook Teams add-In.

Teams Meeting Attendee Types

Teams meetings have different attendee types. Depending on your attendee type, you will have different information and options available during meetings.

- **Internal users:** These are organization users with an account in the same tenant organization. For example, my tenant account is xyz@cyclotron.com.

- **Guest users:** Guest users are invited to one or many teams in your organization. Guest users will have guest accounts in the same tenant.

- **Federated users:** Federated users are users of a different organization (partner or vendor organization) with federation configured between both organizations that use Teams. For example, cyclotron.com and microsoft.com are two different organizations that are federated with each other.

- **Anonymous users:** Anonymous users have no account or an account in a tenant without a federation. Usually these types of users join Teams meetings via a web client.

Remember, that attendee type is determined at join time, and you cannot change that. Suppose a federated user forgets to sign in; they will be considered anonymous when joining Teams meetings. If they want to join a meeting as a federated user, they must sign in first. In that case, they must leave the meeting and rejoin as a federated user. By signing in, it is possible to promote attendees from one attendee type to a different type, such as attendee to the presenter in the meeting.

Meeting Attendees' Experience

Users' experiences will change in a Teams meeting depending on the meeting type and attendee type. For example, beginning with joining a meeting, some users can join a meeting directly, and others might have to wait in the lobby. By default, only internal and guest users can join directly. As a Teams admin, however, you can change the meeting policy to allow everyone to join the meeting directly, irrespective of whether they are internal, guest, or federated users. Anonymous users, however, will not join a meeting directly.

In a meeting, all but anonymous users can mute and remove others and admit users from the lobby to a meeting. Starting a meeting is configurable via policy, and dialing out is also configurable. Only internal users can initiate meeting recordings.

Before and after meetings, internal and guest users can chat in the channel meetings only if they are part of invited teams. Anonymous users cannot see chat, but federated users (tenants in the same region) will see chat after joining the meeting and continue seeing it after it. If federated users are tenants in a different region, they will not see any chats.

Which Teams Clients Can Join a Meeting?

Teams has a number of clients that can participate in a meeting.

- **From desktop client:** You can use a Windows or Mac client, or you can use a web client (Edge, Chrome, or Safari).

- **From mobile:** You can use an Android or iOS Teams app to join a Teams meeting.

- **From a desktop phone:** You can use 3rd Party IP Phone (3PIP) phones and phones optimized for Teams.

- **From a PSTN phone:** You can dial in or out from a Teams meeting.

- **From a Native Teams Device:** You can easily join a meeting with a one-touch join experience on your Teams native IP phone or other Teams native devices.

- **From a room system:** You can join a Teams meeting using Teams room or Surface Hub.

- **Cloud video interop:** You can use third-party CVI solutions like Pexip to integrate with existing room systems.

Teams Licensing for Meetings

Regarding licensing, Teams meetings are included in almost all the Teams licenses. If you want to use Teams audio conferencing, which allows you to dial in and dial out from and to phones, this requires an additional license. Audio conferencing is included in the E5 license or is available as an add-on for E1 and E3 licenses.

A Microsoft Stream license, which provides the ability to record Teams meetings, requires an E1, E2, E3, A1, A3, A5, Microsoft 365 Business, Business Premium, or Business Essential license for both the organizer and the user who initiates the recording.

Note   Microsoft is currently providing an add-on Microsoft Teams Audio Conferencing license that includes dial-out capabilities to users in the United States and Canada. These licenses can be assigned to individual users for their audio-conferencing needs. However, it's important to note that dial-out is available only to users in the United States and Canada.

Teams Meeting Delegation

Meeting delegation allows users to schedule a meeting on behalf of other users. To do that, you need to configure a user as a delegate in Outlook and Teams. There are some requirements for delegation. You must have Office 2013 or a newer version and use Exchange Server 2013, Exchange Server 2016, or Exchange Online. In addition, the admin needs to be in the same environment, both on-premises and online. They need to be online in the same tenant for the online environment. A meeting on behalf of another user can be scheduled only with Teams Outlook add-ins.

Recording

To record a Teams meeting, users must have an E1, E3, E5, A1, A3, A5, M365 Business, Business Premium, or Business Essentials license assigned with a Microsoft Streams license.

Finally, the recording user must be enabled for recording and optionally transcription in the meeting policy. This cannot be an anonymous, guest, or federated user in the meetings.

Microsoft Teams Meeting Networking Considerations

Microsoft Teams supports real-time audio and video calls or meetings with optimal call quality. Call quality, however, depends on underlying network quality. Suppose a network is planned well with sufficient bandwidth. In that case, all required communication is allowed through an egress firewall, and the network has no packet loss and latency; teams calls or meetings will work seamlessly with optimal quality. If there is a blockage of Teams traffic with a high packet drop and latency rate, however, the Teams call experience will be poor, and some Teams features will not work as expected.

Where Teams Meetings Are Hosted

Network planning is critical before deploying a Teams meeting workload. To plan for Teams meeting use, you must understand the different components involved. First, the meeting service resides in the Office 365 data center where Teams is deployed. The meeting service mixes and distributes media (audio, video, application, and desktop sharing) for meetings. Each endpoint (internal and external) sends all media to the meeting service, and then each client receives all media they are attending.

In a Teams meeting, Microsoft will be served locally to end users. That means the meeting will be homed in the data center closest to the first user joining. This is a benefit because if you are a multinational organization with users on multiple continents, the Teams meeting is independent of your tenant location, and users will have the meeting in their region. For example, suppose the Cyclotron tenant is provisioned in the United States and the first users join the meeting from Europe. In that case, the meeting will be homed in a European Teams meeting service Office 365 cloud data center. Teams meetings in regions are highly beneficial because they will reduce latency compared to meetings held in a U.S. Microsoft data center. So, Teams meeting is independent of tenant location, and users will always have meetings within their region.

Networking Considerations for Teams Meeting Deployment

You already know that Teams is a cloud-only service, which means the Teams client is registered against a Teams service in the cloud, and Teams meeting attendees have to join the meeting through Teams service in the cloud. Therefore, all Teams signaling and media traffic traverses through the corporate network to the Internet to the Microsoft cloud network. That's why your Teams meeting planning for networking must include these three network segments, as shown in Figure 4-8.

- **Corporate network (on-premises network):** This is where a user resides in the corporate network to send all traffic to the Teams service in Office 365. First, real-time media traverse the local network, where you have complete control. You should configure this to meet the requirements of Microsoft Teams and prioritize traffic accordingly.

- **Interconnect network:** This is the Internet. If you have ExpressRoute deployed, this is an Internet service provider (ISP) connecting the enterprise network to the Microsoft 365 network. You cannot configure or change it because the Internet is unmanaged. However, you can talk to the ISP to optimize peering by reducing hops with the Microsoft Office 365 network or switch to a different ISP.

- **Office 365 global network:** This is a Microsoft-managed, low-latency network optimized for Microsoft Teams.

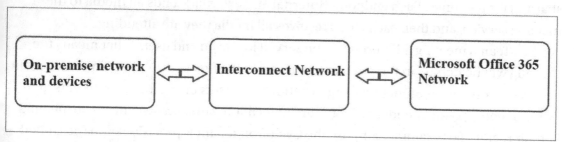

Figure 4-8. Teams traffic traversing across the networks

Allowing Teams Inbound and Outbound Traffic Through Firewall Configuration

Most Microsoft Teams connectivity failures or packet drops are related to a firewall. To handle Teams meetings correctly, you as an admin must allow a number of IP subnets, URLs, and FQDNs on your firewall with some ports and protocols. All the IP subnets, URLs, and FQDNs are listed at `https://aka.ms/o365ip`.

You must also open ports 80 and 443/TCP for all the Teams signaling uses. For media traffic, you must open UDP ports from 3478 to 3481 as preferred and 443/TCP as a fallback. Remember, UDP is always preferred for a better experience than TCP for real-time communications. Ensure the UDP traffic is enabled and avoid proxy servers that might enforce Teams media to TCP traffic.

It is recommended that you bypass Teams traffic from any packet inspection or security stack that might add latency or hold the packet for inspection. If you use VPN connections for remote users, split tunnel the traffic for Microsoft 365 Teams.

Managing a Teams Meeting

Let's look at how to manage a meeting.

Meeting Configuration

In managing a Teams meeting configuration, some global meeting settings apply to all users and all meetings. Meeting policies can be assigned on a per-user basis. By default, all users are assigned with the global policy unless you, an admin, assign a specific policy to be used.

The meeting organizer's policy will be applied to a meeting, so if the organizer has certain rights, all the attendees can use the same feature functionality. Meeting configuration policies can be configured in the Microsoft Teams admin center and by using Windows PowerShell.

Meeting Settings Applied to All Meetings

You can configure several global meeting settings that apply to all users. You can allow or block anonymous participants from meetings, customize meeting invites, and specify network settings, such as QoS marking and customized port ranges.

Meeting Policies Assigned to Users

Meeting policies assigned per user means you can create policies that allow more features to a set of users and restrict some features to specific users per custom requirements. You can configure users to schedule meetings if they can do ad hoc meetings, use Outlook add-ins, or schedule channel or private meetings. The best recommendation is to enable all of these features to provide the maximum opportunity to collaborate, but you should consider your organization's policy.

You can allow features such as transcripts, recording, audio, and video. You can set bandwidth limits and configure contact sharing; for example, whether users share an entire screen, an app only, or this is disabled entirely. You can configure users to allow them to request control for internal users, external users, or both. You can also enable or disable PowerPoint sharing, whiteboards, and shared notes.

You can configure users to schedule and join webinars by allowing meeting registration for better meeting engagement. Additionally, meeting policies allow for customizing recording options, such as enabling recording, setting default expiration time, storage, meeting options, and live captions.

For participants and guests, you can turn on or off the ability of anonymous users to dial out from meetings and start meetings. You can also set lobby settings, such as allowing everyone, everyone in your organization, or everyone in your organization and federated organizations.

Remember that the Global (Org-wide default) policy is created by default, and all the users within the organization will be assigned this meeting policy. As a Teams admin, you can decide if changes must be made to this policy, or you can create one or more custom policies and assign those to users as appropriate.

Creating and Managing Meeting Policy

You can create a new meeting policy or manage the existing meeting policy using the Teams admin center. To create a new meeting policy, follow the steps given next. A meeting policy has different sections: meeting scheduling, meeting join and lobby, meeting engagement, content sharing, recording and transcription, and audio and video.

1. Log in to the Teams admin center. In the left navigation pane, select Meetings. Select Meeting Policies. Click + Add to create a new meeting policy.

2. Once the New Meeting Policy page opens, enter a meaningful name for the new policy and optionally enter a description. In the meeting scheduling section, select whether to turn the following options on or off:

   - **Private meeting scheduling:** Users can schedule private meetings with this setting turned on.

   - **Meet now in private meetings:** This option controls whether users can start an instant private meeting.

   - **Channel meeting scheduling:** Meeting organizers can allow users to schedule channel meetings within channels they belong to with this setting.

   - **Meet now in channel meetings:** This setting enables meeting organizers to allow users to start instant meetings within channels they belong to.

   - **Outlook add-in:** Organizers can schedule private meetings from Outlook by turning on this setting.

   - **Meeting registration:** This option allows organizers to require registration for participants to join a meeting.

   - **Who can register:** This determines who is eligible to register for meetings.

   - **Attendance report:** Organizers can turn attendance reports on or off with this setting.

   - **Who is in the attendance report:** This setting controls whether participants can share their attendance information in the Attendance Report.

   - **Attendance summary:** This option controls whether to show attendance time information, such as join times, leave times, and in-meeting duration, for each meeting participant

Figure 4-9 shows all options in the meeting scheduling section set to On.

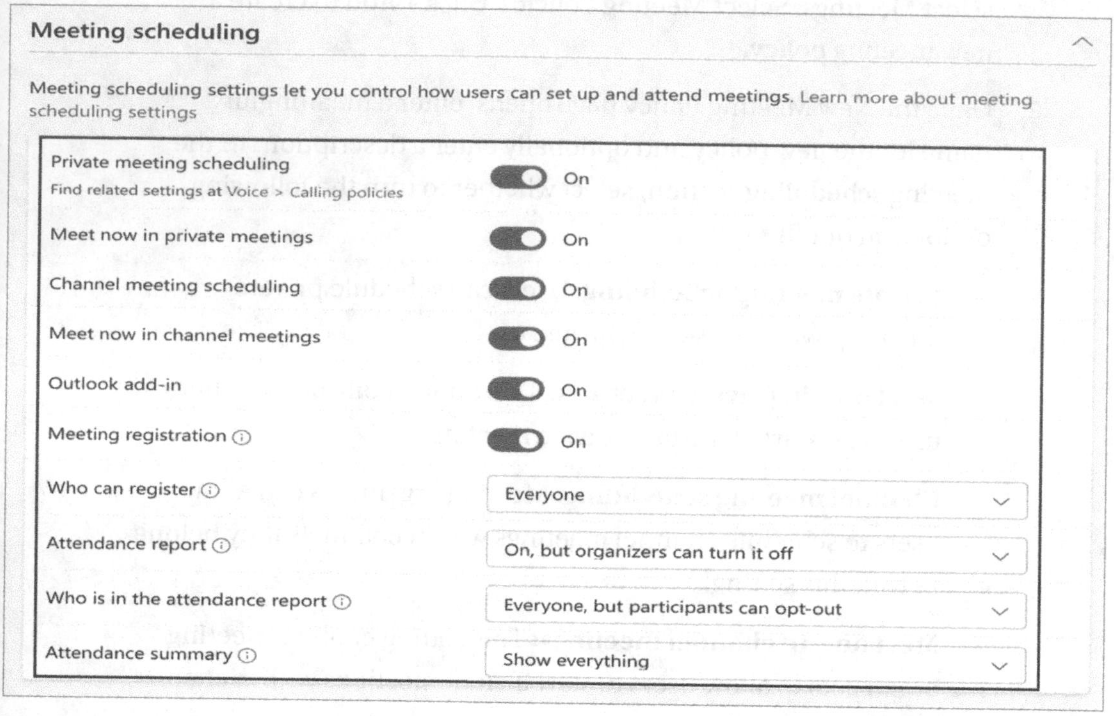

Figure 4-9. *Meeting policy meeting scheduling settings*

For example, Allow Meet Now is a policy applied before starting the meetings and has a per-user model. This policy controls whether the user can start a meeting in a Teams channel without the meeting having been previously scheduled. If you turn this feature on, when a user posts a message in a Teams channel, the user can select Meet Now to initialize an ad hoc meeting in the channel.

3. In the Meeting Join and Lobby section, turn the following options on or off:

    Anonymous users can join a meeting: When this setting is on; anyone can join Teams meetings, including Teams users in other organizations.

Anonymous users and dial-in callers can start a meeting: If you turn on this setting, anonymous users and dial-in users (those who join through a phone call) can start a meeting even if no one else is there.

Who can bypass the lobby: This setting allows you to control who can join a meeting directly and who must wait until they are admitted. This setting controls the default value of who can bypass the lobby in Meeting options; organizers and co-organizers can change this when they set up Teams meetings.

People dialing in can bypass the lobby: Controls whether people who dial in by phone join the meeting directly or wait in the lobby, regardless of who can bypass the lobby setting.

Figure 4-10 shows a summary of the "Meeting join & lobby" settings.

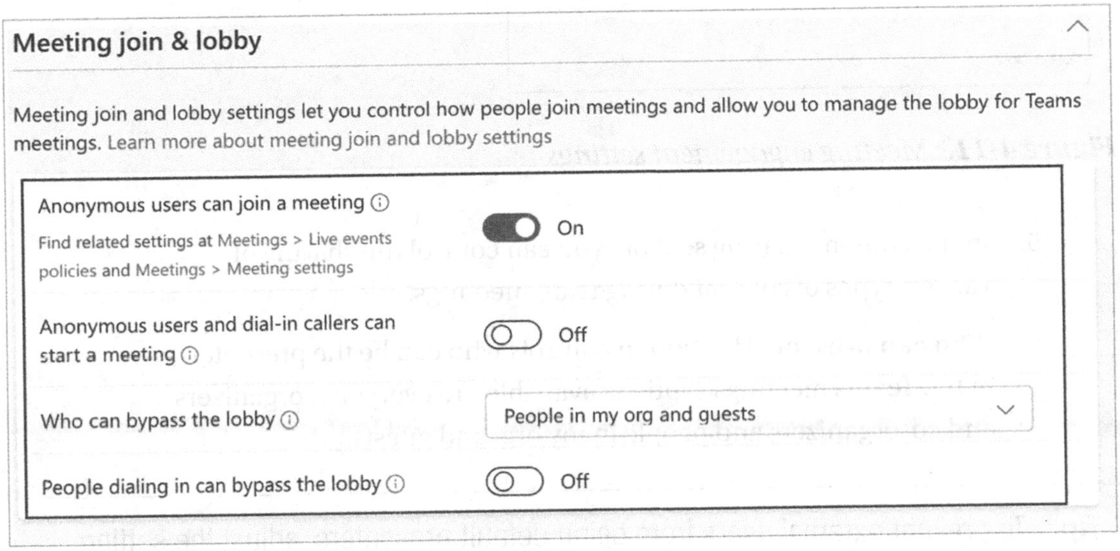

Figure 4-10. Meeting join & lobby settings

4. The Meeting Engagement section, shown in Figure 4-11, will help the admin control how people interact with meeting in an organization. The options available are as follows:

Meeting Chat: This feature allows the admin to decide who can participate in the meeting chat.

Q&A: When turned on, organizers can enable a question-and-answer feature for their meetings.

Reactions: In Teams meetings, this feature allows users to use live reactions such as Like, Love, Applause, Laugh, and Surprise.

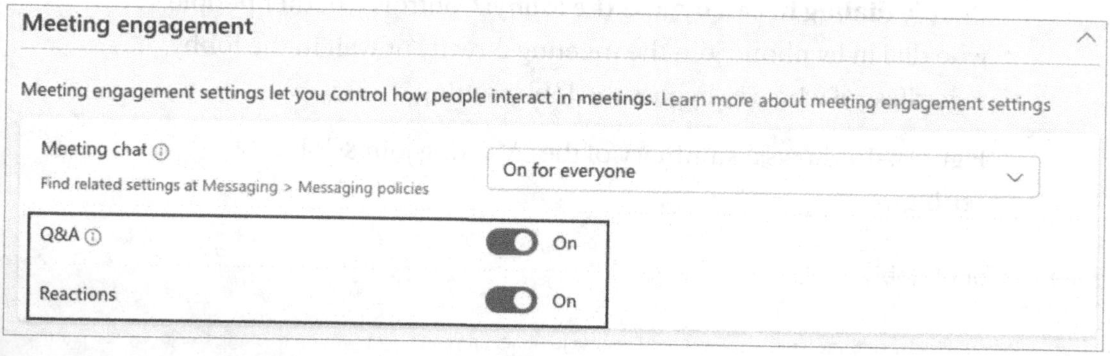

Figure 4-11. Meeting engagement settings

5. In the content-sharing section, you can control the sharing of various types of content during team meetings.

Who can present: This option controls who can be the presenter in the Teams meetings. Options available are everyone, organizers and co-organizers and people in my org, and guests.

Tip   To prevent external users from being default presenters, adjust the setting called "People in my organization and guests."

Screen sharing mode: This controls whether desktop and window sharing is allowed in the user's meeting.

Participants can give or request control: This setting allows users to choose whether to give control of the shared desktop or window to other participants in the meeting.

External participants can give or request control: You can control whether external participants, anonymous users, and guests can take control of shared screens during Teams meetings. Both organizations must enable this feature for an external participant to take control.

PowerPoint Live: This feature lets the meeting organizer decide if users can share PowerPoint slide decks during the meeting.

Whiteboard: This feature determines if a user can share the whiteboard during a meeting. Participants not part of the organization, such as guests and anonymous users, will follow the same rules inherited from the meeting organizer.

Shared notes: This feature allows attendees to share notes during a meeting. See Figure 4-12.

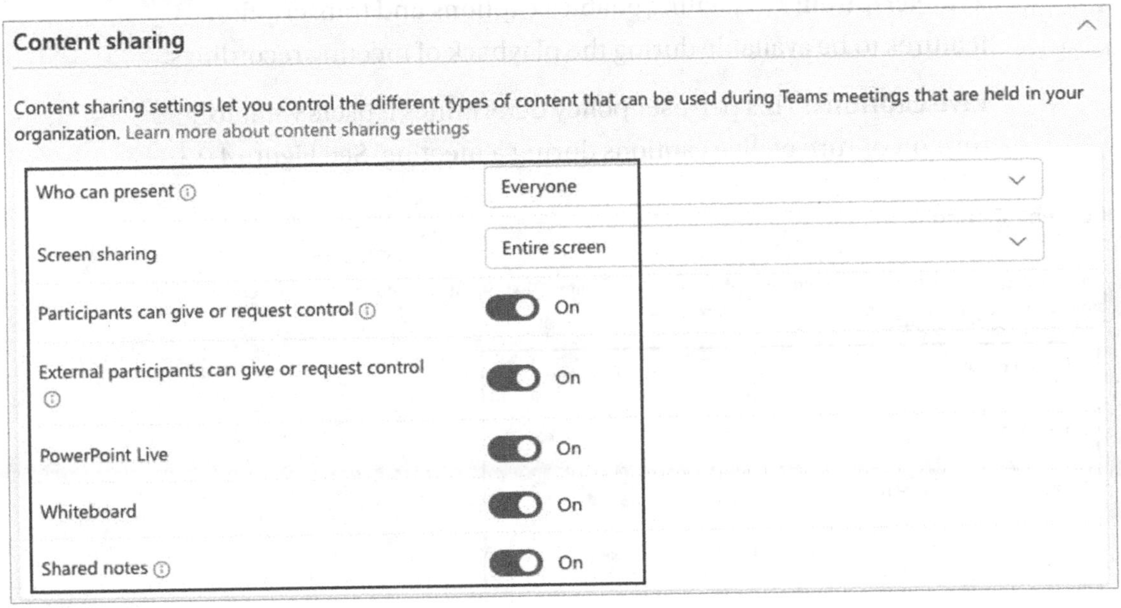

Content sharing

Content sharing settings let you control the different types of content that can be used during Teams meetings that are held in your organization. Learn more about content sharing settings

Who can present ⓘ	Everyone ⌄
Screen sharing	Entire screen ⌄
Participants can give or request control ⓘ	On
External participants can give or request control ⓘ	On
PowerPoint Live	On
Whiteboard	On
Shared notes ⓘ	On

Figure 4-12. Content sharing settings

6. The recording and transcription sections allow you to manage the capabilities and features related to recording and transcribing.

Meeting recording: When turned on, users can record their Teams meetings and group calls.

Note   To record a meeting, the organizer and the person who initiated the recording must be permitted to record.

Recordings automatically expire: This feature allows you to set up automatic recording expiration after the number of days set in the default expiration time setting.

Default expiration time: You can set up the default meeting expiration time from 1 to 99999 days. By default, it is set to 120 days within the org-wide policy.

Store recordings outside your country or region: To store meeting recordings outside your country or region, enable the meeting recording and this setting.

Transcription: This setting enables captions and transcription features to be available during the playback of meeting recordings.

Live captions: This per-user policy determines if users want to turn on or turn off live captions during a meeting. See Figure 4-13.

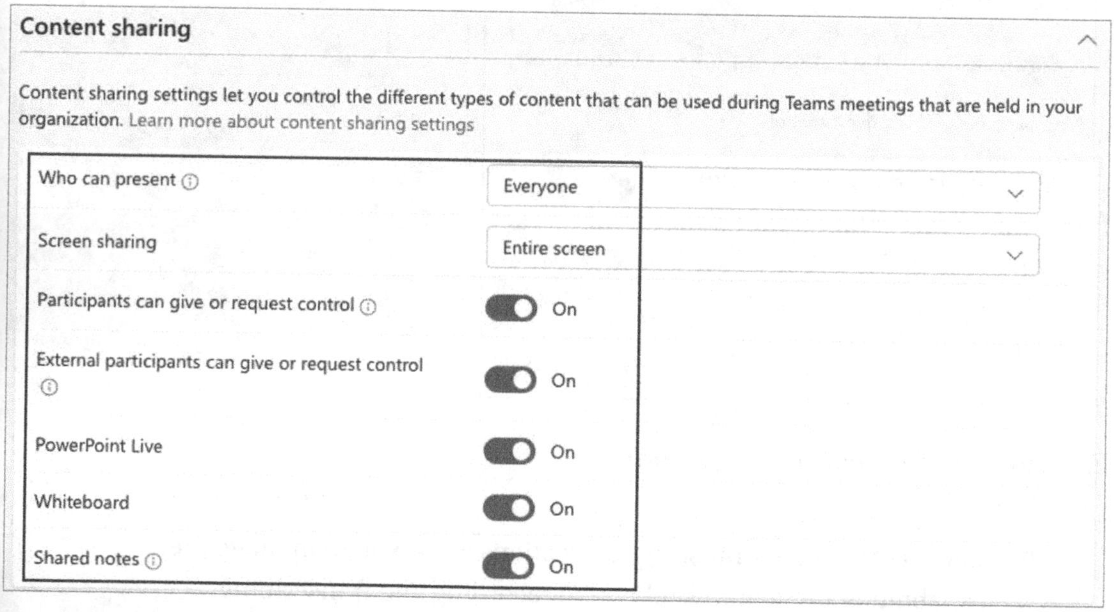

Figure 4-13. *Recording and transcription*

Additional attributes are available for recording and transcription through PowerShell. These attributes include the following:

- Allow cart caption Scheduling

- Channel record download

- Enroll user override

- Live interpretation enabled type

- Meeting invite languages

- Speaker attribute mode:

- Room attribute user override

7. Audio and video settings let you turn on audio and video capabilities within a Teams meeting.

Mode for IP audio: This feature allows you to control whether you can turn on or off audio (incoming and outgoing) during meetings and group calls.

Mode for IP video: This feature allows you to control whether you can turn on or off video (incoming and outgoing) during meetings and group calls.

IP video: This option allows the user to determine if video can be enabled during meetings, one-on-one calls, and group calls. If using Teams on a mobile device, this option controls the ability to share photos and videos during a meeting.

Local broadcasting: Capture and broadcast audio and video using NDI Technology

Media bit rate (Kbs): This option controls the quality (media bit rate) of audio, video, and screen sharing during calls and meetings. This is a great option to configure for low-bandwidth sites in your organization.

Network configuration lookup: If enabled, the roaming policies in the network topology will be verified.

Participants can use video effects: This feature allows them to choose whether to customize their camera feed with video backgrounds and filters.

Live streaming: This allows users to stream their Teams meetings using RTMP. See Figure 4-14.

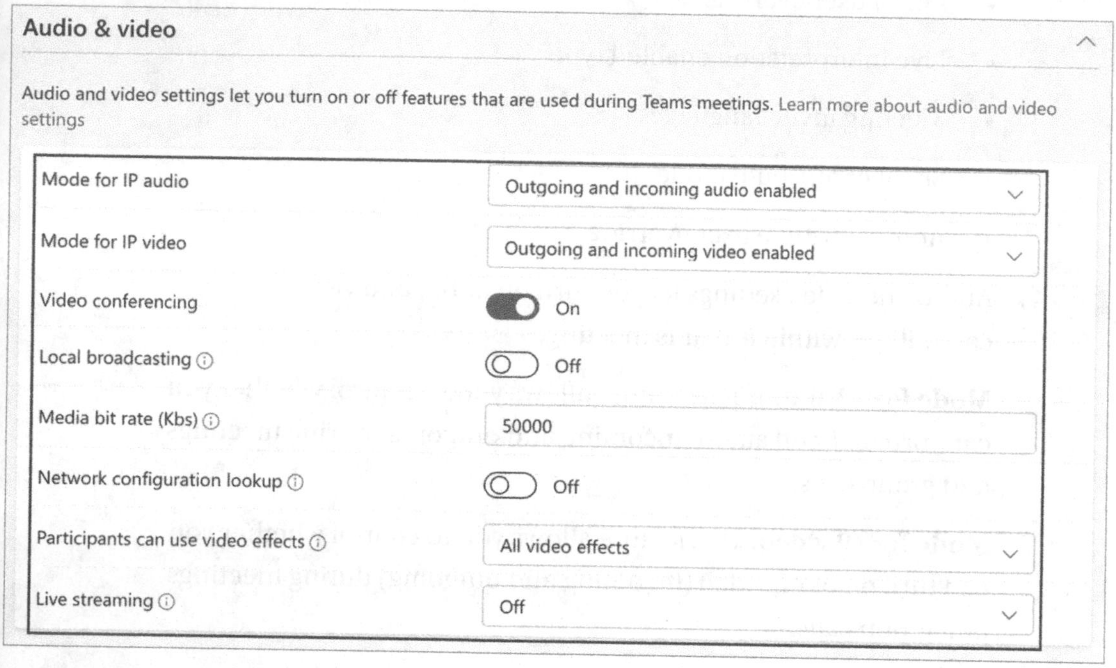

Audio & video

Audio and video settings let you turn on or off features that are used during Teams meetings. Learn more about audio and video settings

Mode for IP audio	Outgoing and incoming audio enabled
Mode for IP video	Outgoing and incoming video enabled
Video conferencing	On
Local broadcasting ⓘ	Off
Media bit rate (Kbs) ⓘ	50000
Network configuration lookup ⓘ	Off
Participants can use video effects ⓘ	All video effects
Live streaming ⓘ	Off

Figure 4-14. Audio and video settings

Once you have finished entering your settings, click Save to commit the changes.

Checking Teams Meeting Quality

To check the quality of Teams meetings, there are two tools you can use. The first is Call Quality Dashboard (CQD), which gives aggregated views of call quality and can be used to investigate quality per building, subnet, or any other metric that makes sense in your scenarios. You can use the CQD to proactively identify quality issues by looking at the lowest-quality site and determining how to improve call quality. To access the CQD, log in to the Teams admin center and click Call Quality Dashboard. You should sign in again to the CQD.

Call analytics is the second tool you can use. This allows you to view individual calls and see the quality of a specific call for both one-to-one calls and Teams meetings. Call analytics can be used reactively to troubleshoot individual calls that a user reports as a poor call quality experience. To access call analytics, log in to the Teams admin center and select Users. Find the individual user whose call quality you want to check and then click Call History. Select the individual call to check call quality, as Figure 4-15 shows.

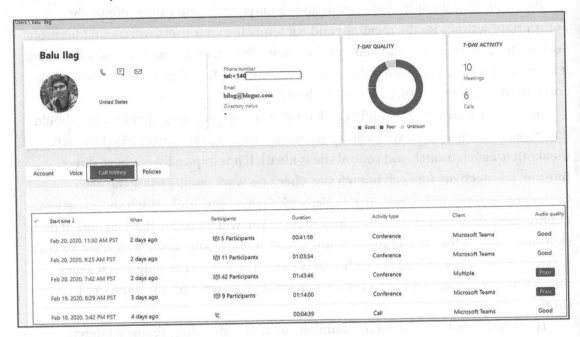

Figure 4-15. *Call analytics*

Microsoft Teams Audio Conferencing

You have already learned how Microsoft Teams meetings work; how Teams provides audio, video, and content sharing through the data network (VoIP); and how the Teams client allows users to join meetings.

This topic covers Teams Audio Conferencing (dial-in), including how Teams Audio Conferencing works, how to acquire a conference bridge, Audio Conferencing licensing, dial-out limits, and more. Teams Audio Conferencing allows attendees to join Teams meetings through dial-in to a Teams conference bridge number with a conference ID through a regular phone (landline or mobile phone). Teams Audio Conferencing is also known as Teams *dial-in conferencing*. For example, users can use Audio Conferencing to attend meetings over a regular phone by dialing into the meeting.

As a Teams admin, you can customize Teams meeting modalities and experiences per your organization's requirements. For example, you can turn certain types of meetings on or off in addition to disabling modalities such as video or screen sharing. Because there is integration between Microsoft 365 tools such as Microsoft Outlook, users can use an add-in to schedule Teams meetings directly from their Outlook calendar.

Based on your organization's needs and requirements, you can configure the appropriate settings for the meetings and conferencing your users will use in Microsoft Teams. Because this communication workspace offers so many options and advantages, it is crucial for you, as a Teams admin, to review and confirm that your environment is configured correctly to provide users the best possible experience.

Before deploying Teams Audio Conferencing across your organization, you should ensure all user locations have Internet access to connect to Microsoft 365 (Internet breakout for each branch and central site is ideal). If it is impossible to have direct Internet connectivity for each branch site, check network quality using the O365 Connectivity Tool or Microsoft Teams Network Assessment Tool, which shows network quality, including packet loss, jitter, and latency. You will therefore have an idea of users' experience when they use Teams meetings. Additionally, you must check whether your network is ready to deploy Microsoft Teams meetings. Before learning about Teams Audio Conferencing, as a Teams admin, you must know what phone numbers Teams supports.

This topic covers Teams service numbers in detail, including Teams conference numbers and the numbers used for the auto attendant and call queue, including toll and toll-free numbers.

Teams Audio Conferencing Licensing Requirements

To use Teams Audio Conferencing, your organization needs an additional license on top of the Microsoft Teams license. Microsoft 365 Audio Conferencing (Teams Audio Conferencing) licenses are available as part of an Office 365 E5 subscription or as an add-on license to an existing subscription like E1 or E3. Microsoft is offering a free Microsoft Teams Audio Conferencing license that includes dial-out capabilities to users in the United States and Canada. These licenses can be assigned to individual users for their audio conferencing needs. However, it's important to note that dial-out is available only to users in the United States and Canada. Users in other regions must be assigned communication credits to dial out from Teams meetings.

Teams Audio Conferencing Requirements

Teams Audio Conferencing involves the Audio Conferencing licenses, the conference dial-in bridge (phone numbers for dial-in), and communications credits for dialing out from Teams meetings. As part of the Teams Audio Conferencing license, Microsoft provides dedicated dial-in bridge numbers (an admin must acquire the dial-in numbers from Microsoft) and shared conference numbers. Suppose your organization uses a legacy solution like Skype for Business (Lync) On-Premises or Online with enterprise voice and dial-in conferencing with their conference bridge numbers. In that case, the organization might use the existing conference bridge for Teams meetings when upgrading from Skype for Business to Microsoft Teams. Microsoft allows using these service phone numbers by porting them from your current service provider to Microsoft 365. This means you can use Microsoft-provided conference bridge numbers, either dedicated or shared or porting your existing service numbers

As a Teams admin, you must configure a Teams conference bridge number. Conferencing bridge numbers allow users to dial into meetings through a landline or mobile phone. When configuring Teams Audio Conferencing in your Microsoft 365 environment, you will receive conference bridge numbers from Microsoft for an Audio Conferencing bridge (a conferencing bridge can contain one or more phone numbers). These conference bridge numbers are used when the users dial into a Teams meeting (the phone number should be included in every Microsoft Teams meeting invite). When an organization enables the audio conference license, shared audio conference bridge numbers are automatically assigned to their tenant. However, a dedicated conference bridge number (toll or toll-free) is available based on request. As an admin, you can obtain a toll or toll-free conference number from Microsoft by using the Teams admin center or creating a ticket with the PSTN Service desk by going to https://pstnsd.powerappsportals.com/create-ticket/.

As a Teams admin, you can continue using the default settings for a conferencing bridge, or you can change the phone numbers (toll and toll-free) and other settings (e.g., the PIN or the languages used). However, you must first decide if you need to add new conferencing bridge numbers, which number should be your default, whether you need to modify the bridge settings, and whether you must port numbers to use with audio conferencing.

Adding Dedicated Conference Bridge Numbers

You must perform the following steps to add a dedicated conference bridge number:

1. Log in to the Teams admin center, and in the left pane, select Meetings. Then select Conference Bridges. On the Conference Bridges page, click + Add.

2. From the + Add drop-down list, select either Toll Number or Toll-Free Number, as shown in Figure 4-16.

3. On the Add Phone Number page, select the phone number you want to add, and then click Apply.

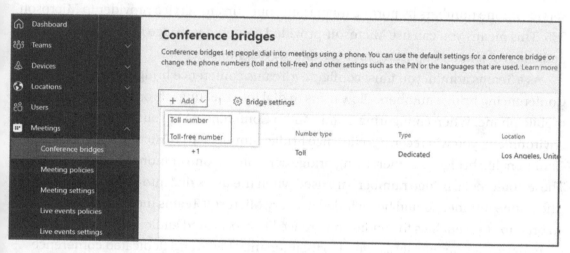

Figure 4-16. Adding a conference bridge number

Setting a Default Conference Bridge Number

To configure a default number for your conference bridge, perform this procedure:

1. On the Conference Bridges page, in the main pane that shows all the conference bridge phone numbers, select the phone number you want to configure as your default.

2. Click Set As Default on the menu bar, as shown in Figure 4-17.

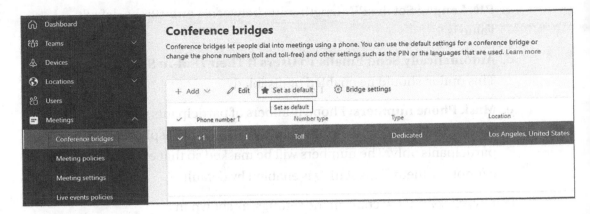

Figure 4-17. Setting a default conference bridge

Configuring and Managing Teams Conference Bridge Settings

To configure conference bridge settings, follow these steps:

1. Log in to the Teams admin center and select Meetings. Select Conference Bridges, and click Bridge Settings on the Conference Bridges page.

2. You can set the following options in the Bridge Settings window to configure bridge settings:

    a. **Meeting Entry And Exit Notifications:** You can turn this setting on or off, depending on whether you want users who have already joined the meeting to be notified when someone enters or leaves the meeting. If this setting is on, you can choose from the following options.

    b. **Entry/Exit Announcement Type:** Select one of the following options.

        i. **Names Or Phone Numbers:** When users dial into a meeting, their phone number will be displayed when they join.

        ii. **Tones:** When users dial into a meeting, an audio tone will be played when they join.

      c. **PIN Length:** Set the PIN length value between 4 and 12; the default value is 5.

      d. **Automatically Send Emails To Users If Their Dial-in Settings Change:** This option should be enabled or disabled.

      e. **Mask Phone numbers:** Phone numbers of participants who join a Teams meeting via audio conferencing will be fully displayed to internal participants only. The numbers will be masked so that external participants cannot see them. This setting is enabled by default.

3. Finally, click Apply to confirm the settings, as shown in Figure 4-18.

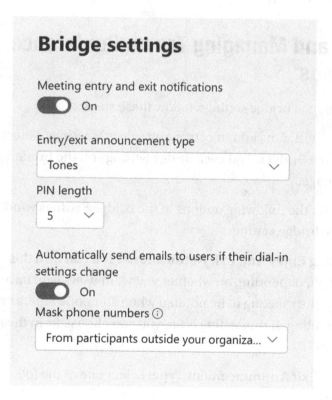

Figure 4-18. *Conference bridge settings*

Setting Up and Managing Communications Credits for Audio Conferencing

Before setting up communications credits, a Teams admin must understand what communications credits are and how they will help. So far, you have learned about Teams meetings and Audio Conferencing, and you know Teams Audio Conferencing allows users to dial out from a meeting to add someone to the Teams meeting. Dialing out from Teams meetings has some limitations, however. Users can dial out from Teams meetings only to certain countries, and the number of minutes is limited. To use Audio Conferencing, each organization has to buy an add-on license to use dial-in and dial-out functionalities in Teams meetings. Limited dial-out minutes are allowed with each Audio Conferencing license subscription.

A Microsoft 365 Audio Conferencing license subscription offers 60 minutes per user per month that can be used to dial out to non-Premium numbers in any of the Zone A countries (Australia, Austria, Belgium, Brazil, Bulgaria, Canada, China, Croatia, Czech Republic, Denmark, Estonia, Finland, France, Germany, Greece, Hong Kong, Hungary, India, Ireland, Italy, Japan, Luxembourg, Malaysia, Mexico, Netherlands, New Zealand, Norway, Poland, Portugal, Puerto Rico, Romania, Russia, Singapore, Slovak Republic, Slovenia, South Africa, South Korea, Spain, Sweden, Switzerland, Taiwan, Thailand, United Kingdom, United States). Microsoft considers the number of Audio Conferencing licenses as the *tenant dial-out pool.* The total number of Audio Conferencing licenses multiplied by 60 minutes will be the monthly dial-out minute pool for the organization. For example, the Cyclotron organization has purchased 50 Audio Conferencing subscription licenses. It has 30 users in the United States, 10 in the United Kingdom, and 10 in India. All these Audio Conferencing subscription licenses are assigned to the users. All 50 users share a pool of 50 users × 60 minutes = 3,000 conferencing dial-out minutes per calendar month that can be used to place outbound calls to nonpremium numbers in any of the Zone A countries (refer to https://docs.microsoft.com/en-us/microsoftteams/audio-conferencing-subscription-dial-out), regardless of where the meeting organizer is licensed or physically located. For example, as a meeting organizer, Cyclotron User B in India can dial out to any of the Zone A countries up to the minute pool limit (i.e., 3,000 minutes).

Note   All dial-out calls exceeding 3,000 minutes per calendar month are billed per minute using communications credits at Microsoft-published rates to that destination.

As an admin, you need to set up communications credits if you would like to use toll-free numbers with Microsoft Teams. Microsoft recommends that you set up communications credits for your Calling Plans (domestic or international) and Audio Conferencing users who need the ability to dial out to any destination. Many countries and regions are included, but some destinations might not be included in the Calling Plan or Audio Conferencing subscriptions. Suppose you don't set up communications credits billing and assign a Communications Credits license to your users. You run out of minutes for your organization (depending on your Calling Plan or Audio Conferencing plan in your country or region). Those users won't be able to make calls or dial out from Audio Conferencing meetings.

Communications credits provide a convenient way to pay for Audio Conferencing and Calling Plan minutes. It ensures users have the ability to add toll-free numbers to use with Audio Conferencing meetings, auto attendants, or call queues. Toll-free calls are billed per minute and require a positive communications credits balance. Dialing out from an Audio Conferencing meeting to add someone else from anywhere in the world requires dial-out credit. Additionally, communications credits get used when users dial any international phone number when they have a Domestic Calling Plan subscription or dial international phone numbers beyond what is included in a Domestic and International Calling Plan subscription. Another important use case for communications credits is dialing out and paying per minute once you have exhausted your monthly minute allotment.

Assigning Communications Credits to a User

You can assign Communications Credits licenses to individual users as an admin by logging in to Microsoft 365 admin center. Navigate to Users. Select Active Users and then select the particular user and enable a Communications Credits license for that user.

Checking Communications Credits Plans and Pricing

Before setting communications credits, you must check the plans and pricing. To do so, log in to the Microsoft 365 admin center (`https://portal.office.com/adminportal/home?add=sub&adminportal=1#/catalog`) and navigate to the Marketplace and validate the subscription plans.

Setting Up Communications Credits for a Tenant

Next you need to know how to set up communications credits for your organization. To do so, follow this procedure:

1. Log in to the Microsoft Office 365 admin center (`https://admin.microsoft.com/Adminportal/Home?`) with your work or school account. Click Billing and then select Purchase Services. Scroll down and select Add-Ons.

2. Select Communications Credits. Enter your information on the Communications Credits subscription page, and click Next.

3. In the Add Funds Field, enter the amount you want to add to your account.

4. Microsoft recommends enabling the Auto-Recharge option. It automatically refills your account when the balance falls below your set threshold. If you don't enable this setting, once the funds are used, calling capabilities enabled using communications credits will be disrupted (e.g., inbound toll-free service). Auto-recharge avoids manually adding a communications credits balance each time your balance reaches zero. This feature is selected in the example in Figure 4-19, and $100 in funds has been added for the Cyclotron organization.

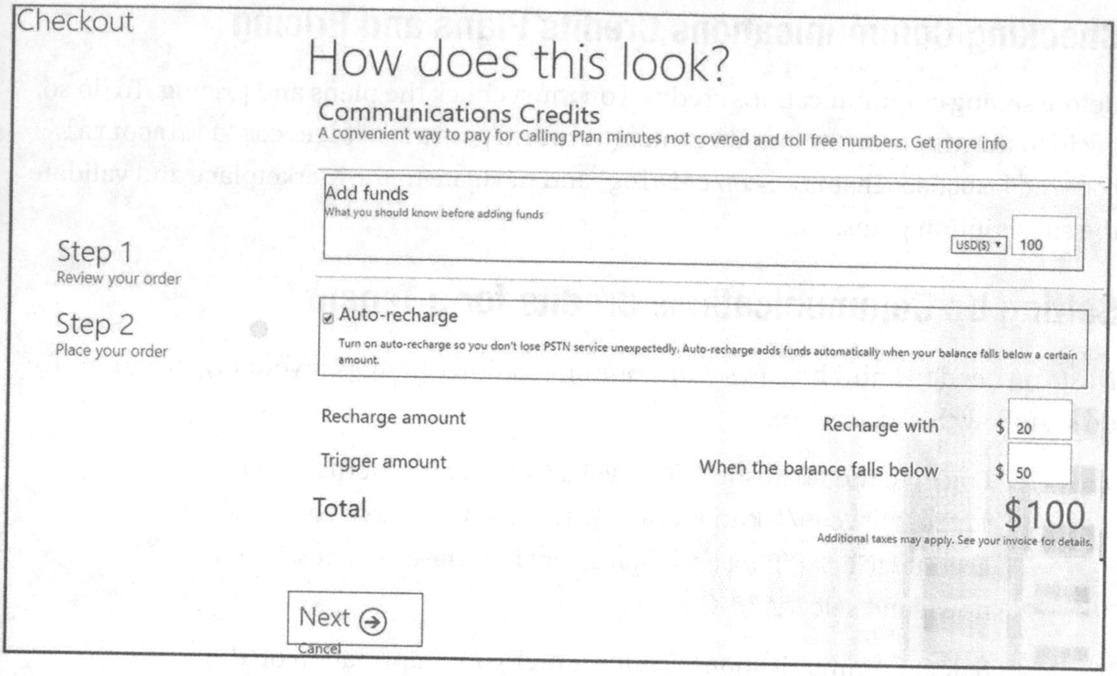

Figure 4-19. Communications credits

Note   Remember the funds will be applied only to communications credits at Microsoft's published rates when the services are used. Any funds not used within 12 months of the purchase date will expire and be lost, so set the credit level based on your usage.

---

5.   Monthly billing for communications credits will be applied only if the allotted funds have been used. To learn how to check your monthly usage, read the next section.

6.   Finally, enter your payment information and click Place Order.

Checking a Tenant's PSTN Usage

Every organization will have a different usage rate because usage is dependent on call volume and rates the provider charges. As an admin, you must get this usage data from your current PSTN service provider. For organizations using Skype for Business Online and

Microsoft as a PSTN service provider, you can get usage data by reviewing it in the Microsoft 365 admin center (Analytics and Reports ➤ Usage Reports ➤ PSTN Usage Details).

When setting up communications credits, you must examine your organization's call usage details to determine your needed amounts. You can get call usage information by reviewing the PSTN usage details report. This report lets you export the call data records to Microsoft Excel and create custom reports.

Managing an Individual User's Conference Bridge Number and Language for Teams Meetings

To manage an individual user's conference bridge number, log in to the Teams admin center and navigate to Users. Find the individual user whose conference bridge number you want to check, and then under Account, view the Audio Conferencing settings for the individual, as shown in Figure 4-20.

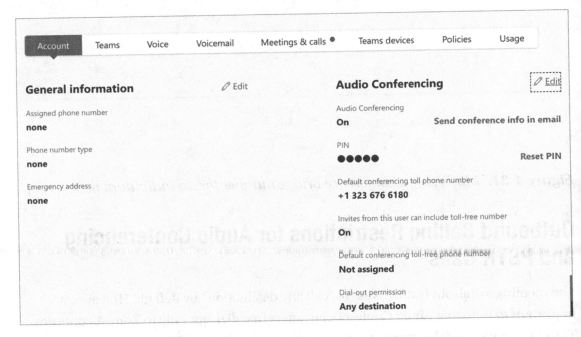

Figure 4-20. Audio Conferencing settings

Under Audio Conferencing, click Edit to modify the settings. On the Audio Conference page, turn on Audio Conferencing, modify the Toll Number or Toll-Free Number values, and modify the Dial-Out From Meetings setting if required. Figure 4-21 shows the settings for this example.

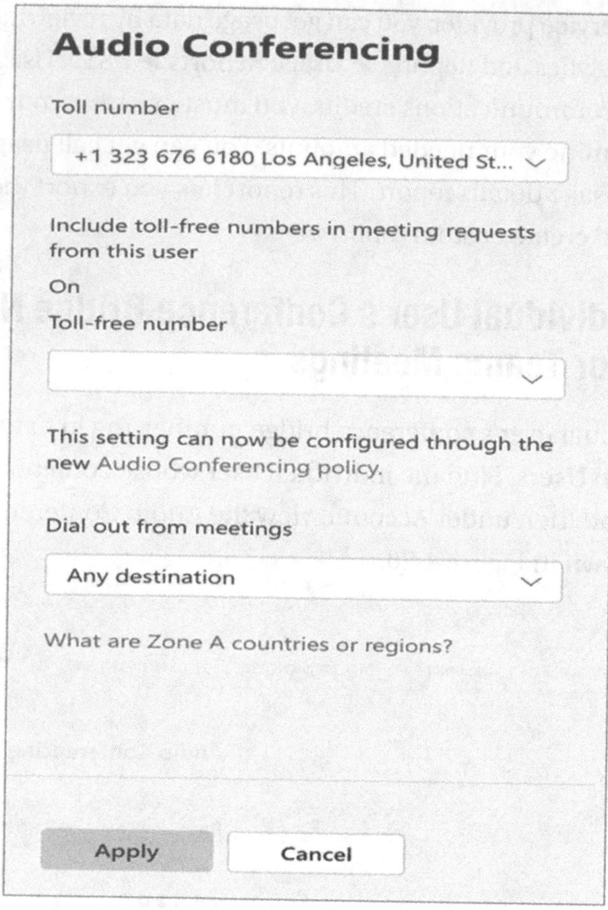

Audio Conferencing

Toll number

+1 323 676 6180 Los Angeles, United St... ⌄

Include toll-free numbers in meeting requests
from this user

On

Toll-free number

⌄

This setting can now be configured through the
new Audio Conferencing policy.

Dial out from meetings

Any destination ⌄

What are Zone A countries or regions?

[Apply]   [Cancel]

Figure 4-21. Modifying a conference bridge number for an individual user

Outbound Calling Restrictions for Audio Conferencing and PSTN Calls

The meeting's dial-out feature is set to "call any destination" by default. However, it's important to note that Audio Conferencing offers free dial-out only to Zone A countries. The organization will be charged pay-per-minute rates for countries outside Zone A based on the specific country. These charges will be deducted from the communication credits. Sometimes, the admin may want to restrict users from dialing out to countries outside of Zone A to prevent unnecessary costs. This can be achieved by changing the user's audio conferencing settings using Windows PowerShell.

```
Grant-CsDialoutPolicy -Identity <username> -PolicyName <policy name>
```

The following table provides an overview of each policy.

PowerShell Cmdlet	Description
`Identity='tag:DialoutCPCandPSTN International'`	A user in the conference can dial out to international and domestic numbers, and this user can also make outbound calls to international and domestic numbers.
`Identity='tag:DialoutCPCDomestic PSTNInternational'`	A user in the conference can dial out only to domestic numbers, and this user can make outbound calls to international and domestic numbers.
`Identity='tag:DialoutCPCDisabled PSTNInternational'`	A user in the conference can't dial out. This user can make outbound calls to international and domestic numbers.
`Identity='tag: DialoutCPC InternationalPSTNDomestic'`	A user in the conference can dial out to international and domestic numbers, and this user can make outbound calls only to domestic PSTN numbers.
`Identity='tag: DialoutCPC InternationalPSTNDisabled'`	A user in the conference can dial out to international and domestic numbers, and this user cannot make any outbound calls to PSTN numbers besides emergency numbers.
`Identity='tag:DialoutCPCand PSTNDomestic'`	A user in the conference can dial out only to domestic numbers, and this user can make outbound calls only to domestic PSTN numbers.
`Identity='tag:DialoutCPCDomestic PSTNDisabled'`	A user in the conference can dial out only to domestic numbers, and this user cannot make any outbound calls to PSTN numbers besides emergency numbers.
`Identity='tag:DialoutCPCDisabled PSTNDomestic'`	A user in the conference can't dial out, and this user can make outbound calls only to domestic PSTN numbers.

(*continued*)

PowerShell Cmdlet	Description
Identity='tag:DialoutCPCandPSTN Disabled'	A user in the conference can't dial out, and this user can't make any outbound calls to PSTN numbers besides emergency numbers.
Identity='tag:DialoutCPCZone APSTNInternational'	A user in the conference can dial out only to Zone A countries and regions, and this user can make outbound calls to international and domestic numbers.
Identity='tag:DialoutCPCZone APSTNDomestic'	A user in the conference can dial out only to Zone A countries and regions, and this user can make outbound calls only to domestic PSTN numbers.
Identity='tag:DialoutCPCZone APSTNDisabled'	A user in the conference can dial out only to Zone A countries and regions, and this user can't make any outbound calls to PSTN numbers besides emergency numbers.

For example, if you have a requirement to prevent your users from dialing out to an international PSTN call but allow them for conferencing, assign a dial-out policy with the attribute DialoutCPCandPSTNDomestic. Note that if you assign this policy to U.S. users, they cannot dial out to outside the United States including Canada.

Configuring and Managing Meeting Policies

Teams meeting policies provide a way to permit or restrict features that will be available to users during the meetings and audio conferencing. Before proceeding, it's important to determine whether you want to customize the global meeting policies and/or if you require more than one meeting policy. You must now identify which user groups will be assigned to specific meeting policies. Finally, you must determine whether your organization must purchase and deploy room system devices for your conference rooms.

As a Teams administrator, you are responsible for managing meeting policies, which control the features of meetings scheduled by users within your organization. These policies are created and managed by you and are then assigned to specific users. You can manage meeting policies through the Microsoft Teams admin center or Windows

PowerShell. These policies directly affect the user's meeting experience before, during, and after the meeting ends. There are three different ways in which meeting policies can be applied.

- **Per meeting organizer:** All meeting participants receive the policy of the organizer.

- **Per user:** Only the per-user policy applies to restrict certain features for the organizer or meeting participants.

- **Per organizer and per user:** Certain features are restricted for meeting participants based on their policy and the organizer's policy.

Note   The policy named Global (Org-wide default) is created by default, and all the users within the organization will be assigned this meeting policy by default. The company administrators can decide if changes must be made to this policy, or they can decide to create one or more custom policies and assign those to users. You can refer to the previous section to create a new Teams meeting policy.

Teams Meeting Limitations

Administrators need to be aware that Teams meetings have certain limitations. Understanding these limitations allows them to determine if Teams meetings and audio conferencing suit your organization. One limitation is that Teams doesn't include a personal conference ID feature. However, you can use a meeting URL instead, which never expires. Here are some other limitations to keep in mind:

Feature	Maximum Limit
Number of people in a meeting (can chat and call in)	1000, includes GCC, GCCH, and DoD, but not A1 (300).
Number of people in a video or audio call from chat	20.

(*continued*)

Feature	Maximum Limit
Max PowerPoint file size	2 GB.
Meeting recording maximum length	4 hours or 1.5 GB. When this limit is reached, the recording will end and automatically restart.
Breakout room maximum participants in a meeting	300.
Teams meeting limit	30 hours.
Teams URL	Never expire.

Meeting Type	Expiration Time	Each time you start or update a meeting, expiration extends by this much time
Meet now	Start time + 8 hours	N/A
Regular with no end time	Start time + 60 days	60 days
Regular with end time	End time + 60 days	60 days
Recurring with no end time	Start time + 60 days	60 days
Recurring with end time	End time of last occurrence + 60 days	60 days

Type of Meeting	Number of Participants	Registration Supported
Meetings	Up to 20,000* Participants up to 1,000 have fully interactive equal meeting capabilities. Participants over 1,000 up to 20,000 have view-only capabilities	Yes
Webinars	Up to 1,000	Yes
Live events	Up to 20,000	No

Capability	Organizer	Co-organizer	Presenter	Attendee
Speak and share video	Yes	Yes	Yes	Yes
Participate in meeting chat	Yes	Yes	Yes	Yes
Share content	Yes	Yes	Yes	No
Privately view a PowerPoint file shared by someone else	Yes	Yes	Yes	Yes
Take control of someone else's PowerPoint presentation	Yes	Yes	Yes	No
Mute other participants	Yes	Yes	Yes	No
Prevent attendees from unmuting themselves	Yes	Yes	Yes	No
Remove participants	Yes	Yes	Yes	No
Admit people from the lobby	Yes	Yes	Yes	No
Change the roles of other participants	Yes	Yes	Yes	No
Start or stop recording	Yes	Yes	Yes	No
Start or stop live transcription	Yes	Yes	Yes	No
Manage breakout rooms	Yes	Yes	No	No
Change meeting options	Yes	Yes	No	No
Add or remove an app	Yes	Yes	Yes	No
Use an app	Yes	Yes	Yes	Yes
Change app settings	Yes	Yes	Yes	No

Teams Webinars

Teams Webinars is a meeting service available in the Teams meeting suite in addition to Teams Meeting and Teams Live events. This two-way interactive virtual event gives organizers more control over conversations and participants. Currently, webinars can accommodate up to 1,000 attendees, which are popular among training, product demos, customer events, etc. In this section, we will discuss how an admin can set up webinars for an organization, including scheduling a webinar and registering for one. We'll also cover the features of webinars and the licensing requirements.

Features of Webinars

You may be curious about the benefits of using webinars instead of Microsoft Teams meetings and Microsoft Live events, which have similar features. Webinars are particularly useful when you require a blend of Live events and Teams meetings. They provide superior registration capabilities compared to Teams meetings and offer more customizable event options than Teams Live events, including event-based themes and meeting options.

Here are the main features of webinars:

- Schedule webinars for up to 1,000 attendees

- Registration

- Assign co-organizers

- Restrict the webinars to org-wide only

- Limit the day and time when people register

- Adjust meeting options

Licensing

The Teams license provides access to basic webinars and their capabilities mentioned in the previous section, but a Teams Premium license offers additional robust features.

Teams Premium licensing is necessary to utilize the capabilities of Teams Webinars fully. The disparities in webinar features between Teams and Teams Premium are outlined in the "Teams Premium" section later in this chapter. As an administrator, it is essential to understand your organization's needs and acquire Teams Premium licenses accordingly. Teams Premium is an add-on subscription-based license. Additional details on Teams Premium are outlined in the "Teams Premium" section.

Here are some webinar-related features with Teams Premium as of this writing:

Set up a green room for webinar presenters: Presenters can use this feature to join early and make adjustments to audio, video, and content-sharing options. They can also communicate with other organizers and presenters before attendees join.

Create a webinar waiting list: By enabling the waitlist, the registration for a webinar will remain open even after the event has reached its capacity limit set by the organizer. This feature allows additional individuals to register and be automatically placed on the waitlist. As new spots become available, individuals on the waitlist will be notified and allowed to register for the event. Organizers can manually review the registration information and approve or reject each registration.

Limit the day and time when people register: An organizer can create a registration time limit for participants. Once the registration period has ended, users may either be added to a waitlist (if available) or can no longer register.

Manually approving the registrations: As an organizer, you can view all the registered participants and manually approve each one. This feature helps ensure that you have the exact group of attendees you need for the webinar event.

Send reminder emails to the registrants: When you enable this feature, an automated email will be sent to all attendees to remind them about the event. This helps build excitement and keeps everyone updated.

Manage Attendee views: This feature allows the organizer to manage the attendee view for a more streamlined event. The options include enabling attendees to only view the shared screen and participants, all presenters with their presentations, and more.

RTMP-In: The feature RTMP-In enables organizers to create Teams Webinars using an external encoder that users Real-Time Messaging Protocol (RTMP).

Teams Webinars Administration

If you are a Teams administrator, you can modify webinar settings for your organization using specific commands. Webinars are enabled by default, but admins can validate this by connecting to Microsoft Teams PowerShell module running this PowerShell command:

```
Get-CsTeamsEventsPolicy -Identity Global
```

The command returns the information about the Global policy. Under the attributes listed, Allow Webinar will be set to Enabled. To turn off webinars, use the PowerShell command to set Allow Webinar to Disabled.

```
Set-CsTeamsEventsPolicy -Identity Global -AllowWebinars Disabled
```

Currently, the administrator must also ensure that the "Allow registration" option is enabled in the meeting policies. This can be verified through this PowerShell command:

```
Get-CsTeamsEventsPolicy | select identity, AllowRegistration
```

If "Allow registration" is disabled, enable it using the following PowerShell command:

```
Set-CsTeamsMeetingPolicy -Identity Global -AllowRegistaration $True
```

As an administrator, you can restrict webinar registration to specific users. By default, registration is open to everyone or the public. However, using the PowerShell command, you can change this setting to only allow internal users and guests:

```
Set-CsTeamsEventsPolicy -Identity Global -EventAccessType
EveryoneInCompanyExcludingGuests
```

To change the settings back to everyone, use the following command:

```
Set-CsTeamsEventsPolicy -Identity Global -EventAccessType Everyone
```

This setting is also available via the Teams meeting policy. Use the following command to modify the changes:

```
Set-CsTeamsMeetingPolicy -Identity Global -Whocanregsiter EveryoneInCompnay
```

To revert to settings for everyone, use the following command:

```
Set-CsTeamsMeetingPolicy -Identity Global -Whocanregsiter Everyone
```

The event registration, RTMP-in, and RTMP-out capabilities are managed using meeting policies discussed in Chapter X and Chapter X.

Teams Webinars Scheduling

Let's look at an example. As an organizer, I plan a webinar to inform my organization about the newest Teams updates and give a brief overview of their features and communication tools. My administrator assigned me a Teams Premium license to take advantage of the webinar features with Teams Premium. I want to schedule the webinar for 30 minutes, limit registration time, add co-organizers, enable a green room for the presenters, and enable Q&A. Let's schedule a Teams webinar based on these requirements.

To schedule a Teams Webinar, go to Teams Calendar and click the down arrow located next to the New Meeting button; from the list of options, select and click Webinar, as shown in Figure 4-22.

Figure 4-22. *Scheduling a webinar*

On the details page, as shown in Figure 4-23, under the setup section, enter the title, the start and end time of the webinar event, and the description. Next, add your co-organizers and presenters to the meeting. As it is an internal event, choose your organization from the attendee options. At the bottom of the details page, you will find the default meeting options, which you can modify later as the organizer. Click Save and send invites. Please note that the invites will be sent only to the presenter and the organizers, not to your entire organization.

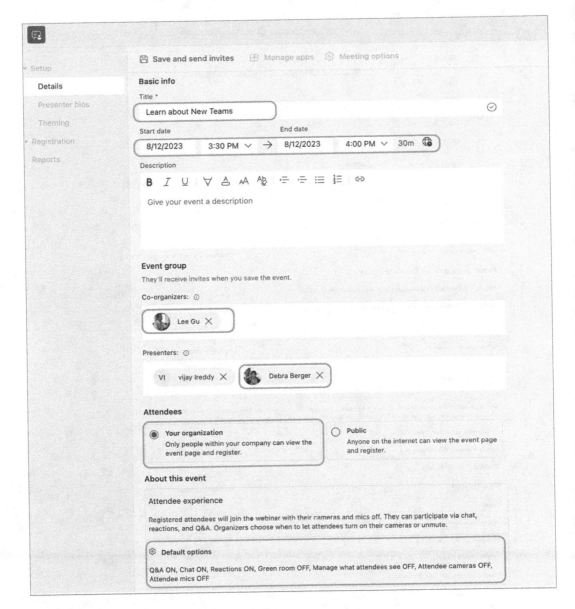

Figure 4-23. *Scheduling a Teams webinar, setup page*

Once the event details are saved, manage apps and meeting options appear on your details screen. As an organizer, I must allow Q&A for all the users and enable a green room as required. These settings can be adjusted in meeting options. As shown in Figure 4-24, click the meeting options, which opens a new browser window with a set of options to adjust. From the list of options, enable Green Room and Q&A and click Save. The detailed meeting options are explained in a later section.

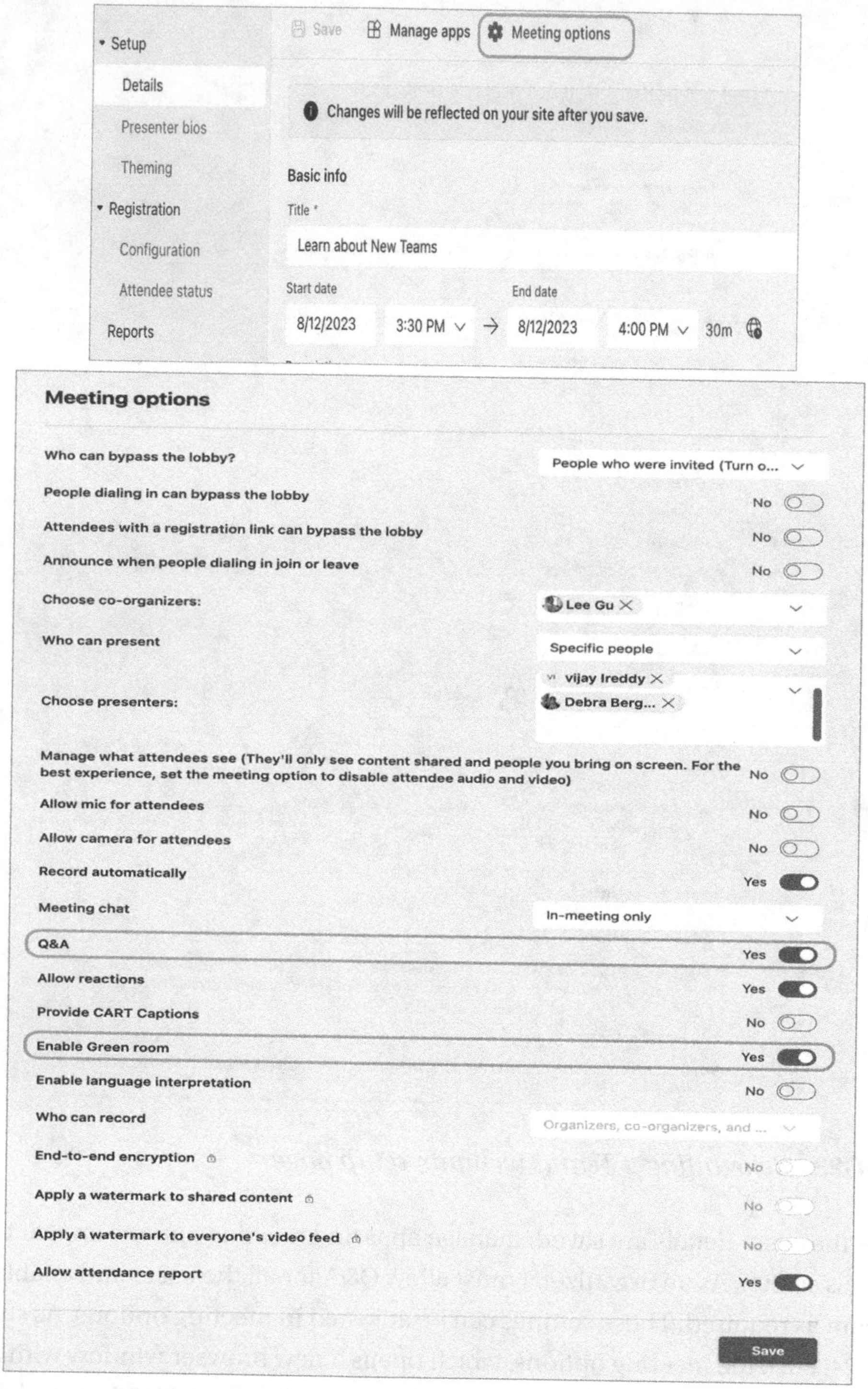

Figure 4-24. *Scheduling a webinar, meeting options*

To update a presenter's bio, return to the setup page and select "Presenter bios." Choose a presenter from the list and click Edit. Add any additional information about the presenter, like bio or photo, and then click Save. For instance, I added more details to a presenter's bio for this event, as shown in Figure 4-25.

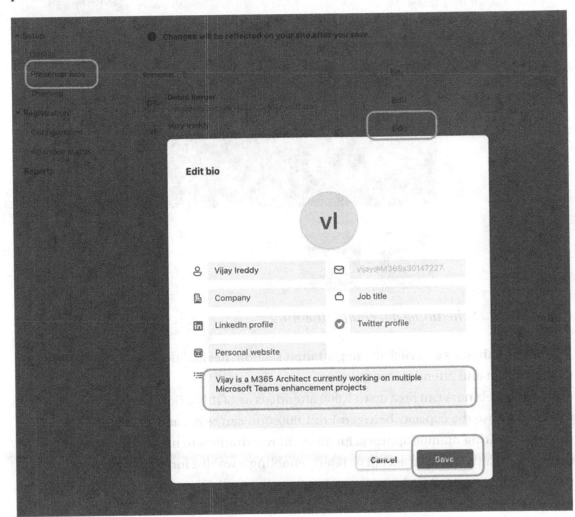

Figure 4-25. *Scheduling a webinar, presenter bio*

Return to the setup section and select Themes. You can choose your organization's banner image and theme color from there. As an organizer, you can customize your banner image, logo, and theme color to personalize the event. The images and theme colors updated here appear on the registration sites and in the emails sent to the attendees. In my current event, as shown in Figure 4-26, I chose a default theme color, banner image, and logo.

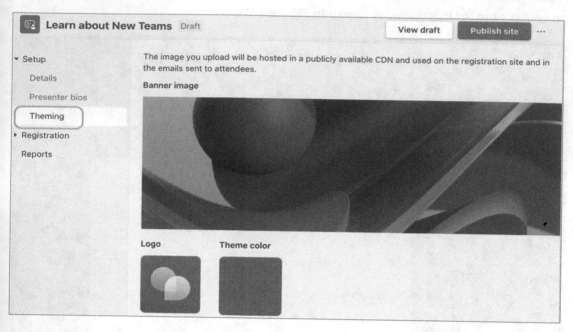

Figure 4-26. *Scheduling a webinar, theming*

Save the themes and click the Registration section. Registration sections contain configuration and attendee status pages.

Teams webinars can host up to 1,000 attendees as of this writing. As an organizer, you can choose the capacity between 1 to 1,000. You can select additional options such as requiring manual approval for all event registrations to manually review each registration and choose to accept or reject, enabling a waitlist for this event, and limiting the registration date. Based on my requirements, I enabled the registration limit for a week, as shown in Figure 4-27.

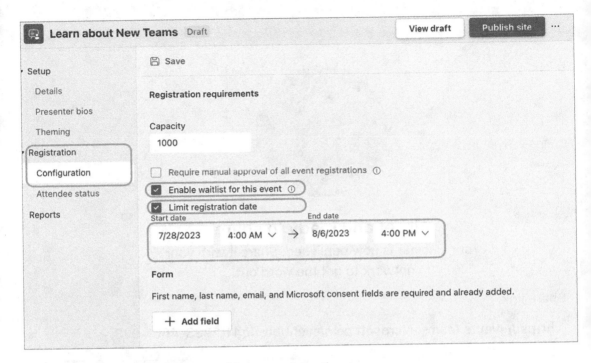

Figure 4-27. *Scheduling a webinar, registration*

The attendance status page displays a roster of users who are either waitlisted, registered, or canceled. You can leave this page for now and come back to it later.

In the reports section, you can find reports related to webinars that can be accessed after the meeting. Typically, the reporting section includes attendance reports, webinar duration, and participant details. Currently, only the organizer has access to these reports.

Validate all the settings and click "Publish site" at the top right. Once the site is published, a sharing link is generated to share the event information with your organization, as shown in Figure 4-28.

All set and ready to share

Your webinar is now published. Share it with your
network to get the word out.

Share link

https://events.teams.microsoft.com/event/bfeffb41-2983-46b1-923

Figure 4-28. *Scheduling a webinar, registration link*

When internal users click the link, they are prompted to sign in with their work
account. After successfully signing in, they are directed to a registration site, as shown
in Figure 4-29. You can find details about the upcoming event on the website, such
as the topic, dates, speakers and bio information, and a registration button. Click the
Register button.

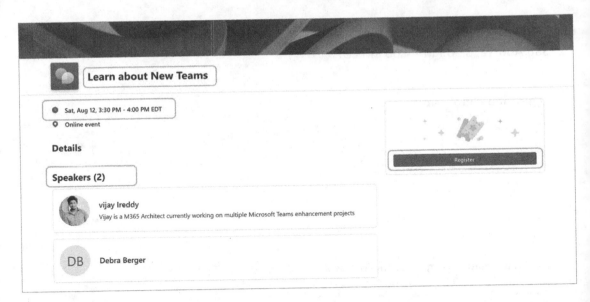

Figure 4-29. Webinar registration

If the webinar is public, you are promoted to enter your first name, last name, and email address; if the webinar is internal and you are signed with your M365 account, your information is prefilled. Accept the privacy terms and click Register. Figure 4-30 shows the webinar registration form.

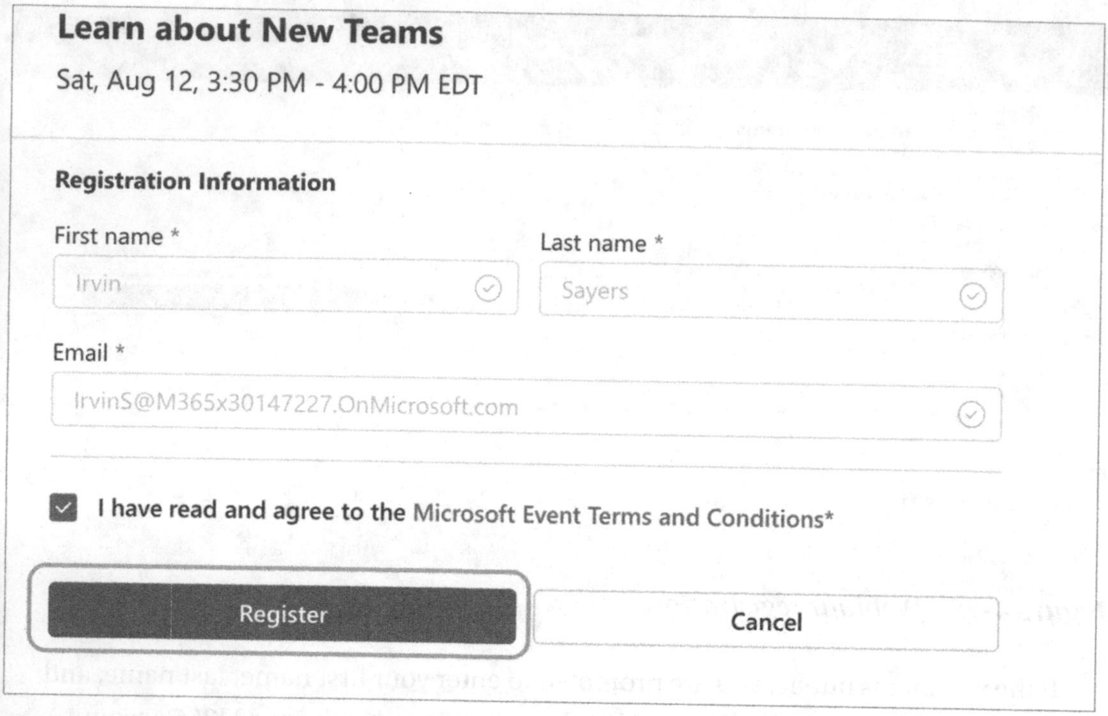

Learn about New Teams

Sat, Aug 12, 3:30 PM - 4:00 PM EDT

Registration Information

First name *

Irvin ⊘

Last name *

Sayers ⊘

Email *

IrvinS@M365x30147227.OnMicrosoft.com ⊘

☑ I have read and agree to the Microsoft Event Terms and Conditions*

| Register | Cancel |

Figure 4-30. *Webinar registration page*

Once the user registers, an email notification with the webinar join-in information is sent to the user's email address, as shown in Figure 4-31. Users can accept the invite in the Teams and Outlook calendars.

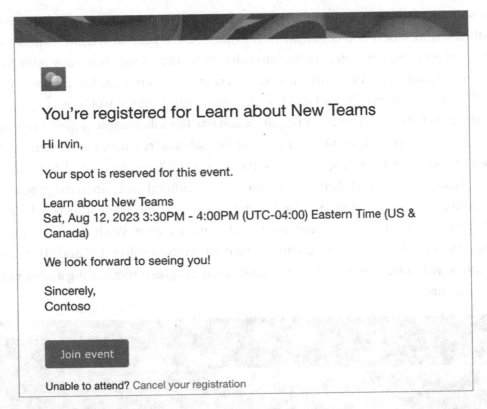

Figure 4-31. *Webinar registration confirmation email*

As an organizer, you can view the list of registered participants by going to the Teams meeting calendar and clicking the scheduled webinar event. Clicking to manage the event opens the scheduling page. To view the list of registered participants, click Registration, then Attendance status, and then Registered, as shown in Figure 4-32.

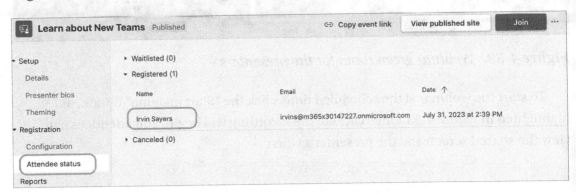

Figure 4-32. *Webinar, attendee registration status*

Presenters can use a green room, a Teams Premium feature, to join a webinar early and adjust audio, video, and content-sharing options. They can also communicate with other organizers and presenters before attendees join. Green rooms are available for the presenters, organizers, and co-organizers. To access the green room for the presenters, ensure the organizer has allowed it in the meeting options for the webinar.

To prepare for a presentation, presenters can use the Join button in their meeting invite to enter the meeting room early and adjust their audio, video, and screen-sharing settings. In the following example, as shown in Figure 4-33, a presenter clicked the meeting link they received when the webinar was scheduled and joined the green room. Once inside, the presenter uploaded a PowerPoint presentation and adjusted their video and background to ensure they were ready to start the webinar. While waiting for the scheduled start time, presenters can interact with attendees using chat and Q&A features and discuss with other presenters and organizers in the green room using audio, video, and screen share.

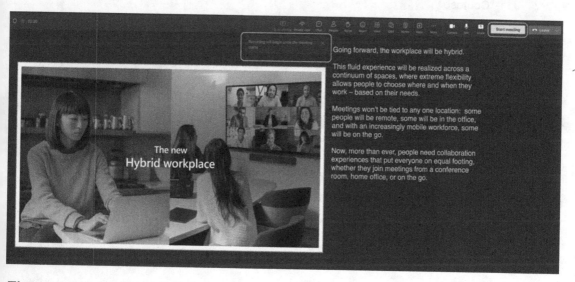

Figure 4-33. *Webinar green room for the presenters*

To start the webinar at the scheduled time, click the "Start meeting" option, as highlighted in Figure 4-33. Once clicked, the recording will begin, and attendees can view the shared screen and the presenter's video.

Meeting Options

Meeting options are available for both Teams meetings and Teams webinars. Additional options become available when an organizer has Teams Premium assigned to them. The following are all the meeting options available. Teams Premium features are indicated by the suffix (P).

- **Sensitivity (P):** Consider using sensitivity labels if your meeting involves sharing confidential information. The details on sensitivity labels are explained in the "Teams Premium" section. The sensitivity labels are preconfigured by the Global admin in the Microsoft Purview Compliance Center. The labels are displayed here for organizers to choose from.

- **Who can bypass the lobby:** If you choose to use the lobby, you and other meeting participants can view a list of people waiting to enter the lobby and decide either to admit or to deny them entry. The Teams administrator configures the default settings for who can bypass the lobby, and Teams meeting organizers can modify these settings.

- **People dialing in can bypass the lobby:** One way to join a Teams meeting is by dialing into the conference bridge, which is explained later in this chapter. To let dial-in users enter the meeting without waiting in the lobby, you can turn on the "People dialing in can bypass the lobby" toggle. The Teams administrator configures the default settings, and the Teams meeting organizers can modify these settings.

- **Announce when people dialing in join or leave:** To receive announcements when people join or leave your meeting via phone (dialing into the conference bridge), toggle on this feature.

- **Choose co-organizers:** To assist in managing a meeting, additional co-organizers may be added. Co-organizers can act as a backup for the organizer to control meeting options and settings. Note that you cannot add an external participant as a co-organizer.

- **Who can present:** With this feature, organizers can assign presenters beforehand or during your meeting to maintain focus and keep things on track. An administrator sets up the default settings, but organizers can modify them if needed. When scheduling a webinar, you can use the option to add presenters. It's important to remember that external participants can be added as presenters in webinars only if the webinar is set to public. However, if these external participants are guests in your organization, they can join, participate, and even present in internal organization webinars.

- **Manage what attendees see (P):** This feature allows the organizer to manage the attendee view for a more streamlined event. The options include enabling attendees to only view the shared screen and participants, all presenters with their presentations, and more.

- **Allow mic for attendees:** Turn the "Allow mic for attendees" toggle on or off to change attendee mic permissions.

- **Allow camera for attendees:** Turn the "Allow camera for attendees" toggle on or off to change attendee camera permissions.

- **Record automatically:** To automatically start recording the meeting when a meeting begins, turn on this option. The recording will continue until it's manually stopped, or the meeting ends.

- **Meeting-chat:** By default, all users invited to a meeting can chat before, during, or after the meeting. However, the organizer can choose to limit chat permissions to specific times using this option. This includes during the meeting only or disabling meeting chat altogether.

- **Allow reactions:** During a meeting, attendees can express their emotions by sending live reactions. Turn on "Allow reactions" to allow this feature inside a Teams meeting.

- **Provide CART Captions:** Communication Access Real-Time Translation (CART) is a service that provides instant text translation of speech by trained captioners. By turning on this feature, as a meeting organizer you can provide CART services to the participants instead of built-in Microsoft Live captions. Please note that a trained captioner is required, and they will need a CART software and CART caption link from the meeting organizer.

- **Enable Greenroom (P):** The green room feature is exclusively available for webinars on Teams Premium. Presenters can use this feature to join a webinar early and adjust audio, video, and content-sharing options. They can also communicate with other organizers and presenters before attendees join. Green rooms are available to presenters, organizers, and co-organizers. Turn on this feature to give green room access to presenters.

- **Enable language interpretation (P):** To have a professional interpreter who can translate the speaker's language into another in real time during your meeting, turn on the "Enable language interpretation" toggle. The professional interpreter will translate the language in real time without disrupting the speaker's original delivery flow. Please note that end-to-end encryption is not available for this feature, and turn off the spatial audio for a more inclusive meeting experience.

- **Q&A:** For active participation during a meeting, you can enable the Q&A feature. This will allow attendees to ask questions, post replies, and even post anonymously.

- **Who can record (P):** When you have a Teams Premium license, you can decide if other internal meeting participants can record the meeting. This feature allows you to choose who is authorized to initiate and manage the recording.

- **End-to-end encryption (P):** Teams Premium offers end-to-end encryption to protect confidential meeting information. Turn this option to encrypt the meeting at the origin and decrypt the data at the destination.

- **Apply a watermark to shared content (P):** This is a Teams Premium feature. When you turn on the "Apply a watermark to shared content" toggle, each meeting participant will see a watermark with their name and email address cast across shared visual content.

- **Allow participants to rename themselves:** To allow participants to modify their display name during a meeting, turn on the "Allow participants to rename themselves" toggle.

- **Allow attendance report:** The attendance reports provide information about the meeting's attendees, such as participants joining and leaving time and the meeting duration. To generate, view, and download attendance reports, turn on the "Allow attendance report" toggle. Please note that only organizers and co-organizers can download the attendance report.

- **Meeting Theme (P):** In Teams Premium, you can use meeting themes to add visuals from your organization, such as logos and brand colors, to your meeting interface. Turn on the Meeting Theme toggle to apply your organization's custom theme for a more personalized, branded meeting experience.

Teams Premium

Due to the global pandemic, meetings and their related tools have become essential for efficient communication among organizations and users. The number of meetings held per day per individual has increased significantly. A survey revealed that organizations have experienced a 252 percent increase in weekly meeting time due to the need to switch through information and solutions, take notes, prepare for meetings, and complete post-meeting work. Organizations have realized that more necessary solutions may be required than meetings such as webinars, virtual appointments, and collaboration tools. As a result of increased security measures, specific confidential meetings require additional precautions to ensure the safety and confidentiality of all participants.

Collaboration and communication became the most needed, and tools like Microsoft Teams helped organizations and users bring them together in a single platform. However, users have struggled to cope with the demanding conditions, resulting in a loss of productivity due to an overload of information from the meetings. By automating and simplifying daily meeting tasks, time spent in meetings can be reduced, and productivity can be increased. To provide advanced meeting capabilities that enable more intelligent, personalized, and secure meetings, Microsoft has introduced Teams Premium. With Teams Premium, users can focus on what matters most, while AI technology handles the heavy lifting. Teams Premium is an all-in-one integrated solution that supports meetings, webinars, and virtual appointments with advanced protection capabilities for highly sensitive meetings.

Teams Premium Features

Attending meetings is essential to stay informed, but sometimes skipping a meeting can help you focus and be more productive. However, reviewing recordings and transcripts to find relevant information can be time-consuming. Teams Premium can help make meetings more productive by doing the following:

- Automatically generating meeting notes and tasks using AI-powered technology from GPT-3.5 by OpenAI.

- Identifying important moments in a recording such as when a user joined and left the meeting, when a screen is shared, and when a user's name is mentioned.

- Ease navigating through meeting recordings using automatically generated chapters based on the topics.

- Providing live translations for captions in the meeting. If the organizer has Teams Premium, the attendees can use live translations of captions for their meeting, even if they don't have Teams Premium.

- Easily schedule the correct type of meeting with the meeting templates and virtual appointments.

- Create custom brandings in webinars, meetings, and Virtual appointments.

- Create custom together mode scenes for your organization.

- Configure watermarking on participants' videos and shared content to protect meetings and limit who can record.

- Enable end-to-end encryption for online meetings (versus just one-on-one meetings and calls) to help protect the most sensitive conversations.

- Microsoft 365 E5 customers who require the highest level of security can now use their existing Microsoft Purview Information Protection sensitivity labels to apply relevant meeting options automatically.

With your existing M365 subscriptions/O365 subscriptions, you can access the basic virtual appointment experience. Advanced virtual appointments capabilities are available with Teams Premium, which will help you with the following:

- Give customers a personalized experience with pre-appointment SMS reminders, a branded lobby room, and post-appointment follow-ups.

- A dashboard that displays both scheduled and on-demand appointments in one place, with the added feature of chatting with clients before their appointments.

- Gain valuable insights and trends about appointments, such as no-shows and wait times.

- Provide a seamless joining experience for mobile customers without needing users to download the Teams app.

The Teams license offered with M365 and O365 subscriptions provides access to basic webinars and their capabilities, but a Teams Premium license offers additional robust features such as the following:

- Set up a green room for webinar presenters feature to join early and adjust audio, video, and content-sharing options. They can also communicate with other organizers and presenters before attendees join.

- Enable a webinar waiting list to allow additional individuals to register and be automatically placed on the waitlist.

- Limit the day and time when people register.

- Manually approve the registrations to ensure you have the exact group of attendees you need for the webinar event.

- Send reminder emails to the registrants before the webinar.

- Manage attendee views for a more streamlined event.

- Use the RTMP-in feature in webinars.

Availability and Licensing

Teams Premium is available to purchase worldwide through all Microsoft purchasing channels. The tenant must be a commercial, worldwide public sector, EDU, GCC, or nonprofit tenant at general release, and the user must have a 0365/ M365 subscription with Teams to use Teams Premium features.

Teams Premium is a per-user, per-month subscription add-on license that requires each user to have a license assigned to access its functionalities.

Here are a few things to keep in mind regarding current limitations:

- When the meeting organizer has a Teams Premium license, there are some specific meeting and event features that will extend the feature benefit to all meeting attendees. This includes organizational users, guests, and external participants even if they aren't licensed with Teams Premium.

- External participants in virtual appointments don't require a Teams Premium license to benefit from Teams Premium advanced virtual appointments.

- For intelligent recap, all the meeting participants need a Teams Premium license.

Teams Premium for Administrators

Teams Premium features are accessible only through Teams Premium Licensing. As an administrator, you must customize the Teams Premium features to meet your organization's requirements before allowing your users to access them. Once your organization has subscribed to Teams Premium licensing, you can unlock the Teams Premium features. As an administrator, you can then configure the following features.

Using End-To-End Encryption on Meetings Up to 50 Participants

Teams meeting by default have encryption enabled by industry standards. Teams Media traffic is encrypted by Secure RTP, a profile of real-time transport protocol that provides confidentiality and authentication. End-to-end media traffic encryption ensures that the traffic is encrypted at the origin and decrypted at the destination. This ensures that nobody can eavesdrop on real-time conversations, except for the meeting or one-on-one call or group call participants. Teams offers end-to-end encryption for one-on-one calls and group calls. With Teams Premium, end-to-end encryption is available for meetings with up to 50 participants. As an administrator, you have to enable this feature for your users, By default, end-to-end encryption for meetings is not enabled. You can enable it in the Teams admin center by using an enhanced encryption policy.

As an administrator, you can also control or configure these settings using Microsoft Teams module Powershell commandlets.

```
Set-CsTeamsEnhancedEncryptionPolicy -Identity Global" -MeetingEndToEnd
Encryption DisabledUserOverride
```

You can also use this command to enable end-to-end encryption for one-on-one calls and group calls using the attribute -CallingEndtoEndEncryptionEnabledType.

Based on these settings, organizers and co-organizers can turn on end-to-end encryption in the Meeting options for each meeting.

Here are some limitations that administrators and end-user must beware of as of this writing:

- Only audio, video, and video-based screen sharing is end-to-end encrypted. Other features such as apps, avatars, reactions, chat, filters, and Q&A are not end-to-end encrypted.

- During an end-to-end encrypted meeting features including recording, live captions, transcription, together mode, large meetings, large gallery view on desktop, and PSTN are unavailable.

- Desktop clients and mobile clients are supported. Channel meetings can also be end-to-end encrypted. Teams Rooms devices and Surface Hub support is coming soon.

- Other platforms are currently not supported including desktop browser.

Please note that end-to-end meeting encryption can be enforced using meeting templates and sensitivity labels.

Tip   Locate the encryption indicator (shield and lock symbol) on your meeting screen to confirm that your meeting is securely encrypted for all the participants. Simply hover over the arrow to view your meeting's unique end-to-end encryption code and ensure that this code is identical for other participants in the meeting.

Adding Watermarks to Meetings

With Teams Premium, users can add watermarks to content shared and participants videos during Teams meetings. However, as an administrator, it's important to note the current limitations of this feature. Currently, watermarks are supported only on Teams desktop clients, Teams mobile clients, and Microsoft Teams Rooms. If you're using any other platform, you will have an audio-only experience when the watermark is used. Watermarks are intended to prevent the unauthorized sharing of confidential information. However, using them during meetings where all participants can directly access the content may not enhance security. Using the combination of watermarks with other Teams Premium protection features like sensitivity labels helps to protect confidential information in meetings. Administrators must also let end users know the limitations of other meeting features when watermarks are turned on. The following meeting features are turned off when watermarks are enabled:

- Meeting recording, including automatic recording and who can record

- Large gallery

- Together mode

- PowerPoint Live

- Whiteboard

- Content from camera

To turn on watermark features from the Teams admin center, follow these steps:

1. Go to Teams Admin Center ➤ Meetings ➤ Meeting Policies.

2. Select the policy to update.

3. To configure the watermark for the attendee video, set Watermark Video to On.

4. To configure the watermark for content shared on the screen, set "Watermark shared content" to On.

5. Use the preview to see how the watermark will look on desktop and mobile devices.

6. Click Save.

You can also turn the watermark on or off by using these PowerShell commands:

```
Set-CsTeamsMeetingPolicy -Identity Global -AllowWatermarkFor
CameraVideo $True
Set-CsTeamsMeetingPolicy -Identity Global -AllowWatermarkFor
ScreenSharing $True
```

Please note that the watermark for meetings can be enforced using meeting templates and sensitivity labels.

Adding Sensitivity Labels

In the previous section, we discussed meeting options. The Teams administrator configures the default settings for meeting options, and the organizer can modify them for each meeting depending upon the meeting requirement. Though this is useful, there are times when the admin needs to ensure that meetings are secured with the admin's configured features, and organizers must keep them the same. With Teams Premium, sensitivity labels can be used to enforce these meeting settings. Microsoft Purview Information Protection offers sensitivity labels that enable you to classify and protect your company's data. Sensitivity labels are usually assigned to documents and emails; in addition to these two, using Teams Premium, sensitivity labels can now be applied to meetings. Sensitive labels protect meeting invites and responses created from Outlook and Teams Calendar and protect Team meetings and chat.

- Meeting organizers can apply sensitivity labels to the Teams meeting invites scheduled in Outlook and Teams. The recipients in your organization will see the sensitivity label.

- All the meeting settings applied to the sensitivity label are enforced when a meeting begins, and internal users can see the labels during the meeting.

The following are meeting settings that you can apply with a sensitivity label:

- Automatically record

- Encryption for meeting video and audio

- Prevent copy of meeting chat

- Prevent or allow copying of chat contents to the clipboard

- Watermark for screen sharing and participants' video

- Who can bypass the lobby

- Who can present

- Who can record

Sensitivity labels can also be applied to Teams meetings using Teams meeting templates. Microsoft recommends configuring and protecting meetings with three tiers of protection. The appropriate level of protection depends on each organization's compliance needs, ranging from no requirements to highly sensitive ones. Microsoft provides basic recommendations for three tiers: baseline protection, sensitive protection, and highly sensitive protection. As an administrator, you can start with these tiers and adjust the configurations to meet the organization's needs. Here are some examples:

Features	Baseline	Sensitive	Highly Sensitive	Highly Sensitive Presentation
Allow camera for attendees	On	On	On	Off
Allow mic for attendees	On	On	On	Off
Apply a watermark to everyone's video feed	Off	Off	On	On
Apply a watermark to shared content	Off	Off	On	On

(*continued*)

Features	Baseline	Sensitive	Highly Sensitive	Highly Sensitive Presentation
End-to-end encryption	Off	Off	On	On
Manage what attendees see	Off	On	On	On
Meeting chat	On	On	In-meeting only	Off
People dialing in can bypass the lobby	Off	Off	Off	Off
Prevent copying chat content to clipboard	Off	Off	On	On
Record meetings automatically	Off	Off	Off	Off
Who can bypass the lobby?	People in my organization, people in trusted domains, and guests	People who were invited	Only me and co-organizers	Only me and co-organizers
Who can present	People in my organization and guests	People in my organization and guests	Only organizers and co-organizers	Only organizers and co-organizers
Who can record	Organizers and presenters	Organizers and co-organizers	Disabled due to watermarking	Disabled due to watermarking

These settings can be managed with a combination of sensitivity labels, meeting templates, and admin settings. Creating a sensitivity label is not covered in this book. Please refer to the following website to learn and configure sensitivity labels for meetings:

https://learn.microsoft.com/en-us/microsoftteams/configure-meetings-three-tiers-protection

Preventing Copying Meeting Chats

If your organization has compliance requirements to prevent copying meeting chats, Teams Premium can make it possible. Administrators can use a sensitivity label to block the copying of chat content. When this label is applied to channel meetings, the label prevents copying chat to the clipboard for all channel chats, even outside channel meetings. For nonchannel meetings, it's enforced only for meetings.

The methods supported to prevent copying chat are as follows:

- Select the text and then right-click and select Copy; or press Ctrl+C.

- Forward messages.

- Share to Outlook.

- Copy link.

Note   Copying using developer tools, third-party apps, or screen captures won't be prevented.

Using Organization-Customized Backgrounds

Custom backgrounds are the images that can be applied to the background of a user's video feed in a Teams meeting. As an admin, you can create custom backgrounds based on your organization themes and make them available for your users to use in Teams meeting at any point in time.

To make custom backgrounds available for your Teams Premium licensed users, you must configure a customization policy in the Teams admin center. Figure 4-34 shows the customization policy. To configure it, follow these steps:

1. Go to the Teams admin center, select Meetings and then Customization Policy.

2. Edit an existing policy or create a new policy by clicking Add.

3. Name the customization policy.

4. Turn on "Use background images for my organization."

5. Click Add.

6. Upload a background image.

7. Click Save.

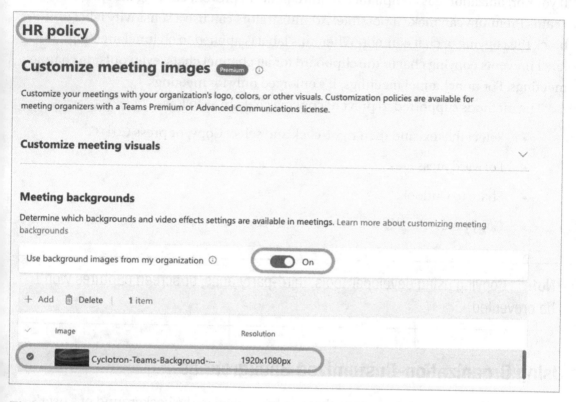

Figure 4-34. Customization policy

Here are the current limitations for the uploads:

- PNG and JPEG image formats for their images

- Images with minimum dimensions of 360 pixels × 360 pixels

- Images with maximum dimensions of 3840 pixels × 2160 pixels

- A maximum of 50 custom background images

Using organization-customized Together mode scenes

With Teams Premium, users can create personalized "together mode scenes" through the Teams Developer Portal. Once created, these scenes can be shared as an app within Microsoft Teams. As an administrator, you must permit users to upload custom apps by managing app permission policies. Refer to this link to create custom-together mode scenes for your meetings:

https://learn.microsoft.com/en-us/microsoftteams/platform/apps-in-teams-meetings/teams-together-mode

Using Organization-Customized Meeting Templates

Meeting templates are available with Teams Premium. Using a meeting template, an administrator can customize the meeting options that the meeting organizer controls typically. Meeting templates ensure a consistent meeting experience for users and also ensure compliance by not allowing organizers to change a few settings. Administrators can lock the template option features so that the meeting organizer can't change it and can unlock others so that meeting options can be changed. Figure 4-35 shows the lock settings. Meeting templates can control the following meeting options:

- Allow mic and camera for attendees

- Allow reactions

- Announce when people dialing in join or leave

- Enable watermark for screen share and for video

- End-to-end encryption

- Lobby

- Manage what attendees see

- Meeting chat

- Q&A

- Recording

- Sensitivity label

The "Sensitivity Label" section mentioned that combining meeting templates with sensitivity labels can help enforce meeting protection. It's important to note that if a meeting invitation has a sensitivity label assigned and meeting templates are used, the meeting options enforced by the sensitivity labels will always take priority. Meeting templates are the most effective way to manage meeting options and ensure compliance for organizations without a Microsoft Purview Compliance Center subscription.

To configure meeting templates, follow these steps:

1. Go to the Teams admin center, click Meetings, and click Meeting Templates.

2. By default, you will see a virtual appointment template. Click Add for a new template.

3. Add a name and description for the new template.

4. Configure the template meeting settings based on your organization's needs.

5. Use the Lock icon to lock any meeting settings that organizers cannot change.

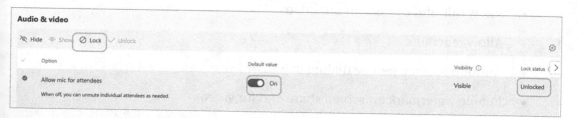

Figure 4-35. *Meeting templates- Lock a setting*

6. After validating all the settings, click Save.

Now that the meeting template is created, you must assign it to the users. Meeting templates can be assigned to the users using the meeting template policies. All meeting templates are available in the Global Meeting template policy by default.

Once the policies get synced, users can use these templates to create meetings. The customized meeting templates are available in the Teams calendar. To use a customized meeting template, follow these steps:

1. Go to the Teams application and click the calendar.

2. Click the down arrow located new to "New meeting."

3. Click the template.

4. The template launches with enforced meeting option settings.

Seeing Organization-Customized Branding

With Microsoft Teams Premium, administrators can create personalized meeting themes that showcase their organization's branding, including their logo, images, and theme colors. Meeting themes are assigned in customization policies, and these policies are assigned to the users. To set customization policies, follow these steps:

1. Go to the Teams admin center, select Meetings, and select Customization Policy.

2. Create a new policy by clicking Add.

3. Add a name to the customization policy.

4. Click Add Theme.

5. Upload the image, logo, and choose the theme color.

6. Click Apply.

7. Turn on "Allow organizer to control meeting theme."

8. Click Save.

The following are the locations where the branding can be found:

Themes	Join Launcher	Meeting Pre-Join	Meeting Lobby	Meeting Stage
Logo	No	Yes	Yes	No
Image	No	Yes	Yes	No
Color	Yes	Yes	Yes	Yes

Teams Phone System Planning

Microsoft Teams provides multiple capabilities, such as chat, audio and video calls, meetings, content sharing, phone calls to external numbers, etc. One feature allows you to use the Teams call interface to make outbound phone calls to internal users, and extensions, and connect with the PSTN. The Microsoft Teams technology that allows call control and PBX capabilities is called the Phone System.

The Teams Phone System permits users to place and receive phone calls, transfer calls, and mute or unmute calls. Teams calling provides multiple features, including call answering and initiating (by name and number) with an integrated dial pad, call holding and retrieving, call forwarding and simultaneous ringing, call history, voicemail, and emergency calls. End users can also use different devices to establish calls, including mobile devices, headsets connected to a computer, and IP phones. This section covers the Teams Phone System, including Direct Routing, Calling Plans, phone number management, and phone call routing policies.

Microsoft Teams natively supports audio and video calls and meetings using a VoIP data network without special licensing. Teams with a Phone System license (add-on) enables calls to landlines and mobile phones by connecting the Teams Phone System to the PSTN. Teams Phone System PSTN connectivity can be established in four ways:

- **Teams Direct Routing:** You can connect your existing on-premises PBX infrastructure with the Office 365 Phone System.

- **Teams Calling Plan:** Using the Calling Plan, users can make and receive phone calls directly through Office 365 Phone System as a telephony provider by purchasing a Microsoft Calling Plan (domestic or domestic and international) for Office 365.

- **Teams Operator Connect:** You can use Microsoft Teams to make and receive calls with Teams-certified telephony providers.

- **Teams Phone Mobile:** Microsoft Teams Phone Mobile allows users to use the same phone number for both their mobile service and desk lines/work. Essentially, their SIM-enabled phone number becomes their Teams phone number.

Teams Phone PSTN Call Flow

As an administrator, it's important to understand the signaling and media path for PSTN calls when troubleshooting. Let's examine how signaling and media call flow works when User A from the Cyclotron tenant makes a PSTN outbound local call from the United States by dialing a 10-digit number from their Microsoft Teams client.

In Microsoft Teams, 10-digit calls are converted to E.164 standard by native or user-defined dial plans. The Teams service only recognizes calls in E.164 format, regardless of the digits dialed. The call is routed to the nearest Microsoft Azure front door. The Teams service performs a reverse number lookup in its database to validate if the number is assigned to a user in the tenant. If not, the Teams service checks if User A has permission to dial out to PSTN numbers. Checkups depend on PSTN connectivity. For Calling Plans, checkups include domestic Calling Plan licenses and dial-out policies. For Operator Connect, checkups include Operator Connect service and dial-out policies. For Teams phone mobile, it validates the Teams Phone Mobile service and dial-out policies. Finally, for Direct Routing, it checks the Online Voice Routing policy and dial-out policies, and if the user is validated to dial outbound, calls are routed to the PSTN carriers.

If you are using the Calling Plans feature, the calls are forwarded to Microsoft's underlying PSTN carrier serving that location. For Operator Connect and Teams Phone Mobile, the calls are sent to the operator's trunk. For Direct Routing, the Teams service checks sends the call to the PSTN gateway associated with the online voice routing policy assigned to User A. Note that the Online voice routing policy must be associated with a PSTN usage that is routable to the PSTN gateway and the session border controller (SBC). The PSTN gateway routes the call to the SBC, and it's forwarded to the PSTN carrier on the defined trunk. The call rings at destination (User B), and User A can hear the early media on their Teams client. Once User B picks up the call, media kicks in.

For Direct Routing, the media flows back through the PSTN network, Direct Routing SBC, Microsoft Phone System, and finally Teams client. For other connectivity models, the media flows through PSTN network, the Microsoft Phone system, and the Teams client. In Direct Routing scenarios, the Teams service bypasses the media when ICE Lite is configured on the SBC. The ICE protocol is used to bypass the media, and User A's Teams client must have direct connectivity with the SBC's external IP address. In such cases, the media flows through the PSTN network, SBC, and the Teams client. When the call is ended by either party (User A or User B), the call termination process follows the reverse path based on the PSTN connectivity models, traversing the same components until the call is fully terminated.

When User A receives an inbound call from User B, the PSTN carriers route the call to the Teams Phone system. In Direct Routing scenarios, calls are sent to SIP trunk/E1/ P1 configured on the SBC and routed to the Microsoft Phone system PSTN gateway using the defined trunk in E.164 format. The Teams service performs a reverse number lookup against the database to validate if the number is assigned to any user. If the number is assigned to User A, the call is forwarded to all Teams clients. Like outbound calls, once User A picks up the call, the media kicks in.

For Direct Routing, the media flows back through the PSTN network, Direct Routing SBC, Microsoft Phone System, and finally Teams client. For other connectivity models, the media flows through the PSTN network, the Microsoft Phone system, and the Teams client. In Direct Routing scenarios, when the media bypass is configured, the media flows through the PSTN network, SBC, and Teams client. When the call is ended by either party (User A or User B), the call termination process follows the reverse path based on the PSTN connectivity models, traversing the same components until the call is fully terminated.

Note   For PSTN calls, clients use UDP 50000–50019 for media traffic and 1024–65535 for SIP signaling.

Configuring and Managing Teams Direct Routing

Direct Routing allows a Teams admin to connect a supported SBC to Microsoft Phone System to enable voice calling features (PSTN calls). For example, you can configure on-premises PSTN connectivity with an SBC to send and receive phone calls from a user with the Teams client. Direct Routing is the other way to connect to the PSTN, where customers interface existing PSTN services to Teams through on-premises SBCs.

Suppose your organization has an on-premises PSTN connectivity solution, such as the Cyclotron organization using the Ribbon SBC to connect an AT&T SIP trunk. In that case, Direct Routing enables you to connect a supported SBC to the Microsoft Phone System. Direct Routing allows you to use any PSTN trunk with your Microsoft Phone System and configure interoperability between customer-owned telephony equipment, such as a third-party PBX, analog devices, and the Microsoft Phone System.

Figure 4-36 shows on-premises PSTN connectivity using the Direct Routing capability with a Microsoft Teams client.

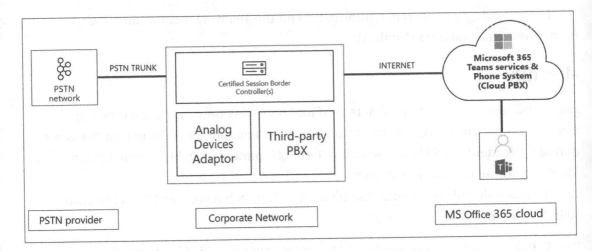

Figure 4-36. *Teams Direct Routing connectivity*

Refer to Chapter 2, which covers Direct Routing requirements, configuring Direct Routing with Windows PowerShell commands, and best practices.

Configuring and Customizing Online PSTN Gateway for Microsoft Teams Direct Routing

One of the main tasks for Teams Phone System Direct Routing configuration is to onboard an on-premises SBC to the Microsoft Teams cloud tenant. To create a new SBC configuration that describes the settings for the peer entity, use the following PowerShell command to create a new Online PSTN gateway:

```
New-CsOnlinePSTNGateway -Fqdn sbc1.cyclotron.com -SipSignallingPort
5061 -MaxConcurrentSessions 100 -Enabled $true
```

This command shows SBC FQDN, SIP signaling port, maximum concurrent sessions, and enabled status; the remaining parameters will stay at their defaults.

When you create an online PSTN gateway, each configuration includes individual settings for an SBC. The SBC configuration setting includes the SIP signaling port, whether media bypass is enabled on this SBC, forward P-Asserted-Identity (PAI), whether the SBC will send SIP options, specifying the limit of maximum concurrent sessions, and much more. One of the important settings that Teams admins can configure for SBC is to set -Enabled to $true or $false. When set to $false, the SBC will continue to handle existing calls, but all new calls will be routed to another SBC in a route (if there is one that lasts).

The following is the detailed information for the Teams Direct Routing SBC parameters that can be customized.

-Identity

Every SBC has a unique name that is used for identifying the SBC. When creating a new SBC, the identity is provided through the -FQDN parameter. If the parameter is not defined, the identity will be copied from the -FQDN parameter, which means that an identity parameter is not mandatory.

For example, this command doesn't define identity but is copied from the Fqdn switch. That means identity is optional.

```
New-CsOnlinePSTNGateway -Fqdn sbc1.cyclotron.com -SipSignallingPort
5061 -MaxConcurrentSessions 100 -Enabled $true
```

-InboundPSTNNumberTranslationRules

While creating an SBC, as an admin you can set the inbound PSTN number translation rules that are applied to PSTN numbers in an inbound direction, as well as in inbound calls coming from carriers to the Teams user.

-InboundTeamsNumberTranslationRules

While creating an SBC, you can set the inbound Teams number translation rules that are applied to Teams numbers (the called numbers) in an inbound direction. This switch gives an ordered list of Teams translation rules that apply to inbound Teams numbers.

-OutboundPSTNNumberTranslationRulesList

While creating an SBC, an admin can set the outbound PSTN number translation rules that are applied to PSTN numbers (the called numbers) in the outbound direction. This switch assigns an ordered list of Teams translation rules that apply to outbound PSTN numbers.

-OutboundTeamsNumberTranslationRulesList

While creating an SBC, you can set the outbound Teams number translation rules applied to Teams numbers (the calling numbers) in the outbound direction. This switch assigns an ordered list of Teams translation rules that apply to outbound Teams numbers.

-SipSignalingPort

This parameter is the listening port used to communicate with Direct Routing services using the Transport Layer Security (TLS) protocol. It must be a value between 1 and 65535. Microsoft recently changed the spelling of this parameter from SipSignallingPort to SipSignalingPort.

-Fqdn

The fully qualified domain name (FQDN) is the name of the SBC. The online PSTN gateway command has only 63 characters to set the FQDN of an SBC, and it is copied automatically to the identity of the SBC field.

-ForwardCallHistory

This command switch indicates whether call history information will be forwarded to the SBC. If enabled, the Office 365 PSTN Proxy sends two headers: History-info and Referred-By. The default value for this parameter is $False.

-ForwardPAI

If the SBC config setting includes ForwardPAI as True, then for each outbound to SBC session, the Direct Routing interface (public IP) will report in P-Asserted-Identity fields the TEL URI and SIP address of the user who made a call. This is helpful when you as a Teams admin set the identity of the caller to Anonymous or a general number of the organization; however, for invoicing reasons, the real identity of the user is required, so the PAI setting controls the forward PAI parameter in an online gateway configuration.

For example, the command looks like this:

```
New-CsOnlinePSTNGateway -Fqdn sbc1.cyclotron.com -SipSignallingPort
5061 -MaxConcurrentSessions 100 -ForwardPAI $true -Enabled $true
```

-Enabled

This parameter is used to enable SBC for outbound calls. Also, this setting allows admins to control the SBC state as active or passive. Admins can use this setting to temporarily remove the SBC from service as it is being updated undergoing maintenance.

Note   If an admin forgets to set this parameter as true, by default SBC will be created as disabled. The default value is -Enabled $false.

Here's an example:

```
New-CsOnlinePSTNGateway -Fqdn sbc1.cyclotron.com -SipSignallingPort
5061 -MaxConcurrentSessions 100 -Enabled $true
```

-ExcludedCodecs

This parameter excludes some codecs when media is being negotiated between the media proxy and the SBC.

-FailoverResponseCodes

Failover response codes are key parameters that have default codes set as (408, 503, and 504). That means you can configure a custom response code or use the default. For example, If Teams Direct Routing receives any 4xx or 6xx SIP error code in response to an outgoing invite, the call is considered completed by default. In the context of an outgoing call from a Teams client to the PSTN number, the call flow will be Teams Client ➤ Direct Routing ➤ SBC ➤ PSTN (telephony network). Setting the SIP codes in this parameter forces Direct Routing, on receiving the specified codes, to try another SBC (if another SBC exists in the voice routing policy of the user).

-FailoverTimeSeconds

This parameter has a default value of 10. Outbound calls not answered by the PSTN gateway within 10 seconds are routed to the next available trunk; if there are no additional trunks, the call is automatically dropped. In an organization with slow networks and slow gateway responses, that could potentially result in calls being dropped unnecessarily. As an admin, you can decide what failure time should be set for the SBC.

-Force

The Force switch specifies whether to remove warning and confirmation messages. It can be useful in scripting to suppress interactive prompts. If the Force switch isn't provided in the command, you are prompted for administrative input if required.

-ForwardPai

This switch suggests whether the P-Asserted-Identity (PAI) header will be forwarded along with the call. The PAI header provides a way to verify the identity of the caller. The default value is $False. Setting this parameter to $true will give the from header anonymously, in accordance with RFC5379 and RFC3325.

-GatewaySiteLbrEnabled

This is another critical setting to enable the SBC to report assigned site location, which is used for location-based routing (LBR). When the SBC has a gateway site and the LBR-enabled parameter is enabled ($True), the SBC will report the site name defined by the Teams admin. On an incoming call to a Teams user, the value of the site assigned to the SBC is compared with the value assigned to the user to make a routing decision. The parameter is mandatory for enabling LBR, and the default value for this parameter is $False.

-GenerateRingingWhileLocatingUser

This parameter is applicable only for Direct Routing in nonmedia bypass mode. Occasionally inbound calls from the PSTN to Teams clients can take longer than expected to be established. This can happen for a variety of reasons. When this occurs, the caller might not hear anything, the Teams client doesn't ring, and some telecommunications providers might terminate the call. This parameter helps to avoid unexpected silences that can occur in this scenario. Once this parameter is enabled for inbound calls from the PSTN to Teams clients, a unique audio signal is played to the caller to indicate that Teams is in the process of establishing the call.

-MaxConcurrentSessions

The alerting system uses this parameter. When any value is set, the alerting system will generate an alert to the Teams admin when the number of concurrent sessions is 90 percent or higher than this value. If the parameter is not set, alerts are not generated. However, the monitoring system will report the number of concurrent sessions every 24 hours.

-MediaBypass

The media bypass parameter indicates that if the SBC supports media bypass, Teams admins can use it for the SBC. Media bypass is useful for sending media directly to SBC from the Teams client instead of sending media through the Teams service. Media bypass increases call quality, so its use is recommended wherever possible.

-SendSipOptions

This parameter describes if an SBC will or will not send SIP options messages. If disabled, the SBC will be excluded from the Monitoring and Alerting system. Microsoft recommends that you enable SIP options, and the default value is True.

There are additional PowerShell commands to manage online PSTN gateway settings such as Set-CsOnlinePSTNGateway, Get-CsOnlinePSTNGateway, and Remove-CsOnlinePSTNGateway.

Figure 4-37 shows the online PSTN gateway PowerShell command parameters.

```
PS C:\> Get-CsOnlinePSTNGateway -Identity sbc1.bloguc.com

Identity                           : sbc1.bloguc.com
InboundTeamsNumberTranslationRules : {}
InboundPstnNumberTranslationRules  : {}
OutbundTeamsNumberTranslationRules : {Remove +, Remove + and Extension}
OutboundPstnNumberTranslationRules : {EU-Service, EU-Emergency, EU-PrefixAll}
Fqdn                               : sbc1.bloguc.com
SipSignalingPort                   : 5061
FailoverTimeSeconds                : 10
ForwardCallHistory                 : False
ForwardPai                         : False
SendSipOptions                     : True
MaxConcurrentSessions              : 200
Enabled                            : True
MediaBypass                        : False
GatewaySiteId                      :
GatewaySiteLbrEnabled              : False
FailoverResponseCodes              : 408,503,504
GenerateRingingWhileLocatingUser   : True
PidfLoSupported                    : False
MediaRelayRoutingLocationOverride  :
ProxySbc                           :
BypassMode                         : None
```

Figure 4-37. *Teams PSTN gateway*

Configuring and Managing Teams Calling Plans

Teams Calling Plan is another way to connect Teams to PSTN using Microsoft as the service provider. Teams provide audio and video calling and meetings using VoIP through the data network, and all these calls and meetings are free. However, making phone calls to external phone numbers or receiving calls from external regular phones to Teams users requires the purchase of a Calling Plan license on top of the Phone System license and Teams license. As an admin, you must know how to purchase and configure Calling Plans for users.

As of this writing, there are two Microsoft Calling Plan options available:

- **Domestic Calling Plan:** Using this plan, Teams licensed users can call out to external phone numbers in the country or region where they are assigned in Office 365.

- **Domestic and International Calling Plan:** Using this plan, Teams licensed users can call out to external phone numbers in the country or region where their Office 365 license is assigned based on the user's location and to international numbers in supported countries or regions. Currently, Calling Plan is available in 196 countries or regions that you can dial into using an international number.

- **Pay-As-You-Go plan:** With this plan, users can make both domestic and international PSTN calls. Unlimited inbound minutes are included for free, while outbound calls are charged per minute using communication credits. There are two options to choose from:

- **Pay-As-You-Go Calling Plan Zone-1:** For users in the United States and Puerto Rico, Canada, and the United Kingdom.

- **Pay-As-You-Go Calling Plan Zone-2:** For users in Austria, Belgium, Croatia, Czech Republic, Denmark, Estonia, Finland, France, Germany, Hungary, Ireland, Italy, Latvia, Lithuania, Luxembourg, Netherlands, New Zealand, Norway, Poland, Portugal, Romania, Singapore, Slovakia, Slovenia, South Africa, Spain, Sweden, and Switzerland.

Note

- Zone 1 licenses are not currently available for sale in the United States and Puerto Rico. However, users of United States and Puerto Rico can still obtain them if purchased in another country.

- Zone 2 licenses aren't currently available for sale in the United States and Puerto Rico.

- Mexico has a separate pay-as-you-go plan.

Figure 4-38 shows the Microsoft-provided PSTN and Calling Plan plus Teams Phone System and the Office 365 cloud where corporate and remote users are connected for Teams services and phone calling capabilities.

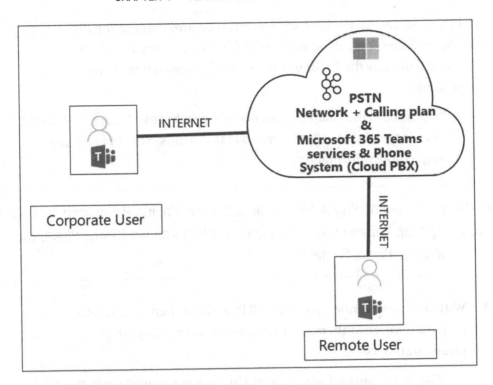

Figure 4-38. Teams Calling Plan

Setting Up a Calling Plan

Teams Calling Plan enables Teams users to make and receive phone call. However, as a Teams admin, you must know how to set up the Calling Plan feature. To set up this feature in your Teams environment, perform the following steps:

1. Check to determine whether Calling Plans are available in your country or region before they are purchased. Calling plans can be purchased depending on availability per country or region. Therefore, when planning for your telephony solution, you should verify whether the country or region used in your Office 365 billing location supports Teams Audio Conferencing.

   a. To check if Calling Plans are available in your country or region, visit this site, which shows the countries where Calling Plans are available: https://docs.microsoft.com/en-us/microsoftteams/country-and-region-availability-for-audio-conferencing-and-calling-plans/country-and-region-availability-for-audio-conferencing-and-calling-plans.

2. Purchase and assign licenses. Once you ensure that Calling Plans are available and can be purchased for your country or region, you should buy the Calling Plan licenses and assign them to your users.

    a. To purchase the Calling Plans license, visit https://docs.microsoft .com/en-us/microsoftteams/calling-plans-for-office-365 to get more information.

Note   Microsoft Teams Phone System licenses and Calling Plans licenses in Office 365 work together. Before looking for the option to purchase Calling Plans, you must first have the Phone System licenses.

---

3. With a phone number, you can call in and out; hence, you must acquire phone numbers. Teams provides several ways to get phone numbers.

    •   **Use the Teams admin center:** This process is used when your country or region supports getting phone numbers through the Teams admin center.

    •   **Port existing phone numbers:** This process is used to port your existing phone numbers from the current carrier to the Office 365 Phone System.

    •   **Use the request number for port numbers:** This process is used when the Teams admin center in your country or region does not support getting phone numbers.

4. Add emergency addresses and locations for the organization.

5. Assign a phone number and emergency address for the user.

Purchasing a Calling Plan for a Teams Organization

Teams Calling Plan requires making and receiving phone calls on users' Teams client. Also, Teams Phone System licenses and Calling Plan licenses work together, so before purchasing a Calling Plan license, your organization must have Phone System licenses. To purchase Phone System and Calling Plan licenses, follow these steps:

1. Purchase a Phone System add-on license (if you are not using an E5 license). To do so, log in to the Microsoft 365 admin center and select Billing. Select Purchase Services and then Add-on Subscriptions. Click Buy Now.

2. After you have finished buying Phone System licenses, you can buy the Calling Plan by logging in to the Microsoft 365 admin center. Select Billing, select Purchase Services, and then click Add-on Subscriptions. Click Buy Now.

Note   Depending on your organization's needs, you can buy and assign different Calling Plans to different users. After you select the calling plan you need, proceed to checkout and purchase it and then you can assign a calling plan to each user in the Microsoft 365 admin center.

Assigning Calling Plans to Users

After acquiring Calling Plan licenses, you as an admin, must assign the Calling Plan license to users using the calling service. To do so, log in to Microsoft 365 admin center and navigate to Users. Select Active Users and then find the user to whom you need to assign a Calling Plan license. Open that user account, select the appropriate license, and click Save Changes. Figure 4-39 shows an account with the Domestic and International Calling Plans assigned.

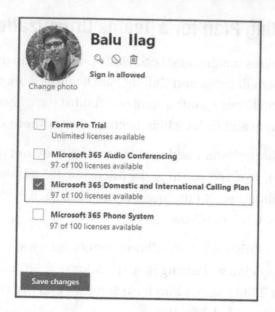

Balu Ilag

Sign in allowed

Change photo

☐ **Forms Pro Trial**
Unlimited licenses available

☐ **Microsoft 365 Audio Conferencing**
97 of 100 licenses available

☑ **Microsoft 365 Domestic and International Calling Plan**
97 of 100 licenses available

☐ **Microsoft 365 Phone System**
97 of 100 licenses available

Save changes

Figure 4-39. Assigning a calling plan

Porting a Phone Number to Microsoft

Porting a phone number to Microsoft involves three steps: porting readiness, port scheduling, and number porting.

Porting readiness includes a checklist of activities to ensure readiness for porting. These typically include the following:

- Identify phone numbers to be ported, including subscriber, toll, and toll-free numbers.

- Identify the losing carrier and the billing address associated with these phone numbers.

- Identify a legal representative or authorized user to sign the LOA forms on behalf of your organization.

- If you are porting outside the United States, identify the migration code, fiscal code, etc. These are included in your carrier monthly bills.

- Fill out the LOA Form to request a port schedule. The form is unique to the country of the port request. Ensure you choose the correct country before you schedule a port. LOA forms from Microsft are available at `https://learn.microsoft.com/en-us/microsoftteams/manage-phone-numbers`.

- Create an emergency address in the Teams admin center. This address is usually the service address associated with your phone number or the location where you plan to service these numbers. Please ensure you enter it accurately, as this address will serve as the emergency address during emergency calls.

Once you confirm that porting readiness is completed, you schedule a port. There are a few things to remember while you are scheduling the port. It is a best practice to schedule porting three weeks in advance as carriers need time to arrange engineers, get approval, or decide if the request is possible. This advance request gives time to manage and resubmit the port request if the carriers reject it. Select a porting time that falls outside of regular business hours to ensure a smooth transition. It would be best if you could schedule it toward the end of the day. In most cases, the Teams admin must assign the phone numbers to the users/call queues/auto attendants. Scheduling outside normal business hours will reduce the end-user impact from making and receiving calls.

To schedule a port, navigate to the Teams admin center, select Phone numbers, and click the port. Choose the country and type of phone number, and hit Next. Enter the Billing Telephony Number setting. The Billing Telephony Number is typically the pilot number for your porting number series/range. You can find this number in the billing summary of your monthly bill. If you have any questions, please get in touch with your losing carrier.

After you enter and click confirm, the system checks with the database and validates the porting availability and the losing carrier. Next, to port your phone numbers, you can either manually enter them separated by commas (,) or upload a CSV file with the numbers prefilled. Click Next and ensure the validation is successful for all the numbers.

Enter the details on the next page like the following:

- Order details
- Port details
- Organization details

- Current service provider details

- Authorized user details

- Service address

- Type of phone number (user usage, service usage)

- Notifications

While entering the authorized user details, you can get the LOA (the LOA is generated based on the details entered in the TAC) sent to the authorized user email for signature or manually upload the LOA. After entering all the details, click Next to upload the LOA if you chose to upload manually. After placing your order, you will receive notifications regarding the status updates, approvals, or rejections to the email address provided during the porting process. If the date and time of the port do not match your order, please contact the PSTN service desk immediately.

You can manually submit porting orders via the PSTN Service Desk. Access it through the Teams admin center; select Phone numbers and create a case. You must prefill the LOA and porting numbers in a CSV file and manually upload them during the port request.

The final stage of number porting is when the losing carrier ports the number to Microsoft. Once the porting order is completed, the notifiers receive an email. The phone number can then be assigned to users or resource accounts in the Teams admin center.

Configuring and Managing Teams Operator Connect

Operator Connect is an additional way to integrate PSTN services into Teams. If your current service provider is part of Microsoft's Certified Operator Connect Program, they can bring PSTN services to Teams using Operator Connect. Operator Connect offers a cost-effective solution for minimizing infrastructure and monthly billing expenses. Instead of billing based on subscriptions, Operator Connect charges your organization based on outbound call usage. This approach helps you save on monthly/annual PSTN bills. Operator Connect might be an effective option if

- You are looking for a cost-saving yet an effective approach.

- Your current service provider is part of the Microsoft Operator Connect program.

- You are looking to bring PSTN services to Teams.

- You don't have Calling Plans available in your region/country.

Figure 4-40 shows a high-level architecture diagram for Operator Connect. The Certified partners connect their SBC as a service (SBCaaS) to Teams. The architecture model utilized direct peering through Microsoft Azure Peering Service, provisioning APIs, and an operator portal for setting up the trunk to Microsoft Teams. This model uses capabilities such as BGP over BFD and end-to-end QoS from the Microsoft Cloud to the operator cloud to strengthen the interconnection. Using the Teams admin center, the initial setup and onboarding are made easier.

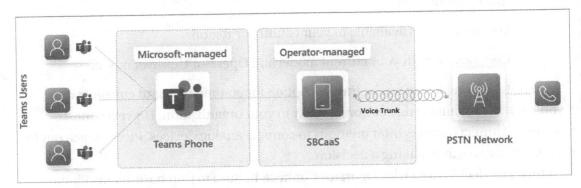

Figure 4-40. *Operator Connect architecture*

Once an operator is onboarded with your tenant, all incoming and outgoing calls will seamlessly go through your Teams to the carrier-managed SBC and then to the PSTN network. This is an all-in-one cloud model; you don't have to manage any infrastructure. This option lets you onboard multiple carriers in a single tenant.

Tip   If your organization is comparing the cost estimates of Operator Connect and Calling Plan subscriptions, please consider including taxes. Calling Plan subscriptions already include taxes, whereas Operator Connect partner bill estimates do not.

Plan for Operator Connect

Operator Connect is a popular option when choosing PSTN connectivity models for Teams Phone. However, it's important to perform readiness checks and requirements mapping to ensure it fits your organization correctly. These checks may include the following:

- Validating If your existing carrier is participating in the Operator Connect program to leverage existing contracts

- Whether the Operator Connect model is providing PSTN connectivity to all your devices

- List of operators available in your country or region

- Cost savings with your current model and Operator Connect model

Operator Connect may not be the best option for connectivity and customization if you have a lot of analog device connectivity in your organization. However, most Operator Connect partners offer methods to connect analog devices. Please reach out to specific carriers before making a decision.

Once you decide to go with Operator Connect, be sure to purchase Teams Phone licenses. These licenses are included with E5 subscriptions or can be bought as an add-on with other subscriptions. Teams Phone licenses add a dial pad to the Teams client. Additionally, ensure that all users using Operator Connect are in Teams Only mode, but the entire organization doesn't need to be in Teams Only mode.

Configure Operator Connect

After completing the readiness requirements and choosing an operator, onboard the operator in the Teams admin center.

1. Go to Voice ➤ Operator and choose an operator from the All Operators tab.

2. Under operator settings, select the country you want to enable with your selected operator.

3. Fill in the contact information and provide the company size.

4. Accept the data transfer notice and add your operator and click Save.

Phone Numbers

Once the Operator Connect is enabled, you must choose whether you acquire new phone numbers from your operator or port the existing number. If your existing carrier is the operator connect partner, raise a support ticket with the carrier to move a phone number from your existing trunk to the Operator Connect trunk.

Acquire New Numbers

To acquire new numbers, you must go to your operator's website. Your operator will provide details of the website. Here is a link from Microsoft that lists operator websites: `https://cloudpartners.transform.microsoft.com/partner-gtm/operators/directory`.

Transfer Your Existing Numbers

To transfer your phone numbers from Calling Plans or your current provider to Operator Connect, you must submit a port order on the operator website with a list of phone numbers and a letter of authorization. After the request is fulfilled, assign the Operator Connect numbers to the users using the following PowerShell command:

```
Set-CsPhoneNumberAssignment -Identity <user> -PhoneNumber <phone number>
-PhoneNumberType OperatorConnect
```

Transferring phone numbers from Direct Routing to Operator Connect can be challenging, depending on whether you manage them on-premises or online. To validate, run the following PowerShell command:

```
Get-CsOnlineUser -Identity <user> | fl RegistrarPool,
OnPremLineURI, LineURI
```

If a user's `OnPremLineUri` attribute contains a phone number, the phone numbers are managed on-premises. The user's phone number must be removed to switch to Operator Connect, requiring scheduled maintenance as the service will be temporarily unavailable.

Here are the steps to assign an Operator Connect number to an on-premises managed Direct Routing user:

1. Set lineuri to Null in your Skype for Business Server by running the following command:

    ```
    Set-CsUser -Identity <user> -LineURI $null
    ```

2. Allow time for changes to sync and validate in an online directory.

    ```
    Get-CsOnlineUser -Identity <user> | fl RegistrarPool,
    OnPremLineURI, LineURI
    ```

3. After the changes have been replicated, execute the command to remove the phone number from Teams.

    ```
    Remove-CsPhoneNumberAssignment -Identity <user>
    -PhoneNumber <pn> -PhoneNumberType DirectRouting
    ```

4. Unassign the voice routing policy.

    ```
    Grant-CsOnlineVoiceRoutingPolicy -Identity <user>
    -PolicyName $Null
    ```

5. Port or acquire the phone numbers and assign them using this PowerShell command:

    ```
    Set-CsPhoneNumberAssignment -Identity <user>
    -PhoneNumber <phone number> -PhoneNumberType
    OperatorConnect
    ```

Teams Phone Mobile

Teams Phone Mobile is another method for providing PSTN services in Teams. Similar to Operator Connect, a list of telecom vendors or operators participate in the Microsoft Teams Phone Mobile program and are eligible to provide Teams Phone PSTN services using this model.

Unlike the Operator Connect model, the Teams Phone Mobile program allows users to use their SIM-enabled phone number as their Teams phone number. This means that users can access their mobile services and Teams using a single phone number. If your organization aims toward a mobile-driven approach, this PSTN connectivity option is the right fit. It is especially useful for salespeople to receive and manage phone calls using their SIM-enabled number and to use the same number for SMS and text messages.

Here are the advantages:

- Single number for mobile and Microsoft Teams allowing users to work from any location securely.

- Users can use unified voicemail, seamless transfers, combined call history, and presence across Teams and native mobile devices.

- Recording and retention of voice calls on native mobile devices.

Architecture

The architecture of Teams Phone Mobile mainly consists of Metaswitch Mobile Control Point (MCP) and Teams-certified mobile interworking SBC. MCP is an application that sits on the carrier-grade application server Rhino. It enhances the user experience by integrating Microsoft Teams into the Mobile Operator's call flow. MCP connects to the Operator's IMS core to determine whether the call should be routed to the mobile operator network and directly to the user's native dialer or routed to Microsoft Teams for applying originating and terminating services for calls made from and to end users. MCP queries the Microsoft Teams phone service if a caller or callee is eligible for Teams Phone Mobile services. If the caller or callee is eligible, MCP adds Microsoft Teams Phone services to the call path. If the user isn't eligible, the call does not reach the Microsoft Teams Phone system, and the MCP ensures the call follows its call path.

The Mobile Interworking SBC ensures that it inserts and removes the ISUP signaling information into SIP signaling messages based on whether calls are routed to the Teams Phone System or the mobile operator. Figure 4-41 shows Teams Phone Mobile architecture.

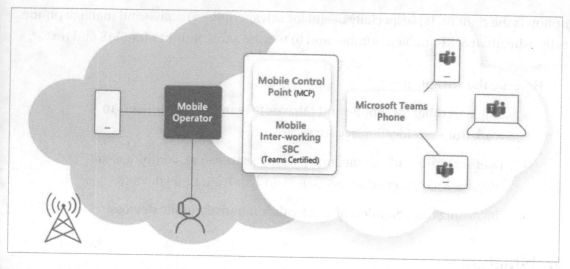

Figure 4-41. *Teams Phone Mobile architecture*

Plan for Teams Phone Mobile

Teams Phone Mobile is a great option for organizations with mobile workforces consisting of frontline workers and sales teams. However, it is essential to validate if Teams Phone is the right method of PSTN connectivity for your organization. The considerations must include the following:

- You want to use a primary company-owned, SIM-enabled mobile number for Teams Phone as a single-number solution.

- Your existing or preferred operator is a participant of the Teams Phone Mobile program.

For users to access Teams Phone Mobile, they need to have the Teams Phone System license and be in Teams-only mode. They also require a Teams Phone Mobile add-on SKU license and an eligible subscription with an operator that supports their SIM-enabled phone numbers for Teams Phone.

Configure Teams Phone Mobile

After completing the readiness requirements and choosing a mobile operator, onboard the operator in the Teams admin center.

1. Go to Voice ➤ Operator and choose an operator from the All Operators tab.

2. Under Operator Settings, select the country you want to enable with your selected operator.

3. Fill in the contact information and provide the company size.

4. Accept the data transfer notice and add your operator and click Save.

Phone Numbers

Once the operator connect is enabled, you must choose whether you acquire new phone numbers from your operator or port the existing number. If you have a company-paid SIM-enabled phone number that you want to add to Teams, contact your operator to confirm your eligibility for the Teams Phone Mobile subscription. Once your operator completes the order, you can assign the numbers to users.

Acquire New Numbers

To acquire new numbers, you must go to your operator's website. Your operator will provide details of the website. Here is a link from Microsoft that lists operator websites: `https://cloudpartners.transform.microsoft.com/partner-gtm/operators/directory`. Order or acquire SIM-enabled mobile phone numbers with Teams Phone service enabled. After completion, view the list of numbers in the Teams admin center under Voice ➤ Phone numbers.

Transfer Your Existing Numbers

To transfer your phone numbers from Calling Plans, ensure you have eligible Teams Phone Mobile subscription and the Teams Phone Mobile add-on licensee. Contact your operator to port your numbers to Teams Phone Mobile on an eligible wireless voice plan that is SIM-enabled. Once the numbers are ported, the operator will upload the numbers in the Teams admin center. Admins can assign the numbers to users using the following Powershell command:

```
Set-CsPhoneNumberAssignment -Identity <user> -PhoneNumber <phone number>
-PhoneNumberType OCMobile
```

It can be challenging to transfer phone numbers from Direct Routing to Teams Phone Mobile, depending on whether you manage them on-premises or online. To validate, run the following PowerShell command:

```
Get-CsOnlineUser -Identity <user> | fl RegistrarPool,
OnPremLineURI, LineURI
```

If a user's OnPremLineUri attribute contains a phone number, the phone numbers are managed on-premises. The user's phone number must be removed to switch to Operator Connect, requiring scheduled maintenance as the service will be temporarily unavailable.

Here are the steps to assign an Operator Connect number to an on-premises managed Direct Routing user:

1. Set lineuri to Null in your Skype for Business Server by running this command:

   ```
   Set-CsUser -Identity <user> -LineURI $null
   ```

2. Allow time for changes to sync and validate in online directory.

   ```
   Get-CsOnlineUser -Identity <user> | fl RegistrarPool,
   OnPremLineURI, LineURI
   ```

3. After the changes have been replicated, execute the command to remove the phone number from Teams.

   ```
   Remove-CsPhoneNumberAssignment -Identity <user>
   -PhoneNumber <pn> -PhoneNumberType DirectRouting
   ```

4. Unassign the voice routing policy.

   ```
   Grant-CsOnlineVoiceRoutingPolicy -Identity
   <user> -PolicyName $Null
   ```

5. Port or acquire the phone numbers and assign them using this PowerShell command:

   ```
   Set-CsPhoneNumberAssignment -Identity <user>
   -PhoneNumber <phone number> -PhoneNumberType
   OperatorConnect
   ```

Configuring and Managing the Call Queue

Microsoft Teams cloud call queues provide multiple features for calling, including a greeting message, music while individuals are waiting on hold, forwarding calls to call agents in mail-enabled distribution lists and security groups, and setting different parameters such as queue maximum size, timeout, and call handling options.

Teams Phone System call queues, and auto attendants must have at least one associated resource account. Basically, a resource account will need an assigned phone number depending on the proposed usage of the associated call queue or auto attendant. You cannot directly give the phone number to a call queue or auto attendant, so the phone number is assigned to a resource account that is associated with call queue or auto attendant. Therefore, the call queue can be dialed directly or accessed by a selection on an auto attendant, and then all calls in the queue will be sent to agents using one of these techniques.

- With attendant routing, the first call in the queue rings all agents simultaneously.

- With serial routing, the first call in the queue rings all call agents one by one.

- With round-robin, the routing of incoming calls is balanced so that each call agent gets the same number of calls from the queue.

- Only one incoming call notification at a time (for the call at the head of the queue) goes to the call agents.

- After a call agent accepts a call, the next incoming call in the queue will start ringing call agents.

As per Microsoft's new requirements, every resource account utilized with a call queue or auto attendant must be licensed with a Microsoft Teams Phone resource account license, regardless of whether it's assigned a phone number or configured for a nested call queue or nested auto attendant.

Note   Call agents who are offline, those who have set their presence to "Do not disturb, "or those who have opted out of the call queue will not receive calls.

Creating a Call Queue

As you learned, a phone number cannot be directly assigned to a call queue; instead, it is assigned to the resource account. That resource account will then be linked to the call queue. That means before creating a call queue, you as a Teams admin must think through the requirements for creating a call queue. The requirements are listed here:

- You must have a resource account created for the call queue.

- When you assign a phone number to a resource account, you can use the free Microsoft Teams Phone Resource Account license.

- Another important requirement is to assign a phone number. Remember that you can assign only toll and toll-free service phone numbers that you got in the Microsoft Teams admin center or port from another service provider to cloud call queues.

- Additionally, communications credits setup in Microsoft 365 is required for toll and toll-free service numbers.

- You can assign multiple resource accounts to call queues, but you cannot assign a single resource account to various call queues.

Follow these steps to create a call queue:

1. Get service numbers from Microsoft or transfer your existing toll or toll-free service numbers before creating your call queues. Once you get the toll or toll-free service phone numbers, they will show up in the Microsoft Teams admin center under Voice ➤ Phone Numbers.

2. Create a resource account. Every call queue must have an associated resource account, which you can associate with the call queue. You should perform the following steps to create a new call queue:

   a. Go to the Microsoft Teams admin center, and select Voice. Select Call Queues, and then click + Add New.

   b. On the Call Queues/Add page, give the call queue a meaningful display name that will be displayed in notifications for incoming calls. Figure 4-42 shows CQ_SipGateway as the queue name.

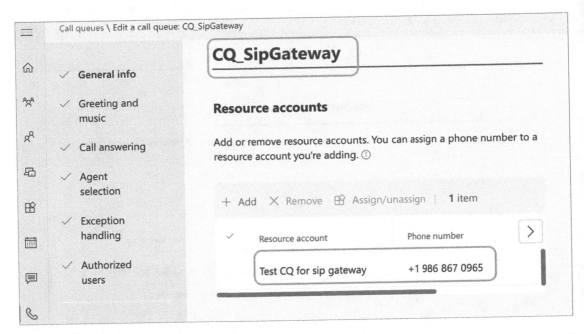

Figure 4-42. *Call queue name and selecting a resource account*

c. Click Add Accounts to select a resource account (it may or may not be associated with a toll or toll-free phone number for the call queue, but each call queue requires an associated resource account). If no resource accounts are listed, you must get service numbers and assign them to a resource account before creating this call queue. In this example, a resource account is created in advance. In Figure 4-43, Test CQ for the sip gateway is assigned with a phone number and assigned to the call queue.

d. To assign a calling ID, click the Add button. This feature allows agents to make outbound calls using either their personal calling ID or the caller ID of a resource account. In this example, we utilize the caller ID of the resource account linked to the call queue. This enables agents to use it as their outbound caller ID.

e. Please choose the preferred language for the agents who will listen to the transcribed voicemail in the call queue. The system will also play prompts to the caller in the selected language. In this example, we choose English (United States). Refer to Figure 4-43 for language selection.

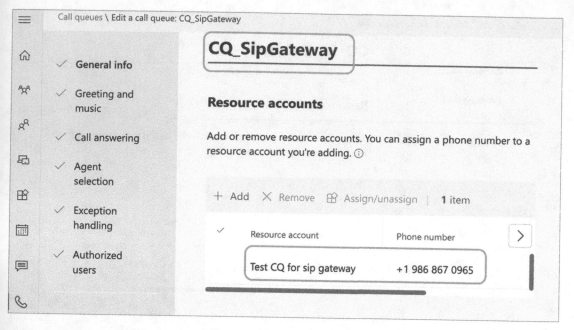

Figure 4-43. Configuring calling ID and language

3. Set the greeting and music that will be played while a call is on hold, as shown in Figure 4-44.

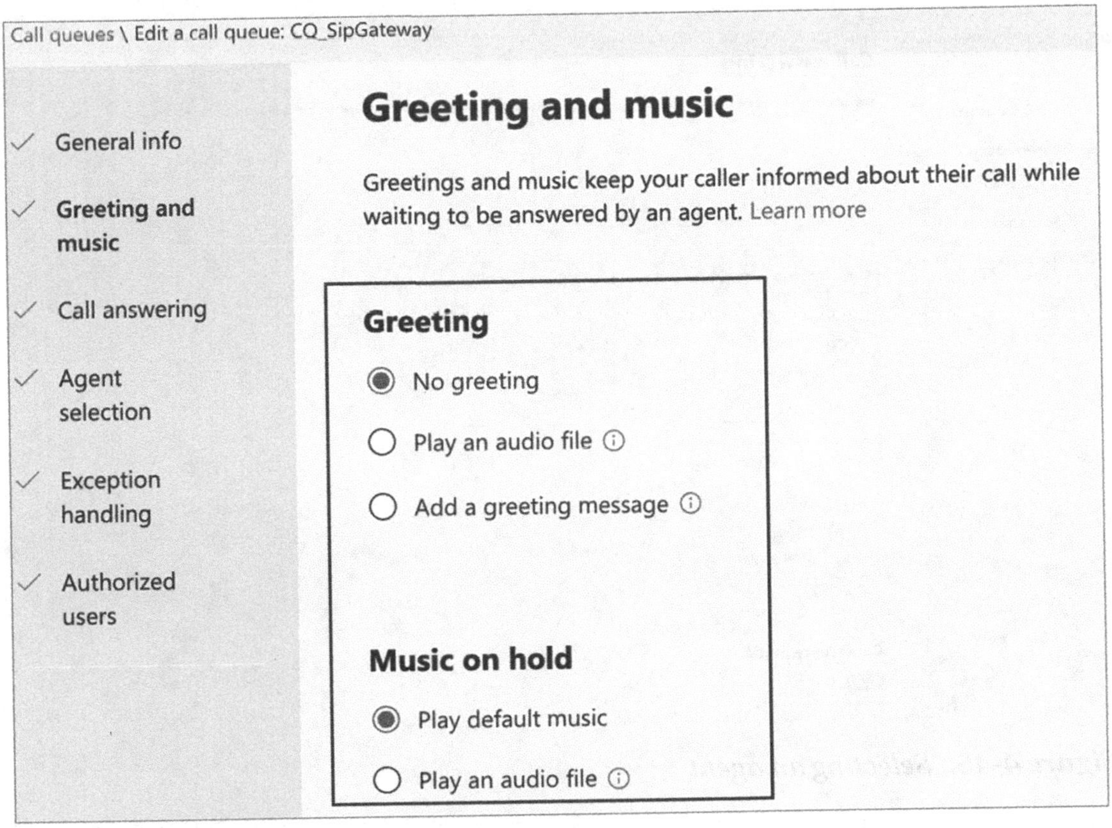

Call queues \ Edit a call queue: CQ_SipGateway

Greeting and music

✓ General info

✓ **Greeting and music**

✓ Call answering

✓ Agent selection

✓ Exception handling

✓ Authorized users

Greetings and music keep your caller informed about their call while waiting to be answered by an agent. Learn more

Greeting

◉ No greeting

○ Play an audio file ⓘ

○ Add a greeting message ⓘ

Music on hold

◉ Play default music

○ Play an audio file ⓘ

Figure 4-44. Selecting a greeting and hold music

4. In the "Call answering" section, add call queue agents and select conference mode.

a. Select the call answering options. You can select a user agent or group. Up to 200 call agents can belong to an Office 365 group, security group, Teams channel, or distribution list. The example in Figure 4-45 shows Christie Cline as the call agent.

b. Turn on the conference mode to reduce the time a caller takes to connect with an agent after the call has been accepted. This is useful if all the agents are in Teams-only mode and using Teams-compatible clients.

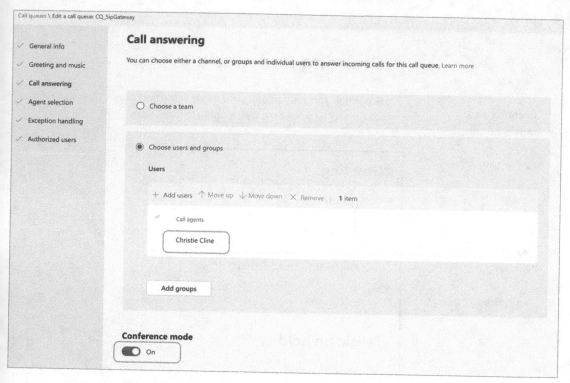

Figure 4-45. Selecting an agent

Note   The call agents that you select must be online users with a Phone System license and Enterprise Voice enabled, online users with a Calling Plan, or Direct Routing with an On-Premises phone number assigned.

---

5. Select a routing method for your call queue distribution method. You can select from the following options:

    a. **Attendant Routing:** This enables the first call in the queue to ring all call agents simultaneously. The first call agent to pick up the call gets the call.

    b. **Longest Idle:** The call routes to the agent who has been idle for the longest time, based on their presence status displayed as "Available." Agents will receive calls only if their presence status is set to Available.

c. **Serial Routing:** Using this option, an incoming call rings call agents one by one, starting from the beginning of the call agent list (agents cannot be ordered within the call agent list). If an agent dismisses or does not pick up a call, then the call will ring the next agent on the list, trying all agents one by one until it is picked up or times out waiting in the queue.

d. **Round Robin:** This method balances incoming calls routing so that each call agent gets the same number of calls from the queue. Figure 4-46 shows the round-robin method selected. "All agents can opt out of taking calls" is set to On, and the "Call agent alert time" setting is 35 seconds.

e. **Presence-based call routing:** By turning on this setting, Calls are routed depending on the agent's presence status. If the agent is available, they will be added to the routing queue using the previous routing methods. However, if the agent's presence is set to any other status, they will not receive any calls until they change their position to available.

f. **Agents can opt out of taking calls:** Enabling this option allows agents to opt out from a specific call queue if they choose to do so. Agents can adjust these settings within their Teams client.

g. **Agent alert time:** The agent alert time is the duration for which a call rings for an agent before being redirected to another agent. Setting the ringing time to 20 seconds is recommended, as this is the default time for Teams. It is recommended to set the ringing time to 20 seconds, as this is the default ring time for Microsoft Teams.

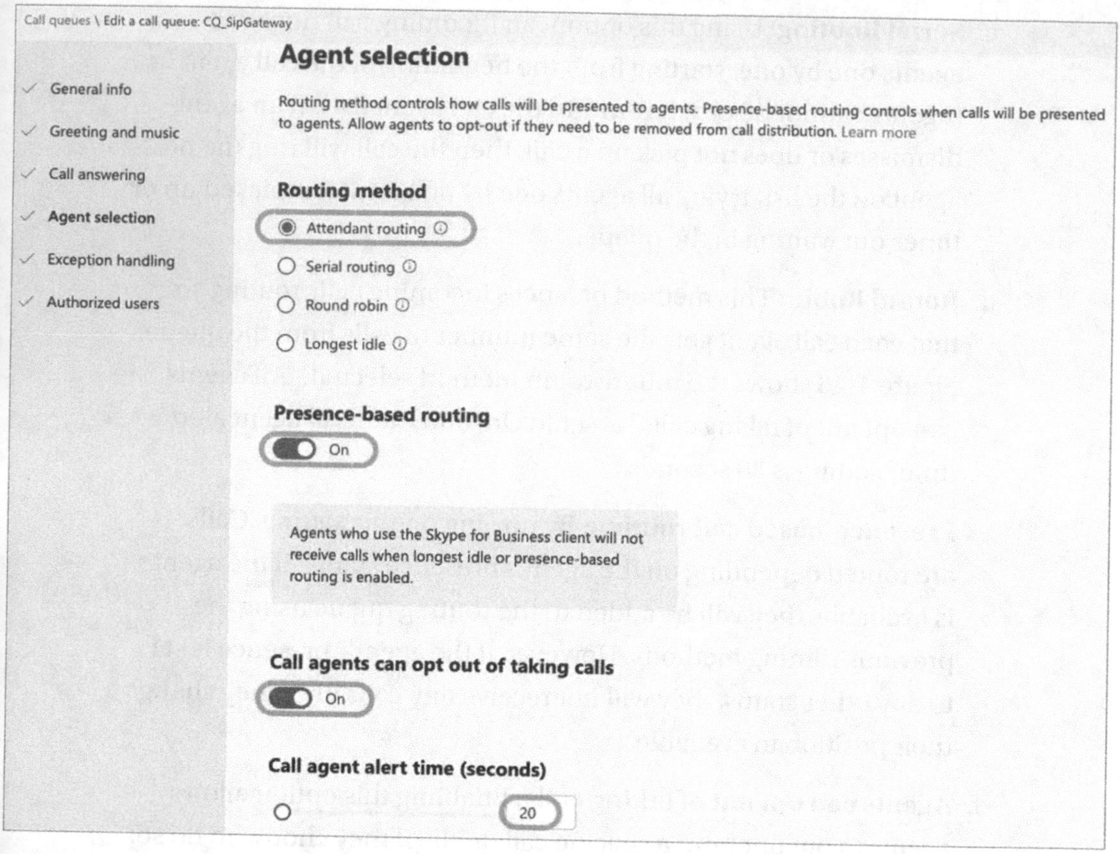

Figure 4-46. *Routing method selection*

6. When it comes to handling exceptions, there are a few settings you can configure. First, you can set Maximum Calls In The Queue. Additionally, you can configure the call timeout and determine how to manage calls when no agents are available in the queue.

   a. **Call Overflow:** Use this setting to set the maximum number of calls that can be in the queue simultaneously (the default is 50, but the value can range from 0 to 200). When the call queue reaches the maximum you have set, you can select what happens to new incoming calls using the following options:

   • **Disconnect:** This option will disconnect the call.

- **Redirect To:** Select one of the following redirect settings using this option:

    1. **Person In Organization:** This selection, shown in Figure 4-47, enables you to select the person to whom the incoming call will be redirected.

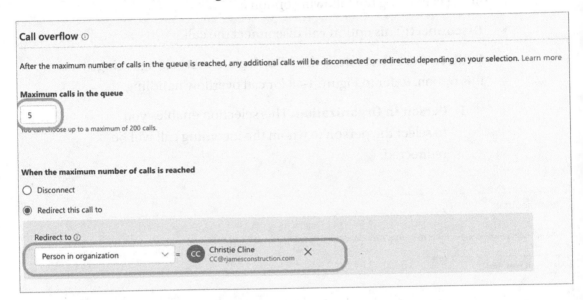

Figure 4-47. *Call overflow handling*

    2. **Voice Application:** You must select the name of an existing resource account associated with either a call queue or an auto attendant.

    3. **External Phone Number:** If you need to redirect a call to an external phone number, you can do so by assigning the resource account with either a Calling Plan license (if you use Calling Plans) or an Online Voice routing policy (if you use Direct Routing).

    4. **Voicemail (Personal):** Use this setting to redirect the call to a user's voicemail.

    5. **Voicemail (Shared):** Use this setting to redirect the call to a Microsoft 365 group's voicemail.

b. **Call Timeout:** Using this setting, you can set up the maximum number of minutes that a call can be on hold in the queue before it gets redirected or disconnected. You can specify the value from 0 seconds to 45 minutes. When the call queue reaches the maximum you have set, you can select what happens to new incoming calls using the following options:

- **Disconnect:** This option will disconnect the call.

- **Redirect To:** Select one of the following redirect settings using this option. Refer to Figure 4-48 for call overflow handling.

    1. **Person In Organization:** This selection enables you to select the person to whom the incoming call will be redirected.

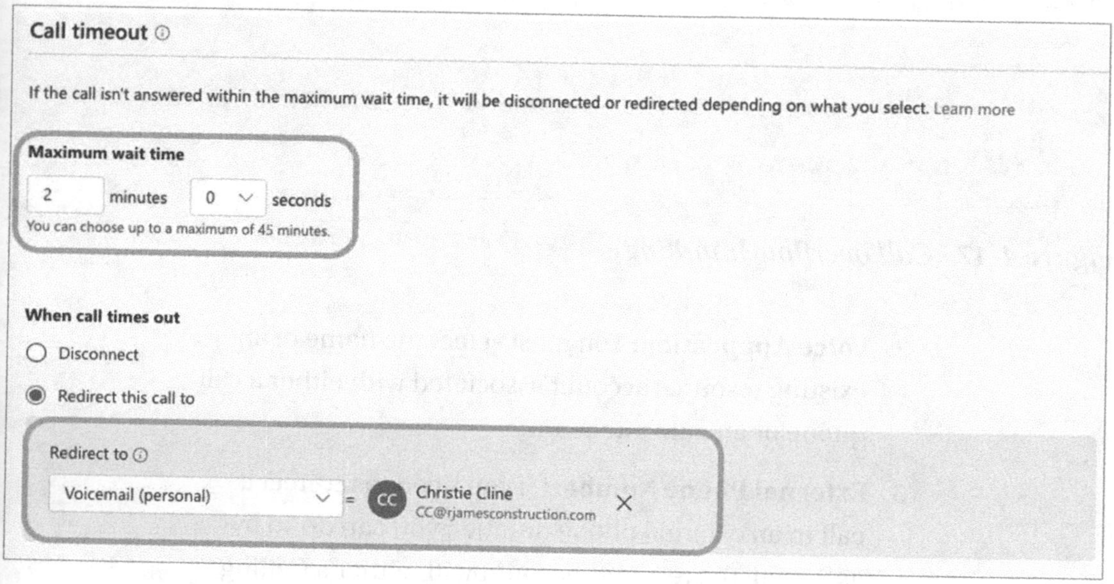

Call timeout ⓘ

If the call isn't answered within the maximum wait time, it will be disconnected or redirected depending on what you select. Learn more

Maximum wait time

| 2 | minutes | 0 ⌄ | seconds |

You can choose up to a maximum of 45 minutes.

When call times out

○ Disconnect

◉ Redirect this call to

Redirect to ⓘ

| Voicemail (personal) ⌄ | = | CC Christie Cline | ✕ |
| | | CC@rjamesconstruction.com | |

Figure 4-48. Call overflow handling

2. **Voice Application:** You must select the name of an existing resource account associated with either a call queue or an auto attendant.

3. **External Phone Number:** If you need to redirect a call to an external phone number, you can do so by assigning the resource account with either a Calling Plan license (if you use Calling Plans) or an Online Voice routing policy (if you use Direct Routing).

4. **Voicemail (Personal):** Use this setting to redirect the call to a user's voicemail.

5. **Voicemail (Shared):** Use this setting to redirect the call to a M365 Group's voicemail.

c. **No Agents Opted/Logged in:** You can use this setting to manage a queue when no agents are logged in or agents are opted out of taking calls from the queue. You can apply this to calls already in the queue and new calls or only the new ones. Configure the call handling under this exception.

- **Queue call:** By selecting this option, the call will remain in the queue.

- **Disconnect:** This option will disconnect the call.

- **Redirect To:** Select one of the following redirect settings using this option:

  1. **Person In Organization:** This selection enables you to select the person to whom the incoming call will be redirected.

  2. **Voice Application:** You must select the name of an existing resource account associated with either a call queue or an auto attendant.

  3. **External Phone Number:** If you need to redirect a call to an external phone number, you can assign the resource account with either a Calling Plan license (if you use Calling Plans) or an Online Voice routing policy (if you use Direct Routing).

4. **Voicemail (Personal):** Use this setting to redirect the call to a user voicemail.

5. **Voicemail (Shared):** Use this setting to redirect the call to a M365 group's voicemail.

7. **Authorized users:** Authorized users are individuals who can manage the call queue settings. Typically, these individuals are supervisors or managers who handle agents. These users must be assigned with Voice application policy to manage the settings. Debra is assigned as an authorized user in the example and added to the HR-Call queue Voice application policy. Debra can manage these settings in the Teams client. See Figure 4-49 and Figure 4-50.

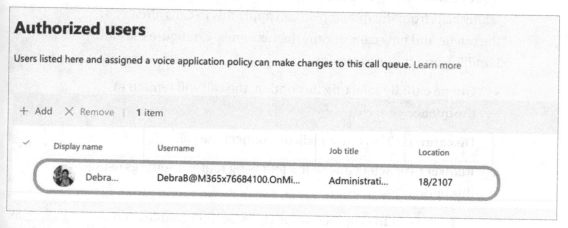

Figure 4-49. *Call queue, authorized users*

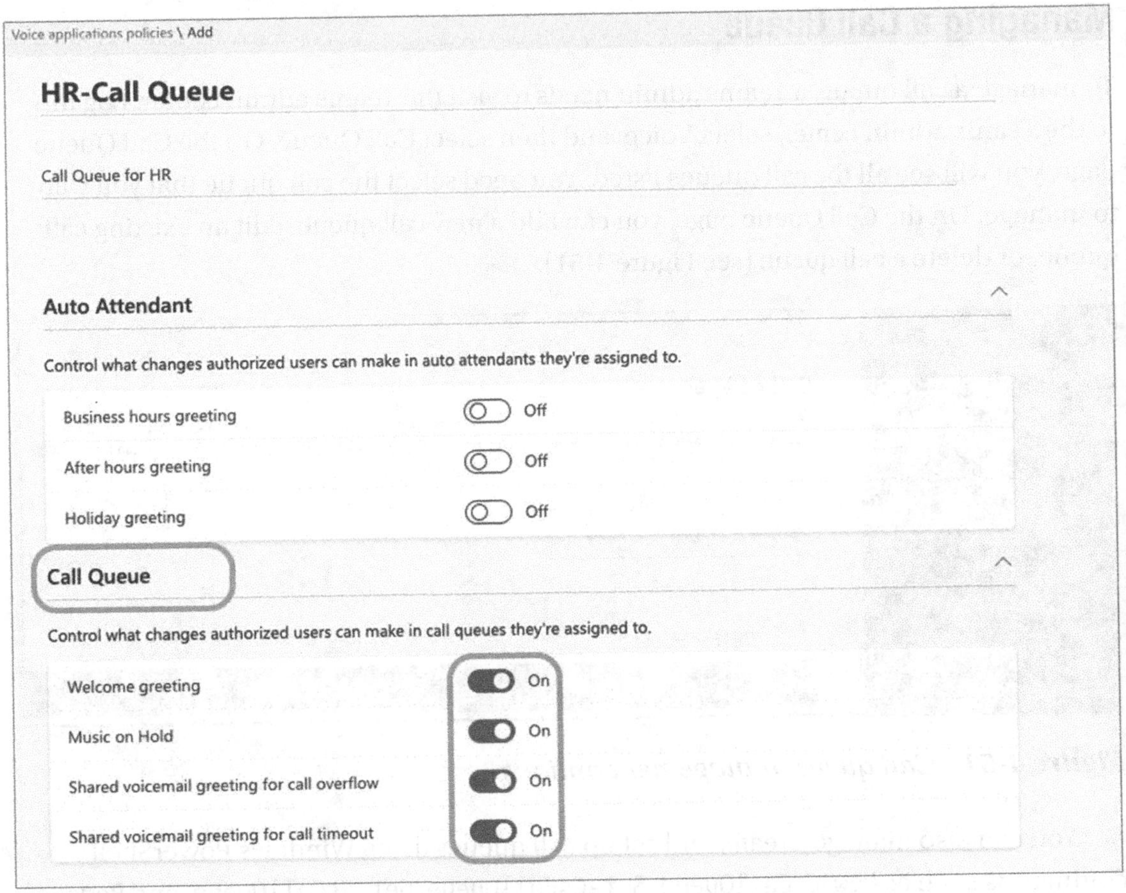

Figure 4-50. *Voice application policy*

8. Verify all the options you selected and then click Save to create the call queue.

9. The call queue might take a while to create. When complete, test the call queue by making a phone call to the resource account service phone number and validate that the call is landing with an agent.

Managing a Call Queue

To manage a call queue, a Teams admin needs to visit the Teams admin center. Log in to the Teams admin center, select Voice, and then select Call Queue. On the Call Queue page, you will see all the call queues listed. You need select the call queue that you want to manage. On the Call Queue page, you can add a new call queue, edit an existing call queue, or delete a call queue (see Figure 4-51).

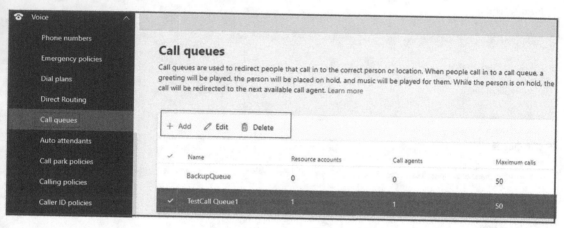

Figure 4-51. *Call queue management options*

You can also manage, create, and set up call queues using Windows PowerShell commands such as `New-CsCallQueue`, `Set-CsCallQueue`, `Get-CsCallQueue`, and `Remove-CsCallQueue`.

Additionally, authorized users can manage the call queues from their Teams desktop client. Please note that they must be added as an authorized user in the call queue and assigned with the voice application policy.

As an administrator, you can validate if a call queue can receive the call by running a diagnostic tool (`https://aka.ms/TeamsCallQueueDiag`).

Managing and Configuring Auto Attendant in Teams

The Teams Phone System provides multiple capabilities, including an auto attendant, which is highly utilized in many customer support organizations. Auto attendants enable external and internal callers to use a menu system to locate and place (or transfer) calls to users or departments in an organization. When people call a number associated with an auto attendant, their options can redirect the call to a user or locate someone else in the organization and then connect to that user.

Microsoft Teams cloud auto attendant features can allow someone to leave a message if a person does not answer the call, and they can provide corporate greetings, custom corporate menus including nested menus (menu inside the menu), and messages that specify business and holiday hours. Auto attendants can also support transferring calls to an operator, other users, call queues, and auto attendants. It also offers a directory search that enables users who call in to search the organization's directory for a name. It also supports multiple languages for prompts, text-to-speech, and speech recognition.

The auto attendant does have some prerequisites before creation.

- An auto attendant must have an associated resource account.

- When assigning a phone number to an auto attendant, you assign it to the resource account associated with that auto attendant; this enables you to have more than one phone number to access an auto attendant.

- A resource account must be assigned with a Microsoft Teams Resource Account license. This license can be acquired for free.

- To get and use toll-free service numbers for your auto attendants, you must set up communications credits.

- A complete auto attendant system usually involves multiple auto attendants and might require only a single assigned phone number for the top-level auto attendant.

- You can assign multiple resource accounts to an auto attendant, but you cannot give a single resource account to multiple auto attendants.

Creating an Auto Attendant with an Existing Resource Account

To create an auto attendant with an existing resource account, follow the procedure in this section. Remember, you cannot directly assign a service phone number to the auto attendant. Assign the number to a resource account associated with the auto attendant.

1. Log in to the Teams admin center and navigate to Voice. Select Auto Attendant and click Add.

2. On the Auto Attendants/Add Auto Attendant page, shown in Figure 4-52, enter a meaningful name and provide the following information:

   - **Operator:** This setting specifies whether a user can request to talk to a person or voice app or if there will be no designated operator. You can refer people to another auto attendant, a call queue, or an enterprise voice-enabled Skype for Business or Teams user.

   - **Time Zone:** This specifies the time zone in which the auto attendant will calculate business hours and holidays.

   - **Language:** This setting specifies the language the system will use.

   - **Enable Voice Input:** This enables voice navigation in the auto attendant menu.

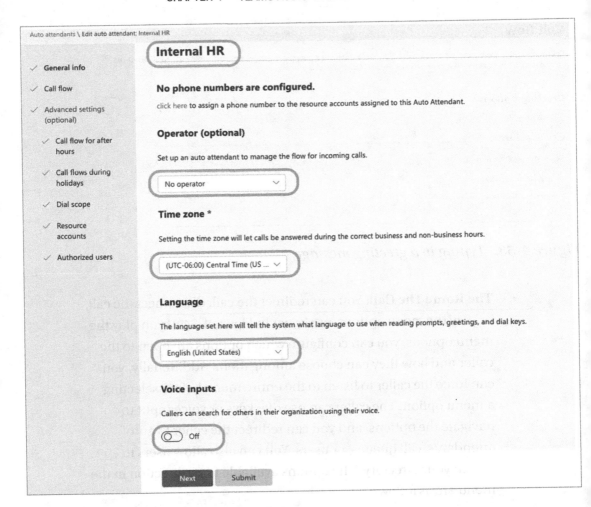

Figure 4-52. *Adding an auto attendant*

3. Click Next. On the page that opens, you are asked to configure the following settings:

- **First Play A Greeting Message:** You can select No Greeting, Play An Audio File, or Type In A Greeting Message. Figure 4-53 shows an example of a greeting message entered.

449

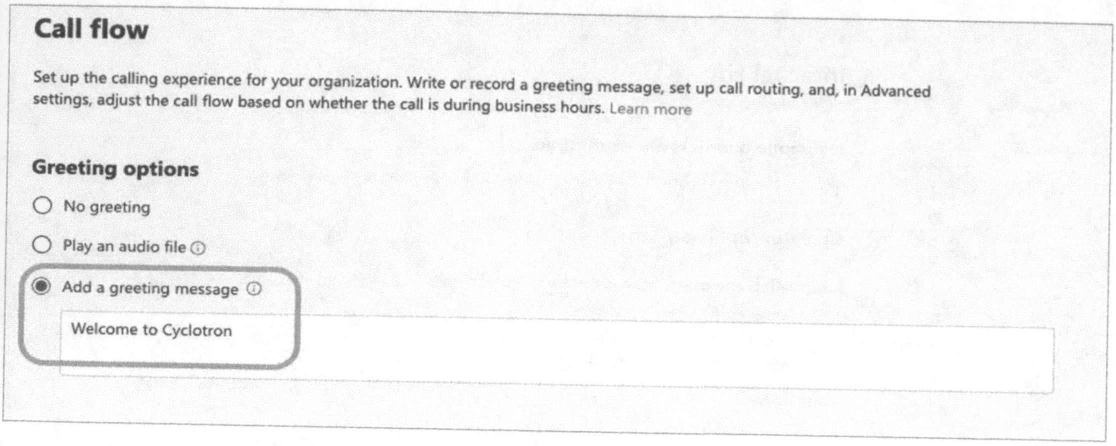

Call flow

Set up the calling experience for your organization. Write or record a greeting message, set up call routing, and, in Advanced settings, adjust the call flow based on whether the call is during business hours. Learn more

Greeting options

○ No greeting

○ Play an audio file ⓘ

◉ Add a greeting message ⓘ

Welcome to Cyclotron

Figure 4-53. *Typing in a greeting message*

- **The Route The Call:** You can redirect the call, disconnect the call, or play the menu options, as shown in Figure 4-54. If you play the menu options, you can configure which options are open to the caller and how they can choose among them. Additionally, you can force the caller to listen to the entire menu before selecting a menu option. The caller can use dial keys or voice input to navigate the options, and you can redirect the caller to auto attendants, call queues, or users. You can also allow users to search your directory. The options available for redirection in the menu are as follows:

- **Person In Organization:** This selection enables you to select the person to whom the incoming call will be redirected.

- **Person In Organization:** This selection enables you to select the person to whom the incoming call will be redirected.

- **Operator:** This setting specifies whether a user can request to talk to a person or voice app or if there will be no designated operator. You can refer people to another auto attendant, a call queue, or an enterprise voice-enabled Skype for Business or Teams user.

- **Voice Application:** You must select the name of an existing resource account associated with either a call queue or an auto attendant.

- **External Phone Number:** If you need to redirect a call to an external phone number, you can assign the resource account with either a Calling Plan license (if you use Calling Plans) or an Online Voice routing policy (if you use Direct Routing).

- **Voicemail (Personal):** Use this setting to redirect the call to a user voicemail.

- **Voicemail (Shared):** Use this setting to redirect the call to a M365 group's voicemail.

- **Announcement (Audio):** Use this setting to play an audio file.

- **Announcement (Typed):** Type in the text message to be played as text-to-speech.

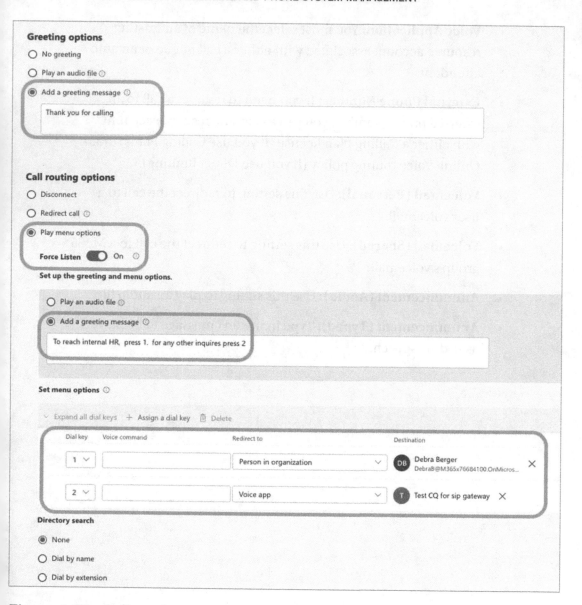

Figure 4-54. *Call routing options*

4. Click Next. On the next page, shown in Figure 4-55, provide the following information:

   a. **Set Business Hours:** Use these settings to specify when the auto attendant will be considered working. If you do not provide business hours, the auto attendant will be set to 24/7 by default.

b. **Set Up After Hours Call Flow:** Select what will happen to the call outside of business hours. If you do not change the default setting, your call will disconnect outside business hours.

c. **First Play A Greeting Message:** Specify a greeting for calls that are received outside of business hours. If you do not change the default setting, your call will not play an outside-of-business-hours greeting.

d. **Call routing options:** After playing the greeting, you have the following options:

- **Disconnect:** This option will disconnect the call.

- **Redirect To:** Select one of the following redirect settings using this option.

   - **Person In Organization:** This selection enables you to select the person to whom the incoming call will be redirected.

   - **Voice Application:** You must select the name of an existing resource account associated with either a call queue or an auto attendant.

   - **External Phone Number:** If you need to redirect a call to an external phone number, you can do so by assigning the resource account with either a Calling Plan license (if you use Calling Plans) or an Online Voice routing policy (if you use Direct Routing).

   - **Voicemail (Shared):** Use this setting to redirect the call to a M365 group's voicemail.

- **Play menu options:** With this feature, you can create a menu that allows callers to select their preferred redirect options based on the menu options provided.

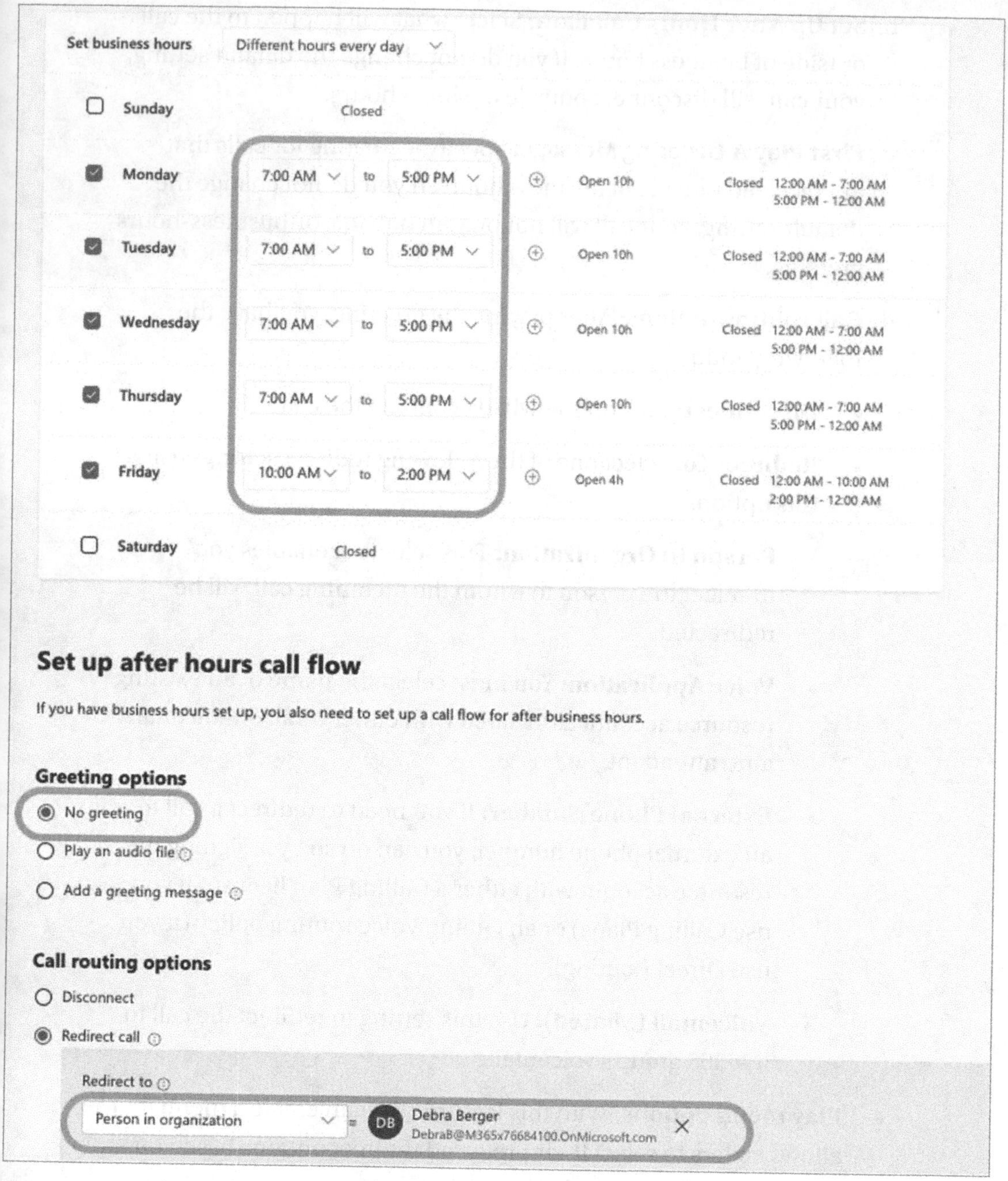

Figure 4-55. *Setting business hours*

5. Click Next. On the next page, you can click + Add to add specific dates as holidays for your auto attendant. Then you will be asked to provide the following information, as shown in Figure 4-56:

    - **Name:** Select the name for the holiday option.

    - **Date:** This is the date for the holiday.

    - **Greeting:** You can elect not to play a greeting and instead play an audio file or use text to speech.

    - **Call routing:** You can decide to disconnect or redirect calls.

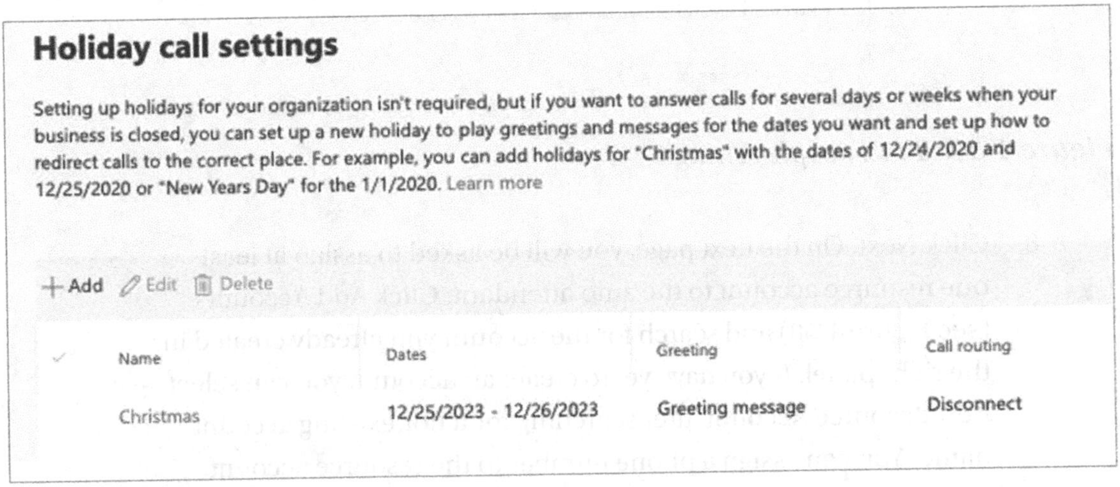

Holiday call settings

Setting up holidays for your organization isn't required, but if you want to answer calls for several days or weeks when your business is closed, you can set up a new holiday to play greetings and messages for the dates you want and set up how to redirect calls to the correct place. For example, you can add holidays for "Christmas" with the dates of 12/24/2020 and 12/25/2020 or "New Years Day" for the 1/1/2020. Learn more

+ Add   ✎ Edit   🗑 Delete

Name	Dates	Greeting	Call routing
Christmas	12/25/2023 - 12/26/2023	Greeting message	Disconnect

Figure 4-56. *Holiday call settings*

6. Click Save to save the holiday. You can add multiple holidays by repeating steps 5 and 6. You can set up to 50 holidays.

7. Click Next. On the page that opens, you can define the scope of users that is searchable by the caller, as displayed in Figure 4-57.

    - **Include:** Select a group of users or all online users. Online users are all those whose accounts are online or have been added using Azure Directory sync. Custom groups can be security, distribution, and Office 365 Groups.

    - **Exclude:** You can select None or Custom User Group. This will exclude those users from being searchable.

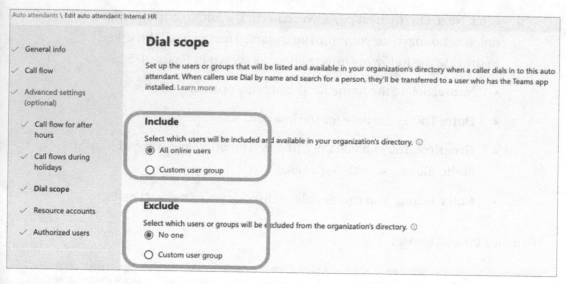

Figure 4-57. *Find people settings*

8. Click Next. On the next page, you will be asked to assign at least one resource account to the auto attendant. Click Add Accounts (see Figure 4-58) and search for the account you already created in the right panel. If you have yet to create an account, you can select Add Resource Account after searching for a nonexisting account name. You can assign a phone number to the resource account.

Auto attendants \ Edit auto attendant: Internal HR

General info

Call flow

Advanced settings
(optional)

Call flow for after
hours

Call flows during
holidays

Dial scope

Resource
accounts

Authorized users

Resource accounts

When you create an auto attendant, you can add a new resource account and assign a phone number to that resource account. Learn more

+ Add   ✕ Remove   ⊞ Assign/unassign   1 item

	Resource account	Phone number	Licensed
✓	HRQueue	⚠ Unassigned	Licensed

Figure 4-58. *Adding a resource account*

9. Next, add authorized users. Authorized users are a list of individuals who can manage the call queue settings. Typically, these individuals are supervisors or managers who handle agents. These users must be assigned with Voice application policy to manage the settings. Debra is assigned as an authorized user in the example and added to the Voice application policy. Debra can manage these settings in the Teams client. Click Submit to create your auto attendant. See Figure 4-59.

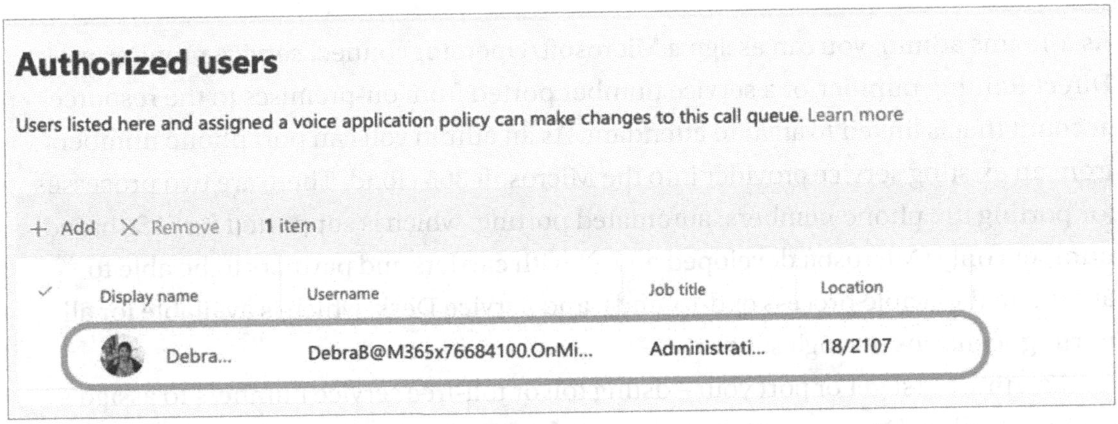

Figure 4-59. *Auto attendants, authorized users*

10. After creating an auto attendant, the next step is to test the auto attendant by calling the resource account phone number that is associated with the auto attendant.

Managing Auto Attendants

As a Teams admin, you must know how to manage auto attendants. To do so, log in to the Teams admin center and navigate to Voice. Select Auto Attendant. On the Auto Attendant page, you will see all auto attendants created in your tenant. You can perform management tasks such as adding new auto attendants, editing existing auto attendants, and deleting auto attendants.

Additionally, authorized users can manage the auto attendants from their Teams desktop client. Please note that they must be added as an authorized user in the auto attendant and assigned to the Voice application policy.

As an administrator, you can validate if an auto attendant is able to receive the call by running a diagnostic tool (https://aka.ms/TeamsAADiag).

Note   You cannot call the attendant if you have not assigned a phone number to your resource account.

Assigning Phone Numbers for an Auto Attendant

As a Teams admin, you can assign a Microsoft/Operator connect service number, a Direct Routing number, or a service number ported from on-premises to the resource account that is linked to an auto attendant. As an admin you can port phone numbers from an existing service provider into the Microsoft 365 cloud. There are two processes for porting the phone numbers: automated porting, which is supported for U.S.-based numbers only (Microsoft developed an API with carriers and partners to be able to automate the whole process end-to-end), and Service Desk, which is available for all porting scenarios through support.

You must first get or port your existing toll or toll-free service numbers to assign a service number. Once you get the toll or toll-free service phone numbers, they show up in the Microsoft Teams admin center under Voice ➤ Phone Numbers. You can identify these numbers by looking for the type listed as Service. You can also update the usage for these phone numbers in the Teams admin center if the phone numbers are available with Calling Plans. If you are using Operator Connect, reach out to your Operator Connect provider to update the usage.

Searching for Users

Callers can search by name or extension when searching for users as part of the auto attendant functionality. This functionality is also known as *directory search*.

- **Dial by Name:** This feature enables the people who call your auto attendant to use voice (speech recognition) or their phone keypad (DTMF) to enter a full or partial name to search your company's directory, locate a person, and then have the call transferred to that person.

- **Dial by Extension:** This feature enables callers to use voice (speech recognition) or their phone keypad (DTMF) responses to enter the phone extension of the user they are trying to reach and then have the call transferred to that person.

The users you want to have located and reached using dial by name or dial by extension are not required to have a phone number or have Calling Plans assigned to them. Still, they must have a Phone System license if they are online users or Enterprise Voice enabled for Skype for Business Server users. Dial by name or extension will even be able to find and transfer calls to Microsoft Teams users who are hosted in different countries or regions for multinational organizations. Given the prerequisites involved, you must explicitly enable dial by name and dial by extension in an auto attendant.

Maximum Directory Size

There is no limit in the number of AD users dial by name, and dial by extension can support when a caller searches for a specific person. The maximum name list size that a single auto attendant can support using speech recognition is 80,000 users.

- **With dial by name**, a caller can enter just one part of the name or full names (FirstName + LastName, and LastName + FirstName). There are various formats that can be used when the name is entered. People can use the 0 (zero) key to indicate a space between the first and last name. When the person enters the name, they will be asked to terminate the keypad entry with the pound (#) key; for example, "After you have entered the name of the person you are trying to reach, please press pound." If multiple names are found, a list of names will be displayed, from which the person calling can select the person they are trying to reach.

- **With dial by extension**, the caller needs the full extension number.

People can also search for others in their company using dial by name with name recognition with speech recognition. When you enable speech recognition for an auto attendant, the phone keypad entry is not disabled, which means it can be used at any time (even if speech recognition is enabled on the auto attendant).

Setting Menu Options

Using the Teams admin center, you can assign functions for the 0–9 dial keys in an auto attendant. Different sets of menu options can be created for business hours and after hours, and you can turn dial on or off by name in the menu options. Keys can be mapped to transfer the calls to any of the following:

- An operator.

- Call queue.

- Another auto attendant.

- Microsoft Teams user with a Phone System license that is Enterprise Voice-enabled or has Calling Plans assigned to them. In cloud auto attendants, you can create menu prompts (e.g., "Press 1 for Marketing, Press 2 for Finance") and set up menu options to route calls. Menu prompts can be created either by using text-to-speech or by uploading a recorded audio file. Speech recognition accepts voice commands, but people can also use the phone keypad to navigate the menu.

Configuring and Managing Emergency Calling

The emergency calling service Enhanced 911 (E911) is the official national emergency service number in the United States. Other countries have similar emergency calling services. In the United States, when someone calls 911, the final destination of that call is a Public Safety Answering Point (PSAP) that dispatches first responders. PSAP jurisdictions usually follow local government (city or county) boundaries. E911 determines location information automatically and routes the call to the correct PSAP, and that's how caller gets the help they need.

Basically, an emergency calling service (in this case, E911) permits an emergency operator to identify a caller's location without asking the caller for that information. When a caller is calling from a client using a VoIP network, that information must be obtained based on various factors. Microsoft Teams offers an E911 calling service through Phone System Calling Plan where Microsoft is the service provider, and through Phone System Direct Routing using your existing on-premises PSTN connectivity to a carrier.

This section provides you with the essential information that you as a Teams admin will need to configure an emergency calling service in your environment.

First you need to understand the different terminology used here. First, the emergency address is a civic address containing the physical or street address of a place of business for your organization. For example, the Cyclotron organization's HQ office address is 537 South Tradition Street, Tracy, CA, 95391. Although not an emergency address, a place can also be used. The site is typically used when an office facility contains multiple floors, buildings, office numbers, and so on. A place is associated with an emergency address to give a more exact location within a building.

Note   There are differences in how you manage emergency calling depending on whether you are using Microsoft Phone System Calling Plans or Phone System Direct Routing using an SBC connected to the PSTN.

E911 Laws in the United States

All Multi-Line Telephone Systems (MLTS) platforms are required to comply with minimum Enhanced 911 rules set by the Federal Communication Commission. This means that every organization in the United States must comply with federal regulations on Enhanced 911. It is now mandatory for organizations across the United States to comply with both Kari's Law and RAY BAUM's Act, which specify direct dialing, notification, and dispatchable location requirements.

Kari's Law

For every phone that can dial into the public switch network, it is required to be able to dial 911, including softphones. Kari's law mandates that MLTS platforms manufactured, imported, offered for first sale or lease, first sold or leased, or installed after February 16, 2020, must allow users to dial 911 directly without the need to dial a prefix to reach an outside line. Additionally, notification must be provided to front desk, security, and administrative personnel when a 911 call is made, including information about the call's location and the phone number that dialed 911.

Note   Kari's law and the commission's rules are forward-looking and do not apply with respect to any MLTS that is manufactured, imported, offered for first sale or lease, first sold or leased, or installed on or before February 16, 2020.

Ray Baum's Act

According to the FCC, all 911 calls must have a "dispatchable location," which means emergency responders should have enough information to locate the person who made the call. Section 506 of Ray Baum's Act defines dispatchable location as this information. The specifics of the dispatchable location will differ depending on where the call is made from, but it may include details. Here's an example:

Street address - 2301 Performance Dr - 4th flr - Room 437/NE Corner

How Is Teams Phone Compliant with These Requirements?

Teams service complies with Kari's law by allowing 911 calls without prefixes or suffixes and without needing to enter the + sign before making the call. Additionally, administrators can configure emergency calling policies to send notifications to the front desk for each location and assign them directly to users or at the network level to dynamically send notifications. To comply with the Raybaums Act, Teams can configure emergency addresses with specific places and locations and assign them to users or networks.

The FCC rules apply to all MTLS systems, including softphones, regardless of their location. This means that even when working remotely, users must provide their accurate location when an emergency call is made from the Teams client. Teams Phone enables users to update their emergency location while working from home, thereby assisting organizations in maintaining compliance with regulations.

How Do Emergency Calls Work for Remote Locations?

Teams Phone enables users to set up emergency addresses while working remotely. Teams use the location services provided by the operating system to suggest an address. The end user can confirm or edit the location or manually enter the address in Teams client.

Once confirmed, the address is saved as the user-confirmed address. Every time the user changes its location, the address is auto-erased. As an administrator, you must enable external lookup mode in the emergency calling policies to allow emergency addresses for the remote location. In the United States, if a user confirms the remote location's address obtained from the operating system or it's edited through autosuggest, the emergency call is routed directly to the PSAP serving the location. If the address is obtained from the operating system and manually edited and confirmed by the user, or if the address is directly edited and confirmed by the user, the call will be redirected to the screening center and transferred to the PSAP. For Canada, calls are screened by the national call center before routing the calls to the nearest PSAP.

How Do Emergency Calls Work with Calling Plans?

Assigning an emergency location to a user when assigned a phone number with a Calling Plan license is mandatory. So, each Calling Plan user is automatically enabled with emergency calling, and the registered address is considered the user's emergency location. It's important to note that the user's emergency address remains the same regardless of whether they change offices or move to different floors within the same building. To address this issue, it's necessary to have a dynamic emergency calling. As an administrator, it's crucial to understand the requirements of your organization and configure your Teams phone to comply with local laws. In the United States, dynamic emergency calling ensures that emergency calls are directed to the nearest public safety answering point without being screened. Here's a breakdown of how emergency calls for Calling Plans are handled based on location:

If a Teams client is located in a tenant-defined dynamic emergency location...	...Route directly to PSAP for users in the...	...United States
If a Teams client is *not* located in a tenant-defined dynamic emergency location...	...Screen call before PSAP routing for users in the....	...United States
If an emergency caller is unable to update their emergency location to the screening center...	...The call will be transferred to the users registered address for users in the...	...United States

(*continued*)

If a Teams client is located in a tenant-defined dynamic emergency location...	...Route directly to PSAP for users in the...	...United States
Regardless of Teams client location...	....Emergency calls are routed directly to the PSAP serving the emergency address associated with the number for users in...	...Canada, Ireland, and the UK
Regardless of Teams client location...	...Emergency calls are routed directly to the PSAP for the local area code of the number for users in the...	...France, Germany, and Spain
Regardless of Teams client location...	...Emergency calls are routed directly to the PSAP for the local area code of the number for users in the...	...Netherlands
Regardless of Teams client location...	...Emergency addresses are configured and routed by the carrier partner for users in...	...Australia
Regardless of Teams client location...	...Emergency calling is not supported for users in...	...Japan

More details are explained in the "Configuring Emergency Calling in Calling Plan Environment" section.

How Do Emergency Calls Work for Operator Connect?

Assigning an emergency location to a user when assigned a phone number with Operator Connect license is mandatory. So, each user is automatically enabled with emergency calling, and the registered address is considered the user's emergency location. When Operator Connect carriers upload phone numbers to your tenant, they will assign each phone number to an emergency location. Depending on the carrier, the emergency address may or may not be altered by the administrator. A dynamic emergency configuration is useful to comply with your location's laws.

For the United States and Canada, dynamic routing is a part of the Operator Connect service. Like Calling Plans, Operator Connect carriers in the United States can route calls based on the current location of Teams clients using dynamic emergency calling instead of the tenant-defined location. For Canada, calls are screened by the national call center before routing the calls to the nearest PSAP. Calls will be routed to the screening center if the dynamic emergency is not configured. If the screening center cannot determine the actual location of the user, calls will be routed to the nearest PSAP service associated with the registered address. For all the other locations, calls are routed based on the emergency calling network of that country or region.

How Do Emergency Calls Work for Teams Phone Mobile?

Like Operator Connect, each Teams Phone Mobile user is automatically assigned an emergency calling when a phone number is assigned. When Team Phone mobile carriers upload phone numbers to your tenant, they assign each phone number to an emergency location. Depending on the carrier, the emergency address may or may not be altered by the administrator. Dynamic emergency configuration is useful for complying with local laws.

For the United States and Canada, dynamic routing is a part of the Teams Phone Mobile service. Like Calling Plans, Operator Connect carriers in the United States can route calls based on the current location of Teams clients using dynamic emergency calling instead of the tenant-defined location. For Canada, calls are screened by the national call center before routing the calls to the nearest PSAP. Calls will be routed to the screening center if the dynamic emergency is not configured. If the screening center cannot determine the actual location of the user, calls will be routed to the nearest PSAP service associated with the registered address. For all the other locations, calls are routed based on the emergency calling network of that country or region. If a user needs to make an emergency call from their SIM-enabled mobile phone, the operator will use either the geographic coordinates or the cell tower handling the call to determine the user's approximate location.

How Do Emergency Calls Work with Direct Routing?

Emergency calling operates differently than other PSTN connectivity modes when using Direct Routing in Teams. As an administrator, you are responsible for setting up emergency call routing policies that specify the emergency numbers and their associated routing destinations. These policies can be associated with either users or sites. If a site is associated with a policy, that site policy will be used for emergency calls. If no emergency call routing policy has been defined for a user or site, that user cannot make emergency calls. With direct routing, the dynamic emergency configuration is useful for complying with local laws.

When using emergency calling with Direct Routing, it is recommended that you use emergency service responders (ERS) or ELIN applications to route the calls to PSAP. Most of the ERS providers in the United States can route calls based on the current location of Teams clients using dynamic emergency calling instead of the tenant-defined location. For Canada, calls are screened by the national call center before routing the calls to the nearest PSAP. Calls will be routed to the screening center if the dynamic emergency is not configured. If the screening center cannot determine the actual location of the user, calls will be routed to the nearest PSAP service associated with the registered address. For all the other locations, calls are routed based on the emergency calling network of that country or region. ERS providers use Pid-flo values from the SIP invite and parse the location information. Most of the Teams-certified SBCs are integrated with ELIN applications.

As an administrator, if you are using ELIN applications to route emergency calls, you must configure the emergency address and the associated phone numbers and upload them to the ELIN applications. More details are explained in the "Considerations for Emergency Phone System Direct Routing" section.

Configuring an Emergency Location in the Teams Admin Center

Teams emergency calling configuration includes multiple steps. One of the most important steps is to add the emergency location addresses in the Teams admin center. To do so, follow this procedure:

1. Log in to Teams admin center. Navigate to Location and then select Emergency Addresses. Click + Add.

2. Enter the name and a meaningful description for an address, as illustrated in Figure 4-60. Once you are finished, click Save to commit the changes.

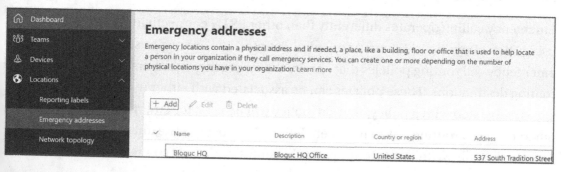

Figure 4-60. *Adding an emergency address*

3.   To add more office addresses, repeat steps 1 and 2. Once all the addresses have been added, you will need to validate the status for each one.

Validating Emergency Addresses

After adding the emergency location addresses, the next step is to assign these emergency locations to the user. However, before giving the emergency addresses to an end user or to a network identifier, you as a Teams admin must validate the addresses.

When you enter an emergency address by using the address map search feature in the Microsoft Teams admin center, the address is automatically marked as validated. Remember, you cannot modify a validated emergency address. If the address format changes, you must create a new address with the updated format. After emergency address validation, the address will be marked as validated, and then you can assign this address to an end user account or network identifier. Figure 4-61 shows that the Cyclotron HQ office address has been validated.

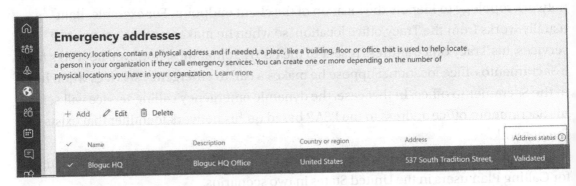

Figure 4-61. Emergency address status

Configuring Emergency Calling in a Calling Plan Environment

You must understand multiple considerations before configuring emergency calling, including emergency addresses, dynamic emergency addresses, and emergency call routing.

As a Teams admin, you must understand how emergency calling will work in Phone System Calling Plan scenarios. (For Phone System Calling Plan, Microsoft will provide phone numbers and work as the service provider.) If you are using Calling Plan, then each Calling Plan user (license assigned) will automatically be enabled for emergency calling and must have a registered emergency address associated with their assigned phone number. Currently, Calling Plan is available in the United States, Canada, and some countries in Europe, the Middle East, and Africa. You can check Calling Plan availability by visiting https://docs.microsoft.com/en-us/microsoftteams/country-and-region-availability-for-audio-conferencing-and-calling-plans/country-and-region-availability-for-audio-conferencing-and-calling-plans.

Note   Calling Plan, by default, provides a native emergency call routing service that routes call based on the Teams users' locations. If you want to route Teams users' emergency calls based on their current locations, use dynamic emergency call routing.

Another consideration is using dynamic emergency calling. This feature allows end users to have their location information sent along with the call to emergency services. To use dynamic emergency calling, a Teams admin must define the organization's network topology to identify the location of the client endpoint. For example, Balu usually works from the Tracy office location, so when he makes a call to emergency services, his Tracy office address is sent to the PSAP. Sometimes, however, he works from a Sacramento office location. Suppose he makes a call to emergency services when he is in the Sacramento office. In that case, the dynamic emergency calling service will send his Sacramento office address to the PSAP based on his network identifier that exists on the network.

As of this writing, Microsoft supports dynamic locations for emergency call routing for Calling Plan users in the United States in two scenarios.

- If a Teams client for a U.S. Calling Plan user dynamically acquires an emergency address within the United States, that address is used for emergency routing instead of the registered address, and the call will be automatically routed to the PSAP in the serving area of the address.

- If a Teams client for a U.S. Calling Plan user doesn't dynamically acquire an emergency address within the United States, then the registered emergency address is used to help screen and route the call. However, the call will be screened to determine if an updated address is required before connecting the caller to the appropriate PSAP.

Emergency call routing to PSAP for Teams Calling Plan is based on factors, such as whether the Teams client dynamically determines the emergency address, whether the emergency address is the registered address associated with the user's phone number, and the emergency calling network of that country.

- If the country is the United States and the Teams client is located at a tenant-defined dynamic emergency location, emergency calls from that client are automatically routed to the PSAP serving that geographic location.

- If a Teams client is not located at a tenant-defined dynamic emergency location, emergency calls from that client are screened by a national call center to determine the caller's location before transferring the call to the PSAP serving that geographic location.

- If an emergency caller is unable to update their emergency location to the screening center, the call will be transferred to the PSAP serving the caller's registered address.

In Canada, Ireland, and the United Kingdom, emergency calls are first screened to determine the user's current location before connecting the call to the appropriate dispatch center. In France, Germany, and Spain, emergency calls are routed directly to the PSAP serving the emergency address associated with the number, regardless of the location of the caller. In the Netherlands, emergency calls are routed directly to the PSAP for the local area code of the number, regardless of the location of the caller. In Australia, emergency addresses are configured and routed by the carrier partner. In Japan, emergency calling is not supported.

Considerations for Emergency Phone System Direct Routing

Microsoft Teams supports emergency calling service through Teams direct routing. Teams allows you to use your existing phone system, including SBC with PSTN connectivity, for inbound and outbound phone calls. As a Teams admin, you must understand how emergency calling works using Direct Routing, and then you can decide to use Direct Routing for emergency calling. You must define emergency calling policies for Direct Routing users using the TeamsEmergencyCallRoutingPolicy PowerShell command to determine emergency numbers and their associated routing destination.

Note   The registered emergency locations are not supported for Direct Routing users.

You can allocate a TeamsEmergencyCallRoutingPolicy to a Teams Direct Routing user account, a network site, or both. When a Teams client starts or changes a network connection, Teams performs a lookup of the network site where the client is located. This lookup is based on the following scenarios:

- If a TeamsEmergencyCallRoutingPolicy is associated with the site, then the site policy is used to configure emergency calling.

- If there is no TeamsEmergencyCallRoutingPolicy associated with the site or if the client is connected at an undefined site, then the TeamsEmergencyCallRoutingPolicy associated with the user account is used to configure emergency calling.

- If the Teams client is unable to obtain a TeamsEmergencyCallRoutingPolicy, then the user is not enabled for emergency calling.

You must understand the considerations and the requirements for emergency calling through Direct Routing. In a Teams Direct Routing scenario, the Teams clients for Direct Routing users can acquire a dynamic emergency address, which can be used to dynamically route calls based on the caller's location.

- For emergency call routing in a Teams Direct Routing scenario, the TeamsEmergencyCallRoutingPolicy mentions an online PSTN usage, which should have the appropriate Direct Routing configuration to properly route the emergency calls to the appropriate PSTN gateway(s) using online PSTN routes. As a Teams admin, you should make sure that there is an OnlineVoiceRoute for the emergency dial string.

- The ability to dynamically route emergency calls for Direct Routing users varies depending on the emergency calling network in each country. Two solutions are available: Emergency Routing Service Providers (ERSPs; U.S. only) and Emergency Location Identification Number (ELIN) gateway applications.

- If you are thinking about using ERSPs, several certified ERSPs can automatically route emergency calls based on the location of the caller.

- If an ERSP is integrated into a Direct Routing deployment, emergency calls with a dynamically acquired location will be automatically routed to the PSAP serving that location.

- Emergency calls without a dynamically acquired location are first screened to determine the current location of the user before connecting the call to the appropriate dispatch center based on the updated location.

Configuring Dynamic Emergency Call Routing Using Direct Routing

Remember that dynamic emergency calling is available through Microsoft Calling Plans and Phone System Direct Routing, and it offers the ability to configure and route emergency calls and notify security personnel based on the current location of the Teams client.

How does dynamic emergency call routing work? For dynamic emergency calling to work, a Teams admin has to define the network topology (adding all user subnets, creating emergency location and assignment, etc.). Based on that network topology configuration, the Teams client provides network connectivity information in a request to the Location Information Service (LIS). The LIS returns a location to the Teams client if there is a match. These location data are transferred back to the client, and then the Teams client includes location data as part of an emergency call. This data is then used by the emergency service provider to determine the appropriate PSAP and to send the call to that PSAP, which lets the PSAP dispatcher find the caller's location to provide the service.

Follow the steps given in the following sections to configure dynamic emergency call routing.

Step 1: Preparation Work

Here is the prep work process:

1. As a Teams admin, you must configure the network settings and the LIS to create a network and emergency location map. Specific to Direct Routing, additional configuration is required for routing emergency calls and possibly for partner connectivity. You must configure connection to an ERSP (in the United States) or configure the SBC for an ELIN application.

2. At startup and periodically afterward or when a network connection is changed, the Teams client sends a location request that contains its network connectivity information to the network settings and the LIS.

3. If there is a network settings site match, emergency calling policies are returned to the Teams client from that site; if there is a LIS match—an emergency location from the network element—the Teams client it is connected to is returned to the Teams client.

4. Once the user using Teams client attempts an emergency call, the emergency location is conveyed to the PSTN, and then for Direct Routing, you must configure the SBC to send emergency calls to the ERSP or configure the SBC ELIN application.

Step 2: Configuring Network Requirements (Sites and Trusted IPs)

Network settings are used to determine the location of a Teams client, and to obtain emergency calling policies and an emergency location dynamically. You can configure network settings according to how your organization wants emergency calling to operate. Network settings include network region, site, subnet, wireless access points, network switch, and trusted IP addresses. Here are the details:

- The network region includes a set of network sites.

- The network site is where your organization has a physical office, such as an office, a set of buildings, or a campus. These sites are defined as a set of IP subnets.

- A network subnet should be associated with a specific network site. A Teams client's location is determined based on the network subnet and the related network site.

- Trusted IP addresses are a collection of the external IP addresses (public-facing IP addresses also known as NAT IPs) of the organization network and are used to determine if the user's endpoint is inside the corporate network.

When Do I Need to Configure Region, Site, Subnet, and Trusted IP Addresses?

The network setting configuration differs based on the Phone System selection. If you are using Calling Plan for a user and require a dynamic configuration of security desk notifications, then you must configure both trusted IP addresses and network sites. If only dynamic locations are required, then you must configure only trusted IP addresses. If neither is required, then configuration of network settings is not required for Calling Plan.

Specific to Direct Routing users, if dynamic enablement of emergency calling or dynamic configuration of security desk notification is required, then you must configure both trusted IP addresses and network sites. If only dynamic locations are required, then you must configure only trusted IP addresses. If neither is required, then configuration of network settings is not required.

Step 3: Configuring Location Information Service, Emergency Policies, and Enabling Users and Sites

Here are the details about step 3.

Configuring Location Information Service (LIS)

LIS is a repository of network sites and subnets. A Teams client gets emergency addresses from the locations associated with different network identifiers, including network subnets and wireless access points (WAPs). As of this writing, an Ethernet switch/port is not supported, but Microsoft plans to support this in the future.

To configure the LIS with network identifiers and emergency locations, you, as a Teams admin can use Windows PowerShell and the commands discussed next.

Get-CsOnlineLisSubnet can be used for getting an existing LIS subnet, Set allows you to set the LIS subnet, and the Remove switch removes the LIS subnet. Similarly, you can use Get, Set, and Remove switches with -CsOnlineLisPort, -CsOnlineLisSwitch, and -CsOnlineLisWirelessAccessPoint.

As an example, the following command shows the subnet 10.10.10.0 set for the LIS with location ID and description.

```
Set-CsOnlineLisSubnet -Subnet 10.10.10.0 -LocationId b983a9ad-1111-455a-
a1c5-3838ec0f5d02 -Description "Subnet 10.10.10.0"
```

Configuring Emergency Policies

As part of an emergency calling service configuration, you need to set two emergency calling policies: Teams emergency call routing policy (TeamsEmergencyCallRoutingPolicy) and Teams emergency calling policy (TeamsEmergencyCallingPolicy). The emergency call routing policies are applied only to Teams Phone System Direct Routing users, not Calling Plan users.

You can create an emergency calling policy and call routing policy using the Teams admin center and Windows PowerShell.

First, to create or manage emergency calling and routing policies using the Teams admin center, log in to the Teams admin center and navigate to Voice. Select Emergency Policies. Once a policy is created, you can assign it to users and network sites. Users can use the Global (Org-wide default) policy or create and give custom policies. Users will automatically be assigned the Global policy unless you create and assign a custom policy.

Note   You can edit the settings in the Global policy, but you cannot rename or delete it. For network sites, you create and assign custom policies.

Follow this procedure to create a custom emergency calling policy:

1. Log in to the Teams admin center and navigate to Voice. Select
    Emergency Policies, and then click the Calling Policies tab. Click
    Add. Enter a name and description for the policy. The example in
    Figure 4-62 shows Vijay WFH Policy as the policy name.

2. Turn on "External location lookup mode" to allow your end users to configure their emergency address when working from a network location outside the corporate network.

3. On the same page you can set how you want to notify people in your organization, typically the security desk, when an emergency call is made. To do this, select one of the following options under Notification Mode:

   - **Send Notification Only:** A Teams chat message is sent to the users and groups that you specify.

   - **Conferenced In But Are Muted:** A Teams chat message is sent to the users and groups that you specify, and they can listen (but not participate) in the conversation between the caller and the PSAP operator.

   - **Conferenced In And Are Unmuted:** Using this option, users can participate.

   Suppose you selected the Conferenced In But Are Muted notification mode, in the Dial-Out Number For Notifications box. In that case, you can enter the PSTN phone number of a user or group to call and join the emergency call. For example, enter the number of your organization's security desk (this example uses +12090001111 as the security desk number), who will receive a call when an emergency call is made and can then listen in or participate in the call.

4. Search for and select one or more users or groups, such as your organization's security desk, to notify when an emergency call is made. The example in Figure 4-62 lists Adele Vance. The notification can be sent to email addresses of users, distribution groups, and security groups. A maximum of 50 users can be notified.

5. Set the Emergency service disclaimer to show a banner to remind your end users to confirm their emergency location.

Click Save to commit the changes.

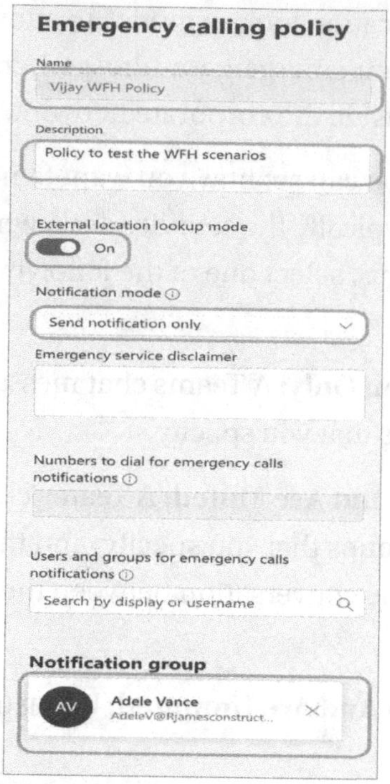

Figure 4-62. *Emergency policies*

You can create a call routing policy by clicking the Call Routing Policies tab.

If you assigned an emergency calling policy to a network site and to a user and if that user is at that network site, the policy assigned to the network site overrides the policy assigned to the user.

You can also use PowerShell to manage emergency call routing and calling policies.

The TeamsEmergencyCallRoutingPolicy is used primarily for routing emergency calls. This policy configures the emergency numbers, masks per number if required, and the PSTN route per number. You can assign this policy to users, to network sites, or to both. (Calling Plan Teams clients are automatically enabled for emergency calling with the emergency numbers from the country based on their Office 365 usage location.) You manage this policy using the New-, Set-, and Grant-CsTeamsEmergencyCallRouting commands. For example, the command shown next first creates a new Teams emergency number object and then creates a Teams emergency call routing policy with this emergency number object.

```
$en = New-CsTeamsEmergencyNumber -EmergencyDialString "911" -EmergencyDialMask
"911;9911" -OnlinePSTNUsage "Local" -CarrierProfile "Local"

New-CsTeamsEmergencyCallRoutingPolicy -Identity "HQ-Emergency" -Tenant
$tenant -EmergencyNumbers @{add=$en} -AllowEnhancedEmergencyServices:
$true -Description "HQ Emergency Route Policy"
```

Note   The OnlinePSTNUsage specified in the first command must previously exist.
You can use the Set-CsOnlinePSTNUsage command for PSTN usage creation.

The resulting object from the New-CsTeamsEmergencyNumber command exists only in
memory, so you must apply it to a policy to be used.

TeamsEmergencyCallingPolicy is another policy required for emergency calling.
It uses Calling Plan and Direct Routing. This policy configures the security desk
notification experience during an emergency call. You can set who to notify and how
they are notified; for example, automatically notify your organization's security desk and
have them listen in on emergency calls. This policy can be assigned to users, network
sites, or both. As an admin, you can manage this policy using the New-, Set-, and Grant-
CsTeamsEmergencyCallingPolicy commands. For example, the PowerShell command
shown here creates a Teams emergency calling policy that has an identity of Cyclotron-
EMS-Policy, where a notification group and number are specified, as well as the type of
notification.

```
New-CsTeamsEmergencyCallingPolicy -Identity Cyclotron-EMS-Policy
-Description "Cyclotron Emergency calling Policy" -NotificationGroup
"alert@cyclotron.com" -NotificationDialOutNumber "+12090001111"
-NotificationMode NotificationOnly -ExternalLocationLookupMode $true
```

Managing Phone Numbers

Let's talk about managing phone numbers.

Acquiring and Managing Teams Service Numbers and User Phone Numbers

Microsoft Teams support service numbers like dial-in conference numbers or auto attendant numbers, as well as user phone numbers like user Teams phone numbers to receive inbound calls and make outbound calls.

- **Teams service** numbers are assigned to services such as Audio Conferencing, auto attendants, and call queues. Service phone numbers, which have a higher concurrent call capacity than user numbers, will vary by country or region and the type of number (whether it is a toll or toll-free number). Admins can acquire service (toll or toll-free) numbers from Microsoft.

- **Teams user phone numbers:** User phone numbers can be assigned to users in the organization for inbound and outbound calling purposes. As an admin, you can acquire Teams user phone numbers from Microsoft or port your existing phone number to Microsoft and use it in Teams Phone System along with Calling Plan.

Getting a Service or Phone Number

An admin can acquire new phone numbers in the Teams admin center. To get a phone number or service number, follow this procedure:

1. Log in to the Teams admin center; then navigate to Voice and click Phone Numbers.

2. On the Phone Numbers page, under Numbers, click + Add for a new phone number request. Enter a name and description.

3. In the Location And Quantity section, enter the following information, as shown in Figure 4-63:

   - **Country Or Region:** Select country or region.

   - **Number Type:** Select the appropriate option that determines whether the phone numbers are designated for users or for services, such as conference bridge, call queue, or auto attendant.

- **Location:** Choose a location for connecting the new phone numbers. If you must create a new location, select Add A Location and enter the required location's data.

- **Area Code:** Select a valid area code for the country and location.

- **Quantity:** Enter the number of phone numbers that you want for your organization.

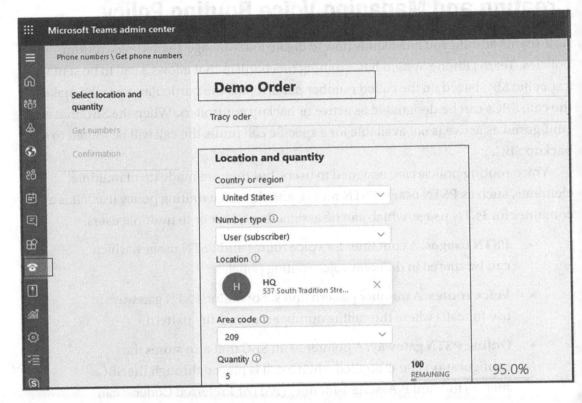

Figure 4-63. *Phone number order*

4.   Click Next to continue. Select the phone numbers you want to apply to your tenant on the Get Numbers page.

5.   Click Place Order to submit the order.

Note   The phone numbers are reserved for only 10 minutes; therefore, if you do not click Place Order, the phone numbers are returned to the pool of numbers, and you have to reorder the phone numbers.

Creating and Managing Voice Routing Policy

As a Teams admin, you must know how to create and manage Teams voice routing policies. Teams Phone System has a routing mechanism that allows a call to be sent to a specific SBC based on the called number pattern plus the particular user who makes the call. SBCs can be designated as active or backup controllers. When the SBC that was configured as active is not available for a specific call route, the call will be routed to a backup SBC.

Voice routing policies are assigned to users, but they are made up of multiple elements, such as PSTN usage, PSTN routes, and the voice routing policy itself. It is a container for PSTN usage, which can be assigned to a user or to multiple users.

- **PSTN usages:** A container for voice routes and PSTN usages, which can be shared in different voice routing policies

- **Voice routes:** A number pattern and set of online PSTN gateways to use for calls where the calling number matches the pattern

- **Online PSTN gateway:** A pointer to an SBC that also stores the configuration that is applied when a call is placed through the SBC, such as forward P-Asserted-Identity (PAI) or Preferred Codecs; can be added to voice routes

Follow these steps to create a voice routing policy:

1. First, create PSTN usage (one or more) for the voice routing policy. Remember that, as of this writing, you cannot create a voice routing policy or PSTN usage or routes using the Teams admin center. You will have to use Windows PowerShell. Before running

the following PowerShell command, however, you must connect to Teams tenant by installing and connecting to the Microsoft Teams module; run the following steps:

```
Install-Module MicrosoftTeams
```

```
Connect-MicrosoftTeams
```

2. PSTN usages are the glue that connects a route to the voice routing policy. Use the following command to create PSTN usage for the U.S. East and West regions:

```
Set-CsOnlinePstnUsage -Identity Global -Usage @{Add="US
East and US West"}
```

3. Now create a PSTN route to match the dialed number and use the PSTN gateway. Refer to the following command to create two routes, Tracy 1 and 2, within the U.S. East and West PSTN usages. Remember that the PSTN gateways are already created as part of the Teams Direct Routing configurations.

```
New-CsOnlineVoiceRoute -Identity "Tracy1" -NumberPattern
"^\+1(209|210)
```

```
(\d{7})$" -OnlinePstnGatewayList sbc1.cyclotron.com, sbc2.
cyclotron.com -Priority 1 -OnlinePstnUsages "US East and
US West"
```

```
New-CsOnlineVoiceRoute -Identity "Tracy2" -NumberPattern
"^\+1(209|210)
```

```
(\d{7})$" -OnlinePstnGatewayList sbc3.cyclotron.com, sbc4.
cyclotron.com -Priority 2 -OnlinePstnUsages " US East and
US West"
```

4. The next step is to create a voice routing policy with these created PSTN usages, using these commands:

```
New-CsOnlineVoiceRoutingPolicy "US East and
West" -OnlinePstnUsages "US East and US West"
```

5. Assign the voice routing policy to users. Use this PowerShell command to do so:

```
Grant-CsOnlineVoiceRoutingPolicy -Identity "Balu Ilag"
-PolicyName "US East and US West"
```

You can verify the voice routing policy assigned to the user by running this PowerShell command:

```
Get-CsOnlineUser "Balu Ilag" | select OnlineVoiceRoutingPolicy
```

Tip   As an admin, you can create a voice routing policy with multiple PSTN usages. You can use the preceding PowerShell commands and make a script to assign policies to multiple users.

Summary

In this chapter, we delved into the multifaceted capabilities of Microsoft Teams in handling various communication needs, including persistent chat, audio/video calls, conferences (both dial-in and client join), and phone systems for inbound/outbound PSTN calls. Specifically, the chapter elucidated the workings of Teams conference management, encompassing aspects such as audio conferencing (dial-in), Teams Webinars, Teams Premium, VoIP for internal and external attendees, and comprehensive insight into Teams Phone System management.

The Teams Phone System, a cloud-based innovation, stands out as a replacement for traditional on-premises PBX systems, offering advanced functionalities such as call control, voicemail with transcription, call queues, auto attendants, call park, emergency calling features, enhanced E9-1-1 dialing, caller ID display, direct routing, and interoperability with third-party systems. This intricate orchestration of features collectively streamlines and modernizes communication, making Teams a central hub for collaboration and connection in today's dynamic working environment.

References

- https://support.microsoft.com/en-us/office/meeting-options-in-microsoft-teams-53261366-dbd5-45f9-aae9-a70e6354f88e

- https://learn.microsoft.com/en-us/microsoftteams/limits-specifications-teams

- https://learn.microsoft.com/en-us/microsoftteams/meeting-policies-overview

- https://learn.microsoft.com/en-us/microsoftteams/outbound-calling-restriction-policies

- https://learn.microsoft.com/en-us/microsoftteams/set-up-webinars

- https://www.microsoft.com/en-us/microsoft-365/blog/2022/10/12/introducing-microsoft-teams-premium-the-better-way-to-meet/

- https://www.microsoft.com/en-us/microsoft-365/blog/2023/02/01/microsoft-teams-premium-cut-costs-and-add-ai-powered-productivity/

- https://learn.microsoft.com/en-us/microsoftteams/enhanced-teams-experience

- https://learn.microsoft.com/en-us/microsoftteams/configure-meetings-three-tiers-protection

- https://learn.microsoft.com/en-us/microsoftteams/platform/apps-in-teams-meetings/teams-together-mode

- https://learn.microsoft.com/en-us/microsoftteams/operator-connect-plan

- https://cloudpartners.transform.microsoft.com/partner-gtm/operators/directory

- https://learn.microsoft.com/en-us/microsoftteams/operator-connect-mobile-plan

- https://www.metaswitch.com/products/mobile-control-point

- https://learn.microsoft.com/en-us/azure/communications-gateway/mobile-control-point

- https://techcommunity.microsoft.com/t5/azure-for-operators-blog/supporting-operator-connect-mobile/ba-p/3473944

- https://learn.microsoft.com/en-us/microsoftteams/create-a-phone-system-call-queue?tabs=general-info

- https://www.fcc.gov/mlts-911-requirements

- https://www.911.gov/issues/legislation-and-policy/kari-s-law-and-ray-baum-s-act/#:~:text=What%20is%20Kari's%20Law%3F,dialing%20911%20from%20an%20MLTS

## CHAPTER 5

Microsoft Teams Governance and Life-Cycle Management

In today's rapidly evolving digital landscape, organizations are seeking collaboration tools that offer flexibility, connectivity, and robust security measures. Microsoft Teams stands as a leading solution, providing an integrated platform that allows seamless communication, collaboration, and content sharing. However, the deployment and ongoing management of such a powerful tool involve complex considerations that go beyond mere usability.

Enter the critical realm of governance and Life-cycle management. This chapter delves into the systematic approach needed to guide Microsoft Teams through its entire life cycle within an organization, from initial planning and deployment to ongoing governance, security, compliance, and eventual decommissioning or upgrading.

Governance involves defining the roles, responsibilities, processes, and rules that ensure Teams align with organizational goals and comply with regulatory requirements. It encompasses aspects such as security protocols, user access controls, communication compliance, data protection, and more. Effective governance ensures that Teams is used responsibly and maintains the integrity and confidentiality of organizational information.

Life-cycle management, on the other hand, focuses on the different stages of Teams within the organization. It includes planning, deployment, operation, maintenance, and eventual retirement or transition to new versions or systems. Life-cycle management ensures that Teams continue to serve the evolving needs of the organization and that any changes or updates are carried out smoothly and efficiently.

485

© Balu N Ilag, Durgesh Tripathy, Vijay Ireddy 2024
B. N. Ilag et al., *Understanding Microsoft Teams Administration*,
https://doi.org/10.1007/979-8-8688-0014-6_5

Together, governance and life-cycle management form a comprehensive framework that empowers organizations to leverage the full potential of Microsoft Teams. This chapter will guide you through these critical aspects, providing insights, best practices, and real-world examples to help you navigate the complexities of managing Teams in a responsible, effective, and compliant manner. Whether you are an IT professional, a business leader, or someone interested in understanding the backbone of modern collaboration tools, this chapter offers essential knowledge to thrive in our interconnected world.

This chapter elaborates on the careful planning and implementation of governance, security, and life-cycle management practices; organizations can ensure that Microsoft Teams is used effectively, securely, and in compliance with all relevant legal and organizational requirements. As Teams is built upon Microsoft 365 Groups, earlier known as Office 365 Groups, which provides various governance capabilities, this chapter delves into the necessary steps and considerations for establishing effective governance practices. To ensure consistent and coordinated interactions within Teams and foster confident collaboration, administrators must address important governance aspects. This chapter guides Teams admins through key considerations, including defining who can create teams, handling unused Teams, establishing guidelines for private channel creation, implementing a Teams naming convention, and more.

Moreover, you will gain insights into the diverse features available for Teams governance. These features encompass group creation controls, classification mechanisms, expiration policies, sensitivity labels, data loss prevention policies, and naming policies. Understanding and leveraging these governance features empowers administrators to establish and maintain a well-governed Teams environment. You have already learned that Microsoft Teams is built on Office 365 Groups, which is part of Office 365 and includes multiple tools to design governance capabilities that organizations require. This chapter provides you with a comprehensive overview of Microsoft Teams governance and life-cycle management. Managing governance and life-cycle management for Teams is essential for consistent and coordinated interaction between users and allows them to collaborate with confidence. Prior to deploying Teams, you as a Teams admin must consider things such as who can create Teams, how to handle unused Teams, who can create private channels, what the Teams naming convention is, and so on. Also, you will learn the features that you can use for Teams governance, such as group creation, classification, expiration policy, sensitivity labels, data loss prevention policies, and naming policy.

After completing this chapter, you will understand the following:

- **Governance and life-cycle management:** The chapter will begin with an overview of the concepts of governance and life-cycle management, specifically within the context of Microsoft Teams.

- **Role-based access control (RBAC):** The chapter will discuss how to assign roles and permissions based on job function.

- **Microsoft Teams identity and access management:** Microsoft Teams has strong authentication because it uses smart protection policies and risk assessment to block threats

- **Teams life-cycle management:** We'll discuss strategies for creating, managing, archiving, and deleting Teams in a controlled manner. This might also include advice on using naming conventions and setting up automatic expiration for inactive teams.

- **Microsoft Teams template and their usages:** We'll discuss best practices for creating and using Teams templates to maintain consistent structure and settings across multiple teams.

- **Data governance and retention policy:** This might include topics such as retention policies, data loss prevention, and managing sensitive information.

- **Compliance:** The chapter will explain how to ensure that Teams usage complies with organizational policies and legal requirements, including strategies for eDiscovery and audit logs.

- **License management:** We'll discuss how to handle Microsoft 365 or Office 365 licenses, including assigning and reclaiming licenses as necessary.

- **Apps management in Microsoft Teams:** Apps in Teams help users bring together their workplace tools and services and collaborate with others.

- **Integration with other services:** We'll discuss how to manage Teams' interactions with other Microsoft 365 or Office 365 services, like SharePoint, OneDrive, and Exchange, and how governance and life-cycle policies for these services interact with Teams.

- **Monitoring and reporting:** We'll cover the tools available for tracking Teams usage and performance and how these can be used to ensure compliance with governance policies.

- **Managing internal risk through information barrier in teams:** Information barriers are policies that an admin can configure to prevent certain users from communicating with each other in Microsoft Teams. This feature is used to limit the flow of information within an organization, mainly for legal or regulatory reasons.

- **Creating and managing Office 365 Groups classification:** Office 365 Groups classifications provide a way to categorize and manage groups based on the role they serve within your organization. Classifications are labels that you can create and apply to Office 365 groups (and therefore to Teams because each team in Microsoft Teams is associated with an Office 365 group).

- **Third-party tools for Microsoft Teams governance and life-cycle management**

- **Importance of third-party tool using a case study**

Each of these topics is complex and could be a chapter in its own right. However, a chapter on Teams governance, security, and life-cycle management would likely touch on each of these to provide a comprehensive overview of the subject. So, buckle up and dive into the intricate world of Microsoft Teams Governance and Life-cycle management.

Introduction to Governance and Life-Cycle Management

Why are governance, security, and life-cycle management important in Teams?

In any enterprise, it's important to maintain control and oversight over the tools and services employees use for work, especially communication and collaboration tools. When it comes to Microsoft Teams—a key tool for collaboration in many organizations—governance and Life-cycle management play a crucial role.

Governance refers to the set of policies, roles, responsibilities, and processes that control how an organization's business divisions and IT teams cooperate to achieve business goals and compliance. In the context of Microsoft Teams, governance involves determining who can create teams and channels, the kinds of data that can be shared, and how users can interact within Teams, among other things. Key topics include the following:

- **Policy management:** Defining rules and guidelines for Teams' usage, including creating and enforcing naming conventions, guest access policies, and more

- **Compliance management:** Aligning with legal, regulatory, and business requirements such as GDPR, HIPAA, etc.

- **Auditing and reporting:** Monitoring and logging activities to ensure adherence to organizational policies and legal regulations

Life-cycle management pertains to how resources (in this case, Teams, channels, and associated Microsoft services like SharePoint sites) are managed, from creation to eventual archival or deletion. It involves creating, using, archiving, and deleting teams in a manner that aligns with the company's policies and procedures. This includes the following:

- **Provisioning and deprovisioning:** Creating and managing Teams, channels, and users throughout their life cycle, including onboarding and offboarding

- **Archiving and retention:** Implementing policies for retaining, archiving, or deleting information based on organizational needs and legal requirements

- **Backup and Restore:** Ensuring data can be backed up and restored to prevent accidental loss or to comply with legal requirements

- **Updates and upgrades management:** Managing updates, new features, and changes in Teams to ensure a smooth transition and prevent potential disruptions

Security within Microsoft Teams involves protecting data, managing access, and ensuring privacy. The key aspects include the following:

- **Identity and access management:** Implementing authentication and authorization practices, like multifactor authentication (MFA), single sign-on (SSO), and role-based access control

- **Data security:** Protecting data both at rest and in transit, including encryption practices and securing file sharing

- **Threat protection:** Utilizing tools like Microsoft Defender to protect against malicious activities and threats

- **Information protection:** Applying labels and rights management to control access to sensitive information

- **Guest access and external collaboration:** Managing how external users can access and interact with data within Teams

- **Monitoring and performance management:** Regularly assessing the performance, availability, and user experience and resolving any issues that arise

In summary, introducing governance and life-cycle management in Microsoft Teams is not just about controlling the use of Teams. It's about making Teams a more effective tool for collaboration, while ensuring security, compliance, and efficient resource usage.

Role-Based Access Control

RBAC is a method of managing users' access to resources based on their role within an organization. The principles of RBAC apply to many systems and services, including Microsoft Teams. In the context of Microsoft Teams, RBAC primarily pertains to the Microsoft 365 admin center and to specific Teams settings. Here are some roles and permissions specific to Teams:

- **Teams Service Administrator:** These admins manage the Teams service in the Microsoft 365 admin center and can access all settings related to Teams. They can also create and manage all Teams.

- **Teams Communications Administrator:** These admins manage meetings and calling functionality in Teams.

- **Teams Communications Support Engineer and Specialist:** These are roles with specific permissions to troubleshoot communication issues in Teams.

- **Global Administrator:** They have access to all administrative features and can assign other admin roles. By default, the person who signs up to buy Microsoft 365 becomes a Global administrator.

- **Teams Owner/Member/Guest:** These are roles assigned within specific teams. Owners have more control over the team's settings and membership, while members and guests have fewer permissions.

RBAC helps in managing Microsoft Teams in the following ways:

- **Security:** By granting only the necessary permissions to each role, RBAC helps limit the potential for unauthorized access or changes to settings and data.

- **Efficiency:** RBAC allows admins to manage permissions for groups of users at once, based on their roles, rather than needing to configure permissions for each user individually.

- **Scalability:** As an organization grows, RBAC makes it easier to manage increasing numbers of users and resources. New users can be assigned to roles, automatically granting them the necessary permissions.

- **Accountability:** By defining specific roles and permissions, it's easier to track changes and actions, which can aid in troubleshooting and compliance.

Remember that RBAC in Teams should be planned and implemented carefully, in line with the organization's broader governance policies. It's essential to regularly review and update roles and permissions to reflect changes in users' job functions or organizational policies.

Microsoft Teams Identity and Access Management

Teams identity was already covered in Chapter 2, but a recap is in order. Identity management is crucial for any application or system. If bad actors compromise an identity, your data and content could be misused. Because Teams leverages Azure AD for identity, the investments and improvements in Azure are directly applied to Microsoft Teams.

Microsoft Teams has strong authentication because it uses smart protection policies and risk assessment to block threats. As a Teams admin or security admin, you need to ensure that your organization's users have strong passwords and have MFA enabled. Once you have enabled MFA for SharePoint Online and Exchange Online, you are automatically supported for Teams because Teams uses SharePoint and Exchange extensively. When a user tries to log in to Teams, they will be challenged for the two-factor workflow or a PIN, and both have the same workflow.

Another aspect of identity is what authorized users have access to. This is specifically based on a policy that is defined in conditional access in Azure AD, and Microsoft Teams is part of this feature as well. Figure 5-1 shows conditional access based on the signal that comes from the devices, applications, and users. Microsoft determines the risk score, and as a Teams admin you configure the policies that determine who can access the Teams application based on the conditions applied.

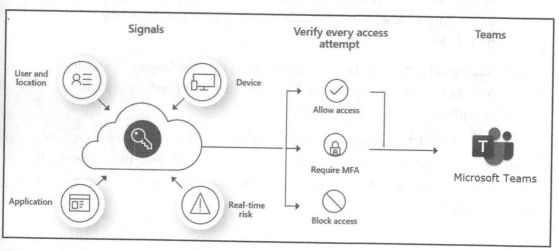

Figure 5-1. *Conditional access workflow*

Remember, the conditional access policies prevent access for authenticated users from unmanaged devices.

Configuring Conditional Access Policy for Microsoft Teams

Azure AD conditional access is a vast topic and includes many facets. For the purposes of this book, I have designed an example conditional access policy. If you are interested in learning more about Azure AD and conditional access, refer to the Microsoft documentation at `https://docs.microsoft.com/en-us/azure/active-directory/ conditional-access/overview`.

Follow this procedure to implement a conditional access policy for Teams:

1. Log in to the Azure AD portal at `https://portal.azure.com`. You must have the appropriate permission (e.g., Global admin role permission) to design conditional access.

2. On the Microsoft Azure home page, navigate to Conditional Access - Policies and open the link.

3. Click + New to create a new conditional access policy. Enter a meaningful name so that the policy can be easily identified. For our test policy, the given name is CA for MS Teams.

4. Under Assignments, select the users and groups to which this policy will apply and then click Done. In the example in Figure 5-2, the user account selected is for Balu Ilag, `bilag@bloguc.com`.

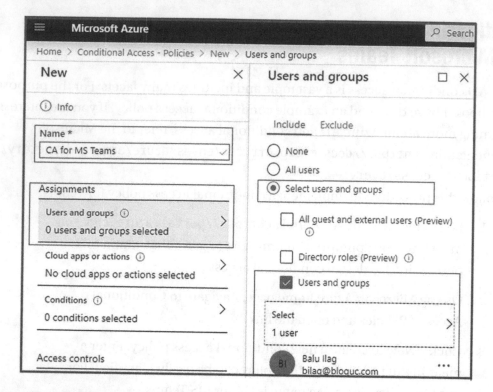

Figure 5-2. *Conditional access policy assignment*

5. In the "Cloud apps or actions pane," select Microsoft Teams as
    a first-party application. Select Microsoft Teams, as shown in
    Figure 5-3, and then click Done.

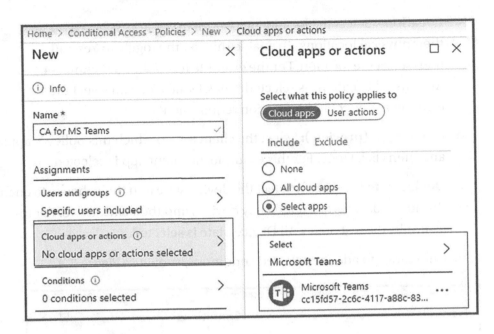

Figure 5-3. *Cloud app as Teams*

6. Select Conditions. In the Conditions pane, you will see different available options.

   a. **Sign-in risk:** This will allow you to select the sign-in risk level: High, Medium, Low, or No Risk. To enable this, set the toggle to Yes and then select the applicable sign-in risk. For the example shown in Figure 5-4, medium risk is selected. You can set risk as per your organization requirements.

   b. **Device platforms:** Select the platform, such as Any Device, or choose a specific platform—Android, iOS, Windows Phone, Windows, and macOS—to which to apply this policy. To enable this, first set the toggle to Yes and then select the platform. For the example test policy shown in Figure 5-4, the Android, iOS, Windows Phone, Windows, and macOS device platforms are selected.

  c. **Locations:** Select the location to control users' access based on their physical locations. To enable this, set the toggle to Yes and then select the location. For the example test policy in Figure 5-4, All Trusted Locations is selected. Click Done. You can select the location as per your organization requirements.

  d. **Client apps (preview):** Select the client app to which this policy is applied and then click Done. For this example, no client app is selected.

  e. **Device state (preview):** Select the device state and then choose to enable this for all devices or exclude any devices and then click Done. For this example, the test policy All Device State is selected.

  f. Click Done to add the selected conditions, shown in Figure 5-4.

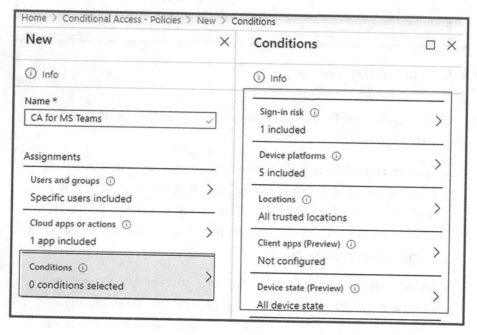

Figure 5-4. *Conditions settings*

  7. Select the access controls to be enforced, like Block or Grant. If Grant is chosen, then select Require Multi-Factor Authentication, Require Device To Be Marked As Compliant, Require Hybrid Azure AD Joined Device, and so on.

8. The session controls enable limited experiences within a cloud app. Select the session usage requirements. For the example shown in Figure 5-5, Sign-In Frequency - 5 days is selected.

9. Click Create, as shown in Figure 5-5, to build this conditional access policy.

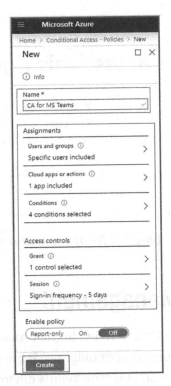

Figure 5-5. *Creating a conditional access policy*

User Experience When User Accesses the Teams Application

Figure 5-6 shows a warning message preventing users from accessing the Teams application from an unmanaged device. This is an example of the granular control that conditional access policy provides, preventing authorized users from accessing the Teams application from an unmanaged device. In this workflow, the first part is authorizing the user, and the second part is applying conditions based on the policy

497

to prevent a user from accessing the Teams app from an unmanaged device. Another valuable condition available through a conditional access policy is the prevention of Teams app access from nonwork locations.

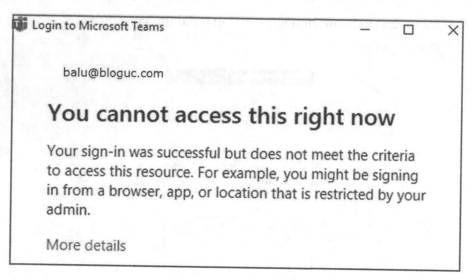

Figure 5-6. *Teams app access blocked from an unmanaged device*

Teams Life-Cycle Management

Microsoft Teams life-cycle management refers to the process of managing Teams from their creation to their eventual archiving or deletion. It involves a series of stages and related administrative tasks, ensuring that the Teams environment remains organized, up-to-date, and compliant with organizational policies. Figure 5-7 Teams life-cycle management.

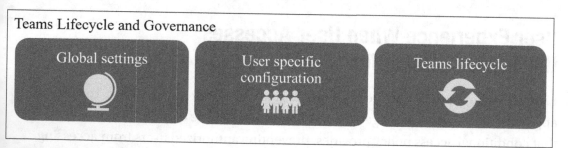

Figure 5-7. *Teams life-cycle and governance*

Here's an overview of the stages in Teams life-cycle management:

- **Planning:** Before a Team is created, there should be a clear purpose or need for it. The nature of the Team (e.g., departmental, project-based), its members, required channels, tabs, and apps should be determined in this stage. Teams can be created based on standardized templates for consistency. Planning sets the stage for the entire life cycle, ensuring alignment with organizational goals, avoiding redundancy, and creating a solid foundation for the team. For example, suppose a company wants to initiate a project for developing a new software product. The planning stage involves defining the project's objectives, identifying key stakeholders, defining team structure, setting permissions, and establishing guidelines for communication and collaboration.

- **Creation:** Once planning is complete, the Team is created based on the specifications. The necessary channels are added, and appropriate members and roles are assigned. This stage involves actually setting up the team in Microsoft Teams, including naming the team, adding members, defining channels, setting up tabs, and integrating any necessary third-party tools. It's important to consider who has the right to create Teams. Some organizations allow any user to create Teams, while others restrict this ability to specific roles. Proper creation ensures that the team has all the necessary resources and structure to function efficiently. For example, using the plan from the previous stage, the project manager creates the new product development team in Microsoft Teams, sets up channels for different development phases, adds team members, and integrates tools like GitHub for code collaboration.

- **Usage:** Once the team is created, it's put to use. Members collaborate, share files, hold meetings, etc. Governance policies and permissions should be enforced to maintain security and compliance during this stage. Proper usage ensures that collaboration is smooth and efficient, boosting productivity and keeping the project on track. For example, team members start collaborating on the code, having daily standup meetings in their designated channels, sharing documents, and providing updates on their progress.

- **Review and update:** Teams should be regularly reviewed to ensure they're still relevant and being used effectively. This could involve reviewing membership, checking activity levels, and updating permissions or settings as needed. Regular review and updates keep the team working efficiently, ensuring that the structure and resources align with the team's evolving needs. For example, a monthly review identifies that a particular channel is not being used, while another is overloaded with messages. Channels are restructured to better suit the team's needs.

- **Archiving:** When a team is no longer actively needed, it can be archived. This preserves the team's content and conversations for reference but prevents any new activity. This is often done for project-based teams once the project is completed. Archiving maintains a record of the work done without cluttering the active workspace. For example, once the software project is completed, the team is archived, preserving all the discussions and documents for future reference but preventing further active collaboration.

- **Deletion:** If a team is no longer needed at all, it can be deleted. This should be done carefully, considering any requirements for data retention. Some organizations may have policies for the automatic deletion of teams after a certain period of inactivity. It is very important to clean up the unused teams, and deletion helps maintain a clean and efficient workspace by removing unnecessary content. For example, a temporary team set up for a one-time event is deleted after the event, as its content is not needed for future reference.

- **Restoration:** If a team is deleted but later needed, it may be possible to restore it, depending on the organization's data retention policies. It is important to know restoration, as it provides a safety net against accidental deletions, ensuring continuity and preserving valuable work. For example, a team that was deleted accidentally is restored, allowing the team to continue their collaboration without losing their prior work. Figure 5-8 shows the Teams life-cycle management stages.

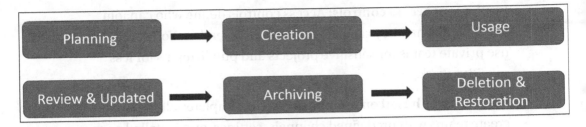

Figure 5-8. Teams life-cycle management stages

In summary, proper life-cycle management in Microsoft Teams ensures that teams are created, used, and retired in an efficient and purposeful manner. Each stage plays a critical role in maintaining a productive and orderly collaboration environment.

Teams Life-Cycle Management Policies

Teams life-cycle management is crucial for maintaining control over the Teams environment, ensuring efficient use of resources, maintaining security and compliance, and preventing the creation of "orphaned" teams or teams sprawl. Automation tools, such as those available in the Microsoft 365 admin center, can help manage a team's life cycle effectively.

Creating and managing Microsoft Teams in a controlled manner involves careful planning, clear governance policies, and routine maintenance. Here are some strategies that can help:

- **Define clear policies for team creation:** Policies should define who is allowed to create new teams. In some organizations, any employee can create a team. In others, only IT or certain managers have this ability. You could also use approval workflows to control the creation of new teams.

- **Use naming conventions:** Naming conventions help keep teams organized and make it easier for users to find the teams they need. For example, include the department name and purpose in the name of each team like Bloguc-HR-Team.

- **Teams expiration:** Create a Teams expiration policy.

- **Implement access controls:** Access controls define who can join a team and what they can do once they're a member. You could use private teams for sensitive projects and public teams for less sensitive work.

- **Create teams based on templates:** Teams templates allow you to create teams with predefined channels, settings, and installed apps, providing consistency across teams.

- **Educate users:** Users should understand how to use teams effectively, which includes knowing your organization's policies for creating and managing teams.

- **Monitor and review teams regularly:** Regular monitoring can help you identify inactive teams or teams that are not following organizational policies. This can be done manually or with the help of Microsoft 365's built-in analytics tools.

- **Archive inactive teams:** Teams that are no longer active should be archived to reduce clutter and confusion. You can set up policies to automatically archive teams after a certain period of inactivity.

- **Implement life-cycle management:** This involves defining the life-cycle stages for a team (e.g., active, archived, deleted), along with the policies and processes for moving a team through these stages.

- **Use automation tools:** Tools like Microsoft 365's group expiration policy can automatically delete teams after a certain period of inactivity, reducing the burden on IT.

Remember, the specific strategies that are right for your organization will depend on your unique needs and context. The key is to have a planned and controlled approach to creating and managing Teams. The following are the most frequently used policies.

Team Creation Policies

Microsoft Teams Team creation policies allow administrators to manage the creation of teams within an organization, giving them control over who can create a team and apply specific settings to those teams. By defining and implementing these policies, administrators can maintain compliance, security, and a coherent structure within the

Teams environment. It ensures that only authorized personnel can create teams and that they do so according to organizational guidelines. Figure 5-9 shows Teams creation policy. Here's how you can create and manage these policies:

1. **Open the Microsoft Teams admin center**: Sign in to the Microsoft Teams admin center with administrative credentials.

2. **Navigate to Teams policies**: Click Teams ➤ Teams policies. Here, you can manage all the existing team creation policies. Figure 5-9 shows the Teams Creation policy, in that you can define the following:

   - Create private channels

   - Create shared channels

   - Invite external users to shared channels

   - Join external shared channels

3. **Create a new policy:** Click Add to create a new policy. You'll be prompted to enter a name and description for the policy, helping identify its purpose.

4. **Define who can create teams:** Under the settings, you can choose whether to allow everyone, specific users, or user groups to create teams. You can add user IDs or groups accordingly.

5. **Set Team settings:** Customize the settings according to your organization's needs, such as defining templates, guest access, naming conventions, and other attributes that must be followed during team creation.

6. **Configure advanced options:** If necessary, you can configure advanced options, such as data classifications and third-party app integrations, to align with your organizational policies.

7. **Save the policy:** Once you've configured all the necessary settings, click Save to create the policy.

8. **Assign the policy to users or groups:** Navigate to Users or Groups and select the individuals or groups to whom you want to apply this policy. Click Policies and then select the newly created team creation policy from the drop-down menu. Click Apply.

9. **Verify the policy implementation:** It's a good practice to verify the policy implementation by logging in as a user to whom the policy is assigned and ensuring that the restrictions or permissions are correctly applied.

10. **Monitor and adjust as necessary:** Continuously monitor these policies, and adjust them as your organization's needs change. You can go back to the Teams policies in the admin center and edit or remove policies as necessary.

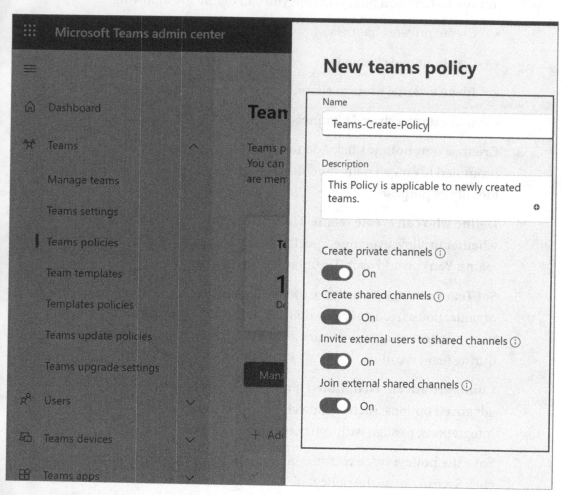

Figure 5-9. *Teams creation policy*

Teams creation policies in Microsoft Teams provide a powerful way for administrators to control and standardize the way teams are created within the organization. Following this guide, you can implement customized policies that align with your organization's goals and compliance requirements, ensuring a secure and efficient collaboration environment.

Archiving and Deleting Teams Management in Microsoft Teams

Over time, a team that was created in Microsoft Teams may become inactive or unnecessary. As a Microsoft Teams admin or team owner, you may need to archive or delete a team that's no longer required. Here's how to manage those scenarios.

Archiving a Team

When you archive a team, the team's activities cease. While the private channels within the team are also archived, you retain the ability to modify members and roles and view all team activities. Follow these steps to archive a team:

1. **Open the admin center:** Select Teams.

2. **Choose the team:** Click the team name you want to archive.

3. **Archive the team:** Select Archive. A confirmation message will appear.

4. **Option to make SharePoint site read-only:** If needed, you can select the option to make the associated SharePoint site read-only for team members (owners can still edit).

5. **Confirm archiving:** Click Archive. The team's status will change to Archived, and it will temporarily appear in "Hidden teams" at the bottom of the team's list. It can later be found under Archived in the "Manage teams" view. Figure 5-10 shows Teams archive option.

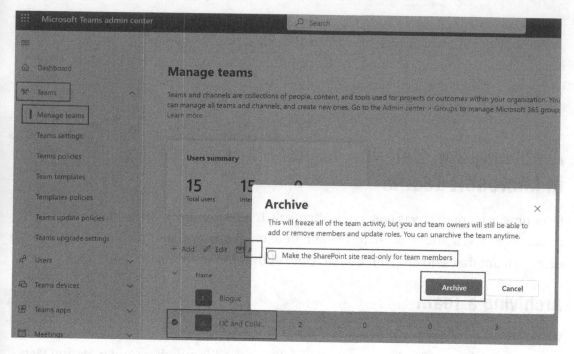

Figure 5-10. *Teams archive*

Important Note   Archiving enables the team to be reactivated in the future. If you think you may need the team later, consider archiving instead of deleting.

Making an Archived Team Active

To reactivate an archived team, follow these steps:

1. **Open the admin center:** Select Teams.

2. **Choose the archived team:** Click the archived team's name.

3. **Restore the team:** Select Restore. The status will change to Active, but it won't be automatically moved back to "Your teams."

Deleting a Team

If you're sure that a team will not be needed in the future, you can delete it. Here's how:

1. **Open the admin center:** Select Teams.

2. **Choose the team:** Click the team name you want to delete.

3. **Delete the team:** Select Delete. A confirmation message will appear.

4. **Confirm deletion:** Click Delete again to permanently delete the team.

Important Note   Deleted teams cannot be directly restored. Always consider archiving before deleting.

Restoring a Deleted Team

Deleted teams can be restored by restoring the associated Microsoft 365 group within 30 days (soft-delete period).

Use the Microsoft 365 admin center to restore the group associated with the deleted team. Restoring the group will also restore the team's content, including channels, tabs, and private channels.

Important Note   By default, a deleted Microsoft 365 group is retained for 30 days, after which it cannot be restored. Learn more by reading "Restore a Deleted Group."

In summary, archiving, reactivating, and deleting teams in Microsoft Teams enable admins to effectively manage their organization's collaboration space. Always consider the implications of archiving or deleting a team and use the appropriate method to align with your organization's requirements.

Best Practices for Archiving and Deleting

Archiving and deleting teams in Microsoft Teams should be managed carefully to ensure that organizational data is handled correctly and resources are used efficiently. Here are some strategies:

- **Define archiving and deletion policies:** First, establish clear criteria for when a team should be archived or deleted. This might be based on the team's activity level, the duration of inactivity, or the completion of the project or purpose the team was created for.

- **Use Teams life-cycle management tools:** Microsoft provides tools within Teams and the broader Microsoft 365 admin center to help manage the life cycle of teams. For example, you can set an expiration policy that automatically deletes teams after a certain period of inactivity, with reminders sent to team owners to renew the team if it's still needed.

- **Implement a regular review process:** Regularly review your Teams environment to identify teams that are inactive or no longer needed. The usage reports in the Microsoft 365 admin center can help identify inactive teams.

- **Archive before deleting:** Archiving a team before deleting it gives you a safety net in case the team is needed again. An archived team is read-only, preserving its content but preventing any new activity. If it turns out the team is still needed, it can be reactivated.

- **Educate team owners:** Make sure team owners understand the criteria for archiving and deleting teams and how to do it. They're often in the best position to know when a team is no longer needed.

- **Use a gradual approach:** When a team is to be deleted, consider first advising members that the team will be deleted on a specific date, giving them a chance to save any needed information elsewhere. Then archive the team, and only after some time has passed, delete it.

- **Understand data retention policies:** When a team is deleted, its associated data in SharePoint and Exchange is also deleted by default, subject to your organization's data retention policies. Make sure you understand these policies and how they impact the archiving and deletion of teams.

- **Regular cleanup:** Regular cleanup activities should be performed to remove unnecessary clutter, which includes removing old files, conversations, and obsolete Teams.

Remember, the specific processes and criteria for archiving and deleting teams should align with your organization's broader IT, security, and compliance policies.

Naming Conventions in Microsoft Teams

Naming conventions in Microsoft Teams are rules or guidelines for how Teams should be named. They can help keep teams organized, make them easier to find, and provide some context about the team's purpose, membership, or associated projects.

Here are some guidelines and best practices for Teams naming conventions:

- **Consistency:** Consistency is key when it comes to naming conventions. The rules should be easy to understand and apply consistently across all Teams.

- **Context:** Include elements in the name that provide context about the team's purpose, such as the department name, project name, or geographical location.

- **Avoid special characters:** Certain special characters can cause issues with integration with other systems. It's often best to stick to alphanumeric characters.

- **Length:** Keep team names as short as possible while still being descriptive. Very long team names can be cumbersome and might get cut off in the Teams interface.

- **Avoid duplicates:** The naming convention should help avoid duplicate names, which can be confusing. This can be especially important in larger organizations where many teams might be created for similar purposes.

Here are some examples of naming conventions for different use cases:

- **Departmental teams:** For teams created for specific departments, you might include the department name and function. Examples: Marketing-Communications and HR-Payroll.

- **Project teams:** For teams created for specific projects, you might include the project name and the department responsible. Examples: ProjectX-Development and WebsiteRevamp-Marketing.

- **Geographical locations:** For teams that are geographically specific, include the location in the team name. Examples: Sales-EastCoast and Support-London.

Remember, naming conventions should be decided in alignment with your organization's broader governance policies, and you should educate users on the importance of following them. Microsoft 365 also allows for enforcing naming policies (such as prefixes or suffixes and blocked words) through the Teams admin center to help maintain consistent naming conventions.

Additionally, note that Teams are built on Microsoft 365 Groups, and the naming policy affects not just Teams but also the associated SharePoint sites, Exchange Online shared mailboxes and calendars, and Planner. Therefore, the naming strategy should be comprehensive and in line with the broader Microsoft 365 governance strategy.

Creating and Managing Office 365 Groups Naming Policy Applicable to Teams

When a user creates an Office 365 Group or Microsoft Teams team (which creates an Office 365 group in the back end) for their professional use, then the expectation is that they should use a meaningful name. Out of the box, users can use any name while creating a group, but if your organization requires a specific naming format, you as an admin can achieve this using a group naming policy that implements a consistent naming strategy for groups created by users. The naming policy will be able to help users identify the function of the group, membership, or the person who created the group. The policy is applied to groups that are created across all Office 365 apps, including Outlook, Teams, SharePoint, Planner, and Yammer. It applies to group names and group aliases, as well.

When creating a naming policy, you must be aware that the maximum group name length is 53 characters, including the prefixes and suffixes. Prefixes and suffixes can contain special characters in the group name (and group alias), and if they contain special characters that are not allowed in the group name, they will be removed and applied to the group alias. This will result in group prefixes and suffixes that will be different from the ones applied to the group alias. Finally, be aware that if you are using Yammer Office 365 connected groups, avoid using the following characters in your naming policy: @, #, [,], <, and >. If these characters are in the naming policy, regular Yammer users will not be able to create groups.

The Office 365 Group naming policy includes a prefix-suffix naming policy. You can use prefixes or suffixes to describe the naming convention of groups. For example, if you configure GRP as a prefix, then the Marketing group will be named GRP Marketing. Custom blocked words is another important features, as it allows an admin to specify a variety of words that will be blocked in groups created by users, such as CEO, CFO, Invoice, Billings, Payments, HR, and so on.

Working with Prefixes and Suffixes in a Group Naming Policy

Specific to the naming policy, prefixes and suffixes can be either fixed strings or user attributes. When using fixed strings, it is advised that an admin assign short strings that will help differentiate groups in the global address list (GAL). Some of the frequently used prefixes and suffixes are keywords such as Ext_name, Int_name, Grp_Name, #Name, or _Name.

Using attributes, you can use attributes that can assist in identification of which user has created the group, like [Department], and where it was created from, like [Country]. For example, a naming policy of GRP [GroupName] [Department] will result in the following if the group is named My Group and the user's department is Marketing: GRP My Group Marketing. Attributes supported in Azure AD are [Department], [Company], [Office], [StateOrProvince], [CountryOrRegion], and [Title]. Unsupported user attributes are considered fixed strings (e.g., [postalCode]). Also, extension attributes and custom attributes are not supported. It's advisable to use attributes that have values filled in for all the users in your organization and not to use attributes that have longer values.

Creating and Managing a Group Naming Policy in an Office 365 Tenant

A naming policy provides a way to standardize Office 365 Groups naming, and it allows you to block certain names as well. You can configure naming policy using the Azure AD admin center and Windows PowerShell. To create a naming policy, follow this procedure:

1. Log in to the Azure Active Directory admin center (https://aad. portal.azure.com/) as a global administrator. In the left pane, select Azure Active Directory. Under Manage, select Groups. In the Settings section, select Naming Policy. Open the Group Naming Policy tab, as shown in Figure 5-11.

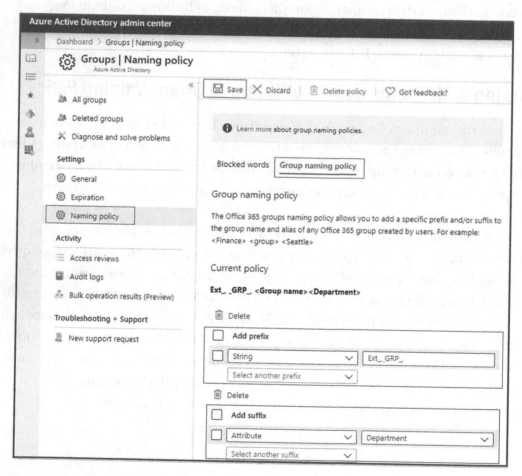

Figure 5-11. *Creating a naming policy*

2. In the Current Policy section, select whether you would like to require a prefix or suffix (or both) and select the appropriate check boxes. For either of these settings, choose between Attribute and String. Figure 5-12 shows the Ext_ and GRP_ prefixes and a Department suffix selected.

Creating an Office 365 Groups Naming Policy Using Windows PowerShell with Azure AD Module

Before creating a new policy, you must check if any existing Office 365 groups naming policy is available. Install the latest Azure AD PowerShell module (if it is not already installed). Open Windows PowerShell as an administrator and connect to Azure AD, and then run this command:

```
$Setting = Get-AzureADDirectorySetting -Id (Get-AzureADDirectorySetting |
where -Property DisplayName -Value "Group.Unified" -EQ).id
```

```
$Setting.Values
```

In the output, check the values for `CustomBlockedWordsList`, `EnableMSStandardBlockedWords`, and `PrefixSuffixNamingRequirement`.

Execute the next PowerShell command to create the naming policy in the existing PowerShell module that is connected to the Azure AD:

```
$Setting = Get-AzureADDirectorySetting -Id (Get-AzureADDirectorySetting |
where -Property DisplayName -Value "Group.Unified" -EQ).id
```

Set the group name prefixes and suffixes; for example, the prefixes `Ext_` and `GRP_`:

```
$Setting["PrefixSuffixNamingRequirement"] ="Ext_[GroupName]","GRP_[GroupName]"
```

To configure custom blocked words that you want to restrict—for example, Invoices, Payroll, and CEO—run this command:

```
$Setting["CustomBlockedWordsList"]="Invoices,Payroll,CEO"
```

You can modify the setting in the Azure AD directory by running this command:

```
Set-AzureADDirectorySetting -Id (Get-AzureADDirectorySetting |
where -Property DisplayName -Value "Group.Unified" -EQ).id
-DirectorySetting $Setting
```

513

Managing the Naming Policy

You can add or remove a naming policy using Azure AD. To add or remove a naming policy, log in to Azure AD and then open the Naming Policy page to add or modify the policy. If you are removing an existing policy, then it will ask for confirmation. Once you confirm the deletion, the naming policy is removed, along with all prefix-suffix naming policies and any custom blocked words.

Adding Custom Blocked Words Under the Naming Policy

In a naming policy, custom blocked words are those users are not permitted to use when creating a group. You can also list several blocked words, which need to be separated by a comma. The blocked words check is done on the group name when it is entered by a user. For example, if a user enters CEO and Prefix_ as the naming policy, Prefix_CEO will fail. A substring search is not conducted, so users can use common words like Pilot even if *lot* is a blocked word.

To add a custom blocked word, log in to Azure AD. Under Manage, select Groups. In the Settings section, select Naming Policy, and then click the Blocked Words tab, as shown in Figure 5-12.

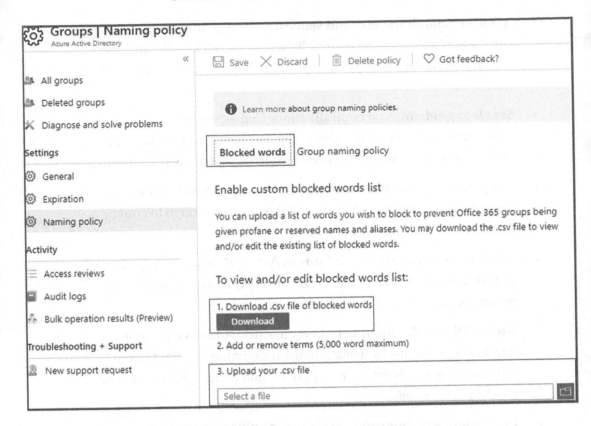

Figure 5-12. *Custom blocked words*

Naming Conventions Best Practices

Naming conventions are critical in Microsoft Teams to maintain consistency, clarity, and ease of navigation within the organization. Following a standardized naming convention helps users find and recognize teams and channels more easily. Here are some best practices for implementing naming conventions in Microsoft Teams:

- **Use prefixes to define categories:** Use clear and consistent prefixes that define the category or department associated with a team or channel. For example, use HR_ for Human Resources or PROJ_ for project-related teams.

- **Include a location (if applicable):** For organizations spread across multiple locations, including the location in the team name can aid in identification such as in NYC_Sales or LA_Marketing.

515

- **Avoid special characters and spaces:** Special characters and spaces can create confusion and compatibility issues. Stick to alphanumeric characters and use underscores (_) or hyphens (-) as separators if needed.

- **Set clear guidelines on capitalization:** Consistent use of capitalization can enhance readability. Decide on a capitalization rule, such as title case or all caps for prefixes, and apply it uniformly.

- **Keep names concise but descriptive:** Names should be short enough to be easily readable but still descriptive enough to convey the purpose of the team or channel.

- **Avoid acronyms unless well-known:** Acronyms can be confusing unless they are well-known and universally understood within the organization.

- **Utilize Microsoft's naming policies feature:** Admins can enforce naming conventions by using Microsoft's naming policies feature. This allows administrators to require certain prefixes or suffixes and block specific words.

- **Implement a review process:** Consider implementing a review or approval process for new team or channel names to ensure compliance with the naming conventions.

- **Provide clear documentation and training:** Make sure all team members understand the naming conventions by providing clear documentation and training if necessary.

- **Consider legal and compliance requirements:** Ensure that your naming conventions comply with legal requirements and internal policies, especially if they relate to sensitive or confidential information.

A coherent and consistent naming convention in Microsoft Teams promotes an organized and efficient environment, minimizing confusion and aiding collaboration. By developing and enforcing a thoughtful naming strategy, organizations can streamline communication and foster a more productive workspace.

Setting Up Microsoft Teams with Automatic Team Expiration

In modern workplaces, collaboration is often fluid, evolving with the ebb and flow of projects and initiatives. Microsoft Teams is designed to facilitate this dynamic collaboration, allowing the creation of teams and channels as needed. However, this ease of creation can lead to an overabundance of inactive or obsolete teams, cluttering the system and complicating management. Enter Automatic Team Expiration—a feature designed to manage the life cycle of teams, keeping the environment clean and efficient.

How to Set Up Automatic Team Expiration

In Microsoft 365, you can set up a group expiration policy that automatically deletes teams (and their associated Microsoft 365 groups) after a certain period of inactivity. Automatic Team Expiration enables administrators to set an expiration time frame for teams. Once the expiration date is reached, owners will be prompted to renew the team if it is still needed. If no action is taken, the team will be archived or deleted.

Here are the steps to configure this:

1. In the Microsoft 365 admin center, go to Groups ➤ Active groups.

2. Select Expiration under Settings.

3. Set the group lifetime in days (the period of inactivity after which a group is considered for deletion).

4. Specify whether owners receive notifications about upcoming deletions and how many days in advance they're sent.

5. Specify whether group owners can renew their groups and whether they can do so upon receiving an expiration notification.

Creating and Managing an Office 365 Group Expiration Policy That Applies to Associated Content

Microsoft Teams is built on Office 365 Groups, and every team has groups associated with it. This means whenever a user creates a new team, an Office 365 group is automatically provisioned. Therefore, as the number of teams grows, the Office 365 group count automatically grows as well. As a Teams admin, you must manage these groups to control their expansion. In many cases, users create a team for a specific task, but after that task is completed, the team and Office 365 group remain active but unused. For example, User A created a team for implementing Microsoft Identity Manager in the Bloguc organization. When the project ended, User A forgot to delete that project team. That means the Office 365 Groups and Teams content still exist. Such use cases will increase the group (and team) count, which adds to management overhead and eventually makes IT administration difficult.

To manage Office 365 Groups regardless of a team's association, you need a method to clean up the unused groups and simplify management. The best solution is to set a group expiration policy, which helps to remove unused groups from the directory system. The group expiration is turned off by default in Office 365. When you decide to implement group expiration, you need to enable the feature for your organization tenants and specify an expiration period for the Office 365 group. Once you set up group expiration, when the expiration date for a group approaches, an email notification is sent to the group owners (whoever created or was set as an owner of the group) to determine if group renewal is required for an additional period. If the group is not renewed, it will be deleted automatically.

Note   If group expiration policy changes are made by an admin, the Office 365 expiration period will be recalculated for the groups.

Important   When an Office 365 group expires, all the group's associated content will be deleted, including Outlook, Planner, and SharePoint. However, there is an option to recover content for up to 30 days from the expiration date.

Note   Renewal notifications are emailed to group owners 30 days, 15 days, and 1 day prior to group expiration. Group owners must have Exchange licenses to receive notification emails. If a group is not renewed, it is deleted along with its associated content from sources such as Outlook, SharePoint, Microsoft Teams, and PowerBI.

To configure the Office 365 group expiration policy, perform these steps:

1. Log in to the Azure Active Directory admin center (`https://aad.portal.azure.com/`) as a global administrator. In the left pane, select Azure Active Directory. Under Manage, select Groups, and then select Expiration to open the expiration settings page, shown in Figure 5-13.

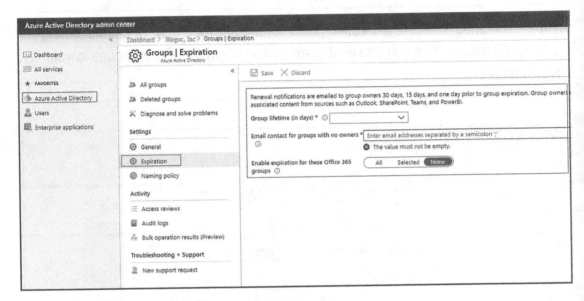

Figure 5-13. *Group expiration settings page*

2. On the Expiration page, you can specify several options.

    - **Group Lifetime (In Days):** This option sets the group lifetime in days with choices of 180, 365, or Custom. The Custom setting requires a lifetime of at least 30 days. The example in Figure 5-14 shows a setting of Custom and 90 days.

    - **Email Contact For Groups With No Owners:** Specify an email address where the renewal and expiration notifications should be sent when a group has no owner. If the group does not have an owner, the expiration emails will go to a specified admin. Figure 5-14 shows the contact email account for groups with no owner.

- **Enable Expiration For These Office 365 Groups:** Select the Office 365 Groups for which you would like to configure this expiration policy. The options are All, for all the groups within your organization; Selected, for only specific groups; and None, which turns this off entirely. For this example, in Figure 5-14, the Selected option is chosen, and the group Test is specified.

Note   You should set the expiration policy for a test group first. Once this setting is properly tested, then you can enable expiration policy for all the groups in your organization.

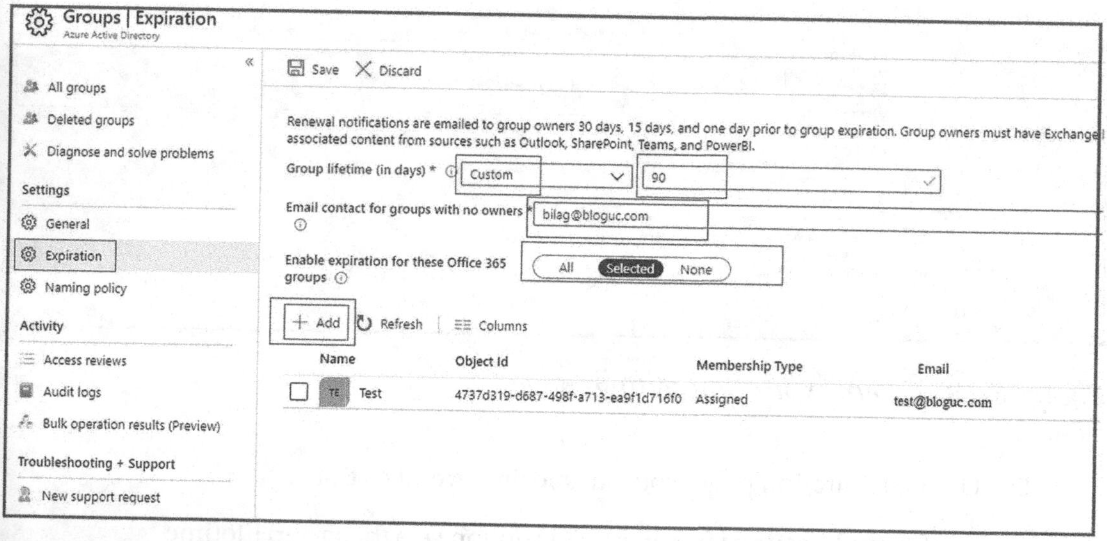

Figure 5-14. *Group expiration settings*

3. After finishing the configuration, click Save.

Remember that group expiration is a feature that is incorporated in an Azure AD Premium subscription. An Azure subscription license is necessary for the admins who are going to configure the settings and the members of the affected groups. Specific to the management aspect, you as a Teams admin (with Office 365 global admin group permission) can create, view, modify, or delete the Office 365 Groups expiration policy settings and users can renew or restore an Office 365 Group that they own.

Best Practices on Teams Auto Expiration

Here are more best practices:

- **Align with organizational policies:** Ensure that the expiration settings align with company data retention and governance policies.

- **Communicate with team owners:** Inform team owners about the expiration policy and the process for renewal to avoid unexpected deletions.

- **Regular monitoring:** Regularly monitor the expiration statuses and act on any teams that are in the process of expiring.

- **Consider activity:** Implement logic that takes into consideration the activity within the team. Some organizations may choose to only expire teams that have been inactive for a specified period.

- **Backup critical data:** Before a team's expiration, ensure that critical data and content are backed up, if necessary.

- **Customize notifications:** Customize notification emails to include specific instructions or links to organizational guidelines on team management.

- **Training and documentation:** Provide training and documentation to team owners on how to manage team expiration, including renewal procedures.

How Group Expiration Works with the Retention Policy

When you as a security admin set up a retention policy in the Microsoft 365 Security & Compliance Center for groups, then the expiration policy works in association with retention policy. Once a group expires, the group's conversations in Outlook and files in SharePoint Online are kept in the retention container for the duration (number of days) specified in the retention policy. The users will not see the group or its content after expiration, however. That's why a user must monitor the group expiration notification and act in a timely manner instead of losing control of their content.

How Group Owners Receive Expiration Notifications

Specific to the group expiration notification, when a group is about to expire, group owners will be notified via email, irrespective of how the group was created, whether through SharePoint, Planner, Teams, or any other Office 365 application. If the group was created via Teams, the group owner will receive a notification to renew through the activity section in the Microsoft Teams client. The group owner will receive the group expiration notification before 30 days, and if it is not renewed, an additional renewal email will be sent 15 days before the expiration. In the event the group is still not renewed, one more email notification will be sent the day before the expiration.

If no one renews the group before it expires, it will be automatically deleted, but the admins will still be able to restore the group within 30 days after the expiration date. It is important to understand that not every admin can restore the expired group, as specific permissions are required to restore a group: Global administrators, Group administrators, Partner Tier2 support, and Intune administrators can restore any deleted Office 365 Group.

When the specified period of inactivity is reached, an expiration notification is sent to the team owner, asking them to renew the team if it's still needed. If the team isn't renewed, it's deleted, along with its associated resources.

Aside from automatic expiration, there are other options to manage inactive teams:

- **Manual archiving or deletion:** Admins or team owners can manually archive or delete teams based on their knowledge of the team's status.

- **Regular reviews:** Regular reviews of Teams usage can help identify inactive teams that might need to be archived or deleted.

- **Usage analytics:** The usage analytics reports in the Microsoft 365 admin center can help identify inactive teams.

The following are best practices for managing inactive teams:

- **Educate team owners:** Make sure team owners understand the automatic expiration policy and know how to renew their teams if necessary.

- **Set an appropriate expiration period:** The right expiration period will depend on your organization's needs. Too short, and team owners might be annoyed by frequent renewal requests. Too long, and you might end up with many inactive teams.

- **Consider the impact of deletion:** Remember that when a team is deleted, its associated resources (like SharePoint sites and files) are also deleted by default. Make sure you understand your organization's data retention requirements before setting up automatic deletion.

- **Regular auditing:** Conduct regular audits to identify and clean up teams that are no longer in use.

Remember that these settings and practices should align with your broader governance policies for Microsoft 365 and Microsoft Teams. It's also important to note that the group expiration policy feature is available only with certain Microsoft 365 subscriptions (like Azure AD Premium P1).

Microsoft Teams Template and Their Usages

Microsoft Teams templates are predefined structures for teams that can be used to create new teams. A template defines the structure of a team by including preset channels, apps, and tabs that cater to a specific workspace requirement.

Teams templates can streamline team creation, ensure consistency across teams, speed up user onboarding, and encourage the adoption of best practices. Instead of starting from scratch every time, you can use a template that has the essential components already configured.

Microsoft provides several out-of-the-box templates for common team types, like project management, events, or departmental collaboration. In addition, organizations can create their own custom templates tailored to their specific needs.

Here are some real-world use cases for team templates:

- **Departmental teams:** You could create a template for each department in your organization, with channels, tabs, and apps that that department typically uses. For example, a Marketing template might include channels for Social Media, Content Creation, and Brand Guidelines, along with tabs for marketing project plans or brand assets.

- **Project teams:** A project team template might include channels for different stages of the project, like Planning, Execution, and Review. It might also include tabs for a project plan, budget, or other essential project documents.

- **Event planning teams:** An event planning template might include channels for different aspects of event planning, like Venue, Promotion, and Logistics. It could also include tabs for the event schedule, budget, or registration information.

- **Classroom teams:** For educational institutions, a classroom template could include channels for different subjects or weeks of the semester. It might also include tabs for assignments, readings, or class discussions.

By using team templates, organizations can standardize the setup of similar teams, which not only saves time but also helps ensure best practices are followed, promotes more effective collaboration, and improves the overall Teams experience.

Create Microsoft Teams Templates

Using Microsoft Teams templates involves two key steps: creating the template (done by an admin) and using the template to create a team (done by any authorized user).

Step 1: Creating a Teams Template

Remember that only Teams admins can create templates. Here's how:

1. In the Microsoft Teams admin center, select Teams ➤ Team Templates.

2. Click Add. See Figure 5-15.

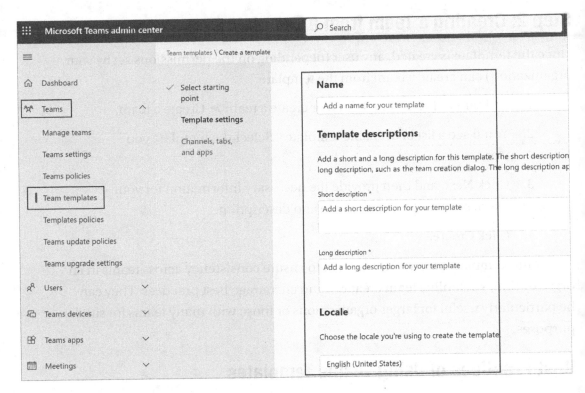

Figure 5-15. Teams template

3. Enter a name and description for the template. Select the language, and then click Next.

4. Choose the settings you want for the template, such as the team's privacy level (public or private), whether to allow guests, and the team picture. Refer to Figure 5-15 for Teams template creation.

5. Set up the structure for your team by adding channels. For each channel, you can specify whether it's shown by default and whether users can remove it.

6. If desired, add apps to the template. These will be added to any team created from the template.

7. When you're done, click Submit. The new template is added to the list in the Team Templates page and is available for users to create teams from.

Step 2: Creating a Team from a Template

Once the template is created, any user (depending on the permissions set by your organization) can create a team from the template:

1. In Teams, click Teams ➤ Join or create a team ➤ Create a team.

2. You'll see a list of available templates. Select the template you want to use.

3. Click Next, and then provide the necessary information for your team, such as the team's name and description.

4. Click Create.

Teams templates are a powerful tool to ensure consistency across teams in an organization, streamline team creation, and encourage best practices. They can be particularly useful for larger organizations or those with many teams for similar purposes.

Best Practices of Using Teams Templates

Teams templates can streamline the creation of new teams, encourage consistency, and help adopt best practices. Here are some best practices for creating and using Teams templates:

- **Align with organizational needs:** Templates should be created based on the unique needs and structures of your organization. This could be based on departmental needs, project structures, locations, or any other organizational structure.

- **Use descriptive names and descriptions:** The name and description of the template should clearly indicate its purpose, making it easy for users to choose the correct template when creating a new team.

- **Include essential channels and tabs:** The structure of the template (including channels and tabs) should be well thought out. Include channels and tabs that are likely to be needed by every team using the template. This can ensure consistency and help users get started quickly.

- **Incorporate useful apps:** Including useful apps in the template can enhance the productivity of the teams using it. For instance, a project management template might include Planner or a departmental team might include Power BI for reporting.

- **Maintain simplicity:** While it's important to include essential elements, be careful not to make the template too complex. Too many channels or tabs can be confusing and discourage users from adopting the template.

- **Educate users:** Users should be educated about the purpose of each template, when to use them, and how they work. This will help ensure templates are used effectively and consistently.

- **Review and update regularly:** As your organization evolves, your Teams templates should evolve too. Regularly review and update templates to ensure they continue to meet the needs of your organization.

- **Test before deploying:** Always test a new template before deploying it organization-wide. This can help you identify any issues or shortcomings early.

By following these best practices, you can leverage Teams templates to promote consistency, improve productivity, and make it easier for users to collaborate effectively in Teams.

Data Governance and Retention Policy

Data governance and retention policies in Microsoft Teams help organizations comply with industry regulations and internal policies by ensuring that certain types of data are retained for a specified period or deleted as required. These policies apply to Teams chat and channel messages.

Here's a brief description:

- **Retention policies:** These are used to ensure that data is retained for compliance, regulatory, or other business reasons. For example, you might need to retain financial data for a certain number of years for auditing purposes.

Retention policies in Teams can be configured in the Microsoft 365 compliance center. You can set these policies to retain data for a specific period, after which the data can be deleted. These policies can be applied at multiple levels such as the entire organization, specific locations, or specific users.

When a retention policy is in place, Teams chat, channel messages, and channel conversations are preserved, and users can continue to work with this content during the retention period. After the retention period expires, data is deleted and is recoverable for an additional 30 days.

- **Data governance:** This refers to the overall management of the availability, usability, integrity, and security of the data used in an enterprise. It involves protecting critical data, managing data growth, and enabling business users to find the information they need.

  In Microsoft Teams, data governance might involve managing where data is stored, how it's secured, who has access to it, and how it's disposed of.

  Data in Teams resides in different services depending on its type. For example, chat data is stored in a mailbox backed by Exchange Online, and files that users share in a chat are stored in OneDrive for Business, while files shared in a channel conversation are stored in SharePoint. Each of these services provides its own data governance capabilities, like data loss prevention (DLP), eDiscovery, legal hold, etc.

Remember, the specific settings and policies you choose should align with your organization's broader IT, security, and compliance requirements. It's also worth noting that data retention and data governance in Microsoft Teams require appropriate Microsoft 365 licensing.

Microsoft Teams retention policies are beneficial for several reasons:

- **Compliance and regulation:** Different industries have various regulations for how long certain types of information must be retained. Retention policies can help ensure that your organization stays compliant with these rules.

- **Litigation support:** In case of litigation or disputes, relevant data, including communications, might be required as evidence. A retention policy ensures that such data is not prematurely deleted.

- **Operational efficiency:** By automatically deleting data that's no longer needed, retention policies can help manage storage and improve system performance.

- **Information management:** Retention policies can help ensure that outdated information is removed, reducing clutter and making it easier for users to find the information they need.

Retention Policies for Teams

In Microsoft Teams, retention policies are very useful for retaining Teams or chat data, as well as defining deletion policies. For most organizations, the volume and complexity of data increases daily, including email to documents to instant messages, and many more. Efficiently managing or governing these data is important because as a Teams admin, you should comply proactively with industry regulations and internal policies that require you to retain content for a minimum period of time. For example, the Sarbanes-Oxley (SOX) Act might require you to retain certain types of content for seven years. Teams is already certified by more than 42 regional or national and industry-specific regulations.

This can also help reduce your risk in the event of litigation or a security breach by permanently deleting old content that you are no longer required to keep. Teams also helps your organization share knowledge effectively and be more responsive by ensuring that your users work only with content that is current and relevant to them.

Specific to the retention policy, it helps organizations either retain data for compliance (namely, preservation policy) for a specific period or remove data (namely, deletion policy) if it is considered a liability after a specific period. Retention policies are available in the Security & Compliance Center, and they work across the different workloads and data types, such as Exchange email, SharePoint document libraries, and OneDrive for Business files.

As you know, Teams chat conversations are persistent and retained by default in Exchange Online. With the addition of retention policies, administrators can configure retention policies (both preservation and deletion) in the Security & Compliance Center for Teams chat and channel messages.

Creating and Managing Retention Policies

Let's talk about creating and managing retention policies.

Managing Retention Policies

You can manage retention policies using Office 365 Security & Compliance Center, or you can use PowerShell. To manage Teams retention policies, log in to the Office 365 Security & Compliance Center, and navigate to Information Governance. Select Retention, as shown in Figure 5-16.

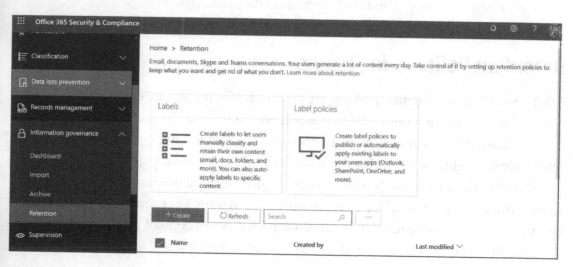

Figure 5-16. *Retention policy*

Microsoft Teams retention policies support different tasks, such as preservation, that allow an organization to keep Teams data for a specified duration and then do nothing. Another policy preserves and then deletes the Teams data. This kind of policy allows an organization to keep Teams data for a specified duration, and then it will be deleted. In addition, there is another policy that allows deletion of Teams data after a specified duration.

So far, advanced retention policy doesn't support Teams chat and Teams channel message locations, but Microsoft might support advanced retention policy for Teams chat and channel messages in the future.

Creating a Teams Retention Policy

As a Teams admin, you must know how to create retention policies for Teams private chats (one-to-one chat and group chat) and Teams channel messages. In many instances, organizations consider private chat data as more of a liability than channel messages, which are usually more project-related conversations. To create a retention policy, follow this procedure:

1. Log into Office 365 Security & Compliance Center (https://protection.office.com/homepage) and navigate to Information Governance. Select Retention and then click Create Policy. Figure 5-17 shows settings for retention policy creation.

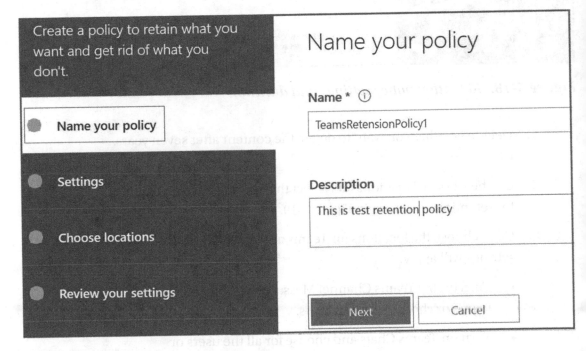

Figure 5-17. *Creating a retention policy*

2. Enter a meaningful name and description for the retention policy. Click Next.

3. On the Settings tab, define retention policies for these locations. Set how long you want to retain the content. For example, Figure 5-18 shows that the content will be retained for seven years.

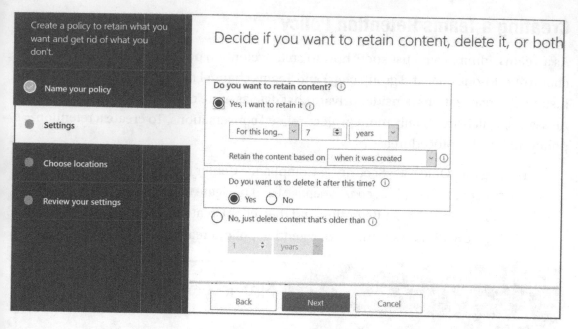

Figure 5-18. *Retention policy settings and duration*

4. Decide whether you want to delete the content after seven years. Click Next.

5. On the Choose Locations tab, select the appropriate applications for retention, as shown in Figure 5-19.

6. Next, choose the locations for Teams and to which teams these settings will apply.

    - Turn on the Teams Channel Messages setting and choose for all teams or choose specific teams.

    - Turn on Teams Chats and choose for all the users or exclude users.

7. When you turn on Teams channel messages, you can specify teams to which this policy will apply. For example, for teams X, Y, and Z, the admin can set the deletion policies for one year (by selecting those teams individually) and apply a three-year deletion policy to the rest of the teams. Click Next to review the settings.

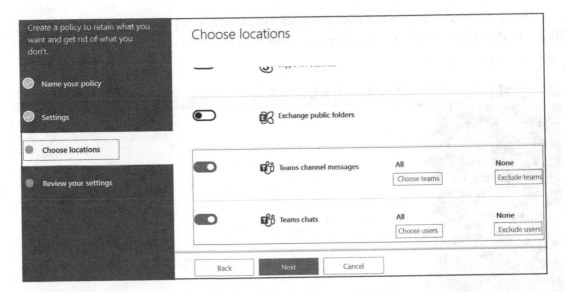

Figure 5-19. *Choosing a location for retention*

8. On the next tab, review all the settings and click Create This
    Policy, as shown in Figure 5-20.

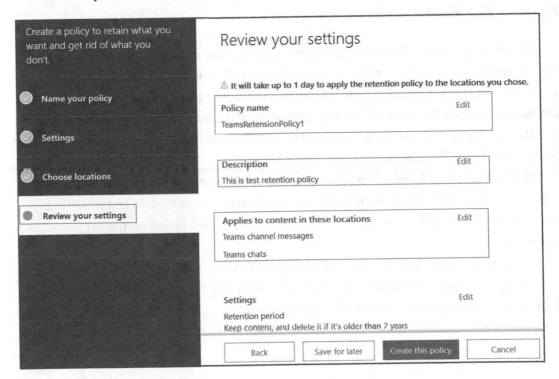

Figure 5-20. *Reviewing the tetention policy*

After policy creation you can see the policy created and its last modified date, as illustrated in Figure 5-21. In this example, Teams chats and Teams channel messages will be maintained for seven years.

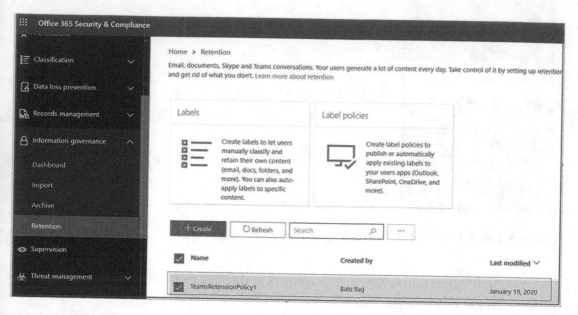

Figure 5-21. Retention policy created

Retention policies allow you to preserve your data for a specific amount of time and then delete the data after that period. Microsoft Teams supports retention policies as short as one day. Retention policies can be configured to retain data for a specific amount of time so that even if the user deletes the data, admins still have access to it. Another policy is to delete data, so if a user wants to delete data after a specific period of time, then you will be able to do this.

You as a Teams admin can create a retention policy based on when the information is created, or you can create policies based on when information was last modified. Microsoft provides the flexibility to create retention policies based on the organization's requirements.

Remember, retention policies should align with your broader compliance, regulatory, and organizational requirements. Consulting with legal and compliance experts is recommended when setting these policies.

Best Practices of Teams Retention Policies

Teams retention policies allow organizations to manage the preservation and deletion of chat and channel messages in Microsoft Teams. When creating these policies, you can define how long to retain data and whether to automatically delete the data after the retention period.

Here are some best practices for Teams retention policies:

- **Understand your compliance needs:** The first step in creating a retention policy is understanding your organization's compliance needs. This could involve legal requirements for data retention, industry-specific regulations, or internal policies.

- **Be specific with your policies:** You can create retention policies for the entire organization, specific locations, or specific users. It's often beneficial to have different policies for different types of data or departments. For example, you might need to retain financial data for a longer period than general communication.

- **Use both preservation and deletion policies:** It's essential to balance the need to preserve data for compliance with the need to delete data for operational efficiency. Retention policies in Teams allow you to do both.

- **Regularly review and update policies:** The retention policy should not be a set-and-forget affair. It should be reviewed and updated regularly to make sure it aligns with any changes in your organization's needs or regulations.

- **Educate users:** Make sure users are aware of the retention policies and understand what they mean. This can help avoid confusion and ensure that users don't unknowingly rely on Teams for long-term storage of critical information.

- **Coordinate with other policies:** Be aware of how your Teams retention policies interact with other policies like those for SharePoint or Exchange, where Teams data is also stored.

- **Test your policies:** After setting a retention policy, it's a good idea to verify that it's working as expected. You can do this by checking that data is being retained or deleted as specified by the policy.

Remember, the creation and management of retention policies should be done in consultation with your legal, compliance, and IT teams. It's also important to note that Teams retention policies require an appropriate Microsoft 365 or Office 365 license.

Data Loss Prevention Policies

Data loss prevention (DLP) in Microsoft Teams is a feature designed to detect sensitive information in Teams conversations and prevent it from being shared or leaked unintentionally. This sensitive information could include credit card numbers, Social Security numbers, or other types of personally identifiable information (PII).

Benefits of Teams DLP policies include the following:

- **Compliance:** DLP helps organizations comply with industry regulations and laws by preventing the leakage of sensitive data.

- **Prevention of data breaches:** DLP policies can detect and prevent sensitive information from being shared unintentionally, reducing the risk of data breaches.

- **Education:** DLP policies in Teams can be configured to notify users when they're about to share sensitive data, educating them about data handling best practices and the potential risks.

- **Visibility and control:** DLP provides insights into where sensitive data is being shared and by whom, allowing organizations to monitor and control data sharing.

How Do Microsoft 365 Data Loss Prevention Policies Work in Microsoft Teams?

DLP in Microsoft Teams offers a vital security measure by defining policies to prevent sharing sensitive data within Teams channels or chat sessions. The following are various examples illustrating how DLP works in Microsoft Teams.

Example 1: Message Protection

Suppose an individual attempts to share sensitive data in a Teams chat or channel with guests (external users). With a proper DLP policy in place, such messages sent to external users are automatically and swiftly deleted according to your DLP configuration.

Note   DLP in Microsoft Teams prevents sharing with the following:

- Guests in teams and channels

- External participants in meetings and chats

DLP for external chats functions if both parties use Teams Only mode with Microsoft Teams native federation. Messages in interoperation with Skype or non-native federated chat sessions are not blocked by DLP for Teams.

Example 2: Document Protection

Imagine someone trying to share a sensitive document with guests via a Microsoft Teams channel or chat. If there's a DLP policy preventing this, the document won't open for the recipients. The policy must encompass SharePoint and OneDrive. This example highlights DLP for SharePoint in Microsoft Teams and mandates Office 365 DLP licensing (within Office 365 E3) but not Office 365 Advanced Compliance.

Example 3: Protection in Shared Channels

In shared channels, the host team's DLP policy applies. Consider a shared channel owned by Team A with DLP policy P1. The sharing can occur in three ways.

- **With a member**: Invite a user without making them a member, and P1 will cover them.

- **Internally with another team**: Share with another team within the organization; P1 applies to all.

- **Cross-tenant with a team**: Share with an external team; P1 applies to all, regardless of the external team's DLP policy.

Example 4: Protection During External Chats

Using the external access feature in Microsoft Teams allows users from different Microsoft 365 organizations to join the same chat. Each participant's DLP policies are enforced according to their respective organizations. For example, Contoso's DLP policies apply to its users, while Fabrikam's apply to theirs. Additional details are available in the guide on managing external meetings and chats.

Note   Non-E5 customers can utilize the 90-day Microsoft Purview solutions trial to further explore how additional Purview functionalities can assist in handling data security and compliance needs. Begin now at the Microsoft Purview compliance portal trials hub, where details about signing up and trial terms are provided.

These examples and guidance offer a comprehensive understanding of how DLP can be customized and employed in Microsoft Teams to secure sensitive information, whether in messages, documents, shared channels, or external communications.

DLP Licensing Requirements for Microsoft Teams

Microsoft's DLP abilities extend to Microsoft Teams, encompassing various communication methods such as chat and channel messages, including those in private channels. The DLP licensing structure for Microsoft Teams is as follows:

1. **Comprehensive DLP coverage:**

    a. **Office 365 E5/A5/G5:** Full DLP functionality

    b. **Microsoft 365 E5/A5/G5:** Includes all DLP features

    c. **Microsoft 365 E5/A5/G5 Information Protection and Governance:** Incorporates extensive data protection

    d. **Microsoft 365 E5/A5/G5/F5 Compliance:** Along with F5 Security & Compliance, offers all-inclusive compliance and security options

2. **Limited DLP coverage:**

    a. **Office 365 and Microsoft 365 E3:** Offers DLP protection specifically for SharePoint, OneDrive, and Exchange. This protection includes files shared through Teams as well, since Teams leverages SharePoint and OneDrive for file sharing.

3. **Special requirement for Teams Chat:**

    a. **E5 License:** Support for DLP protection in Teams Chat is exclusive to those with an E5 license.

These licensing options offer varying levels of DLP capabilities to meet different organizational needs, ranging from comprehensive protection across all Teams communications to more targeted coverage for specific services like SharePoint and OneDrive. The choice of license can be tailored to align with the particular security and compliance requirements of your organization.

Managing Information Protection Using Data Loss Prevention

In any application, an identity is considered a front door. Once you secure the front door, then you will be dealing with how to control the flow of information, and Teams is no exception. Microsoft Teams achieves information protection through the Office 365 DLP stack. DLP enables Teams and security admins to create policies to determine what is considered sensitive or nonsensitive information. Microsoft makes this easier for admins by providing more than 80 predefined rules. An admin can leverage these existing predefined rules or create new custom rules or policies that an organization wants. You can monitor content, detect policy violations, and remediate violations as per the requirement.

Once you create policies, Teams monitors the content, and whenever a policy violation is detected, the end user gets notified, or you can set the policy to prevent access as well.

DLP Policies in Action

You can create DLP policies for different kind of workloads and enable them for Exchange, SharePoint, or Teams. There is only one portal to create DLP policies for all Office 365 applications, which means you don't have to switch among different portals for different applications.

As an example, two users from Bloguc organizations are trying to share content. The sender is trying to send some content, but the Bloguc organization has already implemented a DLP policy that blocks the content because it includes sensitive information. The notification message to the sender, shown in Figure 5-22, says, "This message was blocked," and also indicates why the content was blocked.

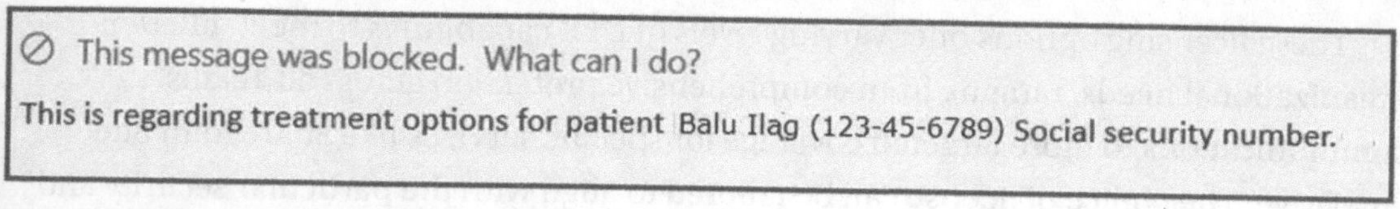

⊘ This message was blocked. What can I do?

This is regarding treatment options for patient Balu Ilag (123-45-6789) Social security number.

Figure 5-22. *DLP policy blocked notification*

The sender is also given the option to override the policy conditions and send the message or report it to a security admin. Figure 5-23 shows the override options.

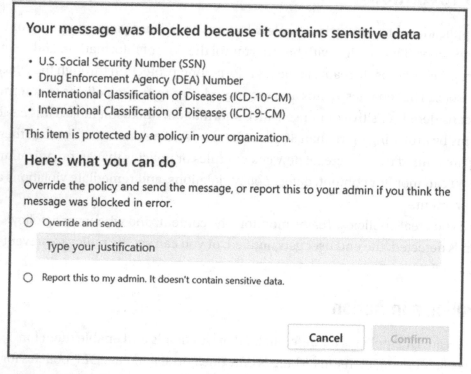

Your message was blocked because it contains sensitive data

- U.S. Social Security Number (SSN)
- Drug Enforcement Agency (DEA) Number
- International Classification of Diseases (ICD-10-CM)
- International Classification of Diseases (ICD-9-CM)

This item is protected by a policy in your organization.

Here's what you can do

Override the policy and send the message, or report this to your admin if you think the message was blocked in error.

○ Override and send.

Type your justification

○ Report this to my admin. It doesn't contain sensitive data.

Cancel   Confirm

Figure 5-23. *DLP policy override options*

The receiver will just get the message saying, "This message was blocked due to sensitive content," as displayed in Figure 5-24.

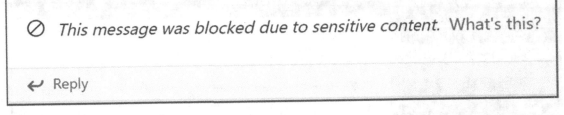

Figure 5-24. *Message blocked due to sensitive content*

This is considered a passive DLP solution, not active. You might wonder why it is considered passive. The reason is that when someone sends sensitive content, the receiver will see the content for a few seconds before it is removed from view. If you want to learn more, refer to the Microsoft documentation about DLP policies at `https://learn.microsoft.com/en-us/purview/dlp-microsoft-teams`, which helps explain why the message was blocked.

DLP policies are useful and provide a solution for preventing the accidental sharing of critical information about confidential projects, both internally and externally.

As of this writing, to leverage DLP policies, both the sender and receiver should be moved to TeamsOnly mode. If the sender is in Island mode and the receiver is in TeamsOnly mode, then the DLP policy will not work the way it should. In addition, the time taken to block the content and generate the warning message is quite lengthy. Microsoft is working to reduce this delay.

Creating a DLP Policy for Microsoft Teams

Teams or security admins can create new or DLP policies or modify existing ones; however, you must have permission to execute the modification steps outlined here. Remember, by default, an organization's tenant admin will have access to the Security & Compliance Center, and they can give Teams or security admins and other people access to the Security & Compliance Center, without giving them all of the permissions of the tenant admin. To create a DLP policy, follow this procedure:

1. Log in to Office 365 Security & Compliance Center by browsing to `https://compliance.microsoft.com`. Select Data Loss Prevention and then select Policy. Click + Create A Policy. Figure 5-25 shows the Create A Policy option.

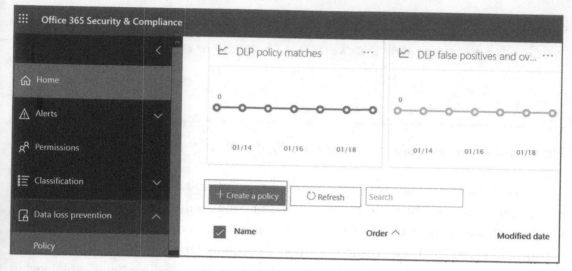

Figure 5-25. *DLP policy creation options*

2. Select a template, and then click Next. In the example shown in Figure 5-26, the U.S. Personally Identifiable Information (PII) Data template is selected.

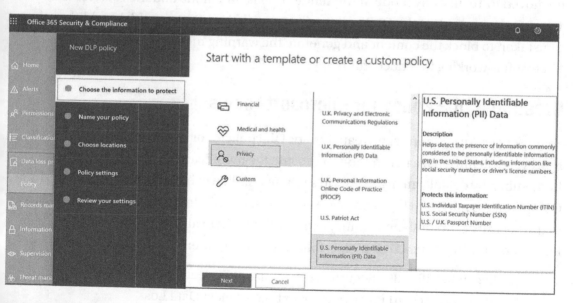

Figure 5-26. *Choosing an available DLP template*

3. On the next page, enter a name and description for the policy,
    and then click Next. Figure 5-27 shows the name given is
    U.S. Personally Identifiable Information (PII) Data- Bloguc Org,
    and the description identifies this policy correctly.

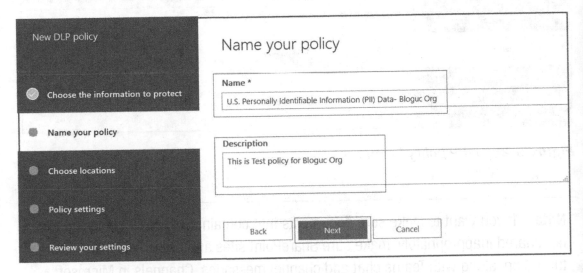

Figure 5-27. *DLP policy name and description*

4. On the next page, the Choose Locations tab, keep the default
    setting that includes all locations, or select Let Me Choose
    Specific Locations, and then click Next. For the example shown in
    Figure 5-28, the default selection that includes Exchange email,
    Teams chats, channel messages, and OneDrive and SharePoint
    documents is selected. If you have selected specific locations,
    select them for your DLP policy, and then click Next.

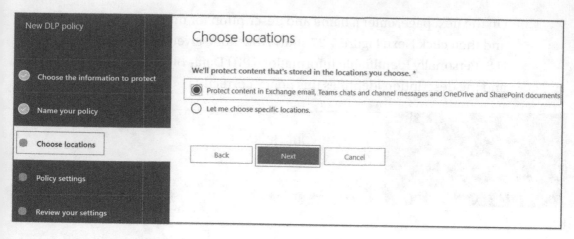

Figure 5-28. *DLP policy locations*

Note   If you want to make sure documents that contain sensitive information are not shared inappropriately, make sure SharePoint sites and OneDrive accounts are turned on, along with Teams chat and channel messages. Channels in Microsoft Teams are strongly dependent on Exchange Online functionality. Make sure that the Exchange email location is also enabled for the policies that should be applied for the content of the channels.

5.   On the next page, the Policy Settings tab, under Customize The Type Of Content You Want Io Protect, keep the simple default settings or choose Use Advanced Settings, and then click Next. If you choose to use the advanced settings, you can create or edit rules for your policy. For this example, shown in Figure 5-29, the default setting is retained to keep the policy simple.

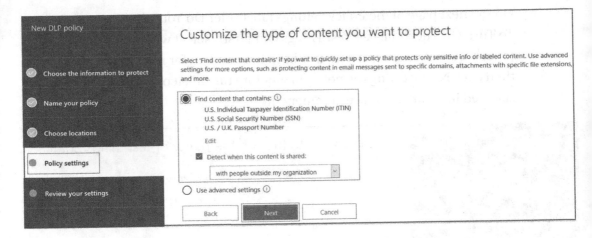

Figure 5-29. *DLP policy settings*

6. On the next page of the Policy Settings tab, under What Do You
    Want To Do If We Detect Sensitive Info?, review the settings.
    (Here's where you can select to keep default policy tips and email
    notifications or customize them.) When you are done reviewing
    and editing the settings, click Next. For this example, all the
    default settings are retained, as shown in Figure 5-30.

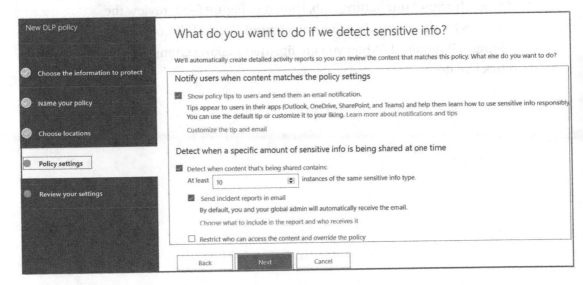

Figure 5-30. *Policy settings for sensitive information*

7. On the next page of the Policy Settings tab, under Do You Want To Turn On The Policy Or Test Things Out First?, select whether to turn the policy on, test it first, or keep it turned off for now, and then click Next. Testing the policy first before turning it on, as selected in Figure 5-31, is recommended.

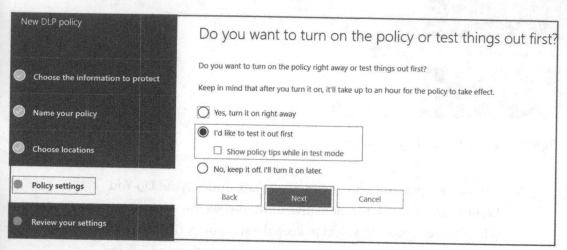

Figure 5-31. *Policy setting for testing*

8. On the Review Your Settings tab, shown in Figure 5-32, review the settings for the new policy that you created. Select Edit to make changes if required. When you are finished making changes, click Create.

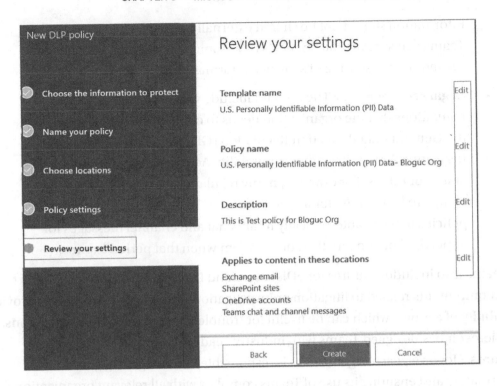

Figure 5-32. Reviewing settings

The DLP policy could take some time to populate, so sometimes it takes up to an hour for your new policy to work. You can make changes in the policy that you created to customize the policy per your organization's requirements.

Remember, DLP policies should align with your organization's broader IT, security, and compliance requirements. Always consult with your legal, compliance, and IT teams when setting these policies.

Compliance

Microsoft Teams compliance with organizational policies and legal requirements refers to how Microsoft Teams aligns with and supports an organization's internal rules, as well as external laws and regulations.

- **Organizational policies:** These might include data handling policies, communication and collaboration policies, IT policies, and more. For example, an organization might have a policy that sensitive information should not be shared externally. Features like DLP in Teams can support such policies by automatically detecting and preventing the sharing of sensitive information.

- **Legal requirements:** These could include various laws and regulations that the organization needs to comply with, such as the General Data Protection Regulation (GDPR) in Europe, Health Insurance Portability and Accountability Act (HIPAA) in the United States, or others. For example, many regulations require certain types of data to be retained for a specific period. Teams supports retention policies that can automatically retain chat and channel messages for a specified period and then delete them when that period expires.

Teams also includes features for eDiscovery and Legal Hold, which can support legal requirements related to litigation or investigation. Audit logs in Teams can provide traceability of actions, which can be useful for troubleshooting and for investigations.

Microsoft has designed Teams with industry-leading compliance and security standards. However, each organization is responsible for configuring Teams appropriately and ensuring its use of Teams complies with all relevant organizational policies and legal requirements. Also, it's important to note that some compliance features in Teams require specific Microsoft 365 or Office 365 licenses.

Compliance use cases in Microsoft Teams refer to the ways in which Teams can help organizations meet their compliance and regulatory requirements. Here are some examples:

- **Data retention:** Organizations in regulated industries often need to retain certain types of data for a specified period. Microsoft Teams supports configurable retention policies that can automatically retain chat and channel messages for a required period and then delete them when that period expires.

- **eDiscovery and Legal Hold:** In the case of litigation or investigation, organizations may need to search for and preserve electronic data related to the matter. Teams support eDiscovery for searching across Teams data. It also allows for Legal Hold, where data pertaining to specific users or cases can be preserved beyond its average retention period.

- **DLP:** DLP policies in Teams can prevent sensitive information from being shared inappropriately, either within the organization or externally. DLP can detect sensitive information such as credit card numbers, Social Security numbers, or other types of personally identifiable information (PII) in Teams chats and channel messages.

- **Information barriers:** For organizations that need to avoid conflicts of interest by limiting which individuals can communicate and collaborate with each other, Teams supports information barriers. This feature allows administrators to define policies that prevent certain groups of users from communicating with each other.

- **Audit log:** Teams activities such as creating or deleting a team, adding or removing a team member, and others can be traced in the audit log. This can be helpful for troubleshooting and for investigations.

- **Communication compliance:** This feature in Microsoft 365 allows organizations to monitor and control inappropriate behaviors in company communications across Teams and other Microsoft 365 services. It can help organizations enforce code of conduct policies and prevent harassment and other problematic behaviors.

Remember, while Teams includes many features to support compliance use cases, each organization is responsible for ensuring its usage of Teams complies with all relevant laws and regulations. It's also important to note that some Teams compliance features require specific Microsoft 365 or Office 365 licenses.

eDiscovery and Audit Logs

eDiscovery and audit logs are essential elements of the compliance and security features in Microsoft Teams. This section highlights some strategies for using them effectively.

eDiscovery

Before setting up eDiscovery in Teams, it's crucial to understand your organization's legal and regulatory requirements.

- **Use advanced eDiscovery features when necessary:** Microsoft 365's advanced eDiscovery solution provides additional capabilities such as near-duplicate detection, email threading, and machine learning-based predictive coding. These can be helpful for larger, more complex investigations.

- **Leverage legal hold:** When you anticipate litigation or an investigation, placing users or content on a legal hold ensures relevant data is preserved. This includes Teams chat and channel messages.

- **Conduct regular eDiscovery training:** Ensure the individuals responsible for conducting eDiscovery (often in your legal department) are trained in how to use the eDiscovery tools in Teams.

- **Regularly review and update your eDiscovery processes:** Laws and regulations change, and so might your organization's needs. Regularly reviewing and updating your eDiscovery processes can help ensure they continue to meet your needs.

Audit Logs

Ensure that Unified Audit Log (UAL) is enabled for your Microsoft 365 tenant. This is where Teams logs its audit events.

- **Understand what's logged:** Not all actions in Teams generate an audit event. Make sure you understand what's logged and what isn't.

- **Regularly review audit logs:** Regular review of your audit logs can help detect unusual or inappropriate activity and can provide useful data for troubleshooting.

- **Use audit log retention policies:** You can specify how long audit logs are retained to meet your organization's needs and compliance obligations.

- **Leverage automation:** Use automated tools, like the Microsoft 365 security and compliance center, to set up alerts for specific types of activities.

Remember, effective use of eDiscovery and audit logs in Teams requires a good understanding of your organization's legal and regulatory environment, as well as a strong collaboration between your IT, legal, and compliance teams. Some features of eDiscovery and audit logs require specific Microsoft 365 or Office 365 licenses.

Setup eDiscovery for Teams

Setting up eDiscovery in Microsoft Teams involves several steps and requires an appropriate Microsoft 365 or Office 365 E3 license at a minimum (some features require E5). Here's a general guide on how to set up eDiscovery for Teams:

1. **Access Compliance Center:** First, sign into the Microsoft 365 compliance center at `https://compliance.microsoft.com`. You'll need an account that has the necessary permissions to create and manage eDiscovery cases (like an eDiscovery Manager).

2. **Create a case:** In the left navigation pane, click eDiscovery ➤ Core eDiscovery. Click "+ Create a case." Give the case a name and description, then click Save. See Figure 5-33.

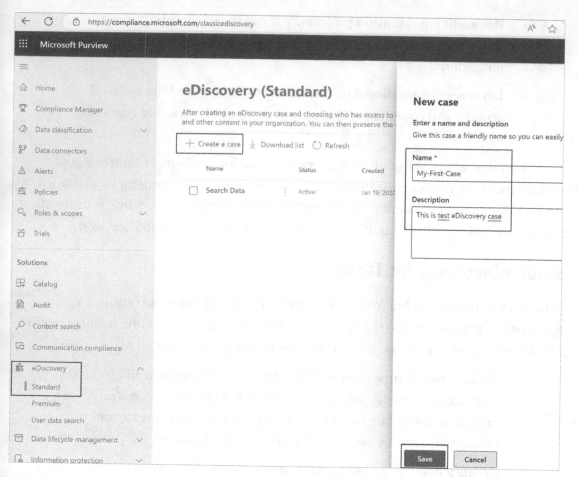

Figure 5-33. *eDiscovery case creation*

3. **Create a hold (optional):** If you want to preserve Teams data
   related to the case, you can create a hold. In the case page, click
   Holds ➤ + Create. Give the hold a name and description, and
   then click Next. In "Choose locations," select "Teams chats" and/
   or "Teams channel messages" as appropriate, and then specify the
   users or teams you want the hold to apply to. In "Hold settings,"
   specify whether to hold all data or only data meeting certain
   search criteria. Then click Finish.

4. **Create a Search:** To search for data relevant to the case, click
    Searches ➤ + New search. In "Choose locations," select "Teams
    chats" and/or "Teams channel messages" as appropriate, and
    then specify the users or teams you want to search. In "Enter
    keywords," specify the search criteria. Then click Search. After the
    search is complete, you can view and export the results.

Creating and Managing eDiscovery for Teams

From a manageability and content discovery perspective, Microsoft has provided
some tools that Teams admins can use to retrieve information such as who is creating
content, monitoring, or reporting. Using Teams, you can discover the content through
eDiscovery and put some users on a legal hold so that they cannot tamper with content
that was created in Teams. For example, if User A is under litigation and they shared the
information with an external user, then you as an admin have the workflow that will help
to export the content and hand it out.

Create eDiscovery Workflows for Teams

You can access eDiscovery through the Office 365 Security & Compliance Center.
The advanced eDiscovery workflow is available in Office 365, and Teams is one of the
primary applications that can be used. In eDiscovery, you can search content that was
created in Teams and content that was exchanged in conversation, including one-to-one
chat, group chat, and channel chat. All these contents are discoverable to you as a Teams
admin and security admin.

To use the eDiscovery search, first log in to `https://compliance.microsoft.com`
and then navigate to eDiscovery. Select "User data search," as shown in Figure 5-34. Click
"+ Create a case" to create a case for eDiscovery.

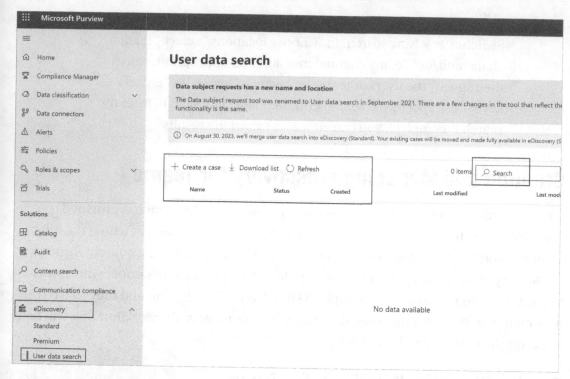

Figure 5-34. *eDiscovery search*

Microsoft has updated the eDiscovery search capability to show the threaded conversation view when a security admin searches in eDiscovery.

There is another feature, redaction, that Microsoft added in eDiscovery search, displayed in Figure 5-35. How does it work? Here is an example: You search some content that is required, and the requested content is one conversation. However, the search results show three threads of conversation. A security admin can activate redaction for the two conversation threads that are not required so that only the required details are shared. You can manage the existing search cases that you have previously created under eDiscovery.

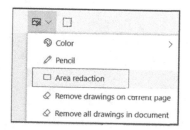

Figure 5-35. *Redaction feature*

Remember, eDiscovery in Teams should be performed in consultation with your legal and compliance teams. They can help ensure that the eDiscovery process aligns with your organization's legal and regulatory requirements. The specifics of setting up eDiscovery may vary depending on these requirements and your organization's internal policies.

Setting Up an Audit Log for Teams

Setting up audit logs for Microsoft Teams involves several steps. You need to ensure that you have the necessary permissions (you need to be a global admin or have relevant audit role assignments such as Compliance admin or Compliance data admin).

Here's how you can set up and use audit logs:

1. **Enable unified audit logging:** Audit logging might not be enabled by default in your Microsoft 365 organization. To enable it, you need to go to the Microsoft 365 compliance center (`https://compliance.microsoft.com/`) and navigate to Audit under Solutions. If it's not already enabled, there will be an option to turn it on. Figure 5-36 shows audit search option.

2. **Access audit logs:** After ensuring audit logs are enabled, you can access them in the Microsoft 365 compliance center. Go to Audit under Solutions, and then click Search in the Audit Log section.

   a. **Search the audit logs:** Here you can search for specific activities. You can set filters such as date range, users, activities (like Created team, Added member to team, etc. for Teams), or even specific file, folder, or site names.

   b. **Interpret audit log data:** The search results provide a wealth of information, including date and time of the event, user who performed the action, the action itself, and the target object. You can view details about an event by clicking a search result.

   c. **Export the search results:** If you need to further analyze the data or archive it, you can export the search results to a CSV file by selecting Export ➤ Download all results.

d. **Set up audit log alerts:** You can also set up alerts for certain activities. This can be done in the "Alert policies" section of the Microsoft 365 compliance center. Click "+New policy" and define the conditions that will trigger the alert.

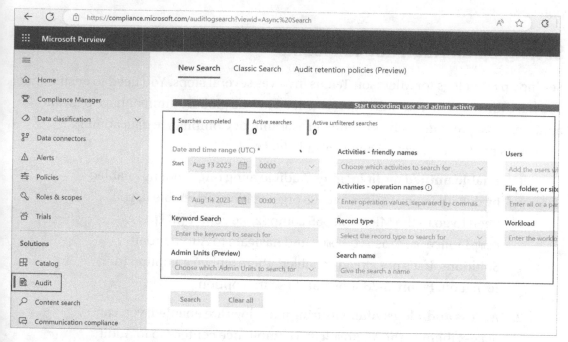

Figure 5-36. *Audit search*

Remember, accessing audit logs requires an appropriate Microsoft 365 or Office 365 license, and the retention period for audit logs is 90 days for most subscriptions (though longer retention periods may be available with certain subscriptions or add-ons). Regular review of your audit logs can help detect unusual or inappropriate activity, provide useful data for troubleshooting, and support compliance efforts.

Best Practices for Setting Up eDiscovery and Audit Logs in Teams

Setting up eDiscovery and audit logs in Microsoft Teams can significantly enhance your organization's security, compliance, and governance. Here are some best practices for implementing these features.

eDiscovery best practices:

- **Understand your requirements:** Before setting up eDiscovery in Teams, understand your organization's legal and regulatory requirements related to eDiscovery.

- **Hold regular training:** Conduct regular training for those responsible for eDiscovery (often your legal and compliance teams) to ensure they understand how to use the tools effectively.

- **Use legal hold:** In the event of anticipated litigation or investigation, use legal hold to preserve all relevant Teams data.

- **Hold regular reviews:** Regularly review and update your eDiscovery processes and procedures to ensure they continue to align with any changes in your business or regulatory environment.

- **Collaboration:** Maintain close collaboration between your IT, legal, and compliance teams to ensure effective and compliant use of eDiscovery tools.

Audit log best practices:

- **Enable unified audit logging:** Ensure that unified audit logging is enabled for your Microsoft 365 tenant.

- **Hold regular reviews:** Regularly review your audit logs to detect unusual or inappropriate activity and to provide useful data for troubleshooting.

- **Understand what's logged:** Not all actions in Teams generate an audit event. Make sure you understand what's logged and what isn't.

- **Set up audit log alerts:** Set up alerts for specific activities to stay informed of actions that are important or may pose a risk to your organization.

- **Use retention policies:** Implement retention policies for your audit logs that align with your organizational and regulatory requirements.

- **Use role-based access control (RBAC):** Ensure that only authorized individuals have access to audit logs to maintain security and compliance.

Remember, these are best practices and may need to be adjusted based on your specific organizational needs and compliance requirements. Always consult with your legal and compliance teams when setting up and managing these features.

Effective License Management

Managing licenses in Microsoft 365 requires an understanding of your organization's needs and the tools Microsoft provides for license management. Here's how to manage and assign licenses, including for Microsoft Teams, and reclaim unused licenses:

Managing and assigning licenses:

- **Access the Microsoft 365 admin center:** Sign into the Microsoft 365 admin center using your admin account.

- **Navigate to active users:** In the admin center, select Users ➤ Active users. Here, you can see a list of all active users in your organization and their license status.

- **Assign a license:** To assign a license to a user, select the user from the list. In the user pane, click Licenses and Apps. You will see a list of available licenses. Check the box for the license you want to assign (e.g., Microsoft 365 Business Basic, which includes Teams), and then click "Save changes."

Reclaiming unused licenses:

If you have licenses that are not currently in use, you can reclaim them to save costs and ensure effective license management.

- **Identify unused licenses:** In the Microsoft 365 admin center, go to Reports ➤ Usage. The usage reports can help you identify which users are not using their assigned licenses.

- **Unassign unused licenses:** To unassign a license from a user, go to Users ➤ Active users, select the user, then click Licenses and Apps. Uncheck the box for the license you want to unassign, and then click Save changes." The license can now be assigned to another user.

Effective License Management Tips:

- **Regular audits:** Regularly review your license usage to ensure all assigned licenses are being used effectively.

- **Automate license management:** Consider using automated tools or scripts to manage license assignments, especially in larger organizations.

- **Group-based licensing:** Use Azure Active Directory's group-based licensing for large-scale, automated license management. This allows you to assign licenses to groups, and any user added to the group will automatically receive the relevant license.

- **Plan for changes:** Be aware that license requirements may change as your organization grows or as Microsoft updates its offerings. Plan for these changes to avoid disruption.

- **License management tools:** Consider using third-party tools designed to streamline the process of managing Microsoft 365 licenses, if the built-in tools don't meet all your needs.

Remember, effective license management requires regular review and proactive management. Make sure to stay up-to-date with Microsoft's licensing changes and best practices.

User Provisioning for Microsoft Teams

Microsoft Teams user provisioning refers to the process of creating, managing, and maintaining user accounts, roles, and access rights in Microsoft Teams. Provisioning ensures that each user has the appropriate rights and permissions based on their role in the organization and includes the creation of Teams, channels, and settings for features like chat, calls, meetings, and live events.

Teams user provisioning typically includes the following processes:

- **Creating user accounts:** This involves setting up new users in the system with their necessary credentials.

- **Assigning roles:** Each user may have a different role with different permissions. Some users may be team owners, some may be team members, and others may have guest access.

- **Setting permissions:** Different users will have different levels of access based on their roles and the organization's needs. This could include things like the ability to create teams and channels or to access certain files.

- **Managing the user life cycle:** Provisioning also involves deactivating or deleting accounts when a user leaves the organization or when a temporary project is completed and the associated Teams and channels are no longer needed.

- **Creating and managing teams and channels:** Provisioning also involves creating and setting up teams and channels, including setting up the necessary permissions for each team or channel.

Yes, license assignment is a part of user provisioning. A Microsoft Teams license needs to be assigned to a user before they can use Teams. This license assignment provides the necessary rights for users to access the services included in the Microsoft 365 or Office 365 suite, such as Microsoft Teams, SharePoint, OneDrive, and more.

It is important to note that Teams user provisioning should be managed carefully to ensure compliance with security policies and regulations and to ensure the efficient use of resources. Organizations often use automated solutions or scripts to manage the provisioning process, especially in large enterprises with a significant number of users.

Before using Microsoft Teams and its features, each user must provision for Teams; without provisioning, users cannot avail themselves of Teams features. Teams user provisioning involves enabling Teams licenses as well as add-on licenses, including Phone System and Office 365 Audio Conferencing and granting the required policies.

Enabling a User Teams License

To enable a Teams license for a user, as well as add-on licenses, follow this procedure:

1. Log in to Office 365 admin center and navigate to Users. Select Active Users and find the user to whom you need to assign a license. You can then enable all necessary licenses. Figure 5-37 shows user Balu Ilag with all required licenses needed to use Teams as a unified communication and collaboration tool.

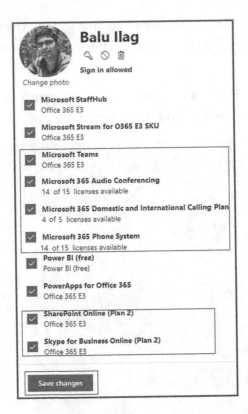

Figure 5-37. *Enabling licenses for a user*

As a Teams admin, you can manage user accounts in the Office 365 admin center for modifying users' display attributes and passwords (depending on the organization topology). You can use the Teams admin center to assign and manage any Teams-specific policies such as meeting policy, live event policy, Teams policy, and so on. You can refer to Chapter 1 for an overview of licensing.

Assigning a Meeting Policy to a User Account Using the Teams Admin Center

You can assign or remove any policy from a user account using the Teams admin center. This includes meeting policies, message policies, live event policies, emergency calling policies, and so on. Follow the steps to assign a Teams meeting policy. After you create a meeting policy, the next step is to assign the policy to a user. You can assign a meeting policy within the Teams admin center in both the Users and Meeting Policy sections. Follow this procedure to assign a meeting policy in the Users section.

1. Log in to the Teams admin center, and navigate to Users. Select the users to whom you want to apply the policy and then click Edit Settings.

2. In the Edit User Policies window, shown in Figure 5-38, select the required meeting policy, and then click Apply.

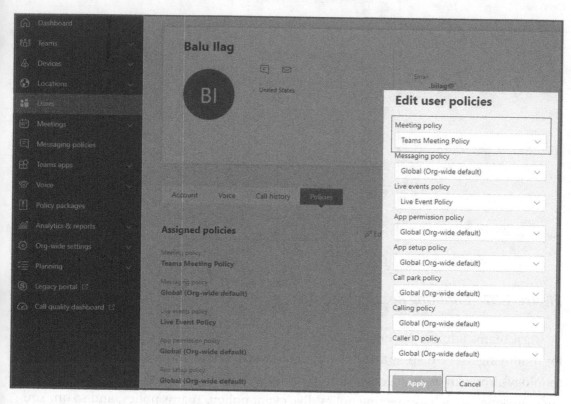

Figure 5-38. *Assigning a meeting policy*

You can also assign a meeting policy in the Meeting Policies section. To do so, log in to the Teams admin center and then navigate to Meetings. Select the required meeting policy and then click Manage Users. In the Manage Users windows, select the user to whom to assign the policy, as shown in Figure 5-39. Click Apply.

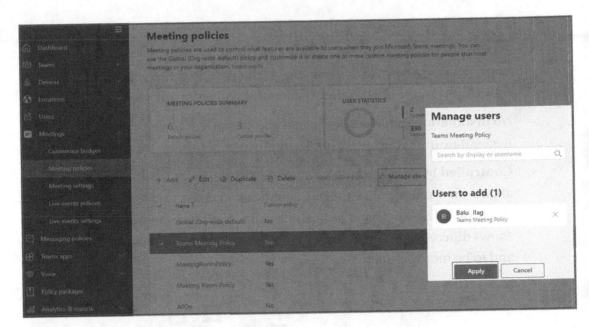

Figure 5-39. *Assigning a policy using the Meeting Policies section*

Apps Management in Microsoft Teams

Microsoft Teams is equipped with a broad range of apps that integrate seamlessly within the platform, providing various tools and services. These apps offer diverse functionalities to assist users in collaboration and task management. The following are some examples of how these apps are utilized:

- **Pinned calendar app:** Allows users to schedule, view, and manage events, making collaboration quick and efficient

- **Bots functionality app:** Provides automated updates or notifications about specific services, like monitoring the quality of a web service within a Teams channel

- **Task management app:** Enables users to share, assign, and track tasks within a channel, fostering team coordination

Here are some characteristics of Microsoft Teams apps:

- **Web-based and lightweight:** These apps resemble web-based SaaS apps, requiring no local deployment. They operate within specified scopes and access organizational data only with admin consent.

- **No installation required:** Adding an app to the Teams client doesn't necessitate installing binary files, simplifying the process for users.

- **Controlled by admins:** Admins can set governance processes that align with organizational policies, standards, and risk profiles, ensuring balance between user needs and compliance. Figure 5-40 shows different apps in Teams for communication, for collaboration, and to be more productive.

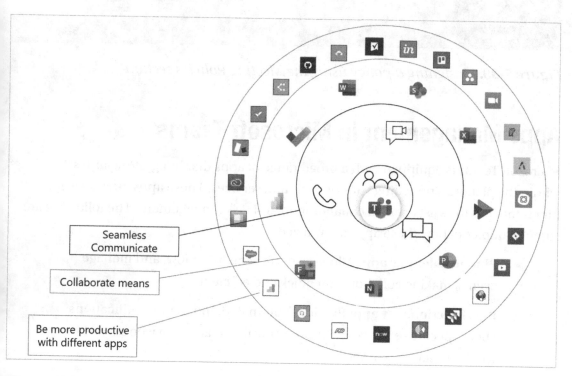

Figure 5-40. *Microsoft Teams Apps for communication and collaboration*

These are types of apps in Microsoft Teams:

- **Core apps:** These are integral to Teams and provide fundamental functionalities. For example, they include Calendar, Files, Activities, and more.

- **Microsoft-created apps:** Developed by Microsoft, these apps extend Teams' capabilities and offer specialized functions. For example, these include Planner, Power BI, SharePoint, and more.

- **Third-party apps (validated by Microsoft):** Created by external partners, these apps undergo validation by Microsoft to ensure quality and security. For example, these include Trello, Adobe Creative Cloud, GitHub, and more.

- **Custom apps created by your organization:** These are tailor-made apps designed to meet specific organizational needs. For example, these include internal tools for HR management, custom workflow automation, etc.

Here are some access and governance apps:

- **Access:** Users can access these apps across various contexts, including meetings, chats, and channels.

- **Admin control:** Through the Teams admin center, administrators can implement enterprise-grade controls and configurations to govern app availability, alignment with organizational requirements, and security.

Microsoft Teams apps offer a rich and dynamic environment for collaboration and productivity. By blending core functionalities, Microsoft-created tools, validated third-party solutions, and custom organization-specific apps, Teams provides a flexible, secure, and robust platform that meets the daily needs of diverse organizations.

Microsoft Teams Apps Life Cycle

Microsoft Teams enriches collaboration and communication through an extensive app catalog. This offers the ability to incorporate various third-party and Microsoft apps, ensuring a more integrated and productive experience within the Teams platform. The life cycle of these apps is streamlined through a structured process to provide better control and efficiency. Figure 5-41 shows Teams apps management life-cycle phases. Here's a breakdown of the phases involved in the life cycle:

1. **Start with the user needing an app:**

   - **Understanding the need:** The life cycle begins by identifying the users' requirements. A particular need might prompt the exploration of a new app, whether it's a productivity tool, a communication enhancement, or a specialized function relevant to specific tasks.

2. **An app is requested:**

   - **Formal request process:** Users or teams may request an app through a designated process, providing details about why the app is required, its intended use, and the expected benefits.

3. **App evaluation:**

   - **Assessment and compatibility check:** Before deployment, the requested app is evaluated to ensure it meets the organizational standards, security requirements, and compatibility with existing systems.

   - **Approval or rejection:** Based on the evaluation, the app may be approved for deployment or rejected if it doesn't align with the organization's policies or needs.

4. **App deployment:**

   - **Configuration and integration:** Once approved, the app is configured, customized if necessary, and integrated within the Teams environment.

   - **User training and support:** Education and support may be provided to users to ensure they can utilize the app effectively.

5. **Managing and monitoring:**

   - **Ongoing oversight:** Continuous monitoring and management of the app ensure that it performs optimally and adheres to compliance standards.

   - **Updates and maintenance:** Regular updates, patches, and maintenance keep the app up-to-date and secure.

6. **End of life : removing access to an app:**

   - **Retirement or replacement:** When an app reaches the end of its life cycle, perhaps due to obsolescence or the availability of a better solution, access to the app is removed.

   - **Data preservation and transition:** Steps may be taken to preserve essential data and transition to a new app if necessary.

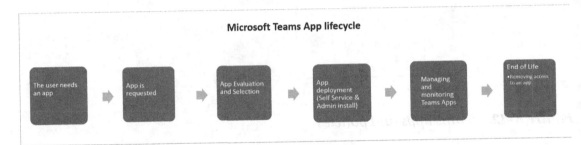

Figure 5-41. *Microsoft Teams app life-cycle phases*

The defined life cycle ensures a methodical approach to the deployment and management of applications within Microsoft Teams, aligning with organizational goals, security protocols, and user needs. It also helps in making informed decisions at each stage, from initial request to eventual retirement, thus promoting an effective and efficient app management system within Microsoft Teams.

Teams Apps and Policy Management

As a Teams admin, you must be aware of the apps that Teams has. Microsoft Teams apps offer multiple features that allow your organization to maximize its Teams experience. These apps include the functionality of tabs, messaging extensions, connectors, and bots provided by Microsoft, built by a third party, or created by developers in your organization. You can manage the apps using the Teams apps section in the Teams admin center, where you can set policies to manage apps for your organization. For example, you can set policies to control what apps are available to Teams users, and you can customize Teams by including the apps that are most important for your users. Figure 5-42 shows the available options to manage apps, manage permission policies, and set up new custom policies.

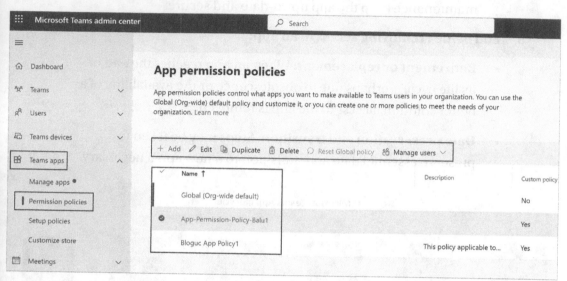

Figure 5-42. *Teams apps and policies*

Teams Apps Permission Policies

Using app permission policies, you can block or allow apps either organization-wide or for specific users. When you block an app, all collaborations with that app are disabled, and the app will no longer appear in Teams. For example, you can use app permission policies to disable an app that creates a permission or data loss risk to your organization.

Managing the Custom App Setup Policies

Admins can use the Teams admin center to manage or edit a policy, including the Global (Org-wide default) policy and custom policies that admins have created. Follow this procedure to manage policies:

1. Log in to the Teams admin center, and navigate to Teams Apps. Select Setup Policies and then select the policy you want to work with. Click Edit to manage the policy settings.

2. On the edit page, make the changes that you want. You can add, remove, and change the order of apps and then click Save.

Assigning a Custom App Setup Policy to Users

You can use the Teams admin center to assign a custom app setup policy to individual users, or you can use the Skype for Business Online PowerShell module to assign a custom policy to groups of users, such as a distribution group or security group. There are multiple ways to assign an app setup policy to your users in the Teams admin center. You can assign users either in Setup Policies or in Users in the Teams admin center.

To assign policies to users using the Teams admin center, follow these steps:

1. Log in to Teams admin center and navigate to Teams apps. Select Setup Policies.

2. Select the custom policy and then click Manage Users.

3. On the Manage Users page, search for the user by display name or by username, select the name, and then click Add. Repeat this step for each user who you want to add.

4. Once you are finished adding users, click Apply.

Creation and management of custom policies for apps was covered in Chapter 2.

Integration with Other Services

Microsoft Teams integrates with many other applications, both within the Microsoft 365 suite and in external applications. In this section, we'll discuss how to manage Teams' interactions with other Microsoft 365 or Office 365 services, like SharePoint,

OneDrive, and Exchange, and how governance and life-cycle policies for these services interact with Teams. How governance and life-cycle policies for these services interact with Teams can be complex and depends on the specifics of the integrated application. However, here are some general points to consider:

- **SharePoint:** Every team in Teams is connected to a SharePoint site. Files shared in Teams are stored in SharePoint, so SharePoint governance and life-cycle policies can impact Teams. For example, SharePoint retention policies will affect files shared in Teams.

- **OneNote:** Teams can integrate with OneNote for shared note-taking. Like SharePoint, OneNote content is subject to retention policies, so if you delete a team in Teams, any associated OneNote content will be handled according to the retention policy.

- **Office 365 Groups:** Every team in Teams is built on an Office 365 group. The life cycle of the team is tied to the life cycle of the group. Deleting the group will delete the team, and group expiration policies can be used to manage inactive teams.

- **External apps:** Teams can integrate with a wide range of external apps. Governance and life-cycle policies for these apps may not be directly linked to Teams. For example, if a team in Teams is deleted, data in an external app that was linked to the team may not be deleted. The specifics depend on the external app and how it integrates with Teams.

Here are some best practices for managing Teams integrations:

- **Understand the integration:** Before integrating an app with Teams, understand how the app works, how it integrates with Teams, and how governance and life-cycle policies for the app interact with Teams.

- **Review and update policies:** Review your governance and life-cycle policies regularly, and update them as needed to account for new integrations.

- **Train users:** Make sure users understand how to use integrated apps in Teams and any governance or life-cycle considerations.

- **Monitor and audit usage:** Use auditing and monitoring tools to track how integrated apps are being used in Teams, and to identify any potential issues or risks.

- **Plan for deprovisioning:** When a team is disbanded or a user leaves the organization, have a plan for how to handle their data in integrated apps.

Remember, managing integrations effectively requires a good understanding of both Teams and the apps you're integrating. Collaboration between your Teams admin, other IT staff, and compliance personnel can be crucial.

Monitoring and Reporting

Monitoring and reporting in the context of Teams life-cycle management refers to the continual tracking, analyzing, and reporting of Teams usage, performance, and compliance within your organization. It plays a vital role in understanding the effectiveness of Microsoft Teams and helps in making data-driven decisions about its management.

Here's a closer look at what these activities might involve.

Monitoring

Monitoring in Teams is about constantly observing and checking the Teams environment over a period for any significant events or changes. It includes the following:

- **Activity monitoring:** This involves tracking activities like team creation, membership changes, channel activities, guest activities, etc.

- **Performance monitoring:** This includes monitoring call and meeting quality, network performance, system uptime, etc. Microsoft provides a Call Quality Dashboard for these purposes.

- **Security monitoring:** This involves monitoring for any security threats or violations, like suspicious login attempts or potential data breaches.

Reporting

Reporting in Teams is about generating structured updates or results derived from the gathered data. It includes the following:

- **Usage reports:** These provide insights into how people in your organization are using Teams, such as how many people are actively using Teams, which features they use, how often they use Teams, etc.

- **Audit reports:** These track detailed activity in your Teams environment and help you understand what changes were made, who made them, and when they were made.

- **Compliance reports:** These reports help to ensure your Teams environment adheres to your internal policies and external regulations.

- **Performance reports:** These include statistics like call and meeting quality, network performance metrics, etc.

All these monitoring and reporting activities help to manage the life cycle of Teams more effectively. For example, they can help you identify teams that are inactive and can be archived or deleted, spot patterns of usage that might require changes in training or policies, and ensure security and compliance. They also assist in forecasting growth and identifying potential issues before they become problems.

Tools Available for Teams Usage and Performance

Microsoft provides several tools for tracking the usage and performance of Microsoft Teams. These can be very helpful for administrators to manage and improve their Teams deployment:

- **Microsoft 365 admin center reports:** The Microsoft 365 admin center provides usage reports that give you insights into how your organization is using Microsoft 365 services, including Teams. You can view data such as the number of active users, the number of meetings held, the number of calls made, and more.

- **Teams admin center:** The Teams admin center provides a wealth of information about Teams usage in your organization. For example, you can see which teams are most active, which channels are being used the most, and more.

- **Call analytics:** Call analytics in the Teams admin center provide detailed information about call and meeting quality. You can see information about individual calls and meetings, including detailed statistics about network quality.

- **Call Quality Dashboard (CQD):** The CQD provides more detailed, aggregate information about call and meeting quality in your organization. You can use it to identify trends, troubleshoot problems, and monitor the impact of changes to your network.

- **Power BI Teams usage report:** The Teams usage analytics, available as part of the Power BI pack, allows you to drill down into Teams usage data and generate customized reports.

- **Security & Compliance Center:** The Security & Compliance Center includes audit logs that can help you track activities in Teams for security and compliance purposes.

- **Microsoft 365 Compliance Center:** This center provides tools for data investigations, content searches, and more. It is particularly useful for eDiscovery, DLP, retention, and compliance purposes.

- **Azure AD reports:** Azure AD provides sign-in and audit logs that can be used to track Teams usage, including sign-in activities and changes in user roles or privileges.

These tools can help you gain a deep understanding of how Teams is being used in your organization, help you manage Teams more effectively, and help ensure a high-quality Teams experience for your users.

Compliance and Governance Policies for Teams Monitoring and Reporting Policies

Microsoft's monitoring and reporting tools are a fundamental part of enforcing and checking compliance with governance policies in Microsoft Teams. They provide the visibility needed to understand how your organization is using Teams and whether usage aligns with your policies.

Here's how you can use these tools to ensure compliance:

- **Microsoft 365 admin center reports:** Use these reports to monitor overall usage of Teams and ensure it aligns with your policies. For example, if you have a policy that certain teams should be active daily, you can use the activity reports to check this.

- **Teams admin center:** This can be used to ensure compliance with policies on team creation and naming. For example, you can view all teams and check that their names follow your naming conventions.

- **Call analytics and Call Quality Dashboard:** These tools can be used to ensure compliance with quality of service policies. If you have a policy requiring a certain level of call quality, you can use these tools to verify that quality levels are being met.

- **Power BI Teams usage report:** The customizable reports can help monitor compliance with a wide range of policies. For example, you could create a report to check compliance with a policy requiring regular usage of Teams for collaboration.

- **Security & Compliance Center:** This is key for enforcing security and data protection policies. You can use the audit log to monitor for actions that violate your policies, like sharing sensitive data outside the organization.

- **Microsoft 365 Compliance Center:** You can use this to enforce retention policies, manage data loss prevention (DLP) policies, and conduct eDiscovery activities. These features can help ensure your Teams data complies with data protection and legal requirements.

- **Azure AD reports:** Sign-in reports and audit logs can be used to enforce policies related to access and identity management.

These tools, combined with clear governance policies and regular reviews, can help ensure that your Teams deployment remains compliant with your organization's governance requirements. Keep in mind that the enforcement of policies also requires action based on the insights gathered from these tools, such as user education, remediation activities, or potential policy updates.

Managing Internal Risk Through Information Barrier in Teams

Microsoft Teams, as part of Microsoft 365, empowers organizations to foster communication and collaboration across various groups and domains. However, there may be scenarios requiring the restriction of communication and collaboration between certain groups to prevent conflicts of interest or safeguard sensitive internal information. Information barriers (IBs) come into play in such scenarios, providing a structured way to manage these restrictions.

IBs are policies enforced within Microsoft Teams, SharePoint Online, and OneDrive for Business to control communication between specified groups of users. They can be set up by a compliance administrator or an IB administrator.

Here are some scenarios for using IB policies:

- **Preventing conflicts of interest:** They can ensure that day traders do not communicate or share files with the marketing team.

- **Maintaining educational integrity:** Instructors in one school cannot communicate or share files with students in another school within the same district.

- **Protecting confidential information:** Finance personnel handling confidential data must not communicate or share files with particular groups.

- **Safeguarding trade secrets:** Internal teams with sensitive materials should not call or chat with certain groups within the organization.

- **Restricting specific collaborations:** A research team can only call or chat with a product development team.

The configuration of IB involves several key steps:

1. **Learn about information barriers:** Understand what IB is and how it aligns with organizational needs.

2. **Configure prerequisites and permissions:** Set the necessary permissions and ensure that all prerequisites are met.

3. **Segment users in your organization:** Identify and segment users into specific groups based on criteria such as roles, departments, or any other relevant classification.

575

4. **Create and configure IB policies:** Define policies that outline the allowed or restricted communication and collaboration between the segmented groups.

5. **Apply IB policies:** Implement the policies within Microsoft Teams, SharePoint Online, or OneDrive for Business to ensure compliance.

Note For those without an E5 subscription, a 90-day Microsoft Purview solutions trial is available to explore additional capabilities related to data security and compliance.

Microsoft's IBs provide a robust and flexible framework for managing communication and collaboration restrictions within an organization. Whether it's avoiding conflicts of interest, protecting sensitive information, or adhering to regulatory requirements, IBs enable organizations to define and enforce precise controls over interactions between different user groups. This ensures integrity, confidentiality, and compliance with organizational policies and legal obligations.

Managing Internal Risk Through Information Barriers in Teams

Managing internal risk is another important consideration. DLP prevents the compromise of sensitive information, but organizations are subject to different kinds of risk, such as IP theft, or content leaks, insider trading, and conflicts of interest. Figure 5-43 shows several types of risk that organizations are subject to.

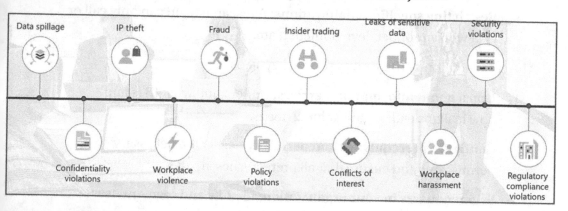

Figure 5-43. *Risks that organizations face*

One of the major tools that Teams uses to mitigate risk is the IB. An IB is often called an *ethical wall*, a barrier in your organization created between different departments or internal units. For example, if you have groups of users that are not supposed to interact with other groups of users, you as a Teams or security admin can create segments and prevent these segments from talking to each other.

This setup is typically used in regulated industry, education, and financial sectors. Basically, IBs build logical boundaries to prevent communication between Group A and Group B. For example, investment bankers cannot find or communicate with financial advisors, but both groups can communicate with human resources (HR). The investment bankers cannot communicate with financial advisors because of potential influence issues. The Microsoft Teams solution is the creation of IB segments, which ensure that you as an admin can put investment bankers in one segment and financial advisors in another segment. IB policies will prevent communication between the segments. Both segments, however, can communicate with the HR team without any barriers. This process is illustrated in Figure 5-44.

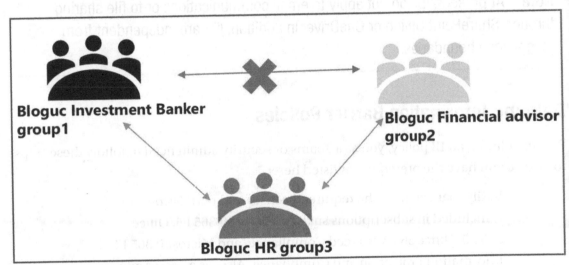

Figure 5-44. *Information barriers between groups*

Information Barrier Policies

IB policies allow you to control communication and collaboration in Microsoft 365 workloads between two groups of people. You can set IB policies to prevent a day trader from calling someone on the marketing team or to keep finance personnel working on confidential company information from receiving calls from certain groups within the organization. Perhaps the organization wants to allow a research team to call or chat online only with the product development team.

Who Can Set Up Information Barriers Policies?

The tenant admins, compliance administrator, or IB administrator can define policies to allow or prevent communications between groups of users in Microsoft Teams. IB policies can be defined to prevent or allow communications in Microsoft Teams. Such policies can prevent people from calling or chatting with those they shouldn't or enable people to communicate only with specific groups in Microsoft Teams. With IB policies in effect, whenever users who are covered by those policies attempt to communicate with others in Microsoft Teams, checks are performed to prevent (or allow) communication, as defined by IB policies.

Note   At present, IBs do not apply to email communications or to file sharing through SharePoint Online or OneDrive. In addition, IBs are independent from compliance boundaries.

Defining Information Barrier Policies

Before defining an IB policy, you as a Teams or security admin need to follow these steps to ensure you have the prerequisites listed here:

1. Verify that you have the required licenses and permissions. IB is included in subscriptions such as Microsoft 365 E5, Office 365 E5, Office 365 Advanced Compliance, and Microsoft 365 E5 Information Protection and Compliance. Also, as a Teams admin you must have one of the following role permissions to define or edit IB policies:

   - Microsoft 365 global administrator

   - Office 365 global administrator

- Compliance administrator

- IB Compliance Management (this is a new role)

2. Validate that the directory includes data for the segmenting users. Make sure that your organization's structure is reflected in directory data. To do this, make sure that user account attributes, such as group membership, department name, and so on, are populated correctly in Azure AD (or Exchange Online).

3. Before you define your organization's first IB policy, you must enable scoped directory search in Microsoft Teams. Wait at least 24 hours after enabling scoped directory search before you set up or define IB policies.

4. To look up the status of a policy application, audit logging must be turned on. We recommend doing this before you begin to define segments or policies.

5. Before you define and apply IB policies, make sure no Exchange address book policies are in place. (IBs are based on address book policies, but the two kinds of policies are not interchangeable.)

6. As of this writing, IB policies are defined and managed in the Office 365 Security & Compliance Center using PowerShell commands. No GUI is available.

7. When your policies are in place, IBs can remove people from chat sessions they are not supposed to be in. This helps ensure your organization remains compliant with policies and regulations. Use the following procedure to enable IB policies to work as expected in Microsoft Teams.

Defining an IB policy is a three-part process.

1. Segment the users in your organization by determining what policies are needed, and then make a list of segments. Identify which attributes to use and then define segments in terms of policy filters.

2. Define the IB policies, but do not apply them yet. Select from two kinds: block or allow.

3. Apply the IB policies involving tasks such as setting policies
    to active status, running the policy application, and viewing
    policy status.

There are many steps involved in defining IB policies, and they change frequently.
Refer to the Microsoft official documentation at `https://docs.microsoft.com/en-`
`us/microsoft-365/compliance/information-barriers-policies?` for up-to-date
information.

Creating and Managing Office 365 Group Classification

Microsoft Teams is built on Office 365 Groups. Office 365 Groups has multiple
capabilities, and one of them is classification, which is often used in organizations
to classify content. As an admin, you can determine and add information about the
group purpose. For example, your organization decides to inform users what type of
documents are stored within the Office 365 Group. This type of group functionality is
called *group classification*. You as an admin can configure group classification so that
when users in your organization create a group, they can choose a classification such as
Standard, Internal, or Confidential.

Note   Office 365 Groups classifications do not exist by default. Admins will need
to create the group classifications so that users can apply them when they create
a group.

Enabling and Configuring Office 365 Groups Classifications

Remember, group classification is not enabled by default. Before users can apply
classifications to Office 365 Groups, you as an admin need to configure the
classifications using Azure AD Windows PowerShell commands. First, install the latest
AzureADPreview module using the following PowerShell commands:

- Remove any earlier version of AzureADPreview using this command:

  ```
  Uninstall-Module AzureADPreview
  ```

  ```
  Uninstall-Module azuread
  ```

- Install the latest version of AzureADPreview using this command:

  ```
  Install-Module AzureADPreview
  ```

To configure the classifications Standard, Internal, and Confidential, use the following command:

```
$Template = Get-AzureADDirectorySettingTemplate | Where {$_.DisplayName -eq
"Group.Unified"}
if (!($Setting=Get-AzureADDirectorySetting|Where {$_.TemplateId -eq
$Template.
Id})) {$Setting = $Template.CreateDirectorySetting}
$setting["ClassificationList"] = "Standard, Internal, Confidential"
```

As the next step, you must associate a description with each classification using the settings attribute ClassificationDescriptions, where the classification should match the strings in the ClassificationList. For example, to add a description to the classifications Standard, Internal, and Confidential, run the following command:

```
$setting["ClassificationDescriptions"] = "Standard: General communication,
Internal: Company internal data, Confidential: Data that has regulatory
requirements"
```

To validate that the classification configuration is added correctly to the group, you need to run the $Setting. Values command.

To commit the setting to Azure AD and make sure the classifications can be applied by your users, you need to run this command:

```
Set-AzureADDirectorySetting -Id $Setting.Id -DirectorySetting $Setting
```

Note   The classification settings update could take an hour before they are available for all users, so be patient after configuring the classification.

Configuring Classifications from Outlook and the Teams Client

After enabling Office 365 Groups classifications, you as an admin can assign the classification to a group from Outlook or the Teams client. To do so, log in to Microsoft Teams client and select Teams. Select Join Or Create and then select the appropriate classification, as shown in Figure 5-45.

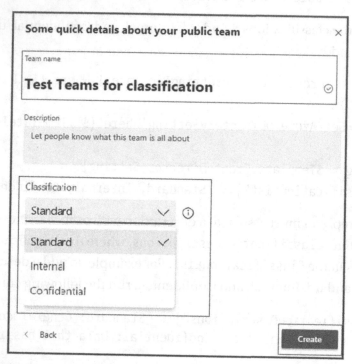

Figure 5-45. *Classification options*

You can also configure classifications on Office 365 Groups using Windows PowerShell. To set a classification to an Office 365 group, you use the Set-UnifiedGroup command with the -Classification parameter. For example, to set a Confidential classification on the group SecretData@bloguc.com, run this command in Exchange Online PowerShell:

```
Set-UnifiedGroup "SecretData@bloguc.com" -Classification "Confidential"
```

You can also create a group and assign a classification during the group creation process. For example, to create a new private group named HRDepartment@bloguc.com with a classification of Internal, run the following cmdlet:

```
New-UnifiedGroup "HRDepartment@bloguc.com" -Classification
"Internal" -AccessType "Private"
```

Third-Party Tools for Microsoft Teams Governance and Life-Cycle Management

Microsoft 365 has quickly become a go-to platform for businesses seeking to streamline communication and collaboration. However, from an IT admin's perspective, managing Microsoft Teams, SharePoint Online, and Viva Engage Communities can pose several challenges. First, understand the Microsoft Teams management and governance challenges from the information technology (IT) and security admin perspective. Here are some of the key challenges they often face:

The Complexity of Managing Large-Scale Deployments

Microsoft 365 is designed to be a highly collaborative and multi-functional platform. This can create complexity when deploying at scale, especially for large organizations with multiple sites, teams, and numerous channels.

- **Governance:** Establishing and enforcing governance policies can be a challenge. This includes managing who can create new sites/teams or channels, maintaining naming conventions, and ensuring appropriate access levels to prevent unauthorized access to sensitive data.

- **Life-cycle management:** Managing the life cycle of Teams, sites, and communities, from creation to archiving or deletion, is a task that requires attention. It can be challenging to keep track of inactive teams or channels and decide when they should be archived or deleted to maintain a clean and efficient Microsoft 365 environment.

- **Security and compliance:** Protecting sensitive data and ensuring compliance with various regulations is a significant challenge. This includes managing guest access, external file sharing, and ensuring that data handling practices align with GDPR, HIPAA, and other relevant regulations.

- **User training and adoption:** Ensuring that all users understand how to use Teams or SharePoint effectively can be time-consuming. This includes training on best practices for collaboration and how to use various features and ensuring that users understand governance policies and security protocols.

- **Monitoring and reporting:** Keeping track of Microsoft 365 usage, user activities, and overall performance can be challenging but is crucial for ongoing management and optimization. IT admins need to monitor user activity, manage system performance, and generate reports to understand how Teams and sites are being used within the organization.

- **Provisioning and deprovisioning:** Quickly setting up new users and removing access for departing employees is another common challenge. This includes assigning licenses, setting up appropriate access levels, and ensuring that departing employees no longer have access to sensitive information.

Third-Party Tools to Solve the Challenges

The utilization of third-party tools like TeamsHUB, Sharegate, and Syskit Point adds a layer of automation, control, and efficiency in managing Microsoft Teams. They fill the gaps in native functionalities, thus helping in achieving robust governance and life-cycle management.

TeamsHUB:

- **What it does:** TeamsHUB automates various aspects of Teams life-cycle management, such as creating, archiving, deleting teams, and doing backup and monitoring activities.

- **Key features:** It can automate team creation with approval workflows, management of members, channels, and settings, comprehensive reporting, archiving, backup and restoration, and deletion of inactive teams.

- **Why it's important:** TeamsHUB streamlines the entire life cycle of a team, reducing administrative burden, ensuring compliance, and improving overall efficiency.

Sharegate

- **What it does:** Sharegate helps in managing and securing Teams deployment. It simplifies the process of migration, security, and compliance.

- **Key features:** It can migrate between SharePoint versions, cloud management, permissions management, reporting, and monitoring.

- **Why it's important:** Sharegate provides a unified platform for control and visibility over Teams, SharePoint, and OneDrive, making it easier for admins to maintain governance policies.

Syskit Point

- **What it does:** Syskit Point offers control and insights into Microsoft 365 environments, assisting in governance, security, and user adoption.

- **Key features:** it offers user activity monitoring, permissions management, external sharing insights, audit log, compliance reporting, and more.

- **Why it's important:** Syskit Point provides a centralized view of all activities, ensuring that admins have the necessary insights to implement governance policies effectively.

Case Study: Bloguc Organization

Let's understand the importance of Third-Party Tools through a case study.

Background

The Bloguc organization, a thriving tech company, is faced with challenges in managing the burgeoning number of teams within Microsoft Teams. The complexities of creating, monitoring, archiving, and deleting teams, along with ensuring compliance and proper access control, are taxing their administrative resources. The manual handling of these tasks leads to delays and the possibility of errors, which can impact security and efficiency.

Challenges Faced by the Bloguc Organization

These are the challenges:

- **Complex team life-cycle management:** Constant creation and archiving of project-based teams lead to clutter and inefficiency.

- **Compliance issues:** Ensuring that all teams adhere to corporate policies and legal regulations was becoming strenuous.

- **Lack of automation:** Manual processes were slow and prone to human error.

- **Visibility and control:** There was difficulty in gaining insight into user activities and permissions across all teams.

How TeamsHUB by Cyclotron Solved the Problems

TeamsHUB by Cyclotron is designed to automate and streamline Microsoft Teams governance and life-cycle management. It's tailored to help organizations like the Bloguc organization by providing centralized control, automation, compliance management, and insightful reporting.

It offers automated team creation and management.

- **Situation:** The Bloguc organization needed to create multiple teams for various projects.

- **Solution:** TeamsHUB allowed the organization to automate the creation of teams with specific templates, ensuring consistency. Approvals were built into the workflow, maintaining control.

- **Example:** A new project team required the creation of a specific channel, adding members with specific roles, and setting particular permissions. TeamsHUB automated this process, reducing the setup time from hours to minutes.

It offers comprehensive reporting and monitoring.

- **Situation:** Visibility into team activities, permissions, and compliance was a challenge.

- **Solution:** TeamsHUB provided detailed reporting and real-time monitoring of all activities within Teams.

- **Example:** Bloguc could now track inactive teams, review user activities, and audit permissions, ensuring that only authorized personnel had access to sensitive information.

It offers archiving and deletion of inactive teams:

- **Situation:** Inactive teams were cluttering the environment, leading to confusion and potential security risks.

- **Solution:** TeamsHUB's archiving and deletion feature allowed Bloguc to automatically archive or delete teams based on specific criteria.

- **Example:** Teams that were inactive for 60 days were automatically archived, keeping the environment clean and secure.

It offers compliance management:

- **Situation:** Ensuring that all teams followed legal and organizational policies was essential for Bloguc.

- **Solution:** TeamsHUB's compliance features enabled Bloguc to implement and enforce specific policies across all teams.

- **Example:** Customizable templates ensured that every team created met the regulatory requirements specific to Bloguc's industry.

TeamsHUB by Cyclotron became an indispensable tool for the Bloguc organization, transforming their Microsoft Teams governance and life-cycle management processes. It automated routine tasks, ensured compliance, provided essential visibility, and empowered Bloguc to manage their growing Teams environment efficiently. By aligning with Bloguc's specific needs, TeamsHUB helped them to focus on their core business without worrying about administrative overhead, all while maintaining a secure and well-governed collaboration environment. Third-party tools like TeamsHUB, Sharegate, and Syskit Point play a pivotal role in enhancing the governance and life-cycle management of Microsoft Teams. They bring automation, control, transparency, and efficiency, allowing organizations to align their Teams environment with their specific policies and needs. By leveraging these tools, organizations can create a well-governed, secure, and compliant collaboration environment that is agile and responsive to their evolving business requirements.

Summary

This chapter provided an in-depth exploration of governance practices for Microsoft Teams, which is built upon Office 365 Groups and offers a variety of governance features. The chapter outlined the critical aspects of Teams governance, including the management of user provisioning, conditional access policy, information protection using data loss prevention, eDiscovery, data governance, and internal risk through information barriers. The chapter also covered essential considerations that administrators must evaluate, such as who can create Teams, how to manage unused Teams, the implementation of naming conventions, sensitivity labels, and expiration policies. Furthermore, the chapter introduced third-party tools designed to automate governance and life-cycle management, exemplified by a detailed case study on the Bloguc organization. These insights equip Teams admins with the tools and knowledge to establish and maintain a well-governed Teams environment, ensuring consistent and coordinated interactions and fostering confident collaboration.

This chapter was a comprehensive overview of the topic and should provide you with the necessary knowledge and skills to effectively manage Microsoft Teams in an enterprise environment.

References

1. Security in Teams: https://learn.microsoft.com/en-us/microsoftteams/security-compliance-overview

2. Microsoft Insider risk solution: https://learn.microsoft.com/en-us/purview/insider-risk-solution-overview

3. Microsoft eDiscovery Solution: https://learn.microsoft.com/en-us/purview/ediscovery

4. Auditing solution: https://learn.microsoft.com/en-us/purview/audit-solutions-overview 3

CHAPTER 6

Migrating Skype for Business On-Premises to Microsoft Teams Online

Balu N Ilaga* Vijay Kumar Ireddy

In this comprehensive chapter, we explore the crucial process of migrating from Skype for Business or Lync On-Premises to Microsoft Teams, particularly focusing on the Phone System, otherwise known as Enterprise Voice. The process of transitioning your organization's communication system can seem daunting, but with careful planning and strategic execution, it can be accomplished smoothly and efficiently.

We dive into the key aspects of the migration process, beginning with a deep understanding of your current setup and the requirements for the new system. We then introduce different migration approaches that you can select based on your organizational needs and goals. These range from running Skype for Business and Teams simultaneously, gradually shifting specific workloads from Skype to Teams, and finally introducing Teams as a collaboration and meetings tool while retaining Skype for Business for chats and calls.

Through real-world examples and clear, step-by-step guidance, this chapter demystifies the migration process, ensuring you can leverage Microsoft Teams to its full potential while minimizing disruption to your users. By the end, you will possess the knowledge to determine the most suitable migration path, manage the transition, and utilize Teams as a robust tool for collaboration and communication within your organization.

Migrating from Skype for Business (Lync) On-Premises environment to Microsoft Teams involves a well-thought-out process that requires detailed planning and efficient execution. With Microsoft Teams bringing unprecedented collaboration and communication capabilities, it is natural for organizations to want to move their existing on-premises setup to the cloud-based Microsoft Teams environment. This chapter aims to provide insights into various migration approaches, the workflow involved, and the tasks that you need to undertake for a smooth transition.

We'll cover the following migration approaches:

- **Side-by-side with Notify:** Also known as the Island mode, this approach is all about running both Skype for Business and Teams simultaneously. Users are notified about Teams and can use both platforms until the organization is ready for a complete transition.

- **Side-by-side with Notify and Shift:** In this model, Teams is introduced alongside Skype for Business. After initial familiarization, specific workloads are gradually shifted from Skype to Teams.

- **Skype for Business with Teams collaboration:** This approach is about introducing Teams as a collaboration tool (for channels, applications, and files), while Skype for Business remains the primary tool for communication (chats, meetings, and calls).

- **Skype for Business with Teams collaboration and meetings:** Teams and Skype for Business are used together, with Teams serving as the primary tool for collaboration and meetings and Skype for Business for chats and calls.

The following is the migration workflow:

1. **Environment assessment:** The first step in migration is understanding the size and scope of your current Skype for Business environment. Assess the features, integrations, and customizations in use.

2. **Planning and preparations:** Design a migration strategy that suits your organization's needs such as identifying the key stakeholders and forming a migration team, developing a migration plan with clear milestones and timelines, and deciding on the migration approach (e.g., phased migration, hybrid deployment, or cutover migration). Also, consider factors such as user training, communication plans, and setting realistic

timelines. Don't forget to prepare a rollback plan in case things go wrong. Finally, ensure that your current infrastructure meets the requirements for Teams. This includes network, bandwidth, and hardware requirements.

3. **Environment configuration:** Set up your Microsoft Teams environment correctly. This includes configuring network settings, security, compliance, and governance policies. Decide on the coexistence mode you'll use during the transition. There are different modes such as Islands, Skype for Business with Teams Collaboration, and Teams Only.

4. **Pilot migration:** Start with a small group of users. Monitor the process, rectify any issues, and refine the strategy based on feedback and results.

5. **User training and adoption:** Provide training resources for your users to familiarize them with Teams. Encourage them to start using Teams for meetings, chats, and collaboration.

6. **Gradual rollout:** Once the pilot phase is successfully completed, gradually increase the number of users migrating to Teams. Keep communicating the changes and provide user training as necessary. Keep an eye on the migration progress and address any issues promptly.

7. **Post-migration activities:** Monitor the Teams environment and solve any teething problems. Collect user feedback and make the necessary adjustments. Remember, migration isn't the end but the start of a new journey. Once all users are successfully migrated and comfortable using Teams, you can begin decommissioning Skype for Business.

In conclusion, migrating from Skype for Business On-Premises to Microsoft Teams is a significant move that requires careful planning and execution. With the right approach, workflow, and tasks checklist, your organization can smoothly transition to Teams and start enjoying the benefits of a modern collaboration platform. The next chapter will guide you through Teams troubleshooting approaches, which will prove handy post-migration, ensuring your team's work is unhindered and productive.

So far, you have learned about Microsoft Teams as an application, including its service architecture, data storage, how the different Teams components communicate to each other, Teams policy management, Teams Phone System management, organization preparation and readiness, the underlying network readiness, and so on. Now we'll look at what you must understand to plan and execute a seamless migration from Skype for Business on-premises to Microsoft Teams.

In this chapter, you will discover how Teams can benefit your organization, including IT and end users. You will also learn about the different migration paths and how to decide which path is appropriate for your organization and its considerations. In the end, you will be able to oversee an actual user migration through PowerShell commands and tools. We also cover best practices, guidance, and technical tips and tricks on your Teams migration journey.

Getting Ready for Microsoft Teams

As part of a user migration, a Teams admin needs to spread awareness about Teams and its features. While using Microsoft Teams, every user can access the chats, meetings, calls, content, apps, and workflow integration opportunities. Users will be able to participate in collaborative workspaces easily. Teams are a hub for teamwork and provide the most robust platform to improve organizational productivity. Teams also provide a toolset for communication and collaboration, including persistent chat, calls, meetings, PSTN calling, and so on, that a team requires to be successful in its professional journey. It provides an integration of Office and third-party apps that users work with every day. Teams is part of Office 365; hence, it includes enterprise-grade security and compliance with customization and management features.

First, understand why we must consider migrating users from Skype for Business to Microsoft Teams. Ever since Microsoft launched Teams, it has continued to build new capabilities, functionalities, and features within Teams to enable end users to communicate and collaborate more effectively in new ways every single day. That is performance by design. It has positive effects on communication and collaboration in organizations. Teams functionality extends beyond what Skype for Business can do. Teams has advanced features and provides modern experiences. Teams combines chat, video, calling, collaboration, and app integration into a single, integrated hub that allows state-of-the-art, cross-platform, and mobile experiences. Teams provides better performance by design in terms of call and meeting quality, and it has reimagined a client built on a cloud infrastructure.

You, as an admin, must get ready for Teams, as it brings several benefits to businesses and end users. Organizations using Teams can make decisions more efficiently using enhanced meeting experiences with collaboration. In addition, they can engage in information sharing while keeping privacy a top priority using private channels within the project team. All Teams capabilities are available through a mobile client that boosts productivity as users can attend meetings and share documents even if they are not in the office. From an end-user perspective, they can join Teams meetings quickly with optimal audio and video quality. When users share the desktop in a meeting, Teams allows sharing control with user photos to quickly identify who has control. In a meeting, users can use a background blur feature so that they can work from anywhere. They can record meetings through cloud recording. In chat, users can use inline message translation, emojis, and GIFs.

For the IT organization, Teams provides a single integrated platform for all productivity needs with end-to-end security and administrative controls. It brings a robust and highly available solution with improved performance and less downtime. In addition, it supports tabs, bots, and connectors for third-party integration. Before user migration, admins must prepare the network environment, prepare the on-premises phone system SBC with Teams Direct Routing or Microsoft Phone System Calling Plan, create required to call routing policies, test inbound and outbound phone calls, test meetings, and so on.

Preparing for the Transition to Microsoft Teams

As a Teams administrator, part of your role in user migration involves actively promoting the utility and benefits of Microsoft Teams. This platform is a veritable powerhouse for organizational collaboration, offering a comprehensive range of features such as chat, meetings, and voice and video calls, as well as a multitude of app and workflow integrations. Microsoft Teams not only facilitates seamless teamwork but also serves as a centralized hub aimed at amplifying organizational productivity. With the inclusion of Office and third-party app integrations, the platform is designed to serve all the professional communication and collaboration needs a team might have. Furthermore, Teams is integrated within the Office 365 ecosystem, providing enterprise-level security, customizability, and administrative control.

Why Transition from Skype for Business to Microsoft Teams?

Microsoft Teams has eclipsed Skype for Business in terms of capabilities and user experience since its launch. It's not merely a static platform but continues to evolve, adding new features and functionalities aimed at optimizing user engagement and operational effectiveness. This innovation is by design and leads to palpable enhancements in the quality of intra-organizational communication and collaboration. Unlike Skype for Business, Teams amalgamates chat, video conferencing, voice calling, file collaboration, and application integration into a unified, user-friendly interface. This provides a more dynamic, cross-platform experience that's mobile-friendly, along with superior call and meeting quality, all backed by robust cloud infrastructure.

Benefits for Administrators and End Users

For you, the administrator, preparing for the Microsoft Teams transition is crucial, given its myriad advantages for both corporate operations and individual users. Organizations that adopt Teams experience improved decision-making efficiency, courtesy of enhanced meeting functionalities and collaborative tools. The platform also offers unique features such as private channels, allowing for secure, role-specific information dissemination. For mobile users, all these capabilities are condensed into a mobile app, empowering them to participate in meetings and collaborate on documents remotely.

From an end-user standpoint, Teams offers features such as intuitive controls for screen sharing during meetings, the ability to blur the background to maintain professionalism while working remotely, and cloud-based meeting recordings. The chat interface supports inline message translation and allows for a more engaging conversation through the use of emojis and GIFs.

IT Preparations Before User Migration

Before transitioning users to Microsoft Teams, IT administrators have several preparatory tasks to complete. These include readying the network environment, setting up the on-premises phone system SBC via Teams Direct Routing or Microsoft Phone System Calling Plan, and implementing call routing policies. This also involves running tests for both inbound and outbound phone calls and ensuring the seamless functioning of meetings. Teams provides a unified solution with comprehensive security features and administrative controls, promising greater performance and lesser downtime. It also accommodates third-party integrations via tabs, bots, and connectors, offering a complete package for productivity.

Interpreting the Migration Roadmap and Coexistence Strategies

Let's talk about the migration roadmap.

Navigating the Technical Jargon

Before diving into the migration pathway, it's crucial to familiarize yourself with the terminology that will be used. Terms like *user upgrades* and *user migration* are often used interchangeably in this context. Furthermore, understanding concepts such as Teams migration coexistence mode, Teams island mode, Skype for Business collaboration mode, Skype for Business with Teams collaboration mode, meeting-first mode, and Teams-only mode are vital. These so-called *user coexistence modes* are pivotal in deciding how incoming calls and chats are routed and which application a user utilizes for initiating conversations, starting calls, or scheduling meetings. Each coexistence mode offers a unique suite of features. The user coexistence modes shown in Figure 6-1 are used to determine both the routing of incoming calls and chats and the app that is used by the user to initiate chats and calls or to schedule meetings. Each mode comes with a distinctive feature set.

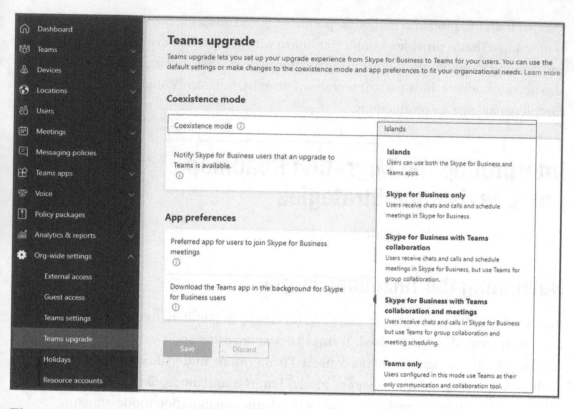

Figure 6-1. *Teams upgrade coexistence mode list*

Beyond Technology: The Human Element of Migration

It's important to recognize that transitioning from Skype for Business to Teams isn't merely a technological shift; it's about the people who will use these platforms for collaborative tasks. The success of any organization relies heavily on its members coming together to work both efficiently and effectively. The essence of teamwork lies not just in whom you connect with but also in why and how you form those connections.

Comparing Skype for Business and Microsoft Teams

While Skype for Business serves as a competent unified communications platform, offering chat, meeting, and call functionalities, Microsoft Teams takes this a step further. It evolved into a centralized hub that empowers users to connect, communicate, and collaborate, all from a single, unified interface. This amplifies the platform's utility, making it indispensable for modern collaborative work environments. Figure 6-2 shows the difference between the two tools and their features.

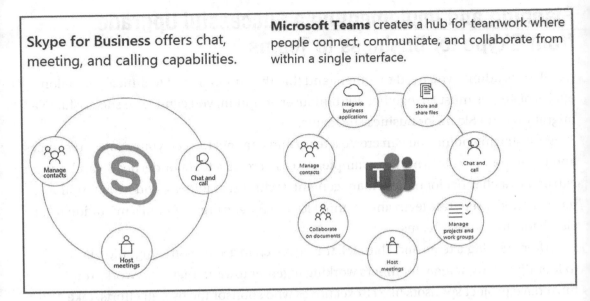

Skype for Business offers chat, meeting, and calling capabilities.

Microsoft Teams creates a hub for teamwork where people connect, communicate, and collaborate from within a single interface.

Figure 6-2. Skype for Business and Teams features comaprison

Structured Planning for Seamless Migration

A well-thought-out strategy must be in place to ensure a smooth migration, balancing technical and user readiness. After completing the preliminary steps, including network readiness and proof of concept (POC), it's essential to keep the lines of communication open with users. This involves frequent updates about what back-end tasks are being performed as part of the transition from Skype for Business to Teams.

Adopting Flexible Migration Approaches

Microsoft provides a versatile set of options for running Teams in tandem with Skype for Business. The quicker you can educate the users about Teams and encourage them to begin using its features, the smoother the transition will be. A logical starting point could be the "island mode," where users are given the freedom to use both Skype for Business and Teams in parallel. This allows them to continue their routine tasks such as calls, chats, and meetings through Skype for Business while progressively shifting collaborative activities to Teams. This dual-system approach could serve as a useful steppingstone for ultimately moving to a Teams-only environment.

Planning and Implementing a Successful Upgrade from Skype for Business to Teams

As a Teams admin, you need to understand that the adoption and technical migration efforts of Teams must go together. Without user adoption, you cannot be successful in a migration from Skype for Business to Teams.

As a starting point, you can create a team and channel to keep your project resources and team members in sync. For example, you can create a team underneath, and you can create a channel for project management, technical readiness, and user adoption. I have created a separate team and channel for the Bloguc organization's migration from Skype for Business to Teams.

After creating a team and channel, the next step in a successful migration is to identify the right team members working together toward migration work. You must have project sponsors like IT executives who sponsor the overall efforts, take accountability, and set the organization's goals. You also need a project team with technical expertise who plans network readiness and executes the upgrade plan. You need a user change management team who drives adoption work, including end-user readiness. Additionally, it requires a project lead who will coordinate and report to the executive sponsor with an upgrade status.

Always start with a framework and scope the overall work and responsibilities. The user readiness team might indicate that in 30 days, every user will have access on Teams with the phone system, and every user will be upgraded to Teams-only mode for chats, calls, meetings, Phone System, and content collaboration all in Teams, and the Skype for Business client will be used only to join Skype meetings. If the technical team comes back and says only the pilot will roll out initially, then user migration might happen in phases after 60 days. This shows a complete disconnect, and that is why scoping with the timeline is particularly important. Throughout the preparation and migration work, check the Teams usage continually before and after the user upgrade.

Skype for Business to Microsoft Teams Upgrade Mode

Many coexistence modes are used to determine both the routing of incoming calls and chats and the app that is used by the user to initiate chats and calls or to schedule meetings. Here is the list of coexistence modes considered in migration paths:

- *Island mode:* In this mode, users can use both the Skype for Business and Teams client apps for all the features these tools provide. In island mode, each client application operates as a separate island. Skype for Business talks to Skype for Business, and Teams talks to Teams. Users are expected to run both clients at all times. They can communicate natively in the client from which the communication was initiated.

- *Skype for Business only mode:* Using this mode, users receive chats, take calls, and schedule meetings in Skype for Business. Users continue to use only Skype for Business. They do not use Teams for chat, meeting, and calling capabilities; they do not use Teams for teams and channels. This mode can be used before starting a managed deployment of Teams to prevent users from starting to use Teams ahead of them being ready. This can also be used to enable authenticated participation in Teams meetings for Skype for Business users, provided the users are licensed for Teams.

- *Skype for Business with Teams collaboration (Teams Collab) mode:* Using this Teams coexistence mode, users receive chats, handle calls, and schedule meetings in Skype for Business, but they use Teams purely for the group collaboration. That means no chat, no calls, and no meetings in Teams. In this collaboration mode, Skype for Business remains unchanged for chat, calling, and meeting capabilities, and Teams is used for collaboration capabilities only, such as teams and channels, access to files in Office 365, and applications. This mode is a legitimate first step for organizations still relying on Skype for Business that want to provide a first insight into the collaboration capabilities of Teams for their users.

- *Skype for Business with Teams collaboration and meetings mode:* Using this mode, users participate in chats and calls in Skype for Business, but they use Teams for group collaboration and meeting scheduling.

- *Teams-only mode:* This is the final stage, when Skype for Business users are ultimately migrated to Teams only. Users configured in this mode, with Teams as their only communication and collaboration tools, receive chats, handle calls, engage in content collaboration, and schedule meetings in the Teams app only. The Skype for Business client is used only to join Skype for Business only meetings.

These coexistence modes all have different feature sets and can be used based on your organization's needs and requirements.

Teams Upgrade Coexistence Modes Are Available as a Deployment Path

When you plan to upgrade users to Teams, the starting point in all cases includes Skype for Business (On-Premises) only mode, and the endpoint is always all users using Teams-only mode. A planned deployment path is the most critical success factor in a Teams migration scenario.

User migration from Skype for Business to Teams is pretty straightforward, as it involves applying a few policies. Once the user is updated to Teams-only mode, and Skype for Business is used only for meetings, users must use the Teams app for all kinds of communication. All routing automatically happens for chat, calling, meetings, external access (federation), and phone system (PSTN); the workload will be moved completely to Teams. However, if users are not ready for the upgrade because they haven't used Teams for any kind of communication and they are not familiar with Teams, you might not have success. Before migration, users must be familiar with Teams to have a successful adoption.

There are multiple considerations when you are deciding on an upgrade path, such as what the interoperability experience looks like. Make sure the feature overlap between Skype for Business and Teams is acceptable to users. You can either move all users at one time or by site or region, depending on what will work better for your organization. You might move collaboration features first and then meetings and then the phone system (PSTN); or you could move all features together. These are some of the decisions you, as the Teams admin, must make before starting the migration.

- By default, users get the full side-by-side experience, which means both the Skype for Business and Microsoft Teams clients are working for chat, calling, and meetings. Skype for Business and Microsoft Teams do not work together in this scenario, and there will be no interoperability between these two clients.

- Another consideration is whether you want to move users to Teams with all the features at once or first move meetings and then move users to Teams with the phone system (PSTN), chat, calling, and so on. That decision will dictate the coexisting experience; for example, some users might be using Teams-only mode, while the rest of the users are using Skype for Business and Teams in island mode using one path.

- You also need to decide if your organization is ready for the default experience or an interoperability experience.

- The last thing you need to consider is how long you want the interoperability experience or the user upgrade duration to be.

After you make all these decisions, the next step is to choose an appropriate upgrade mode for your organization's users. All the coexistence modes represent steps on the path toward Teams-only mode, where the entire workload is handled in Teams, and the legacy Skype for Business client launches only to join Skype for Business.

Identifying the Appropriate Coexistence Mode for Users

Let's talk about the different modes.

Understanding TeamsOnly Mode

For organizations that haven't installed Skype for Business Server on-premises, all their users will operate under the TeamsOnly mode by default. This also sets the tenant's effective mode to TeamsOnly. Verification of this can be done through the TeamsUpgradeEffectiveMode property, accessible via Teams PowerShell. It's worth noting that prior to Skype for Business Online's discontinuation on July 31, 2021, it was possible to alter the coexistence mode for either individual users or the entire tenant. However, this option no longer exists except for organizations maintaining an on-premises Skype for Business Server setup.

Coexistence Modes for On-Premises Deployments

In situations where an on-premises Skype for Business Server exists, the global tenant policy for TeamsUpgradePolicy can vary and may include modes such as SfBOnly, SfBWithTeamsCollab, and SfBWithTeamsCollabAndMeetings. Users can also be allocated a specific TeamsUpgradePolicy, superseding the organization's overarching tenant policy. For cloud-based users, TeamsOnly is obligatory, while on-premises users can select from any mode other than TeamsOnly. Admins should bear these stipulations in mind while charting out their migration strategy to ensure a seamless transition.

Exploring Island mode for Teams and Skype for Business

Island mode is generally recommended for both online and on-premises configurations. This mode functions by default, requiring no special adjustments from administrators. However, the potential for feature overlap between Skype for Business and Teams—specifically in chat, calling, and meetings—may cause some confusion among users. Therefore, initial user education is crucial to make them aware of the duplicate functionalities.

All coexistence modes can be customized on a per-user or tenant-wide basis, either through the Teams Admin Center or by employing Windows PowerShell connected to the Skype for Business Online PowerShell module.

Understanding Feature Overlap in Island mode

In island mode, both the Teams and Skype for Business clients function independently, offering distinct capabilities for chat, calling, and meetings. Teams additionally handles content sharing and collaboration functionalities.

Steps for Effective Transition

User awareness remains pivotal for a smooth transition. An active user education campaign, potentially involving mass communication like emails or large gatherings, is highly advisable. You should provide ample information about Teams' wide-ranging features. Once users are comfortable and actively using Teams, you may then proceed to move them exclusively to TeamsOnly mode, provided that all backend preparations, like network readiness and phone system integrations, are complete. It's recommended to run a TeamsOnly mode proof of concept (POC) for at least 15 to 30 days prior to full-scale user migration, which could be executed regionally or for the entire organization at once.

Remember, if the adoption of Teams is managed effectively and gains widespread user acceptance, a wholesale migration to Teams can be done without toggling between coexistence modes. Figure 6-3 shows the overlapping features of Teams and Skype for Business.

Figure 6-3. Teams side-by-side with Skype for Business

Note   Teams calling features are VoIP only until you move to the Teams-only mode.

Features Available in Island Mode

In the island coexistence mode, users can run both applications with all features available. Specific to the calling and chat features, users will use these features separately in both clients, as described here.

- All users in island mode can receive chats and calls in the same client as the one used by the originator. That means Skype for Business (SfB) users communicate with Skype for Business users, and Microsoft Teams users communicate with Microsoft Teams users for chat, calls, and meetings.

- Users can initiate calls and chats from either client, and the receiver receives it on the same type of client.

- Another important overlap feature is real-time presence status. Both of the clients have separate presence status, and they cannot share their presence status.

- There will be no interoperability between SfB and Teams client for calling, chat, presence, and meetings.

- For external access (federation), chat and calls land in the SfB client only.

- Phone System (PSTN) calls (inbound and outbound) land in the SfB client only.

There are some features specific to meetings.

- Online meeting scheduling is available on Microsoft Teams as well as Skype for Business on both clients.

- In island mode, will see the Outlook meeting add-ins for the Teams as well as Skype for Business clients.

- End users can join meetings from the respective clients. Teams meetings are joined via the Teams client, and SfB meetings are joined via the SfB client. There are no cross-meeting joins.

There are some issues to be aware of when using islands coexistence mode.

- Because both the Teams and SfB client features overlap for chat, calls, and meetings, users have to use the SfB client for SfB meetings and the Teams client for Teams meetings. Chats and calls will land on the originating clients. There is no interoperability between these two clients (until Teams users are moved to Teams-only mode). For example, if the user Balu sends chat messages using SfB to the user Chanda, the same chat message will land on Chanda's SfB client. If the user Balu sends a chat message through a Teams client, then it will land on Chanda's Teams client. If Chanda is not running Teams client, then she will receive a missed notification after some time as the default behavior. For meetings, scheduling and joining is available in both clients.

- User migration all at once by region or site is the best option for an optimal user experience and simplified user adoption. I recommend preparing the environment properly with network readiness and implementing Phone System (PSTN) integration through Direct Routing, voice policies, dial plans, or choose a Phone System Calling Plan so that you can move all your users at once. Large, complex organizations might have to run POC, however, and choose the region or site approach as per the organization and the deployment complexity involved.

- Chat messages and calls from federated users will be received on the Skype for Business client until the users move to Teams-only mode.

- Phone System (PSTN) calling capabilities will be available only when users move to Teams-only mode. Island mode Teams users cannot use PSTN calling in the Teams client; it has to be in the SfB client only.

- Skype dominates an additional but essential consideration for the microphone and speaker device controls, as the Human Interface Device (HID) control for the Skype for Business client is used until the users migrate to Teams-only mode.

- The last consideration is conference and meeting room devices, which must be upgraded or replaced or onboarded on Teams before the user migration so that when users are migrated to Teams, they can use a meeting room to join or host Teams meetings.

Some considerations have to be taken into account for Skype for Business Online organizations and some for Skype for Business On-Premises organizations, as enumerated next.

Understanding Routing Parameters for All the Modes

In the previous section, you learned about the functioning of chats and calls for users in island mode. If you are already in island mode, it is important to first understand how call routing, chat functionality, and presence work for different modes. You should choose a specific mode as your org-wide default when migrating users to Teams-only mode. This will help ensure a smooth transition for your team.

The terminologies used for routing are native and interop. If a direct conversation is possible within the tenant, it's referred to as *native*; if not, Microsoft uses *interop*.

Routing-Call and Chat

When it comes to routing chat and calls, several factors come into play, including the coexistence mode of the recipient, the client used by the sender, and whether the conversation is in-tenant or federated. If you are sending a message to a TeamsOnly user, it will always route to Teams. If you are sending a message to a Skype for Business user, it will always route to Skype for Business. And if you are sending a message to an islands user, it will always route to the same client from which it was sent. To make it easier to understand, Table 6-1 explains how call and chat routing works within the tenant.

Table 6-1. *Intenant Routing to a TeamsOnly Recipient*

Mode	Originator Client	Skype for Business homed	Route-->	TeamsOnly Recipient
TeamsOnly	Teams	Online	|	Teams
Islands	Teams	On-premises	|	Teams
	Skype for Business	On-premises	|	*Teams*
Skype for Business	Skype for Business	On-premises	|	*Teams*

In-tenant Routing to an Islands Recipient

Mode	Originator Client	Skype for Business homed	Route-->	Islands Recipient
TeamsOnly	Teams	Online	|	Teams
Islands	Teams	On-premises	|	Teams
	Skype for Business	On-premises	|	Skype for Business
Skype for Business	Skype for Business	On-premises	|	Skype for Business

In-tenant Routing to an SFB recipient

Mode	Originator Client	Skype for Business homed	Route-->	Skype for Business Recipient
TeamsOnly	Teams	Online	|	*Skype for Business*
Islands	Teams	On-premises	|	**Not Possible**
	Skype for Business	On-premises	|	Skype for Business
Skype for Business	Skype for Business	On-premises	|	Skype for Business

Federated routing scenarios:

Federated Routing to a TeamsOnly recipient

Mode	Originator Client	Skype for Business homed	Route-->	TeamsOnly Recipient
TeamsOnly	Teams	Online		Teams
Islands	Teams	On-premises		Not Possible
	Skype for Business	On-premises		*Teams*
Skype for Business	Skype for Business	On-premises		*Teams*

Federated Routing to an Island recipient

Mode	Originator Client	Skype for Business homed	Route-->	Islands Recipient
TeamsOnly	Teams	Online		*Skype for Business*
Islands	Teams	On-premises		Not Possible
	Skype for Business	On-premises		Skype for Business
Skype for Business	Skype for Business	On-premises		Skype for Business

Federated Routing to an SFB recipient

Mode	Originator Client	Skype for Business homed	Route-->	Skype for Business Recipient
TeamsOnly	Teams	Online		*Skype for Business*
Islands	Teams	On-premises		Not Possible
	Skype for Business	On-premises		Skype for Business
Skype for Business	Skype for Business	On-premises		Skype for Business

Based on the coexistence mode of the user, the presence status is displayed differently. Some users may have both a Skype for Business and a Teams presence, while others may have only a Teams presence or only a Skype for Business presence. Here is how the presence is shared based on the user's coexistence mode:

- If a user is in TeamsOnly mode, then any other user (whether in Teams or Skype for Business) will see that TeamsOnly user's Teams presence.

- If a user is in any of the Skype for Business modes (SfbOnly, SfbWithTeamsCollab, SfbWithTeamsCollabAndMeetings), then any other user (whether in Teams or Skype for Business) will see that Skype for Business user's Skype for Business presence.

- If a user is in Island mode, the presence in Teams and presence in Skype for Business are independent (the values need not match), and other users will see one or the other presence of the island user, depending on whether they are in the same tenant or in a federated tenant and which client they use. See Table 6-2.

Table 6-2. *In-Tenant Presence*

Watcher	Route-->	Islands	Publisher	Teams Only
Client			Skype for Business	
Skype for Business	|	Skype for Business	Skype for Business	Teams
Teams	|	Teams	Skype for Business	Teams

Federated presence

Watcher	Route-->	Islands	Publisher	Teams Only
Client			Skype for Business	
Skype for Business	|	Skype for Business	Skype for Business	Teams
Teams	|	Skype for Business	Skype for Business	Teams

Considerations for Skype for Business On-Premises Organizations

The following are some considerations to be aware of:

- Using Skype for Business On-Premises only, you cannot move or upgrade users to Teams-only mode. You must enable Skype for Business Hybrid first, which is required to start moving users to Teams-only mode. As part of the hybrid configuration, you must sync all msRTCSIP attributes from on-premises Active Directory Domain Services (ADDS) to Online in Azure AD. Refer to the Microsoft documentation at https://docs.microsoft.com/en-us/skypeforbusiness/hybrid/configure-federation-with-skype-for-business-online to learn how to enable a Skype for Business Hybrid configuration.

Note   Users with Skype for Business On-Premises could use Teams, but they cannot be in Teams-only mode.

- If Skype for Business On-Premises users are enabled with enterprise voice, then you must have an enterprise license such as E3 with add-on licenses for Phone System and Audio Conferencing or E5 with an Audio Conferencing license. Without a proper license, you cannot migrate users from Skype for Business to Microsoft Teams-only mode.

- Another consideration is that the Skype for Business On-Premises user will not have interoperability, so there will be no external access (federation) from their Teams client (they must use the Skype for Business client for external access).

- As a prerequisite for Microsoft Teams, all the corporate network locations from which users are accessing Office 365 services (Teams) must have Internet access, so they can connect to Office 365 services for web (signaling) traffic. In addition, ensure that UDP ports 3478 through 3481 and IP subnets (13.107.64.0/18 and 52.112.0.0/14) are opened for Teams media traffic in all locations.

- Additionally, implement QoS and split-tunnel VPN for the Teams audio/video call, conferencing, and desktop sharing scenarios. Refer to Chapter 3 for network readiness and QoS and VPN split tunneling implementation.

Configuring Coexistence (Migration) Mode

As part of Skype for Business to Teams migration, as an admin you need to configure the coexistence mode for your tenant organization as well as individual users. You can select the same coexistence mode for all users and upgrade to Microsoft Teams all at once, or you can migrate a group of users from the same region or site, configuring different coexistence modes for different groups of users.

To set upgrade coexistence mode for all users using the Teams admin center, follow this procedure:

1. Log in to the Teams admin center, and navigate to Teams. Select Teams Upgrade settings.

2. On the Teams Upgrade settings page, from the Coexistence Mode options, select one of the following coexistence modes for your organization, as shown in Figure 6-4:

    - Islands

    - Skype for Business only

    - Skype for Business with Teams collaboration

    - Skype for Business with Teams collaboration and meetings

    - Teams only

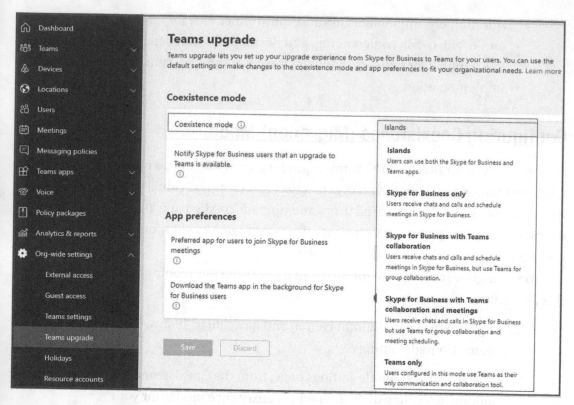

Figure 6-4. *Teams coexistence modes*

3. You can then enable Notify Skype For Business Users That An
    Upgrade To Teams Is Available when not selecting Teams-
    only mode.

4. On the same Teams Upgrade page, you can set the Preferred App
    For Users To Join Skype For Business Meetings option (Skype
    Meetings App or Skype for Business), and you can also enable
    the Download The Teams App In The Background For Skype For
    Business Users option.

5. Finally, click Save to commit your changes.

You, as an admin, can select the Teams coexistence mode for an individual by following these steps:

1. Log in to the Microsoft Teams admin center and navigate to Users. Find and select the user for whom you would like to set the upgrade options.

2. On the User page, on the Account tab, under Teams Upgrade settings, click Edit. On the Teams Upgrade page, select one of the options for the selected user, Use Org-wide Settings, and choose one of these upgrade options:

   - Islands

   - Skype for Business only

   - Skype for Business with Teams collaboration

   - Skype for Business with Teams collaboration and meetings

   - Teams only

3. Click Apply. If you select any coexistence mode (except Use Org-wide Settings), you will have the option to enable notifications in the user's Skype for Business app, which will inform the user that the upgrade to Teams is coming soon. To do so, turn on the Notify The Skype For Business User option.

4. Finally, click Apply to commit the changes.

As an admin, you have the leverage to set the upgrade option using Windows PowerShell. To manage the transition from Skype for Business to Teams, you can use the Grant-CsTeamsUpgradePolicy command. This allows us to apply TeamsUpgradePolicy to individual users or to configure the default settings for an entire organization. For example, to configure the user bilag@bloguc.com to Teams in island mode and to notify the user, run the following PowerShell command:

```
Grant-CsTeamsUpgradePolicy -PolicyName IslandsWithNotify -Identity
"bilag@bloguc.com"
```

To configure a TeamsOnly policy for the entire organization, run the following command:

```
Grant-CsTeamsUpgradePolicy -PolicyName TeamsOnly -Global
```

User Migration from Skype for Business On-Premises with Enterprise Voice to Teams-Only Mode

The process for the on-premises users who are enabled for enterprise voice is explained in this section. The user must be synchronized with Azure AD for the msRTCSIP attribute. The Skype for Business On-Premises environment must be configured for a hybrid with a split domain in place. This means the same domain will be available in On-Premises as well as Online.

Users can be in any coexistence mode except Teams only. First, check the existing configuration using the following PowerShell command, and check that the user is enabled on-premises with a Direct Inward Dial (DID) number assigned.

```
Get-CsOnlineUser bilag@bloguc.com | Select Display*,*interp*,*voice* | fl
```

As part of user provisioning, the user must have the required license assigned, such as E1/E3 plus add-on licenses for Phone System and Audio Conferencing, or E5 with the Phone System and Audio Conferencing licenses assigned.

The next step is to verify the user's enterprise voice, onpreLineURI, voicemail, and so on. Here is the list of attributes and their expected status: EnterpriseVoiceEnabled = $true, HostedVoicemail = $true. You can change that status using the command Set-CsUser bilag@bloguc.com –HostedVoicemail $true.

```
Get-CsOnlineUser -Identity bilag@bloguc.com | Select
Display*,*upgrade*,*voice*, *LineUri* | fl
```

Additionally, you need to assign a voice routing policy and dial plan to the user. As an admin, you can check your existing Skype for Business On-Premises voice policy and replicate a similar PSTN route and usages with the online PSTN gateway, which you set up as part of Teams Direct Routing configuration (refer to Chapter 4). If you are using Calling plans or Operator Connect, ensure that the service is available in the Teams Admin Center and emergency addresses are created.

Grant the user a previously created online voice routing policy (Grant-CsOnlineVoiceRoutingPolicy) using PowerShell and then verify the policy assignment using the PowerShell command Get-CsOnlineUser. For Calling Plans or Operator Connect, the Online Voice routing policy is not required.

You can do staging work, including the voice routing policy, tenant dial plan, online PSTN gateway (with FQDN), calling policy, location-based routing (LBR), and Teams emergency routing policy, ahead of user migration. This work will not disturb the users' existing call flow or any other features.

Redirect the DID from the existing SBC through Teams Direct Routing. For example, configure the SBC to route incoming DID calls to the Direct Routing trunk(s) instead of the Skype for Business Mediation Server and then configure the SBC to route outbound calls to the PSTN provider (SIP trunk or PRI line) accordingly. This is the first step that is disruptive to the user and will start the outage window. Before making call routing changes from Skype for Business mediation pool to Microsoft Teams DR in SBC, all the users for the particular must be migrated to Teams-only mode.

If you are using Calling Plans or Operator Connect with existing numbers, make sure porting is scheduled with the operator ahead of time. On migration day, unassign the numbers in Skype for Business and reassign the numbers in Teams afterward performing the Move-csuser command.

The final step is to upgrade the user to Microsoft Teams. You can perform a single step move with Server 2019 or Server 2015 CU8+ using the following command to move the user to Teams-only mode:

```
Import-Module SkypeOnlineConnector
$Creds = Get-Credential
$sfbSession = New-CsOnlineSession -OverrideAdminDomain "<YourDomainName>.
onmicrosoft.com" -Credential $Creds
Import-PSSession $sfbSession
$url = https://admin<1a>.online.lync.com/HostedMigration/
hostedmigrationService.svc
Move-CsUser -Identity bilag@bloguc.com -Target sipfed.online.lync.com
-MoveToTeams -Credential $creds -HostedMigrationOverrideUrl $url
```

Notice that before upgrading the user and after the upgrade completes, the TeamsupgradeEffiectveMode shows as TeamsOnly and TeamsUpgradePolicy is UpgradeToTeams, along with other attributes such as enterprise voice, OnPremLineURI, and so on. Figure 6-5 shows all the attributes set up correctly after the user has been migrated to Teams-only mode. Then assign the voice routing policy and tenant dial plan as per the requirements.

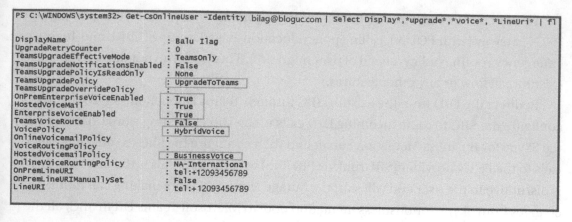

```
PS C:\WINDOWS\system32> Get-CsOnlineUser -Identity bilag@bloguc.com | Select Display*,*upgrade*,*voice*, *LineUri* | fl

DisplayName                        : Balu Ilag
UpgradeRetryCounter                : 0
TeamsUpgradeEffectiveMode          : TeamsOnly
TeamsUpgradeNotificationsEnabled   : False
TeamsUpgradePolicyIsReadOnly       : None
TeamsUpgradePolicy                 : UpgradeToTeams
TeamsUpgradeOverridePolicy         :
OnPremEnterpriseVoiceEnabled       : True
HostedVoiceMail                    : True
EnterpriseVoiceEnabled             : True
TeamsVoiceRoute                    : False
VoicePolicy                        : HybridVoice
OnlineVoicemailPolicy              :
VoiceRoutingPolicy                 :
HostedVoicemailPolicy              : BusinessVoice
OnlineVoiceRoutingPolicy           : NA-International
OnPremLineURI                      : tel:+12093456789
OnPremLineURIManuallySet           : False
LineURI                            : tel:+12093456789
```

Figure 6-5. *User migrated to Teams-only mode*

As part of validation, you can capture the Teams client logs by pressing Ctrl+Alt+Shift+1 on the keyboard while keeping the Teams Windows desktop client on.

As an admin, you must think about how enabling these feature functions affects the users, as they might not be familiar with all the features of Teams. You have to design a user readiness strategy. First, define the value of Teams features for your end users; to do so, understand relevant personas, use cases, and usage scenarios. Remember that business goals (increasing productivity, saving money) are not always user goals.

Is it relevant to measure users' tendency to change? How much change is happening? What is your organizational change culture? Identify the relevant readiness channels, including awareness, training, and support. The most important piece of advice is to communicate early. Don't wait for the completion of the technical readiness stage.

To build and implement your readiness plan, use the following procedure to inform your plan. Make sure to align this with your technical team and project lead.

1. Run the pilot. This allows validation of both technical and user readiness. It also allows the migration to be a formal effort with a defined test plan and clear go/no-go goals. It should also include a good representation of your user base.

2. Plan for coexistence, running Skype for Business and Teams together in your environment using several upgrade approaches (modes) to meet your organization's needs.

3. Finally, perform the upgrade by moving users to Teams-only mode. You can plan for a phased approach that enables you to pause or mitigate if needed. Maintain momentum once you begin to avoid having users in too many modes.

After deployment, create an operational plan. As part of this plan, measure against your defined goals and mitigate as needed. Monitor network health to ensure a positive user experience.

For bulk user migration, you can create your own PowerShell script and then migrate multiple users at once. Here is a simple PowerShell script to migrate users from Skype for Business On-Premises to Teams. The input file is in .csv format with the user UPN, voice routing policy, emergency routing policy, and dial plan.

```
#Script starts
function Select-FileDialog
{
        param([string]$Title,[string]$Directory,[string]$Filter="CSV Files
        (*.csv)|*.csv")
        [System.Reflection.Assembly]::LoadWithPartialName("System.Windows.
        Forms") | Out-Null
        $objForm = New-Object System.Windows.Forms.OpenFileDialog
        $objForm.InitialDirectory = $Directory
        $objForm.Filter = $Filter
        $objForm.Title = $Title
        $objForm.ShowHelp = $true
        $Show = $objForm.ShowDialog()
        If ($Show -eq "OK")
        {
                Return $objForm.FileName
        }
        Else
        {
                Exit
        }
}
Start-Transcript -Path .\UserSfB-Teams_migrate.txt
$creds = Get-Credential
```

```
$sfboSession = New-CsOnlineSession -OverrideAdminDomain "<YourDomainname.
onmicrosoft.com" -Credential $creds
Import-PSSession $sfboSession -AllowClobber
$FileName = Select-FileDialog -Title "Import an CSV file" -Directory "c:\"
$csvFile = Import-Csv $FileName
foreach($entry in $csvFile){
        $user = $entry.sip
        $VoicePolicy = $entry.voicepolicy
        $Dialplan = $entry.dialplan
        $EmergencyPolicy = $entry.emergencypolicy
        $url="https://admin<yourSfBOnline-Tenant>.online.lync.com/
        HostedMigration/hostedmigrationService.svc"
        Move-CsUser -Identity $user -Target sipfed.online.lync.com
        -MoveToTeams -Credential $creds -HostedMigrationOverrideUrl $url
        -Confirm:$False
#Assign Policy
        Set-CsUser -Identity $user -EnterpriseVoiceEnabled $true
        -HostedVoiceMail $true
        Grant-CsOnlineVoiceRoutingPolicy -Identity $user -PolicyName
        $VoicePolicy
        Grant-CsTenantDialPlan -Identity $user -PolicyName $Dialplan
        Grant-CsTeamsEmergencyCallRoutingPolicy -Identity $user -PolicyName
        $EmergencyPolicy
}
Write-Host "Script Completed" -ForegroundColor Yellow
Stop-Transcript
#Script ended
```

Assigning Phone Numbers in Teams

Here are the examples of assigning the phone numbers in Teams based on different PSTN connectivity methods:

```
Set-CsPhoneNumberAssignment -Identity user1@bloguc.com -PhoneNumber
+12065551234 -PhoneNumberType CallingPlan
```

```
Set-CsPhoneNumberAssignment -Identity cq1@bloguc.com -PhoneNumber
+14255551225 -PhoneNumberType DirectRouting
Set-CsPhoneNumberAssignment -Identity user1@bloguc.com -PhoneNumber
+12065551234 -PhoneNumberType CallingPlan
```

Teams-Only Experience for End Users

A Teams-only experience means using Microsoft Teams for everything, including chat, audio and video calls, meetings, and content sharing. Here are the details of the experience a Teams-only user has.

- **For chat and calling:** Teams-only users will receive and initiate all chats and calls in Teams. They can do interoperable IMs or call with any Skype for Business users; also, they will be redirected to Teams if they try to sign in to Skype for Business clients.

- **For meetings:** Users will schedule all new meetings in Teams only. Teams Outlook meeting add-ins are enabled, and the Skype for Business add-in is disabled automatically.

- **For Teams-only users:** All data are migrated to Teams, including existing contacts and buddy lists from Skype for Business, including federated contacts but not distribution lists. Existing Skype for Business meetings (both On-Premises and Online) are converted to Teams meetings.

What Happens to Skype for Business During the Upgrade?

Skype for Business clients get a redirected experience, as shown in Figure 6-6. Skype for Business will go into meeting-only client configuration mode. This gives explicit notification to the user regarding guidance; it provides a secure link to Teams and also enables access to Skype for Business clients.

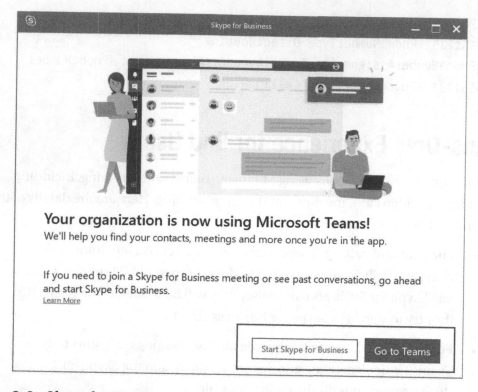

Figure 6-6. *Skype for Business experience after upgrade*

This Skype for Business client is focused primarily on meetings, and it does show meetings, as well as past conversation tabs. However, you cannot initiate chat and calls, and they are disabled. Figure 6-7 shows a meeting calendar to join meetings; however, the chat and call options are gone.

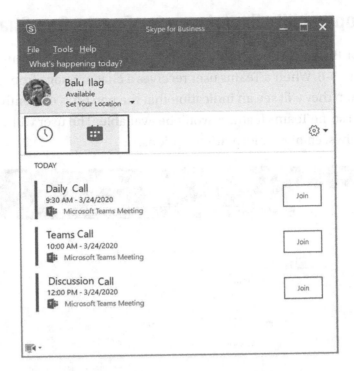

Figure 6-7. Skype for Business experience after upgrade

Regarding meetings, all the previous Skype for Business meetings are migrated to Teams. Users can still attend new Skype for Business meetings scheduled by others; however, they cannot schedule new Skype meetings, and Skype meeting add-ons will automatically be disabled. Therefore, users cannot see the Skype meeting schedule option in an Outlook calendar.

Because all the new meetings scheduled in Teams and Skype for Business (received) are shown, when clicking a Teams meeting in Skype for Business, it redirects to the Teams client. Similarly, selecting a Skype for Business meeting in the Teams app redirects to Skype for Business client.

Client Experiences Between Skype for Business and Teams

When you have a large organization with enterprise voice deployments, and you are choosing a group or site-wise user migration approach, you could have some users on Skype for Business and the rest on Teams. Specific to the federation aspect, when your organization has moved to Teams but your partner organization is still on Skype for Business, what will the experience be like?

Native Interoperability Experience for One-to-One Chat and Call

When a Skype for Business user sends a chat message to a Teams-only user, the result is shown in Figure 6-8. When a Teams user receives a chat message from a Skype for Business user, then they will see an indication that the person is currently using Skype for Business, and some Teams features won't be available. The user will not have the ability to use Giphys, emojis, or formatting options.

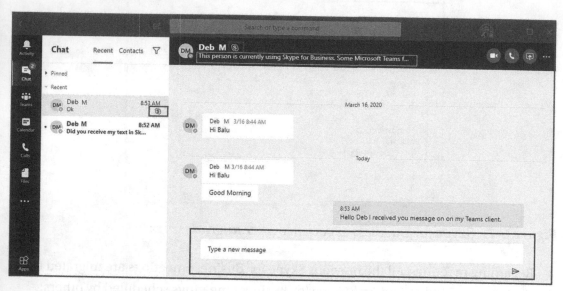

Figure 6-8. *Interoperability message on Teams*

On the Skype side, the experience is similar. A warning text message indicates that the person at the other end is not using Skype for Business, as shown in Figure 6-9.

Figure 6-9. *Interoperability message on Skype for Business*

When the users call, the response is similar, including a warning message that using some Teams features won't be available when using Skype for Business. However, to see the notification, a user must have the latest Skype for Business version of MSI and the Click to Run version.

Native Interoperability Experience for One-to-One Desktop Sharing Between Teams and the Skype for Business Client

When Skype for Business users communicate with Teams users, establishing an interoperability thread communicating via chat, audio, or video, the Skype for Business users are notified the recipient is not using Skype for Business in a yellow banner.

For desktop sharing, when Skype for Business users invoke desktop sharing, usually by clicking a share desktop icon, they are presented with this notification message: "Click to start meeting to share the screen with Teams users." In this example, Skype for Business users talking to Teams users decide to share the desktop; the Skype client shows a notification the meeting will include desktop sharing (see Figure 6-10). The meeting link is shared across the Teams client so that Teams users can join the meeting; however, this is a Skype meeting, so the Skype client will launch, and both users have joined a Skype meeting. If Teams doesn't have a Skype client, then the user can join using a Skype Meeting app in the browser; however, this requires a one-time download.

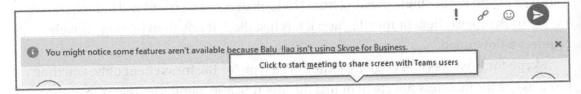

Figure 6-10. *Interoperability experience for desktop sharing on Skype for Business*

The peer-to-peer call desktop is not working for the user to start a meeting. Teams handles that back-end meeting setup on behalf of the user as an automated workflow and invites another participant to the meeting using desktop sharing.

The same things will work when Teams users start a desktop sharing with Skype for Business users. In this case, the Teams user initiating desktop sharing means the meeting URL is shared in Teams across Skype for Business. Skype for Business users can join with the client if the Teams client is not installed, as shown in Figure 6-11.

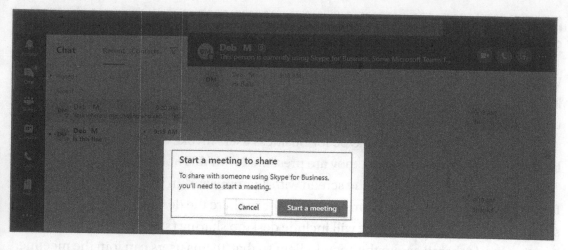

Figure 6-11. *Interoperability experience for desktop sharing on Teams*

Interoperability Meeting Joins Experience

Joining a Skype for Business meeting from Outlook or a Teams client will launch the Skype for Business client or meeting app if it is installed. If not, then joining via web requires a download.

Skype for Business meetings are joined via Skype for Business client only, whether it is a Skype for Business full client or just the Meeting app. Similarly, Teams meetings always join via the Teams client, whether Teams desktop, mobile, or web app only. No cross-platform joining is allowed.

Migration Tips and Tools

In this section, you will learn about the available tools that assist in your Skype for Business to Teams migration efforts and help you troubleshoot meeting migration status.

Teams Meeting Migration Service Tool

The Meeting Migration Service (MMS) tool is a back-end service that triggers when the Move-CsUser command runs using the Skype for Business Online PowerShell module. As an admin, you can check the status of running migrations, manually trigger meeting migrations, and disable migrations altogether. To check the status of meeting migrations, you can use the Get-CsMeetingMigrationStatus command. For example, to get a summary status of all MMS migrations, run the following cmdlet, which provides a tabular view of all migration states:

```
Get-CsMeetingMigrationStatus -SummaryOnly
```

Figure 6-12 shows the meeting migration result.

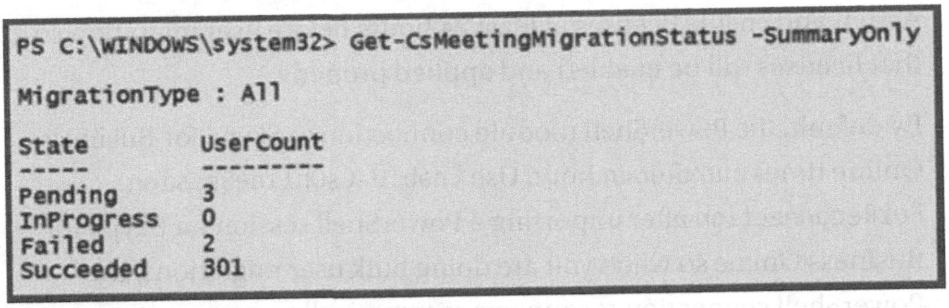

```
PS C:\WINDOWS\system32> Get-CsMeetingMigrationStatus -SummaryOnly

MigrationType : All

State          UserCount
-----          ---------
Pending        3
InProgress     0
Failed         2
Succeeded      301
```

Figure 6-12. *Meeting migration status*

If you would like to check the status of migration for a user, you can use the Get-CsMeetingMigrationStatus command with the Identity parameter. For example, to check the status of migration for the user bilag@bloguc.com, use this command:

```
Get-CsMeetingMigrationStatus -Identity bilag@bloguc.com
```

As part of meeting management, you do enable and disable MMS, but MMS is enabled by default for all organizations. It can also be disabled on different levels, though; for example, it can be disabled entirely for the tenant and disabled only for changes related to Audio Conferencing (where MMS will still run when a user is migrated from on-premises to the cloud or when granted TeamsOnly mode or SfBWithTeamsCollabAndMeetings mode in TeamsUpgradePolicy). To check if MMS is enabled for your organization, run the following command:

```
Get-CsTenantMigrationConfiguration
```

MMS is enabled if the MeetingMigrationEnabled parameter is $true.

Tips for User Migration

The following are some tips:

- Make sure to assign and enable all required licenses, such as Teams license, Skype for Business Plan2, Phone System, and Audio Conferencing, for all users who are being migrated.

- Assign and enable licenses at least 24 hours before user migration so that licenses will be enabled and applied properly.

- By default, the PowerShell module connection to Skype for Business Online times out after an hour. Use `Enable-CsOnlineSession ForReconnection` after importing a PowerShell session for Skype for Business Online so when you are doing bulk user migrations, the PowerShell connection reconnects automatically.

- After migration, user attribute and policy reflection takes a long time. Plan user migration on a Friday so that when users come back on Monday, their accounts will be ready with full functionality, including voice routing policy, dial pad, contact lists, recurring meetings, and so on.

Decommissioning Skype for Business

The final step of migrating from Skype for Business to Teams is decommissioning Skype for Business. Here is a set of prerequisites an admin must complete before decommissioning the Skype for Business footprint:

Step 1: Move all the users to the cloud.

Ensure all the users are moved to Microsoft Teams by running this command:

```
Get-CsUser -Filter { HostingProvider -eq "SRV:"}
```

If any users are returned, move them to the cloud by performing the previous steps mentioned in the document. Then disable the users by running the following command:

```
Get-CsUser -Filter { HostingProvider -eq "SRV:"} | Disable-CsUser
```

Step 2: Disable the hybrid configuration.

Hybrid connectivity is the logical connection between your Teams and Skype for Business on-premises footprint. Before removing the connectivity, ensure that DNS records point to Microsoft Online for all your SIP domains.

Record type	Name	TTL	Priority	Weight	Port	Value
SRV	_sipfederationtls._tcp	3600	100	1	5061	sipfed.online.lync.com
SRV	_sip._tls	3600	100	1	443	sipdir.online.lync.com
CNAME	Lyncdiscover	3600	N/A	N/A	N/A	webdir.online.lync.com
CNAME	Sip	3600	N/A	N/A	N/A	sipdir.online.lync.com

After updating the SIP domains, it is necessary to change the co-existence mode of your organization to Teams-only mode. You can make this change in the Teams admin center by navigating to the Teams upgrade settings and selecting Teams only in the coexistence mode. It is recommended to change this setting using a PowerShell command. When you turn on the Teams-only mode, the system performs a check to validate if all the SIP domains are pointing to Microsoft Online. If any SIP domains are still pointing to on-premises, it will result in an error. The PowerShell tool will show you the exact error and the SIP domain that is still pointed to on-premises. Here are the commands that you need to run:

```
Grant-CsTeamsUpgradePolicy -PolicyName UpgradeToTeams -Global
```

After switching to Teams-only tenant mode, disable the shared SIP space using this command:

```
Set-CsTenantFederationConfiguration -SharedSipAddressSpace $false
```

Finally, disable the communication between on-premises and Microsoft 365 by running the following command:

```
Get-CsHostingProvider|Set-CsHostingProvider -Enabled $false
```

Step 3: Migrate hybrid application endpoints from on-premises to online.

Hybrid application endpoints use both Teams and Skype for Business servers. Examples include endpoints for call queues and auto attendants. Before you can transition these endpoints to online, it is essential to ensure that you have updated the

DNS records for all SIP domains used by the endpoints to point to Microsoft 365. Once you have updated the DNS records, any existing hybrid application endpoints will no longer be discoverable unless you complete this step. Since it is not possible to create online resource accounts if DNS records are pointing to on-premises, it is recommended that you plan to perform both steps 2 and 3 in the same maintenance window.

To migrate the application endpoints, you need to first identify them. Next, create and associate resource accounts in M365 (refer to the call queue and auto attendant section of Chapter 4). After that, remove the phone numbers associated with the hybrid application endpoints and assign them to the M365 resource accounts. Lastly, delete the hybrid application endpoints using this command:

```
Get-CsHybridApplicationEndpoint | Remove-CsHybridApplicationEndpoint
```

Step 4: Remove on-premises Skype for Business deployment.

After removing all the users accounts in step 1 and hybrid application endpoints in step 3, there are the steps you need to perform to properly decommission the SFB server. Skipping any of the steps may result in an error.

1. Check if there are any contacts or applications associated with the Skype for Business Server on-premises deployment.

    ```
    Get-CsMeetingRoom
    ```

    ```
    Get-CsCommonAreaPhone
    ```

    ```
    Get-CsAnalogDevice
    ```

    ```
    Get-CsExUmContact
    ```

    ```
    Get-CsDialInConferencingAccessNumber
    ```

    ```
    Get-CsRgsWorkflow
    ```

    ```
    Get-CsTrustedApplicationEndpoint
    ```

    ```
    Get-CsTrustedApplication
    ```

    ```
    Get-CsPersistentChatEndpoint
    ```

    ```
    Get-CsAudioTestServiceApplication
    ```

    ```
    Get-CsCallParkOrbit
    ```

    ```
    Get-CsUnassignedNumber
    ```

2. Review the output lists from the cmdlets in step 1. Then if objects can be removed, do this only for on-premises objects.

    ```
    Get-CsMeetingRoom | Disable-CsMeetingRoom
    ```

    ```
    Get-CsCommonAreaPhone | Remove-CsCommonAreaPhone
    ```

    ```
    Get-CsAnalogDevice | Remove-CsAnalogDevice
    ```

    ```
    Get-CsExUmContact | Remove-CsExUmContact
    ```

    ```
    Get-CsDialInConferencingAccessNumber |
    Remove-CsDialInConferencingAccessNumber
    ```

    ```
    Get-CsRgsWorkflow | Remove-CsRgsWorkflow
    ```

    ```
    Get-CsTrustedApplicationEndpoint | Remove-CsTrusted
    ApplicationEndpoint
    ```

    ```
    Get-CsTrustedApplication | Remove-CsTrusted
    Application -Force
    ```

    ```
    Get-CsPersistentChatEndpoint | Remove-CsPersistent
    ChatEndpoint
    ```

    ```
    Get-CsCallParkOrbit | Remove-CsCallParkOrbit -Force
    ```

    ```
    Get-CsVoiceRoute | Remove-CsVoiceRoute -Force
    ```

    ```
    Get-CsUnassignedNumber | Remove-CsUnassigned
    Number -Force
    ```

3. Logically remove the Skype for Business Server deployment, except for a single front end, as follows:

    a. Update your Skype for Business Server topology to have a single front-end pool:

        i. In Topology Builder, download a new copy and navigate to the front-end pool.

        ii. Right-click the pool, and then click Edit Properties.

        iii. In Associations, uncheck Associate Edge Pool (for media components) and click OK.

      iv. If there is more than one front-end pool, remove the associations for all remaining pools.

      v. Select Action ➤ Remove Deployment.

      vi. Select Action ➤ Publish Topology.

  b. After publishing the topology, complete the additional steps described in the wizard.

4. Remove Skype for Business Server conference directories.

```
Get-CsConferenceDirectory | Remove-
CsConferenceDirectory -Force
```

5. Finalize the uninstall of your Skype for Business Server deployment.

```
Publish-CsTopology -FinalizeUninstall
```

6. Remove Central Management Store Service Control Point.

```
Remove-CsConfigurationStoreLocation
```

7. Undo Skype for Business Server Active Directory domain-level changes.

```
Disable-CsAdDomain
```

8. Undo Skype for Business Server Active Directory forest-level changes.

```
Disable-CsAdForest
```

Managing Attributes After Decommissioning

When your Skype for Business users move to the Teams cloud, they still keep certain settings (known as msRTCSIP attributes) from your local server network (on-premises Active Directory).

These settings, like the SIP address and phone number, will keep updating to your cloud-based Azure AD. If you need to change these settings, you have to do it on your local network first, and then it will update in the cloud. Keep in mind, if you've completely removed (decommissioned) your local Skype for Business tools, you won't be able to use them to make these changes.

You've got two choices for dealing with this:

- **Do nothing for now**: Keep the users' Skype for Business settings as they are. You can manage these settings using your local network's Active Directory tools. This way, there won't be any service interruptions for users who have moved to the cloud. You can also get rid of your local Skype for Business tools without fully removing them. But, any new users won't have these settings automatically, and you'll need to set them up online.

- **Start fresh**: Remove all the Skype for Business settings from users on your local network. Then manage these settings with online tools. This makes it easier to manage everyone the same way, whether they're new or existing users. But be cautious, as this might temporarily stop the service during the removal process.

Let's break down how to manage attributes after you've decommissioned Skype for Business.

Method 1: Update User Attributes via Active Directory

Even after moving your Skype for Business users to the cloud and taking down your on-premises deployment, you can still manage their settings.

Modifying SIP Addresses or Phone Numbers

Follow these steps:

1. If a user already has a SIP address or phone number in your local (on-premises) Active Directory, any changes to these must be made there first.

2. These updates will then automatically sync to Azure AD.

3. You don't need Skype for Business tools for this; you can make these changes directly in Active Directory. Do one of the following:

   a. Use the Active Directory Users and Computers tool (specifically the MMC snap-in)

   b. Use PowerShell commands.

Note   In Active Directory, go to the user's properties and then the Attribute Editor tab. From there:

- To change a SIP address, edit `msRTCSIP-PrimaryUserAddress`.

- To change a phone number, if it's already set, edit `msRTCSIP-Line`.

If the ProxyAddresses attribute has a SIP address, update it as well, although Office 365 ignores this if msRTCSIP-PrimaryUserAddress is filled.

If a user didn't have a value for `msRTCSIP-Line` before moving to the cloud, you can modify this using the `-PhoneNumber` parameter in the `Set-CsPhoneNumberAssignment` cmdlet via Teams PowerShell.

There's no need to follow these steps for users created after disabling the hybrid setup; you can manage them directly in the cloud.

Note that if you're comfortable maintaining msRTCSIP attributes in your local Active Directory, you can proceed to shut down your Skype for Business servers. However, if you want to erase all these attributes and traditionally uninstall Skype for Business, then opt for method 2.

Method 2: Remove Skype for Business Attributes from Active Directory On-Premises Users

Choosing this approach necessitates extra care and planning. Two types of users must be considered: those with and without the Phone System feature. Users with a Phone System will temporarily lose phone service during this transition.

Here are the preliminary steps:

1. **Pilot test**: Run a pilot test with a few Phone System users before proceeding with larger batches.

2. **Matching SIP and UPN**: The transition is easier if the SIP address and UserPrincipalName match. If not, take additional precautions.

3. **Endpoints**: Before decommissioning Skype for Business, migrate any hybrid application endpoints like Auto Attendants or Call Queues to Microsoft 365.

Here are the data export steps:

- **Confirm on-premises users**: Make sure that no users are homed on-premises by running the relevant PowerShell command.

- **Backup user data**: Export users' SIP address, UPN, and phone numbers using a PowerShell script and save it as SfbUserSettings.csv.

Note   Double-check the exported data and keep a backup.

Here are the batch preparation steps:

1. **Grouping users**: Create CSV files for user groups you want to process in batches, like SfbUsers.csv.

2. **Verify user data**: Confirm the exported data for these specific user groups.

Here are the attribute deletion steps:

1. **Remove Skype attributes**: Delete Skype for Business attributes from Active Directory for the selected user group.

2. **Warning**: Users with a Phone System will lose call capabilities temporarily until step 8 is successfully executed.

Here are the data restoration steps:

1. **Restore SIP in ProxyAddresses**: Use a PowerShell script to add back the SIP addresses to AD's proxyAddresses.

2. **Trigger Azure AD Sync**: Manually start an Azure AD synchronization.

3. **Monitor provisioning**: Check the user provisioning status via Teams PowerShell.

Here are the Phone Number Reassignment steps:

- **Re-assign phone numbers:** Use a PowerShell command to re-assign phone numbers for Phone System users.

Note   For organizations still using Skype for Business endpoints, set -HostedVoiceMail to $true.

Here are the Verification steps:

- **Do a final check**: Use both on-premises and Teams PowerShell commands to verify that all users have been processed correctly.

After completing method 2, refer to the documentation to move hybrid application endpoints and decommission your Skype for Business Server permanently.

Summary

In summary, as an admin, you must build and implement a readiness plan.

As an administrator, your role is critical in migrating from Skype for Business On-Premises to Microsoft Teams Online. The migration can be structured into several sections, with an emphasis on user readiness and the seamless integration of voice services.

Preparatory work: Before migration, stage crucial configurations such as voice routing policy, dial plans, and online PSTN gateways without disrupting existing user functionalities. This step is essential to ensure a smooth transition and should be done in consultation with your technical team and project manager.

The three-phase approach: Then do the following:

- **Pilot testing**: Conduct an initial pilot to validate both technical infrastructure and user readiness. Use a well-defined test plan and clear metrics for success, and make sure your user sampling is representative of your organization as a whole.

- **Coexistence planning**: Operate Skype for Business and Microsoft Teams in tandem using various upgrade strategies tailored to your organization's needs. This concurrent operation offers a cushion for adjustment.

- **Complete the upgrade**: Shift users to a Teams-only environment. Adopt a phased rollout strategy, allowing for pauses or adjustments as needed. Consistency is key; try not to leave users straddling multiple platforms.

Post-deployment: After deployment, do this:

- **Operational planning:** After full deployment, develop an ongoing operational plan.

- **Performance metrics:** Continually measure the outcomes against your predefined goals and make adjustments as needed.

- **Network monitoring:** Regularly scrutinize network health to ensure optimal user experience.

- **User engagement:** Keep users enthusiastic about the new platform to maximize adoption and ROI.

- **Future planning:** Keep an eye on product updates and innovations to continuously optimize and grow.

- **Decommissioning:** Follow Microsoft's guidelines to safely decommission your Skype for Business Server.

By following this structured approach, you can mitigate risks and ensure a successful, efficient transition to Microsoft Teams Online.

References

- Decommission Skype for Business Server - Skype for Business Hybrid | Microsoft Learn:

  ```
  https://learn.microsoft.com/en-us/skypeforbusiness/hybrid/
  decommission-remove-on-prem#remove-your-on-premises-skype-
  for-business-deployment-1
  ```

- Decide how to manage attributes after decommissioning - Skype for Business Hybrid | Microsoft Learn:

  ```
  https://learn.microsoft.com/en-us/skypeforbusiness/hybrid/
  cloud-consolidation-managing-attributes
  ```

- Understand Microsoft Teams and Skype for Business coexistence and interoperability - Microsoft Teams | Microsoft Learn:

  https://learn.microsoft.com/en-us/microsoftteams/teams-and-skypeforbusiness-coexistence-and-interoperability

CHAPTER 7

Microsoft Teams Troubleshooting Approaches

Balu N Ilag[a]* Vijay Ireddy

[a] Tracy, CA, USA

In this chapter, we delve into the various aspects of troubleshooting Microsoft Teams, covering everything from call quality issues to difficulties with meetings and user sign-ins. We also tackle policy-related challenges, tenant and network configurations, and other scenarios that administrators may encounter. It's important to note that Microsoft Teams operates exclusively in the cloud, meaning the scope of troubleshooting for administrators is somewhat restricted compared to legacy systems like Office Communication, Lync, or Skype for Business. Here, the emphasis is largely on client-side troubleshooting using Microsoft-provided data. The chapter zeroes in on three key areas: resolving user login problems, enhancing call quality for individual and group calls, and addressing issues related to Public Switched Telephone Network (PSTN) calls. Additionally, the chapter will introduce various tools that can aid administrators in troubleshooting efforts.

© Balu N Ilag, Durgesh Tripathy, Vijay Ireddy 2024

B. N. Ilag et al., *Understanding Microsoft Teams Administration*,
https://doi.org/10.1007/979-8-8688-0014-6_7

Basic Troubleshooting Approach Specific to Microsoft Teams

Troubleshooting Microsoft Teams is an essential activity for ensuring seamless communication and collaboration within your organization. Despite its robust features, Microsoft Teams can encounter problems. The following is a comprehensive troubleshooting workflow designed to guide you through resolving common issues step-by-step:

1. **Identify the issue:** Begin by collecting detailed information from the affected user about the problem they're experiencing. This step helps define the issue's scope and nature, giving you a better idea of what you're dealing with.

2. **Check for system requirements:** Verify that the user's device— be it a computer or mobile—fulfills the minimum system requirements for Microsoft Teams. Noncompliant hardware or software can be a root cause for performance hiccups.

3. **Verify network connectivity:** Confirm that the user has stable Internet connectivity. Also, review firewall settings and proxy configurations that may be hampering Teams' ability to connect to the internet.

4. **Update Microsoft Teams:** Ensure that the Microsoft Teams application is updated to the latest version. Outdated software can be riddled with bugs that have been fixed in newer releases.

5. **Reboot or reinstall Teams:** Sometimes, the simplest solutions are the most effective. Try restarting the Teams app or even reinstalling it to solve minor glitches.

6. **Check the service status:** Consult Microsoft's service status page to see if there are any ongoing outages or known issues affecting Teams. This can help determine whether the problem is at your end or Microsoft's.

7. **Review error messages:** Take note of any error codes or messages displayed in Teams. These can be valuable leads in identifying the underlying issue.

8. **Test in safe mode:** If the issue persists, run Teams in safe mode to see if third-party add-ins or plugins could be causing interference.

9. **Clear the cache and cookies:** If the application is sluggish or acting erratically, clearing the web app's cache and cookies might bring performance improvements.

10. **Contact Microsoft Support:** When all else fails, it might be time to consult the experts. Reach out to Microsoft Support for more specialized guidance.

11. **Train users:** In some instances, the problem may not be technical but rather user-related. Ensure that your team is well-versed in how to use Teams to its fullest by offering adequate training and resources.

12. **Monitor for recurrence:** After resolving an issue, don't consider it "case closed." Keep an eye on Teams to make sure the problem doesn't recur. Implementing proactive monitoring can go a long way in preventing future disruptions.

Troubleshooting in Microsoft Teams can be complex and varied, depending on the problem at hand. A methodical approach to diagnosis and resolution will increase your chances of effectively addressing issues, thereby minimizing operational disruptions.

Microsoft Teams Foundation Details for Troubleshooting

Microsoft Teams is a feature-rich platform that enables chat, audio and video calls, meetings, content sharing, and application integration. Understanding the foundational aspects of Teams is crucial for effective troubleshooting. Each of these functionalities is reliant on dependent services that interact to form a cohesive user experience.

Interdependent Services and Licenses

The following are the interdependent services and licenses:

- **Voicemail:** For instance, voicemail messages within Teams are dependent on Exchange Online mailboxes. The Teams client connects to these mailboxes, and voicemail playback requires a specific player.

- **PSTN connectivity:** Teams uses next-generation Calling PSTN, and this functionality is enabled through PSTN Connectivity methods and a Phone System license.

- **Licensing:** It's essential to note that a Teams license is required for user provisioning. If the Skype for Business Online Plan 2 license is deactivated, the corresponding user will be de-provisioned in Teams as well.

Directory Services and Attribute Replication

The following are the directory services:

- **Business Voice Directory:** Microsoft maintains a dedicated business voice directory where user attributes are stored. Reverse Number Lookup (RNL) is performed against these attributes.

- **Attribute issues:** If a phone number appears correctly in Skype for Business Online but results in a "404 not found" error during inbound calls in Teams, this suggests that Teams isn't syncing with the Skype for Business Online directory. Understanding where these attributes are stored and how they sync can save valuable troubleshooting time.

Admin Considerations

As an admin, you should ensure that the necessary Teams services, IP addresses, ports and protocols, URLs, and FQDNs are allowed for each feature to function correctly. The process of troubleshooting should involve the use of core tools specific to Microsoft Teams, collecting diagnostic data, and addressing common issues methodically.

Different Teams features rely on various service URLs, making them critical checkpoints during troubleshooting.

- **Authentication:** Teams login is dependent on `Teams.microsoft.com` and `login.microsoft.com`.

- **Chat and presence:** If chat or presence functionalities are not working as expected, ensure the following URLs are accessible:

  - `amer.ng.msg.teams.microsoft.com` (for one-to-one chat)

  - `chatsvcagg.teams.microsoft.com`

  - `presence.teams.microsoft.com`

  - `northcentralus.notifications.teams.microsoft.com`

- **Calling and live events:** These features rely on service URLs like `api.flightproxy.teams.microsoft.com`, `teams.registrar.prod.v2`, and `broadcast.skype.com`.

- **Settings:** Are dependent on the `config.edge.skype.com`, `config.teams.microsoft.com`, and `teams.api.mt.amer.beta` service URLs.

- **Office 365 and Skype for Business:** Service URLs like `bloguc-my.sharepoint.com`, `bloguc.sharepoint.com`, and `outlook.office.com` are essential for voicemail messages.

- **Telemetry:** Data collection and telemetry rely on URLs such as `pipe.skype.com`, `mobile.pipe.aria.microsoft.com`, and `Watson.telemetry.microsoft.com`.

By having a deep understanding of these foundational details, you can troubleshoot more effectively, pinning down the likely sources of any issues that arise.

Microsoft Teams Sign-in Issues

Let's talk about sign-in issues.

How Teams Authentication Mechanisms Work

Microsoft Teams incorporates modern authentication (MA) protocols by default, enhancing security and streamlining the user sign-in process. Modern authentication lays the groundwork for advanced features such as single sign-on (SSO), which considerably simplifies the user experience in a multiservice ecosystem like Microsoft 365.

The Role of Single Sign-On

Single sign-on plays an integral part in the user authentication process within Microsoft Teams. With SSO, a user has to enter their credentials only once—generally when they first log into their Microsoft 365 or Office 365 account. From that point onward, Teams can recognize that the user has been authenticated through the centralized system, negating the need to repeatedly enter login information. This creates a frictionless sign-in experience while maintaining a high level of security.

Hard-Coded Modern Authentication

Because Microsoft Teams is built with Modern Authentication protocols hard-coded into the application, it has a tight integration with Office 365/Microsoft 365 user accounts. Essentially, the Teams app is configured to automatically recognize and authenticate users based on their linked Office 365/Microsoft 365 credentials.

Troubleshooting Sign-i Issues

If a user encounters issues when trying to log into Teams, the problem usually lies with the associated Office 365/Microsoft 365 account. Common issues might include the following:

- Expired or incorrect passwords

- Inactive or unassigned licenses

- Configuration issues or restrictions in the Microsoft 365 admin center

By understanding how authentication works in Microsoft Teams, both users and administrators can ensure a smoother, more secure communication and collaboration experience.

Teams Sign-in Issues and Corresponding Error Codes

If users receive an error code when logging in to Teams, you, as an admin, must take appropriate action. Table 7-1 shows a list of error codes and the actions that should be taken.

Table 7-1. *Teams Known Issues*

Code	Description	Troubleshooting Action
0xCAA20003	You ran into an authorization problem.	Make sure your date and time are set up correctly. Whether your date and time are accurate will affect your ability to connect to secure sites (HTTPS).
0xCAA82EE2	The request has timed out.	Ensure that you are connected to the Internet. Then work with your IT admin to ensure that other apps or a firewall configuration aren't preventing access.
0xCAA82EE7	The server name could not be resolved.	Ensure that you are connected to the Internet. Then work with your IT admin to ensure that other apps or a firewall configuration aren't preventing access.
0xCAA20004	Your request needs to be approved by a resource owner or authorization server.	Contact your IT admin so they can confirm that your organization is complying with Azure AD configuration policies.
0xCAA90018	You're not using the right credentials.	The Windows credentials you signed in with are different than your Office 365 credentials. Try to sign in again with the correct email and password combination. If you continue to receive this status code, contact your IT admin.
none	You'll need to re-enter your PIN using a smart card.	Reinsert your smart card. Also, your smart card certificate might be corrupt. In that is the case, contact your IT admin.

Microsoft Teams sign-in issues are generally broken into several categories.

- Generally, *authentication issues* happen when users might not be entering their sign-in address (email address) or password correctly, and the Teams back-end service might not authenticate the user. This happens for different reasons.

    - The credentials (email address and password) users entered are incorrect; generally, in Teams, we use User Principal Name (UPN) and password.

    - Teams authentication is also dependent on accurate time information on the user's computer, including the affected user's computer, which is configured to the wrong time zone, or maybe the computer clock is incorrectly set.

- *Teams account provisioning* issues occur if users are not be enabled for Teams, or they are enabled but not authorized to sign in. That can check by checked by logging in to the Office 365 portal. Apart from provisioning, the user account might not be synced correctly to Office 365 (directory synchronization is not happening). To check if an account is enabled for Teams and authorized for sign-in, follow these steps:

    a. Log in to the Office 365 portal (https://admin.microsoft.com/AdminPortal/Home#/users) and navigate to Users. Find the affected user and then open the user properties.

    b. Validate that the Teams license is enabled, and check that the user is allowed for login, as shown in Figure 7-1.

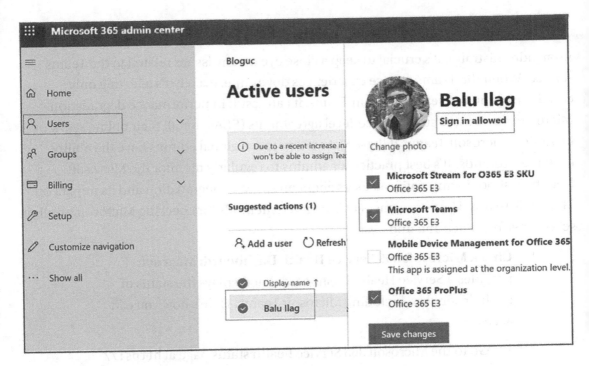

Figure 7-1. *Checking account provisioning*

- *The Microsoft Teams app itself* might have an issue. Perhaps the Teams app is not installed correctly on a user's computer, causing problems with reaching the Office 365/Microsoft services. Maybe the network that the user has connected to has connectivity issues. To resolve the Teams app issue, you could first update Teams and then check that the Internet is working correctly.

- The last category is *Teams back-end cloud service-related issues*. When there are service-related issues, all users in a tenant are affected or some users are affected at the back-end datacenter or region.

- You can collect the Teams diagnostic log and check if there are any issues. When reading these sign-in logs, pay attention to the first few errors or warning messages, as these will indicate the issue.

Teams Service Issues

As an administrator, it's crucial to keep a close eye on any issues related to the Teams service. When the Teams service experiences downtime, even if it's affecting only certain users or app services within Teams, it can result in performance degradation. Microsoft guarantees strict service-level agreements (SLAs) for all their online services, including Microsoft Teams. If these SLAs are not met, global admins have the ability to request refunds. It's best practice for admins to regularly monitor the Microsoft Health Dashboard and notify all users about any service degradation and its impact on Microsoft Teams. Here are some recommended methods for checking Microsoft's online service performance and updates:

1. **Check Microsoft 365 Service Health Dashboard:** Microsoft provides a Service Health Dashboard that displays the status of all their services, including Microsoft Teams. Here's how you can access it:

    - Go to the Microsoft 365 Service health status page at `https://portal.office.com/servicestatus`.

    - Sign in with your Microsoft 365 account.

    - Look for the status of Microsoft Teams. If there's an issue, it will be displayed here.

2. **Check the official Microsoft Teams Twitter account:** The Microsoft Teams Twitter account (`@MicrosoftTeams`) frequently updates about service disruptions, outages, or ongoing issues. They provide valuable information regarding widespread problems.

3. **Check DownDetector or similar websites:** Websites such as DownDetector and Outage.Report collect user feedback to indicate if others are encountering similar problems. You can look up "Microsoft Teams" on these websites to see if there is a surge in reported issues.

4. **Use third-party monitoring tools:** There are third-party monitoring tools available that can alert you in case of any issues with Microsoft Teams or other online services. Some examples of these tools are Pingdom, UptimeRobot, and StatusCake.

5. **Test on different devices and networks:** If you're not sure if the problem is with Microsoft Teams or your Internet, try logging in from different devices such as your computer, phone, or tablet. And check if it works on different networks like your home Wi-Fi, mobile data, or VPN. If it's still not working on any of those, then it's probably something up with Teams itself.

6. **Check for updates or announcements from Microsoft:** Sometimes Microsoft might have announced scheduled maintenance or updates that could impact service availability. Checking the Microsoft 365 blog or announcements might provide additional insight.

Occasional disruptions may occur due to maintenance, updates, or technical issues. Check official channels for status before assuming prolonged outages.

Approaching Teams Issues

Every admin has an individual approach to troubleshooting any issues. Here is the fundamental but beneficial approach that I take whenever dealing with any problem. For example, often admins receive complaints via call, incident report, or email that a user is unable to log in to the Microsoft Teams client. Here is the series of steps you can perform to solve the problem. The most important thing is the approach to the issue.

1. **Understand the problem:** What is not working? Is there any error message provided by the user? If there is not enough information, reach out to the user and make sure you understand the problem first. Once you grasp the problem, move on to step 2.

2. **Check if there is any pattern:** Is more than one user facing the issue? Is the whole site down, or just a single user?

   a. If more than one user is facing a log-in problem, then check if they are located in the same office, on the same network, and so on.

   b. If a single user is affected, check if that user is enabled for Microsoft Teams license. Check if the Teams sign-in ever worked or this is the first time the user is trying to sign in.

      i.   Enabling a Teams license takes up to 12 hours. Typically a license is synced within an hour, but it sometimes takes longer.

     ii.   Check login credentials, as user passwords might have changed, been locked out, or expired.

3. **Check if the problem is with the Teams app:** Try different Teams apps.

    a.   Try with the Teams desktop app (Windows and macOS).

    b.   Use a mobile app (iOS or Android).

    c.   Try with a web browser sign-in using incognito mode (kind of isolated mode).

    d.   If a specific client shows the issue, then clear the client cache and check again.

4. **Check different computers and different networks:** If all Teams apps show an error, then check internal versus external networks (using a mobile hotspot if no external network is available).

5. **Check if Teams login URLs are accessible:** If not, check with your network team to allow Teams communication.

6. If the issue still persists, then you can troubleshoot the issue with the information gathered, or you can open a support case with Microsoft.

Collecting Teams Client Logs

Microsoft Teams has three kinds of log files: debug logs, media logs, and desktop logs. Usually an admin can read debug logs to find the cause of Teams features not working; however, media and desktop logs are needed only if requested by Microsoft Support when you open a support case with Microsoft.

Microsoft Teams makes log collection reasonably easy. Just press a series of keys, and the Teams debug log will be collected and stored in the Downloads folder. Teams have different apps for different platforms, and each Teams app has a different method to collect logs; in addition, their log files are stored in a different location. Here are the details for each Teams app with the process for collecting a log.

First, the Teams debug log is the most common log. It is used for debugging Teams functionality and app-related issues. When you open a case with Microsoft support, they might ask you to generate a debug log. To read this log, you can use any text-based editor.

To generate a debug log for a Teams Windows client, follow this procedure:

1. Log in to the Teams client and then attempt to reproduce the issue, whether it is a call, chat, meeting join, desktop sharing, and so on.

2. While keeping the Teams Windows desktop client open, press Ctrl+Alt+Shift+1 on your keyboard. The Teams debug log is automatically downloaded and saved to the %userprofile%\ Downloads folder, as shown in Figure 7-2.

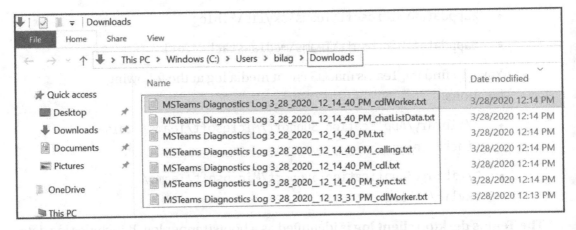

Figure 7-2. *Downloaded Teams debug log*

For a Teams macOS client, follow these steps:

1. Log in to the Teams macOS client and then attempt to reproduce the issue, whether it is a call, chat, meeting join, desktop sharing, and so on.

2. While keeping the Teams desktop client open, press Option+Command+Shift+1 on your keyboard. The Teams debug log will be stored under downloads.

Note   For the web browser, the Teams web app will prompt you to save the debug logs.

The Teams media log includes information about audio and video calling and desktop sharing. This log is needed when you open a Microsoft support case, as it will be inspected by Microsoft Support personnel. You don't have to do anything special to generate this log. It is automatically stored in the following paths.

- You can find the Teams Windows client media log at the following locations:

  - `%appdata%\Microsoft\Teams\media-stack\*.blog`

  - `%appdata%\Microsoft\Teams\skylib\*.blog`

  - `%appdata%\Microsoft\Teams\media-stack\*.etl`

- You can find the Teams macOS client media log at the following locations:

  - `~/Library/Application Support/Microsoft/Teams/media-stack/*.blog`

  - `~/Library/Application Support/Microsoft/Teams/skylib/*.blog`

The Teams desktop client log is identified as a bootstrapper log. It includes log data that occur between the desktop client and the browser. Similar to the media log, this log also is needed primarily when it is requested by Microsoft Support personnel. This log can be viewed via text editors.

To get the desktop log on a Teams Windows client, right-click the Microsoft Teams icon in your application tray, and select Get Logs, as shown in Figure 7-3.

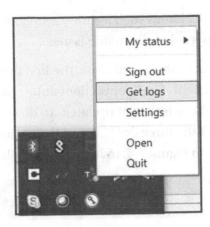

Figure 7-3. *Getting the Teams desktop log*

Teams desktop logs are stored on the path %appdata%\Microsoft\Teams\logs.txt. For the Teams macOS client, from the Help pull-down menu, select Get Logs. Logs are then automatically saved to the path ~/Library/Application Support/Microsoft/ Teams/logs.txt.

Microsoft Teams Client-Side Troubleshooting

This topic covers Microsoft Teams client software installation and connectivity problems. To provide a consistent and positive experience to Teams end users, the client must be properly working without any issues. In this section, you will learn about troubleshooting Teams client installation and update issues, as well as Teams client connectivity issues.

Teams Client-Side Troubleshooting

Microsoft has provided Teams client apps for desktop (Windows and macOS), mobile (iOS and Android), Linux clients, and web clients. Users get similar experiences using these clients.

The Teams client is part of the Office 365 suite, so when the user installs Office 365 ProPlus as Click to Run, the Teams client is automatically installed. Admins can perform a managed Microsoft Installer (MSI) install as well.

If the Teams client is having issues such as not starting, restarting, hanging, and so on, then follow these steps to resolve client-side issues:

1. When the Teams client shows the issue, the first thing to do is update the Teams client. The Teams client auto-updates, but it is best practice to check for client updates. To do so, next to your profile picture, click the three dot (...) and then select Check For Updates, as shown in Figure 7-4, to install any available updates.

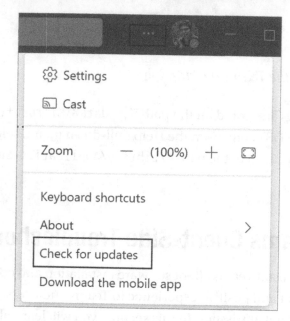

Figure 7-4. *Checking for Teams client updates (desktop client)*

2. If the issue persists after the Teams client updates, the next thing to do is check the client installer log. When the Teams client is installed, the Teams installer logs track the sequence of events. The installer log can be found at `%LocalAppData%\SquirrelTemp\SquirrelSetup.log`. Check this log to see if there is any error message or a call stack near the end of the log. Note that call stacks at the beginning of the log might not mean that an installation issue exists. It can be easier to compare the affected computer log against the log from a successful installation (even on another computer) to see what is expected.

3. If an issue persists, then uninstall the Teams client entirely and then log in to the Teams web client using `https://teams.microsoft.com`. Perform a desktop install by clicking the profile picture and then downloading and installing the Teams desktop app.

Microsoft Teams has various limitations and expiration periods applied for each feature: persistent chat, voice and video calls, meeting, application sharing, file sharing, and so on. In Microsoft Teams, every workload has a different maximum limit set by Teams (back-end) services. Here I elaborate on maximum limits and expirations for Teams meetings, chat, live events, PowerPoint file uploads in a meeting, file store, and so on.

As an admin, you must know when and how Teams expiration and the maximum limit applies. This information will save troubleshooting time, so carefully review these limits and specifications.

Microsoft Teams Meeting Expiration and Time Limits: What You Need to Know

First, it's crucial to understand that a meeting URL in Microsoft Teams is designed to be perpetual; it will never expire. However, this does not apply to PSTN dial-in numbers, CVI coordinates, and specific meeting policies and settings, which do have expiration timelines.

Here are meeting-specific expirations:

- **Meet Now:** These spontaneous meetings will expire eight hours after they start. No extensions are applicable for Meet Now types.

- **Regular meeting without end time:** Such meetings will expire 60 days after their start time. If the meeting is initiated or updated, the 60-day expiration counter resets.

- **Regular meeting with end time:** These expire 60 days after their scheduled end time. Again, starting or updating the meeting resets the 60-day expiration time.

- **Recurring meeting without end time:** These types of meetings will also expire 60 days from their start time, and the counter resets upon each new meeting or update.

- **Recurring meeting with end time:** The expiration for these meetings occurs 60 days after the end time of the last occurrence in the series. The expiration time will reset if the meeting is updated.

It's worth noting that all Microsoft Teams meetings have an overall time limit of 30 hours, irrespective of the meeting type.

By understanding these expiration timelines and time limits, you can better manage your Microsoft Teams meetings, ensuring that you are in compliance with platform policies and making the most out of your collaborative efforts.

Microsoft Teams Meeting and Call Capacity: A Detailed Overview

Depending on your subscription plan, Microsoft Teams offers varied capacity limits for hosting online meetings and video calls. With plans like Microsoft 365 Business Basic, Business Standard, Business Premium, and Microsoft 365 A1, the platform allows up to 300 participants in a meeting. However, if you're subscribed to Microsoft 365 E3/E5, A3/A5, or Government G3/G5 plans, you can extend this limit to host meetings

For direct audio or video calls initiated from a chat, Microsoft Teams allows a maximum of 20 participants.

When it comes to sharing PowerPoint files in Teams, the maximum file size allowed is 2GB.

Teams offers local download availability for meeting recordings that aren't uploaded to Microsoft Stream; these recordings will be accessible for 20 days. Additionally, the maximum duration for a single meeting recording is limited to either 4 hours or 1.5GB. Upon reaching either of these limits, the recording will automatically stop and then restart.

It's important to note that breakout rooms can be created only in meetings with fewer than 300 participants. If you initiate breakout rooms in a meeting, the maximum participant count will automatically be capped at 300.

Note   There is no limit set on how many Teams meeting can be hosted in one Office 365 tenant.

What Is the Maximum PowerPoint Presentation File Size Allowed in a Team Meeting?

Teams allows sharing content in Teams meetings and peer-to-peer calls. You can share and present PowerPoint presentations in a Teams meeting, for example. However, there is a specific file size limit allowed, up to 2GB. You cannot share or upload files larger than 2GB in Teams meetings.

What Is the Maximum Audience Limit of Teams Live Events?

Microsoft Teams live events are used for large broadcast meetings, such as all-staff meetings. The live event audience size maximum limit is 20,000 attendees, and the maximum duration is 4 hours. A user can host concurrent live events in an Office 365 tenant. However, as of this writing, you can host a maximum of 15 concurrent Teams live events in your organization.

What Is the Maximum Limit in Teams and Channels?

Microsoft Teams does have a maximum limit specified for Teams and channels features. Here is the list of features with their limits:

- The maximum number of teams a user can create is 250. Remember, for the 250-object limit, any directory object in Azure AD counts toward this limit. Global admins are exempt from this limit.

- The maximum number of teams a user can be a member of is 1,000. Individual users therefore cannot be part of more than 1,000 teams.

- The maximum number of members in a team is 25,000.

- The maximum number of owners per team is 100. It is a best practice to have at least two owners of a team to handle a single-point failure situation.

- The number of organization-wide teams allowed in any Teams tenant organization is five, so use the organization-wide teams wisely.

- The maximum number of members in an organization-wide team is 10,000, so you cannot have more than 10,000 members in one organization-wide team (the previous limit was 5,000 members).

- The number of teams a global admin can create is 500,000.

- The number of teams an Office 365 tenant can have is 500,000. This limit includes archived teams.

- The number of channels per team is limited to 200, which includes deleted channels. Please note that if you deleted a channel, the channel still counts into the limit until 30 days of the deletion. Please take action when the channel limit comes close to the maximum limit.

- Another significant limitation in Teams is that each team can have a maximum of 30 private channels, so use private channels carefully and create them only when it is required.

Note   In Teams, deleted channels can be restored within 30 days. During these 30 days, a deleted channel continues to be counted toward the 200 channel per team limit. After 30 days, a deleted channel and its content are permanently deleted, and the channel no longer counts toward the limit.

Microsoft Teams Chat Limitations

In Teams, users who participate in chat conversations must have an Exchange Online (cloud-based) mailbox for an admin to search chat conversations. That's because conversations that are part of the chat list are stored in the cloud-based mailboxes of the chat participants. If a chat participant doesn't have an Exchange Online mailbox, the admin won't be able to search or place a hold on chat conversations. For example, in an Exchange hybrid deployment, users with on-premises mailboxes might be able to participate in conversations that are part of the chat list in Teams. However, users need at least an Exchange Online Plan 1 license for Legal Hold and eDiscovery in this case. So, keep this limitation in mind when you are using an Exchange hybrid environment.

Teams chat works on an Exchange back end, so Exchange messaging limits apply to the chat function within Teams as well. The maximum number of people in a private chat is 250.

If you have more than 20 people in a chat conversation, then the chat features such as Outlook automatic replies, Teams status messages, typing indicator, video and audio calling, sharing, and read receipts are turned off.

Another limitation is for files. The maximum number of file attachments in a chat conversation is 10. If the number of attachments exceeds this limit, then the chat participants will see an error message. The maximum chat size is approximately 28KB per post.

Teams Emailing a Channel Limitation

Sending an email to a team is a frequently used feature. If users want to send an email to a channel in Teams, they use the channel email address. When an email is part of a channel, anyone can reply to it to start a conversation. Here are some of the applicable limits for sending email to a channel:

- The message size limitation is 24KB. If the message exceeds this limit, a preview message is generated, and the user is asked to download and view the original email from the link provided.

- The next limitation is for attachments. The number of file attachments is limited to 20. If the number of attachments or images exceeds this limit, the user will see an error message.

- The attachment size of each file is up 10MB. You cannot attach a file larger than 10MB while sending to Teams.

- The limitation for the number of inline images is 50.

Note   Message size, file attachment, and inline image limits are the same across all Office 365 licenses.

What Is the Limitation for Teams Channel Names?

Microsoft Teams channel names cannot contain characters or words such as ~ # % & * { } + / \ : < > ? | ' ", . or characters in the ranges 0 to 1F and 80 to 9F.

Additionally, the words forms of CON, CONIN$, CONOUT$, PRN, AUX, NUL, COM1 to COM9, LPT1 to LPT9, desktop.ini, and _vti_ are not allowed. Also, Teams channel names cannot start with an underscore (_) or period (.), or end with a period (.).

Teams Client Connectivity Troubleshooting

Sometimes users face connection issues when trying to connect to Teams. The problem often occurs when the client cannot connect with the Microsoft cloud. Here are some tips to try when users face connectivity issues:

- Check if the Internet connection is working fine if you are working from home.

- If users face network issues from office locations, a majority of Teams connectivity issues are due to the corporate firewall or proxy blocking Teams service URLs, FQDNs, IP addresses, or ports. It is worth verifying that the required URLs, FQDNs, and IP addresses are allowed through a corporate firewall or proxy. To get a list of Teams URLs, FQDN, IP addresses, and ports, visit the Microsoft document at `https://support.office.com/article/Office-365-URLs-and-IP-address-ranges-8548a211-3fe7-47cb-abb1-355ea5aa88a2`.

- Quit the Microsoft Teams application and relaunch Microsoft Teams.

- Signing out of Microsoft Teams and resigning in with username and password.

- Clear the cache from your device. Clearing the cache for Windows and Mac are explained in the earlier section.

- If you are still facing the issue, log in to the web client by going to `https://teams.microsoft.com/`. If you are able to sign in to the web client, uninstall the Teams client and reinstall it.

Troubleshooting Audio and Video Call Quality in Microsoft Teams

Microsoft Teams offers real-time voice and video interactions through its VoIP features, along with various other functionalities. However, users may encounter issues such as audio disruptions, video pixelation, or disconnections during calls and meetings. Most of these problems stem from network inefficiencies or limitations on the user's device. Understanding and proactively addressing these issues can enhance the user experience and encourage the continued use of Microsoft Teams for organizational communication.

Common Issues and Their Causes

Here are some common issues:

- **Jitter:** This occurs when media data arrives at inconsistent rates, leading to incomplete or garbled audio. It's as if words or syllables get swallowed during the conversation.

- **Packet loss:** This refers to instances where segments of data are lost during transmission. This not only degrades the quality of the voice but can make speech almost unintelligible.

- **Latency:** Also known as round-trip time (RTT), latency results in a noticeable delay between the sender and receiver. This can lead to awkward conversational overlaps as both parties may begin speaking simultaneously due to the lag.

These issues generally arise from network complications such as high packet loss, latency, and jitter, which could also be compounded by resource limitations on the user's device.

Solutions for Better Quality

To rectify these quality concerns, consider implementing quality of service (QoS) settings, which can help prioritize Teams traffic over your network. By doing so, you allocate dedicated bandwidth for Teams' real-time applications, mitigating the impact of other bandwidth-consuming activities such as large file transfers or video streaming.

Here are some steps administrators can take:

- **Immediate issue resolution:** As soon as quality issues are reported or noticed, immediate action should be taken to identify the root cause. Diagnostic tools can help isolate the issue to either network conditions or user device constraints.

- **Consult network admin:** Collaboration with network administrators is essential for optimizing network settings. They can adjust firewall configurations and routing settings to reduce latency, packet loss, and jitter.

- **QoS implementation:** QoS is a vital feature that helps allocate network resources more efficiently. Please refer to Chapter 3 for detailed guidelines on implementing QoS and other advanced solutions such as split-tunnel VPNs.

By addressing these issues strategically, you enhance the overall Teams experience, making it a more reliable tool for both internal and external communications.

Teams Audio and Video Call Quality Issues and Dependency

Let's talk about call quality issues and dependencies.

Network

Optimal call quality in Teams is dependent on good network conditions. The Teams apps will highlight network connectivity issues during the call, as shown in the example in Figure 7-5, which shows poor network conditions. Use a Network Assessment Tool to investigate network conditions and switch connectivity (e.g., wireless to wired) if possible. Expect a higher quality on a managed corporate network than on an unmanaged network like public Wi-Fi.

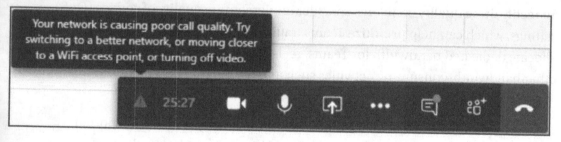

Figure 7-5. Bad network quality in a Teams meeting

Device

For the best audio and video quality, avoid using built-in audio devices; instead, use a USB device listed at https://www.microsoft.com/en-us/microsoft-teams/across-devices/devices. These devices are certified for the best audio and video quality. Here are a few best practices for troubleshooting devices:

- If a computer does not recognize a USB device, then connect the device to a different USB port, as the port might have an issue.

- Try connecting the device directly to the computer; avoid a USB hub for the headset or camera.

- Installing the latest device driver might remediate some audio and video quality issues. Using a headset on the microphone/line-in port of your computer is not a suitable replacement for a USB device, as these devices are also dependent on the computer's audio devices.

- Using a USB headset (headphones) prevents your microphone from picking up audio from your computer or background noise. Sometimes the sound is amplified and passed in and out frequently, resulting in unpleasant, loud static or scream. Remember, using a headset helps to eliminate sources of echo as well.

- If you are unable to use a headset, try to put as much distance as possible between your speakers and microphone to minimize any background noise.

- If you are planning to use a built-in audio device (considering the previously mentioned problems), set up your audio device correctly to manage your Windows audio device.

  a. First search for *Manage Audio Devices*. Select Recording and then select the playback device (headset) that you want to set as default for Teams as well as the computer. For example, in Figure 7-6, I selected Microphone Array (Realtek High Definition Audio).

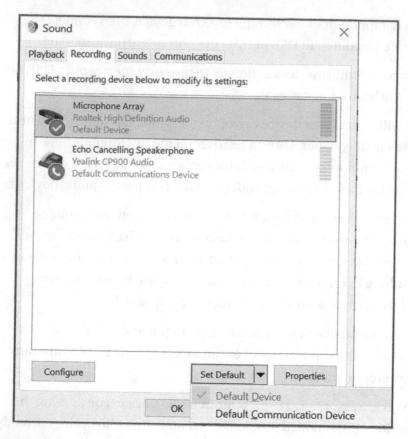

Figure 7-6. *Selecting a device and setting it as the default*

b. Click Properties to set the advanced options. Select the
   Enhancements tab and then select the Acoustic Echo
   Cancellation (AEC) and Far Field Pickup (FFP) check boxes, as
   shown in Figure 7-7.

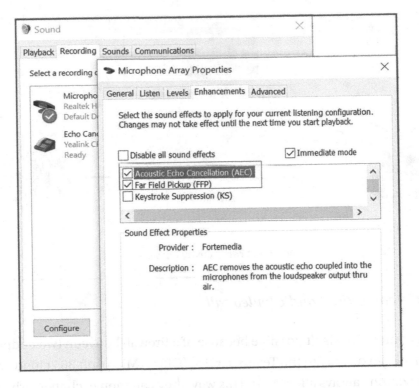

Figure 7-7. Properties for a recording device

How Teams Audio and Video Calls Work

Teams allow one-to-one audio and video calls as well as multiparty meetings. First, understand how a one-to-one audio and video calls work. For example, user Balu is calling user Chanda. Teams clients always send their chat service (signaling) traffic to the Teams service (Office 365 cloud) over 443/TCP. Refer to `https://learn.microsoft. com/en-us/microsoft-365/enterprise/urls-and-ip-address-ranges?view=o365- worldwide#skype-for-business-online-and-microsoft-teams` for port numbers and FQDNs used by Teams.

Teams audio/video and desktop sharing media traffic will prefer a direct connection over UDP. Teams prefer the most direct connection possible. To establish a connection in Teams, leverage the Interactive Connectivity Establishment (ICE) protocol to find the most optimal path to send media. In the example shown in Figure 7-8, direct connectivity between user Balu's computer and user Chanda's computer is possible, and both clients can send media directly between them.

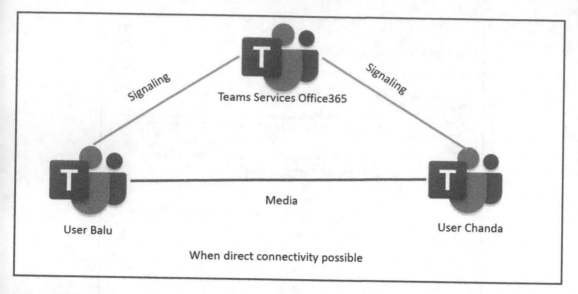

Figure 7-8. *Teams direct audio/video call*

If direct connectivity isn't possible because of a firewall between two endpoints, chat and content still go directly to the Teams service (Office/Microsoft 365 cloud) via 443 (most organizations always allow 443). This way, they can then exchange private chat, files, and so on. They also contribute to the same channels; as you can see in Figure 7-9, the firewall between them is not a problem for signaling traffic.

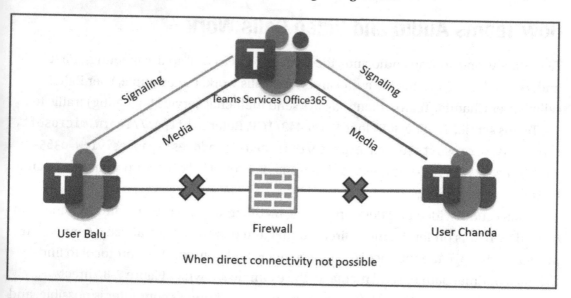

Figure 7-9. *Teams audio/video call via relay*

However, when they start the audio/video real-time session, the firewall blocks their traffic because a direct connection is not possible. In this situation, Teams uses a relay. Basically, user Balu will establish a connection with Office/Microsoft 365, and user Chanda will also establish a connection with Office 365 for this session. Office 365 Relay will proxy any real-time traffic to another relay to another user. User Balu and user Chanda can talk to each other even though there is no direct connectivity. Office/Microsoft 365 functions as a relay for the media traffic, if direct connections are not possible. This media path is not optimal because all client traffic has to go to the Office/Microsoft 365 relay first and then to other users, so this will affect latency and network jitter, but at least Teams allows audio and video instead of no call, which is important.

Teams typically use UDP on ports 3478-3481. If UDP is unavailable, Teams can fall back to TCP on port 443, but with suboptimal call quality.

There are some built-in tools in the Teams service that help you identify a call quality problem. For any issue, without identifying it, you cannot resolve it. Teams provide two tools, Call Analytics and Call Quality Dashboard (CQD), to use when you encounter call quality problems.

Call Analytics

This is my favorite tool, and I frequently use this when I troubleshoot individual users' call quality issues. Call Analytics provides detailed information about the user of the device connected, networks (internal or external, wired or wireless), and connectivity related to specific calls and meetings for each user in a Microsoft Teams or Skype for Business account. You, as an admin, can use Call Analytics to troubleshoot call quality and connection problems experienced in a specific call or meeting using the Teams admin center.

To access Call Analytics that can help you to identify and eliminate problems, follow these steps:

1. Log in to the Teams admin center and navigate to Users. Find the user who encountered a problem and then select that user to open the user's account properties. On the user page, on the right side, you can find the user's quality, activity, and active meetings. Click the quality to check the user's last 7 days' quality or troubleshoot live meetings by clicking "view active meetings."

2. Click "Meetings & calls," which will show the detailed call history for the user, including the recent meetings and the past meetings. This section shows one-to-one calls and meeting audio quality. Figure 7-10 is a sample "Meetings & calls" tab.

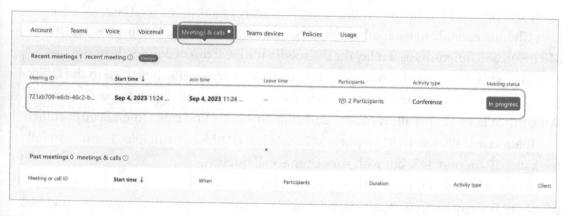

Figure 7-10. *Call Analytics*

3. When you select a particular meeting or call, you will see the call quality details, including device, system, connectivity, and network details. For example, in the example shown in Figure 7-11, I selected a call between Balu and Reva, which was marked as having poor audio quality. Clicking Network, it shows the average packet loss was more than 14 percent, which is very high, and the maximum packet loss rate was more than 25 percent, which is why the audio quality is marked as poor. The statistics also include network quality, including RTT (latency), jitter, and packet loss.

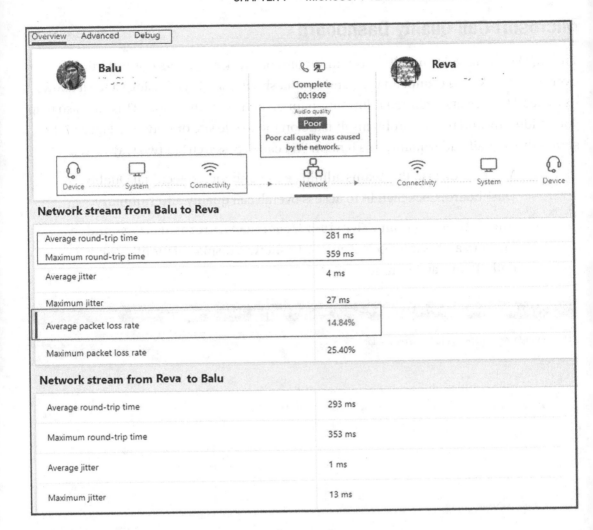

Figure 7-11. *One-to-one call network statistics*

4. If you are interested in doing a deeper dive, then click the
    Advanced tab or Debug tab, both of which show more details
    on what IP address, protocol, and port were used for the media
    session.

Microsoft Call Quality Dashboard

The CQD is designed to help Teams admins and network engineers optimize their overall network. You cannot analyze and troubleshoot a single call using CQD. It allows us instead to look at combined information for an entire organization. This can also help you to identify and reduce problems that are on the whole site or network. Figure 7-12 shows the overall audio quality in a tenant. You can access CQD in two ways.

- You can log in to the Teams admin center and then select Call Quality Dashboard. Click Sign In to access overall call quality and summary.

- Alternatively, you can visit https://cqd.teams.microsoft.com/ and log in to access the CQD. Figure 7-12 shows a display of monthly and daily Teams audio trends.

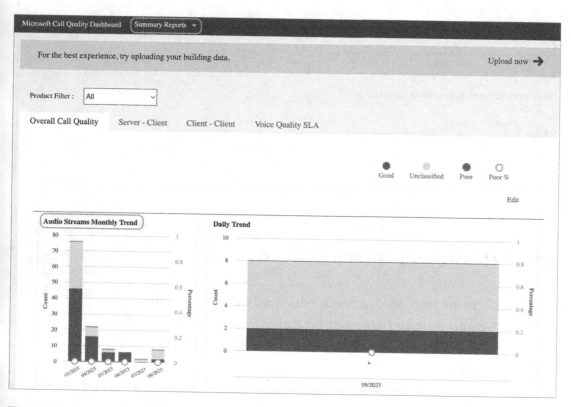

Figure 7-12. *CQD displaying overall call quality*

The Call Quality Dashboard offers basic reporting features that allow administrators to review the quality of audio, video, and client connectivity during meetings. However, to fully utilize the potential of this dashboard, administrators can upload building data. This building data, in the form of a CSV file, contains essential information about a building's location, subnets, and subnet masks associated with it. By uploading this data, administrators can better understand the call quality metrics and how they relate to a building's network infrastructure.

To upload the building data to the call quality dashboard, follow these steps:

- Navigate to `https://cqd.teams.microsoft.com/` and log in using Teams admin credentials. Table 7-2 lists the roles that grant admin permissions to upload tenant data.

Table 7-2. *Teams Role and Permission to Upload Tenant and Report View*

Roles	View reports	View EUII fields	Create reports	Upload building data
Global Administrator	Yes	Yes	Yes	Yes
Teams Service Administrator	Yes	Yes	Yes	Yes
Teams Communications Administrator	Yes	Yes	Yes	No
Teams Communications Support Engineer	Yes	Yes	Yes	No
Teams Communications Support Specialist	Yes	No	Yes	No
Skype for Business Administrator	Yes	Yes	Yes	Yes
Global Reader	Yes	Yes	Yes	No
Reports Reader1	Yes	No	Yes	No

- To upload tenant data, click the settings and select "upload tenant data." Then, choose Building as the data type file. Before selecting a file, ensure that the building data file is complete. The CSV file must be filled with accurate information to reflect the data. Her Table 7-3 shows the file format for the CSV file.

Table 7-3. *Building Data Format*

Column name	Data Type	Example	Guidance
NetworkIP	String	192.168.1.0	Required
NetworkName	String	USA/Seattle/SEATTLE-SEA-1	Required[1]
NetworkRange	Number	26	Required
BuildingName	String	SEATTLE-SEA-1	Required[1]
OwnershipType	String	Contoso	Optional[4]
BuildingType	String	IT Termination	Optional[4]
BuildingOfficeType	String	Engineering	Optional[4]
City	String	Seattle	Recommended
ZipCode	String	98001	Recommended
Country	String	US	Recommended
State	String	WA	Recommended
Region	String	MSUS	Recommended
InsideCorp[2]	Bool	1	Required
ExpressRoute[3]	Bool	0	Required
VPN	Bool	0	Optional

- Please make sure to fill in all the necessary information for each site, and use CIDR subnets. Remember to use 1 and 0 to indicate YES or NO in the last three columns

Once the document has been filled in correctly, remove the headers (first row), save the file as a CSV, and upload the data. Finally, select the desired date and click Upload. Keep in mind that it may take up to 24 hours, and sometimes 48 to 72 hours, for the data to be displayed. If you encounter any errors while uploading the file, ensure that the headers have been removed.

Administrators can view building network data after 24 hours and select from available reports. Once the CQD dashboard with building data becomes available, it can be used as a data source to connect with intelligent tools like Power BI. Power BI is a powerful tool that can help create interactive and insightful dashboards. By creating a call quality dashboard with Power BI templates, administrators can easily visualize and analyze call quality data in an effective manner. Microsoft provides Power BI templates, including quality of experience reports, auto-attendant and call queue historical reports, devices reports, summary reports, etc. Administrators can download Power BI templates from the Microsoft download center (`https://www.microsoft.com/en-us/download/details.aspx?id=102291`). If administrators are planning to use these templates, here are recommended steps:

1. Check if your computer already has the folder named `[Documents]\Power BI Desktop\Custom Connectors`. If you can't find it, create this folder now. Once done, download or use the connector file (`*.pqx` file) that you have received and place it in the Custom Connectors directory you created in earlier

2. Next, launch Power BI Desktop and select File ➤ Options and settings ➤ Options ➤ Security. Under Data Extensions, locate the option that says "(Not Recommended) Allow any extension to load without validation or warning" and select it. By doing so, you will be able to load the connector file without any issues. Refer to Figure 7-13 to see the security options in Power BI.

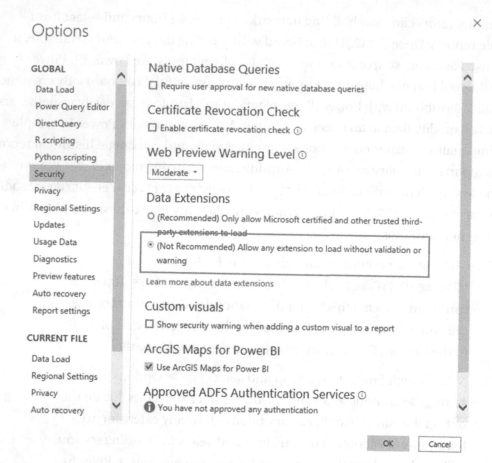

Figure 7-13. *Power BI security options*

3. Select the OK button and then restart Power BI Desktop. Next, navigate to File and select Open Reports, followed by Browse Reports. Change the file type to Power BI Template files (*.pbit). Finally, locate and select the QER template you downloaded, and then click Open.

4. If you are prompted, sign in to the Microsoft Call Quality Dashboard using your administrative credentials that have access to the CQD. Once you have signed in, the template will open, and you will be connected to the CQD. You can confirm that you are connected to the CQD by checking the Fields pane for a list of dimensions and measures.

Teams Phone System Call Troubleshooting

Microsoft Teams only supports E.164 format numbers, so make sure to configure E.164 format phone numbers.

Customizing Call Features in Teams Client

In Teams client, you can configure how you want to handle incoming calls. To do so, log in to the Teams (desktop) client and then click your profile picture. Click Settings and then click "Calls, In" to configure how you want to handle calls. You might want to ring calls to your Teams client, or you might want to forward phone calls to a different phone number. Here are the steps:

1. When you select the Calls Ring Me option, you can also choose the Also Ring option to simultaneously ring another phone number.

2. Select If Unanswered, and then select Send To Voicemail, Another Number Or Call Group, or Do Nothing, which is the default.

3. If you opt to redirect to another number, then enter the period after which you want to redirect this call. The example in Figure 7-14 shows 40 seconds. The default is 20 seconds before the unanswered call is forwarded to a PSTN number.

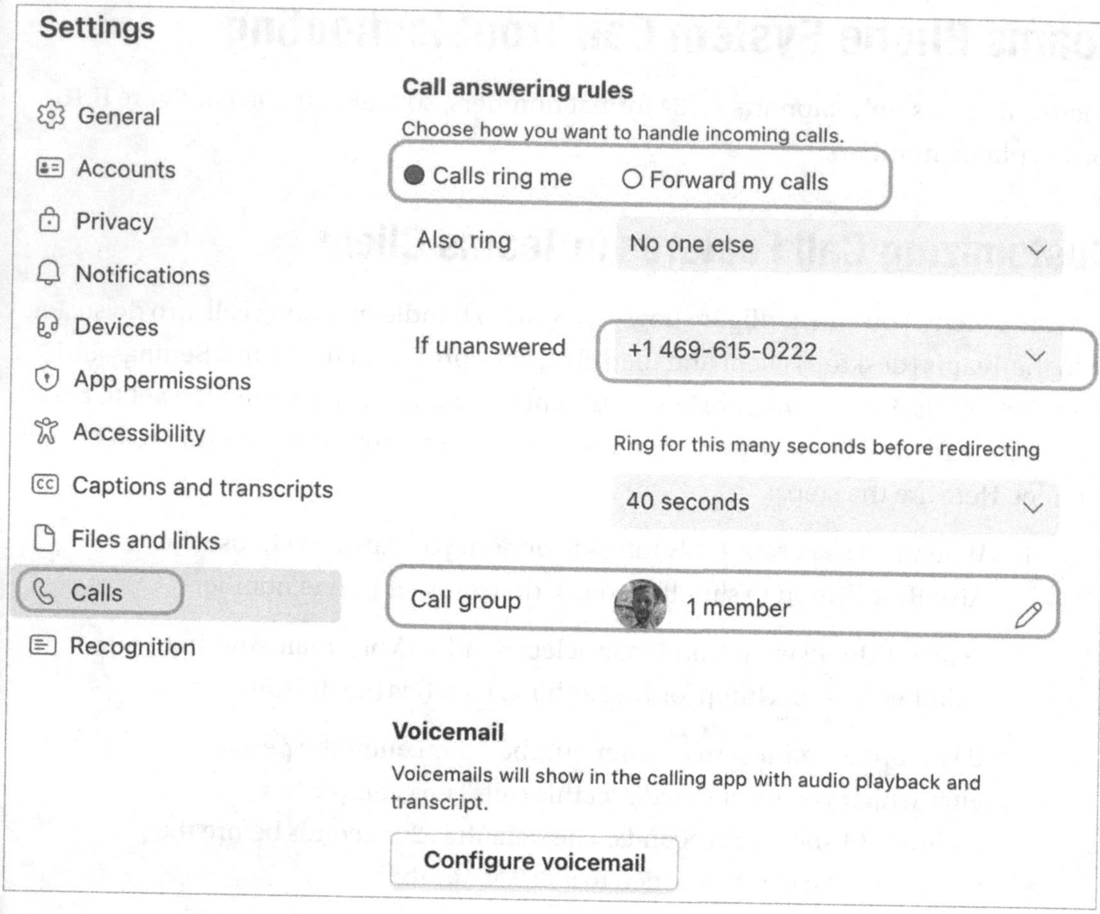

Figure 7-14. *Call answering options*

All these features matter for the user experience, and the settings are quite self-explanatory.

Phone Dial Pad Is Missing in Teams

In Teams, if a dial pad is missing, users cannot make outbound calls (but users can receive inbound calls). There are some prerequisites that need to be fulfilled to have a phone dial pad in the Teams client. Ensure the following things are in place to use a phone dial pad in Teams:

1. Users must have a valid Teams Phone System (Microsoft 365 Phone System) license assigned.

2. Users should have enterprise voice enabled. If not, then run this PowerShell command to enable the user for enterprise voice in Teams:

    ```
    Set-CsUser -Identity "<User name>"
    -EnterpriseVoiceEnabled $true -HostedVoiceMail $true
    ```

3. If you are using Teams Direct Routing, then make sure users have an OnpremiseLineURI number assigned or Microsoft Calling Plan and online phone number assigned to the user.

4. To work with outbound calls, assign a voice routing policy with proper PSTN usage and routes.

Troubleshooting Call Failures with Call Analytics

Whenever Teams client attempts a phone call, it captures some call quality and diagnostics information. That information is used by the Teams service and analyzed by Teams Call Analytics. Teams Call Analytics is the best tool to check call failures.

To access Call Analytics, you must have the appropriate permissions. To access Call Analytics, log in to the Teams admin center, navigate to Users, and then find the user you want to access. Once the user page opens, click Call History and then find the PSTN call that has a problem. For example, Figure 7-15 shows a short call that has an issue.

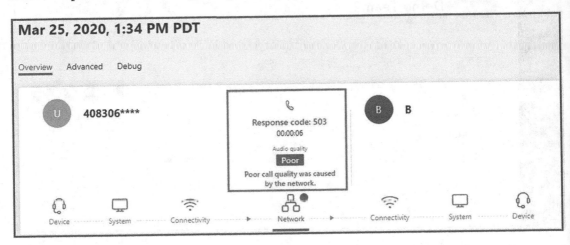

Figure 7-15. *Teams PSTN call*

There are different call failures and codes you might see in Call Analytics such as Response code 486, Response code 408, Failed destination does not exist, 404 not found, and so on.

Unable to Connect to Voicemail in Teams

If you are unable to connect to voicemail using the Teams client, then the first thing you can do is download the Teams diagnostics log. For Windows, press Ctrl+Alt+Shift+1; for macOS, use Command+Option+Shift+1. Open the downloaded log file and search for Voicemail-List, and then review any ERR messages. That is your signal to troubleshoot the issue further.

Understand that Microsoft Teams is tightly integrated with Exchange (Outlook), and if there is an issue, then Teams and Outlook connectivity will be broken. Check that Outlook is connecting, and check the user credentials.

Restoring a Deleted Channel

A team owner can restore a deleted channel. To restore a deleted channel, navigate to Teams. Then next to the team's name, click more options (...), and select Manage Channel. Click the Channels tab and then expand the Deleted section. Click Restore, as shown in Figure 7-16.

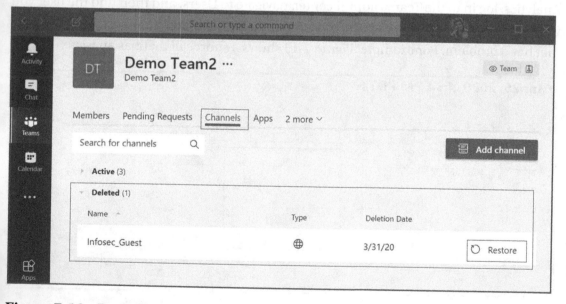

Figure 7-16. *Restoring a deleted channel*

Available Tools for Effective Troubleshooting

Microsoft Teams is dependent on different Office 365 services, such as SharePoint Online, Exchange Online, Skype next-gen, OneDrive for Business, and so on. Therefore, if a dependent service fails, it directly affects Teams performance. This makes checking Teams service health, network connectivity, and performance very important.

Verifying the Teams Service's Health Using the Health Tool

To ensure the overall health of Microsoft Teams, you can use Service Health, Message Center, and Directory Sync status subtools provided by Microsoft. You can find Service Health for Microsoft Teams on the main page of the Office/Microsoft 365 admin portal. It is highly recommended that you frequently check and validate Teams through Service Health. In case you encounter any issues with the Teams service, it is important to first confirm that the Teams service is healthy before doing any further troubleshooting.

Microsoft Teams is built on top of Office 365 services, so when checking Service Health, consider checking the status of Exchange, SharePoint, and OneDrive for Business. Service Health issues for these other services do not automatically mean that Teams is affected (e.g., Address Book downloads in Exchange are unavailable), but you should review the advisories for those affected services to determine if there is an impact to Microsoft Teams.

As an admin, it is important to stay up to date with Microsoft Teams' service improvements and feature updates. To do this, keep an eye on the Microsoft's official documentation, notifications, and alerts. If there is any service degradation, you will receive a message, notification, or alert. Therefore, it is essential to check the Message Center regularly, which is located in the Office 365 admin center under Health. You can access the Message Center by navigating to Health and then selecting Message Center, as shown in Figure 7-17.

Figure 7-17. *Message center showing active and unread messages*

Checking Teams Service Health

Frequently checking the health of Teams and dependent services is highly recommended. You can automate service health notification by setting email, so whenever service degradation happens, you will receive an email alert. To set an email for notification, log in to the Microsoft admin center and navigate to Health. Select Service Health, and then click Customize. In the email window, turn on "send me email notifications about Service Health" and add two email addresses that can receive a proactive notification via email, as shown in Figure 7-18.

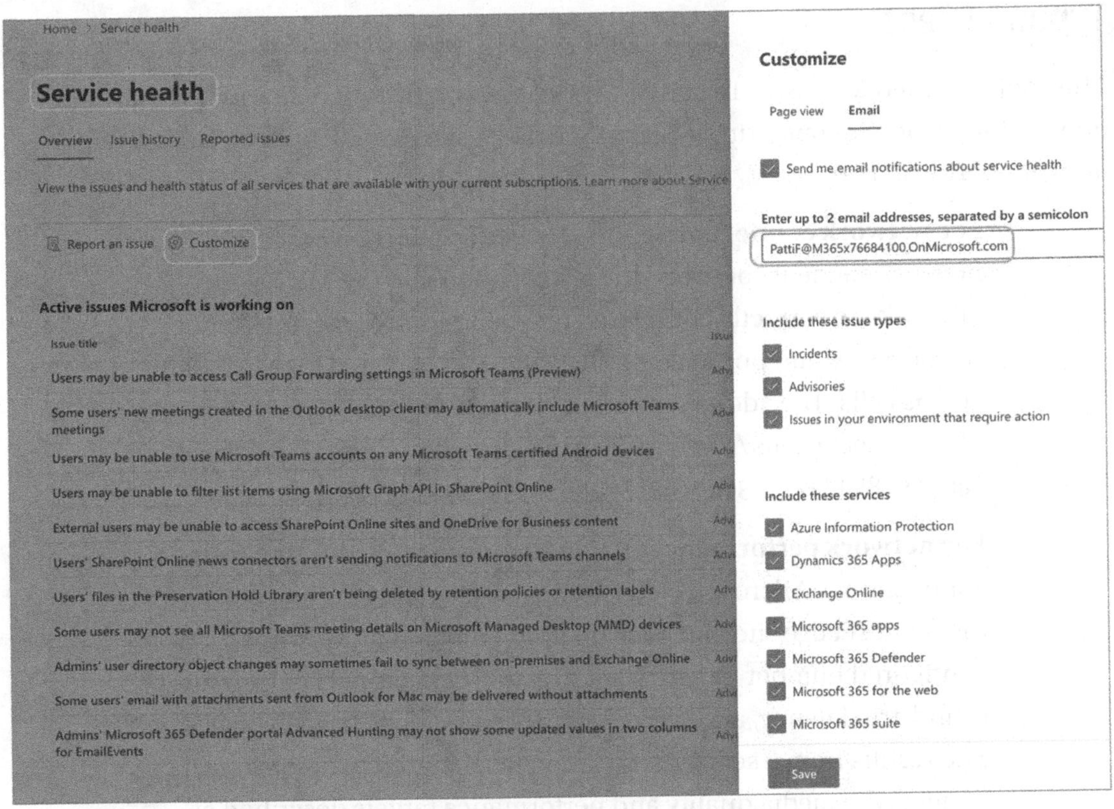

Figure 7-18. *Service Health email notification settings*

Once you add a new email address or change the existing email address, it could take up to 8 hours for these changes to take effect. Sometimes it can take up to 12 hours to apply a policy, although in general they take an hour. Microsoft has a 24-hour SLA for any policy changes to apply because the Teams service resides in Office/Microsoft 365 cloud, and user objects might be on-premises.

Microsoft Teams Network Assessment Tool

When a user reports connectivity and quality issues during Teams calls, you can use the Network Assessment Tool to test network connectivity and quality from the user's location to Teams media services. This tool is very useful in analyzing network quality by running a set of packets to the closest edge site and back for approximately 20 seconds, for a configured number of iterations. The Network Assessment Tool helps in analyzing the connection to Microsoft Network Edge (peering point).

Types of Test

This tool is named Microsoft Teams Network Assessment Tool. You can run this tool on Windows 8 or later operating systems. It helps test network connectivity as well as network performance.

- **For network connectivity:** This tool verifies the network and network elements between the test location and the Microsoft network are correctly configured to enable communication to the IP addresses and ports (using UDP and TCP) needed for Microsoft Teams calls. The addresses and ports are listed at `https://support. office.com/en-us/article/Office-365-URLs-and-IP-address- ranges-8548a211-3fe7-47cb-abb1-355ea5aa88a2#bkmk_teams`.

- **For network performance:** To check the network, this tool tests the connection to Microsoft Network Edge by running audio packets to the nearest edge site and back for approximately 17 seconds for a configured number of iterations. The tool collects packet loss, jitter, round-trip latency, and packet reorder percentage from each call. The results from a set of test calls can be analyzed to determine if it meets the media quality and performance targets described at `https://support.office.com/en-us/article/Media-Quality- and-Network-Connectivity-Performance-in-Skype-for-Business- Online-5fe3e01b-34cf-44e0-b897-b0b2a83f0917`. These targets and testing apply to Microsoft Teams calls only.

Using the Network Assessment Tool

It's a general recommendation to run the Microsoft Teams Network Assessment Tool from each network or subnet location that will support Teams users to validate port connectivity and media quality.

The Teams Network Assessment Tool should be run from a Windows 8 PC or later OS versions. The following conditions should be met to ensure the tool provides accurate results:

- Download and install the tool from the Microsoft download center at `https://www.microsoft.com/en-US/download/details.aspx?id=103017`.

- Windows updates disabled

- Sleep mode disabled

- PC should be idle with no users using the PC during testing

- PC can be locked but not logged off during testing period

- Security software scanning disabled

Additional details about the tool can be found in the Teams Network Assessment Tool installation folder in a Word file named `Usage.docx`.

The Network Assessment tool can run connectivity checks to ensure all required outbound ports to Microsoft Teams are open. If the connectivity checks report blocked ports, those ports should be opened on the firewall before running the media quality tests with the Network Assessment Tool. To run the port connectivity checks, follow these steps:

1. Open a PowerShell session browse to the installation location, typically `C:\Program Files (x86)\Microsoft Teams Network Assessment Tool`.

2. Run the following command:

```
PS C:\Program Files (x86)\Microsoft Teams Network Assessment Tool> .\NetworkAssessmentTool.exe
```

3. After approximately two minutes, results like the following should be displayed: Refer to Figure 7-19 for the Network Assessment Tool results.

```
Microsoft Teams - Network Assessment Tool

Starting Relay Connectivity Check:
UDP, PseudoTLS, FullTLS, HTTPS connectivity will be checked to this relay (VIP) FQDN: worldaz.tr.teams.microsof
t.com
If user wants to check connectivity to a particular relay (VIP) IP, please specify in NetworkAssessment.exe.con
fig.

Connectivity check source port range: 50000 - 50019

Relay : 52.115.63.8      is the relay load balancer (VIP)
Relay : 52.115.63.8      is reachable using Protocol UDP and Port 3478
Relay : 52.115.63.8      is QOS (Media Priority) enabled
Relay : 52.115.63.8      is the relay load balancer (VIP)
Relay : 52.115.63.8      is reachable using Protocol PseudoTLS and Port 443
Relay : 52.115.63.8      is the relay load balancer (VIP)
Relay : 52.115.63.8      is reachable using Protocol FullTLS and Port 443
Relay : 52.115.63.8      is the relay load balancer (VIP)
Relay : 52.115.63.8      is reachable using Protocol HTTPS and Port 443
Relay : 52.115.63.104    is the actual relay instance (DIP)
Relay : 52.115.63.104    is reachable using Protocol UDP and Port 3478
Relay : 52.115.63.104    is the actual relay instance (DIP)
Relay : 52.115.63.104    is reachable using Protocol UDP and Port 3479
Relay : 52.115.63.104    is the actual relay instance (DIP)
Relay : 52.115.63.104    is reachable using Protocol UDP and Port 3480
Relay : 52.115.63.104    is the actual relay instance (DIP)
Relay : 52.115.63.104    is reachable using Protocol UDP and Port 3481

Relay connectivity and Qos (Media Priority) check is successful for all relays.

Starting Service Connectivity Check:
Service verifications completed successfully

Service connectivity result has been written to: C:\Users\JasonHindson\AppData\Local\Microsoft Teams Network As
sessment Tool\service_connectivity_check_results.txt
```

Figure 7-19. *Network Assessment Tool results*

4. Analyze the results and address any unreachable ports with appropriate network team resources

Once the port connectivity checks have completed successfully, you should test the media quality. Follow these steps to run the media quality tests:

1. Open a PowerShell session browse to the installation location, typically C:\Program Files (x86)\Microsoft Teams Network Assessment Tool.

2. Run the following command:

```
PS C:\Program Files (x86)\Microsoft Teams Network Assessment Tool> .\NetworkAssessmentTool.exe /qualitycheck
```

3. Refer to Figure 7-20 for the Network Assessment Tool results.

```
Microsoft Teams - Network Assessment Tool


Initializing media flow.

****************
Starting new call

Media flow will start after allocating with relay VIP FQDN: worldaz.tr.teams.microsoft.com
If user wants to allocate with a particular relay VIP IP address, please specify in NetworkAssessment.exe.config.

Waiting for call to end after 30 seconds, displaying call quality metrics every ~5 seconds.
Change the 'MediaDuration' field in the NetworkAssessmentTool.exe.config file to change the media flow duration.

TIMESTAMP is in UTC. LOSS RATE is in percentage, out of 100.
LATENCY and JITTER are in milliseconds, and are calculated as averages in ~5-second windows.
PROTOCOL displays whether UDP, TCP (PseudoTLS/FullTLS), or HTTPS protocol was used to allocate with the relay server.
Note that for PROTOCOL, UDP protocol is attempted first to connect to the relay, by default.
LOCAL ADDRESS is the local client IP and port that media is flowing from.
REMOTE ADDRESS is the peer (relay server) destination IP and port that media is flowing to.
IS PROXIED PATH shows whether a proxy server is used to connect to the relay, only applies to TCP/HTTPS connections
LAST KNOWN REFLEXIVE IP shows what your latest public (NAT translated) IP and port is that the relay sees during media f
low.
[If LOSS RATE is 100%, the output lines here will be in red]

Quality check source port range: 50000 - 50019

Call Quality Metrics:

2021-05-14 20:04:52        Loss Rate: 0        Latency: 25.7      Jitter: 5        Protocol: UDP
Local IP: 192.168.0.208:50014                  Remote IP: 52.115.223.102:3478
Is Proxied Path: False                         Last Known Reflexive IP: 71.146.175.10:50014

2021-05-14 20:05:00        Loss Rate: 0        Latency: 29.31     Jitter: 47.71    Protocol: UDP
Local IP: 192.168.0.208:50014                  Remote IP: 52.115.223.102:3478
Is Proxied Path: False                         Last Known Reflexive IP: 71.146.175.10:50014

2021-05-14 20:05:08        Loss Rate: 0        Latency: 28.2      Jitter: 148      Protocol: UDP
Local IP: 192.168.0.208:50014                  Remote IP: 52.115.223.102:3478
Is Proxied Path: False                         Last Known Reflexive IP: 71.146.175.10:50014

2021-05-14 20:05:15        Loss Rate: 0        Latency: 25.97     Jitter: 29       Protocol: UDP
Local IP: 192.168.0.208:50014                  Remote IP: 52.115.223.102:3478
Is Proxied Path: False                         Last Known Reflexive IP: 71.146.175.10:50014

Call Quality Check Has Finished
```

Figure 7-20. *Network Assessment Tool results*

The configuration file included in the installation folder of the Teams Network Assessment Tool can be modified to adjust the length of the media test. The default value is 300 seconds. The configuration filename is `NetworkAssessmentTool.exe.config`. The following setting controls the duration:

<add key="MediaDuration" value="300"/>

Change the value 300 to the desired test call duration length, save the file, and run the quality test. The quality test can be interrupted at any time by pressing Ctrl+C within the PowerShell window.

Network Planner

Network Planner is a new tool that is available in the Teams admin center. It can be found by going to Planning ➤ Network planner. In just a few steps, the Network Planner can help you determine and organize network requirements for connecting Microsoft Teams users across your organization. When you provide your network details and Teams usage, the Network Planner calculates your network requirements for deploying Teams and cloud voice across your organization's physical locations.

1. Go to the Network Planner in the Microsoft Teams admin center.

2. On the Network Plan tab, click "Add a network plan."

3. Enter a name and description for your network plan. The network plan will appear in the list of available plans. Refer to Figure 7-21 to see the Network Planner tool.

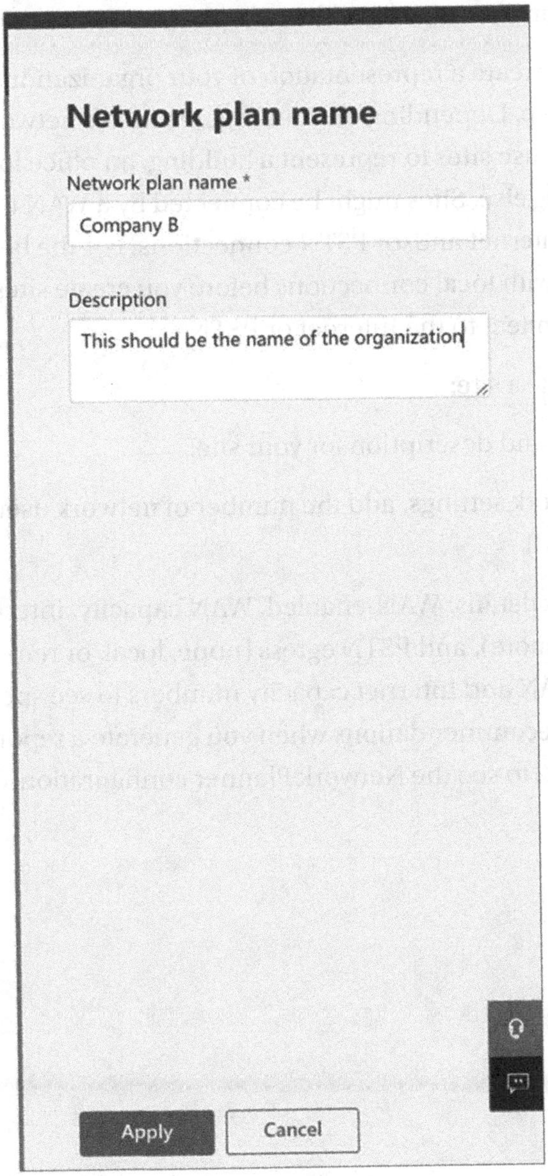

Figure 7-21. Network Planner tool

4. Click the plan name to select the new plan.

5. Add sites to create a representation of your organization's network setup. Depending on your organization's network, you may want to use sites to represent a building, an office location, or something else. Sites might be connected by a WAN to allow sharing of Internet and/or PSTN connections. For the best results, create sites with local connections before you create sites that remotely connect to the Internet or PSTN.

Here's how to create a site:

1. Add a name and description for your site.

2. Under Network settings, add the number of network users at that site (required).

3. Add network details: WAN-enabled, WAN capacity, internet egress (Local or Remote), and PSTN egress (none, local, or remote). You must add WAN and Internet capacity numbers to see specific bandwidth recommendations when you generate a report. Refer to Figure 7-22 to see the Network Planner configuration.

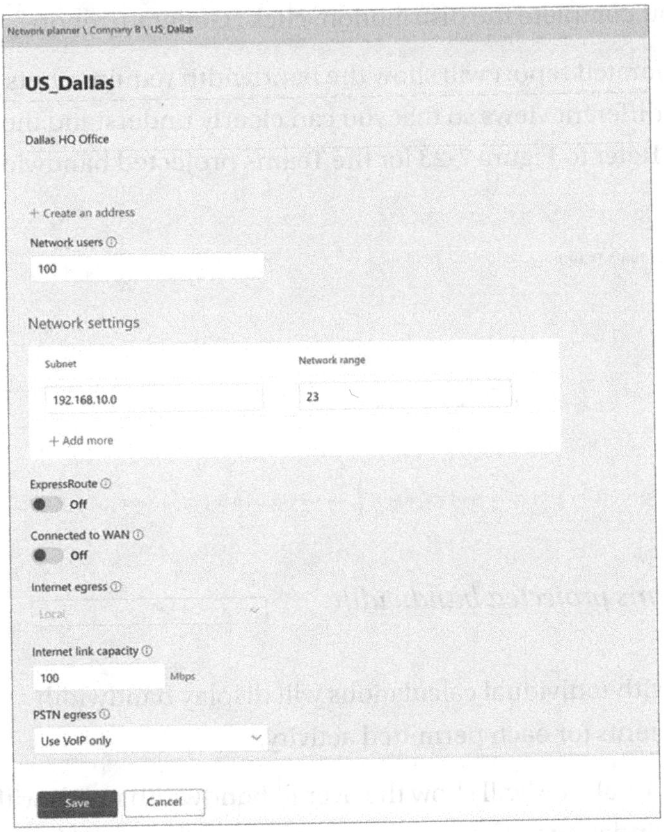

Figure 7-22. *Network Planner Configure*

4. Click Save.

Here's how to create a report:

1. After you add all sites, you can create a report, as follows.

2. On the Reports tab, click "Start a report."

3. For each site you create, distribute the number of users across the available personas. If you use the Microsoft recommended personas, the number will be distributed automatically (80 percent office worker and 20 percent remote worker).

4. After you complete the distribution, click "Generate report."

5. The generated report will show the bandwidth requirements in several different views so that you can clearly understand the output. Refer to Figure 7-23 for the Teams projected bandwidth.

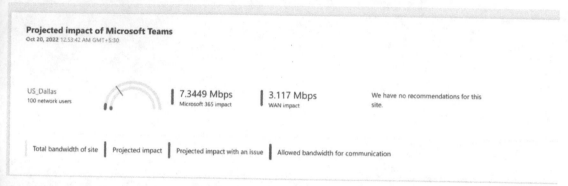

Figure 7-23. *Teams projected bandwidth*

6. A table with individual calculations will display bandwidth requirements for each permitted activity.

7. An additional view will show the overall bandwidth needs with recommendations.

8. Click Save. Your report will be available on the reports list for later viewing.

Office Connectivity Tool

The Microsoft 365 admin center contains a network connectivity test tool as an adjunct to the insights and details available in the Health ➤ Connectivity section of the admin center. The Microsoft 365 network connectivity test tool is located at https:// connectivity.office.com. Results from this tool can be collected in three different methods:

- Enabling Windows Location Services on Windows endpoints

- Adding locations and subnets manually into the tool

- Manually running tests through https://connectivity.office.com

For fewer office locations, it's recommended to run the test manually in multiple locations. To run the test manually, the following actions are required:

1. The user connects to `connectivity.office.com` and signs in by clicking "sign in" in the top-right corner of the page.

2. The user clicks the auto detect location or update the location manually. Refer to Figure 7-24 for Microsoft 365 network connectivity tests.

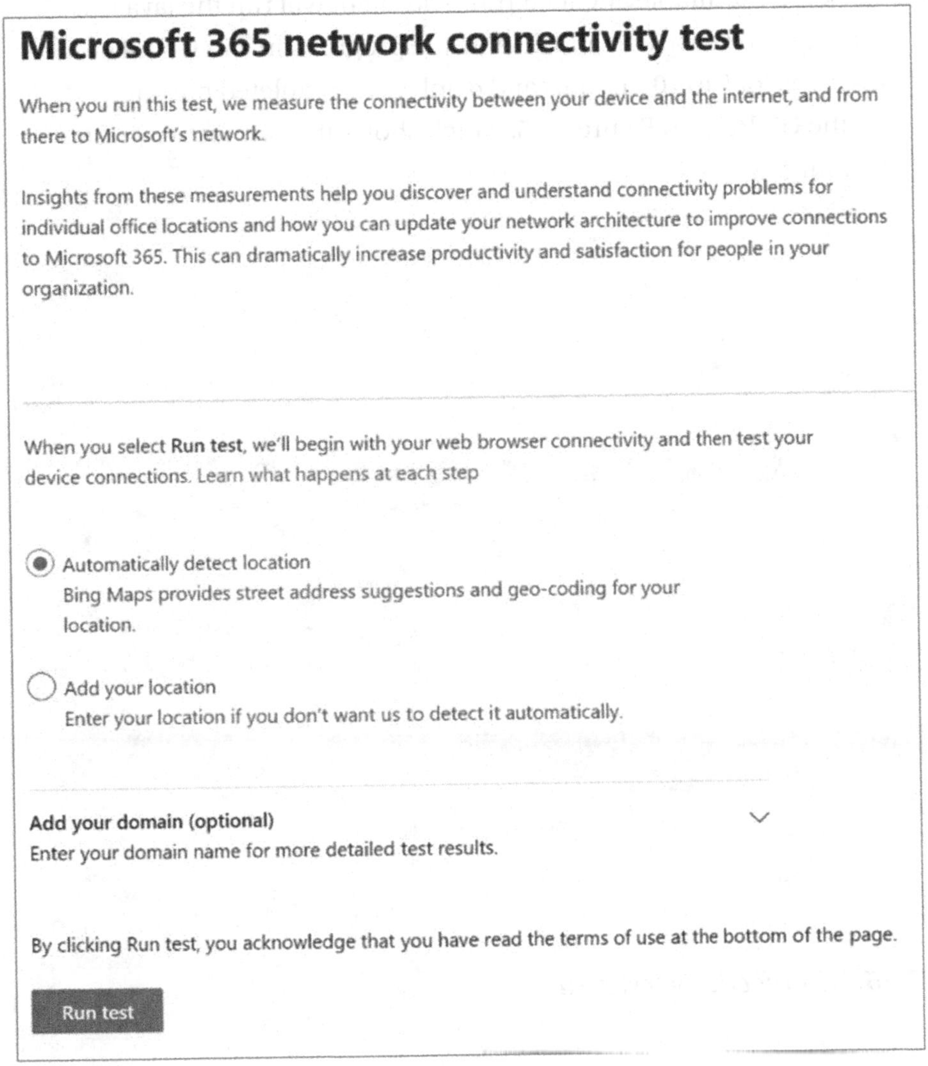

Microsoft 365 network connectivity test

When you run this test, we measure the connectivity between your device and the internet, and from there to Microsoft's network.

Insights from these measurements help you discover and understand connectivity problems for individual office locations and how you can update your network architecture to improve connections to Microsoft 365. This can dramatically increase productivity and satisfaction for people in your organization.

When you select **Run test**, we'll begin with your web browser connectivity and then test your device connections. Learn what happens at each step

◉ Automatically detect location
  Bing Maps provides street address suggestions and geo-coding for your location.

◯ Add your location
  Enter your location if you don't want us to detect it automatically.

Add your domain (optional)   ⌄
Enter your domain name for more detailed test results.

By clicking Run test, you acknowledge that you have read the terms of use at the bottom of the page.

Run test

Figure 7-24. M365 network connectivity test

3. When you click the "Run test" button, it shows the running test page and identifies the office location. You can type in your location by city, state, and country or choose to have it detected for you. If you detect the office location, the tool requests the latitude and longitude from the web browser and limits the accuracy to 300 meters by 300 meters.

4. The browser auto downloads an executable.

5. Click the executable and let it run. The client will run the Java test scripts in the back end and display the progress on client UI. The test runs for 5 to 10 minutes and displays a completed message on the UI. Refer to Figure 7-25, which shows the connectivity tests running.

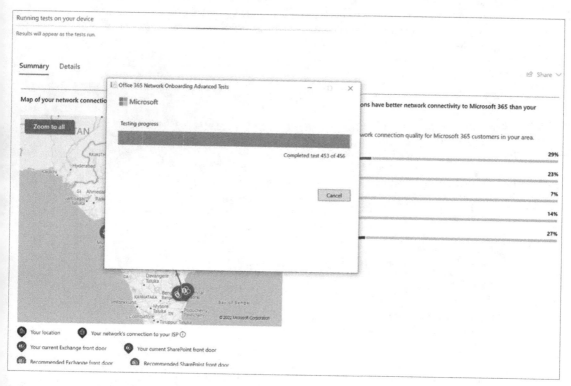

Figure 7-25. *Connectivity test result*

6. Depending on the .NET version installed on the test machine, the client application throws an error to install the 6.0 or above .NET desktop app version app. Please ensure you have installed the desktop version (windowsdesktop-runtime-6.0.9-win-x64.exe) of the runtime from the download page.

7. Once the tests are completed, hit the close button, and come back to the browser. The test results are displayed in the browser. Click the details tab to ensure tests are completed successfully. Refer Figure 7-26 shows a successful test result.

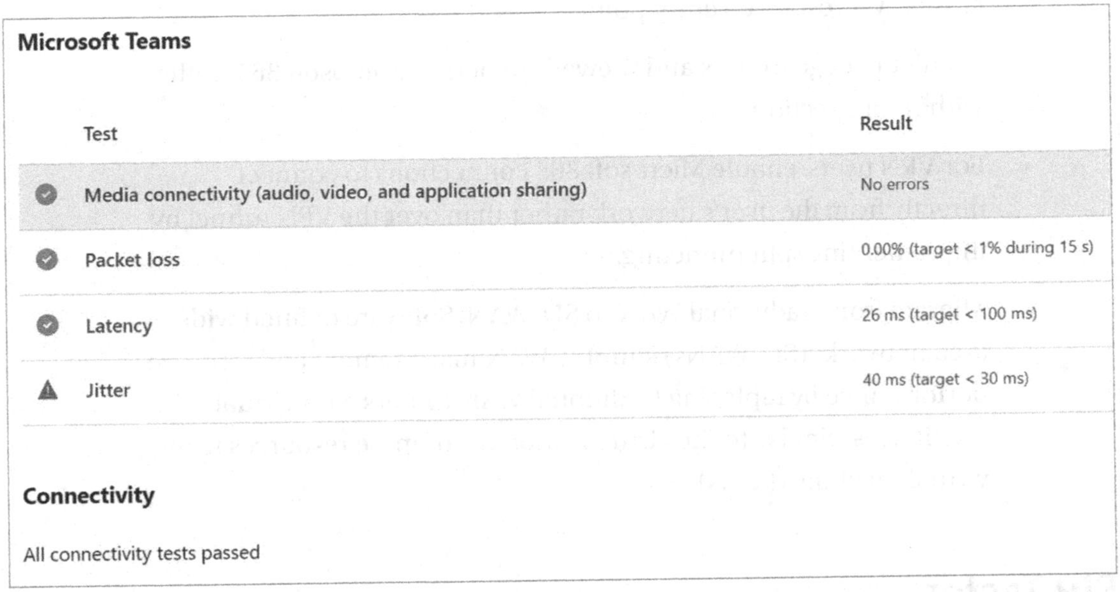

Microsoft Teams	
Test	Result
✓ Media connectivity (audio, video, and application sharing)	No errors
✓ Packet loss	0.00% (target < 1% during 15 s)
✓ Latency	26 ms (target < 100 ms)
⚠ Jitter	40 ms (target < 30 ms)
Connectivity	
All connectivity tests passed	

Figure 7-26. *Test result*

8. Post validation, share the results by clicking the Share button. Share the results to the admin email address.

Network Optimization Methods

Here are the high-level recommendations to optimize the network for better connectivity and network performance:

- Provision local DNS servers in each location and ensure that Microsoft 365 connections egress to the Internet as close as possible to the user's location.

- If your corporate network has multiple locations but only one egress point, add regional egress points to enable users to connect to the closest Microsoft 365 entry point.

- Configure edge routers and firewalls to permit Microsoft 365 traffic without inspection.

- For VPN users, enable Microsoft 365 connections to connect directly from the user's network rather than over the VPN tunnel by implementing split tunneling.

- Migrate from traditional WAN to SD-WAN. Software defined wide area networks (SD-WANs) simplify WAN management and improve performance by replacing traditional WAN routers with virtual appliances, similar to the virtualization of compute resources using virtual machines (VMs).

SIP Tester

The SIP tester for Direct Routing is a PowerShell script tool that allows testing of Direct Routing SBC connections in Teams. Testing Direct Routing is quite complicated, but using the SIP tester tool makes it easier. This tool allows us to test the basic functionality of a customer-paired Session Initiation Protocol (SIP) trunk with Direct Routing, such as outbound and inbound calls, simultaneous ring, media escalation, and consultative transfer.

This SIP tester tool provides the ability to test real accounts in a Teams organization's indirect routing scenarios. Microsoft has written a web service that tests the Teams client login against one configured with SBC Direct Routing. You can automate this PowerShell script to make daily calls and checks to determine if SBC is working correctly.

To download the SIP tester tool, visit the Microsoft site at `https://docs.microsoft.com/en-us/microsoftteams/sip-tester-powershell-script`.

You can read further documents that come along with a script to understand the requirement to create test users, which will be used for basic call testing scenarios.

Refer to my blog at `https://bloguc.com` for more Teams client service troubleshooting information and best practice guidance.

Troubleshooting IM and Presence

Presence is an important feature of a user's profile in Microsoft Teams, which is also available across Microsoft 365 or Office 365. It helps other users to know about the user's current availability and status. By default, users within your organization using Teams can see if other users are available online in almost real time. However, sometimes users may face issues with the presence feature, such as Outlook and Teams presence not syncing, presence not updating correctly, or showing as unknown. Most of these issues can be resolved by updating the Microsoft Teams clients.

Presence sync is dependent on where a user's mailbox is hosted. If the user's mailbox is hosted online, then the presence gets synced seamlessly. However, if a user has a mailbox hosted on-premises, there may be a delay of up to an hour in the presence syncing. Microsoft offers a self-diagnostic tool to validate the user's presence status. Administrators can enter the username or email address of user-facing issues and run tests. The diagnostic tool is available through this link:

`https://admin.microsoft.com/AdminPortal/?searchSolutions=Diag%3A%20Teams%20Presence#/homepage`.

Users may face difficulty in identifying the presence of other users on Microsoft Teams. In such cases, it may appear that the user is offline, which usually happens when the user sets their presence status to "Appear offline" or if there is a network communication issue. If this issue occurs frequently, as an administrator, it is recommended to verify if the contact is active on Microsoft Teams and Azure AD/AD and to ensure that the user has network connectivity to the Microsoft endpoints. If you are unable to determine the issue, it is advised to raise a support ticket with Microsoft.

Finally, during the scenarios of co-existence, based on the user's co-existence mode, presence will vary as follows:

- If a user is in TeamsOnly mode, then any other user (whether in Teams or Skype for Business) will see that TeamsOnly user's Teams presence.

- If a user is in any of the Skype for Business modes (SfbOnly, SfbWithTeamsCollab, SfbWithTeamsCollabAndMeetings), then any other user (whether in Teams or Skype for Business) will see that Skype for Business user's Skype for Business presence.

- When a user is in island mode, their presence in Teams and presence in Skype for Business can be different from each other, and it's perfectly normal. Other users will see either the Teams or Skype for Business presence of the island user, depending on whether they are in the same tenant or in a federated tenant and which client they use.

- Within the same tenant, a Teams user can see the presence of an island user.

- When a user in a federated tenant views the island user's presence in Teams, they will see their Skype for Business presence.

- From Skype for Business, any other user will see the island user's Skype for Business presence (both in-tenant and federated).

Troubleshooting Chat Issues in Microsoft Teams

Users of Microsoft Teams may occasionally experience issues related to the chat feature. Common problems include the disappearance of the chat icon from the navigation pane or the inability to access the chat during a meeting. Here we outline the typical causes of these issues and what to check to resolve them.

Missing Chat Icon in Navigation Rail

One frequent issue is that the chat icon goes missing from the left-hand navigation rail. If this happens, there are several things to consider:

- **Messaging policy:** Ensure that the chat functionality isn't disabled in your organization's Teams messaging policy. If chat is allowed, the icon should normally be visible.

- **User actions:** Users might have unintentionally "unpinned" the chat app from the navigation rail. It's a good idea to verify whether this is the case and, if so, re-pin the chat application.

Meeting Chat Access Issues

Another common problem is that some users can't access the chat during a Teams meeting. This can happen for various reasons:

- **Administrator settings:** The meeting chat could be disabled by the system administrator through a specific meeting policy. This setting can be verified and updated by the administrator as needed.

- **Meeting organizer control:** Sometimes, the meeting organizer might have altered the default meeting options, affecting chat accessibility.

- **High attendee count:** If a user joins a meeting with more than 1,000 participants, they might face limitations on accessing the chat feature.

- **External users and forwarded links:** It's worth noting that external participants and those who join through a forwarded meeting link might also have restricted chat access.

By identifying the root cause of these chat-related issues, users and administrators can take appropriate actions to rectify them, ensuring a more seamless communication experience within Microsoft Teams.

Summary

Microsoft Teams serves as a comprehensive solution for unified communications and collaboration. However, like any sophisticated platform, it is not entirely immune to issues. This chapter provides an in-depth guide to various approaches for effective troubleshooting of Microsoft Teams, ensuring a seamless experience for end users.

One of the fundamental steps in avoiding common Teams problems is to adequately prepare your network environment. This includes configuring your corporate firewall to allow Teams services, IP addresses, ports and protocols, URLs, and FQDNs. Such preparedness ensures that each feature within Teams operates as expected.

This chapter emphasized the importance of employing the right set of tools for diagnostics and troubleshooting:

- **Call Analytics:** This tool offers detailed information on call history, providing deep insights into individual call records. It is especially useful for identifying issues related to call quality.

- **Call Quality Dashboard (CQD):** The CQD provides a broader view by allowing you to analyze call data in aggregate. It is invaluable for spotting trends and systemic issues within your organization's Teams usage.

- **Network Assessment Tool:** This is an essential tool for evaluating your network's capacity to handle Teams traffic, particularly focusing on audio and video quality.

Collecting diagnostic information from Teams clients can offer insights into common problems that users may face. These could range from chat-related issues to audio-video quality problems in calls and meetings. Understanding how to collect this information is key to quick and effective problem resolution.

Not all troubleshooting tools are suited for every problem. Knowing which tool to use in specific scenarios is crucial for efficient problem-solving. For example, while Call Analytics might be perfect for diagnosing issues on an individual level, CQD could be better suited for a holistic organizational assessment.

Understanding the intricacies of Microsoft Teams and knowing how to wield its troubleshooting tools are essential skills for administrators and IT professionals. Whether you're trying to get ahead of issues by setting up your network correctly or dealing with user-reported problems, the strategies and tools discussed in this chapter will equip you with the knowledge you need for effective troubleshooting.

CHAPTER 8

Teams Reporting and Monitoring

In today's digitally connected enterprise environment, reporting and monitoring are crucial elements in ensuring optimal system performance, enhancing user experience, and driving strategic decision-making. In the world of Microsoft Teams, these elements are no different. This chapter aims to introduce and explain various Microsoft Teams reporting and monitoring tools, including the Teams usage reports, custom Power BI reports, Call Analytics, and the Call Quality Dashboard. Understanding these tools is integral for admins and management to ensure smooth operations, gain insightful data, and guide strategic planning.

Monitoring and reporting are integral aspects of Microsoft Teams administration. These functionalities offer in-depth insights into user activities, performance metrics, and call quality, aiding administrators in managing the service more effectively. Microsoft Teams provides various tools, such as the Teams admin center, Microsoft 365 admin center, and PowerShell, to facilitate advanced reporting and real-time monitoring.

Here are the key features:

- **User activity reports:** Helps track the usage patterns of individuals or teams, revealing the most frequently used channels, apps, and features

- **Performance metrics:** Monitors CPU, memory usage, and network statistics related to Microsoft Teams usage

- **Call analytics:** Provides detailed statistics for individual calls and meetings, useful for troubleshooting poor call or meeting experiences

- **Real-time monitoring:** Live dashboards for tracking ongoing meetings and call quality

© Balu N Ilag, Durgesh Tripathy, Vijay Ireddy 2024
B. N. Ilag et al., *Understanding Microsoft Teams Administration*,
https://doi.org/10.1007/979-8-8688-0014-6_8

- **Compliance and security monitoring:** Tracks login attempts, data sharing, and other security-related activities

- **Power BI Connector for Teams and CQD**

In this chapter, we will cover the following topics:

- **Introduction to reporting and monitoring:** We cover the importance and role of reporting and monitoring within Microsoft Teams.

- **Teams usage reports:** We cover the built-in usage reports available in the Microsoft Teams admin center. We cover what data these reports provide, how to access them, and how they can be used to monitor user engagement and usage patterns.

- **Custom Power BI reports:** We cover how admins can leverage Power BI to create custom reports, providing more specific or complex data analysis. We also cover how to connect Power BI with Microsoft 365 usage analytics and how to use it to gain deeper insights.

- **Teams Call Analytics:** We cover the Call Analytics tool within Teams, which provides detailed information on individual calls and meetings. We also cover what data is provided and how this tool can be used for troubleshooting specific issues reported by users.

- **Call Quality Dashboard (CQD):** We cover the Call Quality Dashboard, which provides aggregated data on call and meeting quality at an organizational level. We explain how to use the dashboard to identify and address systemic issues affecting call quality.

- **Call quality troubleshooting using the CQD:** We describe the process of troubleshooting.

The chapter concludes by reinforcing the importance of effective reporting and monitoring in ensuring a positive Microsoft Teams experience and setting the stage for the next topic of discussion.

Microsoft Teams Analytics and Reporting

The new analytics and reporting features in the Microsoft Teams admin center offer robust insights into user engagement and system performance within your organization. These analytics enable you to understand how your team interacts through messages, channels, and device usage, thereby helping you tailor business strategies, training programs, and communication initiatives.

The following roles are eligible to access these reports:

- Global Administrators

- Teams or Skype for Business Administrators

- Global Readers (access limited to tenant-level aggregate data)

To access a report, go to the Microsoft Teams admin center and select "Analytics & reports" and then View Reports; then select the specific report you want to run.

Note   The Microsoft Teams admin center reports are distinct from the Microsoft 365 reports available in the Microsoft 365 admin center.

The Microsoft Teams admin center offers a variety of reports, constantly updated for different organizational needs.

- **Teams Usage Report:** Metrics for active users, channels, messages, and privacy settings

- **Teams User Activity Report:** Detailed user-level statistics including message counts and meeting participation

- **Teams Device Usage Report:** Breakdown of device types used to access Teams

- **Teams Live Event Usage Report:** Metrics around live event views, start times, and statuses

- **Teams PSTN Reports:** Multiple reports related to public switched telephone network (PSTN) usage

- **Teams Information Protection License Report:** Data related to licenses and change notifications

- **Teams Virtual Appointments Report:** Metrics for virtual appointments, including attendee details and wait times

Figure 8-1 shows the list of reports.

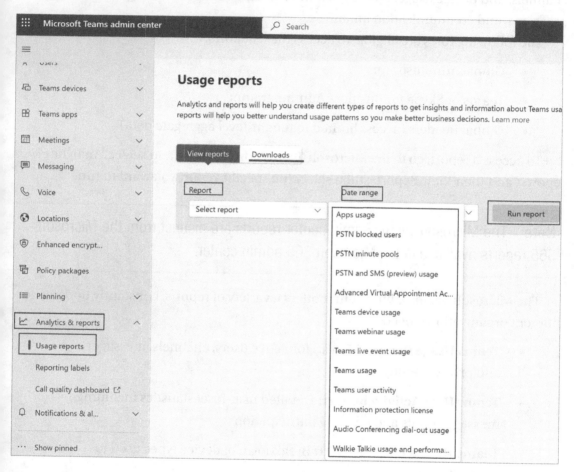

Figure 8-1. *Usage report list and options*

Microsoft Teams Usage Activity

The Microsoft Teams Usage Activity section is part of the Microsoft 365 dashboard. It gives you a quick look at how people in your company are using Microsoft Teams. You can see things such as how many people are active, how many messages are being sent, and how many meetings are happening.

Here's how to access the report:

1. Go to the admin center and click Reports.

2. Then click Usage.

3. On this page, find the Microsoft Teams card and click "View more."

You'll find different graphs and tables showing you various details.

- **Channel usage:** This graph shows how often different channels are being used.

- **Team usage:** This one shows how many different teams are active.

The report also has more specific details for each team such as when was the last time someone did something in a team, how many people are active, etc.

- **Customizing the view:** You can pick what details you want to see by selecting "Choose columns."

- **Saving the report:** If you want to look at this data later, you can download it as an Excel file. This lets you sort and filter the information however you want.

- **Time range:** You can look at activity from the last week up to the last 6 months. But if you pick a specific day to look at, you'll see only up to 28 days from today's date.

Note that the information might take up to 48 hours to show up. So if you're looking for what happened on September 1, you might not see it until September 3. Also, the data is checked daily for the last three days to make sure it's accurate.

The Teams usage chart gives you information on different kinds of teams and activities. Here's what each term means:

- **Private teams:** Teams that are invite-only

- **Public teams:** Teams anyone can join

- **Active private teams:** Invite-only teams that people are currently using

- **Active public teams:** Open teams that people are currently using

These are the metrics for individual teams:

- **Team ID:** The unique number or name that identifies each team

- **Internal Active Users:** People in your organization who have done something in Teams recently, not including guests

- **Active Guests:** People not in your organization who have been active in Teams

- **External Active Users:** People from outside your organization who are active but are not logged in as guests

- **Active Channels:** Channels in active teams that people are currently using

- **Active Shared Channels:** Channels that are active and are shared with people outside the team

- **Total Organized Meetings:** All the meetings set up by a user

- **Posts:** Number of new messages

- **Replies:** Number of responses to messages

- **Mentions:** Number of times people are tagged

- **Reactions:** Number of emojis or likes on messages

- **Urgent Messages:** Number of messages marked as urgent

- **Channel Messages:** Unique messages in team chats

- **Last Activity Date:** The most recent date someone in the team did something

---

Note   These counts include only those activities done directly in Teams, not through other services or apps connected to Teams.

If you're an admin and you want to make this data anonymous, you can do the following:

1. Go to the Microsoft 365 admin center.

2. Navigate to Settings ➤ Org Settings.

3. On the Services tab, click Reports.

4. Choose "Display anonymous identifiers" and save the changes.

This will hide names, emails, and other personal information in the reports.

Understanding Microsoft Teams User Activity Reports in Simple Terms

The Microsoft 365 dashboard lets you see how people are using Microsoft products, including Teams, in your company.

This is how you find the report:

1. Go to the admin area and click Reports.

2. Then click Usage.

3. Next, click "View more" under the Microsoft Teams section.

In this report, you'll see various tabs. Click "User activity" to see what people are doing in Teams. You can choose which details to show in the report. You can also download the data to look at it in Excel.

This is what the key terms mean:

- **Username:** This is the email of the person using Teams.

- **Tenant name:** This is company where the user works.

- **Is external:** This shows if the user is from outside your company.

- **Channel messages:** This is how many messages a person sent in Teams chats.

- **Posts:** This is first message in a chat.

- **Replies:** These are the responses to those first messages.

- **Urgent messages:** These are messages marked as important.

- **Total meetings:** This is the total number of meetings the user joined.

- **1:1 calls:** These include direct calls between two people.

- **Last activity date:** This is the last time the user did something in Teams.

These are other activities:

- **Audio duration:** Total time spent on audio calls

- **Video duration:** Total time spent on video calls

- **Screen share duration:** Total time spent sharing screens

---

Note   This report doesn't include data from other apps that might be connected to Teams.

By understanding these terms, you can get a better idea of how people in your company are using Microsoft Teams.

Setting Up the Power BI Connector for Microsoft Teams' Call Quality Dashboard: A Simple Guide

This section shows how to set up the Power BI Connector for tracking call quality on Microsoft Teams. Be aware, the data source used in the report needs to be updated every two months. For the limitations of this tool, visit the Microsoft website.

Here is how to install the tool:

1. **Create a folder:** Check if you have a Custom Connectors folder in your Documents folder under Power BI Desktop. If not, create one.

2. **Download a file:** Get the connector file (a *.pqx file) and put it in the folder you just made.

3. **Open Power BI:** Launch the Power BI Desktop application.

4. **Change the security settings:** Go to File ➤ Options and Settings ➤ Options ➤ Security. Here, allow any extension to load without any warning (though it's not recommended).

5. **Restart Power BI:** Close and re-open the program.

6. **Load the template:** Go to File ➤ Open Reports ➤ Browse Reports. Change the file type to Power BI Template files (*.pbit), find the template you downloaded, and open it.

7. **Sign in:** Use your Azure AD credentials to sign in to the Call Quality Dashboard.

8. **Final check:** If you see various dimensions and measures in the Fields pane, you're good to go.

If a new version comes out, just replace the old `*.pqx` file with the new one in the Custom Connectors folder.

Here are some common issues and fixes:

- **Expired data source:** The report uses a free database that needs to be updated every two months. Set a monthly reminder to do this.

- **Error messages:** If you get errors, make sure you're using the December 2020 version of Power BI or later. If you have the right version but still see errors, reinstall the connector file.

- **Web settings:** When you publish the report online, you may need to update some credentials. Go to Datasets in Power BI Online, find your report, click the three dots for the menu, and update the credentials.

By following this simplified guide, you should be able to set up and use the Power BI Connector for the Microsoft Teams Call Quality Dashboard effectively.

Microsoft Teams App Usage Report

The App Usage Report in Microsoft Teams helps you understand which apps people are using. You can find out about Microsoft apps like Viva Learning, third-party ones like Polly, and custom business apps.

You can use it to find out the following:

- The number of apps installed by users

- The apps that are actually being used, sorted by type

- The usage on different platforms: Windows, Mac, web, or mobile

- The number of active users and teams for each app

Note   The report doesn't include data on custom apps that are side-loaded.

To see these reports, you need to be an admin. In the Teams admin center, do the following:

1. Go to Analytics & reports ➤ Usage reports.

2. Choose "Apps usage" under the Report section.

3. Pick a date range and click "Run report."

You'll see the following in the report:

- **Time range:** You can see trends over 7, 30, 90, or 180 days.

- **Data delay:** The report might be one to two days behind.

- **Graphs:** Hover over the dots on the graph to see specific numbers for that date.

- **Filters:** You can filter the data to see specific types of apps.

- **Table info:** The table breaks down usage by each app.

  - **App ID:** Unique identifier for the app

  - **App name:** The app's name

  - **Publisher:** Who made the app

  - **Teams and users:** How many are using it

  - **Platforms:** Where it's being used

  - **Last used:** The last time someone used it

- **Customize the table:** You can click "Edit columns" to change what's displayed.

- **Download:** You can save the report as a CSV file for more detailed analysis.

To manage apps, go to Manage Apps in the Teams admin center. You'll need the app name or external app ID for this.

By understanding how to read and use the Teams App Usage Report, you can get a clearer picture of app utilization in your organization.

Microsoft Teams Device Usage Report

The Microsoft 365 Reports dashboard lets you see how people in your company are using different Microsoft products, including Teams. The Teams Device Usage Report helps you know what devices (such as computers and phones) people are using for Teams.

Here's how to access the report:

1. Go to the admin center and click Reports ➤ Usage.

2. On the main page, click "View more" on the Teams activity card.

You can do the following:

1. Choose the "Device usage" tab to see what devices people are using.

2. You can customize the report by clicking "Choose columns."

3. You can also download the data into an Excel file for more analysis.

You can look at data from the last week, month, or even half a year. If you pick a specific day, you'll see info for up to 28 days from today.

Here's what the report tells you:

- **Username:** The person's name

- **Windows:** Shows if they used Teams on a Windows computer

- **Mac:** Shows if they used Teams on a Mac computer

- **iOS:** Shows if they used Teams on an iPhone or iPad

- **Android:** Shows if they used Teams on an Android phone

- **Chrome OS:** Shows if they used Teams on a Chromebook

- **Linux:** Shows if they used Teams on a Linux computer

- **Web:** Shows if they used Teams on a web browser

- **Last activity date:** Shows the last time the person did something in Teams

- **Is licensed:** Shows if the person is allowed to use Teams

This report is a handy tool for understanding what devices are popular for Teams in your company.

Microsoft Teams PSTN Blocked Users Report

The PSTN Blocked Users Report in Microsoft Teams helps you find out who in your company can't make phone calls using Teams. You can see details like their phone number and why they can't make calls.

Here's how to get access to the report:

1. Go to the Microsoft Teams admin center.

2. Click "Analytics & reports" and then "Usage reports."

3. Find and click "PSTN blocked users."

4. Click "Run report."

Here's what the report tells you:

- **When was it made:** The report is usually a day or two behind real-time activities.

- **Graph info:** The graph shows dates on the x-axis and the number of blocked users on the y-axis. Hover over any point to see how many users were blocked on a specific date.

- **Table details:** The table lists everyone who can't make phone calls. Here's what the columns mean:

  - **Display Name:** The person's name. Click it to go to their settings.

  - **Phone:** Their assigned phone number.

  - **Blocked Reason:** Why they can't make calls.

  - **Blocked Action:** Shows if they are blocked or unblocked from making calls.

  - **Blocked Time:** When they were blocked.

You can customize this table to see only what you need.

- **Edit Columns:** Click this to add or take away information from the table.

- **Full Screen:** Click this if you want to see the report in full-screen mode.

This report is a useful tool for managing phone call permissions in your company.

Microsoft Teams PSTN Minute Pools Report

The PSTN Minute Pools Report in Microsoft Teams shows you how many calling minutes your company has used this month. It tells you what type of call plans are being used, how many minutes you have left, and where the calls are being made from.

Here's how to access the report::

1. Open the Microsoft Teams admin center.

2. Click "Analytics & reports" and then "Usage reports."

3. Choose "PSTN minute and SMS(preview) pools" and hit 'Run report."

Here's what is on the report:

- **Report date:** The data in the report is usually a day or two old.

- **License activity:** Click a call plan (or "license") to see how it's being used.

- **Graph info:** The x-axis shows countries, and the y-axis shows minutes. Hover over the bars to see the minutes used in each country.

- **Filters:** You can choose what to see on the graph. Click terms like "Unused," "Domestic users," "No data," or "International used" to filter the view.

- **Table details:** Here's what the columns mean:

  - **Country or Region:** Where the calls are being made

  - **Capability Description:** The type of call plan, like "Domestic and international calling plan (1200 domestic minutes)"

  - **Total Minutes:** All the minutes you can use this month

  - **Minutes Used:** Minutes already used this month

- **Minutes Available**: Minutes left for this month

- **Capability**: The specific plan or license being used for the call, like "MCOPSTN1 - Domestic Calling Plan (3000 min US / 1200 min EU plans)"

You can customize this table.

- **Edit Columns:** Use this to add or remove information in the table.

- **Full Screen:** Click this to make the report bigger on your screen.

This report helps you keep track of your company's call usage.

Microsoft Teams PSTN and SMS Usage Report

This report in Microsoft Teams tells you about the calls and audio meetings happening in your company. If you use Microsoft for phone services, you'll see details on the Calling Plans tab. If you use your own phone services, you'll find information under Direct Routing.

Note   If you use Telstra or Softbank for your calls, this report won't show you anything. You'll need to contact them for your call details.

Here's how to access the report:

1. Go to the Microsoft Teams admin center.

2. Click "Analytics & reports" and then "Usage reports."

3. Choose "PSTN and SMS (preview) usage."

4. Pick a time range for the report, either the last 7 or 28 days, or set your own range.

5. Click "Run report."

Here's what the report includes:

- **Time range:** The data shows trends over the last 7, 28, or custom range of days.

- **Report date:** Data may be one to two days old.

- **Graph:** The x-axis shows the time range you chose; the y-axis shows the total number of calls. Hover over a point to see the call count for that day.

- **Table:** This is the meat of the report. It tells you the following:

    a. **Time stamp:** When the call started.

    b. **User info:** Who made or received the call. Click the name to see more settings.

    c. **Call details:** Where the call came from or went to, and what it cost.

    d. **Call types:** What kind of call it was (like a conference call, transferred call, etc.).

    e. **More:** Duration of the call, if it's local or international, and so on.

- **Customize the table:** Click "Edit columns" to pick what information you want to see.

- **Filter:** You can sort the report by username or type of call.

- **Full screen:** Make the report bigger to see details more easily.

- **Export:** You can save the report to look at later. Just click Export to Excel and then Download.

This report helps you understand how your team uses calls and meetings so you can make better decisions.

Direct Routing PSTN Usage Report

The Direct Routing PSTN Report in Microsoft Teams shows you details about phone calls made or received in your organization using your own phone service.

Here's what you will find on the report:

- **Time period:** You can look at data for the last 7 or 28 days.

- **Report date:** Each report has the date it was made. Data might be one to two days old.

- **Graph info:** The graph shows the total number of calls over your chosen time period. Hover over a point to see details for that day.

- **Detailed table:** This table tells you more about each call.

  - **Time stamp:** When the call started.

  - **Display name:** The name of the person or bot involved. Click it to go to their settings.

  - **SIP address:** Contact address of the person or bot in the call.

  - **Caller/callee number:** Who made and received the call.

  - **Call type:** Tells you the type of call (inbound, outbound, emergency, etc.). For example:

    - If a user got an incoming call, it's labeled "dr_in."

    - If a bot made an outgoing call, it's labeled "dr_out_bot."

- **Edit columns:** You can choose which details to show in the table.

- **Full screen:** Click to see the report in full-screen mode.

- **Download:** You can download the report for offline use or billing.

Here is some additional information:

- **Caller/Callee fields:** These can show different types of phone numbers or even text, depending on your setup. For example, it could show Internal Revenue Service instead of a number for spam calls.

That should give you a more straightforward understanding of what the Direct Routing PSTN Report is and what information you can get from it.

Phone Number Obfuscation Based on Location

Privacy regulations require that phone numbers from outside the customer's organization be partially concealed. The last three or four digits are replaced with asterisks (e.g., +123 456789***). For calls coming in, the number of the person calling is obscured; for calls going out, the recipient's number is obscured. This applies to PSTN and Direct Routing reports in the tenant's admin center, data exports, and call logs accessed via Microsoft Graph. Different rules may apply in Call Analytics and the Call Quality Dashboard.

The rules vary based on the country or region where the organization is located.

Country/Region	Digits to Obscure
Belgium	3
Switzerland	4
Germany	3
Denmark	3
...	...

Shared Correlation ID Details

The Shared Correlation ID appears only in the downloaded Excel report and signifies related calls. Here are some examples:

- **Scenario 1:** PSTN User 1 calls Teams User 1; no Shared Correlation ID.

- **Scenario 2:** Teams User 1 calls PSTN User 1; no Shared Correlation ID.

- **Scenario 3:** PSTN User 1 calls Teams User 2; a Shared Correlation ID indicates related calls.

Data Retention Policies

Data retention varies based on location-specific regulations.

Country	PSTN Plans	Direct Routing
Canada	150 days	150 days
Switzerland	365 days	365 days
Germany	365 days	100 days
...	...	...

The rules also apply to data exports and logs in the tenant's admin center and Microsoft Graph. The retention duration defaults to the tenant's location if a user's location isn't specified.

Exporting Call Data

Click Export to Excel and then Download on the Downloads tab. The process may take varying amounts of time depending on the data size. The downloaded ZIP file will include `PSTN.calls.[UTC date].csv` and `DirectRouting.calls.[UTC date].csv` for PSTN and Direct Routing data.

Additional fields are not visible online.

A `parameters.json` file for selected export ranges and capabilities.

The exported data complies with the RFC 4180 standard and can be read by Excel or other compliant editors. Specific details on columns, data types, and their meanings are also provided in the exported report. The data can be retained for up to one year or five months for PSTN and Direct Routing reports, respectively, unless otherwise restricted by local laws.

Audio Conferencing Dial-Out Usage Report

The Audio Conferencing Dial-Out Usage Report in the Microsoft Teams admin center helps you understand how much you're spending on audio calls and how much the service is being used. It shows details about money spent and call minutes used. This helps you plan how much money you'll need for future calls.

Here's how to access the report:

1. Open the Microsoft Teams admin center.

2. Click "Analytics & reports" and then "Usage reports."

3. Find and click the Audio Conferencing Dial-Out Usage Report.

Here's how to pick a date and country:

- You can choose to see data from the last 7 or 28 days or pick your own date range.

- You can also filter the report by country.

The report has three main sections, each showing different charts and details.

- **Cost Tab:** Shows how much money was spent on calls
- **Minutes of Use Tab:** Shows how many minutes were used in calls
- **Dial-Out Calls Tab:** Shows the total number of calls made

All the information takes about one to two days to show up in the report.

Important Note   The person who set up the meeting is listed as the one who used the minutes and spent the money, even if they didn't make the calls.

Here are the tab details:

- **Cost tab:** A graph shows spending over time, and a section below the graph shows the total cost of calls.

- **Minutes of the Use tab:** A graph shows minutes used over time, and a section below the graph shows the total minutes.

- **Dial-Out Calls tab:** A graph shows the number of calls over time, and a section below the graph shows the total number of calls.

The table at the bottom breaks down usage by each person. It shows the following:

- Who organized the meeting
- Their username
- How many minutes they used
- How much they spent

You can search and export date using this report.

- You can search for a specific user's data.
- You can click a meeting organizer's name to see more details.
- You can download any of these reports as a CSV file for further study. Just click Export to Excel and then download the file when it's ready.

Microsoft Teams Live Event Usage Report

The Teams Live Event Usage Report helps you understand what's happening with live online events in your company. It shows you details like when an event started, how many people watched it, and who organized it.

Here's how to access the report:

1.   Open the Microsoft Teams admin center.

2.   Click "Analytics & reports" and then "Usage reports."

3.   Choose "Teams live event usage."

You can use certain filters on this report.

- You can look at data from a specific time period, even up to a year.

- Optionally, you can also filter the report to show events organized by a specific person.

Here's what's on the report:

- **Trends:** You can look at event data from the last 7 or 28 days or pick your own date range.

- **Up-to-date info:** The report updates almost instantly when you refresh the page.

- **Graph details:** The graph shows the number of people who watched the events during your chosen date range.

- **Table info:** The table under the graph breaks down each event by the following:

  - Event name

  - Start time

  - Status (if the event has happened yet)

  - Who organized it

  - Who presented it

  - How many people watched it

- If it was recorded or not

- What tool was used to produce it

If an account no longer exists, it shows as --.

- **Customize the table:** You can add or remove columns to see only the details you want.

Important Notes

- The report can show up to 100 events at a time. Use date filters to see more.

- People who are present without logging in and those who watch a recorded event are not counted.

Clicking an event name gives you a detailed summary and allows you to see or download files related to that event, such as transcripts and recordings.

If your company uses special tools like Microsoft eCDN, Hive eCDN, or Kollective eCDN, you can get even more detailed reports.

Microsoft Teams Webinar Usage Report

The Webinar Usage Report in Microsoft Teams helps you understand your company's webinars. It shows useful details such as the webinar title, when it started and ended, and who was involved in organizing or presenting it.

Here's how to access the report:

1. Open the Microsoft Teams admin center.

2. Click "Analytics & reports" and then "Usage reports."

3. Select "Webinar usage reports."

Here are the date and organizer options:

- You can choose a specific time range for the data, even up to a year.

- If you want, you can also show only those webinars organized by a particular person.

Here's what's on the report:

- **Trends:** You can choose to see data from the last week or the last month, or you can pick your own dates.

- **Up-to-date info:** The report updates almost instantly each time you refresh the page.

- **Chart info:** The graph shows the total number of views. You can hover over any point to see the number of views on a particular date.

- **Table details:** The table below the graph gives you more information about each webinar, such as the following:

  - Unique webinar ID

  - Webinar title

  - Start and end times

  - Names of the organizer, co-organizer, and presenters

  - Whether the webinar is open to everyone in the organization or is private

If an account is deleted or no longer exists, it will show as --.

Important Note   The report will show a maximum of 100 webinars. If you want to see more, you'll need to use date filters to narrow down the list.

Microsoft Teams Information Protection License Report

This report helps you understand how different apps are using Microsoft's special APIs that need a paid license. It shows data only for apps using these APIs in a specific way (model=A). It won't show anything for other models or trial versions.

Here's how to see the report:

- **Access:** You need to be a Teams admin to view this report.

- **Steps:** Open the Microsoft Teams admin center, click "Analytics & reports," click "Usage reports," and click Pick Information Protection License.

You have the following options:

- **Time frame:** Choose the date range you're interested in.

- **App selection:** You can pick a specific app to focus on.

You'll see the following:

- **Categories:** The report shows data like how many users have a license, who doesn't, and the API usage limits.

- **Export and tabs:** You can download the data or switch between tabs to see different types of API usage.

Here's what is on the report:

- **Trends:** See app and API usage trends for up to the last three months.

- **Apps:** Lists all the apps using these special APIs.

- **Licensed users:** Shows how many users have a valid license.

- **Unlicensed users:** Shows how many don't.

- **API limits:** Shows the maximum API calls allowed before extra charges apply.

- **Actual API use:** Shows how much of the API limit has been used.

You can also see specific details such as the following:

- Who triggered notifications

- Who updated messages

- How many messages were exported

Here are some additional tips for this report:

- **Download:** You can download the data for offline checking. It downloads only the tab you are currently looking at.

- **Hide/show data:** You can choose what data labels to show in the charts.

- **API types:** Each tab gives details on a specific type of API such as notifications or message exports.

If you want to hide user-specific information such as names and emails, here are the steps:

1. You need to be a global admin.

2. Go to the Microsoft 365 admin center, click Settings, click Org Settings, and click Reports.

3. Choose to display anonymous identifiers.

Click "Save changes," and this will make reports anonymous in both the Microsoft 365 and Teams admin centers.

Microsoft Teams SMS Notifications Usage Report

This report helps you understand how your organization is using SMS (text messages) to remind people about their virtual appointments. It covers text reminders sent in the Virtual Appointments app and in the Teams healthcare records system.

You must be one of the following: Global admin, Teams admin, Global reader, or Report reader.

Here's how to view the report:

1. Open the Microsoft Teams admin center.

2. Select "Analytics & reports" and then "Usage reports."

3. Choose SMS notifications usage.

4. Pick 7 days, 30 days, or 90 days for the timeframe.

5. Run the report.

Here's what's on the report:

- **Chart overview:** A chart shows how many texts were sent each month.

- **Table details:** The table gives you the nitty-gritty about each text.

Here are the key parts of this report:

- **Date:** Shows when the report was made. It's usually updated every 24 to 48 hours.

- **Chart axes:** The chart's x-axis shows the months, and the y-axis shows the number of texts sent.

- **Filter options:** You can choose to see only texts related to virtual appointments or healthcare records.

- **Table info:** You'll see the exact time a text was sent, where it came from, the type of text (reminder or confirmation), and whether it was delivered or not.

These are the different delivery statuses:

- **Delivered:** The text reached the phone.

- **Not Delivered – Blocked by recipient:** The person opted out of texts.

- **Not Delivered – Invalid phone number:** It had the wrong number format.

- **Not Delivered - Phone number doesn't exist:** The number isn't real or allocated.

- **Not Delivered - Blocked phone number:** The number is on a spam list.

- **Not Delivered - Unreachable phone number:** The phone was off or had no signal.

- **Not Delivered - Spam detected:** A filter caught it as spam.

- **Not Delivered - Recipient blocked:** The number is blocked from receiving any texts.

- **Not Delivered - Other error:** Miscellaneous errors.

Now you can better track and understand how your organization is using SMS notifications for virtual appointments.

Custom Power BI Reports

Let's talk about custom Power BI reports.

Custom Power BI Reports: Leveraging Power BI for CQD Analysis in Microsoft Teams

In July 2022, a new Quality of Experience Report (QER) template was introduced for Power BI query templates in the CQD of Microsoft Teams. This template was designed to replace the older CQD Power BI templates from 2020. Although the older templates will remain accessible for demonstration, they are no longer maintained or updated. It's recommended to transition to the QER template for ongoing support. Note that this does not affect the CQD Teams Auto Attendant & Call Queue Historical Report.

For those interested in employing Power BI to analyze CQD data in Microsoft Teams, you can download the specialized Power BI templates provided by Microsoft. Upon opening these templates, you'll be prompted to authenticate using your CQD admin credentials. These templates are customizable and can be shared across your organization, provided users have both a Power BI license and CQD admin access.

Before you can start utilizing these Power BI templates (PBIT files), you'll need to install the Power BI Connector for Microsoft CQD. This is done by utilizing the MicrosoftCallQuality.pqx file that comes as part of the download package.

Ensure you have the appropriate CQD role permissions to access these Power BI reports.

Let's talk about the available templates.

QER.pbit is an all-in-one report template that offers a variety of functionalities.

- Search by meeting URL, conference ID, and more

- Meeting and user health details

- Metrics for media setup, reliability, and different types of media (audio/video/sharing)

- Insights into VPN impact, top problem areas, daily reports, and general usage statistics

- User feedback and network metrics

QER MTR.pbit is optimized for Microsoft Teams Rooms and covers MTR overview, network, and device health metrics.

QER PS.pbit is designed for Microsoft Teams Phone System deployments and includes the following:

- Direct Routing and Phone System Reports

- SBC and PSTN overviews

CQD Teams Auto Attendant & Call Queue Historical Report.pbit focuses on the following:

- Call analytics for auto attendants and call queues

- Agent activity timelines

For deprecated templates, users can still find information on PSTN Direct Routing, help-desk reports, and more, but these are no longer updated.

For further details on each template and how to maximize your reporting experience, you can refer to the respective guides provided by Microsoft.

Installing and Setting Up Microsoft Call Quality Connector for Power BI

Before taking advantage of Power BI's query templates for Microsoft Teams' CQD, you must first install the Microsoft Call Quality Connector for Power BI. This connector comes in the form of a MicrosoftCallQuality.pqx file, which is included in the download package. Then follow these steps:

1. **Locate or create a Custom Connectors folder:** Check if you already have a [Documents]\Power BI Desktop\Custom Connectors folder on your computer. If it doesn't exist, create one.

2. **Download and move the connector file:** Download the connector file, which will have either a .mez or .pqx extension, and move it to the Custom Connectors directory.

3. **Security settings:** If the connector file has a .mez extension, you'll need to modify your security settings. Follow the guidelines provided in the custom connector setup documentation for this step.

4. **Version updates:** If a newer version of the Microsoft Call Quality connector becomes available, replace the older file in the Custom Connectors directory with the new version.

Here's how to set up the connection:

1. **Initiate a connection:** Open Power BI Desktop, navigate to the Home tab, and click Get Data.

2. **Choose a data source:** In the Get Data window that appears, go to Online Services and then select Microsoft Call Quality (Beta). Click Connect to proceed.

3. **Authenticate:** You'll be prompted to sign in. Use the same credentials that you normally use for the Call Quality Dashboard.

4. **Data connectivity mode:** A prompt will appear giving you a choice between two data connectivity modes. Choose DirectQuery and confirm with OK.

5. **Load a data model:** A final window will display the data model for the Call Quality Dashboard. At this stage, you'll see only the data model, not the actual data. Click Load to finalize the setup.

6. **Query building:** With the data model loaded on the right side of your Power BI window (though no data will be visible yet), you can now proceed to construct queries to retrieve data.

If you encounter any unclear steps during setup, a more comprehensive guide can be found in the "Quickstart: Connect to data in Power BI Desktop" documentation.

Building queries in Power BI for Microsoft Teams data involves a series of steps from connecting your data source to visualizing the information. Here's a step-by-step guide on how to go about it:

1. **Connect to a data source:** Open Power BI and navigate to the Home tab. Click Get Data and select the appropriate data source. For Teams data, you might connect to Microsoft's Graph API, SQL databases, or other relevant sources where your Teams data is stored.

2. **Authenticate:** Follow the authentication prompts, entering the credentials used for your Teams account or another relevant service.

3. **Import or use DirectQuery:** Choose whether to import the data into Power BI or use DirectQuery to query the data directly from the source.

4. **Select tables and columns:** Once you're connected, you'll see a navigator panel showing available tables and columns. Select the ones relevant to your Teams analysis.

5. **Load data:** Click Load to bring the data into Power BI. It will appear in the Fields pane on the right side.

6. **Create basic queries:** Navigate to the Data view by clicking the table icon at the left. Here you can create new columns, filter data, or perform basic transformations using the formula bar and Power Query Editor.

7. **Make DAX queries:** For more advanced queries, you can use Data Analysis Expressions (DAX) in the formula bar to create new measures, calculated columns, or calculated tables.

8. **Query parameters and variables:** If your query needs to be dynamic, consider adding parameters or variables.

9. **Choose visualizations:** Switch back to Report view by clicking the bar chart icon at the left. Drag and drop the fields onto the report canvas and choose the type of visualizations (charts, tables, etc.) you'd like to use.

10. **Publish and share:** Once your query and visualizations are set up, click Publish to share the report with others in your organization who have a Power BI license.

For more complex scenarios such as timeseries analysis, user behavior funnels, or anomaly detection, you might want to use advanced DAX functions or even R/Python scripts, which can be run within Power BI.

By following these steps, you can build a range of queries to analyze your Microsoft Teams data, all tailored to your specific needs.

Creating a Focused Report Using Drill-Through in Power BI for Microsoft Teams

Drill-through functionality in Power BI offers a streamlined way to dive deeper into your Microsoft Teams Call Quality data. Once you've set up your basic query via the Microsoft Call Quality connector, implementing drill-through is fairly straightforward.

1. **Add a new page for focused reporting:** Create a new report page where you'll house your drill-through queries.

2. **Define the drill-through dimension:** On this new page, select the data dimension you plan to use for drill-through. Then drag it to the Drill-through area in the Visualizations pane.

3. **That's It!** Now, any other query on different report pages that uses the same dimension to drill down to this more focused report, applying the selected dimension's value as a filter automatically.

When using the Microsoft Call Quality connector, it's advisable to design your queries to be drill-through-friendly. Instead of loading a large dataset and filtering it down, start with more general queries and use drill-through to focus on more specific, high-cardinality data. For instance, start by identifying problematic regions or countries and then drill down to subnets within those areas for more details.

Here are some limitations:

- **Calculated columns:** Generally this is not supported in DirectQuery mode.

- **Aggregations:** These are built in, so manually adding or modifying aggregations usually leads to errors.

- **Custom visuals:** Compatibility is not guaranteed with all custom visuals, especially those requiring calculated columns.

- **Cached data reference:** This is not supported in DirectQuery mode.

- **Relative data filtering:** This is supported only with the Start Time and End Time dimensions.

- **Measurement-only queries:** This is not supported. Always include at least one dimension in your visualizations.

- **Government cloud support:** This is limited to Power BI Desktop and requires an appropriate Power BI U.S. government license.

Most limitations are inherent to either DirectQuery connector capabilities in Power BI or the design fundamentals of the CQD data model.

By understanding both the capabilities and limitations of the Microsoft Call Quality connector and Power BI's drill-through functionality, you can create more targeted and insightful reports.

Utilizing the CQD PSTN Direct Routing Report in Microsoft Teams

The CQD PSTN Direct Routing Report for Microsoft Teams is part of our downloadable Power BI query templates. This comprehensive report enables you to closely monitor the usage and performance metrics of your Public Switched Telephone Network (PSTN) services. With this tool, you can gauge service reliability, Session Border Controller (SBC) status, network metrics, and the Network Effectiveness Ratio metric among other parameters. This report is pivotal for troubleshooting issues such as call drops, understanding volume changes, and assessing the overall call impact.

The report is divided into four main sections.

- PSTN Overview

- Service Details

- Network Effectiveness Ratio

- Network Parameters

These are the key features:

- **Flexible analysis:** You can dissect data by various metrics such as call type, SBC, and geographic region of both the caller and callee. The report offers data aggregation for the previous 7, 30, or 180 days.

- **Trend monitoring:** Evaluate both short-term and long-term service reliability with hourly and daily trends. This dual approach lets you spot real-time incidents as well as long-term health trends.

- **Drill-through capabilities:** The report allows for a deeper dive into metrics such as Service Detail and Network Effectiveness Ratio. Simply click the data point you're interested in for more specific information.

For example, let's say you want to examine all inbound calls passing through a specific SBC with the United States as the internal region.

- **Call type filtering:** Use the top-level filters to select ByotIn as the call type, the specific SBC, and US for the internal region.

- **Usage trends:** 180-day trend information is available.

- **Network metrics:** Data on Post Dial Delay, Latency, Jitter, and Packet Loss for the past 180 days is shown.

- **Service capacity:** You'll see charts displaying the maximum volume of concurrent calls and daily active users over the past 180 days.

- **Quality metrics:** You can examine the primary reasons affecting call quality during this period.

Here are the service details:

- **Total attempted calls:** This is the sum of all calls attempted, both successful and failed, in the selected period.

- **Total connected calls:** This is the sum of all successfully connected calls.

- **Total minutes:** This is the cumulative minute usage.

- **Daily active users:** This is the number of unique users who made at least one successful call on a given day.

- **Concurrent calls:** This is the peak number of simultaneous calls in a minute.

- **User feedback:** Rate My Call scores are included, where a rating of 3 to 5 is deemed good, and 1 to 2 is poor.

By understanding and utilizing these metrics, the CQD PSTN Direct Routing Report provides you with the insights needed to optimize your telephony services in Microsoft Teams.

Teams Call Analytics

Let's talk about Call Analytics.

Configuring Call Analytics for Microsoft Teams

As an administrator of Microsoft Teams, you have the capability to employ per-user call analytics for identifying and resolving issues related to call quality and connectivity for individual users. This is a step-by-step guide on how to fully leverage the Call Analytics feature.

Assign targeted roles like help-desk agents to certain individuals to permit them to access user-specific call analytics. Note that these roles are restricted from accessing the broader Teams admin center.

These are the permissions levels:

- **Tier 1 support:** Assign the Teams communications support specialist role to provide limited access to call analytics.

- **Tier 2 support:** Assign the Teams communications support engineer role for comprehensive access to call analytics.

You can use the Azure AD for assigning roles.

Here's how to update the location information:

1. **Uploading a data file:** Populate per-user call analytics with building, site, and tenant information by uploading a .tsv or .csv data file.

2. **Mapping the IP address to the location:** Once uploaded, this data can be utilized to correlate IP addresses to physical locations, assisting admins and support staff in identifying trends or common issues among users in a specific location.

3. **Existing data use:** If you're already using Teams or Skype for Business, you can repurpose existing tenant and building data files from the CQD.

4. **Download:** Navigate to the Microsoft Teams admin center, go to Analytics & reports ➤ Call Quality Dashboard ➤ Upload now. Click Download next to the desired file in the "My uploads" list.

5. **Upload:** For uploading this new file into call analytics, consult the guidelines in Add and Update Reporting Labels.

Once the setup is complete, you can commence using per-user call analytics. For a deep dive into troubleshooting, refer to the guide "How to Use Per-User Call Analytics to Troubleshoot Poor Call Quality."

By following these steps, you prepare your Microsoft Teams environment for effective troubleshooting and analytics, making it easier for support roles to identify and resolve issues that users may encounter.

How to Use Call Analytics to Troubleshoot Poor Microsoft Teams Call Quality

Welcome to the deep dive into the world of Call Analytics for Microsoft Teams. As anyone who's worked remotely can tell you, the quality of your calls and meetings can make or break your day. If you're a Teams administrator or someone designated as a Teams communications support specialist or engineer, you have tools at your disposal to solve these issues. This blog post is designed to walk you through how to use Call Analytics to improve the individual call or meeting experience for Microsoft Teams users.

Note   This guide assumes you've already set up Call Analytics in Microsoft Teams. If you haven't done so, check out our guide on setting up Call Analytics for Teams.

Call Analytics is a feature within Microsoft Teams that offers granular information about each user's calls and meetings. It's not just about basic data—this feature provides comprehensive analytics on devices, networks, connectivity, and even building or site information if you've uploaded that data. Whether it's poor audio quality or connectivity issues, Call Analytics can help you get to the root of the problem.

To access this treasure trove of information, navigate to the Teams admin center. On the Users tab, select a user profile and then go to the Meetings & Calls tab. This will display all calls and meetings for that user within the past 30 days. For more granular data, you can click any given session to see detailed media and networking statistics.

Teams Communications Support Specialist (Tier 1)

- Handles basic call-quality issues

- Collects relevant data and escalates to the support engineer for further investigation

Teams Communications Support Engineer (Tier 2)

Accesses detailed call logs and performs in-depth analysis to solve complex issues.

Activity	Information	What Tier 1 Sees	What Tier 2 Sees
Calls	Caller Name, Recipient Name, Caller Phone Number, Recipient Phone Number	Limited Data	Detailed Data
Meetings	Participant Names, Participant Count, Session Details	Limited Data	Detailed Data

Note   For security reasons, certain sensitive information such as full phone numbers will be obfuscated.

Troubleshooting Steps

Here are the troubleshooting steps:

1. **Locate the user in question:** Log in to the Teams admin center and use the user search to find the user whose calls you want to investigate.

2. **Dive into specific calls or meetings:** Under Meetings & Calls, you'll find a list of sessions the user has been part of. Click any to get more details.

3. **Inspect the Advanced tab:** Look for indicators in yellow and red. Yellow signifies a minor issue, and red points to a major problem, often the main reason for the poor call quality.

Refer to Figure 8-2 for user call analytics information.

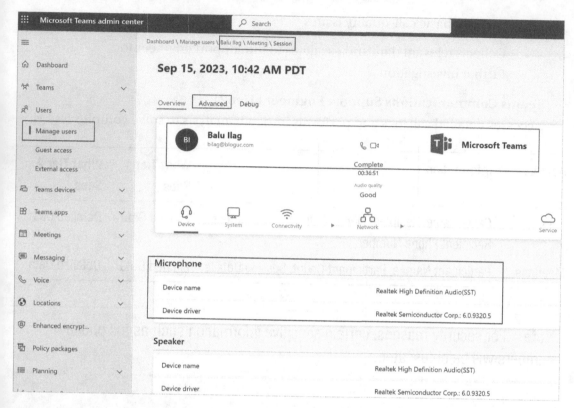

Figure 8-2. *Teams Call Analytics*

Anything in yellow means monitor it, but it's not critical
Anything in red re quires immediate action.

4. **Understand quality of experience (QoE) data:** In some cases,
   quality of experience data might not be available, usually due to
   dropped calls or terminated client connections. For those with
   QoE data, pay attention to the following:

   - **Call setup errors:** If error codes like Ms-diag 20-29 appear, the
     call setup failed.

   - **Network issues:** Watch for packet loss, jitter, and other network
     problems.

   - **Device malfunctions:** Check whether a device is functioning
     properly.

Call Analytics is a robust tool for troubleshooting and enhancing the Teams calling and meeting experience. While the data is immensely detailed and valuable, always remember to consult Microsoft Support for complex issues, especially before making judgments based on advanced telemetry and diagnostic data.

Call Quality Dashboard

The Teams Call Quality Dashboard serves as an organization-wide monitoring tool for evaluating the quality of calls and meetings on Microsoft Teams, as well as Skype for Business Online and Skype for Business Server 2019. Accessible via `https://cqd.teams.microsoft.com`, the CQD offers a near-real-time data stream, updating call records usually within 30 minutes after a call concludes.

The CQD adheres to Microsoft 365's standards for managing end-user identifiable information (EUII), ensuring data security and compliance. The dashboard aims to assist Teams and Skype for Business administrators, along with network engineers, in keeping tabs on performance metrics. CQD allows for a synergistic approach with individual user call analytics, helping to pinpoint whether poor call quality is an isolated or systemic issue.

The dashboard is also instrumental in offering insights into several quality metrics including overall call quality, server-client interactions, and voice quality service-level agreements (SLAs). It further provides the capability to upload building or endpoint data. Doing so enables location-enhanced reports, which can refine the analysis of call quality and reliability down to a user's specific building or network endpoint. To activate these specialized views, administrators need to upload the necessary data via the CQD Tenant Data Upload page.

To initialize the CQD in Microsoft Teams, visit `https://cqd.teams.microsoft.com` and log in using your administrative credentials. Alternatively, navigate to the Teams admin center and choose "Analytics & reports," followed by the Call Quality Dashboard option. Figure 8-3 shows the CQD Summary reports.

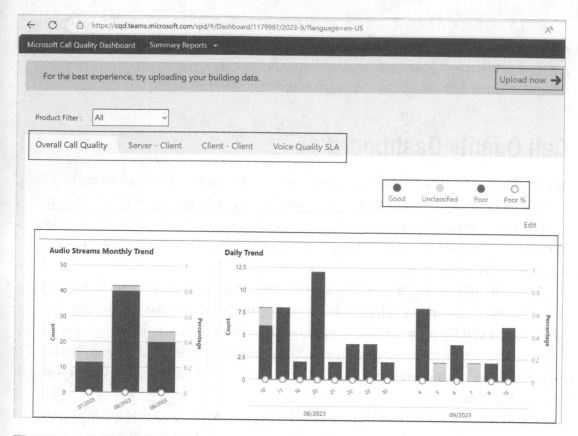

Figure 8-3. *CQD Summary Report*

Once you land on the dashboard page, log in using your either Global Administrator or Microsoft Teams Administrator account. The CQD provides a holistic view of call and meeting quality, encompassing Microsoft Teams as well as Skype for Business Online and Skype for Business Server 2019.

Note that if you're using Skype for Business Server 2019, you will need to set up the Call Data Connector beforehand.

Designate roles to individuals requiring access to the CQD, keeping in mind that roles differ in their access levels to various functionalities such as viewing reports, accessing end-user identifiable information (EUII), or uploading building data. Roles that can access the CQD range from Global Administrators and Teams Administrators to more specialized roles like Teams Communications Support Engineer.

Important Note   If EUII isn't visible and you possess a role with the appropriate access level, be aware that CQD retains EUII for only 28 days, deleting anything older.

For a comprehensive understanding of these roles and their capabilities, refer to the Office 365 admin roles documentation. Once you've logged into the CQD for the first time, it will commence the data collection and processing activities.

Microsoft advises uploading tenant and building data for an optimal experience with the CQD. Tenant data comes in two forms: building and endpoint files.

Getting Started

You can download a sample template from `https://github.com/MicrosoftDocs/OfficeDocs-SkypeForBusiness/blob/live/Teams/downloads/locations-template.zip?raw=true`. For building mapping help, read the "Create a building map for CQD" guide (`https://learn.microsoft.com/en-us/microsoftteams/cqd-building-mapping`).

Uploading Data

Here's how to upload data:

1. Navigate to the CQD from the Teams admin center.

2. Click the gear icon in the top-right corner.

3. Choose Tenant Data Upload from the Summary Reports page.
    Figure 8-4 shows a tenant data upload.

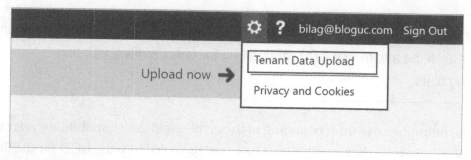

Figure 8-4. *Uploading tenant data*

4. If this is your first CQD visit, you'll receive a prompt to upload building data.

5. On the Tenant Data Upload page, click Browse to select a data file.

6. Set the start date and optionally an end date.

7. Click Upload.

Before uploading, the system validates your file. If the file fails validation, an error message will appear for troubleshooting. For instance, an error could occur due to an incorrect number of columns.

Upon successful upload, the uploaded files are listed in the "My uploads" table. It might take up to four hours for the file to be fully processed.

If you've uploaded a building file already and need to make changes, download the original file, amend it, delete the existing file in CQD, and then re-upload.

File Requirements

Here are the file requirements.

Building Data File

- Format: .tsv or .csv

- No table header

- 15 columns in specified order and format (see detailed guide)

- Examples and specifics can be found in the detailed guide.

Endpoint Data File

- Format: .tsv or .csv

- No table header

- 7 columns, only String data type allowed, 64 character limit

- Further examples and specifics can be found in the detailed guide.

The following are some special considerations:

- Supernetting is supported but not recommended.

- The VPN column is optional.

- Only one active building file can exist in CQD at a time.

For missing subnets, follow these steps:

1. Go to the Missing Subnet Report on the Quality of Experience Reports page.

2. Download the original building file.

3. Append new subnets.

4. Re-upload with a start date set to at least eight months prior.

Note   For a comprehensive view of the report, add your tenant ID as a query filter for Second Tenant ID.

This condensed guide is meant to provide an overview. For further details and advanced configurations, consult the comprehensive guide.

Teams CQD Data and Report

The CQD updates call records within 30 minutes after a call ends. However, this near-real-time data is retained for only a limited period.

Choose from various methods to access CQD data:

- **Teams admin center:** This offers basic, noncustomizable call quality data on the Users page.

- **CQD portal:** This features customizable, detailed reports and filters.

- **Power BI:** You can view and download customizable templates for data analysis.

- **Graph API:** This is an advanced method for in-depth data analysis and integration.

Quick-start with two CQD templates: All Networks and Managed Networks. Follow the menu steps to import them.

End-user identifiable information (EUII) is stored for 28 days, after which it becomes anonymized.

You need the following admin role permissions:

- **Roles with EUII access:** Global Admin, Teams Service Admin, etc.

- **Roles without EUII access:** Reports Reader, Teams Communications Support Specialist

The CQD supports rolling-trend reports for various time spans. Use date parameters in URLs for specifying the last day in the trend.

These are the types of reports:

- **Summary reports:** These provide a snapshot of call quality.

- **Detailed reports:** These provide in-depth analysis.

- **Location-enhanced:** These require tenant data upload.

- **Reliability reports:** These include all media types.

- **Quality drill-downs:** These break down data by multiple dimensions.

- **Help-desk reports:** These include user-specific call and meeting data.

- **Client version reports:** These track usage by app versions.

- **Endpoint reports:** These measure call quality by device.

If default reports aren't sufficient, create custom ones or use Power BI templates.

Ensure there are no overlaps in subnet information when uploading building files, as this may cause incorrect mappings.

Call Quality Troubleshooting Using the CQD

To ensure optimal performance in Microsoft Teams, it's essential for IT administrators and support engineers to have a proactive strategy for monitoring and sustaining call and meeting quality. The CQD is your go-to tool for this purpose, with a particular focus on enhancing audio quality as a pathway to improving video and content sharing experiences as well.

Monitoring Categories and Best Practices

After deploying Microsoft Teams for meetings and voice services, it's crucial to maintain regular checks on various aspects of call and meeting quality. Here's a breakdown:

Call Quality

- Segment metrics based on internal (e.g., VPN, Wi-Fi, wired) and external calls.

- Further classify metrics by building or network.

- Monitor calls made through VPN, TCP, UDP, or proxy.

Call Reliability

- Address any network or firewall issues.

- Evaluate the rates of call setup and drop failures.

- Determine where most of these failures occur.

User Experience

- Leverage Rate My Call data to gauge the user's real-world experiences.

- Pinpoint the source of poor experiences.

- Link poor experiences with metrics on call quality, reliability, and devices.

741

Devices

- Analyze which audio and video devices are most frequently used and their effects on call quality.

- Ensure that drivers for audio, video, USB, and Wi-Fi are up-to-date.

Clients

- Study the types and versions of client software in use and their impact on call and meeting quality.

Common Issues and Remediations

Several factors can degrade user experiences.

- Firewall or proxy misconfigurations

- Weak Wi-Fi signals

- Limited bandwidth

- VPN issues

- Outdated client versions and drivers

- Unsuitable audio devices

- Faulty subnets or network devices

Prioritize resolving these issues to sustain high-quality experiences across Teams.

Leveraging CQD Templates for Efficient Assessment

Two predesigned CQD templates are available: one for monitoring all networks and another specific to internal networks. Although the All Networks template can show building and network data, you can enhance this by uploading custom building and location information. This enables CQD to provide more granular and informative reports, differentiating between internal and external subnets.

By systematically addressing the areas outlined in this guide, you'll be well-equipped to ensure a consistently high-quality experience for all Teams users.

Quality in Microsoft Teams revolves around both service metrics and the user's experience.

Service metrics are client-specific metrics collected during each call. These include factors like the following:

- Poor stream rates (incoming and outgoing)
- Setup failure rate
- Drop failure rate

The Poor Stream Rate (PSR) metric focuses on the proportion of low-quality streams in your organization, aiming to pinpoint areas for improvement.

In CQD, one important metric is the Audio Poor Percentage. PSR comprises five network metrics such as jitter, packet loss, and round-trip time. A stream is tagged as poor if it surpasses the set limits for any of these metrics.

Why Use Streams Over Calls?

Streams offer insights into which part of a call—outgoing or incoming—affected quality. Stream direction can pinpoint issues from problematic devices to network limitations. By focusing on stream data, you can delve into the root cause of poor call quality.

Setting Up Targets

Setting quality and reliability targets is crucial for ensuring consistent call quality. Here are some suggested targets:

Network Type	Quality Targets (Audio Poor Stream Rate)	Reliability Targets (Setup & Drop Failure Rate)
Overall	3.0%	1.0%, 3.0%

User Experience Metrics

User experience can be subjective but is equally important. The Rate My Call (RMC) feature helps collect user feedback to complement service metrics.

Device and Client Preparedness

Keeping both client software and devices updated is crucial for optimal user experience. These are categories for quality management:

- **Network:** Focus on PSR, TCP usage, and the network environment.

- **Endpoints:** Use up-to-date clients and quality audio devices.

- **Service management:**

  - **Microsoft's role:** Maintain Teams and Skype services.

  - **Your role:** Keep your organizational settings, like firewalls, updated.

Regularly review and adjust your quality management practices to ensure the best call and meeting experiences.

Ongoing Improvements

Microsoft is continually refining its reporting capabilities, adding new metrics, features, and additional reports over time.

If you're a Global Administrator and want to anonymize identifiable information in reports, navigate to the Microsoft 365 admin center. Go to Settings, click Org Settings, and go to the Services tab. Select Reports. From there, select "Display concealed user, group, and site names in all reports."

By configuring these settings, you'll anonymize data both in Microsoft 365 and Teams admin center reports.

By leveraging the analytics and reporting features in Microsoft Teams, administrators can gain a more nuanced understanding of user engagement and system performance. This data is critical for optimizing workflows, ensuring efficient resource allocation, and promoting effective communication within the organization.

Summary

This chapter served as a comprehensive guide for administrators and team leads seeking to understand and optimize the performance and usage of Microsoft Teams within their organization. The chapter introduced the pivotal role of reporting and monitoring in ensuring seamless communication and collaboration through Teams. It then delved into various tools and methodologies, from built-in Teams Usage Reports for gauging user engagement to the more advanced custom reporting capabilities offered through Power BI. For those concerned with call and meeting quality, the chapter discussed both individual-level analytics and broader organizational metrics through Teams Call Analytics and the Call Quality Dashboard, respectively. It also offered a robust guide for troubleshooting call quality issues, harnessing the analytical power of both CQD and Call Analytics.

In conclusion, the chapter emphasized that effective reporting and monitoring are not just optional but essential for a successful Microsoft Teams experience, thereby setting the stage for deeper explorations into Teams functionalities.

CHAPTER 9

Microsoft Teams for Education: Setup, Usage, and Management

Microsoft Teams for Education is a specialized version of Microsoft Teams that is designed to meet the unique needs of educators and students. Microsoft Teams is a platform designed to simplify communication, collaboration, and sharing of resources among users. It is an online communication tool that allows students and teachers to work together and stay connected. In the education sector, Teams has emerged as a powerful platform for remote learning, with numerous features designed to support online education. In this chapter, we use the terms *educator* and *teacher* interchangeably, *IT administrator* and *management* interchangeably, as well as *scholar* and *student* interchangeably.

This chapter aims to explore the use of Microsoft Teams in education, focusing on its functionalities, features, and benefits. In particular, we will discuss how educators and school IT administrators can control Teams to ensure student safety, how students can turn in their assignments using Teams, and how educators can monitor and grade student progress in Teams.

Microsoft Teams for Education Overview

Microsoft Teams for Education is a powerful communication and collaboration platform designed specifically for educational institutions. It is part of the Microsoft Office 365 suite of tools and allows teachers, students, and administrators to communicate, collaborate, and share resources in a single platform.

© Balu N Ilag, Durgesh Tripathy, Vijay Ireddy 2024
B. N. Ilag et al., *Understanding Microsoft Teams Administration*,
https://doi.org/10.1007/979-8-8688-0014-6_9

With Microsoft Teams for Education, educators can create virtual classrooms, assign and grade assignments, and provide feedback to students. Students, on the other hand, can access course materials, collaborate with classmates, and submit assignments. Microsoft Teams for Education provides a centralized hub for all classroom activities and streamlines communication between teachers and students. Here are some key features of Microsoft Teams for Education:

- **Virtual classrooms:** Educators can create virtual classrooms within Teams and invite students to join. They can share course materials, conduct online lectures, and facilitate discussions with students.

- **Assignments and grading:** Teachers can create assignments within Teams and assign them to individual students or groups. They can grade assignments and provide feedback to students, all within the same platform.

- **Collaboration:** Microsoft Teams for Education provides a platform for students to collaborate with each other on group projects or assignments. They can share files, co-author documents, and provide feedback to each other.

- **OneNote integration:** Microsoft Teams for Education integrates with OneNote, a note-taking application, to provide students with a digital notebook. This allows students to take notes and organize their course materials in one place.

- **Meetings:** Teachers and students can schedule online meetings within Teams to discuss course materials or assignments. This feature also allows for screen sharing and recording of meetings.

- **Security and privacy:** Microsoft Teams for Education complies with industry standards for security and privacy. It provides control over who can access course materials and allows for secure communication between teachers and students.

Before Teams deployment, make sure you do the following:

- Deploy School Data Sync to automate the creation of Teams and simplify the process for educators. Contact `https://aka.ms/ sdssupport` for deployment assistance.

- Configure the correct ports and protocols for Teams to ensure proper functionality. Refer to the Office 365 "URLs and IP address ranges" documentation for more information.

- Prepare your school's network for Teams to ensure a smooth and stable user experience. This may include reviewing bandwidth requirements and adjusting network settings as needed.

- Choose the appropriate team type for your needs. Teams for Education offers four team types, each with different features and use cases. Refer to the "Choose a team type to collaborate in Teams" documentation to learn more about each type and determine which one is best suited for your needs.

Microsoft Teams: The All-in-One Hub for Everyone in Education

Microsoft Teams serves as a unified platform that connects all aspects of education, providing a digital space where everyone can collaborate, communicate, and innovate. This section covers how various educational stakeholders benefit from using Teams. Figure 9-1 shows all the involved parties.

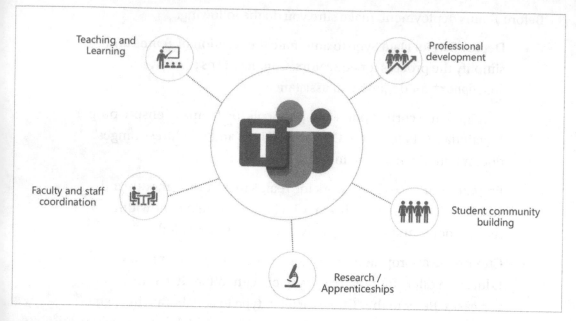

Figure 9-1. All-in-one hub for everyone in education

Teaching and Learning

Teams offers a dedicated space where teachers and students can engage in real-time or asynchronous learning. Teachers can distribute assignments, offer feedback, and facilitate group projects, all in one platform. Students, in return, can ask questions, submit their work, and collaborate with their classmates. It's a complete digital classroom environment where both teaching and learning can happen seamlessly.

Faculty and Staff Coordination

The platform is not just for teachers and students; it's also an administrative tool. Staff can coordinate everything from admissions to event planning. Teams channels can be designated for specific departments or tasks, and important documents can be shared securely. Whether it's the finance department working on budgets or staff organizing an event, Teams keeps everyone in sync.

Professional Development

Teams offers a space for professional learning communities (PLCs) and other staff development initiatives. Here, educators can share teaching resources, discuss educational strategies, and even invite experts for special webinars or workshops. Teams can also be used to track professional development milestones, making it easier for administrators to gauge and support staff progress.

Student Community Building

Apart from academics, Teams can be a hub for extracurricular activities. Student organizations, clubs, and teams can have their own channels. This feature fosters a sense of community and belonging among students. They can share updates, plan events, or even run virtual meetings, bridging the gap between in-person and digital interactions.

Research/Apprenticeships

For higher education and research institutions, Teams provides a collaborative environment where complex projects can be managed. Whether it's a long-term research project or a short-term apprenticeship, participants can share data, run virtual lab meetings, and keep everyone updated on progress. Teams can host files, data sets, and other research materials, making it easier for involved parties to collaborate.

In summary, Microsoft Teams is an all-encompassing hub tailored to meet the diverse needs of everyone involved in the educational process, from classroom instruction and administrative work to professional growth and community engagement.

How Microsoft Teams Helps Teachers and Schools

Microsoft Teams is a tool that helps teachers and school staff work together easily. It's a place where teachers can chat, share information, and make plans. Teams helps teachers create better learning experiences and saves time on school tasks.

In Teams, teachers can use class teams to talk with students, share study materials, and grade assignments. Students can use programs such as Word, PowerPoint, Excel, and OneNote that they already know. Teachers can also use OneNote Class Notebooks to plan lessons and give feedback. This helps make schoolwork easier for both teachers and students.

Teams isn't just for teachers and students. School staff can also use it to work on projects or school-wide plans. It's a place where everyone in the school can find important forms, policies, and instructions. School leaders can use it to give private feedback and training plans for teachers. Online meetings can happen in Teams too, even if people are in different locations.

Finally, learning how to use Teams in school helps prepare students for the future. Many businesses use Teams, so students will already know how to use tools they will likely see in their jobs. This gives students a head start in being ready for the work world.

How Do I Get Microsoft Teams?

Microsoft Teams for education is free for students as well as teachers. However, they have used a valid education domain email address. Students and teachers from K-12 to the collegiate level can use Teams for free with an eligible active school email. Refer to Figure 9-2 to download Microsoft Teams: `https://go.microsoft.com/fwlink/p/?LinkID=869426&clcid=0x409&culture=en-us&country=US&lm=deeplink&lmsrc=groupChatMarketingPageWeb&cmpid=directDownloadWin64`.

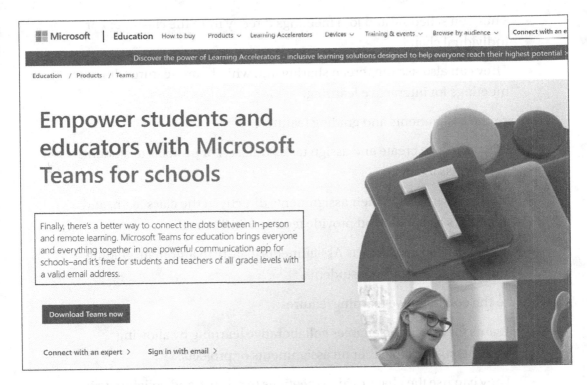

Figure 9-2. *Downloading Teams now*

For institutions, there are different plans. You can compare the different plans and choose one suitable for your institution. You can get complete information about all the different license plans for education and comparison. Refer to `https://edudownloads.azureedge.net/msdownloads/Microsoft-Modern-Work-Plan-Comparison-Education_11-2021.pdf`.

If you want to try or buy the Microsoft 365 suite, then visit `https://www.microsoft.com/en-us/microsoft-365/try?ocid=cmmjmzkagvx&rtc=1`.

Microsoft Teams Functionality and Features For Education

Here's the chat and meetings features:

- Educators and students can use chat and video meetings to communicate and collaborate in real time.

- They can schedule and join meetings directly from the class team or individual chat.

- They can also use the screen sharing and whiteboard features during meetings for interactive learning.

Here are the assignments and grading features:

- Educators can create and assign tasks, quizzes, or projects to students in the class team.

- Students can turn in their assignments directly in the class team, and educators can grade and provide feedback in Teams.

- Educators can also use the Assignments feature to automate grading and provide feedback to students.

Here are the collaborative learning features:

- Teams for Education enables collaborative learning by allowing students to work together on assignments or projects.

- They can use the chat or video meetings to discuss and collaborate in real time.

- They can also use the Files feature to share and collaborate on documents, presentations, or spreadsheets.

Here are the Class Notebook features:

- Class Notebook is a digital notebook that enables educators to organize and distribute course content to students.

- It includes sections for notes, handouts, quizzes, or assignments, which students can access and work on.

- Educators can also provide feedback and grade students' work in the Class Notebook.

Configure Microsoft Teams for Education

Enabling Microsoft Teams for an education institute requires careful planning and execution to ensure that the Teams environment is secure and complies with the institution's policies and regulations. By following these step-by-step instructions, educational institutes can enable Microsoft Teams and provide their students and faculty with a powerful collaboration platform for remote learning and communication.

Enabling Microsoft Teams for an education institute involves a series of steps that need to be completed in a specific order. The following is a detailed step-by-step guide on how to enable Microsoft Teams for an education institute.

Creating a Microsoft Teams Account for Education

Creating a Microsoft Teams for Education account generally involves a few more steps than creating a standard Teams account. This is because Teams for Education is designed to be used in a school or university setting and has features that support classroom collaboration, assignments, and grading. The following are the general requirements to create a Microsoft Teams for Education account:

- **Access to Microsoft 365 Education plan:** Teams for Education is available as part of the Microsoft 365 Education package, which requires a valid school email address.

- **Admin rights:** If you are an IT administrator at an educational institution, you may need to set up Teams for your faculty, students, and staff.

Step 1: Verify Eligibility

Before enabling Microsoft Teams for an education institute, it is essential to verify the eligibility requirements. Microsoft Teams for Education is available for primary and secondary schools, colleges, universities, and other academic institutions that are accredited and recognized by the relevant authorities. You can visit `https://www.microsoft.com/en-us/education/products/office` to check your institute eligibility. Figure 9-3 shows the eligibility verification by entering the institute email address.

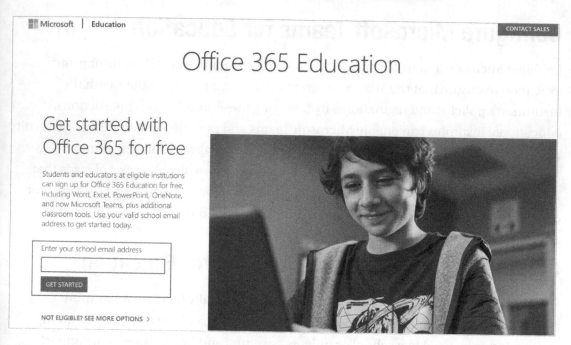

Figure 9-3. *Microsoft 365 Education Account verification*

Step 2: Create a Microsoft 365 Education Account

The next step is to create a Microsoft 365 Education account. To do this, follow these steps:

1. Go to the Microsoft Education page and then click Get Started. Refer the Figure 9-4 for education account setup.

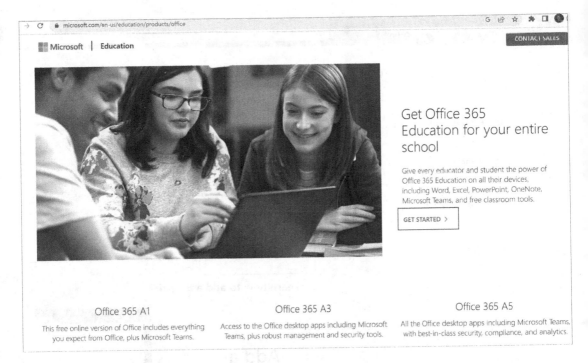

Figure 9-4. *Microsoft 365 Education Get Started page*

2. Provide the required information, including the name of the institution, country, and primary contact.

3. Choose the number of licenses needed for your institution and select the appropriate license type.

4. Agree to the terms and conditions and click Create account.

Step 3: Verify the Domain

After creating the Microsoft 365 Education account, the next step is to verify the domain. This is necessary to ensure that only authorized users can access the institution's Teams account. To verify the domain, follow these steps:

1. Sign into the Microsoft 365 Education account using the primary contact's email address and password.

2. Click Settings and then Domains. Figure 9-5 shows the "Add a domain" page.

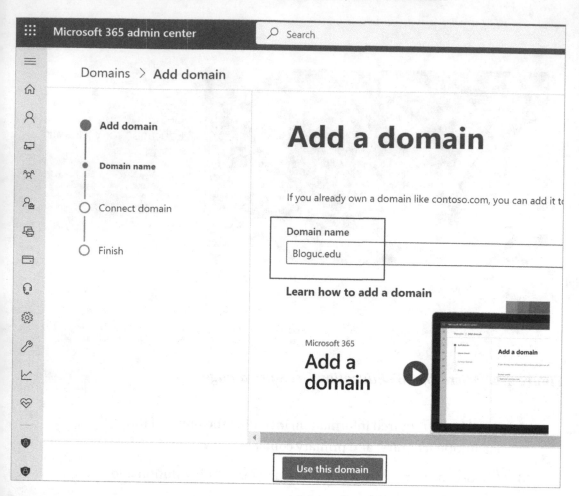

Figure 9-5. Adding a domain

3.   Enter the domain name for the institution and click "Use this domain."

4.   Follow the on-screen instructions to verify the domain.

Step 4: Create Users and Assign Licenses

Once the domain is verified, the next step is to create users and assign licenses. To do this, follow these steps:

1.   Click Users and then "Active users."

2.   Click "Add a user."

3. Provide the required information, including the user's name and email address.

4. Assign the appropriate license type and click "Add user." Refer to Figure 9-6, and add the user and license.

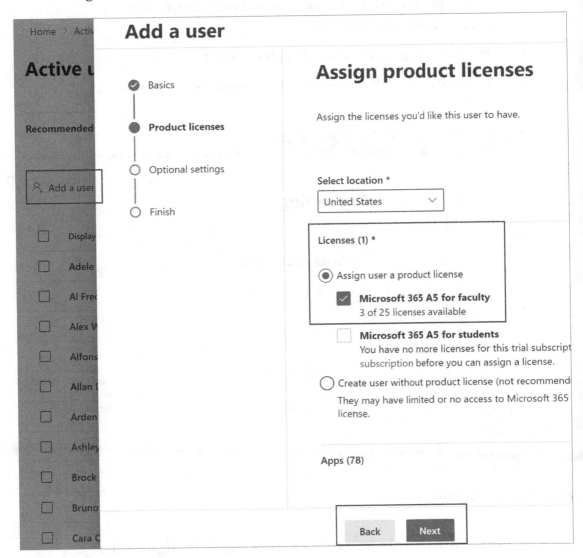

Figure 9-6. *Adding a user and license*

Step 5: Enable Teams for the Institution

After creating users and assigning licenses, the next step is to enable Teams for the institution. To do this, follow these steps:

1. Sign into the Microsoft 365 Education account using the primary contact's email address and password.

2. Click Admin to go to the Office 365 admin center

3. Then go to Settings ➤ Org Settings ➤ Microsoft Teams. Refer to Figure 9-7.

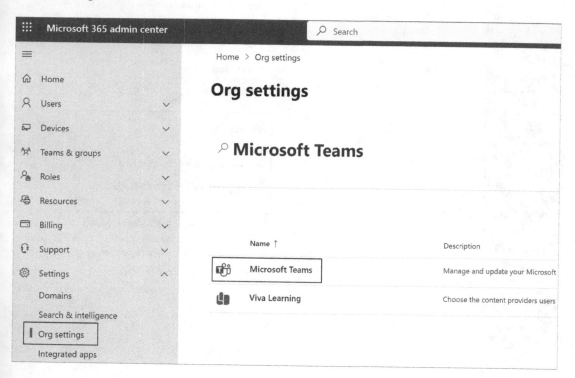

Figure 9-7. *Enabling Teams*

4. Click "Go to the old admin center Settings page" to navigate to the non-preview settings page and select Microsoft Teams from within the Settings ➤ Services list.

5. On the Microsoft Teams settings screen, select the license that you want to configure, Student or Faculty and Staff. Select Faculty and Staff.

6. Select to turn on Microsoft Teams for each license type in your organization.

7. Then click Save to complete the steps.

Step 6: Set Up Policies and Permissions

The final step is to set up policies and permissions for the institution. This is necessary to ensure that the Teams environment is secure and complies with the institution's policies and regulations.

Teams for Education Policy Wizard: Ensuring a Safe and Productive Learning Environment

The Microsoft Teams for Education Policy Wizard is your one-stop solution to efficiently manage policies for both students and educators in your institution. With this tool, you can effortlessly implement the most relevant policies that contribute to a secure and enriching educational environment.

Why Policy Control Is Essential

Policies in Microsoft Teams help you control the application's behavior and available features to different users. These can range from calling and meeting policies to messaging policies. Customizing these policies based on your institution's requirements is vital for controlling user interactions and keeping the digital learning space secure.

Focused Learning: Student vs. Educator Policies

To maintain an optimal learning environment, you'll want to adjust policies for both students and educators. Typically, policies for students are more restrictive to minimize the risk of unauthorized access or distractions. On the other hand, educators often require more permissive policies to perform tasks such as scheduling meetings and sharing educational content effectively.

Running the Wizard

Note the following about running the wizard:

- The wizard categorizes policies based on the type of educational institution—be it Primary, Secondary, or Higher education.

- For students, the wizard modifies the Global (Org-wide default) policies with settings tailored for student safety.

- For educators and staff, the wizard creates and assigns custom policies that meet their specific needs.

One-Time Setup

You need to run the wizard only once. Any new students or staff added later will automatically be assigned the appropriate default policies, saving you time and effort in manual setup.

Automatic Updates

New Teams features will have their EDU-relevant default policy settings added automatically, keeping your environment updated without requiring admin intervention.

Important Note   While the wizard will meet the needs of most educational organizations, you still have the option to manually create and manage policies for more specific requirements.

Getting Started: Steps to Run the Wizard

Here are the steps to run the wizard:

1. Open the Microsoft Teams admin center and navigate to Home.

2. Click Quick Setup under the "Easy policy setup for a safe learning environment" tile.

3. Choose your institution type.

4. Select the groups containing your educators and staff.

5. Review and apply your settings.

The changes may take some time to propagate, especially for larger groups, but rest assured, they are applied in the background.

After successfully running the wizard, don't forget to check the "What to do after running the wizard" section to ensure that you're making the most of your Teams for Education experience.

Supervised Chats in Microsoft Teams: Balancing Safety and Personalized Learning

Digital communication within educational institutions must prioritize student safety while allowing meaningful interactions. While disabling private chats in Microsoft Teams is a common practice to prevent inappropriate behavior, it often eliminates the space for one-on-one student-teacher interactions. Supervised chat in Microsoft Teams is the answer to this dilemma.

How Supervised Chat Works

Supervised chat enables authorized educators to initiate private chats with students, ensuring that students can't start new chats without an educator present. Once a chat is initiated, educators or "supervisors" can't exit, and participants can't remove them. This ensures a safe and monitored communication space.

Note   This feature applies only to new private chats created after enabling supervised chat, not to existing chats, meeting chats, or channels.

Here are some scenarios when a supervised chat becomes indispensable:

- One-on-one follow-up sessions between educators and students who may hesitate to ask questions publicly

- Educators reaching out to students individually to discuss assignments or class participation

- Monitored student group discussions

- Enabling nonteaching staff to interact with students in a supervised setting

Setting Up Supervised Chat

Let's talk about how to set up supervised chat.

Chat Permission Roles

Before activating supervised chat, define the chat permission roles for each user, aligning with one of three categories:

- **Full permissions:** Best suited for educators, these users can initiate and supervise chats.

- **Limited permissions:** Ideal for nonteaching staff who need supervised access to students but full access to other staff.

- **Restricted permissions:** Designed for students, allowing them to engage only in chats started by users with full permissions.

To assign roles, navigate to the Teams admin portal and find the Chat permissions role policy under your "Messaging policy" options. You can also use PowerShell commands for role assignment.

Enabling Supervised Chat

After setting up roles, turn on supervised chat by toggling the Role-based chat permissions policy in Teams settings. PowerShell commands can also be used for this.

Ongoing Maintenance

Post-activation, ensure the following:

- New users are assigned appropriate roles (by default, they are set to restricted).

- If a "full permission" user leaves or is removed, another user with full permissions must replace them to continue the supervised chats.

Note   Guests in your tenant are automatically assigned a limited role, and supervised chat is an all-or-nothing feature—it cannot be partially implemented across your user base.

Teams Control for Educators and School IT for Student Safety

As an educator or IT administrator, controlling the use of Teams in your institution is crucial to ensuring student safety. Microsoft Teams has numerous controls that can be customized to fit the specific needs of your institution. The platform includes a range of features and tools that enable teachers and students to collaborate, communicate, and learn in a virtual environment. Some of the key topics that are covered under Microsoft Teams for Education include the following:

- **Class creation and management:** Teachers can create virtual classrooms, manage class rosters, and assign tasks and assessments to students.

- **Communication and collaboration:** Microsoft Teams for Education provides a range of communication and collaboration tools, such as video conferencing, chat, and file sharing, that enable students and teachers to work together in real time.

- **Learning management system integration:** Microsoft Teams for Education can be integrated with popular learning management systems (LMS), such as Canvas and Blackboard, to provide a seamless learning experience for students.

- **Assignments and assessments:** Teachers can create and assign assignments and assessments to students and can use the platform's grading and feedback tools to provide feedback and track progress.

- **Accessibility and inclusion:** Microsoft Teams for Education includes features that support accessibility and inclusion, such as live captions and transcripts, translation capabilities, and support for assistive technologies.

- **Security and compliance:** Microsoft Teams for Education is designed to meet the security and compliance needs of educational institutions, with features such as data encryption, multifactor authentication, and compliance with international standards such as GDPR and FERPA.

Overall, Microsoft Teams for Education is a comprehensive platform that enables teachers and students to collaborate and learn in a virtual environment, with tools and features that are specifically designed to support the needs of the education community.

How to Manage Your Team and Set Rules in Microsoft Teams for Educators

Here's how to manage your team and set rules:

- **Changing roles and deleting members:** After making a team, teachers can change what role a member has or even remove them.

  To change someone's role, click the three dots next to the team name and click Manage Team. To make someone an owner, find their name, click the drop-down arrow next to Member, and choose Owner. If you need to kick someone out, just click the 'X' next to their name. Figure 9-8 shows Teams permission role and Team management options.

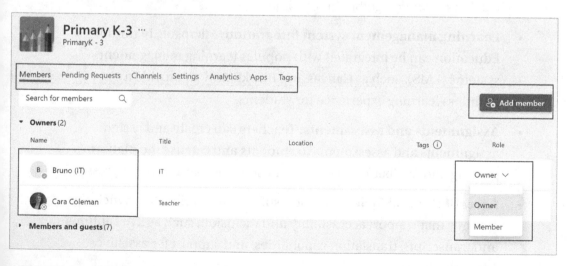

Figure 9-8. *Teams role setting*

- **Starting and managing conversations:** You can chat with students and other teachers on the Posts tab.

  This is a good way to talk about class topics, set rules, and help students be good digital citizens. But sometimes, you might need to make sure chats stay respectful and on-topic.

  You can stop certain students or even the whole class from posting messages using the Manage Team option.

- **Setting up team rules:** In the Manage Team menu, teachers can change a lot of settings. First, go to Settings. Here, you can decide what members can and can't do, such as making or deleting chat channels, tabs, and apps. In the @mentions area, you set who can tag the whole team or a specific channel. And if you like fun, you can allow students to use GIFs, stickers, and memes in the "fun stuff" area. Refer to Figure 9-9 for the Teams management settings.

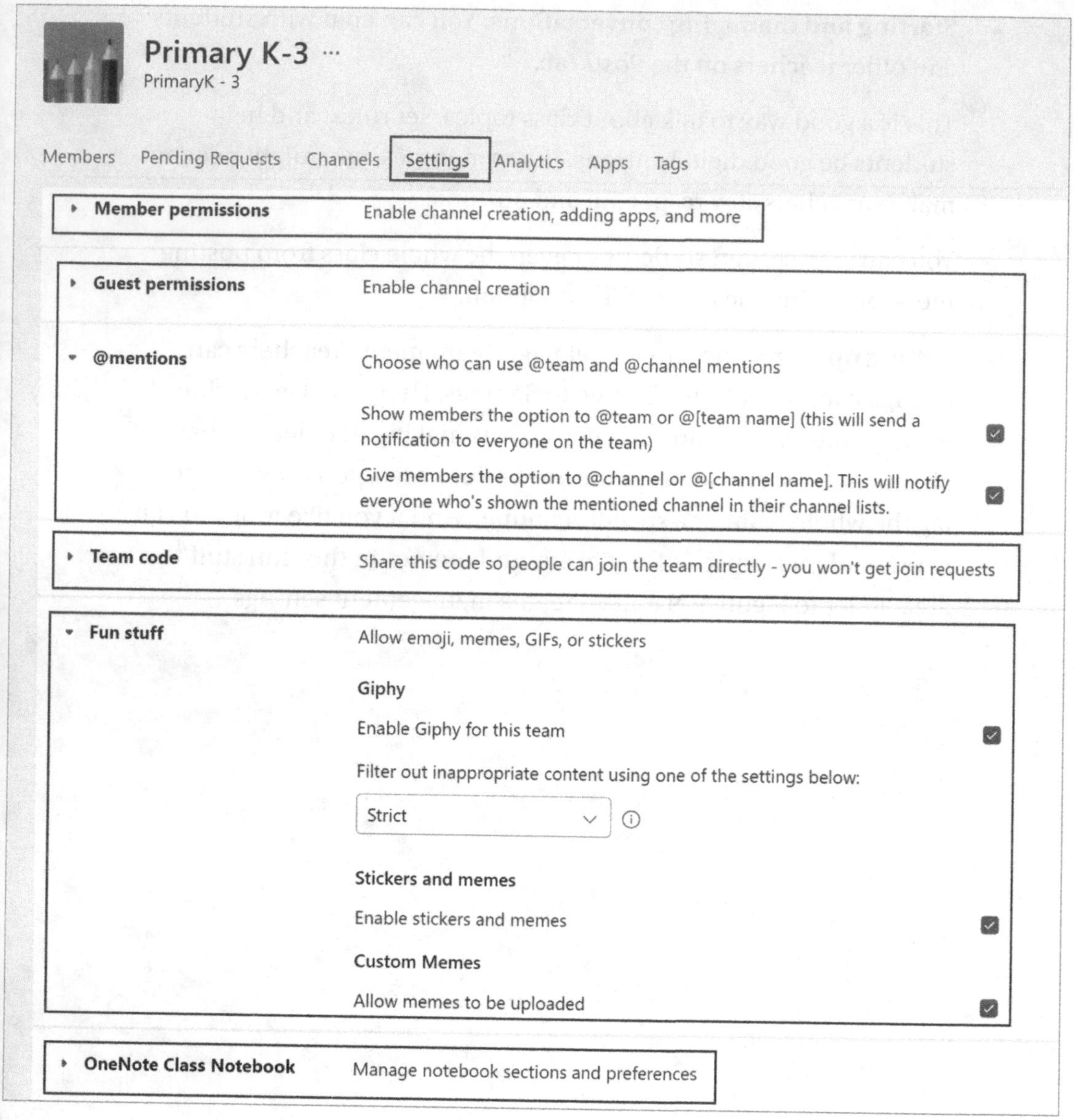

Primary K-3 ⋯
PrimaryK - 3

Members   Pending Requests   Channels   Settings   Analytics   Apps   Tags

▸ **Member permissions**   Enable channel creation, adding apps, and more

▸ **Guest permissions**   Enable channel creation

▾ **@mentions**   Choose who can use @team and @channel mentions

Show members the option to @team or @[team name] (this will send a notification to everyone on the team) ☑

Give members the option to @channel or @[channel name]. This will notify everyone who's shown the mentioned channel in their channel lists. ☑

▸ **Team code**   Share this code so people can join the team directly - you won't get join requests

▾ **Fun stuff**   Allow emoji, memes, GIFs, or stickers

Giphy

Enable Giphy for this team ☑

Filter out inappropriate content using one of the settings below:

Strict ⌄ ⓘ

Stickers and memes

Enable stickers and memes ☑

Custom Memes

Allow memes to be uploaded ☑

▸ **OneNote Class Notebook**   Manage notebook sections and preferences

Figure 9-9. *Teams management settings*

Setting Up Parent Connection in Microsoft Teams for Education

The Parent Connection feature in Microsoft Teams for Education allows educators to securely communicate with students' parents and guardians. This guide is designed for IT professionals in educational settings to assist in setting up Parent Connection effectively.

The following are the benefits of Parent Connection:

- There is real-time communication between educators and guardians via chat, email, and calls.

- If the guardian is not on Teams, they receive an email invitation.

- Features like supervised chat are supported.

- There are restrictions in place for guardians' interactions within Teams.

PBX capabilities and PSTN connection are required for call functionalities. Plans like Microsoft 365 A1 and A3 lack PBX and PSTN, requiring additional licensing.

Data Synchronization

Let's talk about data synchronization.

The Graph API can be used to populate parent and guardian contact information, or School Data Sync (SDS) can be used.

- SDS ensures that the Teams' guardian contact data stays up-to-date.

- If a guardian is removed from a student's records, chat owners are alerted.

Here's how to set up SDS:

1. Fill out the RFA process at FastTrack or open a support ticket.

2. For parent contacts, use the SDS CSV format v1 or v2.1.

3. Populate `User.csv` and `Guardianrelationship.csv` with the relevant information.

Here are some important policies:

- Class team owners must have chat and external access enabled.

- Private meeting scheduling and anonymous join options must be enabled.

Parent and Guardian Access Limitations

Guardians have restricted access and can engage only in specific chats. External individuals can also see the online status of your organization's members, which can be disabled.

Best Practices for Sharing Student Information

IT admins should instruct class owners on the best practices for sharing student data securely.

Blocking a Parent or Guardian

Educators can block and remove a guardian from the chat as needed.

Configuring External Access via PowerShell

Here's how to configure external access via PowerShell:

1. Install the latest Teams PowerShell module.

2. Use admin credentials to run specific PowerShell commands to enable or disable user-level policies.

Enabling the Parents App

The Parents app can be enabled or disabled at both the tenant level and the user level through the Teams admin center.

Setting Preferred Contact Method

Admins can opt for either email or SMS as the primary contact method for sending Parent Connection invites. Refer to Figure 9-10 for parent and guarding settings.

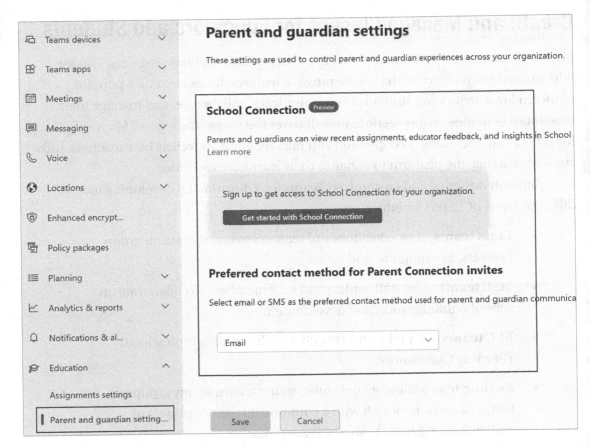

Figure 9-10. *Parent and Guardian settings*

Important Notes

- If opting for SMS, ensure that phone numbers are in the E.164 format.

- Mobile carrier SMS rates may apply to recipients.

For more detailed steps and PowerShell commands, consult the respective sections.

Create and Manage Classes for Educators and Students

Microsoft Teams is a powerful tool that is useful not only for businesses but also for educational institutions. With its wide range of features, it has become a popular platform for teachers and students to communicate, collaborate, and manage their classroom activities. In this section, we will cover the various aspects of Microsoft Teams for Education, including class creation and management, as well as how teachers and students can use the platform to enhance their learning experience.

Microsoft designed and customized Teams for Education by developing four different types of Teams for educators.

- **Class teams** allow educators and learners to collaborate on group projects, assignments, and more.

- **Staff teams** allow staff leaders and staff members to collaborate on school administration and development.

- **PLC teams** allow educators to collaborate within a Professional Learning Community.

- **Anyone teams** allow school clubs, sports teams, or any group of learners and school staff with a common interest or project to collaborate. Figure 9-11 shows Team types.

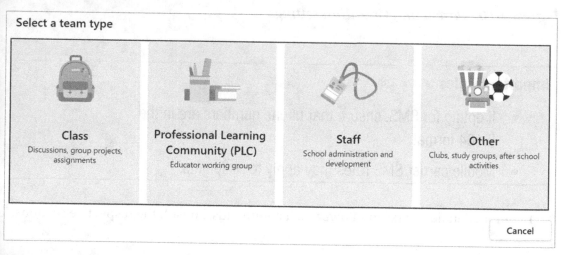

Figure 9-11. Team types

Creating a New Team

To create a team, follow these steps:

1. Log in to the Teams client using your account.

2. Select the "Join or create a team" button at the top of the Teams app.

3. Then, select "Create team" and choose the type of team to create. Figure 9-12 shows the team type.

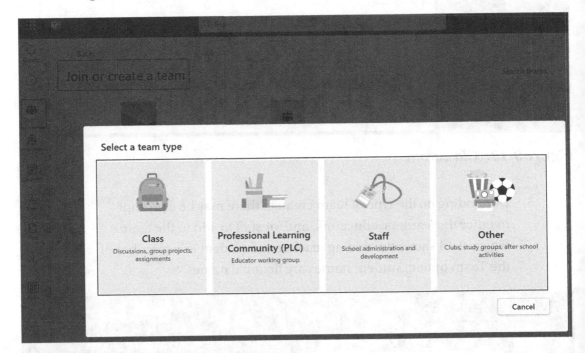

Figure 9-12. *Teams creation: types*

4. For this book demo, select the Class Team type. Next, name the team, and if desired, add a description. Figure 9-13 shows a class team.

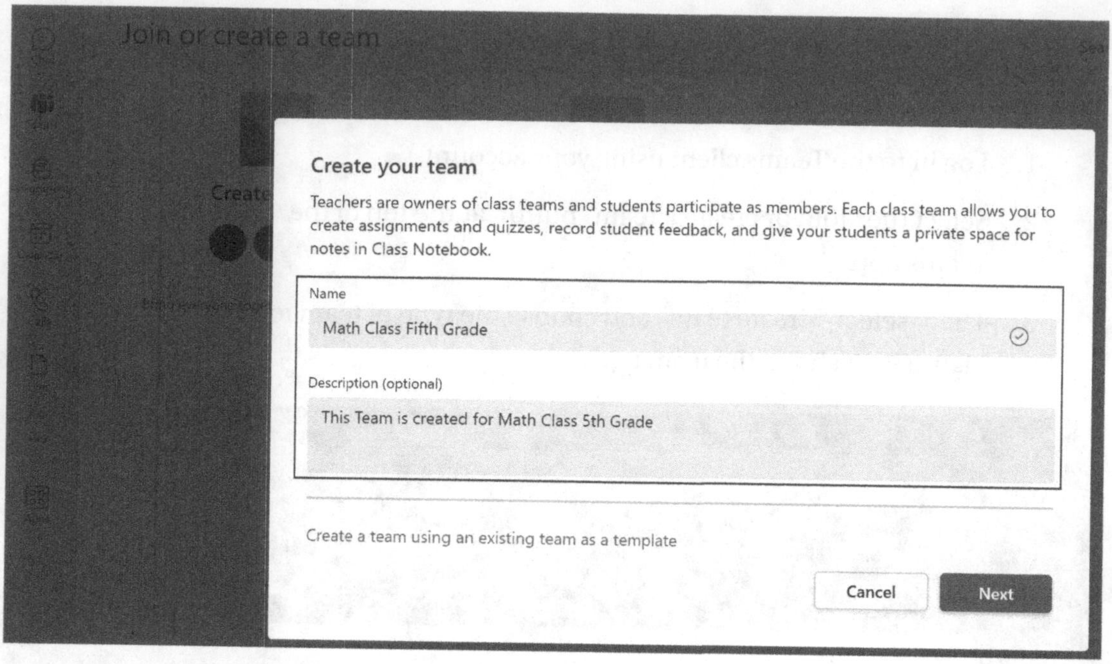

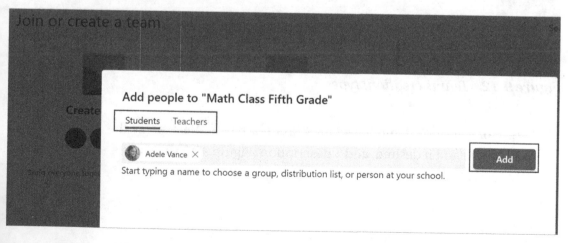

Figure 9-13. *Class team*

5. Depending on the type of team created, there may be a prompt
   to enter the learners, educators, and/or staff to add to the team.
   Figure 9-14 shows the adding teacher and student as a member of
   the Team option; student names are fictional names.

Figure 9-14. *Adding the student and teacher to the team*

6. When entering learners and co-educators in a class team, they'll
    be given specific permissions based on their status as a learner or
    educator.

7. Members are added to the team by typing a name to choose a
    group, distribution list, or person at the school.

8. Finally, Figure 9-15 shows the Home page, Class Notebook,
    Classwork, Assignments, Grades, Reflect, Insights, and Parents
    options. Also, you can upload class materials and set up a Class
    Notebook.

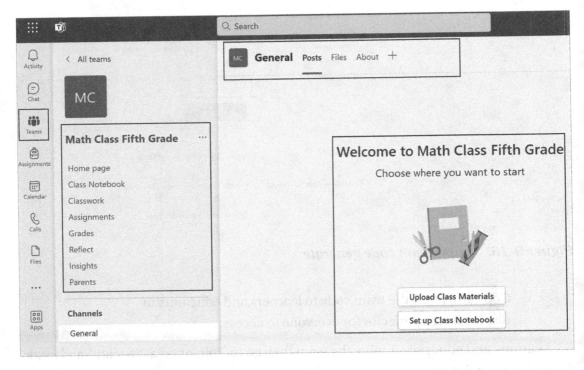

Figure 9-15. *Class team created*

Lettings Others Join Your Team

If it's preferable for learners and staff members to join the team, rather than entering
their names, generate a team code.

1. Click the ellipsis next to the name of the team and choose Manage
    Team and then select Settings.

2.   Once in the settings, click "Team code" and then click Generate.
     Figure 9-16 shows the team code generation.

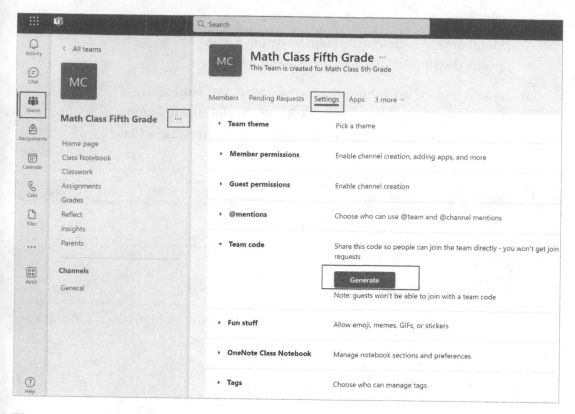

Figure 9-16.   *Teams team code generate*

3.   Copy and email the team code to learners and educators or
     display it on a projector for everyone to access.

Learners and educators joining the team then go to "Join or create a team" and enter
the code to join the team.

Creating and Managing a Class

Creating a class in Microsoft Teams is a straightforward process.

1.   Once a teacher has logged in to their Microsoft Teams account,
     they can navigate to the Teams tab and click the "Join or create a
     team" button.

2. From there, they can select "Create a team" and choose Class as the team type.

3. This will prompt the teacher to enter the name of the class, as well as a description and any other relevant details.

4. Once the class has been created, the teacher can add students to the team.

5. This can be done by clicking the "Add member" button and entering the student's email address.

Note   The teacher can also invite co-teachers or other staff members to the team if necessary.

After the students have been added, the teacher can create channels within the team. Channels are a way to organize conversations and resources around specific topics or activities. For example, a class may have a channel dedicated to homework assignments, another for class discussions, and another for group projects.

Teacher and Student Roles/Activities

Microsoft Teams offers a range of features that can be used by both teachers and students to enhance their learning experience. Here are some of the most important activities that can be done on the platform:

- **Assignments:** Teachers can create and assign homework and other assignments to their students using the Assignments feature. This feature allows teachers to set deadlines, attach files, and give feedback on completed work. Figure 9-17 shows the Assignments tab and options.

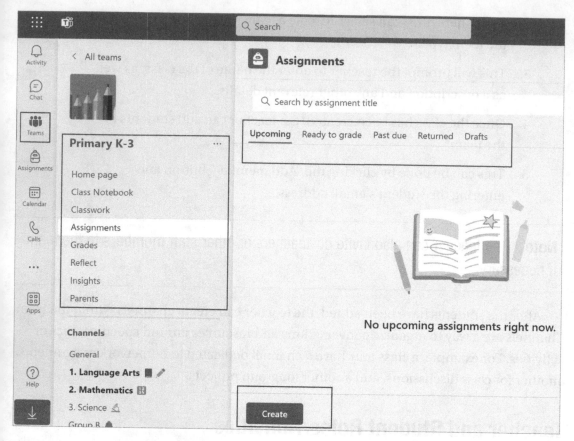

Figure 9-17. *Assignment option*

- **Meetings:** Teachers can schedule and host virtual meetings with their students using the Meetings feature. This can be used for lectures, group discussions, or one-on-one meetings with students.

- **Collaboration:** Students can collaborate with their peers on group projects using the Files feature. This feature allows students to create and edit documents, presentations, and spreadsheets in real time.

- **Communication:** Teachers and students can communicate with each other using the Chat feature. This can be used for quick questions or discussions that do not require a virtual meeting.

- **Quizzes and Tests:** Teachers can use the Forms feature to create quizzes and tests for their students. This feature allows teachers to create multiple-choice questions, true/false questions, and other types of assessments.

Student Role

Microsoft Teams has several features that make it easy for students to turn in their assignments. The following are the two main ways that students can turn in their assignments in Teams:

1. **Assignments Tab:** The Assignments tab in Teams enables educators to create, distribute, and grade assignments. Students can turn in their assignments through the Assignments tab, which allows them to attach files, add comments, and submit their work for grading.

2. **OneDrive:** Students can also turn in their assignments by saving their work to their OneDrive and sharing it with their teacher through Teams. This method is useful when the teacher does not use the Assignments tab to distribute assignments.

Teacher Role

Microsoft Teams has several features that enable educators to monitor student assignments and progress and grade them. Some of these features are as follows:

- **Assignment grading:** The Assignments tab in Teams allows educators to grade student work, provide feedback, and return the graded assignments to students.

- **Insights:** The Insights feature in Teams allows educators to track student engagement with Teams. Insights provide data on student activity, such as how many messages they have posted, how many meetings they have attended, and how much time they have spent on Teams.

- **OneNote:** Teams integrates with OneNote, a digital note-taking tool, allowing educators to create and share notes with students. OneNote also enables educators to provide feedback to students and track their progress.

Microsoft Teams for Education: Usage and Management

In today's digital age, technology has become an integral part of education, and it has become essential for educators and students to have a platform that can facilitate remote learning, communication, and collaboration. Microsoft Teams is a robust collaboration platform that enables educators and students to work together, communicate, and learn effectively, irrespective of their physical location. This chapter aims to provide a comprehensive guide on Microsoft Teams for Education, including setup, usage, and management.

Meeting Overview

Creating a Teams meeting is super flexible—you don't even have to open the Teams app to start one. Whether you want to jump right in or plan for later, there are plenty of options. Here's how:

- **Directly in Teams:** Use the Calendar tab on the left sidebar. You can start a meeting right away or schedule one for later.

- **Through Outlook:** Go to the Calendar tab and create a meeting. The settings here are similar to Teams.

- **In a chat:** Use the meeting icon in the Chat tab to set up a meeting with everyone in that chat conversation.

Always rename your meeting to reflect its purpose so everyone knows what it's about.

You can customize these settings:

- **Who can join easily:** You can decide who gets to skip the waiting room.

- **Presenter controls:** Choose who can unmute, turn on cameras, or chat.

- **Invitation controls:** Allow or disallow meeting rescheduling or forwarding the invites.

You can always change these settings during the meeting too.

These are settings for channel meetings:

- **Public or private:** If the meeting is in a channel, anyone with access to the channel will automatically be invited.

- **Invite more people:** Even for channel meetings, you can invite more people as long as the channel isn't private.

Tip   Hover over icons if you forget what they do; a pop-up will remind you.

So, whether it's a quick catch-up or a planned event, Teams and Outlook have got teachers covered for any kind of meeting setup.

Creating Meetings in Microsoft Teams?

Microsoft Teams is part of the larger Microsoft Office family, making it simple to set up meetings either for right now or later on. You can create meetings in both Outlook and Teams, letting you start instantly, schedule for a future time, or even send meeting invites through email. Clicking Meet Now takes you straight into a Teams meeting. Figure 9-18 shows Teams meeting creation.

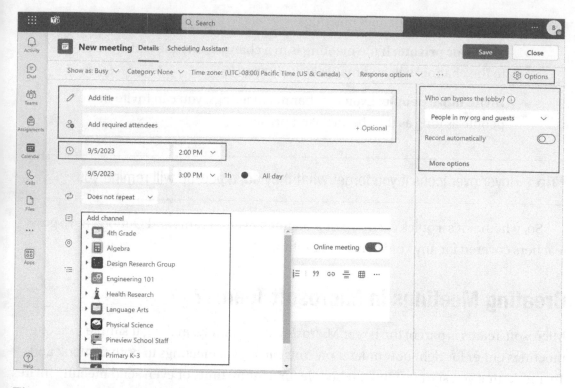

Figure 9-18. *Teams meeting creation*

Creating a meeting in Outlook is as simple as sending an email. Think of the meeting's title as the email's subject line. The people you have to invite are like the email's "to" field, while optional guests are similar to the "cc" field.

To make things more efficient, you can set meeting options in advance. In the settings, you can decide who can skip the waiting area (the "lobby"), who can unmute themselves, and who can chat. You can even stop people from forwarding the invite to keep your meeting secure. All of this is super useful when you don't have the Teams app open.

In Teams itself, there are multiple ways to create a meeting.

- Click the calendar icon on the left sidebar to start a meeting right away or plan one for later. Here, you also have the choice to link the meeting to a channel, automatically inviting everyone who can access that channel.

- You can require people to register in advance to join the meeting.

- Another way is through the chat icon on the left sidebar. You can
  either start a meeting right away or schedule one for later. Anyone
  involved in the chat will automatically get an invite.

Lastly, you can create meetings in specific channels within Teams. Just choose to start the meeting immediately or schedule it for later.

Both channel and chat-based meetings keep a running log of all comments, organizing them in a threaded conversation within that channel or chat.

To sum it up, Microsoft Teams is designed for easy communication, and it keeps all related content neatly organized.

Teams Meeting View Options

Teams has many ways to make your meetings better. You can see people in different styles on your screen. For a small group, use the 3x3 Gallery view to see up to nine people. For bigger groups, Large Gallery shows up to 49 people.

Want to feel like you're in the same room? Try Together mode. This puts everyone in a virtual space like a classroom or a stadium. You can even change the background scene by clicking a pencil icon.

If you're teaching and need to focus, use Focus mode. This makes everything else go away, so you only see the main screen and not the small pictures of everyone else.

To keep your class in check, use Hard Audio Mute. This lets you mute everyone so they can't talk until you allow it. This helps when you need everyone to pay attention.

Worried about security? Teams has got you covered. You can use a special waiting room called the *lobby*. This lets you decide who can join the meeting. Also, you can make your meetings even more secure by creating them in Outlook and making it so the invite can't be forwarded to others.

Customize Learning Experiences with Breakout Rooms in Teams

In the world of education, there are various methods of instruction: teaching the whole class, one-on-one sessions, and small group collaborations. Microsoft Teams caters to all these needs, and breakout rooms are its answer to facilitating small group interactions during virtual lessons.

The concept of breakout rooms emerged in response to educator requests for more versatile small-group capabilities, like private channels. Breakout rooms offer a virtual space where educators can segment the larger class into smaller groups for targeted discussions and team-based activities. Figure 9-19 shows breakout room options.

Figure 9-19. *Teams breakout room options*

Here's what you can do with breakout rooms:

- **Select the number of rooms:** Decide how many breakout rooms you'll need based on the activity or discussion topics.

- **Group assignments:** You can let the system auto-assign learners to different rooms, or you can do it manually based on specific needs or criteria.

- **Room transfers:** If necessary, you have the flexibility to move students from one room to another even after the groups have been formed.

- **Group announcements:** Broadcast messages or instructions to all breakout rooms simultaneously, ensuring everyone is on the same page.

- **Room visits:** Educators can jump between rooms to monitor progress, provide clarification, or facilitate discussions.

- **Wrap-up feature**: When it's time to reconvene, you can automatically close all breakout rooms, bringing everyone back to the main virtual classroom.

Breakout rooms in Teams make it easier than ever to diversify instructional methods, allowing for more tailored and interactive learning experiences.

Streamlining Large-Scale Online Events with Class Teams

For educators exploring options for hosting larger gatherings such as the following, class teams provides the perfect platform to make these events happen online:

- Parent-teacher nights

- School announcements

- Student performances

- Extensive lectures

With the capability to host up to 10,000 attendees, setting up a live event is a straightforward process. You can also enhance participant safety by establishing specific access protocols and permissions.

As the host of a live event, educators can customize their sessions in multiple ways.

- **Control the number of presenters:** Decide who can actively present or speak during the event, ensuring a focused and well-organized presentation.

- **Engage with Q&A sessions:** Open the floor for questions to make the event interactive and address any queries or concerns attendees may have.

- **Record events:** Choose to record the live event, making it accessible for later viewing for those who couldn't attend in real time.

- **Set caption language:** Preconfigure the language for live captions, improving accessibility for a diverse audience.

Class teams allow for versatile event hosting, including turning traditional in-person events such as research presentations, science fairs, or student government speeches into accessible online experiences. This capability extends the reach of these events, enabling students who can't attend in person, as well as parents and community members, to stay engaged and informed.

Assignments and Grading

As part of the assignment and grading, educators can create and assign tasks, quizzes, or projects to students in the class team. Students can turn in their assignments directly in the class team, and educators can grade and provide feedback in Teams. Educators can also use the Assignments feature to automate grading and provide feedback to students.

Microsoft Teams for Education offers a robust set of tools designed to streamline the assignment and grading processes, making life easier for both educators and students. The following are some of the key features that facilitate these important educational tasks.

You can create and assign tasks.

- **Task creation by educators:** One of the most useful features is the ability for educators to create various types of assignments—be it tasks, quizzes, or long-term projects. Educators can craft these assignments with rich detail, including guidelines, due dates, and attached resource materials like PDFs or links to supplementary content.

- **Assigning to a class team:** Once created, these assignments can be directly assigned to students within the class team. This eliminates the need for external platforms or email chains, making the assignment process smoother and more organized.

Here are submission and grading details:

- **Student Submission:** Students have the advantage of submitting their assignments right within the Teams environment. They can upload files, write text responses, or even share links as their submissions. This centralizes the process, making it easier to keep track of who has submitted what and when.

- **Educator grading:** After submission, educators can go through each student's work to grade it. Teams offer various marking options, including numerical scores, letter grades, or customized feedback. This makes the grading process more flexible and tailored to the educational context.

- **Feedback provision:** Beyond just giving a grade, educators can provide personalized feedback. Teams allow for inline comments on student work, making it easy for students to understand what they did well and where they need improvement.

Here are some automation and advanced features:

- **Automated grading:** One standout feature is the Assignments tool's ability to automate some grading tasks. For multiple-choice quizzes or tests, the platform can automatically grade submissions as soon as they are turned in, speeding up the feedback loop for students.

- **Feedback automation:** Educators can also create preset comments for common issues or achievements, making it quicker to provide consistent feedback to multiple students.

- **Integrated rubrics:** For more complex assignments, Teams supports the integration of grading rubrics. These rubrics can be custom-built within the platform or imported from external sources, providing a structured framework for grading and feedback.

By incorporating these features, Microsoft Teams for Education makes the process of assigning tasks and grading them a more streamlined and efficient experience for educators and students alike.

Assignments in Microsoft Teams for Education

The assignments and grades functionalities in Teams for Education give educators the ability to assign tasks, homework, or tests to students. Instructors can manage due dates, provide detailed instructions, attach necessary resources, employ grading rubrics, and monitor both class and individual student progress through the Grades tab.

To configure assignment-related settings, administrators should go to the Teams admin center and navigate to Education ➤ Assignment Settings. Refer to Figure 9-20 for the assignment setting; you can enable integration with Turnitin.

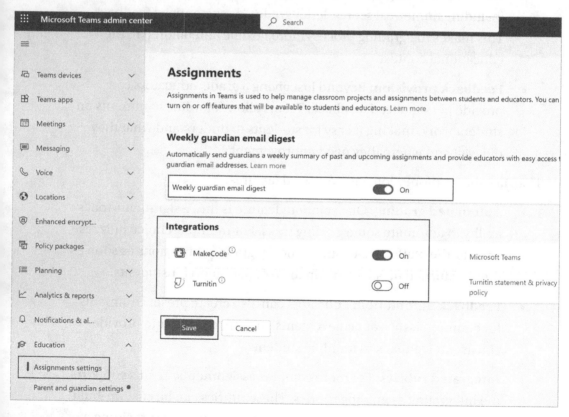

Figure 9-20. *Assignment settings*

Guardian Weekly Digest

By default, the guardian email setting is turned off. When enabled, parents or guardians receive a weekly email digest that provides an overview of the past and upcoming assignments. To set up this feature, follow these steps:

1. Activate Parent and Guardian Sync via School Data Sync (SDS).

2. In the Teams admin center, switch on the Guardian Setting.

3. Verify that the student's profile in SDS has an email tagged as Parent or Guardian.

Note   Teachers can opt out of this feature through their own class team settings.

MakeCode Integration

Microsoft MakeCode, a block-based coding platform, can be enabled in the Assignments section of the Teams Admin Center. This feature is off by default. Once activated, it may take a few hours for settings to apply.

Turnitin Integration

Turnitin is an external service that helps maintain academic integrity. To integrate Turnitin into Teams Assignments, follow these steps:

1. Obtain a Turnitin subscription.

2. Input your Turnitin API key and API URL in the Teams admin center.

3. Save the settings and allow a few hours for activation.

Data Management

Student and teacher files related to assignments are stored in SharePoint document libraries. IT administrators can use the Content Search tool to find assignment-related data stored in SharePoint.

Some assignment-related data, like grades and feedback, are not stored in SharePoint. Administrators or teachers may need to navigate directly to the specific assignment to access this data.

You have bulk data operations as well.

- **For students:** Use scripts to bulk export or delete student assignment data by providing the user ID.

- **For teachers:** Bulk data export options are available, but bulk deletion is not an option due to shared data.

To remove assignments and grades, follow these steps:

- **For individual users:** Navigate to the Teams admin center, select Teams apps and then Permission policies and block assignments and grades for specific users.

- **For the entire tenant:** Go to the Teams admin center, select "Teams apps" and then "Manage apps" and change the status of Assignments and Grades to Blocked.

Diagnostic Tools

A built-in diagnostic tool is available for troubleshooting issues related to the Assignments feature. Data such as the group ID, tenant ID, and assignment ID can be gathered and provided to Microsoft Support agents as needed.

To access the tool, press Ctrl+/ on the desktop and Web, or touch and rotate the screen with two fingers by 45 degrees on mobile devices.

Note   Diagnostic data is not automatically sent to Microsoft and must be manually provided to support agents.

Collaborative Learning

Teams for Education enables collaborative learning by allowing students to work together on assignments or projects. They can use chat or video meetings to discuss and collaborate in real time. They can also use the Files feature to share and collaborate on documents, presentations, or spreadsheets.

Deep Dive into Collaborative Learning with Teams for Education

Collaborative learning is not just a buzzword; it's an educational approach that enables students to engage with each other, share ideas, and build a deeper understanding of subjects. Microsoft's Teams for Education serves as a powerful platform to facilitate this mode of learning by offering a suite of features specifically tailored for educational environments. The following are some key aspects that illustrate how Teams for Education makes collaborative learning more efficient, interactive, and fruitful.

Working on Assignments or Projects Together

Teams for Education allows students to partner up or form groups for various tasks, be it assignments, quizzes, or long-term projects. This collaboration isn't limited to a single class but extends to multidisciplinary efforts as well. Educators can set up a shared space, usually a channel within the Teams environment, where students can access all the resources they need to complete their work. This feature minimizes the time and effort needed to organize, thereby enabling students to focus more on the content and collaborative aspects of their tasks.

Real-Time Discussions Through Chat or Video Meetings

Communication is the backbone of collaboration, and Teams for Education provides two robust options for this: chat and video meetings. Students can use the chat feature for quick queries, sharing references, or even casual conversations that can spark innovative ideas. On the other hand, video meetings provide a more immersive interaction, replicating the dynamics of in-person group meetings. These meetings can be scheduled or started spontaneously and can include features such as screen sharing, whiteboarding, and breakout rooms for smaller group discussions, allowing for a multifaceted exchange of ideas.

File Sharing and Collaborative Document Editing

Collaboration often requires students to work together on documents, presentations, or spreadsheets. The Files feature in Teams provides a centralized space where these documents can be uploaded, accessed, and edited by all group members. What sets Teams apart is its seamless integration with Microsoft Office 365, allowing real-time co-editing of Word documents, PowerPoint presentations, and Excel spreadsheets. This functionality means that students can see each other's edits and contributions as they happen, leading to a fluid and dynamic collaborative process.

In summary, Teams for Education is more than just a digital classroom; it's a comprehensive, integrated platform designed to enhance collaborative learning. By offering diverse ways for students to interact and work together, it enriches their educational experience, making learning more engaging and effective.

Class Notebook

Class Notebook is a digital notebook that enables educators to organize and distribute course content to students. It includes sections for notes, handouts, quizzes, or assignments, which students can access and work on. Educators can also provide feedback and grade students' work in Class Notebook.

What Is a Class Notebook?

A Class Notebook is an innovative digital tool that serves as an all-in-one hub for educational resources, designed to streamline the process of course management for educators. It offers an organized, accessible platform to distribute course materials while also creating an interactive learning environment for students. Figure 9-21 shows the Class Notebook.

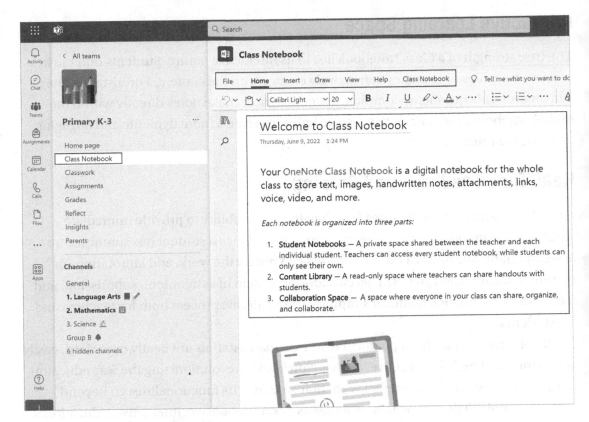

Figure 9-21. *Class Notebook*

Features of a Class Notebook

This section looks at the features of a Class Notebook.

Organized Layout for Multiple Content Types

At its core, a Class Notebook is organized into various sections that can hold different types of educational content. These sections can include notes from lectures, supplementary handouts, quizzes, or specific assignments. This modular design not only makes it easier for educators to keep their course materials organized but also allows students to easily locate and access the resources they need for their studies.

Interactive Learning Space

The true strength of a Class Notebook lies in its interactive nature. Students don't just receive static files or text; they can actively engage with the content. For instance, they can answer quiz questions, complete assignments, or make notes directly within the digital notebook. This interactive feature helps to create a more dynamic and engaging learning experience.

Real-Time Feedback and Grading

One of the most valuable features for educators is the ability to provide immediate feedback and grades within a Class Notebook itself. Once a student has submitted an assignment or completed a quiz, educators can review the work, add annotations or comments, and assign grades. This closed-loop system of assignment, submission, and feedback all within one platform simplifies the academic process both for teachers and for students.

By offering a centralized platform where course materials are neatly organized, easily accessible, and highly interactive, a Class Notebook is revolutionizing the way educators manage their courses and interact with their students. Its functionalities go beyond that of a simple digital repository; it serves as a comprehensive, interactive, educational platform.

Enhance Team Learning with Notebooks in Microsoft Teams

When you start a new Team in Microsoft Teams, a OneNote Notebook tab will appear automatically. To get your notebook up and running, just click the Setup button located in the Notebook tab. You have two choices: start a completely new Notebook or use an existing one as a template.

The staff Notebook app guides you through setting up your notebook. First, it shows you the different sections it's making. Then, you get to organize individual sections in each team member's private area. The app even gives you some ready-made suggestions for section names that you can keep, change, or delete.

After your notebook is set, you'll have access to a shared space for team collaboration, a content library, and private spaces designated for each team member. Your notebook also comes with prefilled sections and pages to make it easier for your team to get started.

Track Assignments with Insights

Microsoft Teams for Education provides insights that allow you to track assignments and monitor student progress. Here are the steps to tracking assignments using insights:

1. Open Microsoft Teams and go to the class team for which you want to track assignments.

2. Click the Assignments tab in the menu on the left.

3. Select the assignment you want to track and click it. Figure 9-22 shows the assignment with status. This figure has a fictional name and phone number that doesn't have any actual name correlation.

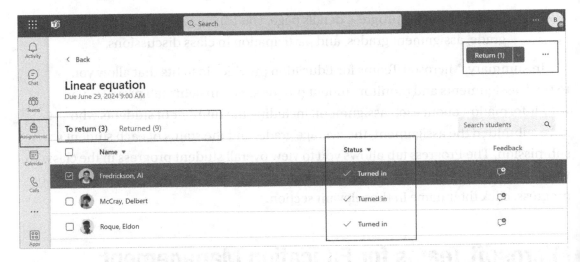

Figure 9-22. *Assignment tracking*

4. On the assignment details page, click the Insights tab.

5. The Insights tab will provide you with information about the assignment, including the number of students who have submitted the assignment, the average grade, and the status of each student's submission.

6. To view more detailed information about a particular student's submission, click the student's name in the "Submission status" section.

7. In the student's submission details page, you can view their submission, provide feedback, and enter a grade.

8. To track overall student progress, click the Progress tab in the menu on the left.

9. The Progress tab provides you with a summary of each student's progress in the class, including their overall grade, the number of assignments they have completed, and their participation in class discussions.

10. To view more detailed information about a particular student's progress, click their name in the Students section.

11. On the student's progress details page, you can view their overall grade, assignment grades, and participation in class discussions.

In summary, Microsoft Teams for Education provides insights that allow you to track assignments and monitor student progress. The Insights tab provides you with information about each assignment, including the number of students who have submitted the assignment, the average grade, and the status of each student's submission. The Progress tab allows you to view overall student progress in the class. To view more detailed information about a particular student's assignment submission or progress, click their name in the relevant section.

Microsoft Teams for Education Management

Microsoft Teams for Education is an integrated digital platform designed to facilitate interactive learning, collaboration, and effective classroom management. It's a part of Microsoft's Office 365 suite and is engineered to function as a virtual classroom that can serve educational institutions of all sizes and types.

IT Management in Microsoft Teams for Education

IT administrators can manage Microsoft Teams for Education at the institution level, including user accounts, access permissions, and security settings. They can also integrate Teams with other education tools, such as learning management systems or student information systems.

Information technology (IT) management in the educational sector has never been more critical, especially with the rise of remote learning and digital classrooms. Microsoft Teams for Education is one such platform that offers an integrated approach to learning management. For IT administrators, this provides a broad range of opportunities to centralize, streamline, and secure educational operations at the institutional level.

Let's look at the key features.

User Account Management

IT administrators can control who has access to Microsoft Teams for Education by managing user accounts. This includes adding or removing accounts for educators, students, and staff. Various access levels can be assigned to different user roles, ensuring that only authorized individuals have access to specific areas of the Teams platform. This centralized control simplifies account management and enhances security.

Access Permissions and Security Settings

Security is a paramount concern in any educational institution, and Microsoft Teams for Education is designed to meet this need. IT administrators can customize security settings to comply with institutional and regulatory standards. This can include implementing two-factor authentication (2FA), setting up firewall rules, and monitoring for any unusual activities within the Teams environment. These settings can be applied universally or tailored to specific teams or user groups.

Integration with Learning Management Systems or Student Information Systems

One of the powerful features of Microsoft Teams for Education is its ability to integrate seamlessly with other educational software. IT administrators can sync Teams with learning management systems (LMSs) like Moodle or Blackboard and student information systems (SISs) such as PowerSchool. This integration provides a unified user experience and streamlines educational processes. For example, grades entered into Teams can be automatically updated in an LMS or SIS, saving educators time and reducing the risk of errors.

Compliance and Data Management

Microsoft Teams for Education also offers compliance features that meet various educational regulations. IT administrators can configure Teams to ensure compliance with laws such as the Family Educational Rights and Privacy Act (FERPA) in the United States or the General Data Protection Regulation (GDPR) in Europe. Additionally, data retention policies can be implemented to control how long data is stored and who has access to it.

Software Updates and Patch Management

Keeping the software up-to-date is crucial for both features and security. IT administrators can manage software updates and patches for Microsoft Teams centrally, ensuring that all users are operating on the most recent and secure version. This level of control minimizes vulnerabilities and ensures that new features and improvements are rolled out consistently across the institution.

Managing an educational institution's IT infrastructure is a complex but crucial task. Microsoft Teams for Education offers a range of features that simplify this work, from user account management to complex integrations with other educational systems. By taking advantage of these features, IT administrators can provide a secure, efficient, and unified digital learning environment for both educators and students.

Security and Compliance

Microsoft Teams for Education is compliant with industry-standard regulations, including GDPR and FERPA. IT administrators can enable or disable specific features, such as file sharing or external access, based on institutional policies and regulations.

In the age of digital transformation, security and compliance are crucial elements for any educational institution. Microsoft Teams for Education, as a leading platform in collaborative learning and remote education, offers an array of features to ensure that educational organizations meet or exceed these requirements. This section explores the various facets of security and compliance within Teams for Education, offering insights to IT administrators and institutional leaders.

Regulatory Compliance: GDPR and FERPA

Microsoft Teams for Education is designed to be compliant with industry-standard regulations like the General Data Protection Regulation (GDPR) in Europe and the Family Educational Rights and Privacy Act (FERPA) in the United States. GDPR safeguards personal data and ensures that organizations follow strict guidelines on how they store, process, and share this data. FERPA similarly provides protections for student education records in the United States, limiting who may access these records and under what conditions.

Being compliant with these regulations assures educational institutions that they are partnering with a platform committed to legal rigor and the protection of sensitive information. Teams' features, such as data encryption and secure data storage, support these compliance efforts, providing peace of mind to educators, students, and parents alike.

Granular Control Over Features

IT administrators have the flexibility to enable or disable specific features based on the policies and regulations of their institutions. For example, file sharing can be either allowed or restricted, depending on the need to control the dissemination of potentially sensitive educational material. Likewise, external access can be toggled on or off, offering the option to restrict Teams' access solely to internal members of the institution or allowing collaboration with external partners, such as guest lecturers or researchers.

This granular control extends not just to data sharing but also to other functionalities like chat, video conferencing, and even the integration of third-party apps. By providing such tailored control, Teams allows educational institutions to enforce their specific usage policies and regulatory obligations effectively.

Security Measures for Data and Communication

Microsoft Teams for Education uses strong encryption protocols for both data at rest and data in transit. This includes encrypting chat messages, video meetings, and shared files. IT administrators can also implement additional security measures, such as multifactor authentication (MFA), to ensure that only authorized users can access the Teams environment.

Monitoring and Reporting

Monitoring features in Teams allow for real-time auditing and activity logs, which can be crucial for tracking any unauthorized or suspicious activities. These features are integral for not only maintaining a secure platform but also for compliance reporting, ensuring that the institution can demonstrate due diligence in the protection of sensitive information.

Security and compliance are foundational elements of Microsoft Teams for Education. With regulatory compliance like GDPR and FERPA, granular controls, robust encryption, and monitoring capabilities, Teams provides a secure and compliant environment for remote learning and collaboration. IT administrators can precisely tailor the platform's features to meet the unique needs and regulatory requirements of their educational institutions, making Teams an ideal choice for a secure, compliant digital learning space.

Analytics and Reporting

Teams for Education provides analytics and reporting features that enable educators and IT administrators to monitor students' activity, usage, and engagement. Educators can use analytics to assess student progress, identify areas of improvement, and provide personalized learning experiences.

Analytics and Reporting in Microsoft Teams for Education

Analytics and reporting are becoming increasingly important in educational settings, especially with the rise of online learning and collaboration platforms such as Microsoft Teams for Education. The ability to accurately gauge student activity, usage, and engagement can have a direct impact on the success of teaching methods, learning outcomes, and overall institutional goals. This article delves into the analytical features of Teams for Education, showcasing how educators and IT administrators can leverage them for better educational outcomes.

Monitoring Students' Activity, Usage, and Engagement

Microsoft Teams for Education offers an extensive range of analytics and reporting features aimed at keeping track of students' online activity, tool usage, and overall engagement within the platform. IT administrators can access detailed dashboards that present metrics such as the number of active users, the time spent on specific tasks, and the frequency of interactions such as posts or file sharing. These metrics offer invaluable insights into how students are utilizing Teams for learning and communication.

Assessing Student Progress

Educators have the option to delve deep into analytics to monitor individual student progress. For example, by analyzing the metrics related to assignment submissions, educators can identify which students are consistently submitting assignments on time and who may be struggling. Understanding students' activity patterns can also be a robust measure of their attention spans and learning preferences, helping educators adapt their teaching methods accordingly.

In addition, Teams can integrate with other analytics tools, enabling a more comprehensive look at student performance, such as quiz scores, participation in discussions, and project contributions.

Identifying Areas for Improvement

While monitoring student performance is crucial, analytics can also help educators identify areas of improvement in their teaching methodology. If the data indicates low engagement during specific lecture topics or a general trend of late assignment submissions, educators can reassess their teaching strategies and make appropriate adjustments. For instance, an educator can modify lesson plans, increase interactivity during live sessions, or provide additional resources to enhance understanding.

Personalized Learning Experiences

The granularity of the analytics provided by Teams for Education allows educators to offer personalized learning experiences for students. By understanding the unique learning styles, challenges, and preferences of each student, educators can tailor their lesson plans, assignments, and feedback to better suit individual needs. Personalized learning pathways can be developed, and resources can be allocated more efficiently, ensuring that each student has the opportunity to succeed.

Analytics and reporting in Microsoft Teams for Education are much more than just numbers on a screen; they are powerful tools for fostering academic growth, enhancing teaching methods, and ensuring effective resource allocation. By enabling real-time monitoring of student activities and providing deep insights into both teaching and learning, these features are instrumental in creating a responsive, adaptable, and effective educational environment.

Simplify Your Data with Power BI and Teams

Teams isn't just for meetings; it's a one-stop place for real-time collaboration. Features like live streaming and video make it easy to connect with your team. Plus, it's accessible to everyone, thanks to features found across Microsoft's product range, including Office 365.

One of these great features in Teams meetings is live captioning. It's really useful for identifying who's speaking during monthly faculty get-togethers, class reviews, or any other staff event. The live captions appear on the screen and show who's talking, making the meetings more accessible for everyone.

Sharing and Working Together on Files in Teams

Teams makes it super simple to share files with students or co-workers. Each team, and even each channel inside a team, gets its own special folder for sharing files. You can work on Word, Excel, or PowerPoint files right there in the Teams app, and everyone can see the changes happening live.

Here's how you can add or make files in this folder:

- **Uploading existing files:** To add a file you already have, go to the Files tab within your team and click Upload. This will bring up a window where you can choose which file (or files) you want to add. Just pick the files and hit Open. Now, everyone in the team can see and use these files.

- **Creating new files:** If you need to make a new file, go to the 'Files' tab and click 'New.' You'll get options to create different kinds of files such as Word, PowerPoint, Excel, or even Forms for Excel and OneNote. Name your new file and click Create. You can start editing it right away in Teams. If you'd rather work in the desktop version of the app, you can easily switch by clicking "Open in Desktop app." Once a file is in the team folder, any team member can view or edit it, making teamwork a breeze.

Hybrid Teaching and Learning Using Microsoft Teams: The Future of Education

In today's rapidly evolving educational landscape, hybrid teaching and learning models are gaining increasing traction. With the advent of technology and the challenges posed by recent global events, schools and institutions are adopting flexible approaches that combine the best of both in-person and online learning. Microsoft Teams serves as a vital platform in this regard, offering a plethora of features to support effective hybrid education.

Hybrid teaching and learning involve a blend of traditional classroom experiences and digital interactions. Students may attend some classes in person while participating in others online through video conferencing, digital assignments, and collaborative projects. This approach provides the flexibility to adapt to different learning environments, making education more accessible and inclusive.

The following sections highlight the hybrid learning features of Teams.

Seamless Integration

Microsoft Teams integrates seamlessly with a host of educational tools and LMSs, providing a centralized platform for both educators and students. This allows for smooth transitions between in-person and online activities, making it easier to implement and manage a hybrid curriculum.

Collaborative Learning Spaces

Teams facilitate collaborative learning by enabling real time interactions through chat and video meetings. Whether in the classroom or logging in from home, students can participate in group discussions, work on shared projects, and receive instant feedback from educators.

Assignments and Grading

The platform supports a comprehensive assignment and grading system. Educators can create tasks, quizzes, or projects and assign them to the class. Students can submit their work directly within Teams, where it can be graded and reviewed. This makes it easier to manage assignments in a hybrid setting, ensuring no student is left behind, whether they are learning remotely or in the classroom.

Breakout Rooms for Group Work

Breakout rooms are a unique feature of Teams that enhances small group instruction in a virtual setting. Educators can divide the class into smaller groups for focused discussions or collaborative tasks, mimicking the small-group dynamics of an in-person classroom.

Analytics and Reporting

For a successful hybrid model, continuous monitoring of student engagement and performance is essential. Teams provide robust analytics and reporting features, allowing educators to track student activity and adapt teaching strategies in real-time.

Accessibility and Inclusion

Microsoft Teams is designed with accessibility in mind, offering features like real-time captioning and screen readers to make learning accessible to everyone. In a hybrid model, these features ensure that all students have equitable access to educational resources, irrespective of their physical location.

Hybrid teaching and learning represent a significant shift in the way education is delivered, requiring platforms that can adapt and provide robust, integrated solutions. Microsoft Teams stands out as an exceptionally versatile platform for hybrid education, offering features that cater to diverse learning needs while maintaining the integrity and effectiveness of the educational process.

Best Practices for Utilizing Microsoft Teams: A Guide for Students and Educators

Here are some best practices for educators:

- **Set clear guidelines and expectations:** From the start, outline your expectations for how Teams will be used for educational purposes. Discuss topics such as etiquette during video calls, expected response times, and guidelines for sharing files.

- **Organize class materials:** Use Teams' file-sharing capabilities to create a well-organized digital library. Create folders for each subject or project and store relevant documents, slides, and worksheets for easy student access.

- **Utilize breakout rooms for small group instruction:** Take advantage of Teams' breakout rooms feature for group assignments or discussions. These can simulate small classroom discussions and are a good way to encourage student engagement.

- **Scheduled check-ins and feedback:** Consistent feedback and timely responses are crucial. Schedule weekly or bi-weekly check-ins to discuss progress, address concerns, and provide feedback.

- **Integrate with other educational tools:** Teams can be integrated with many LMSs and other educational tools. Use this feature to streamline resources and materials across multiple platforms.

- **Engage through polls and quizzes:** Keep the class engaged by occasionally posting quizzes or polls that students can participate in during or outside of live sessions.

- **Monitor analytics for student engagement:** Teams offers analytics that can help you gauge the level of student interaction. Use this data to adjust your teaching methods as necessary.

- **Secure your virtual classroom:** Use the security features available in Teams to create a safe learning environment. This includes setting permissions for which users can join meetings or share content.

- **Accessibility features:** Make use of the built-in accessibility features such as live captions during meetings to make sure your content is accessible to all students.

- **Continual professional development:** Keep abreast of the latest Teams updates and new features that can be used to enhance the educational experience.

Here are some best practices for students:

- **Stay organized:** Use Teams' notebook and file storage capabilities to keep all your class materials in one place. Take advantage of the "Planner" or "Tasks" features to keep track of assignments and due dates.

- **Be present:** Attend all virtual classes just as you would in-person ones. Keep your camera on when possible, as it encourages active participation.

- **Know the tools:** Familiarize yourself with Teams' features. Knowing how to navigate breakout rooms, upload assignments, and use the chat function can greatly improve your learning experience.

- **Respect digital etiquette:** Use professional language in chats and emails, keep yourself muted when not speaking during meetings, and use video responsibly.

- **Engage in discussions:** Whether in the main classroom setting or a breakout room, be an active participant. Share your thoughts, ask questions, and engage with your peers.

- **Use the resources:** Teams offers various tools for collaboration, like file sharing, screen sharing, and a whiteboard. Utilize these features to enhance group projects or study sessions.

- **Seek help when needed:** Don't hesitate to reach out to teachers or peers through the Teams chat if you're struggling with class material or technical issues.

- **Privacy matters:** Be cautious while sharing personal information within Teams. Always ensure you're within a secure and appropriate channel before discussing sensitive topics.

- **Review recorded lessons:** If your teacher makes recorded versions of classes available, make the time to review these, especially if you found certain concepts challenging to understand the first time.

- **Be mindful of notifications:** Teams has a robust notification system to keep you updated. Customize these to fit your needs without becoming a distraction.

By adhering to these best practices, both educators and students can make the most of the versatile, powerful features offered by Microsoft Teams for an enriching, organized, and secure learning experience.

Summary

This chapter offers a comprehensive overview of the various collaboration tools available in Microsoft Teams for Education. Aimed at educators, students, and IT administrators, the chapter delves into features such as virtual classrooms, shared whiteboards, file storage, and breakout rooms. It provides step-by-step guides on how to set up these tools for maximum engagement and learning impact. It also covers best practices for educators to effectively manage their virtual classrooms and facilitate group projects. By the end of the chapter, readers will be equipped with the knowledge and skills to fully leverage Microsoft Teams as a collaborative educational platform.

Also, this chapter guides education IT professionals through the necessary steps for setting up the Parent Connection feature in Microsoft Teams for Education. This tool helps educators securely connect with parents and guardians. IT admins will find information on requirements and how to share valuable resources with guardians and educators for getting started with Parent Connection.

References

- *Microsoft Teams for education*: https://learn.microsoft.com/ en-us/training/paths/master-microsoft-teams-any-learning- environment/

- *Create or join a team*: https://learn.microsoft.com/en-us/ training/modules/structure-teams-channels-tabs-files-apps/ get-started-create-join-team

- *Live events*: https://learn.microsoft.com/en-us/training/ modules/assemble-learners-staff-microsoft-teams-meetings/ host-live-events-stay-connected

CHAPTER 10

Take Your Microsoft Teams Learning to the Next Level and Get Certified

Balu N Ilag[a*]

[a] Tracy, CA, USA

Congratulations! You've arrived at the final chapter! Your journey through the previous eight chapters has been an admirable endeavor, and now it's time to elevate your knowledge by focusing on managing Microsoft Teams certification planning and preparation.

Having devoted significant effort to understanding Microsoft Teams administration, the next logical step is to consolidate your learning by earning a certification. The aim of this chapter is to share some concise planning and preparation strategies for taking the Managing Microsoft Teams certification exam. Embrace this opportunity, and let's prepare for the MS-700 exam together. Once you clear it, you will be awarded the title of Microsoft 365 Certified: Teams Administrator Associate.

The role of a Microsoft Teams administrator, although relatively new, is expansive and complex. It's suitable for professionals with backgrounds in Skype for Business (Lync), Telecom administration, unified communication and collaboration, and support administration. The role encompasses a myriad of responsibilities, such as implementing Teams settings and policies, deploying client software, and efficiently managing Office 365 workloads to facilitate collaboration and communication within an enterprise.

Should you qualify for this role, your responsibilities will include planning, deploying, adapting, and managing all features within Teams. Additionally, you will be tasked with upgrading user workloads from Skype for Business to Microsoft Teams and acquainting yourself with telephony integration, including the Teams Phone System Direct Routing using SBC, Teams Phone System Calling Plan, and Teams Audio (dial-in) Conferencing.

Moreover, your duties will extend beyond mere planning, deployment, and administration. Collaboration with telephony engineers will be essential for integrating advanced voice features into Microsoft Teams. This could involve configuring Teams Direct Routing using SBC, telephony integration, phone number (DID) porting, number translation, voice gateway for analog devices, and more. Collaboration with other administrators, such as security and compliance admins, messaging admins, networking engineers, identity management admins, and audio/video device admins, may also be required.

Before attempting the Managing Microsoft Teams certification exam, an in-depth understanding of Teams components is essential. This includes proficiency in Teams chat, calls, meetings, teams and channels, app policies, and overall administration using the Teams admin center and Windows PowerShell. Crucially, familiarity with managing Teams policy settings through both the Teams admin center and PowerShell is vital. Along with Teams expertise, a foundational grasp of integration points with other apps and services—such as SharePoint, OneDrive for Business, Exchange Online, Azure AD, and Office 365 Groups—is essential (refer to Chapters 1 and 2 for more details).

So buckle up, and let this chapter serve as your roadmap to success as you venture toward becoming a certified Teams administrator. It's time to take your Microsoft Teams learning to the next level!

Introduction to the Exam

As Microsoft Teams continues to become an essential collaboration platform, gaining mastery over its administration has never been more critical. For professionals looking to validate their skills, the "MS-700: Managing Microsoft Teams certification stands as a benchmark. This chapter provides a comprehensive guide to the MS-700 certification, delineating the knowledge required, the distribution of questions across various sections, and strategies to ace the exam.

The MS-700: Managing Microsoft Teams certification is a robust measure of an individual's expertise in Teams administration. Through this chapter, candidates are provided with the vital information required to embark on this certification journey. From understanding the intricacies of Microsoft 365 services to in-depth Insights into the examination sections, this chapter acts as a roadmap for those aspiring to take their Microsoft Teams skills to the next level. Whether you're a seasoned professional or a beginner looking to validate your skills, this guide offers a structured path toward achieving the MS-700 certification.

Candidates aiming for the MS-700 certification must possess the following expertise:

- **Understanding Microsoft 365 services:** A thorough knowledge of Microsoft 365 groups, Microsoft SharePoint Online, OneDrive, Exchange, and Azure Active Directory (Azure AD), part of Microsoft services, is vital.

- **Integration and extension options:** Candidates should be familiar with integrating and extending Teams with other apps such as Microsoft Viva, Power Platform, third-party apps, and custom apps.

The examination is broken down into four main sections, each focusing on a specific aspect of Teams administration. The percentage of questions from each section is as follows:

- **Configure and Manage a Teams Environment (45–50%):** This largest section of the exam focuses on creating and configuring Teams settings, including policies, guest access, security, and compliance.

- **Manage Teams, Channels, Chats, and Apps (20–25%):** This section of the exam emphasizes the management of collaboration within Teams, including the creation, modification, and deletion of teams, channels, chats, and apps.

- **Manage Meetings and Calling (15–20%):** This section of the exam assesses the candidate's ability to handle meeting and call options within Teams, including configurations, policies, and user experiences.

- **Monitor, Report on, and Troubleshoot Teams (10–15%):** This section of the exam tests the skills in monitoring Teams' health, generating reports, and troubleshooting issues.

Strategies and Preparing

The following are tips to prepare:

- **Understand the exam structure:** Familiarize yourself with the four main sections, understanding the percentage of questions from each to prioritize study time.

- **Focus on practical skills:** Hands-on experience with Microsoft 365 services and Teams administration is crucial.

- **Utilize official study materials:** Leverage official guides, courses, and practice exams aligned with the MS-700 certification.

- **Consider third-party tools and training:** Some third-party providers offer specialized training that may complement official resources.

Planning and Preparing for the Managing Microsoft Teams Exam

When sitting for the Managing Microsoft Teams exam, it's crucial to attempt all questions since there is no penalty for incorrect answers. You will be allocated 180 minutes to complete 40 to 60 questions, with some potentially worth multiple points. It's advised to strategically allocate 150 minutes for answering the questions and an additional 30 minutes for instructions, comments, score reporting, and other administrative tasks.

The exam may include a case study that will require you to synthesize information about business and technical requirements, existing environments, and other essential background details. Your ability to understand and integrate information from various sources, pinpoint what is crucial, and make the best decision will be assessed.

Keep in mind that this exam is not a substitute for proper training, and this book alone may not contain everything you need to pass. However, it does provide valuable insights necessary to succeed. The exam is segmented into three primary sections:

- **Planning and Configuring a Microsoft Teams Environment:** This part constitutes 45 to 50 percent of the exam questions. It focuses on preparing the environment before deploying Microsoft Teams. This includes transitioning from Skype for Business to Teams, orchestrating network settings, implementing governance and life-cycle management, managing guest access, overseeing security and compliance, deploying and handling Microsoft Teams endpoints, and finally monitoring and analyzing service usage.

- **Managing Chat, Calling, and Meetings:** This section will account for approximately 30 to 35 percent of the questions. It examines your ability to oversee these essential communication functions within the Microsoft Teams platform.

- **Managing Teams and App Policies:** This final part, comprising 20 to 25 percent of the exam questions, assesses your skill in administering Teams and app policies within the organizational setting.

While this chapter revisits each topic relevant to Teams administration, it does so without delving into exhaustive detail. It serves as an essential guide and supplement to your broader study plan, helping you align your preparation with the specific demands of the MS-700 exam. Make sure to approach this exam with thorough preparation, utilizing this chapter and additional resources to ensure you're ready to showcase your expertise in managing Microsoft Teams.

Focus on Practical Skills: Hands-on Experience

Hands-on experience with Microsoft 365 services and Teams administration is not just an add-on but a core component of your preparation for the MS-700 exam. It bridges the gap between theoretical learning and the practical application of skills that will be assessed in the exam. Integrating hands-on practice into your study routine will enhance your understanding, retention, and problem-solving abilities, setting you up for success in the Managing Microsoft Teams certification exam.

- **Real-world application:** Unlike theoretical knowledge, hands-on experience prepares you for real-world scenarios. You will face questions in the exam that require you to demonstrate a practical understanding of how to plan, configure, and manage a Microsoft Teams environment. This includes a nuanced appreciation of migration, network settings, governance, life-cycle management, security, compliance, and more.

- **Enhanced retention:** Engaging with the actual tools, platforms, and systems will help you remember the functionalities and configurations more effectively. By practicing with real examples, you solidify the concepts in your mind, leading to better performance in the exam.

- **Problem-solving skills:** The MS-700 exam may present you with complex case studies and simulations. Having hands-on experience means that you have faced similar challenges in a practical setting, enhancing your ability to think critically, analyze problems, and arrive at effective solutions.

- **Utilize official study materials:** Leverage official guides, courses, and practice exams aligned with the MS-700 certification. Leveraging official study materials is a strategic approach to preparing for the MS-700 exam. Official guides, courses, and practice exams are crafted to mirror the actual test's content and complexity. By integrating these resources into your study plan, you ensure that your preparation is focused, accurate, and aligned with what you will face on exam day. Make the most of these materials, and complement them with hands-on practice and other supplemental resources to round out your preparation and set yourself up for success in earning the Microsoft 365 Certified: Teams Administrator Associate certification.

  - **Alignment with the exam objectives:** Official materials are designed to align precisely with the exam's objectives and cover the content in the depth and manner required for the test. This ensures that you are studying exactly what you need to know.

  - **Quality and accuracy:** Official resources are typically developed by subject matter experts who understand the intricacies of the technology and the certification exam itself. This means you can trust the quality and accuracy of the information.

  - **Practice exams:** Many official certification preparation packages include practice exams that simulate the actual test experience. These are invaluable in gauging your readiness and identifying areas where you may need additional study.

How to Leverage Official Study Materials

Use the following to help you study:

- **Official guides and textbooks:** Start with the official study guides and textbooks that are recommended for the MS-700 exam. These books often provide comprehensive coverage of the exam topics and include practice questions, exercises, and detailed explanations.

- **Official online courses:** Microsoft and other authorized providers may offer online training courses specifically designed for the MS-700 certification. These courses often include video lectures, quizzes, and hands-on labs, providing a structured and interactive learning experience.

- **Official practice exams:** Utilizing practice exams that are officially endorsed or provided by Microsoft ensures that you are practicing with questions that accurately reflect the style and content of the actual exam. These practice tests are often accompanied by explanations for correct and incorrect answers, helping you understand the underlying concepts.

- **Microsoft learning pathways and documentation:** Microsoft's official documentation and learning pathways can be valuable resources, offering detailed insights into the functionalities and configurations that may be tested in the exam.

- **Utilize official community support:** Engage with official forums and support communities. Interacting with others preparing for the same exam can provide insights, encouragement, and answers to specific questions.

- **Consider third-party tools and training:** Some third-party providers offer specialized training that may complement official resources. Considering third-party tools and training as part of your preparation strategy for the MS-700 exam can add depth and variety to your study plan. By incorporating reputable and specialized third-party resources, you can enhance your understanding, gain different perspectives, and benefit from additional practice opportunities.

Carefully selecting and integrating these tools with official materials ensures a well-rounded and effective approach to preparing for the Managing Microsoft Teams certification exam, setting you on a path to success.

Why Third-Party Tools and Training Can Be Beneficial

Here are some reasons why you might want to use materials from third parties:

- **Different perspectives:** Third-party providers often bring unique approaches and perspectives to the material, which can help you understand the concepts from different angles and deepen your comprehension.

- **Specialized focus:** Some third-party training providers specialize in certain areas of technology or certification preparation, offering in-depth courses, workshops, or tools focused on particular aspects of the exam.

- **Additional practice opportunities:** Third-party tools often include practice exams, quizzes, and exercises that provide more opportunities to test your knowledge and improve your skills.

- **Flexible learning options:** Depending on your learning style and needs, third-party providers may offer flexible training options, such as self-paced online courses, boot camps, one-on-one coaching, or customized study plans.

How to Utilize Third-Party Tools and Training

Here are some tips to finding third-party materials:

- **Research reputable providers:** Not all third-party tools and training are created equal. Look for providers with a strong reputation, positive reviews from previous students, and experience in Microsoft Teams or related technologies.

- **Identify complementary content:** Consider what specific areas you may need additional support or practice in, and seek out third-party resources that address those topics. Some third-party courses may offer unique insights or cover areas not emphasized in official materials.

- **Utilize practice tools:** Practice exams, simulators, and other tools from third-party providers can be valuable additions to your study routine. They offer additional ways to apply what you've learned and gauge your readiness.

- **Consider your budget:** Some third-party resources may come at a cost. Balance the potential benefits against your budget, and consider free trials or samples if available.

- **Integrate with official resources:** Use third-party tools and training to complement, not replace, official study materials. Align your third-party resources with the official exam objectives and guidelines to ensure cohesive preparation.

How to Gain Hands-On Experience

Here's how to gain hands-on experience:

- **Utilize lab environments:** Many online platforms offer virtual labs where you can practice configuring and managing Microsoft Teams and related Microsoft 365 services. These labs simulate real-world environments and are an excellent way to gain practical experience.

- **Experiment with actual tools:** If possible, work with actual Microsoft 365 tools within your organization or a personal environment. Familiarize yourself with the administrative interfaces, settings, policies, and other components.

- **Follow tutorials and guides:** Many online resources offer step-by-step guides to carrying out specific tasks within Microsoft Teams. Following these tutorials will provide you with a structured approach to learning the practical skills needed for the exam.

- **Join community forums:** Engaging with other learners or professionals in community forums can expose you to new challenges and solutions. You can also seek assistance with any specific issues or questions you may have.

Plan Configure and Manage a Teams Environment (45–50%)

By gaining a strong understanding of these topics and actively engaging with practical examples and real-world scenarios, you will substantially increase your chances of successfully passing the MS-700 exam. Be sure to balance your study approach by integrating official resources, third-party training, and hands-on practice.

This section covers overall Teams deployment planning and preparation and configuration in brief detail. If you want to understand each topic in depth, you need to review the relevant chapters earlier in the book. This section of the exam includes the most questions (between 45 and 50 percent). I recommend spending more time on this section to get familiar with each topic mentioned here. Also, review the previous chapters to get comfortable the topic of configuration, specifically the following:

- Upgrade from Skype for Business to Microsoft Teams

- Plan and configure network settings for Microsoft Teams

- Implement governance and life-cycle management for Microsoft Teams

- Configure and manage guest access

- Manage security and compliance

- Deploy and manage Microsoft Teams endpoints

- Monitor and analyze service usage

Upgrade from Skype for Business to Microsoft Teams

If your organization has a Skype for Business environment, the first thing you need to do is think about the upgrade path from Skype for Business to Microsoft Teams and then understand the five coexistence modes. Choose the coexistence mode that will best meet your organizational requirements.

Start an upgrade path with a small group of users; ideally, you can choose IT organization users who understand things and can test things better for you and then gradually expand to the whole organization. I recommend planning an upgrade by region. Migrating users in the same region, on the same Teams mode, works better. If you move half of the users from North America and half from the Asia-Pacific region, then the remaining users will not have a similar experience, causing more confusion. For that simple reason, a region-wide or site-wide approach works better.

You need to select an appropriate upgrade path and coexistence mode to meet your organization's specific needs and requirements. When you migrate pilot users to Teams, they might see issues involving their existing meetings not being migrated to Teams. As an admin, you need to plan to check meeting migration status and troubleshoot meeting migration requests, in case there is an issue. Microsoft has provided the Meetings Migration Service (MMS). Once this service is triggered, the meetings migration process can take up to two hours until it is finalized. It could take longer if the user has many meetings.

Note   If an error occurs during the migration process, MMS will periodically retry up to 9 times during a period of 24 hours.

You also need to understand the user experience. This includes configuring Microsoft Teams upgrade notifications and meeting app options. At the end, you need to configure a coexistence mode for the organization and per user. Figure 10-1 shows the available coexistence modes. You should understand each mode and its details. You can review Chapter 6 for upgrade mode and migration details.

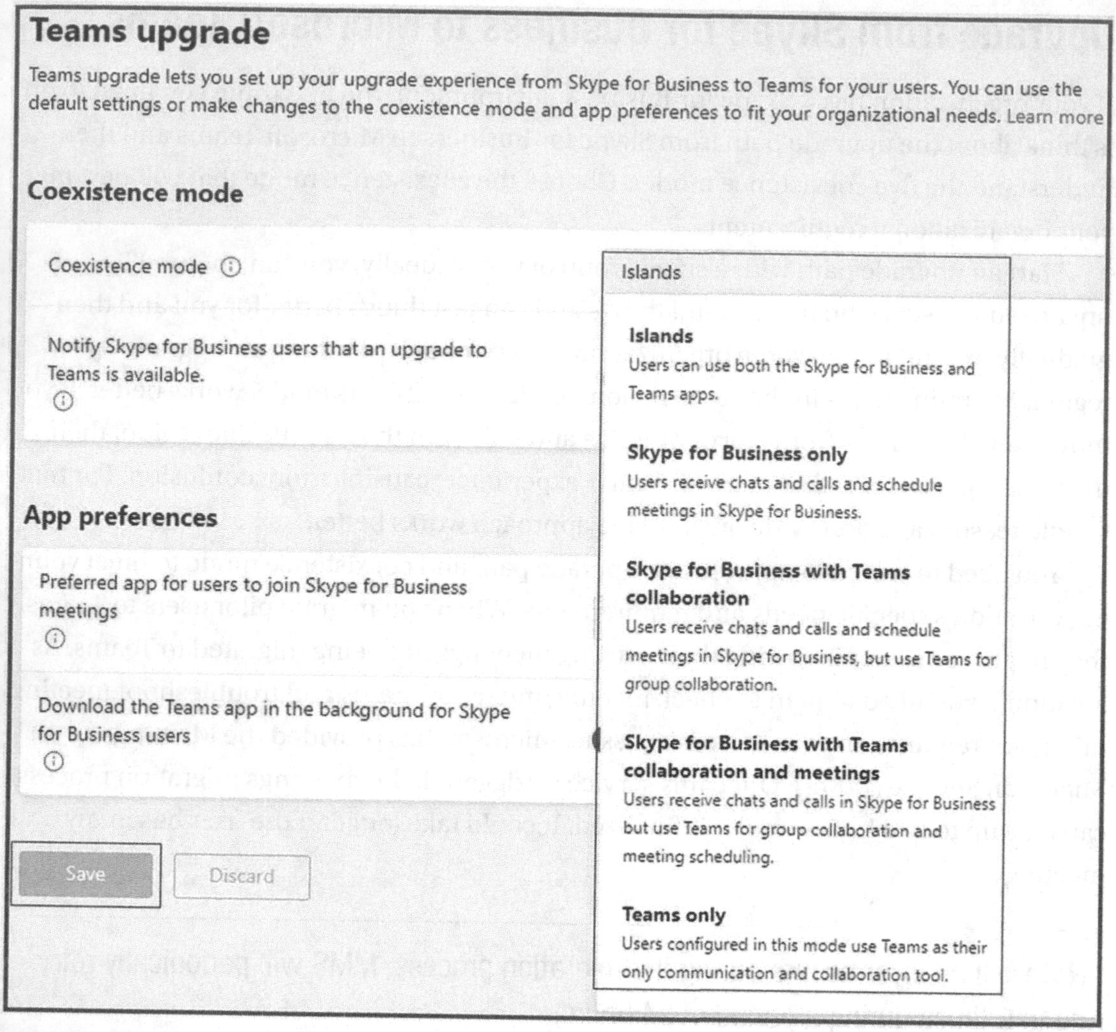

Teams upgrade

Teams upgrade lets you set up your upgrade experience from Skype for Business to Teams for your users. You can use the default settings or make changes to the coexistence mode and app preferences to fit your organizational needs. Learn more

Coexistence mode

Coexistence mode ⓘ

Notify Skype for Business users that an upgrade to Teams is available.
ⓘ

Islands
Islands Users can use both the Skype for Business and Teams apps.
Skype for Business only Users receive chats and calls and schedule meetings in Skype for Business.
Skype for Business with Teams collaboration Users receive chats and calls and schedule meetings in Skype for Business, but use Teams for group collaboration.
Skype for Business with Teams collaboration and meetings Users receive chats and calls in Skype for Business but use Teams for group collaboration and meeting scheduling.
Teams only Users configured in this mode use Teams as their only communication and collaboration tool.

App preferences

Preferred app for users to join Skype for Business meetings
ⓘ

Download the Teams app in the background for Skype for Business users
ⓘ

Save   Discard

Figure 10-1. Coexistence mode

Plan and Configure Network Settings for Microsoft Teams

Configuring network settings for Microsoft Teams is another critical task that admins need to perform. Persistent chat, presence, and instant messaging will work flawlessly out of the box, but as soon as you turn on audio, video, and application sharing, that might not work as required to allow Teams traffic via a corporate firewall with optimized networking. Also, for Teams, optimal call quality requires having enough network bandwidth for audio, video, and application sharing. For example, if there are 5,000 users in the Bloguc HQ office using local Internet and local PSTN for outside phone calls, then how much network bandwidth will you be required to provide for optimal call quality in Teams? Microsoft provides a bandwidth calculator to calculate the required network bandwidth by using a network planning tool, but you must know how to use that Network Planner to calculate network bandwidth capacity for Teams audio, video calls, meetings, and significant events. Basically, the Network Planner will estimate required network bandwidth for the specified number of users.

Another critical area is allowing Teams signaling and media traffic from your organization to Teams Office 365 cloud services. Teams do have multiple service IP subnets, service URLs and FQDNs, and wildcard URLs with required ports and protocols allowed through your organization network firewalls. It is crucial to perform network assessment. Microsoft makes this easier by providing the Network Testing Companion tool for Microsoft Teams and Skype for Business online environments. This tool makes a call and tries to establish a connection by checking the Teams service IP address through establishing connectivity tests. The tool also captures user details like how much packet loss is observed and how much jitter and latency are observed when the network connection is established.

In addition to allowing Teams traffic and assessing bandwidth requirements, implement QoS. Basically, Teams media traffic is audio, video, and application sharing traffic, which is latency, jitter, and packet loss sensitive. Optimizing the network is therefore crucial. QoS is one way to optimize your network bandwidth. You must know where to enable QoS, though. QoS can be implemented through different methods based on different devices. Refer to Chapter 3 for details on QoS implementation. Table 10-1 shows Teams scenarios and port requirements.

Table 10-1. Teams Scenarios and Source and Destination Ports

Teams Scenario	Source IP/Port	Destination IP/Port
Non-real-time traffic	Teams client IP/high ports	Office 365 80 and 443 TCP
Real-time media traffic	Teams client IP 50000–50059 UDP high ports	Transport Relays 3478–3481 UDP

Plan and Configure Network Settings for Teams

Intro text...

- **Calculate network bandwidth capacity for Teams voice, video, meetings, and live events.**

  - **What to study:** Understand the bandwidth requirements for various Teams services, including voice, video, meetings, and live events. Learn how to assess current bandwidth and predict the needs based on expected usage.

  - **How to study:** Consult Microsoft's official documentation to get the recommended bandwidth for different services. Utilize network calculators and perform real-world tests if possible.

  - **Example question:** What is the recommended upload and download bandwidth for Teams HD video conferencing for 50 users?

- **Analyze network impact by using Network Planner.**

  - **What to study:** Learn how to use Microsoft's Network Planner tool to simulate Teams usage and its impact on network resources.

  - **How to study:** Read up on Microsoft's Network Planner documentation and perform practical exercises simulating different scenarios.

  - **Example question:** How do you generate a report for a planned Teams meeting with 100 participants using Network Planner?

- **Specify network ports and protocols used by Teams.**

  - **What to study:** Get to know the specific network ports and protocols that Microsoft Teams uses for communication.

  - **How to study:** Refer to Microsoft's official documentation to understand which ports and protocols need to be open for Teams to function smoothly.

  - **Example question:** Which UDP ports are generally required for Teams video traffic?

- **Specify optimal network architecture for Teams.**

  - **What to study:** Understand how network architecture affects Teams' performance, and learn how to plan an optimized network architecture for Teams.

  - **How to study:** Go through Microsoft's best practices guides and case studies related to network architecture.

  - **Example question:** How can Quality of Service (QoS) policies improve Teams' voice and video performance?

- **Assess network readiness and connectivity by using the Microsoft Teams Network Assessment Tool and Microsoft 365 Network Connectivity Test Tool.**

  - **What to study:** Learn how to use Microsoft's Network Assessment and 365 Network Connectivity Test tools to check if your network is ready for Teams deployment.

  - **How to study:** Familiarize yourself with these tools by running them in your network environment and interpreting the results.

  - **Example question:** What are the key metrics you should monitor when assessing network readiness for Microsoft Teams?

Implement Governance and Life-Cycle Management for Microsoft Teams

Let's assume you are an admin working for a retail organization that has 1,000 stores across the country and your organization happens to have locations with the same Teams structure. You don't want to spend more time repeating the same steps that you follow to create a team channel manually. You can automate the team channel creation process by creating a team template.

Tip   You might get similar scenarios in the exam, so reading the scenario and understanding it is an important step before answering the questions.

"Plan and implement governance and life-cycle management" makes up a significant portion of the "Configure and manage Teams environment" section in the MS-700 exam. These are detailed breakdowns of what you should know for each topic.

- **Identify licensing requirements for advanced life-cycle management of Teams.**

    - **What to study:** Know which Microsoft 365 licenses are necessary for advanced features related to Teams life-cycle management.

    - **How to study:** Check Microsoft's official documentation for licensing prerequisites.

    - **Example question:** Which Microsoft 365 license is required for Teams data retention policies?

- **Identify where Teams stores content.**

    - **What to study:** Understand the different locations where Teams stores data, such as chat content, files, and logs.

    - **How to study:** Study architecture and data storage documentation for Teams.

    - **Example question:** Where are Teams chat histories stored?

- **Plan and manage update policies.**

    - **What to study:** Learn how to manage update policies, including Public Preview, Office Insider, and Targeted Release.

    - **How to study:** Review update cycles and engage in hands-on practice with Teams admin settings.

    - **Example question:** What is the difference between Targeted Release and Public Preview?

- **Create and manage policy packages in Teams.**

    - **What to study:** Know how to create, assign, and manage policy packages that bundle together various policies.

    - **How to study:** Experiment with creating policy packages in the Teams admin center.

    - **Example question:** How do you create a policy package for frontline workers?

- **Plan and configure policy assignment for users and groups.**

    - **What to study:** Understand how to assign policies to individual users and groups.

    - **How to study:** Use the Teams admin center for hands-on practice.

    - **Example question:** How do you assign a messaging policy to a specific group of users?

- **Configure settings for Microsoft 365 Group creation.**

    - **What to study:** Learn how to configure who can create Microsoft 365 groups and what settings they can use.

    - **How to study:** Dive into the settings in the Microsoft 365 admin center.

    - **Example question:** How can you restrict Microsoft 365 group creation to certain roles?

- **Configure an expiration policy for Microsoft 365 Groups.**

    - **What to study:** Know how to set up policies for group expiration and renewal.

    - **How to study:** Use the Microsoft 365 admin center for configuring and testing expiration policies.

    - **Example question:** What happens when a Microsoft 365 group reaches its expiration date?

- **Configure a naming policy for Microsoft 365 Groups.**

    - **What to study:** Understand how to enforce naming conventions and restrict certain words in group names.

    - **How to study:** Configure naming policies via the Microsoft 365 admin center.

    - **Example question:** How do you block inappropriate words in Microsoft 365 group names?

- **Archive, delete, or unarchive one or more teams.**

  - **What to study:** Learn the steps and implications of archiving, deleting, and unarchiving Teams.

  - **How to study:** Review the Teams life-cycle documentation and try archiving and restoring teams in a test environment.

  - **Example question:** How do you restore a deleted Team?

- **Restore or troubleshoot the deletion of a Microsoft 365 group.**

  - **What to study:** Understand how to recover or troubleshoot a deleted Microsoft 365 group.

  - **How to study:** Work with PowerShell and the Microsoft 365 admin center.

  - **Example question:** What are the steps to restore a deleted Microsoft 365 group?

- **Identify when to use access reviews in Azure AD.**

  - **What to study:** Know when it's appropriate to use Azure AD access reviews for Teams members and guests.

  - **How to study:** Review scenarios and documentation related to Azure AD's access reviews.

  - **Example question:** When should you conduct an Azure AD access review for Teams?

- **Perform operations for Teams using PowerShell.**

  - **What to study:** Understand how to perform common Teams operations using PowerShell commands.

  - **How to study:** Work hands-on with PowerShell scripts and Teams cmdlets.

  - **Example question:** How do you retrieve a list of all Teams in your organization using PowerShell?

By thoroughly understanding these topics, you'll be better prepared for the governance and life-cycle management questions that may appear on the MS-700 exam. Don't forget to supplement your studies with hands-on practice, official study materials, and third-party training resources.

Based on the way and the frequency with which your users create teams in your organization, you might need to control team creation. Basically, Microsoft Teams is created based on Office 365 Groups, and you can set up policies for Office 365 Group creation to control team creation.

There are many features that you can use for team governance, such as group creation, classification, expiration, and naming policy, which allows you to undertake seamless life cycle management.

Tip   Be familiar with the group, classification, expiration, and naming policies; you might get an objective or scenario type question on policy on your exam.

Also, be familiar with how to manage Teams during different life-cycle management stages. For example, if a user accidentally deleted a team a week ago, is there still a way to restore the team, and how? The answer is yes. You can restore the team, as there is a 30-day soft deletion period in which a team can be restored. You could encounter such a question on the exam.

Tip   You can create a classification using only Windows PowerShell.

Remember the steps for policy creation and the restore command for group restoration using PowerShell commands, as you will likely be asked questions on this topic on the exam.

First, create team templates, then set up policies for Office 365 Groups. Create and configure Office 365 Groups for Microsoft Teams classifications, expiration policy, and naming policy

To archive, restore, and delete a team, follow this procedure.

- **Office 365 groups creation:** `.\GroupCreators.ps1 | Set-AzureADDirectorySetting`

- **Restore soft-deleted Office 365 groups:** `Restore-AzureADMSDeletedDirectoryObject`

Tip   You can create a naming policy group expiration using the Azure AD admin center.

Remember, you can only create classifications for Office 365 Groups using PowerShell.

Here is the sample PowerShell command:

```
$Template = Get-AzureADDirectorySettingTemplate

$Setting = $template.CreateDirectorySetting()

$setting["ClassificationList"] = "Low Impact, Medium Impact, High Impact"
```

Configure and Manage External Collaboration

The topic "Configure and manage external collaboration" is essential for the Microsoft Teams certification exam, especially the MS-700. The following is a breakdown of each subtopic you should be familiar with:

- **Identify licensing requirements for external collaboration.**

  - **What to study:** Understand the licensing requirements for external collaboration features.

  - **How to study:** Refer to Microsoft's licensing guides.

  - **Example question:** Which license is required to enable guest access in Microsoft Teams?

- **Configure SharePoint Online and OneDrive External Sharing settings.**

  - **What to study:** Learn how to configure external sharing for SharePoint and OneDrive.

  - **How to study:** Practice configuring these settings in the SharePoint admin center.

  - **Example question:** How do you restrict external sharing to specific domains in SharePoint Online?

- **Configure external access in the Microsoft Teams admin center.**

  - **What to study:** Understand how to enable and manage external access in Teams.

  - **How to study:** Navigate to the Teams admin center to explore external access settings.

  - **Example question:** How do you allow external Teams users from a specific domain?

- **Configure external collaboration settings in Azure AD for Guest Access.**

  - **What to study:** Know how Azure AD affects guest access.

  - **How to study:** Experiment with Azure AD external collaboration settings.

  - **Example question:** What are the different guest user permissions in Azure AD?

- **Configure guest access and sharing in various admin centers.**

  - **What to study:** Learn to configure guest access through the Teams admin center, Microsoft 365 admin center, and Azure AD admin center.

  - **How to study:** Conduct hands-on practice with guest settings across these platforms.

  - **Example question:** How do you enable guest access to Teams in the Microsoft 365 admin center?

- **Control guest access to a specific team.**

  - **What to study:** Understand how to limit guest access to certain Teams and how to apply sensitivity labels and Azure AD controls.

  - **How to study:** Experiment with settings within individual Teams.

  - **Example question:** How do you apply a sensitivity label to restrict guest access to a Team?

- **Remove guests from Teams.**

  - **What to study:** Learn how to remove guests from specific Teams or from the tenant.

  - **How to study:** Practice the removal process from Teams and Azure AD admin center.

  - **Example question:** How do you remove a guest user from all Teams in your organization?

- **Configure shared channels for external access.**

  - **What to study:** Understand how to set up shared channels that can be accessed by external users.

  - **How to study:** Review documentation and get hands-on experience.

  - **Example question:** How do you create a shared channel between two organizations?

- **Configure and manage cross-tenant access for B2B Direct Connect.**

  - **What to study:** Learn how to enable and manage cross-tenant collaboration via B2B Direct Connect.

  - **How to study:** Explore the settings in Azure AD for B2B Direct Connect.

  - **Example question:** How do you restrict cross-tenant access to only certain Azure AD groups?

By thoroughly studying these subtopics, you'll be better prepared to answer questions about external collaboration in the MS-700 exam. Keep in mind that practical hands-on experience will complement theoretical knowledge, so practice configuring these settings whenever possible.

Configure and Manage Guest Access

Guest access is frequently used by organization users, and it is a common feature that allows users to work with guest users (external) and add them to the team. The guest user who is from a different organization might be a partner, a vendor, and so on. As a

Teams admin, I frequently use guest access when working on a project that involves an external partner in sharing a document, calling, and chatting with them.

As a Teams admin, you must know how to configure guest access in different places, including Azure AD, the Microsoft 365 admin center, SharePoint, and the Teams admin center. To monitor guest usage, you should know how to use the Azure AD access review, where you can review guest access (see Chapter 2).

Tip   Remember to configure guest access in different admin centers, including Azure AD, Teams admin center, Office 365 Group, and SharePoint admin center.

Be familiar with the following topics, as you might be asked scenario-type questions or settings for these configuration steps.

1. First, configure guest access from the Azure AD portal to allow users to add guests.

2. Then enable guest permissions in Microsoft Teams admin center; this is an organization-wide setting.

3. Then configure guest access for users in Microsoft Teams.

4. Configure meetings, messaging, and calling options for guests; this is another critical setting where you can allow or restrict features.

5. Managing Azure AD access review for guests is an administrator tasks, not the configuration setting. However, as an admin, you must be familiar with the Azure AD access review process.

6. Also, know about the guest removal process as well.

You have to use a different admin center. To enable guest access successfully, you need to enable access in Azure AD, Office 365 Groups, and Microsoft Teams admin center. Additionally, you need to allow external access in SharePoint as well.

Tip   You might be asked how to enable guest access, and you will be given the names of administrative tools. You will need to pick the right tools to enable guest access.

If you want to prevent a Teams member from adding guests to a team, you need to go to Azure AD and turn off the Member Can Invite option.

Manage Security and Compliance

Microsoft 365 provides enterprise-grade security to Teams and compliance capability, including threat protection, information protection, and security management. For example, you as a Teams admin are working in a financial institution like banking, and their users do not allow sharing of confidential data in Teams, such as account numbers, Social Security numbers, and credit card numbers. You need to find a solution. The answer is you need to apply the data loss prevention (DLP) compliance features that allow you to create a policy that can check what is shared in Teams and if the content matches the criteria. It will then delete content and show the information message.

You must know what this compliance feature does and how to apply this feature, including DLP policy, retention policy, sensitivity labels, threat management, and IB policy. You can refer to Chapter 5 for a review.

You must be familiar with the tasks mentioned next, because you might be asked to answer or configure one of the tasks. Chapter 5 provides details about these configuration activities.

1. Assign Microsoft Teams admin roles and remember role names and their list of actions.

2. Create and manage compliance features, including retention and sensitivity policies.

3. Create security and compliance alerts for Microsoft Teams.

4. Create an IB policy.

5. Finally, read security reports for Microsoft Teams.

If you are interested in learning more about the different roles and their activities, refer to the Microsoft document at https://aka.ms/teams-rbac.

Manage Security and Compliance Settings for Teams

By gaining a comprehensive understanding of these topics, you'll be well-prepared for the security and compliance questions that may appear on the MS-700 exam. Always balance your approach by using a mix of official materials, hands-on practice, and third-party resources.

- **Identify licensing requirements for security and compliance features.**

  - **What to study:** Familiarize yourself with the different Microsoft 365 license types and the security and compliance features they include.

  - **How to study:** Refer to Microsoft's licensing documentation for a breakdown of features available with different license types.

  - **Example question:** Which Microsoft 365 license is required to use Advanced Threat Protection in Teams?

- **Specify security and compliance alert policies for Teams.**

  - **What to study:** Understand how to create and manage alert policies in Teams for specific security and compliance events.

  - **How to study:** Hands-on practice via the Microsoft Teams admin center, focusing on configuring alerts for specific scenarios.

  - **Example question:** How can you set an alert for unauthorized access attempts in Teams?

- **Choose appropriate teams administrator roles.**

  - **What to study:** Know the different administrator roles available for Teams and their permissions.

  - **How to study:** Consult official Microsoft documentation to review each role and its capabilities.

  - **Example question:** What are the responsibilities of a Teams Service Administrator?

- **Plan and configure enhanced encryption policies.**

  - **What to study:** Learn how to set up and manage encryption policies for Teams, including end-to-end encryption.

  - **How to study:** Practice configuring encryption via the Microsoft Teams admin center.

  - **Example question:** How do you implement end-to-end encryption for Teams meetings?

- **Plan and configure threat policies in Microsoft 365 Defender.**

  - **What to study:** Understand the threat protection features available in Microsoft 365 Defender and how they can be implemented for Teams.

  - **How to study:** Work through configuring threat policies in Microsoft 365 Defender, with a focus on Teams.

  - **Example question:** How can Microsoft 365 Defender help mitigate phishing threats in Teams?

- **Plan and configure retention policies.**

  - **What to study:** Know how to create retention policies for chats, messages, and shared files in Teams.

  - **How to study:** Perform practical exercises on setting up retention policies through the Microsoft 365 compliance center.

  - **Example question:** How do you set a retention policy for Teams chats?

- **Plan and configure sensitivity labels and policies.**

  - **What to study:** Learn how sensitivity labels can be used to protect sensitive content in Teams.

  - **How to study:** Hands-on practice in creating and applying sensitivity labels via the Microsoft 365 compliance center.

  - **Example question:** What are sensitivity labels, and how are they different from permission levels?

- **Plan and configure data loss prevention (DLP) policies.**

  - **What to study:** Understand the functionalities of DLP in Teams, such as detecting and protecting sensitive information.

  - **How to study:** Set up DLP policies through the Microsoft 365 compliance center and test them in Teams.

  - **Example question:** How can DLP policies prevent the sharing of credit card information in Teams chats?

- **Plan conditional access for Teams.**

  - **What to study:** Learn how to implement conditional access policies for Teams to restrict access based on conditions.

  - **How to study:** Configure conditional access policies via Azure AD and test their impact on Teams.

  - **Example question:** How can you restrict Teams access to only company-managed devices?

- **Plan and configure information barrier (IB) policies.**

  - **What to study:** Understand how to set up Information Barriers to restrict communications between certain groups.

  - **How to study:** Use the Microsoft 365 compliance center to set up and test information barriers.

  - **Example question:** In what scenarios are Information Barriers most useful?

- **Identify appropriate use cases for communication compliance and insider risk management.**

  - **What to study:** Be familiar with what communication compliance and insider risk management can offer in a Teams environment.

  - **How to study:** Study real-world scenarios and consult Microsoft documentation for best practices.

  - **Example question:** What kind of activities could trigger an insider risk alert in Teams?

Deploy and Manage Microsoft Teams Endpoints

The Microsoft Teams app is available for desktop (Windows and macOS), mobile (Android and iOS), Linux clients, and web clients. The end user using Teams on any of these devices will have the same experience. Apart from desktop, mobile, and web clients, there are different devices, like desk phones, conference rooms, and common area phones. Native Teams phones and conference rooms are available that you can use; however, you need to set up resource accounts for these room devices. See Chapter 2 for Teams client deployment.

Tip   You must know Teams app supported platforms and how to deploy the Teams app for a different operating system platforms. You can refer to the mentioned resources.

Here is the secure link to download the Teams app: `https://teams.microsoft.com/downloads`.

- Deploy Microsoft Teams clients to devices, including Windows, VDI (Virtual Desktop), macOS, and mobile devices. Refer to the Microsoft documentation for Teams app deployment for different operating systems at `https://docs.microsoft.com/en-us/microsoftteams/get-clients`.

- Manage configuration profiles (refer to Chapter 2).

- Manage device settings and firmware (refer to Chapter 2).

- Configure Microsoft Teams rooms. Refer to the Microsoft documentation at `https://docs.microsoft.com/en-us/microsoftteams/rooms/rooms-deploy` to configure a Teams room account with prerequisites.

Tip   You might encounter a question on the Teams phone profile setup, so it is essential to be familiar with the process.

To configure the profile, you need to create a profile with custom configurations, such as general setting with device lock setting, language, time and date format, daylight saving time, device settings with a display screensaver, office hours for the device, and network settings with DHCP enabled hostname, IP address, subnet mask, DNS, and gateway. Figure 10-2 shows the profile configuration settings. You must know what customization settings are available in the profile configuration.

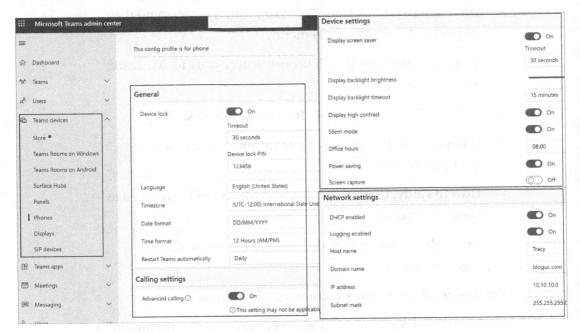

Figure 10-2. *Profile configuration settings*

Manage Teams Clients and Devices

The "Manage Teams clients and devices" section is a crucial area for the MS-700 exam. This topic is dense and covers a variety of hardware and software configurations necessary for Teams administration. Here's a breakdown of the subtopics:

- **Identify licensing requirements for Teams phone and resource accounts.**

  - **What to study:** Know what licenses are needed for Teams phones and resource accounts.

  - **How to study:** Review Microsoft's documentation on Teams licensing.

- **Example question:** What type of license is required for setting up a Teams conference phone?

- **Identify licensing requirements for Teams devices.**

  - **What to study:** Understand what licenses are needed for different Teams-compatible devices.

  - **How to study:** Look at the list of supported devices and their respective licensing requirements.

  - **Example question:** Which license is necessary for Microsoft Teams Room devices?

- **Manage configuration profiles for Teams devices.**

  - **What to study:** Learn how to create and manage device configuration profiles.

  - **How to study:** Use the Teams admin center or PowerShell to configure profiles.

  - **Example question:** How do you set a device profile to Meeting Mode?

- **Configure Teams Rooms accounts and systems.**

  - **What to study:** Be familiar with setting up Teams Rooms, from the accounts to the physical system setups.

  - **How to study:** Refer to Microsoft's Teams Rooms setup guides and get hands-on experience.

  - **Example question:** What are the settings to enable direct guests to join from Cisco WebEx in a Teams Room?

- **Manage device settings and firmware.**

  - **What to study:** Understand how to manage the settings and firmware updates for Teams devices.

  - **How to study:** Use the Teams admin center to check device statuses and perform firmware updates.

  - **Example question:** How do you roll back a firmware update for a Teams phone?

- **Manage Teams device tags.**

  - **What to study:** Know how to create and manage device tags for better organization.

  - **How to study:** Apply tags to devices through the Teams admin center and track their effect.

  - **Example question:** What's the advantage of applying a device tag to Teams phones in a specific building?

- **Provision and configure remote sign-in for new devices.**

  - **What to study:** Learn how to enable remote sign-ins for new devices that are Teams-compatible.

  - **How to study:** Follow Microsoft's guidelines for setting up remote sign-ins and try it out in a test environment.

  - **Example question:** How do you configure a Teams device to allow remote sign-in?

By comprehensively understanding these subtopics, you'll be well-prepared to tackle questions related to managing Teams clients and devices in the MS-700 exam. Hands-on experience will be invaluable, so make sure you get plenty of practice working with Teams devices and their settings.

Monitoring and Analyzing Microsoft Teams Service Usage

After you've set up your Teams environment and welcomed users aboard, it's crucial for administrators to keep an eye on how the platform is being utilized. Microsoft offers a variety of usage reports that help admins gauge how different Teams features—such as teams and channels, voice and video calls, chat messages, and live events—are being used by the workforce.

The following are essential reports for administrators:

- **Microsoft Teams Usage Reports:** Admins should be familiar with these reports that provide specific insights into Teams feature usage.

- **Microsoft 365 Usage Reports:** In addition to Teams-specific reports, admins should also understand usage reports for Microsoft 365 as a whole.

- **Teams Call Analytics:** This is especially useful for understanding one-on-one call dynamics and meeting-related statistics.

- **Call Quality Dashboard:** An essential tool for assessing the quality of calls across the organization.

Important Tip   You may come across exam questions related to troubleshooting individual call quality issues. The key is to employ Teams Call Analytics and interpret these reports to pinpoint any call quality concerns.

Measuring Adoption and Feature Usage

Understanding the level of Teams adoption is essential for the platform's success in your organization. Microsoft's dashboards and reports, accessible through the Teams admin center, can help you evaluate which features are popular and which are underutilized. For example, you may find that chat features are highly used, while call and meeting features are less popular.

Teams Call Analytics is especially useful for understanding one-on-one call dynamics and meeting-related statistics. Figure 10-3 shows Teams individual Call Analytics.

Figure 10-3. *Teams individual Call Analytics*

The Call Quality Dashboard (CQD) is also an invaluable resource for assessing the overall quality of calls in your organization. It can provide metrics on an individual level, as shown in Figure 10-3, and also offer a broader view for the entire organization, as depicted in Figure 10-4.

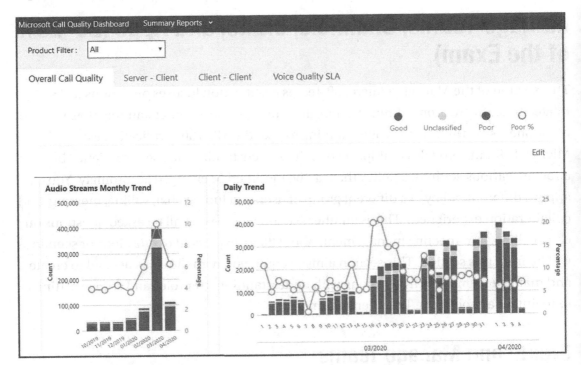

Figure 10-4. *Call Quality Dashboard for the Bloguc organization*

Figure 10-4 shows the CQD for the Bloguc organization.

You can access Teams device and user activity reports for up to 180 days through the Microsoft 365 admin center. If you're focused on analytics, go to the Teams admin center, navigate to Analytics & Reports, and select Usage Report. These reports can cover data for the last 7 or 28 days as of the latest update.

Additional Tip   The exam may include questions about exporting Teams user activity reports for periods exceeding 90 days. In such cases, the Microsoft 365 admin center is your go-to resource for these extended reports.

By comprehensively understanding these topics, you'll be well-prepared to monitor and analyze Teams services effectively, a skill that will not only be useful in practical terms but also valuable for the MS-700 certification exam.

Manage Teams, Channels, Chats, and Apps (20–25% of the Exam)

This section of the Managing Microsoft Teams certification focuses on various tasks related to team creation, administration, and configuration. Understanding these components is crucial for anyone planning to take the MS-700 certification exam. Microsoft Teams provides multiple capabilities to customize the user experience by allowing various settings, a policy that can be modified or changed accordingly. You can apply a different policy to a different group of users, including chat, calling, meeting, and collaboration experiences. This is another section where you will be asked questions on chat, calling, and meeting management. About 20 to 25 percent of questions or scenarios will be from this section. This section aims to equip you with the skills needed to create and manage teams effectively, along with understanding user roles and critical settings to maintain a productive Teams environment.

Create and Manage Teams

This section aims to provide a comprehensive understanding of how to effectively manage channels and chats in Microsoft Teams. The topics cover everything from channel types to policy governance, ensuring you are well-equipped for the certification exam. Mastering these topics is crucial, as they make up a significant portion of the MS-700 exam and are integral to effective Teams management.

Create a team using different methods.

- **Microsoft Teams admin center:** Learn how to navigate the admin center to create a new team and specify its settings.

- **Teams client:** Understand how to utilize the Teams client software for team creation.

- **Teams PowerShell module:** Familiarize yourself with PowerShell commands for team operations.

Create a team from existing resources.

- **Microsoft 365 group:** Learn to convert an existing Microsoft 365 group into a team.

- **SharePoint site:** Understand how to leverage an existing SharePoint site to form a team.

- **Existing team:** Learn how to clone or duplicate existing teams.

Use a Teams templates:

- **Create a team from a template:** Learn to use predefined or custom templates to create teams.

- **Manage templates and policies:** Learn to create, modify, and manage Teams templates, and understand how to set up template policies.

Learn to manage membership and user roles.

- **Manage membership:** Learn how to add or remove members and manage guest access.

- **User roles:** Understand the different user roles within a team— Owner, Member, and Guest.

You should learn about Microsoft Teams admin center management.

- **Manage a team:** Explore the functionalities available in the Microsoft Teams admin center to manage existing teams.

- **Environment settings:** Understand how to configure settings that apply to Teams at an organizational level.

You should know the following privacy and sensitivity settings:

- **Configure Privacy and Sensitivity Settings:** Learn how to set up different privacy levels for your teams. Understand how to set up sensitivity labels and what each label entails.

Manage Channels and Chats

The management of channels and chats is a significant focus within the second section of the MS-700: Manage Microsoft Teams certification. The following is a detailed overview of the topics related to managing channels and chats.

These are recommended channel types:

- **Understand standard channels.**

  - **Description:** These are channels that are open to all team members. Use standard channels for general topics that everyone can contribute to.

  - **When to Use:** These are recommended when you want open, transparent conversations where all team members can participate.

- **Understand private channels.**

  - **Description:** These are limited to a subset of team members and offer more privacy.

  - **When to Use:** These are ideal for discussions that involve sensitive information or a specific subset of team members.

- **Understand shared channels.**

  - **Description:** These are channels that can be accessed by members from multiple teams.

  - **When to Use:** Use them when you have topics or projects that involve members from different teams but don't require a new team.

- **You need to learn how to add, edit, and remove channels.**

  - **Adding channels:** Learn the different ways to add channels via the Teams client and admin center.

  - **Editing channels:** Understand how to rename channels, change channel settings, or add new functionalities.

- **Removing channels:** Familiarize yourself with the process of safely archiving or deleting channels.

- **You need to learn how to manage Teams channel settings.**

  - **Settings management:** Learn how to manage settings like permissions, tabs, and apps for specific channels.

  - **Pinning and following:** Know how to pin important channels and manage notifications settings.

- **Learn about Teams policies for channels.**

  - **Create policies:** Learn how to create new policies for channels, specifying things like who can add or remove channels.

  - **Manage policies:** Understand how to apply, edit, or remove existing policies for better channel governance.

- **Learn how to manage private and shared channel membership.**

  - **Private membership:** Learn how to add or remove members in private channels and manage guest access.

  - **Shared membership:** Understand how to control access to shared channels, which involve members from multiple teams.

- **Learn how to create and manage messaging policies.**

  - **Messaging policies:** Learn how to create policies that govern chat behaviors, like the ability to edit or delete sent messages, use Giphy, or mention everyone in a channel.

  - **Apply messaging policies:** Understand how to assign these messaging policies to users or groups within the Teams admin center.

Manage Apps for Teams

Managing apps for Teams is a vital component in the MS-700: Manage Microsoft Teams certification. Understanding how to oversee app settings, permissions, and policies is crucial for successful Teams management. The following is a detailed look at the subtopics involved:

- **Manage org-wide app settings in the Microsoft Teams admin center.**

  - **Description:** Centralize app control by setting global parameters that affect all Teams apps within your organization.

  - **Key points:** Manage settings such as third-party apps, side-loading of apps, and app-level permissions for the entire organization.

- **Create and manage app permission policies.**

  - **Description:** Define which apps users can or cannot access.

  - **Key points:** Create permission policies to allow or block specific apps. Assign these policies to different user groups based on role or function.

- **Create and manage app setup policies.**

  - **Description:** Configure pre-installed apps and the app menu layout for Teams users.

  - **Key points:** Use setup policies to streamline the user experience by preconfiguring essential apps and pinning them to the sidebar.

- **Manage permissions and consent for apps, including blocking apps.**

  - **Description:** Control how apps access data and which apps can be installed.

  - **Key points:** Set up permission scopes for apps and handle user consent flows. Block unwanted or risky apps.

- **Recommend appropriate extensibility options.**

  - **Description:** Understand and recommend when to use various extensibility features.

  - **Key points:** Choose the right combination of apps, connectors, tabs, meetings, and messaging extensions to achieve specific organizational goals.

- **Manage the purchasing of apps in the Teams App Store.**

  - **Description:** Oversee the procurement process for paid apps.

  - **Key points:** Control purchase permissions, and manage billing and licensing for paid apps in the Teams app store.

- **Customize the appearance of the Teams App Store.**

  - **Description:** Personalize the visual presentation of the Teams app store.

  - **Key points:** Adjust categories, featured apps, and branding to align with organizational needs.

- **Customize the branded experience of an app.**

  - **Description:** Alter how a specific app appears and behaves within Teams.

  - **Key points:** Customize app names, icons, and interactions for a more cohesive branded experience.

- **Upload an app to Teams.**

  - **Description:** Learn the procedure to upload a custom or third-party app to Microsoft Teams.

  - **Key points:** Utilize the Teams admin center or Teams client to upload apps, ensuring they meet organizational compliance and security requirements.

847

Manage Teams Meeting and Calling

The third section of the MS-700 certification exam focuses on the management of Teams meeting and calling features. This topic comprises 15–20% of the exam and covers a wide range of subtopics.

Manage Meetings and Events

Here are the relevant topics:

- **Recommend meeting types.**

    - **Description:** Understand the different types of Teams meetings and events, such as live events, webinars, and virtual appointments, and recommend the best fit for various scenarios.

- **Enable enhanced meeting features.**

    - **Description:** Assign Microsoft Teams Premium licenses to users to unlock additional meeting capabilities.

- **Configure meeting settings.**

    - **Description:** Manage settings like participant roles, permissions, and meeting expiration time.

- **Create and manage meeting templates and template policies.**

    - **Description:** Establish standardized meeting templates and corresponding policies to streamline meeting setup.

- **Create and manage meeting policies.**

    - **Description:** Create policies that dictate the behavior and capabilities during meetings, such as recording options and participant roles.

- **Create and manage conference bridges.**

    - **Description:** Set up and manage dial-in numbers and settings for audio conferencing.

- **Create and manage audio conferencing policies.**

  - **Description:** Create policies governing the use and behavior of audio conferencing, like PIN requirements and participant access.

- **Plan and configure live events settings and policies.**

  - **Description:** Understand how to set up and manage live events, including permissions, recording policies, and attendee management.

Manage Phone Numbers and Services for Teams Phone

Here are the relevant topics:

- **Evaluate PSTN options.**

  - **Description:** Understand and compare different Public Switched Telephone Network (PSTN) options like Calling Plan, Direct Routing, Operator Connect, and Teams Phone Mobile.

- **Add, change, or remove an emergency address.**

  - **Description:** Manage emergency addresses to ensure compliance and user safety.

- **Provision and manage phone numbers.**

  - **Description:** Assign and manage phone numbers for users, services, and conferencing bridges.

- **Assign, change, or remove a phone number for a user or resource account.**

  - **Description:** Manage phone numbers for individual users or resource accounts like conference rooms.

- **Create and manage resource accounts.**

  - **Description:** Create and manage accounts for resources like meeting rooms and equipment in the Teams admin center.

Manage Voice Settings and Policies for Users

Here are the relevant topics:

- **Create and manage voicemail policies.**

  - **Description:** Define voicemail behavior, including message length and retention policies.

- **Configure auto-attendants and call queues.**

  - **Description:** Set up automated attendants for call routing and manage call queues for incoming calls.

- **Create and manage calling policies.**

  - **Description:** Define and manage policies that control calling features available to users, like call forwarding and simultaneous ring.

Monitor, Report On, and Troubleshoot Teams (10–15%)

The fourth section of the MS-700 certification exam centers on monitoring, reporting, and troubleshooting within Microsoft Teams. This accounts for 10–15% of the total exam content. The following is a comprehensive overview of each subtopic.

Monitor and Report on Teams

Here are the relevant topics:

- **Monitor and report on voice and meeting quality.**

  - **Description:** Understand how to use in-built tools and metrics to gauge the quality of voice and video calls. This includes latency, jitter, and other key performance indicators.

- **Report on Teams usage.**

  - **Description:** Access and interpret data on various usage metrics, including team activity, app usage, the number of active users, per-meeting metrics, and storage usage.

- **Monitor and report on the creation and deletion of Teams.**

    - **Description:** Track the lifecycle of Teams—from creation to deletion—and report on them for governance and compliance needs.

- **Monitor and report on guest access.**

    - **Description:** Monitor and report on the activity and permissions of guest users, ensuring compliance with company policies and security measures.

- **Monitor the Microsoft 365 Network Connectivity Test Tool.**

    - **Description:** Utilize the Microsoft 365 Network Connectivity Test tool to assess network performance and address any bottlenecks or issues affecting Teams performance.

- **Manage feedback policies.**

    - **Description:** Set up and manage policies for capturing user feedback within Teams, facilitating continuous improvement.

Troubleshoot Audio, Video, and Client Issues

Here are the relevant topics:

- **Collect client-side logs.**

    - **Description:** Know how to collect logs from the Teams client for diagnostic purposes, aiding in troubleshooting efforts.

- **Clear the Teams client cache.**

    - **Description:** Learn the process to clear the Teams client cache to resolve performance and login issues.

- **Troubleshoot issues by using self-help diagnostics for Teams.**

    - **Description:** Leverage the self-help diagnostic tools available within Teams to identify and resolve common issues affecting audio, video, and client performance.

Manage Chat and Collaboration Features in Microsoft Teams

Microsoft Teams serves as a hub for chat-based workspace and collaboration functionalities. The platform offers a myriad of settings to control user activities in both chat and channel messages, such as message sending and deletion, communications with internal and external parties, email-to-channel capabilities, and third-party file storage integration, among other features.

As a Teams administrator, you're expected to be proficient in various configuration settings. These range from chat messaging policies and federated external access to channel and team management. You should also be comfortable with setting up both standard and private channels, email integrations, external SharePoint and OneDrive access, as well as configuring various cloud storage options for seamless collaboration.

Here are some quick tips for exam preparation:

- **Team and private channel creation:** Familiarize yourself with Office 365 Groups settings, as you will likely face questions related to controlling team and private channel creation.

- **Controlling chat and channel messages:** To regulate chat and channel activities, you'll need to delve into messaging policies found in the Teams admin center. This is where you can set parameters like who can start new posts in specific announcement channels.

- **Email and file storage configuration:** The Teams admin center is also where you can configure email integration and select cloud storage options. Available file storage options that may come up in the exam include Citrix Files, Dropbox, Box, and Google Drive.

By mastering these elements, you'll be well-prepared for the examination and capable of effectively managing a Teams environment.

Messaging policy in the Teams admin center (see Figure 10-5) controls chat and channel messages. There is also a channel setting for messages in the Teams client. For example, if the team's owner wants to have an announcement channel in a team that allows only specific members to start a new post, you will set that here.

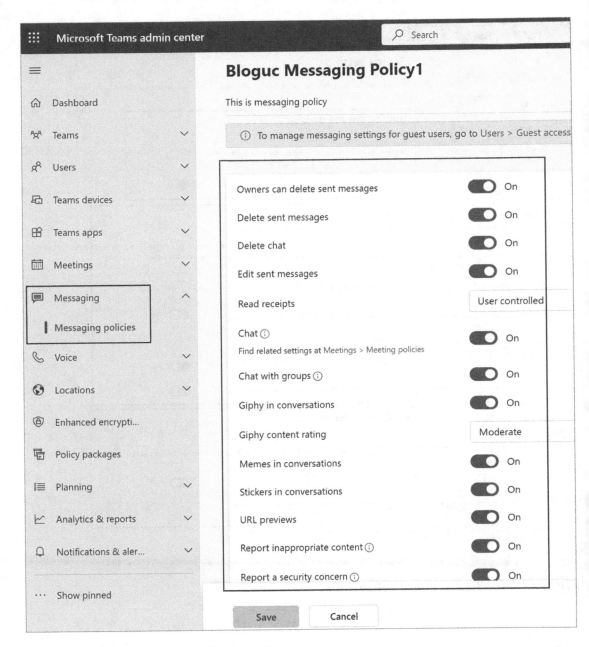

Figure 10-5. Messaging policies settings

To configure email integration, log in to the Teams admin center, where you can set up email integration and cloud file storage, as shown in Figure 10-6.

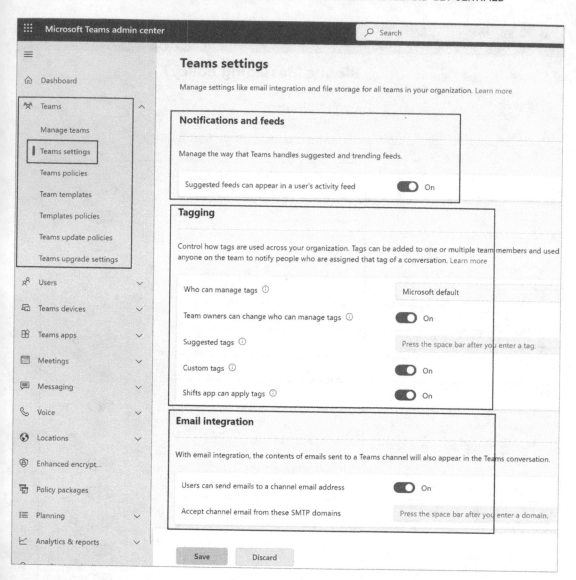

Figure 10-6. Teams email integration

Tip   You might see a question on the exam asking for a list of file storage options. The answer is Citrix files, Dropbox, Box, and Google Drive.

Manage Meeting Experiences

You as a Teams admin can customize Teams meeting management settings by going to the Teams admin center and selecting Meetings. Select the appropriate option and set it accordingly. Meeting settings include allowing anonymous users to join the meeting, whether the user can request or give control, or what the user experience is while using a dial-in conference bridge. These are all features you can configure in a Teams meeting setting, based on your user and organization requirements.

Tip   You might encounter questions about how to allow an anonymous user to join a Teams meeting. The answer is enabling the Anonymous Users Can Join A Meeting option in the meeting settings, as shown in Figure 10-7.

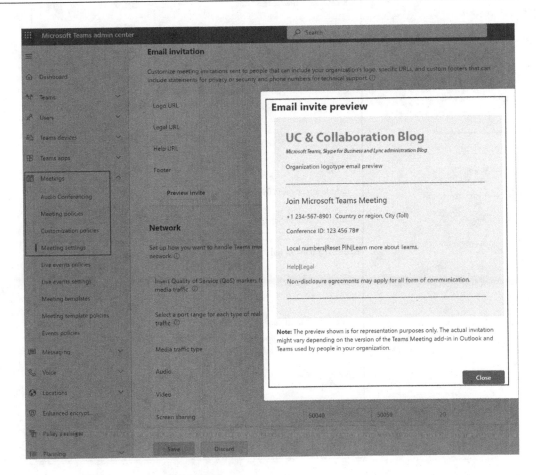

Figure 10-7. *Teams meeting settings*

Meeting settings are set for meetings. You can customize email invitations and enable QoS by adding custom port ranges as per your organization's needs.

Teams meeting policies do have several options you can turn on or off. Meeting policies settings are divided into four categories: General, Audio & Video, Content Sharing, and Participants & Guests, as shown in Figure 10-8.

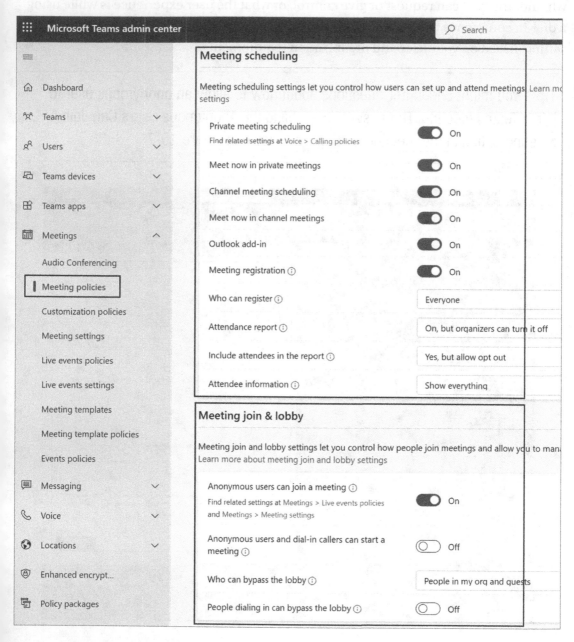

Figure 10-8. Meeting policies settings

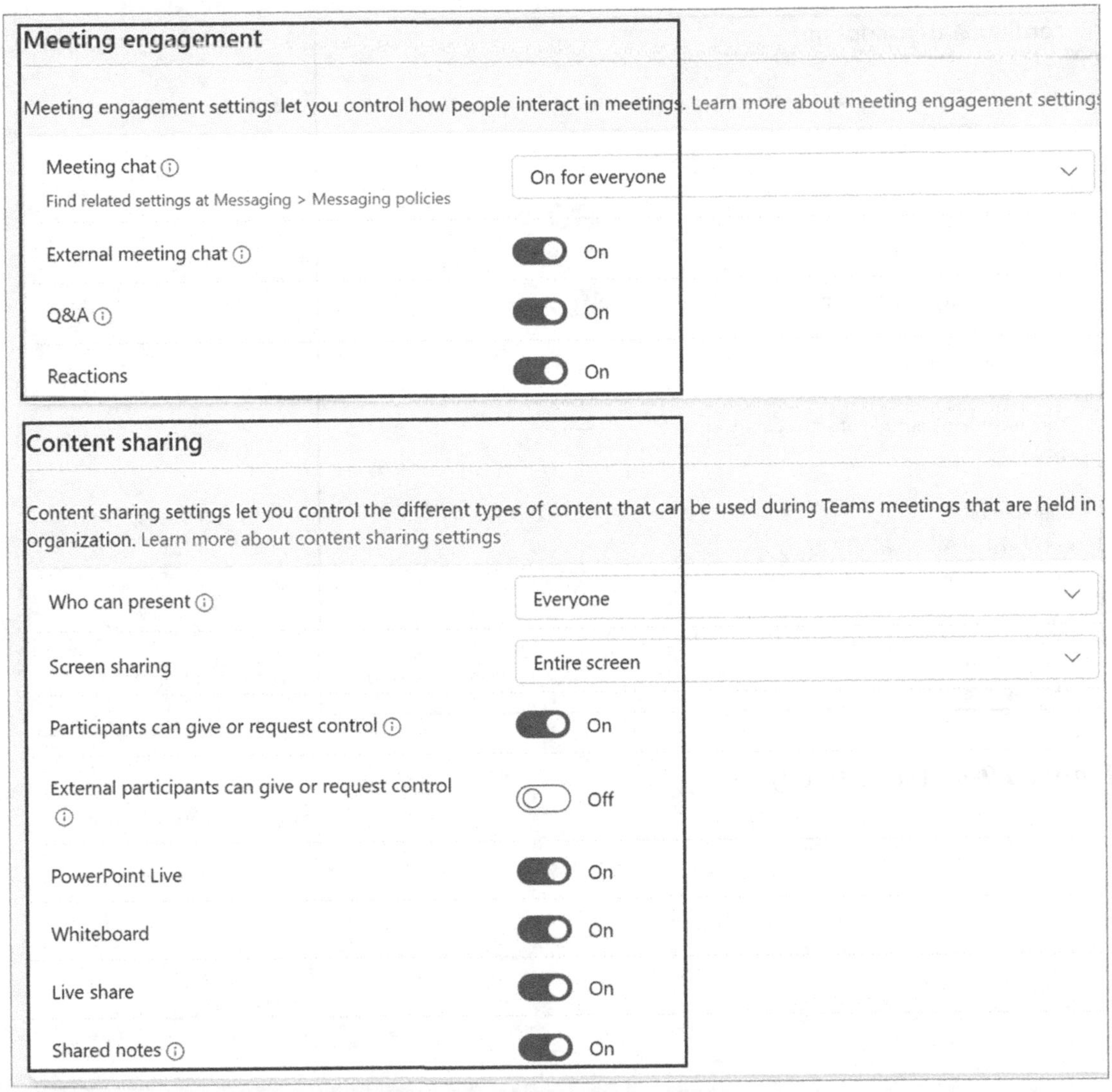

Meeting engagement

Meeting engagement settings let you control how people interact in meetings. Learn more about meeting engagement settings

Meeting chat ⓘ	On for everyone ⌄
Find related settings at Messaging > Messaging policies	
External meeting chat ⓘ	🔘 On
Q&A ⓘ	🔘 On
Reactions	🔘 On

Content sharing

Content sharing settings let you control the different types of content that can be used during Teams meetings that are held in organization. Learn more about content sharing settings

Who can present ⓘ	Everyone ⌄
Screen sharing	Entire screen ⌄
Participants can give or request control ⓘ	🔘 On
External participants can give or request control ⓘ	⚪ Off
PowerPoint Live	🔘 On
Whiteboard	🔘 On
Live share	🔘 On
Shared notes ⓘ	🔘 On

Figure 10-8. (*continued*)

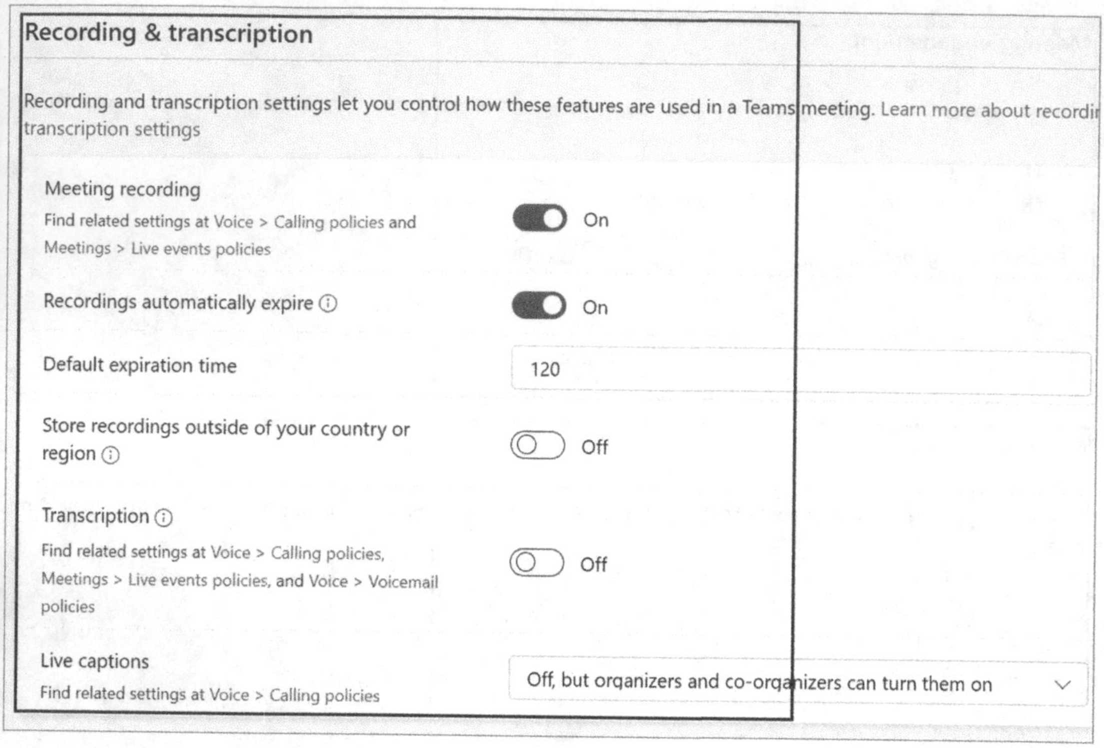

Recording & transcription

Recording and transcription settings let you control how these features are used in a Teams meeting. Learn more about recordir transcription settings

Meeting recording

Find related settings at Voice > Calling policies and
Meetings > Live events policies   On

Recordings automatically expire ⓘ   On

Default expiration time   120

Store recordings outside of your country or
region ⓘ   Off

Transcription ⓘ

Find related settings at Voice > Calling policies,
Meetings > Live events policies, and Voice > Voicemail   Off
policies

Live captions
Find related settings at Voice > Calling policies   Off, but organizers and co-organizers can turn them on

Figure 10-8. (*continued*)

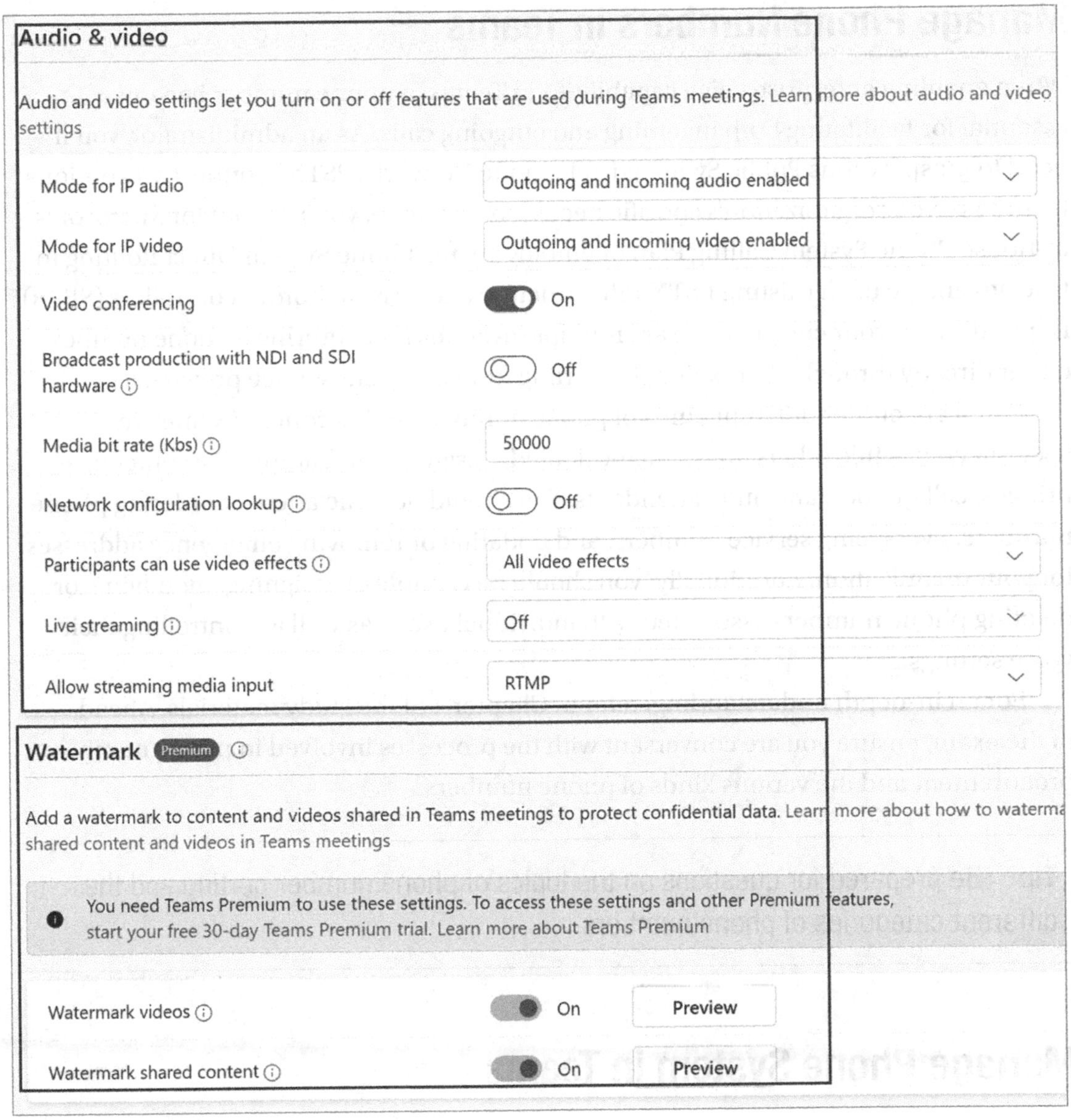

Audio & video

Audio and video settings let you turn on or off features that are used during Teams meetings. Learn more about audio and video settings

Mode for IP audio	Outgoing and incoming audio enabled ⌄
Mode for IP video	Outgoing and incoming video enabled ⌄
Video conferencing	🔘 On
Broadcast production with NDI and SDI hardware ⓘ	⚪ Off
Media bit rate (Kbs) ⓘ	50000
Network configuration lookup ⓘ	⚪ Off
Participants can use video effects ⓘ	All video effects ⌄
Live streaming ⓘ	Off ⌄
Allow streaming media input	RTMP ⌄

Watermark `Premium` ⓘ

Add a watermark to content and videos shared in Teams meetings to protect confidential data. Learn more about how to watermark shared content and videos in Teams meetings

> ● You need Teams Premium to use these settings. To access these settings and other Premium features, start your free 30-day Teams Premium trial. Learn more about Teams Premium

Watermark videos ⓘ	🔘 On Preview
Watermark shared content ⓘ	🔘 On Preview

Figure 10-8. (*continued*)

Manage Phone Numbers in Teams

When enabling enterprise voice capabilities in Teams, a phone number becomes essential for facilitating both incoming and outgoing calls. As an administrator, you'll need to grasp various Public Switched Telephone Network (PSTN) connectivity options tailored to your organization's specific needs. For example, you may opt for Microsoft's in-house Phone System Calling Plan or employ Teams Phone System Direct Routing to take advantage of an existing PSTN infrastructure and session border controllers (SBCs). Depending on your choice, there are multiple avenues for acquiring a phone number, either directly through Microsoft or by porting from a current service provider.

You'll encounter different kinds of phone numbers in this context: some are user-specific, while others are service-oriented, designed for features like conference bridges, call queues, and auto-attendants. You should become adept at ordering phone numbers, overseeing service numbers, and updating or removing emergency addresses for your organization. Additionally, you should be capable of assigning, modifying, or deleting phone numbers associated with individual users, as well as controlling their voice settings.

For an in-depth understanding, refer to Chapter 4 of the study materials. Ahead of the exam, ensure you are conversant with the processes involved in phone number procurement and the various kinds of phone numbers.

Tip   Be prepared for questions on the topics of phone number porting and the different categories of phone numbers.

Manage Phone System in Teams

As an administrator for Microsoft Teams, it's crucial to have a deep understanding of both the Phone System Calling Plan and Phone System Direct Routing to effectively set up and manage call policies. For instance, if a customer dials a hotline number, how is that call processed and routed? Mastery in configuring resource accounts for specialized voice functionalities like call queues and auto-attendants is required. Moreover, the platform offers a range of customizable voice policies, including the ability to alter the display number or caller ID.

In cases where a user experiences issues such as dropped calls, you will need to consult the Direct Routing dashboard to pinpoint possible problems. Your role involves a diverse set of tasks that range from overseeing resource accounts, setting up and managing call queues and auto-attendants, to administering various call and caller ID policies. You should also be competent in interpreting the metrics and warnings on the Direct Routing health dashboard.

For more comprehensive coverage of each of these tasks, Chapter 4 serves as a valuable resource.

Tip 1   Anticipate exam questions on the Phone System Calling Plan and Direct Routing. Ensure you're well-versed in the ins and outs of setting up and administering these features.

Tip 2   The exam may include questions related to the Direct Routing health dashboard, particularly its warnings. Understanding how to interpret these warnings to diagnose potential issues is crucial, so make sure you're familiar with both the setup and the health dashboard.

Managing Teams and Implementing App Policies

This final segment of the Manage Microsoft Teams exam constitutes approximately 20–25% of the test questions. Once Teams is enabled for your organization, your role as an admin extends to effective management of Teams. This includes tasks such as creating teams, creating channels, and integrating Teams with existing infrastructures such as distribution groups, Office 365 Groups, and SharePoint sites. For instance, if a user reports that a team doesn't appear in search results, permissions for that team could be the underlying issue. Therefore, setting appropriate permissions is crucial.

Teams come in different flavors—public teams, private teams, and org-wide teams. You must understand the constraints and features of each type and know how to convert existing teams into an org-wide team. You can expect exam questions related to team management, membership control, and the implementation of Teams app policies.

Management tasks here include the creation of a team, upgrading existing resources into a team, setting privacy levels for a team, and overseeing org-wide teams.

Tip Be prepared for questions related to PowerShell commands that upgrade distribution groups to Office 365 Groups. The relevant command is `Upgrade-DistributionGroup -DlIdentities IT@bloguc.com`.

Once a team is established, controlling its membership is vital. You'll need to make sure active users have appropriate access. Activities such as adding new users or removing those who have left the company can be executed either through the Teams admin center or via Windows PowerShell. Additionally, you can automate membership based on attributes in Active Directory, such as department.

Tip Expect questions on automating membership management. For example, you can create a dynamic distribution group using PowerShell:

```
New-DynamicDistributionGroup -Name "Marketing Group"
-IncludedRecipients "MailboxUsers,MailContacts"
-ConditionalDepartment "Marketing","Sales".
```

Policy implementation for Teams apps is another focus area. You must understand how to restrict custom and third-party apps and how to configure policies for specific scenarios, such as allowing only developers to sideload apps. Understanding how to create and assign a Teams setup policy for particular teams is essential.

By mastering these topics, you'll be better prepared for the exam and more effective in your role as a Microsoft Teams admin.

Recommended Study Resources for Exam Preparation

We strongly suggest that you engage in practical training and acquire hands-on experience prior to taking the certification exam. Our study resources encompass a variety of options, including self-directed learning materials and formal classroom instruction, along with access to comprehensive documentation, community forums, and instructional videos.

Study these resources:

- **Access learning materials:** Links are provided for you to explore various learning paths and documents.

- **Self-guided learning:** Opt for self-paced courses and modules to study at your convenience.

- **Instructor-led training:** Consider enrolling in courses conducted by experienced instructors for an interactive learning experience.

- **Microsoft 365 guidelines:** Gain insights into the comprehensive Microsoft 365 documentation.

- **Microsoft Teams admin manual:** Use a dedicated guide to mastering Teams administration.

- **Intro to Microsoft Teams:** Use a primer to get you started with Microsoft Teams.

- **Post your questions:** Utilize Microsoft Q&A and Microsoft Docs to seek clarifications and answers.

- **Community assistance:** Join the Microsoft 365 Tech Community for peer support and expert advice.

- **Follow Microsoft Learn:** Keep up-to-date with the latest resources and discussions on Microsoft Learn's Tech Community page.

- **Exam prep videos:** Check out the Exam Readiness Zone for videos designed to prepare you for the certification.

- **Explore more on Microsoft Learn:** Browse through additional video series and shows available on Microsoft Learn.

By leveraging these resources, you can ensure that you're well-prepared to succeed in your certification exam.

Summary

The MS-700 certification is a comprehensive guide to mastering the management of Microsoft Teams, one of the leading collaborative platforms. This certification is segmented into several key areas, each targeting different facets of Teams management.

To prepare for the exam, here are some tips:

- Familiarize yourself with Office 365 Groups to handle questions on team and private channel creation.

- Pay attention to messaging policies in the Teams admin center for controlling chat and channel messages.

- Learn about file storage options, including Citrix Files, Dropbox, Box, and Google Drive, as they might appear in exam questions.

By delving into these categories, administrators not only prepare for the MS-700 exam but also equip themselves with the essential knowledge needed to manage Microsoft Teams efficiently. This certification is integral for anyone aspiring to be an expert Teams admin, providing the skills needed to streamline communication and collaboration within any organization.

References

- **Manage Microsoft Teams:** https://learn.microsoft.com/en-us/certifications/exams/ms-700/

- **MS-700 Certifications:** https://learn.microsoft.com/en-us/certifications/resources/study-guides/ms-700

- **Managing Teams:** https://learn.microsoft.com/en-us/training/paths/get-started-managing-microsoft-teams/

Index

A

Access control lists (ACLs), 310
Access reviews, 47, 226, 826, 831
Access token, 49–52
Active Directory container, 311
Active Directory Domain Service (ADDS), 47, 612
Active Directory Federation Services (ADFS), 18
Active private teams, 703
Active public teams, 703
Activity monitoring, 571, 585
Admin center
    accessing, 93
    admin, 92, 93
    admin tools, 92
    analytics and reports tab, 255
        reporting labels, 259, 260
        Teams reports, 259
        usage reports, 256–258
    call quality dashboard (CQD) (see Call quality dashboard (CQD))
    dashboard, 95, 96
    definition, 94
    devices tab (see Devices tab)
    enhanced encryption policies, 244, 245
    live event policies, 88
    live events, 84, 85
    locations tab (see Locations tab)
    log in, 95
    meetings tab (see Meetings tab)
    messaging policies tab (see Messaging policies tab)
    planning tab (see Planning tab)
    policy packages, 245, 246
    Teams apps tab (see Teams apps tab)
    Teams tab, 96
    upgrade settings, 112
        admin, 112
        coexistence mode, 116
        default view, 112, 113
        individual user, 117, 118
        modes, 113–115
        PowerShell, 118, 119
        Skype, 112, 115
    users tab (see Users tab)
    uses, 94, 95
    voice tab (see Voice tab)
Administrators, 22, 41, 45, 46, 93, 267, 373, 397, 596, 839
Adoption strategy, 332
    business objectives and use cases, 332
    training plan, 333
Analytics and reporting, 701, 702
    files, sharing and working, 802
    identify areas of improvement, 801
    Microsoft Teams for education, 800
    monitoring students' activity, usage, and engagement, 801
    personalized learning experiences, 801, 802
    simplify your data, Power BI, 802
    student progress, assessing, 801

C

N

O

P

Q

R

W

X, Y, Z